I MACCABEES

THE ANCHOR BIBLE is a fresh approach to the world's greatest classic. Its object is to make the Bible accessible to the modern reader; its method is to arrive at the meaning of biblical literature through exact translation and extended exposition, and to reconstruct the ancient setting of the biblical story, as well as the circumstances of its transcription and the characteristics of its transcribers.

THE ANCHOR BIBLE is a project of international and interfaith scope. Protestant, Catholic, and Jewish scholars from many countries contribute individual volumes. The project is not sponsored by any ecclesiastical organization and is not intended to reflect any particular theological doctrine. Prepared under our joint supervision, THE ANCHOR BIBLE is an effort to make available all the significant historical and linguistic knowledge which bears on the interpretation of the biblical record.

THE ANCHOR BIBLE is aimed at the general reader with no special formal training in biblical studies; yet, it is written with the most exacting standards of scholarship, reflecting the highest technical accomplishment.

This project marks the beginning of a new era of co-operation among scholars in biblical research, thus forming a common body of knowledge to be shared by all.

William Foxwell Albright
David Noel Freedman
GENERAL EDITORS

Following the death of senior editor W. F. Albright, The Anchor Bible Editorial Board was established to advise and assist David Noel Freedman in his continuing capacity as general editor. The three members of the Editorial Board are among the contributors to The Anchor Bible. They have been associated with the series for a number of years and are familiar with its methods and objectives. Each is a distinguished authority in his area of specialization, and in concert with the others, will provide counsel and judgment as the series continues.

EDITORIAL BOARD

Frank M. Cross — Old Testament
Raymond E. Brown — New Testament
Jonas C. Greenfield — Apocrypha

THE ANCHOR BIBLE

I MACCABEES

A New Translation
with
Introduction and Commentary

by

Jonathan A. Goldstein

DOUBLEDAY & COMPANY, INC.
GARDEN CITY, NEW YORK
1976

"Die Hellenistische Welt um 185 vor Chr." from GROSSER HISTOR-
ISCHER WELTATLAS I edited by Herman Bengton and Vladimir Milojcic,
5th edition. Reprinted by permission of Bayerischer Schulbuch Verlag.

"The Temple and Its Courts as Envisioned by Ezekiel" from S. Yeivin,
"Miqdaš," Enc. Bib., V (1968). Reprinted by permission of Bialik Institute,
Israel.

CARTA'S ATLAS OF THE PERIOD OF THE SECOND TEMPLE, THE
MISHNAH AND THE TALMUD by Michael Avi-Yonah. Copyright ©
Carta, Jerusalem 1966. Reprinted by permission of Carta Publishing Com-
pany, Ltd.

"The Second Temple" from Sepher Yerushalayim, ed. M. Avi-Yonah (Jerusalem and Tel Aviv: The Bialik Institute and Dvir, 1956). Reprinted by
permission of Dvir Publications.

Qadmoniot V, 1972. Map from "Jerusalem Revealed" p. 43 reprinted by permission of the Israel Exploration Society.

Revue Biblique, XXXIII (1924), 381, Fig. 3 "Topographie des Campagnes
Machabéennes" by F. M. Abel. Reprinted by permission of Librairie Lecoffre,
France.

THE MACMILLAN BIBLE ATLAS by Yohanan Aharoni and Michael Avi-
Yonah. Copyright © Carta, Jerusalem 1964, 1966, 1968. Redrawn with permission from Macmillan Publishing Company.

THE WESTMINSTER HISTORICAL ATLAS TO THE BIBLE, Revised
Edition, edited by George Ernest Wright and Floyd Vivian Filson. Copyright
1956 by W. L. Jenkins. Redrawn with permission of the Westminster Press.

Library of Congress Cataloging in Publication Data

Bible. O.T. Apocrypha. 1 Maccabees. English. Goldstein. 1976.
I Maccabees.

(The Anchor Bible vol. 41)
Selected Bibliography: p. 180
Includes index.
1. Bible.   O.T.   Apocrypha   1 Maccabees—Commentaries.
I. Goldstein, Jonathan A., 1929–
II. Title.   III. Series.
BS192.2.A11964.G3   vol. 41 [BS1823]   229'.73'07
ISBN 0-385-08533-8
Library of Congress Catalog Card Number 75–32719

To my parents and my teachers

THE APOCRYPHA

The term Apocrypha (or "Deuterocanonical Books" in Roman Catholic usage) is popularly understood to describe the fifteen books or parts of books from the pre-Christian period that Catholics accept as canonical Scripture but Protestants and Jews do not. This designation and definition are inaccurate on many counts. An apocryphon is literally a hidden writing, kept secret for the initiate and too exalted for the general public; virtually none of these books makes such a pretense. Not only Roman Catholics but also Orthodox and Eastern Christians accept these books, wholly or partially, as canonical Scripture. Roman Catholics do not accept all of them as Scripture, for I and II Esdras and the Prayer of Manasseh are not included in the official Catholic canon drawn up at the Council of Trent. Many Protestant churches have no official decision declaring these books to be non-canonical; and, in fact, up to the last century they were included in most English Protestant Bibles. What is certain is that these books did not find their way into the final Jewish Palestinian canon of Scripture. Thus, despite their Jewish origins (parts of II Esdras are Christian and Latin in origin), they were preserved for the most part in Greek by Christians as a heritage from the Alexandrian Jewish community and their basic text is found in the codices of the Septuagint. However, recent discoveries, especially that of the Dead Sea scrolls, have brought to light the original Hebrew or Aramaic text of some of these books. Leaving aside the question of canonicity, Christians and Jews now unite in recognizing the importance of these books for tracing the history of Judaism and Jewish thought in the centuries between the last of the Hebrew Scriptures and the advent of Christianity.

PREFACE

This book contains my own efforts to solve the problems of the First Book of Maccabees. Although there is merit in presenting a synthesis of the prevailing views in recent and earlier scholarship, the brevity of life forces decisions upon us: I prefer to use my time in studying the problems themselves, rather than how others have tried to solve them. If others have come upon my solutions before me and wish that I had acknowledged the fact, I apologize to them and concede them their claims to priority. In particular I have found many times that a discovery of mine had already been made by Menahem Stern. Wherever I have made use of another scholar's discoveries, I have tried to acknowledge my debt. At the very outset, I wish to acknowledge my debts, too numerous to be itemized, to the giants in the field, Carl Grimm, F.-M. Abel, and especially my teacher, Elias Bickerman. I have also learned much from the studies of my teacher, H. L. Ginsberg. Where I believe my own views to be solidly based, I have presented the evidence for them and have avoided presenting and refuting opposing views, including those of Jochen G. Bunge, whose work, *Untersuchungen zum zweiten Makkabäerbuch* (Diss. Rheinische-Friedrich-Wilhelms-Universität zu Bonn; Bonn: Rheinische-Friedrich-Wilhelms-Universität, 1971), came to my attention when this volume was in press. Otherwise my task would have been endless. A commentary, especially one for the Anchor Bible, should not look like a debate.

I am grateful to the publishers for allowing this book to be a compromise. Originally the First and Second Books of Maccabees were to appear in one volume. The Introduction is still an introduction to both. The size of the present work made it desirable to devote a separate volume to Second Maccabees.

In writing my commentary I faced the problem of how best to arrange comments on longer and shorter passages. A comment on an entire section is called on "introductory NOTE." Comments on passages are arranged in the order of the initial verses. A NOTE on 1:1–5 will appear before a NOTE on 1:2–5. Where two passages have the same initial verse, I comment on the longer one first. A NOTE on 1:1–7 will appear before a NOTE on 1:1–6.

In this volume II Esdras is the Greek translation of the Hebrew books of Ezra and Nehemiah, not the apocalyptic work called "II Esdras" in AB vol. 42.

The reader may find that unfamiliar names and words make my book difficult. I hope that any such problems will be solvable through the use of a collegiate dictionary and the indexes to this book.

I have been unable to find a consistent way to transliterate Hebrew. Ancient Hebrew can be rendered by the standard scholarly system, but that system becomes awkward when used for medieval or modern Hebrew. I do try to spell the author and title of each work always in the same way. Where an author provides a transliteration or translation of a title, I use that.

I am grateful to the University of Iowa for facilitating my research, especially through generous grants and leave from teaching. I am grateful to my parents, Rabbi and Mrs. David A. Goldstein, for unfailing encouragement. My scholarly wife, Helen, made herself available for consultation, and my daughter, Risë, typed parts of the manuscript. I record my thanks here to my two research assistants, Walter Conlon and Bernard Black. I have learned much from conversations with my colleague, George Nickelsburg.

Working with the editors of the Anchor Bible has been a rewarding experience. David Noel Freedman made many valuable suggestions, and Robert Hewetson and Ann Mokrauer prepared the work for publication with intelligence and efficiency.

JONATHAN A. GOLDSTEIN

July 1975

CONTENTS

LIST OF ILLUSTRATIONS

PRINCIPAL ABBREVIATIONS

AB	Anchor Bible, 1964–
ABAW	*Abhandlungen der Bayerischen Akademie der Wissenschaften, Philosophisch-historische Abteilung*
Abel	F.-M. Abel, *Les Livres des Maccabées**
AIPHOS	*Annuaire de l'Institut de philologie et d'histoire orientales et slaves,* Université libre de Bruxelles
AJSL	*American Journal of Semitic Languages and Literatures*
Alon	Gedaliahu Alon, *Studies in Jewish History**
ALQ	*The Ancient Library of Qumran,* by Frank Moore Cross*
ANET²	*Ancient Near Eastern Texts,* ed. J. B. Pritchard*
APOT	*The Apocrypha and Pseudepigrapha of the Old Testament,* ed. R. H. Charles*
ARW	*Archiv für Religiouswissenschaft*
BA	*Biblical Archaeologist*
BANE	*The Bible and the Ancient Near East*
Baron	Salo W. Baron, *A Social and Religious History of the Jews,* 2d ed., rev. & enl. Columbia University Press, 1952–
BASOR	*Bulletin of the American Schools of Oriental Research*
BEFAR	Bibliothèque des Écoles françaises d'Athènes et de Rome
Bengtson, *Strategie*	Hermann Bengtson, *Die Strategie in der hellenistischen Zeit**
Bevan	Edwyn R. Bevan, *The House of Seleucus**
Bickermann, *Gott*	Elias J. Bickermann, *Der Gott der Makkabäer**
Bikerman, *Institutions*	Élie Bikerman, *Institutions des Séleucides** (See Introduction, Part I, n. 57)
BO	*Bibliotheca orientalis*
BZAW	Beihefte zur *Zeitschrift für die Alttestamentliche Wissenschaft*
CAH	Cambridge Ancient History
CBQ	*Catholic Biblical Quarterly*
CD	Documents of the Damascus Covenanters, published in Chaim Rabin, *The Zadokite Documents,* 2d ed. Oxford: Clarendon Press, 1958
CIL	*Corpus Inscriptionum Latinarum*
CPJ	*Corpus Papyrorum Judaicarum,* eds. Victor A. Tcherikover and Alexander Fuks*

* For further reference, see Selected Bibliography.

DAGR   Dictionnaire des antiquités grecques et romaines, eds.
              Ch. Daremberg and Edm. Saglio, 5 vols. in 10. Paris:
              Hachette, 1877–1919
Dan LXX   The old Greek version of Daniel
Dan Th.   Theodotion's Greek version of Daniel
DJD   *Discoveries in the Judaean Desert*. Oxford: Clarendon
              Press, 1955–
DMP   *De Mortibus Persecutorum* (See pp. 92–103)
Du Mesnil, *Études*   Robert du Mesnil du Buisson, *Études sur les dieux
              phéniciennes hérités par l'Empire romain**
EI   *Eretz-Israel*
Eissfeldt   Otto Eissfeldt, *The Old Testament: An Introduction**
Enc. Bib.   Encyclopaedia Biblica. Jerusalem: Bialik Institute,
              1955–   (in Hebrew). References to columns
Enc. Jud.   Encyclopaedia Judaica. Jerusalem: Encyclopaedia Ju-
              daica; New York: Macmillan, 1972. References to
              columns
FGH   *Die Fragmente der griechischen Historiker*, ed. F.
              Jacoby. Berlin: Weidmann; Leiden: Brill, 1923–
Geiger, *Urschrift*   Abraham Geiger, *Urschrift und Übersetzungen der
              Bibel**
Ginsberg   H. Louis Ginsberg, *Studies in Daniel**
Ginzberg, *Legends*   Louis Ginzberg, *The Legends of the Jews**
GKC   *Gesenius' Hebrew Grammar**
Grimm   Carl L. W. Grimm, *Das Erste Buch der Maccabäer**
H   Chapter and verse numbers which differ in the Hebrew
              version from the Greek are designated by an "H."
Hanhart   (See Introduction, Part VIII, n. 2)
Head   Barclay V. Head, *Historia Numorum**
Heuss, *Grundlagen*   Alfred Heuss, *Die völkerrechtlichen Grundlagen der
              römischen Aussenpolitik in republikanischer Zeit**
HTR   *Harvard Theological Review*
HTS   Harvard Theological Studies
HUCA   *Hebrew Union College Annual*
I   First Maccabees
II   Second Maccabees
III   Third Maccabees
IV   Fourth Maccabees
IEJ   *Israel Exploration Journal*
IG   *Inscriptiones Graecae*, Editio major
IG II²   *Inscriptiones Graecae* Editio minor, vols. II–III
IG IV²   *Inscriptiones Graecae*, Editio minor, vol. IV
IGLS   *Inscriptiones grecques et latines de la Syrie*, eds. L.
              Jalabert, R. Mouterde, et al. Paris: Geuthner, 1929–
ILS   *Inscriptiones Latinae Selectae*, ed. H. Dessau, Berlin:
              1892–1916

* For further reference, see Selected Bibliography.

IOS	*Israel Oriental Studies*
J. *AJ*	Josephus *Antiquities of the Jews*
J. *Ap.*	Josephus *Against Apion*
J. *BJ*	Josephus *Bellum Judaicum=The Jewish War*
J. *Vita*	Josephus *Life of Josephus*
JAOS	*Journal of the American Oriental Society*
JE	*The Jewish Encyclopaedia.* New York and London: Funk & Wagnalls, 1901–6
JEA	*Journal of Egyptian Archaeology*
JJS	*Journal of Jewish Studies*
JNES	*Journal of Near Eastern Studies*
JQR	*Jewish Quarterly Review*
JRS	*Journal of Roman Studies*
JTS	*Journal of Theological Studies*
Kappler	(See Introduction, Part VIII, n. 1)
Kolbe, *Beiträge*	Walther Kolbe, *Beiträge zur syrischen und judischen Geschichte**
Latte	Kurt Latte, *Römische Religionsgeschichte**
LCL	Loeb Classical Library. Harvard University Press
M.	*Mishnah*
Mayser	Edwin Mayser, *Grammatik der griechischen Papyri aus der Ptolemäerzeit**
Meyer, *Ursprung*	Edward Meyer, *Ursprung und Anfänge des Christentums**
MGWJ	*Monatschrift für die Geschichte und Wissenschaft des Judentums*
Migne	J.-P. Migne, *Patrologiae Cursus Completus, Series Latina*, Paris, 1843–90, and *Series Graeco-Latina*, Paris 1857–1934
Mørkholm	Otto Mørkholm, *Antiochus IV of Syria**
Mørkholm, *Studies*	Idem, *Studies in the Coinage of Antiochus IV of Syria**
OCD²	Oxford Classical Dictionary*
OGIS	*Orientis Graeci Inscriptiones Selectae*, ed. Wilhelm Dittenberger
P. Dura	Documents in C. B. Welles et al., *The Parchments and Papyri*, Final Report V, Part I of *The Excavations at Dura Europos*
PEQ	*Palestine Exploration Quarterly*
PW	Pauly-Wissowa et al., eds., Realencyclopaedie der Klassischen Altertumswissenschaft. References to columns
Q	I use the customary abbreviations in alluding to texts from Qumran. In most cases where I mention a Qumran text, I give the reader references to the published versions. Exceptions are the following:
	1QH *Hōdāyōt* (Hymns of Thanksgiving). Published in Eleazar L. Sukenik, *The Dead Sea Scrolls of the Hebrew University*, Jerusalem:

* For further reference, see Selected Bibliography.

Magnes Press, 1955, and in Jacob Licht, *The Thanksgiving Scroll*, Jerusalem: Bialik Institute, 1957 (in Hebrew).

1QIs^a   The great Isaiah Scroll from Cave 1. Published in The Dead Sea Scrolls of St. Mark's Monastery, eds. M. Burrows, John C. Trever, and W. H. Brownlee (New Haven: American Schools of Oriental Research, 1950–51), vol. I.

1QM   The War Scroll. Published in Sukenik and in Yigael Yadin, *The Scroll of the War of the Sons of Light against the Sons of Darkness*, Oxford University Press, 1962.

1QpHab   The commentary on Habakkuk. Published in Burrows et al.

1QS   The Manual of Discipline. Published in Burrows et al., Vol. II 2.

4Q175   4Q Testimonia. Published in John Allegro, DJD, V, 1968

QDAP   *Quarterly of the Department of Antiquities in Palestine*
RAC   *Reallexikon für Antike und Christentum*
RArch   *Revue archéologique*
RB   *Revue biblique*
REA   *Revue des études anciennes*
REG   *Revue des études grecques*
REJ   *Revue des études juives*
RHR   *Revue de l'histoire des religions*
Roscher   W. H. Roscher, ed., *Ausführliches Lexikon der griechischen und römischen Mythologie**
RPh   *Revue de philologie, d'histoire et de littérature anciennes*
RQum   *Revue de Qumrân*
Schürer   Emil Schürer, *Geschichte des jüdischen Volkes im Zeitalter Jesu Christi**
SEHHW   *Social and Economic History of the Hellenistic World* by M. I. Rostovtzeff*
Sel.   Seleucid Era
Sel. Bab.   Babylonian Seleucid Era   } See Introduction,
Sel. Mac.   Macedonian Seleucid Era   } pp. 21–24
Sherk   Robert K. Sherk, *Roman Documents from the Greek East**
Studies Smith   *Christianity, Judaism and Other Greco-Roman Cults: Studies for Morton Smith at Sixty*, ed. Jacob Neusner. Leiden: Brill, 1975
Syll.²   *Sylloge Inscriptionum Graecarum*, 2nd ed., W. Dittenberger, editor

* For further reference, see Selected Bibliography.

Syll.[3]	*Sylloge Inscriptionum Graecarum,* 3d ed., W. Dittenberger, editor
TB	Babylonian Talmud
TCAAS	*Transactions of the Connecticut Academy of Arts and Sciences*
Test	Testament of (e.g.) Dan
To.	Tosefta
TP	Palestinian Talmud
VTS	Vetus Testamentum Supplements. Leiden: Brill, 1953–
YGC	*Yahweh and the Gods of Canaan* by William Foxwell Albright*
ZAW	*Zeitschrift für die alttestamentliche Wissenschaft*
ZDPV	*Zeitschrift des deutschen Palästina-Vereins*
ZNW	*Zeitschrift für die neutestamentliche Wissenschaft*

* For further reference, see Selected Bibliography.

INTRODUCTION

I. THE CONTENT AND CHARACTER
OF OUR TWO BOOKS

"Fear not, my servant Jacob" (Isa 44:2).

The faithful Israelite living in Judaea under the rule of the Ptolemies and the Seleucids in the third and second centuries B.C.E. learned from childhood that the LORD's chosen people had nothing to fear if they kept the LORD's commandments. Subjection to the great empires of Persia and the Hellenistic kings had brought stability and security over long periods, which in part compensated for galling exploitation and servitude and for episodes of devastating warfare. Then, under the Seleucid Antiochus IV from 167 to 164 B.C.E., obedience to the LORD's commandments became a crime punished with extreme severity. No harsher trial ever tested the monotheistic faith of the Jews.

The outcome was entirely unexpected: the desperate resistance of the Jews prevailed, and for a time the "yoke of foreign empires" was lifted from the Jews as they became independent under the Hasmonaean dynasty. After the centuries of heartbreaking delay, were the glorious predictions of the prophets of a mighty restored Israel being fulfilled? For the Jews, the events cried out for an interpretation in accordance with the teachings of the Torah and the Prophets. God's favor had departed from Israel in the dark days of the destruction of the two kingdoms. If now God's favor had fully returned after the harshest time of troubles, it was necessary for the people to know how and why; otherwise, they might again lose His favor.

The tradition of the Greek and Roman Christian churches has preserved two Jewish historical works which explain to the chosen people the time of troubles and the victories which followed. Early in the Greek manuscript tradition these works received the titles, First and Second Books of Maccabees. However, in the books themselves and in the earliest sources, "Maccabee" or "Maccabaeus" never occurs in the plural, appearing only as an additional name of the hero Judas. Clement of Alexandria and Origen, the earliest of the Church Fathers to mention the books by name, call them *Ta Makkabaïka,* "Maccabaean Histories," from which title persons who spoke loosely probably turned to call all the heroes in the stories "Maccabees." The first datable occurrence of such use of "Maccabees" for the heroes is in Tertullian *Adversus Judaeos*

4, of ca. 195 C.E. From then on, the Fathers speak of the "Books of Maccabees."[1]

These two books present sharply different accounts; indeed, we shall find that their authors were bitter opponents. The webs of doctrinal subtleties, of charge and countercharge, which characterize the polemics of monotheistic sects against the rivals they call "heretics"—these webs give rise to some of the most complicated puzzles in the history of literature. So it is with our two books. First Maccabees and the original of which Second Maccabees is an abridgment were written in close succession as propaganda after decades of controversy. The difficult task of interpreting such works has been made more difficult by the almost perverse skepticism of scholars toward them since the time of the Renaissance.[2] Propagandists can and do lie, but propagandistic historians lie only where it is to their advantage and only where there is small danger of being exposed. Since each of our two books presents one of two extreme opposing views, they can be made to act as a check one upon the other. Thus, one can sharply restrict the field for imaginative scholarly skepticism which would reject or radically alter their accounts. We begin our study by examining the nature of the books as they have reached us through the tradition of the Church.

The First Book of Maccabees

First Maccabees is a history of the rise of the Hasmonaean dynasty, from the daring deeds of the zealous priest Mattathias to the reign of John Hyrcanus, high priest and prince of the Jews by dynastic heredity. The author sets forth most of the important doctrines of his book in the first two chapters. He begins by setting the scene, the Near East under the rule of the Graeco-Macedonian kingdoms founded by the successors of Alexander the Great: wicked were those kings (I 1:1–9) and wicked was Antiochus IV Epiphanes, who began to reign in 175 B.C.E. and authorized wicked Jews to abandon the restrictions of the Torah and to adopt Greek ways including the educational institutions of the gymnasium (1:10–15; see commentary). As if in punishment for the wickedness of these apostate Jews (1:15, end, 28, 64), a dreadful series of visitations came upon Judaea and Jerusalem (1:16–64).

In 169 B.C.E. after a victorious campaign in Egypt, Antiochus IV marched on Jerusalem and sacked the temple. Two years later, an official

---

[1] "Maccabaean Histories": Clement of Alexandria *Stromateis* i 21.123; v 14.97; Origen *Contra Celsum* viii 46, etc. See Abel, pp. viii–x. The loose usage may appear already at Hippolytus *De Antichristo* 49, where the manuscript tradition has two readings, *Makkabaiois* and *Makkabaïkois*.

First Maccabees goes far beyond the lifetime of Judas Maccabaeus and dwells upon the importance of his brothers, so that its original title could hardly have been "Maccabaean History"; indeed, we know it was not. See Part I, pp. 14–21.

[2] See Part II, n. 2.

of his, the Mysarch, sacked and burned the rest of the city, destroyed its fortifications, slaughtered or enslaved or expelled pious Jews while seizing their possessions, and built a citadel, the Akra, to shelter the community of "sinners" whom he placed in power. Decrees followed in which the king forbade Jews to observe the commandments of the Torah and ordered them to violate its prohibitions; the king appointed officials to enforce the decrees. On 15 Kislev (6 December), 167 B.C.E., an "abomination of desolation" was set up in the temple; sacrifices there to the abomination began on 25 Kislev.

After paying brief respect to the brave but suicidal efforts of pious Jews to disobey the king's decrees, the author introduces the aged priest Mattathias, father of five sons: John, Simon, Judas, Eleazar, and Jonathan. Grieved like all pious Jews, Mattathias withdrew from Jerusalem to the village of Modeïn (2:1–14). There, however, he rose in zeal and dared to use the sword against the king's agents and against their Jewish collaborators (I 2:15–28). Jews knew God had commanded them to destroy all Jewish idolaters (Exod 22:19; Deut 13:7–18). If Jews before Mattathias' act of zeal had no choice but to die (I 1:63) and if Mattathias' act is presented as something exceptional, we may infer that pious Jews were as much bound by their religion not to rebel against the king as they were bound to obey the Torah. Indeed, other evidence shows that pious Jews faced this cruel dilemma. Mattathias dared to assert that a king who commanded the violation of the Torah could no longer be ruling Jews by divine right. If Mattathias had based his ruling on a scriptural text, our author surely would have quoted it. Mattathias justified his act only by his own zeal, comparing it to that of Phineas (Num 25:6–15).[3]

The aged priest made another daring innovation. The royal authorities discovered that to massacre the Pietists who refused to obey the decrees they had only to wait for the Sabbath, when the Pietists would abstain from every form of self-defense (I 2:29–38). Mattathias countered by teaching that self-defense on the Sabbath was permitted. He won over to his view a large number of these "Pietists," whom author names as such, using the Hebrew equivalent Asidaioi (=Ḥăsīdīm; I 2:39–43). We may infer that the Pietists were a well-defined group among the Jews. Indeed,

---

[3] The Pietist belief that God forbade resistance: see in AB vol. 41A commentary on II 1:7 and II 15:10–17. Our author never treats the Psalms as canonical scripture (see NOTE on I 7:16–17). However, some Jewish contemporaries of Mattathias may already have taken Ps 119:126 as justification for resistance, rendering it, "It is time to take action for the LORD, for they have violated Thy Torah." See To. Berakot 7:24; TB Berakot 54a, 63a; Temurah 14b; Yoma 69a (a legend applying the text to a crisis in the time of Alexander the Great). Our author may have drawn on sources who accepted Ps 119:126 as scriptural justification. At I 6:59 one might see a paraphrase of the verse in the heathen government's recognition that the violation of the Torah had caused the rebellion. Note also the use of the Greek words for "time," "law" and "act" at I 2:25–26 and 49–51.

two of the sects famous later among the Jews can be connected with them. The name of the Essenes is simply the Aramaic equivalent *Ḥᵉsayīn*. Scholars have traced the origins of the Pharisees to the Pietists mentioned in First Maccabees, and the term *ḥāsīd* is prominent among the words used by Pharisees of members of their order. The Essenes are the sect whose settlement and library were discovered at Qumran near the Dead Sea.[4]

Mattathias' band began to succeed in enforcing the observance of the Torah and in killing or expelling the royal agents and their Jewish collaborators (2:44–48). On his deathbed, old Mattathias is portrayed as charging his sons to carry on tasks comparable to those of Phineas, Joshua, and David, as if they, too, could earn the rewards received by those ancient heroes. Our author has the dying Mattathias appoint Simon as "father" and "man of counsel" at the same time as he entrusts the conduct of the war to Judas (2:49–70). Nothing indicates that Simon was the eldest. In the list of the brothers at 2:2–5 John appears before Simon. Simon for long years thereafter was to be a loyal subordinate of his brothers, Judas and Jonathan. Nevertheless, he was to be the first to hold power as independent prince and high priest of the Jews.

The story of Mattathias and especially his farewell address are most important for our author's purposes. We must stop to examine them more closely. The author himself says (I 2:26) that the story of Mattathias follows the model of the story of Phineas (Num 25:1–15). Both words and content follow the model. Both narratives take place at a time of God's wrath against Israel (Num 25:3, 11; I 1:64). Just as Phineas in Num 25:7 "saw" that nothing was being done about the mixed marriage that had angered God and "rose and left the congregation," so Mattathias "saw" the apostasy in Judah and Jerusalem and "rose and left" Jerusalem for Modeïn (I 2:1–6; the "seeing" is placed last so that the lament in vss. 7–14 will not interrupt the flow of the narrative). Just as Phineas showed "zeal" and acted on behalf of the "anger" of the Lord (Num 25:11) and stabbed the sinful couple in their illicit bedchamber, the place of their sin (Num 25:8; see the Greek versions) so Mattathias was "filled with zeal and anger" and slew the idolater on the altar, the place of his sin. With the reticence he displays throughout his book, the

---

[4] On the name of the Essenes and the use of it in the Aramaic original of Daniel 11, see Ginsberg, pp. 42–49. On origins of the Pharisees: Baron, II, 342–44, nn. 43–44; Cross, ALQ, pp. 131, 141, n. 66. On *Ḥāsīd* as used by Pharisees: *M. Abot* 2:5; *M. Ḥagigah* 2:7; To. *Soṭah* 13:4, etc. The very name of the Pharisees (*Pᵉrūshīm* or *Pᵉrīshīn*="separatists" or "schismatics") may have been given them by opponents, presumably the Essenes; see Baron, II, 342, n. 43. On the "early *Ḥasidim*" mentioned in rabbinic literature, see E. E. Urbach, "*Ḥasid*," in Encyclopaedia Hebraica, XVII (5725=1964–65), 751–52 (in Hebrew). On Qumran and the Essenes: Cross, ALQ, pp. 52, n. 2, and 70–106; George W. E. Nickelsburg, Jr., *Resurrection, Immortality, and Eternal Life in Intertestamental Judaism*, HTS, XXVI (Harvard University Press, 1972), 144–69.

author lets his Jewish reader draw the inference: as Phineas was rewarded by being made the founder of the high priestly line (Num 25:12–13), so will Mattathias be rewarded.

Less obvious but also surely intentional is the parallel between Mattathias and the two spies Joshua and Caleb (Num 13–14). Though otherwise all Israel were rebels (*apostatai*) against God (Num 14:8), Joshua and Caleb remained loyal; just so, Mattathias exclaimed that though all others in the kingdom would obey the king's command to rebel (*apostênai*) against their religion, he and his family would remain loyal (I 2:19–22). Again the Jewish reader would infer: as Joshua and Caleb were rewarded (Num 14:30; Josh 14:6–15, 19:49–50; Sir 46:1–10), so will Mattathias and his sons be.[5]

Also probably intentional is the author's description of the flight Mattathias led to the mountains in language which recalls the similar act of David (I 2:27–28, 42–43; I Sam 22:1–2, 23:14), especially since both flights are followed by massacres of innocents (I 2:29–38; I Sam 22: 7–19). Both David and Mattathias as fugitive outlaws loyally lead their bands to fight for the sake of Israel (I 2:44–48; I Sam 23:1–5, 25: 14–16) and legislate for Israel's welfare (I 2:39–41; I Sam 30:22–25). Again our author may be hinting that if David was rewarded, so will Mattathias be.

The parallels between the two massacres of innocents are particularly significant. The priests massacred at Nob belonged to a rejected line of high priests (I Sam 3:11–14, 14:3, 22:11, 20; I Kings 2:27). Just so, God showed little if any favor to the Pietists who died in their non-resistance (I 2:29–38) but gave victory to Mattathias, the zealot who dared to make defensive war even on the Sabbath (2:39–48). Indeed, our author stresses that many Pietists endorsed Mattathias' course by joining him and his sons (2:42).[6]

These lessons and others are driven home in Mattathias' farewell address. The author avoids assuming the posture of a propagandist urging the Dynastic claims of the Hasmonaeans. Rather, he has the dying Mattathias give a series of examples of the great deeds and great rewards of ancient Israelite heroes (2:51–60) in order to exhort his sons to do likewise and earn glory and eternal fame (2:51; cf. 2:64). The examples are carefully selected: Mattathias, like Abraham, had been ready to sacrifice his offspring (1:50, 2:17–21). Just as Abraham by such deeds of faith was held to be righteous (Gen 15:6) in the days when Sodom and Gomorrah were destroyed, so the faithfulness of the Hasmonaeans will preserve them from the punishment incurred by the guilt of this "Age of Wrath" (I 1:64; cf. Dan 8:19, 11:36).

---

[5] For Jonathan as Judge: see I 9:73, and cf. I 9:27 with Judg 10:9; I 9:30 with Judg 11:6, 8; and I 9:44 with Josh 3:4–17.

[6] Contrast the misgivings of the Pietist author of Dan 11:34.

Like Joseph, Mattathias resisted temptation to violate the will of God (I 2:17–22); just as Joseph became lord of Egypt, so may descendants of Mattathias become powerful officials of an empire (cf. I 10:19–20, 62–65, 88–89, 11:27, 42–51, 58–60).

Mattathias was a member of the priestly line of Yehoyarib (2:1). Until Antiochus IV appointed an outsider, Menelaus, to the high priesthood (cf. II 4:23–25 with 3:4), the office had long been in the hands of the "Oniad" line, who were descended from Jeshua of the line of Yedayah.[7] Later, when members of the Hasmonaean family were raised to the high priesthood, partisans of the Oniad line and others viewed them as usurpers. Hence, our author takes care to have Mattathias identify the next example, Phineas, as "our forefather," thus asserting for his own priestly line eligibility for the high priesthood equal to that of the Oniads. The examples of Joshua, Caleb, and David follow (I 2:54–57).

Next comes Elijah, who, like Phineas and Mattathias, did deeds of zeal in an age of wrath (I Kings 18, 19:10, 14); therefore, Mattathias' family may look forward to rewards like Elijah's, perhaps the gift of prophesy, if not assumption into heaven. Mattathias' grandson John Hyrcanus, indeed, was granted prophetic revelation.[8]

The author probably viewed even the last two examples, the miraculous escapes of Daniel and Hananiah, Azariah, and Mishael as having been equaled by the many Hasmonaean successes against heavy odds (I 2: 59–60).

The remainder of First Maccabees serves to bear out the predictions ascribed to the dying Mattathias. First Judas, relying on divine aid gained through righteousness and prayer, wins a crescendo of victories and defeats the local Seleucid forces, to the point of dismaying Antiochus IV himself (3:1–28). Shortage of financial resources distracts the king into seeking tribute and booty in the Iranian territories. He leaves Lysias as regent in the western part of the realm and as guardian of the heir to the throne, with ample military resources (3:29–37). Judas and his men with the strength of their faith in God defeat Lysias' subordinates and then repulse Lysias himself at Beth-Zur to make possible the purification of the temple and reestablishment of the cult at the very season in which it had been desecrated three years earlier (3:38 – 4:58). For our author, the purification and the *de facto* end of the persecution came only as a result of military victories. He mentions no diplomacy and no official Seleucid revocation of the decrees. The dedication of the new altar

[7] Ezra 2:36; Neh 7:39, 12:1, 6, 10–11; I Chron 9:10, 24:7. See R. de Vaux, *Ancient Israel* (New York: McGraw-Hill, 1961), pp. 388–403; J. Liver, "The 'Sons of Zadok the Priests' in the Dead Sea Sect," RQum 6 (1967), 18–28.

[8] J. *BJ* i 2.7.68–69; *AJ* xiii 10.3.282, 7.299–300; To. *Soṭah* 13:5 and parallels; cf. Test Levi xviii 6.

was to be celebrated ever after with the annual festival of Hanukkah, the Feast of Dedication (4:59).

Judas, Simon, and Jonathan had striking success in protecting and avenging their Jewish brethren who were attacked by hostile neighboring peoples (I 4:60 – 5:68). A Jewish reader could see that their campaigns ranged as far as Joshua's. Equally striking failures fall to the lot of rival pretenders to national leadership, so as to demonstrate that divine favor rests upon the descendants of Mattathias (5:55–62).

Antiochus IV, repulsed in an attempt to plunder a temple in Elymais, receives the news of Judas' victories and dies of melancholy, repenting of the evil he inflicted upon the Jews and appointing Philip to be guardian of the child heir, Antiochus V (6:1–16). Lysias establishes Antiochus V as king and keeps power himself as guardian (6:17).

At this point the author tells of Judas' attempt to reduce the "sinners" in the Akra by siege and of the expedition of Lysias and Antiochus V to relieve the besieged. In the course of the campaign Judas' brother Eleazar died a hero's death, and a much reduced force of rebel Jews was besieged in Jerusalem. Their situation became desperate because the observance of the sabbatical year left the Jews short of supplies. The besieged were saved by the timely arrival at Antioch of an army under Philip, Antiochus IV's chosen guardian for the child king, to challenge the regime of Lysias. To meet the threat, Lysias and Antiochus V make peace with the rebels, but they wickedly violate their pledge not to destroy fortifications in Jerusalem. On their return to Antioch, they defeat Philip (6:18–63).

However, the victors themselves fell to a new enemy. Antiochus IV had usurped the throne after the death in 175 of his brother, Seleucus IV. Normally, the heir would have been Seleucus' son Demetrius, but at the time Demetrius was a hostage in Rome. Now Demetrius escaped from Rome and took over the Seleucid kingdom. The supporters of the new king Demetrius I executed Lysias and Antiochus V (7:1–4). Led by Alcimus, a claimant to the high priesthood, Jewish enemies of Judas' party successfully appeal to Demetrius for aid. Although Pietists break with Judas to trust Alcimus and the royal agents, they are disabused when sixty of them are crucified by order of the man they trusted (7:5–19). The reader could infer that the Pietists were fools and that Demetrius was a wicked man with wicked subordinates. Indeed, Demetrius continued to support Alcimus as high priest. The royal agent Nicanor in a fruitless effort to capture Judas even threatens a renewed desecration of the temple but is crushed in battle on the day celebrated ever after as the Day of Nicanor (7:20–49). Judas had succeeded as a latter-day Judge of Israel, and there was a brief interlude of peace (7:50; cf. Judg 3:11, 30, etc.). Judas also took the important step of making the first treaty of the Jews with the righteous superpower, Rome, and received Rome's verbal support against Demetrius (I 8).

Demetrius, however, persisted. His general Bacchides after committing atrocities against Jews offered battle to Judas. Though most of his supporters panicked and fled, brave Judas stood his ground and fell, a victim of the cowards among his people, but perhaps also—the author may wish the reader to think—of his own indomitable courage (9:1–22). Repeatedly in the course of his narrative on Judas our author has borrowed language from Samuel and Chronicles to describe Judas' great deeds in the same terms as parallel feats of Saul, Jonathan, and especially David, as if Judas' deeds were equally worthy of winning royal dynastic power for Judas' family.

Judas' death brought not peace but a period of oppression for the pious and a resurgence of the wicked among the Jews (I 9:23–27). At this point, Jonathan arises, the reader can see, as a second Judge. Judas' friends freely choose him. Jonathan's brothers, John and Simon, may have been older, but both deferred to him. At first, Jonathan operates as an outlaw in the Judaean desert. Every Jew knew David had done the same. When his brother John falls victim to Transjordanian marauders, Jonathan proves to be a second Joshua and a worthy son of Mattathias. First he smites the marauders to the east. Then, when Bacchides tries to destroy him on the east bank of the Jordan on the Sabbath, Jonathan follows his father's teaching, fighting his way to cross the Jordan like Joshua so that the dismayed royal authorities, like the ancient Canaanites, fortify Jericho and other towns (9:28–53).

When Alcimus dies in agony of a sudden stroke after an impious act, Bacchides no longer has to protect Alcimus' interests against Jonathan and withdraws for two years (9:54–57). However, after receiving an appeal from Jonathan's wicked Jewish enemies, Bacchides returns, but Jonathan resists so successfully that Bacchides punishes those who had sought his aid and makes peace with Jonathan. Jonathan settles at Machmas, no longer as outlaw but as Judge of his people and punisher of the wicked (9:58–73).

Next, a young man who claimed to be Alexander, son of Antiochus IV, arose as a rival to the wicked Demetrius. Our author never questions the young pretender's claims. As both rivals for the Seleucid throne bid for Jonathan's support with offers of privileges for the Jews and their leader, Jonathan wisely rejects the wicked Demetrius and sides with Alexander. Even so, he is able to use the offers of Demetrius so as to gain possession of Jerusalem except for the Akra and to gain the release of Jewish hostages and to fortify Jerusalem. Only Beth-Zur and the Akra were left as refuges for the wicked. Alexander appointed Jonathan high priest. When Demetrius fell in battle, Alexander became undisputed king.

At the festivities of Alexander's marriage to Cleopatra, daughter of Ptolemy VI Philometor of Egypt, Jonathan received further honors from the new Seleucid king despite the calumnies of "sinners" (10:1–66).

Alexander, however, was soon faced by the rival claims to the throne of Demetrius II, son of Demetrius I (10:67–68). Whatever Alexander's failings, he was no persecutor, and Jonathan was his loyal subject, valiantly defeating the agents of Demetrius to win yet more honor and territory from his king (10:69–89). If Ptolemy VI plotted against Alexander, Jonathan was not involved; Jonathan's respectful conduct toward Alexander's father-in-law, Ptolemy, as the Egyptian king pretended to march on a peaceful visit to Seleucid Syria, was perfectly correct (11:1–7). In the war by which Ptolemy overthrew Alexander and by which Demetrius became undisputed king, Jonathan had no role (11:8–19), being occupied in an attempt to reduce the Akra (11:20–21). Demetrius II moved to support the besieged, but Jonathan's diplomacy brought the king instead to confirm the honors granted by Alexander and add more (11:23–37). Demetrius, however, roused the discontent of his soldiers by dismissing them and soon was faced both by a rival claimant to the throne, the child Antiochus VI, put forward by the general Tryphon, and by a rebellion of the people of Antioch. In return for Jonathan's aid, Demetrius promised to grant all his requests, including the removal of the colony in the Akra, but when Jonathan's men won him victory, the king did not fulfill his promises (11:38–53).

The reader can infer that Jonathan was no longer legally or religiously bound to be loyal to the faithless Demetrius. Indeed, Tryphon's armies captured Antioch from Demetrius and Antiochus VI thereupon successfully offered privileges to Jonathan and gave Simon a high and powerful military post (11:54–59). Jonathan marched victoriously over almost the entire area ruled by David, on both sides of the Jordan (11:60–74). Like David he made alliances with righteous gentiles, with Rome and Sparta (12:1–38). As the loyal defender of Antiochus VI, Jonathan fell victim to the treacherous ambition of Tryphon, who to prepare the way for usurpation lured Jonathan into a trap (12:39–53). The reader is to infer that the kings and regents of the Seleucid empire are not to be trusted.

Simon it was who rose as national leader when Jonathan was trapped and later killed. Simon's conduct was always proper. Even when he delivered Jonathan's sons into Tryphon's hands, he did so because he had no alternative (13:1–30). Simon persevered against the usurper Tryphon and won from Demetrius II, who still had a foothold in the empire, the grant of Israel's independence (13:31–42). Simon and his sons successfully pushed the liberation of territory claimed by the Jews and captured the Akra. Simon also renewed the ties with Rome and Sparta.

Therefore, the people through its national deliberative organs was moved freely to confer upon Simon and his descendants the high priesthood and political and military leadership of the nation (13:43–14:48, 15:15–24).[9]

Simon successfully coped with the usurper Tryphon and with the new Seleucid king, Antiochus VII, only to fall victim with two of his sons to his own treacherous son-in-law (15:1–14, 25–16:18). However, the remaining son John (Hyrcanus) survived to have a successful reign, as is told "in the chronicle of his high priesthood" (16:19–24). Here the author ends his work, for he has established the legitimacy of the Hasmonaean dynasty.

God's favor for the Hasmonaean dynasty is not the only belief the author wishes to teach. Others appear prominently throughout his book. Jews must not "make a covenant with the gentiles" in the sense of adopting their cultural or religious institutions (I 1:11–15, 2:23–27, 42–48, etc.). Although military alliances with them are permitted, Greeks, including Seleucid and Ptolemaic kings, are generally faithless. Righteous gentiles may exist, such as the Spartans and the Romans.

We may infer that our author completely rejected the belief in immortality or resurrection since he does not allude to either even where a believer could hardly have avoided doing so (2:62–64).[10] Our author's hostility to the belief probably goes back to Mattathias, who had to rouse pious Jews to active armed resistance and had to condemn teachings which made unresisting martyrdom the only pious course and promised it would be rewarded. Accordingly, our author is also completely silent on the value of martyrdom. Nowhere does he suggest that the blood of the martyrs rouses God to action. His silence, in contrast to the vehement assertions in Second Maccabees, is eloquent.[11]

Indeed, to our author piety by itself was not enough to bring salvation to the Jews. They must also obey the Hasmonaeans, the stock chosen by God to save them. Pious Jews who did not follow the Hasmonaeans were massacred or, worse, incurred heinous sin as traitors.[12]

Several traits sharply distinguish First Maccabees from the biblical histories. Prophesy is absent from the narrative; so are miracles in the sense of direct supernatural intervention. Even the dying Mattathias' prescient exhortations are not called prophesy. For our author it was an article of faith that prophesy had ceased after Haggai, Zechariah, Malachi,

---

[9] On the dislocation in the text here, see introductory NOTE to I 14:16–24k.

[10] Cf. Ps 115:17; contrast II 7:22–23, 27–29, 12:43–45.

[11] Contrast esp. I 3:46–53 and 4:24–45 with the parallel II 8:17, 28–29. See also Part IV p. 79.

[12] See I 1:63, 2:29–39, 3:42–43, 5:1–2, 54–64, 67, 6:18–19, 7:5–18, 9:5–31, 53–73, 10:61–66, 11:20–21, 70–74, 12:35–38, 13:1–10, 14:4–15, 25–49, 15:21, 16:17.

and had not reappeared during the events covered by his history. The return of prophesy would come shortly before God's ultimate victory.[13] Earlier Jewish writers agreed with our author that miracles had ceased with the passing of the generation which saw the destruction of the first temple and that they, too, would return only as part of the Lord's ultimate victory.[14] There is thus no reason to consider remarkable the absence of miracles and prophesy from First Maccabees.

Our author also knew how hazardous it was to claim openly that the events of his history were fulfillments of prophesy. Jews had erred disastrously in the time of the second temple in seeing fulfillments of prophesy; see e.g. Dan 11:14. Accordingly, our author never claims openly that the achievements of his heroes fulfilled the words of the prophets. He is audacious enough, however, to describe those achievements in words obviously taken from famous prophesies, so as to lead his readers to think that the Hasmonaeans indeed fulfilled them.

First Maccabees differs from the biblical histories, except Esther, also in abstaining from the use of the biblical names of God. Our author uses "Heaven" as a substitute. We may infer that for him, as for many later Jewish authorities, those divine names were too holy to be used. Still more extreme was the author of the book of Esther, who avoids all direct allusions to God, probably for the same reason.[15]

---

[13] I 4:46, 9:27, 14:41; Joel 2:28–29 [3:1–2H]. Our author may well have believed that prophesy returned in the reign of John Hyrcanus; see above, n. 8. Others did see during the events of the revolt against Antiochus a return of prophesy. The probable meaning of Dan 9:24 is that the last prophets are to come before the end of the sabbatical year, 164/3; see Part II, pp. 42–43. The Essenes, believers in the veracity of Daniel, held that prophesy had returned by then, if not earlier; see J. *BJ* ii 8.12.159; i 3.5.78–80; *AJ* xiii 11.2.311–13. Essene reverence for the book of Daniel is attested by the fragments of it found at Qumran and by its influence on other Qumran texts. See Part II, n. 17.

[14] See H. Lesètre, "Miracle," *Dictionnaire de la Bible,* IV 2 (1912), 1118–19. No miracles occur in Ezra, Nehemiah, and Esther. The miracles in Tobit and Daniel occur to men born before the Babylonian exile. Cf. Psalm 85; Dan 9:24–27; Sir 36:1–17, esp. vss. 5 and 15; Enoch lxxxix 56–cx 16; Test Moses iv 8–9; at Joel 2:30–31 [3:3–4H], miracles, like the return of prophesy, lie in the future. Cf. Dan 12:4–6.

[15] On these tendencies with respect to divine names and their later manifestations, see A. Marmorstein, *The Old Rabbinic Doctrine of God* (1927; rep., New York: Ktav, 1968), pp. 17–147; E. Bickerman, "Anonymous Gods," *Journal of the Warburg Institute* I (1937–38), 187–96. The abstention from the use of the divine names is probably connected with Mattathias' ideology of resistance. Pietists may well have tried to "resist" Antiochus by magical use of divine names, a course which Mattathias may have regarded as impious even before the persecutions and as a dangerous self-delusion during them. Even if not impious, successful use of a divine name to defeat an enemy would indeed have been a miracle, and for our author the age of miracles had not yet returned. On magical use of divine names, see J. D. Eisenstein, "Names of God," JE, IX, 164, and Wilhelm Bacher, "*Shem ha-Meforash,*" JE, XI, 263–64. Until God himself chose to announce the return of miracles, such resort to His name might be considered the sin of "putting the Lord to test" (Deut 6:16; Exod 17:7).

Our author wrote his book in elegant biblical Hebrew, taking as his model the historical books of the Bible. The original Hebrew text has long since perished, but the character of the Greek translation through which the book survives is such that the original can be proved to have been Hebrew. Not only is the Greek extremely literal "translatese" of the type used by the translators of the Hebrew Bible, but on occasion the translator has construed an ambiguous Hebrew expression so as to produce an incongruous text which no Greek original could have contained.[16]

On the other hand, the translator's vocabulary goes far beyond that of the Greek versions of the canonical Hebrew books. From his vocabulary we can judge that, had he wished, the translator could have written in normal Hellenistic Greek. Unlike Lysimachus, the translator of the book of Esther,[17] he deliberately turned his back on "Hellenism" to write in the "Jewish-Greek" syntax of the Septuagint.

The Hebrew original was probably available to Josephus as he wrote his *Antiquities*, in which he paraphrased large sections of First Maccabees.[18] However, Josephus was composing an extremely voluminous work which he wished to have in elegant Greek. In rendering the events of the Hebrew books of Samuel, Kings, and Esther, he saved time and trouble by using the available Greek translations and probably by letting trained Greek secretaries restyle them for him.[19] He would be driven to consult the Hebrew text only where he suspected a mistake in the Greek version. His procedure with First Maccabees would have been the same, so that we can expect to find but few traces of Josephus' consultation of the Hebrew.

Whatever the case with Josephus, there can be little doubt that copies of the original Hebrew still existed in the times of Origen (ca. 184 or 185

Perhaps the old tradition at *M. Sanhedrin* 9:6 should be read in this connection: "If one curses through a *qōsēm* . . . zealots smite him to death." On the likelihood that the tradition dates from the time of Mattathias, see Ben-Zion Lurie, *Megillath Ta'anith* (Jerusalem: Bialik Institute, 1964), pp. 20–24 (in Hebrew). Though the Talmuds interpret the passage differently, one would expect *qōsēm* to mean what it does in the Bible, where it is applied to Balaam (Josh 13:22; cf. *qᵉsāmīm* at Num 22:7). Balaam, as a *qōsēm*, was thought to be able to bring disaster upon the Israelites by cursing them, presumably through the power of the name of the LORD. If so, Mattathias and his followers would even outlaw Pietists who sought to "resist" through the power of the divine name.

[16] See NOTE on I 1:29–40; Harry W. Ettelson, "The Integrity of I Maccabees," TCAAS, 27 (1925), 307–14; Paul Joüon, "Quelques hébraïsmes de syntaxe dans le premier livre des Maccabées," *Biblica* 3 (1922), 204–6.

[17] See Elias Bickerman, *Four Strange Books of the Bible* (New York: Schocken, 1967), pp. 218–19.

[18] Josephus paraphrased First Maccabees: see Grimm, pp. xxvii–xxx. Probable use of Hebrew: see NOTES on I 3:15, 34, and esp. on 5:4–5.

[19] See H. St. John Thackeray, *Josephus: the Man and the Historian* (New York: Jewish Institute of Religion Press, 1929), pp. 81–99, 102–20.

to 253 or 254 c.e.) and Jerome (ca. 345 to 419–20). In his commentary on Psalm 1 Origen gave a list of the scriptural books used by the Jews,[20] probably deriving his information from his Jewish neighbors in Caesarea. He writes that the number of the scriptural books handed down among the "Hebrews" is twenty-two, "equal to the number of the letters of their alphabet. According to the Hebrews, the twenty-two books are as follows: the book which with us bears the title 'Genesis' among the Hebrews bears the title '*Brêsith,*' from the opening word of the book, which means 'In the beginning.'" Origen's list continues, giving for each book the Greek title used by Christians and the Hebrew title used by Jews. The passage, with its verbs in the present tense, clearly refers to books existing in Origen's time[21] among Jews who use the Hebrew alphabet and give the books Hebrew titles. The Greek titles had no heterodox connotations for Jews, for those, too, were of Jewish origin. The reason for using Hebrew titles could be only the use of Hebrew books. Hence, when Origen adds at the end of his list of the books of the Hebrew Bible that "Outside these there is the Maccabaean History, which bears the title '*Sarbêthsabanaiel,*'" he must be referring to a Hebrew or Aramaic book he found in the possession of Jews. Origen and his Christian predecessors spoke of only two works called "Maccabaean History" and only one of these, First Maccabees, existed in an early Hebrew or Aramaic version so as to be even remotely associated with scripture by Jews of Origen's time.[22]

Jerome, in his "Helmeted Preface" to the books of Samuel and Kings, probably took Origen's remarks as his model, but the departures from Origen show that Jerome made his own observations.[23] Like Origen, Jerome begins by mentioning the twenty-two letters of the Hebrew alphabet and then lists the twenty-two books recognized by the Jews as

[20] Preserved *apud* Eusebius *Historia ecclesiastica* vi 25.1–2.

[21] Contrast the aorist and perfect participles in Origen's discussion of the origins of the Gospels *apud* Eusebius *Historia ecclesiastica* vi 25.4–6. On the parallels to Origen's statement, at Jubilees ii 23 and at Epiphanius *De mensuris et ponderibus* 4 and elsewhere, see J. T. Milik, "Recherches sur la version grecque du livre des Jubilés," RB 78 (1971), 549–50.

[22] On *Yosippon,* a medieval historical compilation in Hebrew which draws on I, II, and Josephus, see Baron, VI (1958), 188–95, 417–20. The Syriac version of II depends on the recension of the Greek Bible made by Lucian, who died in 311, and hence is later than Origen. See Werner Kappler, *De memoria alterius libri Maccabaeorum,* Diss. Academia Georgia Augusta (Göttingen: Dieterich, 1929), pp. 15–16. Moreover, as we shall see (pp. 25–29), the Hebrew or Aramaic title given by Origen does not fit II.

[23] *Prologus galeatus,* vol. XXVIII, cols. 593–604 Migne. Origen gives *Ammesphekôdeim* as the Hebrew name of Numbers; Jerome gives *Vaiedabber.* Origen gives no collective Hebrew name for the Pentateuch; Jerome gives *Thorath.* Origen gives *Ouammelchdauid* as the title of III–IV Kings [I–II KingsH] and renders it as "David's Kingdom." Jerome gives *Malachim* and may be correcting Origen when he say that the proper title is "Kings" and not "Kingdoms." Comparison of the two texts reveals several other such examples.

scripture along with the Hebrew titles used by them (in the case of the book of the Twelve Prophets, an Aramaic title, *Thare Asra*). Thereupon, Jerome speaks of the books of the list as "all the books we have translated," and goes on to mention the Apocrypha, saying, "Therefore, Wisdom, popularly titled the Wisdom of Solomon, and the book of Jesus ben Sira and Judith and Tobit and the Shepherd are not in the canon. I have found the First Book of Maccabees in Hebrew; the Second is a Greek book as can also be proved from considerations of style alone."[24]

From the context, Jerome's meaning is clear:

1) The Apocrypha do not belong to the twenty-two books translated by Jerome from the Hebrew.

2) Jerome had seen no Hebrew text of the book of Ben Sira or of Tobit or of Judith, though we now know such texts existed before his time.[25]

3) Jerome had seen a Hebrew text of First Maccabees. In this context, which contrasts First Maccabees with Ben Sira, Tobit, and Judith, "I have found . . . in Hebrew" (*Hebraicum reperi*) cannot mean "[Though I have seen no Hebrew copy,] I have concluded that First Maccabees was originally in Hebrew," for then he could as easily have said the same of Ben Sira, Tobit, and Judith.

The Hebrew or Aramaic title given by Origen has long been a puzzle giving rise to farfetched hypotheses. Robert Estienne, who published in 1544 the first edition of Eusebius' *Historia ecclesiastica,* must have had great Hebrew learning, or access to it. The reading *sarbêth sarbane el* of Origen's title in Estienne's edition probably is his own emendation of the manuscript reading *sarbêthsabanaiel.*[26] If so, he came close to guessing the probable solution. In the nineteenth century Abraham Geiger and Senior Sachs both perceived the essential key to the problem.[27] As Estienne may have guessed, the reading of the manuscripts of Eusebius is slightly corrupt. The probable original title was *sphar bêth sabanai el* (in Hebrew or Aramaic consonants, *spr byt srbny 'l*), "Book of the dynasty of God's resisters."[28]

[24] "Igitur Sapientia, quae vulgo Salomonis inscribitur et Jesu filii Sirach liber et Judith et Tobias et Pastor non sunt in Canone. Machabaeorum primum librum Hebraicum reperi; secundus Graecus est, quod ex ipsa quoque *phrasei* probari potest."

[25] Otto Eissfeldt, *The Old Testament: an Introduction* (New York and Evanston: Harper & Row, 1965), pp. 585, 587, 597–99; Sirach *Prologue.*

[26] In the same passage Estienne "corrects" the manuscript readings on the basis of the Masoretic vocalization which was unknown to Origen; e.g. *sepher* and *Ieezkêl* replace the manuscript readings *sphar* and *Iezekiêl.*

[27] Geiger, *Urschrift,* pp. 204–5; S. Sachs, "Le titre du livre des Macchabées," REJ 26 (1893), 161–66.

[28] *"Sphar"* is the Syriac and biblical Aramaic vocalization of *spr* and appears in Origen's list in the Hebrew title of Psalms (*Spharthelleim*). *"Sabanai"* for *"sarbanaï"* is probably a case of phonetic spelling. Origen's informants in Caesarea may well have left *r* unpronounced when it closed a syllable, as did the scribes of Qumran and

In translating this title one must take care to reflect its ambiguity. "God's resisters" can mean either "resisters on behalf of God's chosen cause" or "those who resist God."[29] We shall find that many pious Jews regarded Mattathias as an arch-sinner for his audacious interpretations of the Torah and held his sons to be heinous sinners, too.[30] The title in Origen could have been given the book by enemies of the Hasmonaeans.

Let us trace what can be known of the history of the epithets used to refer to the members of this always controversial dynasty. In First Maccabees there is no special name for the dynasty unless one so takes the tendentious description at 5:62, "the stock to whom it was granted to work the salvation of Israel." The author carefully traces their ancestry to the priestly clan or "course" of Yehoyarib (2:1), as does the official dynastic document he quotes (14:29). The Hasmonaeans may have been pleased to do so because of the prestige of the clan (I Chron 24:7; J. *Vita* 11) and because of the meaning of the name, "the LORD contends [on behalf of the name-bearer]."[31]

Conspicuous by its absence from First Maccabees is the name "Hashmonay." In Josephus and rabbinic sources, the descendants of Matta-

---

Babylonian Jews. Qumran manuscripts frequently omit resh altogether in such cases or have it as a suspended letter; e.g. 1QIs^a 19:6, 23:6, 29:16, 36:2, 39:8, 53:8, 63:8; 11QPs^a 27:9; 1QM 5:3–4, 6:5 and 9, 14:10. See E. Y. Kutscher, *The Language and Linguistic Background of the Isaiah Scroll* (Leiden: Brill, 1974), p. 531. On Babylonian Jewish Aramaic, see J. N. Epstein, *A Grammar of Babylonian Aramaic* (Jerusalem: Magnes Press, 1960), p. 19 (in Hebrew). It is also possible that a learned but uncomprehending scribe omitted the rho and connected the mysterious word with the name Sabannaious at I Esd 9:33 or with Sabanei at II Esd 20:4 (Neh 10:5) or with Sabania at II Esd 20:10 (Neh 10:11).

Abel, p. v, objects that Hebrew '*l* should be represented in Greek by *êl*, not by *el*, for that is the usual practice with theophoric names ending in -*el*. Manuscript *M* of Eusebius does read *basanaiêl*, but the metathesis of consonants does not inspire confidence in the quantity of the last vowel. Hebrew '*l* is rendered in Greek by *el* when unstressed, and similar words have epsilon even when stressed; see A. Sperber, *Historical Grammar of Biblical Hebrew* (Leiden: Brill, 1966), p. 193. In Origen's time -*êl* was pronounced like the English word "eel," and Origen may have used the spelling -*el* to reflect more accurately the pronunciation of his informants. For Hebrew forms like *sphar*, see GKC, § 93*g* (pp. 263, 266).

[29] The root *srb* often has pejorative connotations. See Ezek 2:6; Targum to Ps 78:8; Deut 1:26; and I Sam 15:23.

[30] Part IV, pp. 95, 118.

[31] It is just possible that 2:67 plays upon the meaning of the name, for the Greek *ekdikein* renders the Hebrew root *ryb* at Judg 6:31. However, at 2:67 the verb occurs with the noun *ekdikēsis* as a cognate accusative, and the noun in the Greek Bible never renders a derivative of the Hebrew root *ryb*, so that the Hebrew original of 2:67 probably had the Hebrew root *nqm*.

Scholars have held that Hasmonaean interpolations are responsible for the importance of the clan of Yehoyarib in Chronicles, Ezra, and Nehemiah. Even if those scholars are right, by our author's time (see Part IV), the interpolations were scripture. For a defense of the biblical texts exalting the clan of Yehoyarib, see Jacob Liver, *Chapters in the History of the Priests and Levites* (Jerusalem: Magnes Press, 1968), pp. 33–52, and J. M. Grintz, "From Zerubbabel to Nehemiah," *Zion* 37 (1972), 155–56 (both in Hebrew).

thias are called the "descendants" or "house" of Ḥashmonay,[32] and from
the name we get our adjective "Hasmonaean." The meaning of the name
is unknown. However, the way it is used in Josephus and in early and
correct rabbinic texts, some of which are probably earlier than Josephus,[33] implies that it was Mattathias' additional name as "Macca-

[32] Absence: cf. B. Niese, "Kritik der beiden Makkabäerbücher," *Hermes* 35
(1900), 457–58. Josephus: *BJ* i *Prooem.* 6.19; *AJ* xi 4.8.111; xx 8.11.190, 10.3.238;
Vita 1 4; cf. *AJ* xiv 16.4.490–91, etc. Rabbinic sources: *M. Middot* 1:6; *Seder
'Olam Rabbah* 30, p. 142 Ratner; TB *Shabbat* 21b, *Megillah* 11a; *Menaḥot* 28b;
Soṭah 49b and parallels; *Bereshit Rabbah* 99:2; *Soferim* 20:8; *Midrash Tehillim* to
Ps 30:3 and to Psalm 93 beginning; Targum to I Sam 2:4 and to Song of Songs
6:7; and the prayer *'Al hannissim*. For the correct reading at TB *Megillah* 11a, see
Gedaliahu Alon, *Studies in Jewish History*, 2 vols. (Tel-Aviv: Hakibutz Hameuchad,
1957–58), I, 24 (in Hebrew). For a translation of *'Al hannissim*, see below, n. 33.

[33] The prayer *'Al hannissim* was probably composed in the reign of John Hyrcanus
(134–104 B.C.E.) as I shall argue in a future article. The earliest extant texts of the
prayer are medieval.

Grammatically, *'Al hannissim* is not a complete sentence. It was written as a part
of a sentence of the Prayer of Thanksgiving (*Hoda'ah*). I give here a translation of
the version of the Prayer of Thanksgiving and of *'Al hannissim* in *Maḥzor Vitry*,
ed. S. Hurwitz (Berlin: M'kize Nirdamim, 1889), pp. 67–68. *Maḥzor Vitry* was written before 1105, though the manuscripts of it contain many later additions. In the
translation below, *'Al hannissim* appears after "hopes in you," as in all extant versions. However, as the passage stands, the syntax is obscure. Does *'Al hannissim*
give the reason for the "hopes" which precede it? Or is it connected to "all these" in
the sentence which follows it, giving reasons why God's name will forever be
exalted? To preserve the ambiguity, I have (ungrammatically) printed *'Al hannissim*
as a separate paragraph. One may guess that *'Al hannissim* was originally written to
stand after "tell your praise" or "noon," as part of an enumeration of present and
past miracles.

Translation

We give thanks to You, for You are the LORD our God and the God of our fathers; You are the firm foundation [literally, "rock"] of our lives, our protecting
shield. Throughout all generations we shall give thanks to You and tell Your
praise, because of our lives which are given into Your hands, because of our souls
which are entrusted to You, because of Your miracles which are daily with us, and
because of Your wondrous and beneficent acts which come every day and at every
hour, evening, morning, and noon. O beneficent One—Your mercies have never
ended. O merciful One—Your lovingkindnesses have never ceased. Indeed, we have
always put our hopes in You.

Because of the miracles and because of the deliverance and because of the mighty
deeds and because of the victories and because of the wars, redemption, and deliverance which You wrought for our fathers in days of yore at this season in the
days of Mattathias, son of Yoḥanan, great priest, Ḥashmonay, and his sons, when
the wicked Hellenistic empire rose against them, against Your people Israel, to make
them forget Your Torah and to make them violate the statutes willed by You, and
You in Your abundant mercy stood by them in their time of trouble, pleaded their
cause, judged their suit, and wreaked their vengeance: You delivered the mighty into
the hands of the weak, the many into the hands of the few, the unclean into the
hands of the pure, the wicked into the hands of the righteous, and the arrogant into
the hands of those who were devoted to Your Torah; for Yourself You won renown
in Your world for greatness and holiness, and for Your people Israel You won a
great victory and deliverance to this very day; thereafter, Your children came to the
inner shrine of Your temple and cleansed Your nave and purified Your sanctuary
and kindled lights in Your holy courts and established these eight days of Hanukkah

baeus" was Judas'.[34] Our pattern of given name(s) plus surname did not exist among the ancient Jews, who bore only a given name. The names of Mattathias and his sons were extremely common in Jewish priestly families. Where many persons in a society bear the same name, there must be some way to distinguish one from another. Often the way is to add to the overcommon given name other names or epithets. These additional appellations may describe the person or his feats or his ancestry or his place of origin; they may even be taunt-epithets. Members of Roman aristocratic families had both a given name (*praenomen*) and a surname (*nomen*), but there were so few given names in use that the Romans early resorted to the use of such an additional name (*cognomen*). Even an uncomplimentary cognomen might become hereditary in a Roman aristocratic family.[35]

Our author readily speaks of his heroes as sons of Mattathias, but he avoids mentioning Mattathias' additional name, though Josephus, proud of his descent from the dynasty, uses the name without hesitation. We can guess that our author avoids "Ḥashmonay" because, unlike Josephus, he knew it had uncomplimentary connotations, or perhaps only because it recalled the obscure origins of the dynasty.[36]

On the other hand, Pietist enemies of the dynasty may have chosen to refer to the descendants of the "arch-sinner" Mattathias by calling them "descendants of Ḥashmonay," especially if the name was derogatory.

---

to give You thanks and praise You for Your many miracles and wondrous acts [I omit the words which follow in *Maḥzor Vitry;* they come from another source, *Soferim* 20:8].

Because of all these Your name shall forever and ever be continually blessed, exalted, and extolled, O our King, and all that live shall give You thanks (*selah*). Blessed are You O LORD, Whose name is good and to Whom it is fitting to render thanks.

[34] See on I 2:1–5. In *'Al hannissim* Mattathias appears as "Mattathias, son of Yoḥanan, . . . priest, Ḥashmonay." The style of Alexander Balas at I 10:1 follows a similar scheme (name, patronymic, epithet), as do the styles of Ptolemies III and V (see Friedrich Preisigke, *Wörterbuch der griechischen Papyrusurkunden* [Berlin: Selbstverlag der Erben, 1925–31], III, 34, 36). Still closer is the scheme of the official name of a Roman citizen: praenomen-and-nomen, patronymic, tribe, and cognomen. Josephus nowhere states that "Ḥashmonay" was Mattathias' additional name and may have been ignorant of the fact. On the other hand, he may well be correct in stating that Mattathias' grandfather Simeon (or, less likely, his great-grandfather) bore the name; see *AJ* xii 6.1.265. Giving the grandson the name of the grandfather was common. Josephus erred in naming Mattathias' father as Ḥashmonay at *BJ* i 1.3.36, and at *AJ* xii 6.1.265 corrected his error. See p. 60. On the other hand, the Byzantine writer Georgius Syncellus correctly states that *Asamônaios* was Mattathias' additional name (*Eklogê chronographias*, vol. I, 543 Dindorf).

[35] E.g. Nasica and Naso ("big-nosed"); Dalman and Perles suggested that "Maccabaeus" means "hammer-headed"; see Abel, pp. ii–iii.

[36] There is no evidence to tell us how obscure or how distinguished Mattathias' family was before. If it was obscure, one may compare the example of Augustus, who avoided use of the name "Octavianus" which recalled his relatively obscure origins.

If the members of the dynasty preferred to be called "descendants of Yehoyarib," that name, too, lent itself to derogatory distortions. "Yehoyarib" can mean "the LORD contends [sc. on their behalf]" or "the LORD contends [sc. with those who rebel]."[37]

Such derogatory interpretations were current at the time of Origen and are quoted from Palestinian rabbis at most one generation removed from him (late third to early fourth century C.E.). R. Levi, the older of the two, preserves traditions of families important before the destruction of the temple.[38] The younger, R. Berekhyah, is one of the chief Palestinian transmitters of older material.[39] They are quoted as follows[40]:

> Said R. Levi, "Yehoyarib—the man; Meron—the town; Resisters[41] [Aramaic $m^e sār^e bay$]—He delivered the House over to the enemies [Aramaic $m^e sar\ baytā\ l^e sān'ayya$]." Said R. Berekhyah, "The Lord contended with His children because they rebelled and resisted Him [Heb. $yāh\ hērīb\ 'im\ bānāw\ 'al\ šemārū\ w^e sār^e bū\ bō$]. Yeda'yah, Profound, Sepphoris—the Lord knew [Heb. $yāda'\ yāh$] the profound plot in their heart and exiled them to Sepphoris."

Geiger and Sachs were correct in seeing in this passage the key to the title in Origen, but they could not know the nature of the text on which R. Levi and R. Berekhyah made their punning interpretations.

The two rabbis were interpreting the words of the list of the twenty-four priestly courses set up on stone in Palestinian synagogues after the destruction of the Jewish settlements in Jerusalem and most of Judaea in the 130s as a result of Hadrian's suppression of the second Jewish revolt. The purpose of the list was to preserve the identity of the priestly clans in hopes that the temple cult would be restored. On the list as restored from fragments on stone and from allusions in early medieval poetry ap-

---

[37] $yryb$ means "enemy" at Isa 49:25; Jer 18:19; Hosea 10:6; Ps 35:1.

[38] TP Ta'anit 4:2, p. 68a.

[39] See W. Bacher, *Die Agada der Palästinensischen Amoräer* (Hildesheim: Olms, 1965), III, 348–50.

[40] TP Ta'anit 4:5, p. 68d.

[41] The consonantal text is *msrbyy*. The doubled *y* is anomalous; cf. E. Y. Kutscher, "Studies in Galilean Aramaic," *Tarbiz* 22 (5711=1950–51), 185–90 (in Hebrew). Nevertheless, it is confirmed by the rhyme -*bay* in an early liturgical poem; see Ezra Fleischer, *"Piyyuṭ leyannay ḥazzan 'al mishmarot ha-kohanim,"* Sinai 64 (5729= 1968–69), 184. In a letter of September 2, 1970, E. Y. Kutscher suggested to me that the spelling of the name in the Palestinian Talmud and in the poems based on it is distorted to fit R. Levi's pun, for in Galilean Aramaic, as in the Christian Aramaic of Palestine and in the Elephantine papyri, the absolute state of the word for "house" is *bay*, even though the emphatic state is *bayta*. See Kutscher, "The Hermopolis Papyri," IOS 1 (1971), 116, and n. 45. If his suggestion is correct, the original epithet may have been the normal plural emphatic state, *msrby'*, "the resisters," or even *srbny'*. Unfortunately, not one of the fragments on stone (below, n. 42) preserves the name. In any case, *srnby'* and *msrby'* are synonyms derived from the same root.

pears the number of the course in the sequence of duty at the temple; its name; its nickname, if any; and its place of residence after the Hadrianic persecutions; e.g. "First course: Yehoyarib, Resisters, Meron." Origen probably could have seen such a list in a synagogue of his own city of Caesarea, for fragments of one dating to the third or fourth century have been found there near the ruins of a synagogue.[42]

R. Berekhyah gave an inauspicious meaning to "Yehoyarib." Both rabbis gave inauspicious interpretations to the nickname. It is hard to believe that the nickname was not originally a hostile distortion,[43] though, as often happens,[44] partisans of the Hasmonaean dynasty may have eventually accepted the appellation $m^e s \bar{a} r^e b a y$ or $s a r b \bar{a} n \bar{e} y$ $\bar{e} l$, interpreting it as "resisters on behalf of God." Since the Maccabaean pattern of resistance had proved disastrous in the Jewish revolts against Rome, it is not surprising that among Origen's Jewish informants the book glorifying the dynasty bore the mocking title given it by anti-Hasmonaeans: "Book of the Dynasty of God's Resisters."[45]

In contrast to the highly emotional narrative in Second Maccabees, the author of First Maccabees presents a relatively sober narrative after the pattern of the historical books of the Hebrew Bible, especially the books of Samuel. As we shall see, our author is no more objective and impartial than were his models. Like them, he is an ardent partisan. His work, indeed, is full of emotional outbursts, though, as in Samuel, such outbursts occur as poetic insertions which interrupt the flow of the narrative. Two of these insertions, like the poems of Hannah and David in Samuel, are ascribed to a major character: the lament and the farewell address of Mattathias. The rest are not ascribed to anyone. Some may be poems contemporary with the events; others may be compositions of our author. In most cases the reader has no way of knowing which alternative is correct.[46]

Again following the model of the biblical histories of the kingdoms of Israel and Judah, the author took care to give his narrative a chronological framework. The official dating system in the territories under Seleucid

---

[42] Some of the "nicknames" are derived from the names of families within the courses. See Liver, *Chapters*, p. 47. Inscription: M. Avi-Yonah, "The Caesarea Inscription of the 24 Priestly Courses," EI 7 (1964), 24–28 (in Hebrew), with bibliography of the relevant literature.

[43] "Yehoyarib" could be twisted to give a bad meaning only by an enemy. The root *srb*, however, added only one consonant to the root of "Yehoyarib" and had generally bad connotations.

[44] "Tory" and "Whig" originated as derogatory nicknames given by opponents.

[45] On hostility to the clan of Yehoyarib in rabbinic tradition, see Geiger, *Urschrift*, pp. 204–5; Saul Lieberman, *Tosefta Ki-Fshuṭah* (New York: Jewish Theological Seminary of America 5717=1954–55), part v (*Mo'ed*), pp. 1076–77, 1115 (in Hebrew), and compare the lot of Menelaus' clan of Bilgah, Lieberman, part IV (*Mo'ed*), pp. 908–10 (in Hebrew).

[46] See Part V, n. 34, example 5.

rule was the Seleucid era, which numbered the years from the capture of
Babylon by Seleucus I in August 312 B.C.E. It continued in use long after
the fall of the empire. To understand First Maccabees we must study
carefully the nature of the author's chronology, especially since such
study reveals important facts about the author's sources.

The Seleucid era originated as the numbering of the satrapal years of
Seleucus, the satrap who was to become King Seleucus I. He counted
them from the beginning of the first calendar year after his conquest of
Babylon. At that time Seleucus was legally a subject of the figurehead
king Alexander IV, posthumous son and heir of Alexander the Great.
Alexander IV's regnal years were counted from late summer or early
autumn. Hence, for Seleucus the calendar year began in late summer or
early autumn, and his first satrapal year began by early autumn, 312
B.C.E. For our purposes, we may set the beginning of the Seleucid year at
1 Dios, the first day of the first month of the Macedonian calendar,
which fell in late summer or early autumn. Indeed, from the time of
Seleucus I, Macedonian Dios was equated with Tashritu of the Babylonian calendar, the month in which the autumnal equinox fell, and so
on with the rest of the months of the Macedonian year. In most respects,
for the Seleucids, the Macedonian calendar became identical with the
Babylonian calendar, with its year of twelve lunar months and its addition of an intercalary thirteenth month seven times every nineteen years.
However, the Babylonians and many other peoples subject to the Seleucids refused to have their calendar years begin in the autumn. At Babylon the calendar year began with 1 Nisanu, the month of the vernal
equinox. The Babylonians reckoned the first year of the Seleucid era from
spring 311 B.C.E. Thus, the beginning of the Seleucid year could vary
according to the local calendar. The era which counted the years from
Dios (ca. September–October), 312 B.C.E., we may call the Macedonian
Seleucid era ("Sel. Mac."); the era which counted from Nisan (ca.
March–April), 311 B.C.E., we may call the Babylonian Seleucid era
("Sel. Bab.").[47]

---

[47] See E. J. Bickerman, *Chronology of the Ancient World* (Cornell University
Press, 1968), pp. 22–26, 71; Schürer, I, 33, n. 1; Jeanne and Louis Robert, "Bulletin
épigraphique," REG 65 (1952), 183 (inscriptions listing the Macedonian months in
order). Strange as it may now seem, the beginning of the numbered year did not
have to fall on the first day of the first month. Until 1752 the beginning of the legal
year in Britain fell not on January 1 but on March 25. Surviving ancient legal documents allow us to deduce that the beginning of the Seleucid year fell between 1 Loos
and 30 Dios on the Macedonian calendar (Bickerman, *Chronology,* p. 71). The
statement at *M. Rosh ha-shanah* 1:1, that the (calendar) year begins 1 Tishri
(=1 Dios), in all probability means that the Macedonian Seleucid year began on
that date.

To convert Sel. Mac. dates to years B.C.E., subtract the number of the year from
313 if the date falls within or after the first lunar month after the autumnal equinox
and before January 1; otherwise, subtract it from 312. To convert Sel. Bab. dates to
years B.C.E., subtract the number of the year from 312 if the date falls within or after

Our author himself identifies the system of his year-dates as the Seleucid era[48]; his months bear the names of the Babylonian lunar months. Indeed, we know that during the Babylonian exile the Jews adopted the Babylonian calendar and, with slight phonetic modifications, the Babylonian month-names. However, whereas the Babylonians came to have a regular cycle of adding an intercalary month to the lunar year seven times every nineteen years, we have no information as to how the Jews in the time of our author kept their local version of the Babylonian lunar calendar in step with the solar year as required by the agricultural nature of the Jewish festivals. Several vexatious problems for understanding the events and propaganda of the period become easy to solve if we assume that there was no regular cycle of intercalation and that for all known Jewish groups except the Essenes, the high priest and the Council of Elders proclaimed intercalations when observation or calculation showed them to be necessary. Such a system would never be much out of step with the Seleucid and Babylonian calendars; indeed, no ancient author mentions any discrepancy. In particular, it is safe to assume that our author's calendar was based on a year of twelve lunar months with some kind of intercalation.[49]

In numbering the years, what form of the Seleucid era did our author use? The Jews in Judaea recognized several types of calendar year, each with its own beginning, as can be deduced for the period of the Hebrew Bible from the passages where authors felt it necessary to give both the name and the ordinal number of the month.[50] For a later period, the Mishnah states,[51] "1 Nisan is the new year's day for the [regnal years of] kings. . . . 1 Tishri is the new year's day for [calendar] years."

Even if we could be sure that the Mishnah still represents the practice of the time of our author, for us the Mishnah is ambiguous: Is the year of the Seleucid era a "regnal" year or a "calendar" year? Moreover, assuming that the Jews treated the year of the Seleucid era as a regnal year and had it begin in Nisan, we must still reckon with the possibility that unlike the Babylonians they numbered the years from Nisan, 312, rather than from Nisan, 311, even though they would then be numbering from a date before Seleucus conquered Babylon. This possibility can be ex-

---

the first lunar month after the vernal equinox and before January 1; otherwise, subtract it from 311.

Tables for converting dates on the Babylonian calendar to dates on the Julian calendar: Richard A. Parker and Waldo H. Dubberstein, *Babylonian Chronology*, Brown University Press, 1956.

[48] See I 1:10 and NOTES ad loc. and on I 1:1, *Alexander . . . Chetiim.*

[49] See Bickerman, *Chronology*, pp. 24–26. Hence, the Hasmonaeans and our author did not accept the calendar based on the 364-day solar year which was peculiar to the books of Enoch and Jubilees and to the Essenes of Qumran. The authors of Enoch and Jubilees and of the Qumran texts designate months only by ordinal number, never by a Babylonian name.

[50] I Kings 6:1; Zech 1:7; Esther 2:16 and throughout Esther.

[51] *Rosh ha-shanah* 1:1.

cluded. Elias Bickerman has shown that in official documents Jews in Judaea, like the Babylonians, numbered the years of the Seleucid era from Nisan, 311.[52] Our author surely was a Jew writing in Judaea. The use of two forms of an era is understandable as an accommodation to different customs as to the calendar date of new year's day, but it is hard to understand how two forms of an era could have been used in Judaea if in both forms the year began on the same calendar date.

To decide among the remaining possibilities, we must examine the Seleucid dates given in First Maccabees in the light of information from other sources. Unfortunately, our information is inadequate to provide certainty. Another fact further complicates the problem. We shall see later that our author wrote long after the events and could and probably did make chronological mistakes. Thus, if a hypothetical reconstruction of our author's dating system should result in his giving an erroneous date for an event, that reconstruction is not necessarily wrong. But if our author could make a mistake at any and every point, the number of possible hypotheses becomes unmanageable. How, then, can one come near solving the problem? One can do so only by considering probabilities, by preferring that hypothesis which can best accommodate the available data and which presents the obviously intelligent author of First Maccabees as behaving intelligently: any errors of his should be easily explainable.[53]

Elias Bickerman produced such a hypothesis, and subsequent discoveries have confirmed his conclusions. In the present work we bring evidence to show that if the date in First Maccabees for the eastward march of Antiochus IV (3:37) is 147 Sel. Mac., the date for the Feast of Dedication (4:52) must be 25 Kislev, 148 Sel. Bab. Bickerman demonstrated that in First Maccabees all dates for events of royal Seleucid history, including accessions and deaths of kings and campaigns not involving Judaea, fit the available data, provided we assume that those dates are according to the Seleucid era which numbered the year from Dios, 312 B.C.E. At least two of our author's dates for events of royal Seleucid history (at 6:16 and at 7:1) are correct only on that basis. Bickerman also showed that almost all dates in First Maccabees for events of local Jewish history fit the available information, provided we assume that those dates are according to the Seleucid era which numbered the years from Nisan, 311. The date at 10:21 can otherwise hardly be correct. Finally, Bickerman argued that the date at I 6:20 was erroneous, the result of an explainable miscalculation by our author.[54]

[52] "Ein jüdischer Festbrief vom Jahre 124 v. Chr.," ZNW 32 (1933), 239–41.

[53] The chronological system proposed by Robert Hanhart fails to meet these criteria. See below, n. 54. On the date of First Maccabees, see Part IV. On errors of our author, see below, n. 55.

[54] Bickerman wrote his fundamental studies, "Makkabäerbücher," PW, XIV (1930), 781–84, and Der Gott der Makkabäer (abbr. Gott), pp. 154–57, before important documents and corrected readings became available. Hence, see now J.

It may seem strange that our author could use dates on two different bases. Stranger still, our author appears to have been led into error by the inconsistency of his two sets of dates, as if he himself was unaware of the difference between them. Bickerman[55] saw the solution: similar inconsistencies are found in many ancient writers of history, when they draw on two sources which use different systems of chronology. Our author would thus be shown to have drawn on at least two sources, on a non-Jewish work dealing with Seleucid history which dated according to the Macedonian Seleucid era, and on Jewish records or traditions which dated according to the Babylonian Seleucid era.

On the other hand, First Maccabees was written as a unitary work. The efforts of scholars to prove that the work is of composite authorship can

---

Schaumberger, "Die neue Seleukiden-Liste BM 35603 und die makkabäische Chronologie," *Biblica* 36 (1955), 423–27, but beware of Schaumberger's unsound discussion beginning with the last paragraph on p. 427 and extending through p. 435. For advances beyond Bickerman and Schaumberger, see Appendices I and II. On the dates at I 3:37 and 4:52, see Appendix I.

Bickerman's hypothesis requires setting autumn, 164, to autumn, 163, as a sabbatical year. On the problems involved, see Appendix I and NOTE on I 6:20.

In the present state of the evidence, the ultimate test of Bickerman's hypothesis is the chronological coherence of my interpretations of First and Second Maccabees and Daniel. On the basis of those interpretations I have constructed the chronological scheme presented in Part VII. He who wishes to suggest a rival hypothesis will have to show that it leads to more probable interpretations of the evidence of those books.

Much less probable is the hypothesis of Robert Hanhart, in Albert Jepsen and Robert Hanhart, *Untersuchungen zur israelitisch-jüdischen Chronologie*, BZAW 88 (1964). Hanhart (pp. 57–59) takes as the cornerstone of his chronological system the correctness of the dates at both I 6:20 and II 13:1, even though he himself admits there are inaccuracies in both First (pp. 79–84) and Second (pp. 71–90) Maccabees. His system results in requiring dates in the abridged history in Second Maccabees to be reckoned as Sel. Bab., in defiance of the evidence at II 14:4 (see Appendix II).

Instead of seeing a distinction between Seleucid dynastic dates and local Jewish dates, Hanhart (pp. 56–57) sees a distinction between "secular dates" and "dates of church history." The fact that a Seleucid era is used for both sets of dates may be enough to render such a distinction absurd, and there is nothing to show that such a distinction was even conceivable at our author's time. Hanhart (p. 82) emerges with a general rule very close to ours: "secular dates" in First Maccabees are Sel. Mac., and "dates of church history" are Sel. Bab. However, on his own assumptions, Judas' siege of the Akra is a "secular" event (pp. 67–68), whereas Judas' victory over Nicanor must be an event of "church history" (p. 69)!

Hanhart also believes (pp. 71 and 82, n. 41) that our author could have consciously and deliberately dated events by two forms of the Seleucid era. The hypothesis is improbable in itself and is all the more unlikely because we can show that our author was probably misled several times by the inconsistency of his two sets of dates; see below, n. 55. Hanhart's hypothesis requires dating the sieges of Beth-Zur (I 6:31–49) and of Mount Zion (6:48–61) in 163/2 B.C.E. However, he also accepts our dating of the sabbatical year in 164/3 and is forced to interpret away, implausibly, the evidence at I 6:48 and 53, that the defenders lacked supplies because it was the sabbatical year; see *Untersuchungen*, pp. 67–68.

[55] Our author led into error: see Part V, p. 101, Appendix I, and NOTES on I 6:20, 7:43, and introductory NOTE to I 14. Similar inconsistencies in ancient writers: Bickermann, *Gott*, p. 156.

be refuted. Very early in the history of the transmission of the text, however, and perhaps in the original publication of the Hebrew, one segment of the text (I 15:15–24) was displaced from its original position after 14:24, probably when sheets were fastened together in the wrong order into a scroll.[56]

Scholars have rightly been impressed with the accuracy of First Maccabees, though there are several demonstrable errors in the narrative.[57] The author is generally well informed on Seleucid institutions. He probably intended to add his work to the sacred scriptures of the Jews. However, it was destined to be rejected. The later history of the Hasmonaean dynasty proved false our author's claim that God had chosen Mattathias' line to be both high priests and kings. Belief in the resurrection, denied by our author, became a fundamental of Judaism. Already Josephus was emending the text of First Maccabees and departing from its narrative as he would never have done with sacred scripture. In the times of Origen and Jerome, when the original Hebrew was still being read by Jews, First Maccabees was clearly outside the canon of the Jewish scriptures. The book is never mentioned or quoted by the *tannaim* and *amoraim*. Medieval Jews begin to know its contents from the Latin and Greek versions and from Josephus.

The Church Fathers were inspired by the tales of the courage of the defenders of the faith. The pietistic teachings of Second Maccabees probably led them to expect similar views from our author, so that they failed to perceive his drastic but tacit denial of the resurrection. Hence, though Jews ceased to preserve First Maccabees, the Church treasured the Greek version and from it made others in Latin, Syriac, and Armenian.[58]

---

[56] Composite authorship refuted: Ettelson, TCAAS 27 (1925), 255–380, and below, Part III, n. 8. See also G. O. Neuhaus, "Quellen im 1. Makkabäerbuch," *Journal for the Study of Judaism* 5 (1974), 162–75.

Scroll assembled in wrong order: see introductory NOTE to I 14:16–24.

[57] Errors: see NOTES on 5:6, 6:20, 55–56; on Seleucid institutions: see Hermann Bengtson, *Die Strategie in der hellenistischen Zeit*, 3 vols. (München: C. H. Beck, 1937–52), III, 283 (index of references to First Maccabees); Élie Bikerman, *Institutions des Séleucides* (abbr. *Institutions*), p. 1 and *passim*. [Bickerman spells his name differently when he writes in different languages: in German, Bickermann; in French, Bikerman; in English, Bickerman. The English spelling—Bickerman—is used throughout *except* in citations of his German or French works.]

[58] Josephus' emendations: see Appendix V. Josephus' departures: see e.g. NOTE on 13:39–40. Cf. J. *Ap.* i 8.41. Pietistic teachings of Second Maccabees: pp. 28–33.

A very early medieval Jewish composition drawing on First Maccabees is *Megillat Antiokhus=Sefer Beney Hashmonay*. See the edition of M. Z. Kaddari, *Bar-Ilan*, I (1963), 81–105. On the basis of the Aramaic, Kaddari would date the work within one hundred years after the destruction of the temple (*"Be-eyzoh aramit nikhtebhah Megillat Antiokhus,"* *Leshonenu* 23 [5719=1958], 129–46). Since *Megillat Antiokhus* ends with a description of the practices to be observed on the Feast of Dedication (cf. Esther 9:22), earlier rabbinic authorities would have cited it had it been in existence. The complete silence of the earlier rabbinic sources hence makes so early a date of composition unlikely. Rather, an early medieval author probably used archaic language. The work was known already to Sa'adya Gaon (882–942 C.E.) and

The Second Book of Maccabees

The form of Second Maccabees is strange. The book begins with two letters. The first (II 1:1 to 1:10a . . . "in the 188th year") we shall call Epistle 1 (Ep. 1), and the second (II 1:10b, "The people . . ." to 2:18) we shall call Epistle 2 (Ep. 2). At 2:19 begins a history which the writer in his preface (2:19–32) says is an abridgment of the work of one Jason of Cyrene on Judas Maccabaeus and his brothers, the purification of the "greatest" of temples and the dedication of the altar, and the wars against Antiochus IV Epiphanes and Antiochus V Eupator, and the miraculous divine interventions and glorious victories which then occurred. This history continues until the end of the book at 15:39, where the writer says he has reached the end of his task, "since thereafter the city [Jerusalem] has been in the hands of the Hebrews." The abridger thus implies that the work of Jason of Cyrene extended further, since the task the abridger set himself was to abridge Jason's work. Had he covered Jason's narrative to the end, he would have concluded by writing, "Since Jason ended his work at this point, my work, too, is done." Jason of Cyrene is otherwise unknown to us.

If the two prefixed letters had been omitted, no one would have missed them. Indeed, we shall see that both letters contradict the narrative of the historical work. Let us proceed first to examine the character of the historical work. The narrative should conform to what the abridger says

---

probably also somewhat earlier to the author of the *Halakhot Gedolot* (ninth century). See Abraham J. Wertheimer, *Batei Midrashot*, I (Jerusalem: Mosad Harav Cook, 1954), 311–13 (in Hebrew); and Baron, VI (1958), 167–68, 184–85, 189, 407–8, n. 18, 416, n. 44, 484–85, n. 103.

The author of *Megillat Antiokhus* appears to have known passages from First and Second Maccabees and Josephus, either by hearsay or by having a written text before him. In any case, he proceeded eclectically, regarding as most reliable some garbled Jewish traditions, presumably oral. These he supplemented from the other sources. The setting of the scene in *Megillat Antiokhus* vss. 1–3 is obviously influenced by I 1:1–4 and has no parallel in the other sources. Similarly, the assertion in vs. 37[36] that *informers* reported on the Sabbath-observing Pietists in the caves is directly suggested only by I 2:31 (*anêngelê*). Only in vs. 38[37] and at I 2:33 do the soldiers say to the Pietists in the caves, "Come out to us." Only in vs. 49 and at I 3:46 do the forces led by the Hasmonaeans assemble at Mizpah (*Massêpha*). On the other hand, the use of fire against the Pietists in the caves (vs. 40[39]) is found only at J. *AJ* xii 6.2.274 and at II 6':11. That the Pietists retreated to the wilderness caves for the *purpose* of observing the Sabbath (vs. 37[36]) is asserted only at II 5:11. The prominence of Bacchides, called "Bagris" in *Megillat Antiokhus*, need not imply that the author drew on J. *BJ* i 1.2.35. In oral tradition the name of Bacchides, who in fact was a long and formidable opponent of the Hasmonaeans, may have displaced the other names.

Another very popular medieval work which certainly drew on the Latin versions of First and Second Maccabees and Josephus is *Yosefon* or *Josippon*, written in 953. See David Flusser, "*Yōsēfōn*," Encyclopaedia Hebraica, XIX (5728=1967–68), 656–58 (in Hebrew), and Baron, VI, 189–95, 417–21.

References to First and Second Maccabees in the Church Fathers: Abel, pp. viii–xi.

The old Latin version may have been translated from the Greek by Jews. See below, p. 178.

in his preface. Indeed, though we cannot compare the abridgment with
the lost original, all indications are that the abridgment conforms to
the abridger's description.[59] He added nothing; he only abridged and
restyled. Like the original as described in the preface, the abridged work
has as the chief hero Judas Maccabaeus, focuses much attention on the
temple, regards as among the chief villains the persecuting kings Antiochus IV and V, and makes the narrative teem with miracles, in sharp
contrast to the history without miracles given in First Maccabees. Hence,
we may speak of the content of the abridgment as indeed the work of
Jason of Cyrene. Henceforth we shall call II 3 to 15 "the abridged history."

There are other contrasts between Jason's work and First Maccabees.
Jason takes great pains to illustrate the sanctity of the temple, a point
taken for granted in First Maccabees. Though Jason has heroes other
than Judas, Judas' brothers are not among them. Particularly prominent
is the figure of the high priest Onias III, a man passed over in silence in
First Maccabees. The abridged history, indeed, begins (II 3:1–40) with
a bold assertion of all these points of contrast: because of the merit of
the high priest Onias III in enforcing the provisions of the Torah, miraculous divine intervention prevented Heliodorus, the minister of the Seleucid
king Seleucus IV, from seizing for the royal treasury the money deposited
in the temple.

Well might Jason begin at this point, the first miracle attested for the
second temple, a miracle which ushered in a period which passed belief
both in its disasters and in its triumphs. Wickedness among the Jews enters the narrative in the person of Onias' enemy, Simon of the priestly
course Bilgah, administrator of the temple, who spitefully proposes to
the king's officials that the money on deposit can be seized. Where in
First Maccabees we find only a general mention of wicked men as the
instigators of Hellenization in Jerusalem, Jason of Cyrene traces it first to
the removal of the pious Onias III from the holy city. Onias went to
Antioch to appeal to Seleucus IV to curb the machinations of his enemy
Simon (4:1–6).

In the absence of the pious priest from Jerusalem, his wicked brother
Jason (whom we shall call "Jason the Oniad") supplanted him as high
priest by promising increased revenue to the new king, Antiochus IV
(4:7). At the same time, the wicked Jason purchased from the willing
king a new royal policy toward the Jews as well as important privileges
for himself and his impious followers. No longer would royal policy bind
the Jews to observe the commandments of the Torah. Jews could now introduce Greek political and cultural institutions and have the privileges of

[59] See commentary on II 2:19–32.

"Antiochene" citizenship.[60] Jason himself received the important prerogative of drawing up the list of those so privileged and proceeded to bring his fellow Jews over to the Greek way of life (4:7–12).

The result was that priests ignored the temple cult for the newfangled Greek pastimes, and their neglect of God's laws brought down upon them the just punishment that soon followed: the Greeks whom they aped became the instruments of retribution (4:13–17). The sins grew worse. Jason did not shrink from sending offerings to idols (4:18–20). Nevertheless, punishment was not immediate. After attending to dangers from the direction of Ptolemaic Egypt, Antiochus IV even paid a friendly visit to Jerusalem (4:21–22).

Jason's pontificate lasted three years.[61] Thereupon, however, the still more wicked Menelaus, brother of the troublemaker Simon, supplanted the wicked Jason by offering Antiochus still higher revenue. Jason crossed the Jordan into exile in the Ammanitis. However, Menelaus could not raise the promised amount in taxes. In his peril, he stole from the temple to bribe royal officials. Onias III, ready to expose the thievery, took asylum at Daphne. By yet another bribe Menelaus induced a royal official to lure Onias from asylum and slay him. Antiochus IV, still no enemy of the Jews, had the murderer executed. Menelaus and his followers, however, continued to provoke the wrath of the righteous by plundering temple property. Rioting broke out in Jerusalem. The king summoned Menelaus to render account, but Menelaus again purchased safety by bribing an official, so that the Jewish elders protesting his depredations were themselves outrageously put to death (4:23–50). Wickedness of Jews was reaching its full measure.

Dire omens accompanied Antiochus' "second" expedition to Egypt. In the course of the campaign, a false rumor spread that Antiochus was dead, and Jason the Oniad returned from exile in a brutal but abortive attempt to seize power from Menelaus. Though Menelaus was driven to take refuge in the citadel, Jason was forced to withdraw and later came to a deserved miserable end (5:1–10).

Antiochus, however, inferred that the Jews were in revolt and brutally suppressed them as "rebels" and sacked the temple. Indeed, he had become the "rod of God's anger" against the wicked, but he arrogantly believed that God would not punish infractions against His temple after the sinners had been chastised (5:11–21).

The Jews had more punishment to suffer. First, they were harried by the king's officials. Then, a force under Apollonius the Mysarch perpetrated a massacre at the holy city. Judas Maccabaeus and a small group of companions were driven to flee Jerusalem and take refuge in the wil-

[60] On the meaning of "Antiochene" citizenship, see Part VI, pp. 111–25.
[61] See AB vol. 41A, NOTE on II 4:7–38.

derness (5:21–27). There is no trace in the abridged history that Jason
of Cyrene deigned to mention Mattathias.

The worst was yet to come. The king dispatched an Athenian, Geron, to
force the Jews to violate the Torah. Jerusalem's temple was to be called
the temple of Zeus Olympius; the Samaritan temple on Mount Gerizim
was to be called the temple of Zeus Xenius. All Jewish observance was
forbidden, on pain of death. Martyrdoms were many and Jason describes them vividly so as to display the steadfast piety of the victims and
their faith in resurrection and in divine vindication (6:1 – 7:42).

From First Maccabees one can infer that but for the rise of Mattathias
and his sons the deaths of the martyrs would have been in vain.[62] In
contrast, Jason insists that their martyrdom was not in vain. It brought
God to have mercy on His people (II 7:37–38). Again and again Judas
Maccabaeus and his men prayed for divine aid and received it, as could
be seen from their ever growing successes against the enemy. Throughout, Judas and his men scrupulously observed the commandments of the
Torah, especially the commandment to rest on the Sabbath. The families
of the martyrs received a share of the spoils, as if the martyrs had been
partly responsible for the victories. By their success in vanquishing their
wicked enemies, Judas and his men forced even the wicked general
Nicanor to acknowledge God's power to protect His righteous people
(8:1–36).[63]

In First Maccabees between this expedition of Nicanor and the Feast
of Dedication Judas and his men defeat an expedition led by the regent
Lysias; no expedition of Lysias occupies that position in Second Maccabees.[64] Up to this point, the mention of direct divine intervention
against Antiochus IV and his subordinates is as absent from the abridged
history as it is from First Maccabees. Miracles begin to appear in Second
Maccabees with chapters 9 and 10. To complicate matters, in these
chapters there is a severe dislocation in the narrative.[65] In its original
order, the narrative proceeded with the account of how Judas and his
men recovered Jerusalem and the temple, reestablished the sacrificial
cult, celebrated the occasion after the manner of the festival of Tabernacles, and decreed that the eight-day festival in honor of the purification
of the temple be made an annual observance (II 10:1–8).

Thereupon, the narrative turned to describe the miraculous and grue-
some death of Antiochus IV. God himself brought the wicked king to

---

[62] See pp. 4–7.

[63] On the topical notes at II 8:30–33, outside their chronological setting, see commentary.

[64] On the discrepancy, see Part IV, pp. 83–84.

[65] For proof, see commentary introducing II 9. On the cause of the dislocation, see
Appendix IV, end. Compare the dislocation of I 15:15–24; see p. 26, and introductory
NOTE to I 14:16–24k.

perish in tardy repentance near Ecbatana (II 9). The events which occurred under the regime of the child Antiochus V and his chief minister
Lysias follow. After the death of a minister who might have advocated
a just policy toward the Jews, the Jews have to face wars against neighboring peoples stirred against them by hostile Seleucid officials. There is
a miracle, as Judas, helped by supernatural beings, leads his men to
victory, but members of his family, including his brother Simon, are somehow involved in a scandalous failure (10:9–38).

At this point, Jason of Cyrene places a first expedition of the regent
Lysias, which Judas repulses at Beth-Zur. Thus, it is similar to the campaign of Lysias dated before the Feast of Dedication at I 4:28–35.
However, unlike the report in First Maccabees, Judas here wins with the
help of a supernatural cavalier, and his victory is followed by a formal
place between Lysias and Judas. The peace treaty ends the persecution
and restores the temple to the Jews. As evidence for his account, Jason
presents the official correspondence of Lysias, Antiochus V,[66] and two
Roman ambassadors (II 11).

According to Jason, the regime at Antioch was unable to make its officials and the gentile populations adjacent to Judaea observe the peace.
Jews living in gentile areas suffered atrocities. Judas and his men
avenged the dead and saved the living in a series of expeditions during
which they scrupulously observed the Sabbaths and festivals. Whereas
in First Maccabees (I 5:54) the author proudly notes at the close of
Judas' victorious campaign the remarkable fact that not one man in the
Jewish army was killed, Jason calls attention to the providential miracle
in the course of the very next campaign: on the Jewish side only sinners
fell. Jason lays great stress on the fact that Judas saw to it expiatory sacrifices were offered for the fallen sinners; thereby Jason deduces that heroic Judas, too, shared the belief in the resurrection (II 12).

Jason turns to tell of the expedition of Lysias and Antiochus V, which
he dates in 149 Sel. For the first time in the abridged narrative, an absolute date appears, one which contradicts the account in First Maccabees. According to First Maccabees, the siege of the Akra, to which the
expedition was a response, occurred in 150 Sel. Since Judas' siege of the
Akra was a local event in Judaea, the date in First Maccabees must be
on the Babylonian Seleucid era, so the contradiction cannot be resolved
by juggling the two forms of the era. Jason reports that at the outset of
the expedition Menelaus approached the chief minister and the king hop-
ing to be confirmed as high priest, but instead God saw to it that the two
viewed Menelaus as the cause of the troubles and had him executed at
Beroea in a matter entirely befitting his sins (II 13:1–8).

---

[66] The letter at II 11:27–33 was written in the name of Antiochus V, not Antiochus
IV. See NOTE on I 3:32–33.

The boy-king furiously sought to avenge his father's fate upon the Jews, but brave Judas and his brave men inflict a reverse upon the king's army near Modeïn, a site unmentioned at this point in First Maccabees. At first even treason in their own ranks does not break the brave resistance of the Jews at Beth-Zur, but those besieged there finally withdraw under a truce. Nevertheless, Judas defeats the Seleucid forces (no such victory is claimed in First Maccabees), and the king and his chief minister have to give up all thought of pursuing their campaign on receiving news of the revolt of Philip, a trusted minister at Antioch. Here, too, Jason contradicts First Maccabees, for there the enemy at Antioch is the rival guardian for Antiochus V whom Antiochus IV appointed on his deathbed (I 6:55–56). Though the text here describing how an honorable peace was then made bears the marks of drastic abridgment, it is clear that Jason's narrative, unlike First Maccabees, said nothing of Antiochus V's demolition of Jewish fortifications in violation of his own word. On the contrary, Jason tells us that Lysias even defended the peace with the Jews against the bitter objections of the citizens of Ptolemais (II 13:9–26).

However, Lysias and Antiochus were soon to fall. "Three years later," as Jason misleadingly says,[67] Demetrius I seized power and had the boy-king and his chief minister put to death. A certain wicked Alcimus, who had already been high priest, now sought confirmation in office from Demetrius. To secure the king's support, he denounced both Judas and the Pietists (*Asidaioi*) as rebels and disturbers of the peace of the kingdom. Alcimus complained that he had himself been driven from his high priestly office by their turbulence; Judas must be destroyed. With the concurrence of his advisers, Demetrius sent Nicanor to reinstate Alcimus, destroy Judas, and disperse Judas' followers. To cope with the Seleucid force which had been augmented by Jewish renegades, the Jews first prayed for divine aid, and Judas sent out a force under his brother Simon, who suffered a mild defeat. Jason here may tacitly suggest that only Judas himself was worthy of divine intervention. Indeed, rather than clash with Judas, Nicanor made peace with him and became his friend (II 14:1–25).

Much of this account is in sharp contrast with First Maccabees. There, Alcimus, spokesman of renegades, accuses not the Pietists but only Judas and his brothers. Pietists, but not Judas and his brothers, are so foolish as to trust Alcimus and the Seleucid agents (I 7:5–30).

For Jason, the period of mutual trust ends when Alcimus appeals to Demetrius and accuses Nicanor of treason for showing favor to Judas. Ordered by the king to take Judas prisoner, Nicanor, frightened by his precarious position, turns into an enemy of the Jews and their God.

[67] See Part V, pp. 91–92.

Unable to capture Judas, he threatens to destroy the temple if the Jews do not surrender the man. The Jews respond by turning to prayer; rather than submit to arrest by Nicanor's soldiers, Razis, a venerated Jewish elder, theatrically commits suicide, firm in his belief in the resurrection. Impious Nicanor even orders Jews to violate the Sabbath in pursuit of Judas (II 15:1–5).

Judas, however, bravely prepares for battle and rallies his men with biblical texts and with the report of his own miraculous dream: he saw the pious Onias III praying for the Jewish defenders, and with Onias appeared the prophet Jeremiah, who handed Judas a sacred golden sword with which to defeat the enemy. With prayer Judas and his men went into battle against Nicanor, and in a great manifestation of God's power slaughtered the vast enemy force and its leader, and fixed Nicanor's severed head and hand in sight of the temple he had threatened to destroy. The Jews decided to celebrate the date, 13 Adar, annually as the "Day of Nicanor" (15:6–36).

From then on, says the abridger, the Jews possessed Jerusalem. At this point, therefore, he ends his work (15:37–39). Jason, who told "the story of Judas Maccabaeus and his brothers" (II 2:19), probably continued at least to the death of Judas.[68]

The contrasts of Jason's work with First Maccabees go far beyond miracles and other details of narrative. Where First Maccabees was written to prove the legitimacy of the Hasmonaean dynasty, Jason pointedly makes every effort to show that Judas' brothers were at best ineffective and at worst tainted by treason and sin.[69] Where in First Maccabees there is strong, if tacit, denial of the resurrection, Jason loudly asserts the belief (II 7, 14:46) and goes through logical gymnastics to prove that Judas himself held it (II 12:42–45). Where in First Maccabees, without obedience to the Hasmonaeans piety and even martyrdom are not enough to win God's favor, Jason makes even Judas' victories a result of divine favor won by the martyrs. Where in First Maccabees the commemorative festivals, the Feast of Dedication and the Day of Nicanor, are mentioned, they do not become the focus of attention; in Second Maccabees and perhaps in the complete work of Jason the narrative is organized in two parallel sections, each telling of threat to the temple, martyrdom, triumph, with the first celebration of each festival as the climax.

The author and the translator of First Maccabees carried their rejection of Greek institutions so far that they refused to use the normal Greek language; the author took as his models the biblical historians, not

---

[68] See p. 27; Part IV, p. 80.
[69] II 10:19–22, 12:36–40, 14:17; perhaps also II 12:24, though Jason does not identify the dupes as members of the Hasmonaean family. Greek "Dositheos" and Hebrew "Jonathan" are synonyms ("gift of God"). See also Part III, pp. 59–61; Part IV, pp. 79–80, 85.

Greek writers. Jason, who bore a Greek name and came from the Greek city of Cyrene, wrote his book in a Greek that was considered elegant at the time. He followed the patterns of the popular Greek genre of "pathetic history," of which the abridgment is the sole surviving example, except for fragments. The author of a Greek pathetic history strove to entertain his reader by playing strongly upon the emotions, with vivid portrayals of atrocities and heroism and divine manifestations and with copious use of sensational language and rhetoric, especially when presenting the feelings of the characters.[70]

Again unlike First Maccabees, Jason, a Jewish Greek, gladly notes that Jews can have beneficial covenants with Greeks, even when they are not military alliances, so long as there is no neglect of Jewish law. Such a beneficial covenant added to the merits of Onias III. Even outside Sparta and Rome righteous gentiles exist.[71] Other fundamental differences between the two books remain to be discovered.[72]

What title Jason gave his work is hard to tell. The only clue is the description of the book's content at II 2:19–22, which is much too long to be a title. The title may have been "The History of Judas Maccabaeus and His Brothers," but Jason's emphasis on the temple and his hostility to the brothers argue against it. On the other hand, the title of the abridgment may well have been "The Maccabaean history" (*Ta Makkabaïka*).[73]

Books in the genre of pathetic history often lacked a strict chronological framework.[74] In Jason's abridged work, except for quoted official documents, which would naturally use the Macedonian Seleucid era, there are only two absolute dates (II 13:1, 14:4). Both connect Seleucid kings with events in Judaea, so either form of the Seleucid era might have been used. It can be shown, however, that Jason used the Macedonian form.[75]

Having studied the abridged history, we turn to the letters at the beginning of Second Maccabees. E. Bickermann[76] solved most of the problems of Ep. 1 (II 1:1–10a). His results can be summarized here.

Epistle 1 is an authentic festal letter sent out by Jewish authorities in Jerusalem, calling upon the troubled Jews of Egypt to repent of their

---

[70] On Jason's style, see Jerome, quoted on p. 15–16; Abel, pp. 36–37; Niese, *Hermes* 35 (1900), 300–3; Bickermann, *Gott*, p. 147. On pathetic history, see Polybius ii 56 and Plutarch *Themistocles* 32; cf. Cicero *Orator ad M. Brutum* 37.128; and see also R. Reitzenstein, *Hellenistische Wundererzählungen* (Leipzig: Teubner, 1906), pp. 84–91, and Albin Lesky, *A History of Greek Literature* (New York: Crowell, 1966), pp. 764–66, 768–69.

[71] II 3:1–3, 4:6, 36–38, 49, 10:12–13, 11:13–15, 12:12, 30–31, 14:18–28.

[72] See Part II, pp. 45–54, Part IV, pp. 78–84.

[73] See p. 3.

[74] See Reitzenstein, pp. 84–86.

[75] See Appendix II.

[76] ZNW 32 (1933), 233–54.

sins and observe the "Festival of Tabernacles in the Month of Kislev," i.e. the Feast of Dedication.[77] The letter bears the date 188 Sel. The genre of the festal letter announcing a coming festival and often also calling for repentance can be traced back as far as II Chron 30:1–9 and is well attested in later antiquity among both Jews and Christians.

Bickerman was able to prove that Ep. 1 used the Babylonian form of the Seleucid era, as one would expect of a Jewish document sent from Jerusalem. As a festal letter announcing the Feast of Dedication, Ep. 1 would then date from ca. November, 124 B.C.E. Within Ep. 1, at II 1:7–8, an earlier authentic festal letter is quoted, which we may call Ep. 0. Epistle 0 was sent by the Jews of Jerusalem and Judaea to the Jews of Egypt in the reign of Demetrius II in 169 Sel. Bab., which can only be winter 143/42.

The Jews of Egypt in 124 faced trouble, as Ptolemy VIII Euergetes II gained the upper hand in his dynastic war with his sister Cleopatra II, who had received Jewish support.[78] Moreover, the Jews of Jerusalem could accuse their brothers in Egypt of sin for continuing to tolerate and use, contrary to Deut 12:4–14, the Jewish temple of Onias IV at Leontopolis. In founding that temple, Onias IV, son of Onias III, probably held that God had long since removed his presence from Jerusalem, so that the temple there was no longer the place which the Lord had chosen as the sole center for sacrificial worship. Certainly Onias IV quoted Isa 19:19 as prophetic justification for his temple, which he founded in the reign of Ptolemy VI Philometor, who died in 145, before the date of Ep. 0.[79] Hence, Ep. 0, calling upon Egyptian Jews to observe the Jerusalem temple's Feast of Dedication, was probably propaganda against the Oniad temple of Leontopolis, as much so as Ep. 1 with its allusion to the sin of the Egyptian Jews.

We learn from Josephus that Onias IV stood high in the favor of Ptolemy VI and Cleopatra II. Only with the death of Ptolemy VI and with Cleopatra's loss of power in late 143 or early 142 did an anti-Oniad message like that of Ep. 0 have a prospect of success in Egypt. Hence, Ep. 0 probably represents the earliest call from Jerusalem to Egyptian Jewry to observe the Feast of Dedication.[80]

Unlike the abridged history, Ep. 1 is a translation from a Hebrew or Aramaic original[81] and can hardly have been an integral part of Jason's work, though Jason probably used it as a source.[82] Moreover, it is im-

---

[77] Cf. II 10:5–8; I 4:59.

[78] See Bickermann, ZNW 32 (1933), 251–54, and my article, "The Tales of the Tobiads," in *Studies Smith*, Part III, pp. 85–123.

[79] J. *AJ* xiii 3.1–3.62–73; *BJ* vii 10.2–3.421–32; Hans Volkmann, "Ptolemaios 24," PW, XXIII[II] (1959), 1717.

[80] Bickermann, ZNW 32 (1933), 253–54.

[81] ZNW 32 (1933), 245–46.

[82] Compare II 10:3, 5 end – 6, with II 1:8–9.

probable that either Jason or the abridger prefixed Ep. 1 to his book. According to Ep. 0 as quoted in Ep. 1, the rebellion of Jason the Oniad against the Seleucid kingdom was the sin which brought on the dreadful visitations.[83] According to Jason of Cyrene and his abridger, Jason the Oniad was partly to blame, but his deadly sin was not his rebellion—a mere episode—but his Hellenization of Jerusalem, and even in the sin of Hellenization Jason's guilt was overshadowed by the crimes of Menelaus and his henchmen (II 4:13–50, 13:3–8).

Epistle 2 (II 1:10b–2:18) is written in idiomatic Hellenistic Greek. Nevertheless, one can prove that it cannot have been prefixed to the historical work by the author or the abridger. Epistle 2 is another piece of anti-Oniad propaganda, forged in Egypt around November, 103 B.C.E., as a supplement to Ep. 1, in order to prove to the Jews of Egypt that God did indeed have his presence at Jerusalem and to call upon the Jews of Egypt, again sorely troubled, to observe the Feast of Dedication. Thus, Ep. 2 again teaches the illegitimacy of the Oniad temple of Leontopolis.

There is a probable explanation for the presence of Epp. 1 and 2 at the head of Second Maccabees. It is that at some time after 78/7 B.C.E. someone wished to give the Jews of Egypt a scroll with narrative and festal letters for the Feast of Dedication analogous to the scroll of Esther for Purim and analogous to Third Maccabees for the Egyptian Jews' own festival of deliverance. By prefixing Epp. 1 and 2, which by then circulated together, to the abridged history, he accomplished his purpose.[84]

Hence, Second Maccabees may be a liturgical text, even though Jason of Cyrene and his abridger had no intention of writing sacred scripture. Greek-speaking Jews of Alexandria might consider Second Maccabees holy, but it could never be so for Jews whose language was Hebrew or Aramaic. The great wars of the Jews with Rome and the inroads of Christianity were to leave few Jews who could consider a Greek work as holy. Hence, although the theology of Second Maccabees was so acceptable to Jews that martyr tales in rabbinic literature are probably influenced by it, the book was preserved only by the Church. Medieval Jews were glad to draw on its narrative for inspiration when they rediscovered it in the possession of their Christian contemporaries.[85]

---

[83] See on II 1:7.

[84] See Appendices III and IV.

[85] Allusions to Second Maccabees in the Church Fathers and in early medieval Jewish works: above, n. 58. Martyr-tales in rabbinic literature: TB *Giṭṭin* 57b, *Midrash Ekha Rabbah* 1:50 (to Lam 1:15). Other sources listed by Gerson D. Cohen, "The Story of Hannah and Her Seven Sons in Hebrew Literature," in the *Mordecai M. Kaplan Jubilee Volume* (New York: Jewish Theological Seminary of America, 1953), Hebrew Section, pp. 109–10, n. 3. Cohen, pp. 109–22, gives a thorough treatment of these texts and a list of the medieval works based on them.

II. THE EXTANT SOURCES OF FIRST AND SECOND MACCABEES

Even if they had been written by contemporaries of the events, both books of Maccabees would have had to draw on oral or written sources, since no one could have been eyewitness to everything. The author of First Maccabees implies that he based his narrative upon written sources (I 9:22). Oral sources and lost written sources are difficult if not impossible to trace. Both books, however, present some of their sources almost as they found them, in the documents they quote and even in the documents they paraphrase. The hyperskeptical scholarship which began with the Renaissance tended to reject these documents as spurious. Scholars of the past one hundred years have vindicated almost all of them. One can now confidently assert that neither Jason of Cyrene nor the author of First Maccabees forged a document. All the documents in First Maccabees are authentic. Jason of Cyrene regarded as authentic the letter of Antiochus IV, forged by the regime of Lysias (II 9:19–27),[1] and the forged Ep. 2 was not part of Jason's work.

To prove each document authentic would multiply the size of what already promises to be a long book. I treat advances beyond earlier scholarship in the commentary. For the rest, the reader should consult earlier works.[2] The general principles used in proving the documents authentic are simple. The style and vocabulary used by government bureaus tended to change over the years. Ancient forgers even when they had access to early authentic documents seldom if ever appreciated such changes. Nor was it easy for a later writer, particularly a Jew without access to Seleucid archives, to make a detailed forged document fit into its intended historical background. Every document quoted by our two

---

[1] See commentary in AB vol. 41A.

[2] See R. Laqueur, "Griechische Urkunden in der jüdisch-hellenistischen Literatur," *Historische Zeitschrift* 136 (1927), 231–41; Ettelson, TCAAS 27 (1925), 342–75; Bickermann, PW, XIV, 785–87, 789–90, and especially his "Une question d'authenticité: les privilèges juifs," *Université libre Bruxelles: Annuaire de l'Institut de philologie et d'histoire orientales et slaves* 13 (1953), 11–34, which includes an explanation of the factors which led to the almost perverse skepticism. Against the recent skepticism of Otto Mørkholm (pp. 162–65), see commentary at 12:20–23 and on the documents of II 11.

historians can be shown to be written in the correct style and vocabulary of its period. Many of the documents go into great detail; yet, so far as we know, every detail can be fitted into the historical background. A very strong suggestion of authenticity lies in the fact that the content of most of the quoted documents really runs counter to the propagandistic thrust of the work which quotes them. Thus, the documents of Seleucid concessions to the Hasmonaeans in First Maccabees nevertheless all assert Hasmonaean subjection to the Seleucid kings. The document at I 14:27–49 conspicuously fails to view the Hasmonaeans as liberators of Israel. None of the documents quoted by Jason really proves his points. The ultimatum at II 11:27–33 is the reverse of the concession of a badly defeated regime, and even the other documents of II 11 do not justify the inference at 11:12–15, that Lysias was badly defeated and granted concessions in accordance with Judas' demands. Judas is not mentioned in the correspondence. Similarly, there is no trace of repentance or desperation in the forged letter of Antiochus (II 9:19–27; see commentary), which Jason accepted as genuine and used to prove his account (9:1–18, 28) of the king's dreadful end. A forger's work at least gives the appearance of proving the forger's point.

A group of literary sources certainly contemporary with the events narrated in our two books and probably known to both authors has survived. The entire group belongs to the genre known as "apocalyptic," which sprang up during Antiochus' persecutions among Jews who strove to strengthen their people's faith in the hour of unbearable trial. The writer of an apocalyptic work took the events of his own time and placed them in some providential scheme of history and gave predictions of a glorious future. Such writers did not presume to pose as prophets. Prophesy had departed from Israel, to return in God's own time.[3] They did not publish their works in their own name but ascribed them to such ancient worthies as Enoch, Moses, and Daniel. Even then, the prophesies usually were not the unaided inspiration of the writer but represented the results of his laborious "scientific" study of the words of the Torah and the Prophets.

Such writers worked under severe constraints. Both they and their audience were interested not in remote periods but in the present and the immediate future. In their writings they would have the ancient worthy they chose as spokesman predict events down to the dreadful visitations of the immediate present, often with great specificity so as to show his great prophetic power, and then they would have him go on to predict a glorious deliverance. If the glorious deliverance did not occur (and it never did, since it included such things as an eternal empire for the righteous or the resurrection of the dead), one can usually date such

[3] See Part I, pp. 12–13.

a work by the last historical event clearly described. Let us proceed to examine three such works.[4]

1. The Testament of Moses

Although a patristic text cites it under the title "Assumption of Moses," the work as we have it, a farewell charge of Moses to Joshua, is better called the "Testament of Moses." Like many apocalyptic works, it has suffered interpolations by authors who tried to bring it up to date and keep its predictions true. However, much or all of Test Moses vi – vii can be shown to consist of such revisions,[5] and then it becomes easy to interpret the work.

The writer has Moses survey for Joshua the history of the Israelites from the conquest of Canaan. At iii 14 he reaches the Babylonian exile and at iv 7 the return to Jerusalem. Thereupon the faithful will grieve because valid sacrifices will be impossible (iv 8). There will be sectarian divisions and "whoring after strange gods" and pollution of the altar by unfit priests who are "slaves, the sons of slaves,"[6] and also bribery and injustice. Then there will be dreadful visitations inflicted by sinful rulers; worst of all, a powerful ruler will try by torture to force Israel to violate the Torah (v 1–6, viii 1–5).

"Taxo,"[7] a Levite with seven sons, from a family long innocent of sin,

[4] I shall deal elsewhere with the apocalypse at Jubilees xxiii 16–31. I shall show that it dates from the time of Hellenization under the high priests Jason and Menelaus, before Antiochus IV published his decrees in 167 B.C.E. banning Jewish observances. For the present, see Nickelsburg, *Resurrection*, pp. 31–33, 46–47.

[5] Patristic text: Gelasius Cyzicenus *Commentarius Actorum concilii Nicaeni* ii 18, quoted at Schürer, III, 294. See R. H. Charles, APOT, II, 407–9; cf. Eissfeldt, p. 623.

On the interpolations, see J. Licht, "Taxo, or the Apocalyptic Doctrine of Vengeance," JJS 12 (1961), 95–103; Nickelsburg, *Resurrection*, pp. 43–45; and my "The Testament of Moses: Its Content, Its Origin, and Its Attestation in Josephus," *Studies on the Testament of Moses*, ed. George W. E. Nickelsburg, Jr., Septuagint and Cognate Studies, No. 4 (Cambridge, Mass.: Society of Biblical Literature, 1973), pp. 43–47.

[6] Menelaus came from the priestly course of Bilgah and cannot have been of slave descent (II 3:4, 4:23). "Slaves, the sons of slaves" may be a later anti-Hasmonaean interpolation, referring to the charge that John Hyrcanus or Alexander Jannaeus was descended from a woman who had been a captive; see Part IV, pp. 68–69. Perhaps any non-Zadokite priest could have been called a "slave" in comparison to a Zadokite. See also Lieberman, *Tosefta Ki-fshuṭah*, Part IV (*Mo'ed*), pp. 908–10 (in Hebrew). The unfit priests are called "priests who are no priests"; cf. II 4:13.

[7] The question of the origin and meaning of the name is a difficult one. Our sole text for the Testament of Moses is a Latin translation of a Greek version of the Hebrew or Aramaic original. Hence, "Taxo" may reasonably be taken as a Latin transliteration of Greek *taxôn*, the future participle of the verb *tassein*, "to order." Although the future participle is rare or absent from the Greek translations of the Hebrew Bible, a Greek translator of the time of the Hasmonaeans or later could have used it to render a Hebrew or Aramaic participle; see F.-M. Abel, *Grammaire du grec biblique* (Paris: Gabalda, 1927), pp. 265–66. The Greek translator may

will rouse the vengeance of the Lord by suffering martyrdom in a cave in resolute refusal to transgress, and the glorious deliverance will follow (ix 1 – x 10).

The author of the Testament of Moses knows of the Hellenizing priests, the persecutions, and the efforts, based on scriptural texts, to "seek justice" from God by suffering martyrdom.[8] He believes that the glorious deliverance is imminent. He does not argue against advocates of resistance by armed force. Hence, he wrote in 166 or early 165, the time of mass martyrdom, before Mattathias' and Judas' policy of resistance had begun to make progress.

The Testament of Moses probably was known to both our authors. Both agree with it in regarding the persecution as punishment for the sins of the Hellenizers. Jason shares the idea that the divine vengeance is roused by wholesale martyrdom. The story of the martyrdom of the woman and her seven sons (II 7) may well be an effort to make the disappointing prophesy of Test Moses ix 7 – x 1 prove true after all.[9]

The Testament of Moses is interesting for other beliefs it displays. According to it, the second temple is not fully "the place which the Lord hath chosen" (see Deut 12:4–14), for fully valid sacrifices cannot be offered there (iv 8).[10] The eschatology of the work does not include a resurrection but only the glorification of Israel and the punishment of the gentiles.

2. Enoch lxxxv–xc

The author of Enoch lxxxv–xc gave a schematic view of the history of the world from the creation. At lxxxviii 67 he spoke of the destruction of the first temple. From lxxxix 68 to xc 8 he described the helplessness of the Jews, sheep under the oppressive domination of foreign beasts and birds of prey, for seventy periods of presumably seven years each.[11]

---

have wished to stress that the person described as "the orderer" was yet to come. Or he may have felt the increasingly future force of the Hebrew and Aramaic participles; see M. H. Segal, *A Grammar of Mishnaic Hebrew* (Oxford: Clarendon Press, 1927), pp. 157–59; E. Y. Kutscher, *"Aramit,"* Enc. Bib., I (1955), 589 (in Hebrew).

Hebrew *ḥōqᵉqē* at Judg 5:9 is rendered by a derivative of *tassein*, so scholars have tried to connect Taxo with the *mᵉḥōqēq* in the literature of the Essenes of Qumran. On the possibility, see M. Delcor, "Contribution à l'étude de la législation des sectaires de Damas et de Qumrân," RB 62 (1955), 61–66. One might note that *taxis* renders Hebrew *tōrāh* at Prov 31:24[26], so that Taxo might be the *mōreh* (teacher) of the Qumran texts. See also NOTE on 2:28–38.

[8] See NOTE on 2:28–38. The expectation of rousing God's vengeance by martyrdom, both in the Testament of Moses and at II 7:6 and 8:3, is derived from Deut 32:36 and 43. Indeed, the entire Testament of Moses is based on Deuteronomy 31–34. See Nickelsburg, *Resurrection*, pp. 29–30.

[9] See NOTES on 2:28–38 and II 7:1.

[10] See my article in *Studies on the Testament of Moses*, pp. 48–50.

[11] Cf. Dan 9:24; see below, pp. 43–44.

The seer's treatment of the last period of the seventy seems to have been written in several stages. In the first stage, the seer knows only of plural horned lambs or rams who unsuccessfully resist the birds of prey (xc 9a) and pray loudly for help (xc 11); these lambs or rams will receive divine aid, as God will destroy the oppressors (xc 17–18). These horned rams probably represent militant Pietists, who tried to resist Jason and Menelaus (II 4:39–50, 5:5–7), and the royal officials who carried out the persecution (I 2:29–38; II 6:11).

In the second stage, the seer speaks of an invincible single horned ram, who will win repeated victories for the Jews (xc 9b–10, 12–16). Mattathias' activity was on too small a scale to fit the description in Enoch, so the great horned ram must be Judas Maccabaeus. The plural horned rams run to join Judas (xc 10; cf. I 2:42) but are not mentioned as participating in his struggles. Finally, says the seer, all Jews will join in a complete victory, probably the victory over Nicanor (xc 19). The seer knows of Judas' many mighty struggles but not of his death. He believed that invincible Judas would live to see the glorious deliverance. Hence, he wrote before Judas' death in spring, 160 B.C.E. There is a possible faint allusion to the work in First Maccabees. Jason or one of his sources almost certainly used it.[12]

---

[12] See NOTE on 9:7–10, and Part V, pp. 96–97.

Several strange aspects of Enoch xc suggest that it was composed in at least three stages. The singular pronouns in xc 12, referring to the single horned ram, are very awkward after the mention of the plural rams in xc 11. The great single ram is not mentioned in xc 17–19, and the plural rams are not mentioned in xc 12–16. The loud prayers of the plural rams in xc 11 appear useless in their present context, but could well have roused the recording angel, if xc 17 originally followed xc 11. Very strange is the way in which the foreign oppressors are "completely" destroyed several times over in xc 15 (?), 18, and 19. On our hypothesis, everything becomes understandable. Originally, the seer predicted ultimate victory for the battered Pietists (xc 9a, 11, 17–18). The career of Judas Maccabaeus led him to add xc 9b–10, 12–16. He appears to have taken note of every stage of Judas' progress, and ultimately he was able to work even xc 17–18 into Judas' career. How did he proceed?

The seer chooses to represent by ravens officials of low rank in the Seleucid and Ptolemaic empires; often such low officials were members of the conquered peoples. The highest royal Macedonian officials the seer represents as eagles, and those of intermediate rank as vultures and kites.

In xc 12 we find ravens, probably the local officials Apollonius and Seron, fruitlessly trying to defeat Judas Maccabaeus. In xc 13–14, the original text probably had local officials (Philip, as at II 8:8) seeking help from higher officials and receiving it through the campaign of Gorgias and Nicanor, in the course of which Judas mysteriously learned of Gorgias' stratagem (I 4:1–3). The seer ascribes Judas' information to the action of a supernatural being.

In xc 15 the seer probably alludes to the sudden withdrawal of Lysias after the battle which ended his expedition of 164 (I 4:34–35), a battle at which Pietists reported a supernatural apparition (II 11:8–13). In xc 16 the seer alludes to the wars with neighboring peoples (I 5) and to the campaign of Lysias and Antiochus V, in which collaborationist Jews ("sheep of the field") participated and Judas was hard pressed (I 6:21–54). Finally he found it possible to make xc 17–18 allude to Judas' surprising escape from siege and to the destruction of Lysias and Antiochus V

Again the author's beliefs are interesting. He has no reservations about the rightness of Judas' resistance. Unlike the author of the Testament of Moses, the author of Enoch lxxxv–xc believed that the second temple was as much God's temple as the first, though the priests of the second temple did not properly observe the laws of purity, so that all offerings there were ritually impure (lxxxix 73). Later, both the Pharisees and the Essenes were to think the same of the Sadducean priests. We cannot tell whether the seer meant to predict a resurrection.[13]

3. Daniel 7–12

Far more complicated and controversial are the apocalypses in Daniel 7–12. They require extensive study.[14] Here we may summarize the results of the research. The chapters show no doubt of the continued holiness of Jerusalem and of the full validity of the temple cult.[15] Chapter 7 was written as a Jewish apocalypse in two stages, the earlier dating from the reign of Seleucus IV (187–175). Otherwise, all the chapters date from the period of the persecutions and Judas' wars, and all may be by the same apocalyptic seer.

The author of Daniel 7 in its final form knows that Antiochus IV conquered Egypt, which was then under three rulers. He knows that Antiochus spoke arrogant words against God, massacred saintly Pietists, and issued decrees abolishing Jewish observances and substituting others. However, he does not know of the desecration of the temple. He predicts continued power for Antiochus for three and a half years, until the beginning of the sabbatical year in late September or early October, 164 B.C.E. Then will come a glorious deliverance, an eternal kingdom of the saints. Hence, the seer measured his three and a half years from an event of about April, 167. I shall show in my commentary on Daniel that the event was the expedition of the Mysarch (I 1:29–35; II 5:24–26). Though the seer made his predictions "scientifically," on the basis of his own study of scripture, the march of events soon began to prove them false.

Antiochus did not enjoy undisturbed power for three and a half years.

(I 6:55 – 7:4). The finality of the destruction mentioned in xc 18 suggests that the seer thought no more struggles would follow. However, when Nicanor's expedition came (I 7:26–48), the seer added xc 19, with its references to the miraculous sword (II 15:15–16) and to the rising of the village Jews who cut down the fugitives (I 7:46).

[13] On Judas' resistance, contrast the beliefs of some of the author's contemporaries, below, pp. 43–44, and commentary on II 1:7 in AB vol. 41A. Charles is probably wrong in rendering Enoch xc 33 as a reference to resurrection. The word he translates by "destroyed" probably means "perishing" or "lost." Cf. Ezek 34:16 and Isa 27:13. Also, in Enoch xc 38, the word Charles translated by "generations" may mean "families."

[14] I shall deal elsewhere in detail with the book of Daniel.

[15] I 7:25: God must have been "present" in some sense in Jerusalem to be the target of Antiochus' blasphemies; cf. 8:11–14, 25, 9:25–27, 11:28, 31, 36, 38, 12:11.

The Hasmonaean revolt brought some relief to the pious. Hence, the extended "prophesy" in Dan 10–12:3 knows of the "little help" of the Hasmonaean revolt (11:34) after a year of unrelieved persecutions (11:33), but not of Antiochus IV's march eastward, which probably began before the end of June, 165.[16] As a prelude to the glorious deliverance, the seer predicts totally unhistorical, severe troubles for the Jews and a totally unhistorical death for the persecuting king (11:40–12:1). The deliverance includes the resurrection of the righteous Pietists (12:2–3). The seer hardly welcomed the Hasmonaean revolt. Earlier rebels he condemned as sinful "men of violence" (11:14), and the Pietists who joined Judas are by no means praised (11:34b; contrast 11:35).

These prophesies, too, were based on scripture, and they, too, began to prove false. The seer who wrote Daniel 9 took the deliverance predicted in Daniel 7 and shifted it from the beginning of the sabbatical year in autumn, 164 B.C.E., to the end of the sabbatical year in autumn, 163. The beginning of the sabbatical year saw only the destruction of the "abomination of desolation" (9:27). The seer also set forth a detailed divine scheme (9:24–27) of history, of seventy weeks of years, from the time of dreadful sins denounced by Jeremiah to the time of deliverance. The seer explained the terrible sufferings of the saints under Antiochus IV not as expiation of present sin but as the last stage of the expiations for the heinous sins denounced by Jeremiah. I shall deal elsewhere with the difficult problems of Dan 9:24–27.

Even the additional year purchased by the ingenious concepts of Daniel 9 did not save the prophesies from the danger of being proved false. A seer produced Daniel 8 just in time to show that Daniel had predicted the arrival at Jerusalem on January 28, 163, of the news of the death of Antiochus IV. Furthermore, taught the seer, the death of Antiochus IV was not the immediate prelude to the resurrection; it was only a vindication of God and His temple, eleven hundred and fifty days after the desecration of 15 Kislev (December 6), 167 (Dan 8:13–14, 23–25). As for the Seleucid persecutor king who would conquer Egypt only to perish shortly before the resurrection (11:40–12:2), he would have to be a successor of Antiochus IV.

As the sabbatical year 164/3 wore on, it saw the dismaying victories of Lysias and Antiochus V over hitherto invincible Judas. By June 27, 163 B.C.E., twelve hundred and ninety days after the desecration of the temple, the seer saw the coming of the troubles foreseen at 11:41 and 12:1. He predicted that Judas and his men would be crushed (12:7), but the glorious deliverance and resurrection would occur by the Day of Remembrance (Rosh ha-shanah), on the faulty Jewish calendar then in use, by August 12, 163 B.C.E., thirteen hundred and thirty-five days after

16 See introductory NOTE to I 3:27–37.

the desecration (12:11–12). Clearly, for the seer, Judas and his men were only a "little help" and were no essential part of the scheme of salvation. The seventy periods of Dan 9:24 reappear at Enoch lxxxix 59, but at Enoch xc 9–16 the author insists on Judas' invincibility. Hench, Enoch lxxxv–xc may have been written to contradict the view of the seer of Daniel, that Judas was unimportant.

The seer was able to see to it that his creations in Daniel 8–10 and possibly 12:4–13 were published in writing in acceptable Hebrew. The overprecise prophesies of 11:1 – 12:3, which were always in danger of being proved false, he probably spread orally, improvising modifications when necessary and keeping his own notes in Aramaic. The frequent alterations left his notes a chaos for any other reader. The seer probably died in 164/3 or soon after, and his followers, unwilling to alter his notes, reverently left them as they were, only translating them literally into wretched Hebrew so as to have the inspired words of Daniel in the language of his brother prophets.

The impact of Daniel 7–12 on our two authors was profound. Let us turn to examine it. Contemporaries and near contemporaries understood more of these strange chapters than did later generations. As long as men were alive to remember the suspicious circumstances of the successive revelations, some loyal Jews could accept the popular tales of Daniel 1–6 and reject Daniel 7–12. The disordered and obscure text quickly gave rise to diverse interpretations. The oracles appear to have been controversial when our two historians wrote, since neither mentions them by name. The two sects which were to be hostile to the Hasmonaeans, the Essenes and the Pharisees, accepted the oracles. The Hasmonaeans readily understood how the oracles of Daniel first condemned by implication their use of force, then considered them to be but a little help, and finally predicted their doom. Ideological considerations can explain the omission from Mattathias' speech in First Maccabees of Daniel's promises of resurrection and an eternal Jewish empire.[17] When, however, Mattathias

---

17 Essenes and Pharisees: their acceptance of the veracity of Daniel is widely attested. Thus, Josephus, an admirer of both sects, strongly endorses the oracles; see Part III, nn. 3 and 5. Rabbinic literature, the work of the heirs of the Pharisees, contains no trace of any doubt of the veracity of Daniel. Fragments of copies of the book of Daniel have been found at Qumran. See *Qumran Cave I*, eds. D. Barthélemy and J. T. Milik, DJD, I (1955), 150–52 (Dan 1:10–17, 2:2–6, 3:22–30); and *Les 'petites grottes' de Qumrân*, eds. M. Baillet, J. T. Milik, and R. de Vaux, DJD, III (1962), 114–16 (Dan 8:20–21, 10:8–16, 11:33–36, 38). Barthélemy, DJD, I, 150, noted that canonical texts from Qumran were written on parchment in columns twice as high as they were broad, whereas the Daniel fragments from Cave I had columns that were almost square and those from Cave VI were written on papyrus. Accordingly, he suggested that the Essenes of Qumran did not treat Daniel as canonical. One could also note that no commentary on Daniel has been discovered at Qumran. However, to speak of a "canon" in the time of the Qumran scribes is anachronistic. In any case, "canonical" works now are known to have been written at Qumran in square or broad columns and on papyrus. See DJD, III, 62–69 (Jeremiah), 71–74

speaks of Hananiah, Mishael, and Azariah in the fiery furnace and of Daniel in the lions' den (I 2:59–60), his silence on Daniel 7–12 is surely eloquent: for the author of First Maccabees, those chapters are a forgery.

The published text of Dan 11:25–30 from the first was probably as we have it. No ancient author ever thought of trying to reconstruct the author's meaning from the clues in the disordered text.[18] As the text stands, it has Antiochus IV turning against the "Holy Covenant" and "acting" at the end of both his Egyptian expeditions, of 169 and 168 B.C.E. The attempts of pagan potentates to violate Jerusalem and the temple were matters which pious Jews faithfully recorded. If the enemy somehow failed, Jews knew their God had revealed His power, as He had against Sennacherib and Heliodorus. If the enemy succeeded, Jews knew that their God had failed to act because of their sins, as in the time of Nebuchadnezzar and Antiochus IV. Jewish tradition as we find it in I 1:20–29 and II 5:11–24 agrees that Antiochus in person violated Jerusalem and the temple only once. How, then, should Dan 11:28–30 be interpreted? The author of First Maccabees seems to take delight in proving the oracles of Daniel false. Though he surely detested the official chroniclers of Antiochus IV, he took the trouble to go to a Seleucid source for the date of Antiochus' first expedition against Egypt. Our author's narrative at first (I 1:17–20, 24a) reads like a paraphrase of Dan 11:25–26, 28, perhaps in order to expose the seer's errors, for with great detail our author shows how Antiochus plundered the temple, though Dan 11:28 seems to reveal nothing of the kind.

On his second expedition, in 168, Antiochus overran all Egypt and even Alexandria was almost in his grasp when he was confronted by a Roman ultimatum to withdraw. Unwilling to contend with the superpower, he grudgingly complied, as is reflected in Dan 11:29–30a. Thereupon, Dan 11:30b apparently has Antiochus acting in fury against the Holy Covenant.[19] In First Maccabees, on the other hand, the author appears pleased to pass over Antiochus' second expedition in silence, as if it had no tangible effect on the Jews.

Especially strange is the order of Dan 11:31–39. At 11:39, the seer alludes unmistakably to the expedition of the Mysarch in 167 B.C.E.:

(Ruth), 112–14 (Song of Songs), and 169–71 (Deuteronomy), all with square or broad columns, and 107–12 (I and II Kings), on papyrus. The lack of a commentary on Daniel may be accidental; Daniel is not the only canonical book for which no commentary has been found at Qumran. It is also possible that commentaries to Daniel were deliberately kept unwritten, as secrets of the sect. See also J. A. Fitzmyer, "Some Observations on the Targum of Job from Qumran Cave 11," CBQ 36 (1974), 505–6.

On Mattathias' speech: see Part I, pp. 12–13.

[18] See also NOTE on I 1:20, *with a strong army*.

[19] See Mørkholm, pp. 88–96, and cf. J. *AJ* xii 5.3.246; for the probable original meaning of Dan 11:30b, see NOTE on I 1:29–40.

"He [Antiochus IV, the King of the North] shall bring into the citadels of the pious the people of a strange god . . . and place them in power over the Many and distribute land for a price."[20] At 11:36–38, the seer alludes to the decrees which came *later* in 167 B.C.E.,[21] outlawing orthodox Jewish observance and imposing a different "Jewish" cult[22]: "The king shall act arbitrarily and arrogantly lord it over every god. Concerning the God of gods he shall say things past belief. Yet he shall prosper until the Wrath [of God] shall come to an end, for utter ruin shall have been accomplished. Though he shall pay no heed to the gods of his forefathers, and to the Delight of Women or any other deity he shall pay no heed, for he shall lord it over them all, yet he shall [claim to] show honor to the God of the pious on His altar base, and he shall honor a God whom his forefathers did not recognize, with gold and silver and precious stones and costly gifts." At 11:31, the seer alludes to the desecration of the altar on 25 Kislev, 167 B.C.E. At 11:32–33, he alludes to the persecutions which continued into 166 B.C.E. and beyond; and at 11:34–35 he alludes to the Hasmonaean uprising and to the sufferings of the Pietists, which occurred in the course of the persecutions. Thus, if the verses alluded, as they should, to events in chronological order, we would have them in the order 30, 39, 36–38, 31–35.

It is easy to suggest how the present order may have come about. To the seer, Antiochus' withdrawal from Egypt in 168 upon receiving the Roman ultimatum appeared to be the fulfillment of Num 24:24, and the oppression of Hebrews by the Mysarch in 167 seemed to be one more sign of the approaching End. Hence, originally in Daniel the seer probably had only vss. 11:30 and 39, followed immediately by the expected eschatological events in vss. 40 ff. However, as history took unexpected turns, the seer crowded into the margin of his manuscript first vss. 36–38, and then vss. 31–35, wherever they would fit. He died before he could leave to posterity a text written in proper order.

At the time of our two authors, however, probably no one was aware how the text of vss. 31–39 had grown. Hence, Dan 11:39 was not taken to refer to the expedition of the Mysarch, and it became easy to infer from vss. 30–31 that the expedition of the Mysarch and the desecration of the temple followed almost immediately upon Antiochus' withdrawal from Egypt in 168. The author of First Maccabees seems pleased that he can contradict the apparent meaning of Dan 11:30–31 by informing his readers that the Mysarch came in 167, two years after the sack of 169, and that the Mysarch's expedition and the desecration were two separate events.

---

[20] On "shall bring into" and "the pious," see Ginsberg, pp. 42–43, 46–49. On "the Many" as an expression for "Jews," see Cross, ALQ, pp. 231–34, and cf. Isa 53:11–12 and Dan 12:3.

[21] On the dates of the Mysarch's expedition and the decrees, see p. 42.

[22] See Part VI, pp. 140–58.

Our author goes on contradicting the seer: the entire account of Mattathias and Judas shows that they were no "small help," and at I 2:42 the pious do not "slip" into joining the Hasmonaeans as Dan 11:34[23] would have it. They join Mattathias boldly and zealously *after* his pronouncement allowing defensive warfare on the Sabbath.

Between the king's return from Egypt in 168 B.C.E. (11:30) and the unhistorical final war (11:40–45), the seer predicted *at most* two expeditions sent out by the king against the Jews (11:31–35 and 11:39). Otherwise Antiochus only blasphemes or performs incomprehensible acts of worship (11:36–38). The seer completely failed to foresee Antiochus' expedition to the eastern satrapies, unless "toward the east" at Dan 8:9 is a clumsy allusion to it.

The author of First Maccabees may have had evidence that in sending the expedition of Nicanor and Gorgias against the Jews Lysias was following instructions which Antiochus had left before his march eastward. Even without such evidence, our author would have been delighted to mention a third expedition ordered by the king against the Jews, since' the seer predicted at most two. Our author goes further. I 3:36 is an imitation of Dan 11:39. Since no one at the time thought of applying Dan 11:39 to the Mysarch's expedition, for our author it could be only a false prophesy, that the king's orders to subjugate the Jews and distribute their land to gentiles would be fulfilled.

The rededication of the temple on 25 Kislev 164 B.C.E., three years after the desecration, confounded all of the seer's predictions. Our author takes care to give the date at I 4:52.

The predictions of Dan 11:40–43 were so obviously unfulfilled that believers had to apply them to a time other than the reign of Antiochus IV. In I 5 our author was probably aware that his narrative belied Dan 11:41. He certainly contradicted Dan 11:44–45. Not reports from the east and north, but the renown of the victories of Judas and his brothers (to the south of Antioch!) drove Antiochus to undertake his eastern campaign (I 3:26–37) in the course of which he died; the expedition occurred not shortly before the resurrection but in the mundane year 147 Sel. (166/5; I 3:37); the king died not shortly before the resurrection, but in the mundane year 149 Sel. (164/3; I 6:16); the king perished not in the area between the Mediterranean, the Dead Sea, and the temple mount but in "Persis" (I 6:5; note the emphatic "there" at I 6:16), after hearing dismaying reports, again not from the east and north but from the west (I 6:5–7).

Judas himself, whether he was hiding in the mountains or besieged in Jerusalem, probably understood the seer's prediction (Dan 12:7), that before the end of the sabbatical year he would be defeated. His unexpected deliverance gave him the great satisfaction of proving the seer's

23 Dan Th. 11:34, *en olisthrêmasin.*

prediction false. When Antiochus V thereafter perfidiously breached the walls of the temple mount and returned to Antioch to be victorious over the rebel Philip, Judas still had a considerable consolation: clearly no eschatological triumph had occurred with the end of the sabbatical year. The seer was wrong on all counts. The author of First Maccabees was probably pleased to flaunt the facts (I 6:49, 53–63).[24]

After telling of Judas' death, our author or his source bitterly reflected on the falsity of Dan 12:7–12 and probably also on the falsity of Jubilees xxiii 26–31 and Enoch xc 16–38. The sufferings of pious Jews under Alcimus' regime, which certainly did not outlaw Jewish religion, cannot have been as bad as under Antiochus IV's persecutions, yet the author at I 9:27 speaks of "the worst troubles to afflict Israel since the cessation of prophesy." Perhaps he attempts here, by use of an ironic paraphrase of Dan 12:1, to make vivid the falsity of the seer's prophesies. It is hard to see how any author, however prejudiced, could write thus, unless he was bitterly commenting on the falsity of Dan 12:7–12. Judas and his men, "the hand of the Holy People," had been smashed. Yet no glorious resurrection and no kingdom of saints had followed, but only renewed strength and impunity for the "wicked" in their outrages against the "true upholders of the Torah." Prophesy had ceased; the seer of Daniel was a fraud. Josephus, who believed in the seer's veracity, may have perceived the author's bitter meaning. He replaces "since the cessation of prophesy" by "since their return from Babylon."[25]

Our author never mentions directly the visions of Daniel. Potential and actual supporters of the Hasmonaean dynasty believed in the visions and could have been antagonized by a direct attack. It was enough to let the facts refute the seer.

Jason of Cyrene, on the other hand, believed in the veracity of Daniel, so much so, that he frequently follows the seer's prophesies against all other sources or tries to shield the prophesies from those who would prove them false.[26] Jason, too, never mentions Daniel's visions directly, for by his time the faithful, like Jerome in his *Commentary on Daniel*, could not be sure whether the words referred to the persecution of the 160s B.C.E. or to the troubles of the Last Age. To cite Daniel directly as having predicted an event was to risk a wrong resolution of the ambiguity. Jason could not or would not acknowledge that Daniel disparaged his

---

[24] Another reason for the Hasmonaean spokesman to stress the sabbatical year was the refutation which the course of events gave to the quietist teaching of "O Israel, observe the Sabbath and the sabbatical year, and God will protect you."

[25] *AJ* xiii 1.1.5.

[26] In contradicting I 1:10 by proving that Antiochus IV was not wicked to the Jews from the beginning (see Part IV, p. 78), Jason does not contradict Daniel. At Dan 7:8, 20–21, 24–25, Antiochus IV at first is a typical Hellenistic conqueror and only later turns to wickedness with his presumptuous acts against the Jews and their God. The case is similar at Dan 8:9–12, 23–25. Even at Dan 11:21 Antiochus IV is not originally wicked but only contemptible.

hero, Judas. Perhaps for Jason the "little help" was Mattathias, whom indeed he thought beneath mention.[27]

Jason probably took even the point at which his book began with Daniel. Daniel had predicted an Era of Wrath, to last for seventy sabbatical weeks of years. At the beginning of the last of these hebdomads would come the death of the "anointed" priest, Onias III, and within the last hebdomad would come the Oniad Jason's bloody but abortive coup (Dan 9:24-26). One cannot tell whether Jason of Cyrene recognized the allusion to Menelaus' intrigues and sacrileges at Dan 11:22-24.[28] In any case, Jason of Cyrene shared the seer's pietist belief, that throughout the Era of Wrath Jews were condemned by their God to obey their heathen rulers. Hence, Jason had to justify the revolt of his hero, Judas Maccabaeus. He could do so if he could find a sign that the divine sentence upon the Jews had at least in part been lifted before Judas' revolt. Characteristic of the Era of Wrath was the absence of miracles.[29] The return of miracles would be the sort of sign Jason required. Some Jews had seen a miraculous divine intervention in the repulse of Heliodorus from the temple. The merit of the high priest, Onias III, was said to have been a factor in the miracle. Thus, for Jason, the merit of Onias III lifted part of the divine sentence and allowed Judas to end the Era of Wrath. This is the probable reason for Jason's glorification of Onias III. Jason shows no sign of having noticed that the seer alluded to the attempt of Heliodorus with no reference whatever to any miracle (Dan 11:20). Ben Sira glorifies Simon II, not Onias III.

The author of First Maccabees welcomed the opportunity to show that the two visits of Antiochus IV to Jerusalem implied by Dan 11:28 and 30 could not be reconciled with the single violation of the temple and the holy city known to tradition. If we assume that Jason of Cyrene was aware of the difficulties posed by the prophesies of Daniel and did the best he could to protect their veracity from challenge, many strange features of Second Maccabees become easy to understand. Let us see what results from the assumption. In the case of the king's visits to Jerusalem, Jason found that he could indeed narrate two and place each

[27] See Part IV, p. 79.
[28] Put a period after $w^e y i \check{s} \check{s} a b \bar{e} r \bar{u}$ in Dan 11:22, and then read $w^e g a m \ n^e g \bar{i} d \ b^e r \bar{i} t \ min \ hithabb^e r \bar{u} t \ . . .$, and for $l \bar{a} h e m$ (Aramaic: $l h w n$) in 11:24 perhaps read $l^e y \bar{a} w \bar{a} n$ or $l \bar{o}$ (Aramaic: $l h$). The resultant text then means, "And also a Jewish high priest through association with the king shall work treachery and thus rise to rule over Israel. In time of peace he shall come against the riches of the city and do what his ancestors had not done: he shall squander the property as spoil and plunder to the Greeks [or "to him" (sc. the king)], and he shall plot against the pious until the appointed time." For $n \bar{a} g \bar{i} d$ as high priest, see on II 3:4. For "a small people" as Israel, see Deut 7:7. For $m^e d \bar{i} n \bar{a} h$ as "city" rather than "province" see Lam 1:1. For "squander" $(y i b z \bar{o} r)$ one might read "loot" $(y \bar{a} b \bar{o} z)$, although that is not necessary. For $m i b s \bar{a} r \bar{i} m$ as a mistranslation of Aramaic $h s y n$, "Pietists, the pious," see Ginsberg, pp. 42-49.
[29] See Part I, pp. 12-13.

after a military operation against Egypt as required by Dan 11:25–30. Jason told of one visit (II 4:21–22) in which the king "acted" benevolently to Jerusalem, after attending (presumably by proxy) a deceitful feast in Egypt, so as to fit Dan 11:27–28; and he told of another visit (II 5:11–21) in which the king acted in wrath, so as to fit Dan 11:30. Although the events of Antiochus' peaceful visit to Jerusalem when Jason the Oniad was high priest scarcely fit the context of Dan 11:28, Jason of Cyrene appears to have regarded parts of Dan 11:25–28 (perhaps only the order of the events) as oracular secrets. He met the seer's obscurity with his own vagueness at II 4:21–22: "Antiochus saw to his own security on the side of Egypt" (with or without a lucrative military campaign?) and "thus" (how? the Greek is *hothen*) on his return passed through Joppe, Jerusalem, and Phoenicia.[30]

Accordingly, for Jason the campaign of 169 B.C.E. was indeed Antiochus IV's second departure against Egypt.[31] The text of Daniel, however, was still embarrassing. Jason vividly described Antiochus' rage (II 5:11), probably drawing on Dan 11:30, but there the king's rage against the holy covenant comes not in 169 but after the king received the Roman ultimatum of 168. Jason could not solve this difficulty. He could try to conceal it. Antiochus' campaigns against Egypt were famous. To an unwary reader, "second departure against Egypt" would indeed mean the campaign of 168. To maintain the ambiguity, Jason omitted the date and suppressed his own natural bent to give a detailed description of the causes of his characters' emotional outbursts. Though Polybius and Daniel describe Antiochus' emotional turmoil upon receiving the Roman ultimatum, Jason carefully refrains from mentioning the ultimatum.

Again, to maintain the ambiguity and protect the veracity of Daniel against such attacks as at I 1:29–64,[32] Jason gives no date for the operations of the Mysarch and speaks vaguely of the "defilement" the Mysarch caused in Jerusalem (II 5:27) and uses the same word "defilement" for the desecration of the temple on 25 Kislev (II 6:2), as if the Mysarch had earlier perpetrated some similar desecration.[33] Though an unprejudiced reader would take Dan 11:31 as ignoring the Mysarch's expedition or as confounding it with the desecration of 25 Kislev, Jason thought that the seer knew that the two were separate events. In so thinking, Jason, as we have seen, was correct, but he probably did not suspect that Dan 11:39 referred to the Mysarch's expedition. As Jason viewed it, the desecration came "a short time" after the Mysarch's expedition (II 6:1).

---

[30] Cf. the view of Kolbe and Bévenot, quoted by Abel, p. 348.

[31] *aphodos;* so read at II 5:1 with manuscripts A and 93.

[32] See pp. 45–46.

[33] Perhaps he was punning on the Mysarch's title (*mysos* in Greek means "defilement").

We shall find that his "short time," by his own calculations, was probably at least six or seven months.[34]

Our assumption has led us to conclude that Jason knew the king's sack of Jerusalem occurred in 169 and the desecration of the temple in 167, but he wrote obscurely to protect the veracity of the book of Daniel. If we proceed without our assumption and use only the information in II 5–6, Jason's vagueness leaves it possible that the sack occurred in 169 or 168, with the desecration falling "later," in 169, 168, or 167. However, by reckoning backwards from the first usable absolute date in the abridged history (II 11:33), one can again make it almost certain that Jason, like First Maccabees, dated the desecration in 167.[35]

[34] See pp. 52–53.

[35] Between the Feast of Dedication and Lysias' first expedition, which he knew ended in Xanthicus (February–March), 164 B.C.E. Jason narrated (II 10–11): the rise of Lysias; the fall of Ptolemy Makron; a campaign against Idumaea in which there was a siege; the campaign against the first Timotheus, which was closely followed (II 11:1) by Lysias' first expedition. According to Jason the rise of Lysias took place immediately upon the arrival at Antioch of the news of Antiochus IV's death; there could be no delay in appointing an executive to act for a child-king. The fall of Ptolemy Makron must have occurred soon, too; Lysias had immediately to consolidate his position against rivals. The campaign against Idumaea in First Maccabees immediately after the spread among the gentiles of the news of the rededication and is closely followed by the campaign against the first Timotheus (I 5:1–8), just as it is in II 10:14–37. Nothing indicates that a winter intervened between any of the events. Hence probably for Jason as for First Maccabees they occupied less than one year. Since for Jason they were all over by February–March, 164, he can hardly have believed that the dedication occurred in December, 167, two years after a desecration in 169. One who wishes to dismiss the fact that no intervening winter is mentioned may suggest that Jason believed the events after the Feast of Dedication occupied fourteen months, with the Feast of Dedication falling in 166. Then, however, the desecration would fall in 168, and the three and a half years of Dan 7:25, 9:27, and 12:7, if measured from the descration, would end in June, 164, in a non-sabbatical year and at a time when no memorable events are recorded in First or Second Maccabees or alluded to by Daniel. If the three and a half years were measured from about six months earlier, presumably from the Mysarch's expedition, they would end in December, 165. They would end one year after the hypothetical date of the Feast of Dedication, in the midst of the events of II 10–11, well before the miraculous apparition mentioned at II 11:8, which brought Lysias' defeat and "suit for peace." A believer in the truth of Daniel's prophesies would find such a chronology embarrassing; see pp. 52–53.

As we shall see (Part IV, p. 82), Jason eagerly contradicted the date for the Feast of Dedication in First Maccabees. From this fact, one more argument can be derived to show that Jason could not have dated the desecration in 168, an argument which does not depend on Daniel. The basis for Jason's chronology against that of First Maccabees is the assumed date in February–March, 164, of the letter at II 11:22–26. If the dates at I 1:54 and 4:52 are interpreted as Macedonian Seleucid dates, the desecration and dedication according to First Maccabees fall in December, 168 and 165, with a three-year interval ending well before the supposed date of the letter of Antiochus V, and thus the chronology of First Maccabees could have been harmonized with the evidence which Jason brought to refute it. Jason, who knew and used the Macedonian Seleucid era, would have said something to exclude such a harmonization if he had thought it possible.

The Roman ultimatum followed closely upon the Roman destruction of the Antigonid kingdom of Macedonia. Greeks and Romans regarded both events as epoch-making. The year in which they fell was one of the best-known dates in the Graeco-Roman world.[36] Surely Jason knew it, too. He and the abridger are able to give dates for far more obscure events of Seleucid history (II 13:1, 14:4). Hence, it is hard to believe Jason's vagueness was not deliberate, and our assumption, that he was vague to protect the veracity of Daniel, gains confirmation.

A pious writer who could not reject any of his contradictory sources could only take refuge in vagueness. Josephus had a different solution for these difficulties, but he, too, took refuge in vagueness here and in similar situations.[37]

Whereas the author of First Maccabees flaunted the date of Antiochus' departure eastward and ascribed the expedition of Gorgias and Nicanor to the instructions left by the departing king, Jason probably avoided mentioning the departure that had confounded the predictions of the seer and ascribed the expedition of Gorgias and Nicanor to Lysias' response to the local Seleucid agent's calls for help, perhaps on good evidence.[38]

On the other hand, sometimes Jason could use the testimony of Daniel to advantage against an opponent. Thus, Jason is delighted to contradict (II 13:1) the erroneous date at I 6:20[39] for the year of Judas' siege of the Akra and the Seleucid expedition which broke it. Jason may have derived his correct date from some non-Jewish historian. But he could have also derived or supported that date from interpretations of the book of Daniel. He probably did not know that Dan 11:22–24 predicted an end for the pontificate of Menelaus by the end of the sabbatical year 164/3. But he may have had his own peculiar interpretation of the prophesies at Dan 8:9–14, 24–26, and 9:27. Jason found the prophesies of Daniel 8 a difficult problem. On Jason's chronology, Antiochus IV was dead before 15 Xanthicus, 148 Sel.=March 12, 164 B.C.E., long before the end of the twenty-three hundred days and nights after the desecration by which time, according to Dan 8:14, the Holy would be vindicated. The only later event by which the Holy could be said to be vindicated was the offer of sacrifice at Jerusalem by the Seleucid king himself (II 13:23; cf. I 6:62). Jason dated the desecration of the temple to 25 Kislev (December 16), 167 (II 10:5). Thus, for Jason, the expedition of Lysias and Antiochus V would have ended twenty-three hundred days and nights

36 Polybius iii 3.8–9: xxix 27.11–13; Mørkholm, pp. 94–96.

37 See Appendix V; commentary, NOTE on I 1:33–40, end; and my article in *Studies Smith*, Part III, pp. 121–23.

38 See Part V, pp. 97, 103. (II 8:1–17 derived from *DMP*); see also Part III n. 10.

39 See NOTE ad loc.

after the desecration, that is to say, on February 8, 163 B.C.E.=23 Shebat,[40] 149 Sel. Mac., precisely the year given at II 13:1.

Equally a problem for Jason was the three and a half years predicted as the duration of the time of troubles at Dan 7:25 and 9:27. Like the Revised Standard Version, Jason may have understood Dan 9:27 to mean, "until the decreed end is poured out on the desolator"; he may have interpreted the "desolator" to mean Menelaus, who was executed, according to him, at the beginning of Lysias' and Antiochus V's campaign. If so, Jason of Cyrene believed that Menelaus' execution came three and a half years after some point in Antiochus IV's attacks on Jews and Judaism mentioned in Daniel 7 and 9. That point for Jason could not have been the desecration of 25 Kislev since by his chronology the entire expedition of Lysias and Antiochus V was over about three years and three months after the desecration. But the slaughter of the saints at Dan 7:25 and perhaps even the interruptions of the sacrificial cult at Dan 9:27 to Jason indicated the murderous and defiling expedition of the Mysarch.[41] The expedition of Lysias and Antiochus V as narrated by Jason must have lasted at least three months, the time required to force the defenders of Beth-Zur to give up under siege despite having received supplies. If the Mysarch's expedition is the starting point for the three and a half years, on Jason's chronology it must have occurred at least six to seven months before the desecration, with Menelaus' death falling three and a half years later, in the autumn or winter of 164/3 B.C.E.[42]

If we have reconstructed it correctly, Jason after all his labor would still have found his own interpretation of Dan 9:27 embarrassing because Menelaus' death should have ended the dreadful three and a half years. Hence, Judas' plight as narrated in I 6:47–54 was unacceptable to Jason. On the contrary, Judas must have won a victory, as we find at II 13:22. Also unacceptable were the references to the sabbatical year, for two reasons. First, observance of the sabbatical year should bring God's aid to the saints, not hinder them.[43] Second, to have mentioned the sabbatical year might cast discredit on the prophesies of Daniel which predicted

---

[40] Cf. *Megillat Ta'anit* 28 Shebaṭ. *Megillat Ta'anit* is a list in Aramaic of thirty-six dates on which Jews were forbidden to fast. It was probably compiled during the great Jewish revolt against Rome, between 67 and 70 C.E. After the completion of the Palestinian and Babylonian Talmudim, a rather unreliable commentary on *Megillat Ta'anit*, the "scholia," was written in Hebrew. Some of the dates are festivals commemorating events mentioned in First and Second Maccabees. Thus, *Megillat Ta'anit* is an important historical source for the period. Hans Lichtenstein, "Die Fastenrolle," HUCA 8–9 (1931–32), 257–351, gives a critical edition of the list and the scholia and a discussion of the historical problems.

[41] See pp. 50–51.

[42] "Super-Hasmonaean" Josephus characteristically contradicts him, but Josephus' evidence may well have been as poor as Jason's; see commentary on II 13:3–8.

[43] Cf. Geiger, *Urschrift*, p. 218.

that it would be a turning point. Hence, although Jason was well enough informed on Jewish law to know that 149 Sel. Mac. was a sabbatical year, he does not mention the fact.

Finally, if Daniel's prophesy was to be true at all, Judas' "victory" after Menelaus' death had to be a real turning point, not a compromise which allowed Antiochus V to show that he was powerful enough to violate his agreement by breaching the walls of the temple mount. Hence, Jason does not mention the perfidy of Antiochus V. Rather, the king humbled himself, honored the temple, and withdrew, thus "justifying the Holy" as predicted at Dan 8:14. Because of the obvious drastic abridgment of Jason's account at II 13:18–26, we cannot tell whether Jason tried further at that point to vindicate the veracity of Daniel.[44]

Our reconstruction of Jason's interpretations of Daniel would explain the sudden appearance of absolute dates in the abridged history at II 13:1 and 14:4 after their complete absence from the narrative of the earlier chapters (the dates in II 11 are in the quoted documents, not in the narrative). At that point it became safe to include absolute dates. On Jason's reconstructed interpretation, the latest historical event predicted by Daniel was the expedition of Lysias and Antiochus V, and Daniel had "predicted" its date "correctly." The true date of Alcimus' approach to Demetrius I (II 14:4) conflicted with none of the prophesies cherished by Jason.

For believers, as for Jerome,[45] all prophesies of Daniel unfulfilled by the end of the sabbatical year in early autumn 163 B.C.E. were prophesies to be fulfilled in the distant future, when God should see fit to bring the End.

---

[44] But see on II 5:24–27.
Once he had established Antiochus V's withdrawal as a real turning point, Jason may have been led by his knowledge of the Jewish religious year to believe that the turning did come at the "end of the year," as predicted in Daniel's prophesies; not, however, at the end of the sabbatical year, which by then was long since over, but at the end of the year for tithing the produce of fruit-trees, 1 or 15 Shebaṭ (M. Rosh hashanah 1:1). Megillat Ta'anit dates Antiochus V's withdrawal from Jerusalem on 28 Shebaṭ. Jason, who probably dated it 23 Shebaṭ (p. 53), may have conjectured that the truce and negotiations which brought the king's withdrawal began about 15 Shebaṭ.
Other attempts by Jason to defend the veracity of Daniel: see NOTES on II 2:20; 5:24–27.
[45] See Jerome Commentarii in Danielem, Prologue and on 7:14b and on 11:24–12:12.

III. JOSEPHUS AND THE WORK
OF ONIAS IV

We have now established that First and Second Maccabees represent opposing views and draw on a variety of earlier sources and that the earlier
sources in antiquity received varying interpretations. As time passes, such
literature of controversy becomes more and more difficult to understand
for readers who do not know the background of the issues which agitated
a bygone age. Nevertheless, an intelligent person studying the problems
with the help of other sources still surviving in his time could achieve
much. If, however, his own convictions would not let him accept an interpretation which would solve a problem, that problem would be insoluble for him.

Such an intelligent man was the much maligned historian Josephus.
Within the limits of time imposed by the huge scope of his work he was
a careful writer. Though his theological position blinded him to certain
possibilities, as a historian he was worthy at least of standing in the
same rank as nineteenth- and twentieth-century historians of the Hasmonaean period who so disparage him. We have observed that he used
First Maccabees.[1] We shall see that he studied both First and Second
Maccabees in the light of Daniel and Greek and Roman sources and in
the light of other sources no longer available to us.

What were the presuppositions of Josephus?

1) He was a proud descendant of Jonathan, the Hasmonaean, and a
defender of the honor of the Hasmonaean line through the reign of John
Hyrcanus and even of later members, though he recognized the grave
failings of Alexander Jannaeus and his successors.[2]

2) By the time he wrote the *Antiquities* and the *Life* he was a convinced Pharisee, but even earlier in life he had been sympathetic to both
the Pharisees and the Essenes.[3] Hence, he believed in immortality and
resurrection.[4]

---

[1] Part I, p. 13.

[2] *Vita* 1.2–5; *AJ* xii 6.1.265 – xiii 10.7.300, esp. xiii 300, xiii 11.3.318–19, 15.3.394 –
16.1.406, 16.6.430–32, xiv 16.4.490–91, xv 3.3.51–52, etc.

[3] *Vita* 2.10–12, 5.21; *BJ* ii 8.2–14.119–66.

[4] *BJ* ii 8.14.163, iii 8.5.372–75; *AJ* xviii 1.3.14—see L. H. Feldman's note *c* ad
loc., *Josephus*, IX, LCL, no. 433 (1965), p. 13; *Ap.* ii 30.218.

3) He believed in the veracity of Daniel 7–12.[5]

4) He was proud of the martyrs and believed in the value of martyr-dom.[6]

In addition, Josephus was a proud Jew writing to win admiration for his people from Greek and Roman readers. If he did not have firm evidence, he would avoid presenting an account which contradicted reputable Greek or Roman writers.[7]

All these tendencies can be found in both the *War* and the *Antiquities.* The *Antiquities,* however, show much more clearly than the *War* the operation of the tendencies and the sources used by Josephus. Let us, therefore, examine the *Antiquities* first. Josephus' convictions were not necessarily compatible with one another. In particular, pride in the Hasmonaean dynasty could well be in conflict with Josephus' other beliefs. There can be no doubt of his commitment to Hasmonaean pride. In the *Antiquities* he made First Maccabees his principal source for the entire period covered by it.[8] First Maccabees, however, rejects Daniel 7–12 and the belief in the resurrection and suggests that martyrdom can be in vain. First Maccabees contradicts Greek and Roman writers and holds that the Hasmonaeans, God's chosen stock, are nearly infallible. Josephus knew how fallible they proved to be. All these considerations led Josephus to modify not only the style but the content of First Maccabees when he adapted the work for his *Antiquities.*[9] The modifications show conclusively that he had at his disposal the content of Second Maccabees and possibly the complete work of Jason of Cyrene.[10]

---

[5] *AJ* x 11.7.267–81, xii 7.6.322.

[6] *Ap.* i 8.43, ii 30.219, 32.232–35, 38.277; *BJ* ii 8.10.151–53, i 1.2.34–35; *AJ* xii 5.4.255–56, 6.2.272–75, 3.281–82.

[7] Cf. *AJ* xii 9.1.358–59.

[8] Even beyond I 13:42 or 14:16; see Part I, n. 55, and commentary, NOTES on 13:31–52, 14:16–24k, and 15:1–14, 25–26.

[9] Examples of modifications in the light of later Hasmonaean fallibility: I 2:51–68 versus *AJ* xii 6.3.279–84 (see Part IV, p. 74); I 5:62 versus *AJ* xii 8.6.352 (see Part IV, p. 74).

[10] See commentary in AB vol. 41A to II 7:1 (most conclusive), to II 5:14, 6:12 – 7:42, 8:30, 10:6–7, 13:3–8, 23; and NOTES on I 1:57–64, 2:38, 3:18–22, 5:8, 7:43–46. See also Appendix V and my article in *Studies Smith,* Part III, pp. 85, 116–23. The verbal echoes of II 7 and other passages show that Josephus possessed Jason's Greek work or the abridgment, not merely Jason's hypothetical Hebrew or Aramaic source(s).

Possession of Jason's complete work is suggested by the following:

1) Jason took an interest in the fate of the Samaritan temple (II 6:2) and probably included at least some of the material of *AJ* xii 5.5.257–64. However, Josephus may well have taken the information from the book of Onias IV. See p. 50.

2) Josephus' contemporary, the author of Fourth Maccabees, may have drawn on the unabridged work of Jason. The expansion in Fourth Maccabees of the account of the martyrdoms of the mother and her seven sons in II 7 may be the author's own, but the author also knows of Antiochus IV's march against the Persians as following upon the king's failure to force the Jews of Jerusalem to change their religion (IV 18:5). First Maccabees tells of resistance in Judaea, not in Jerusalem, as the cause which drove the king to march eastward (I 3:1–31). Second Maccabees omits

On the other hand, Josephus' narrative shows that he considered Jason's work unreliable.[11] Josephus accepted only Jason's respect for the martyrs[12] and his detailed reprobation by name of Menelaus. Josephus rejected outright Jason's veneration for Onias III[13] and his aspersions on the Hasmonaeans. Wherever he could, Josephus contradicted Jason's attempts to refute First Maccabees, especially on points of chronology. However, he could not defend the chronology of First Maccabees where it contradicted a reputable Greek or Roman historian[14] or his own understanding of Daniel.[15] Josephus' attempts to contradict Jason allow us to describe those parts of his account as "super-Hasmonaean," as being even more effectively pro-Hasmonaean than First Maccabees. Josephus' "super-Hasmonaean" propaganda deserves close analysis.[16]

We may summarize here the results of such investigation. Josephus, in presenting a pro-Hasmonaean rebuttal to the work of Jason of Cyrene, sought to prove that all of the later Zadokite-Oniad high priests, including Onias III, were insignificant or contemptible men. In so doing, he had to refute not only Jason of Cyrene but other propagandists for the Zadokite line.[17] By careful analysis of Josephus' account one can prove that he probably drew on a propagandistic history written by Onias IV.[18] This Onias, who normally would have succeeded his father, Onias III, as high priest, instead was pushed aside by the successive royal appointments of Jason, Menelaus, and Alcimus to the pontificate. Onias IV thereupon took service under Ptolemy VI Philometor, who allowed him to found a Jewish temple at Leontopolis in Egypt.

---

the notice of the eastward march, perhaps because the abridger left it out. However, it is likely that Jason deliberately refrained from giving the place of the martyrdoms (see commentary on II 7:1) and probably avoided mentioning the expedition which Daniel failed to predict, until he had to speak of it in connection with the king's death (II 9:1). Hence, the author of Fourth Maccabees may have derived his knowledge of Antiochus' march eastward from a source other than Jason and probably did infer for himself that Jerusalem was the place of the martyrdoms.

See E. Bickerman, "The Date of IV Maccabees," *Louis Ginzberg Jubilee Volume* (New York: American Academy for Jewish Research, 1945), pp. 105–12. On the divergences between Second and Fourth Maccabees, see Moses Hadas, *The Third and Fourth Books of Maccabees* (New York: Harper, 1953), pp. 92–95, 162–66.

3) See NOTE on I 9:19–21.

[11] Cf. Geiger, *Urschrift*, p. 229.

[12] See commentary on II 6:12–7:42.

[13] On Josephus' treatment of Onias III, see my article in *Studies Smith,* Part III, pp. 116–23.

[14] See NOTE on I 12:39–40.

[15] See Appendix V.

[16] See my article in *Studies Smith,* Part III.

[17] The Essenes of Qumran also place great importance on the Zadokite line, but their veneration was directed to members of the family acceptable to them. They may well have been hostile to Onias IV, the probable founder of the Sadducees. See Part IV, pp. 70–71.

[18] See my article in *Studies Smith,* Part III.

Between 131 and 129 B.C.E. Onias IV published a work proving (1) that Jews could rightfully collaborate with Greeks, but only with the Ptolemaic empire, not with the wicked Seleucids; (2) that his righteous father, Onias III, had won great benefits for the Jews through his friendly relations with the Greeks, even with Seleucids, though his true loyalties were to the Ptolemies; proof of the merit of Onias III was God's miraculous defense of the temple in Jerusalem; (3) that his own Tobiad kinsmen, Joseph and Hyrcanus, and even his sinful uncle, Jason, had pursued a similar phihellenic and pro-Ptolemaic policy, to the great advantage of the Jews, but their policy had been thwarted by wicked pro-Seleucid Tobiads and by the wicked usurper of the high priesthood, Menelaus, so that disaster came upon the Jews; and (4) that the last surviving link to Israel's original cult institutions, other than the Torah, was the Oniad line of high priests. The divine presence had never returned to the temple in Jerusalem, so that it was no more holy than the temple of Leontopolis. One can also show that Onias IV was interested in the history of the Samaritans. In his eyes their temple on Mount Gerizim could have some legitimacy.

Josephus was quick to see that Onias' work was a source of Jason of Cyrene's glorification of Onias III. The clues are still visible in Second Maccabees. Though Jason of Cyrene believes passionately in the sanctity of the temple in Jerusalem, he begins his book with the strange assertion (II 3:1) that the only Onias' piety (not divine providence!) gave the holy city the blessings of peace.[19] Oddly, too, he goes on to say (II 3:2) that "another unexpected result" (*synebaine kai*) was that the Seleucid kings themselves were brought to honor the temple, as if it were strange that Seleucid kings should show such respect. We can see here, at the beginning of the story of the miraculous repulse of Heliodorus, the hand of an anti-Seleucid propagandist. Conclusive proof that Jason of Cyrene drew on Onias IV's work lies in the mention of Hyrcanus the Tobiad at II 3:11. Hyrcanus is nowhere else mentioned in Second Maccabees and need not have been mentioned at II 3:11. Indeed, as Josephus knew,[20] Hyrcanus was viewed by the Seleucid authorities as a rebel whose goods were forfeit, so that by mentioning Hyrcanus the high priest impaired his own plea that the deposits in the temple were inviolable. Jason of Cyrene could mention Hyrcanus here only if he was copying the propaganda of Onias IV, which sought to show how God favored both Onias III and Hyrcanus.

Normally Jason of Cyrene was a loyal partisan of Jerusalem who probably considered the Samaritans as beneath mention. They are unmentioned at II 15:1–2, where one might expect at least a derogatory reference to them. Probably, he referred to the Samaritan temple at II 6:2 only because he was drawing on Onias IV.

The views which Jason of Cyrene shares with Onias IV were repugnant to Josephus. To refute Jason, Josephus needed only to refute Jason's source. Much to his satisfaction, on careful study of Onias' work, Josephus thought he could prove that the author had deliberately distorted the facts. Better yet, Josephus thought the truth could be reconstructed from Onias' distorted account, a truth which proved the unworthiness of the Oniad high priests, at least from Onias II on, and in particular showed that the pontificate of Onias III had in no way been remarkable. In fact, if Jason could claim that incompetent Joseph and Azariah were Hasmonaeans,[21] Josephus or his source could retaliate by taking advantage of the fact that Menelaus' Hebrew name was probably Onias son of Simon to turn Menelaus into an Oniad, a brother of Onias III and Jason, the sons of Simon II.[22]

Throughout his narrative, Josephus reasserts the version of First Maccabees against the version of Jason,[23] except for the account of Antiochus'

[21] II 8:22–23; see commentary and Part I, n. 69.

[22] *AJ* xii 5.1.238, xx 10.3.235–36. Two brothers could bear the same name if they were half brothers or if "Onias" was a name each assumed upon investiture as high priest, like the names of the popes. Every King of the Ptolemaic dynasty bore the name "Ptolemy," even brothers who shared the throne, like Ptolemy VI and Ptolemy VIII. Antiochus IV had an older brother Antiochus.

[23] *AJ* xii 6.1–3.265–84 with I 2 *against* the silence of Jason on Mattathias.

AJ xii 7.3.298 with I 3:38–39 (Lysias in fulfillment of the king's command sends out the expedition of Nicanor and Gorgias) *against* II 8:8 (Ptolemy the son of Dorymenes sends it out in response to Philip's call for help).

AJ xii 7.5.313 with I 4:26–35 (Lysias' first expedition occurs before the Feast of Dedication and ends with his defeat but with no treaty) *against* II 11 (Lysias' expedition occurs after the Feast of Dedication and ends with the treaty stopping the persecution).

AJ xii 7.6.320 with I 1:59, 4:52 (Feast of Dedication three years after the desecration) *against* II 10:3 (two years after).

AJ xii 8.1–6.327–53 with I 5 (wars with neighboring peoples uninterrupted by an expedition of Lysias; no distinction between the two Timothei) *against* II 8:32, 10:10 – 12:45 (expedition of Lysias occurs in midst of neighbor wars; Timothei carefully distinguished at 8:32, 10:24).

AJ xii 9.1–2.354–59 with I 6:1–17 (Antiochus IV dies after Lysias' first campaign, after trying to rob a temple in Elymais) *against* II 9 (the king dies before Lysias' campaign, after trying to plunder Persepolis).

AJ xii 9.3–7.362–82 with I 6:18–63 (expedition of Lysias and Antiochus V provoked by siege of Akra in 150 Sel; Seleucid forces badly defeat Judas, who is hampered by observance of sabbatical year; Judas in Jerusalem rescued by arrival of Philip, Antiochus IV's choice to replace Lysias as regent; even so, Antiochus V destroys fortifications at Jerusalem) *against* II 9:28–29, 13:1–26 (expedition of 149 Sel. unprovoked; Jews defeat Seleucid forces; no mention of sabbatical year; Seleucid forces withdraw because of revolt of minister Philip at Antioch; the Philip who was chosen by Antiochus IV was a fugitive in Egypt; Antiochus V showed only kindness to Jerusalem).

actions against Jerusalem, where Josephus was constrained by his belief in the veracity of Daniel to emend the version of First Maccabees.[24]

We turn now to examine Josephus' brief sketch of Hasmonaean history in the *War*.[25] Striking is the obvious inaccuracy of the account. Josephus himself years later in writing his *Antiquities* felt compelled to correct the flagrant errors in the *War*.[26] The errors are not of the sort that would arise from tendentious interpretation of inadequate sources. They are all of the kind that a learned person might make if he could no longer consult books he had once read: confusion of Onias-Menelaus with Jason and with Onias IV[27]; placing the persecution immediately after the sack of Jerusalem[28]; giving the name "Bacchides" to an official important in the early stages of the persecution[29]; having Mattathias become acknowledged leader of the Jews after driving Seleucid troops out of Judaea[30]; giving Judas as Mattathias' eldest son; having Judas make his alliance with Rome early in his career and having him repulse a second invasion led by Antiochus IV[31]; placing the occupation of the Akra by Seleucid troops after the repulse of this invasion and immediately before the purification of the temple[32]; giving the three and a half years of Dan 7:25, 9:27, and 12:7, as the duration of the interruption of Jewish sacrifices between Antiochus IV's sack of Jerusalem and Judas' purification of the temple and reinstitution of sacrificial worship[33]; having Judas fall to Antiochus V's generals at Akedasa[34]; having John fall a few days later to collaborationists[35]; and confusing Alexander Balas with Antiochus VI.[36] All these

---

AJ xii 10.1.391 with I 7:6 (Alcimus accuses his whole nation) *against* II 14:6 (Alcimus accuses the pietists and Judas).

AJ xii 10.2–3.393–400 with I 7:8–25 *against* silence of Jason.

AJ xii 10.4.405 with I 7:29–32 *against* II 14:12–30.

AJ xii 10.6.412 with I 7:50, 9:23–27, *against* II 2:22, 16:37.

With I and against II Josephus mentions the Akra from the time it was built, not first with the victory over Nicanor; see commentary on II 5:24–27.

Josephus also contradicts (*AJ* xii 8.7.383–85) Jason's dating of the death of Menelaus at the beginning of the expedition of Lysias and Antiochus V (II 13:1–8).

[24] See Appendix V.

[25] *BJ* i *Prooem.* 7.19, 1.1.31 – 2.3.54.

[26] The *War* was published between 75 and 79 C.E.; see Thackeray, *Josephus*, pp. 34–35. Josephus finished the *Antiquities* in 93/4 (*AJ* xx 12.1.267).

[27] *BJ* i 1.1.31, 33; corrected: *AJ* xii 5.1.237–40, 9.7.387–88.

[28] *BJ* i 1.2.34; corrected: *AJ* xii 5.4.248.

[29] *BJ* i 1.2–3.35–36 (cf. II 8:30); corrected: *AJ* xii 6.2.270.

[30] *BJ* i 1.3.37; corrected: *AJ* xii 6.2.278–86.

[31] Eldest son, at *BJ* i 1.3.37; corrected: *AJ* xii 6.1.266, 4.283–84. Judas' acts, at *BJ* i 1.4.38; corrected: *AJ* xii 10.6.414–19, 7.2.297, and 9.1.354–57.

[32] *BJ* i 1.4.39; corrected: *AJ* xii 5.4.252; see commentary, NOTE on I i: 33–40.

[33] *BJ* i *Prooem.* 7.19 and 1.1.32 and 4.39; corrected: *AJ* xii 7.6.320.

[34] *BJ* i 1.6.47; corrected: *AJ* xii 10.1.389–90.

[35] *BJ* i 1.6.47; corrected: *AJ* xiii 1.2.10–11.

[36] *BJ* i 2.1.48–49; corrected: *AJ* xiii 2.1–2.35–45 and 6.1.187. Thackeray twice mistranslated *ho Antiochou pais* ("the son of Antiochus") as "the young Antiochus." Josephus at this point may have forgotten the name of Alexander Balas, who claimed

errors could have been made by a modern reader of First and Second Maccabees who had not thoroughly mastered the books. On the other hand, it is hard to ascribe such mistakes to a careful historian working with written sources in front of him.

Indeed, all peculiarities of Josephus' account in the *War* down to the death of Simon can be explained if Josephus wrote it relying on his memory of the content of First Maccabees and the works of Jason of Cyrene and Onias IV, none of which was then in his possession,[37] and also relying on his own interpretations of the prophesies of Daniel. So strong are the traces of the polemic interests of these Jewish sources that one cannot attribute the account in the *War* to a non-Jewish source, except through the unnecessary and improbable hypothesis that some gentile author tried to synthesize the accounts of First Maccabees, Jason of Cyrene, and Onias IV, or others like them, and was then copied by Josephus.[38]

As a descendant of the Hasmonaeans Josephus could have heard and remembered true traditions preserved nowhere else. An example might be at *BJ* i 1.5.45, where Josephus says that after the battle of Beth-Zechariah Judas withdrew to the province of Gophna (cf. I 6:47).

---

to be the son of Antiochus IV. Tryphon was the guardian of Alexander Balas' son, Antiochus VI. Josephus may have failed to perceive other instances where the narrative of First Maccabees contradicted his in the *War*. See commentary, NOTES on I 15:1–14, 25–26, 16:1–7, and 16:16.

[37] Josephus tells us he had copies of "sacred books" (*Vita* 75.418), but he did not regard any of the three Jewish histories of the Hasmonaean period as sacred.

[38] Hence, the widely accepted theory of Hölscher, that Josephus drew the sketch of Hasmonaean history in the *War* from the gentile historian Nicolaus of Damascus, is false. See Hölscher, "Josephus 2," PW, IX (1916), 1942–49.

IV. THE DATE AND SETTING OF FIRST AND SECOND MACCABEES IN THE POLEMICS OF THE HASMONAEAN PERIOD

First Maccabees cannot have been complete before the last decade of the second century B.C.E. At I 8:10 Judas, who was killed in 160 B.C.E., is moved to admire the Romans because of their victory over the Achaean League and their destruction of Corinth in 146 B.C.E. Only a member of a later generation could commit so flagrant an anachronism. Moreover, the author refers to the reign of John Hyrcanus, who died in 104 B.C.E., as if that prince was dead (I 16:23–24; compare the numerous instances of the formula in the books of Kings).

The author of Ep. 2, with his erroneous account of the death of Antiochus IV,[1] cannot have known either First Maccabees or the complete or abridged work of Jason. On the other hand, he probably knew Hebrew. Not only is this suggested by his pose as the learned scribe of the Council of Elders and of Judas, writing to the learned Aristobulus. There are other indications: he gives a forced Hebrew etymology of a foreign word[2] and may have been familiar with the Hebrew book of Esther,[3] which was first translated into Greek in 78/7 B.C.E.[4] Hence, neither the Hebrew nor the Greek of First Maccabees was available in Egypt to the author of Ep. 2 as he wrote. The author of Ep. 2 takes pains to state (II 2:13–15) that the authorities in Hasmonaean Jerusalem will supply copies of the books important for Jewish religion, which they have collected. Hence, we may infer that the books of Maccabees were not available in Jerusalem, either, at the time of Ep. 2 (late 103 B.C.E.).

If they knew of Ep. 2, both Jason of Cyrene and the author of First Maccabees had good reason to ignore it as a forgery because of the error

---

[1] See Appendix III, beginning. On the problems of Ep. 2 see Appendices III and IV and commentary.

[2] See in AB vol. 41A commentary on II 1:36.

[3] See commentary on II 1:10 and 1:18.

[4] See E. Bickerman, "The Colophon of the Greek Book of Esther," JBL 63 (1944), 339–62.

on the death of Antiochus. In addition, Jason could have rejected it as pro-Hasmonaean propaganda.[5]

Neither First Maccabees nor the work of Jason of Cyrene can have been written after Pompey's conquest of Jerusalem in 63 B.C.E. According to II 15:37, Jerusalem had been in Jewish hands from the death of Nicanor down to the time of writing. The pro-Hasmonaean patriot who wrote First Maccabees showers praise on Rome as a righteous republic and friend of the Hasmonaeans and the Jews, with no suggestion that one day Rome will be an enemy (I 8, 12:1–4, 14:24, 40, 15:15–24). Hence, both books were written between 103 and 63 B.C.E.[6]

We can be more precise. Josephus did his utmost to collect instances of Roman favor to the Hasmonaean dynasty, but before Pompey's intervention in Judaea he can report nothing after the Roman alliance and declaration of 132 B.C.E. in favor of John Hyrcanus (AJ xiii 9.2.259–66). Josephus missed a later instance, probably of 113–112, because he wrongly supposed the document dealt with Hyrcanus II, not with John Hyrcanus I.[7] Thereafter, however, there is no trace of benevolent intervention by Rome. John Hyrcanus and his heir might well be grateful for the support he received from the superpower, but after three decades of no Roman action whatever, what Hasmonaean propagandist would have praised Rome so highly?

Furthermore, there is no hint that the authors knew the inglorious history of Rome which, from 91 B.C.E., before the eyes of all in the eastern Mediterranean world belied the encomium at I 8:1–16. Rome incurred disgrace through the Social and Mithradatic wars, the long inability to cope with the Cilician pirates, and the careers of Sulla, Sertorius, and Pompey. Hence, First Maccabees can hardly have been written after 90 B.C.E. By that time, Alexander Jannaeus' struggle against the Pharisees had long since begun.[8] Other evidence, too, suggests for First Maccabees a date before the end of the reign of Alexander Jannaeus.[9]

Finally, the abridgment of Jason's work probably existed shortly after 78/7 B.C.E., for that is the probable date at which Epp. 1 and 2 were prefixed to the abridgment.[10]

A date in the reign of Alexander Jannaeus fits well the propagandistic thrust of both books and the history of the times. We shall show that

[5] See Appendix III, end.

[6] See also introductory NOTE to I 8:1–16. "In Rome" at I 14:16 is probably an interpolation; see commentary.

[7] J. AJ xiv 10.22.247–55; see M. Stern, "The Relations between Judea and Rome during the Rule of John Hyrcanus," Zion 26 (1961), 12–21 (in Hebrew).

[8] The civil war lasted six years before the Pharisees sought the aid of the Seleucid Demetrius III Eucaerus, who was deposed and handed over to Mithradates II of Parthia by 87 B.C.E. See J. AJ xiii 13.5.376 – 14.3.385; BJ i 4.4–5.91–95; Ralph Marcus, Josephus, VII, LCL, no. 365 (1943), p. 421.

[9] See NOTE on I 8:14

[10] See Appendix IV.

First Maccabees is pro-Hasmonaean propaganda and the work of Jason an anti-Hasmonaean reply, both written in the reign of Alexander Jannaeus. To do so we must show first how the need for such pieces of propaganda grew up among the Jews and then how First Maccabees and Jason's work fulfilled that need.

Jewish Opposition to the Hasmonaeans

From the first, the Hasmonaeans were ready to kill apostate Jews, who had no choice but to oppose them. Some of the residents of the Akra, however, may have been pietists innocent of apostasy, but if so, they lost influence with Jews because of their "treason."[11] In any case, apostates and the men of the Akra and their descendants were of no importance for the later controversies over Hasmonaean legitimacy.

Onias IV and his adherents, soldiers serving the Ptolemaic enemies of the Seleucid empire, may well have viewed with favor the activity of Mattathias, Judas, and Jonathan the "Judge." When, however, Jonathan became high priest, these proponents of the Oniad-Zadokite line had to oppose him.[12]

Other loyal Jews, however, indeed men of extreme piety, opposed the Hasmonaeans from the very time of Mattathias' act of zeal, in particular the group called the Pietists (*Ḥasidim*). The Pietists were quietists who believed that it was a heinous sin to rebel against the heathen kings who ruled over them by the grace of God.[13] The Pietists were ready to lay down their lives in their belief in the promises of the prophets, that God would come to the rescue of faithful Sabbath-observers (I 2:29–38; II 6:11).[14] If they were then massacred, they turned to their faith in resurrection (Dan 12:2–3; II 7:9, 11, 14, 23, 29, 36). They now clung to this belief, whether or not it was a recent development in Judaism, for only it could justify their martyrdom.

In contrast, Mattathias dared to rebel and even to fight on the Sabbath and probably condemned as false the belief in the resurrection.[15] Though large numbers of *Ḥasidim* were eventually to join Mattathias (I 2:41), the pious quietists who were ready to die, steadfast in their faith, surely thought his teachings impious and his actions heinous sins. They probably called him a "man of violence,"[16] doomed to destruction.[17] The author

[11] See II 14:3; I 7:5; Ps 73:15 with commentary to I 7:16–17; and pp. 64–65.
[12] See Part III, pp. 57–61.
[13] See Part I, pp. 5–6, 7, 9, 12, 17–21, 32.
[14] See commentary, NOTE on I 2:28–38.
[15] See Part I, pp. 5–6, 12.
[16] Cf. Dan 11:14; CD 1:18–19.
[17] CD 1:13 – 2:1 can be read as a description of Mattathias and Judas ("the man of scoffing"?) who preached violation of the Sabbath by defensive warfare and tried to humble the lofty kingdom (CD 1:15, 18–19) and went beyond the borders of the promised land to invade the land of the gentiles (CD 1:16) and opposed the legitimate high priest Alcimus. Judas and his brothers all died by the sword (CD 2:1;

of Dan 11:34 gives but faint praise to the "little help" and disapproves of the Pietists who slipped into joining the Hasmonaeans. Hence, among the "troublers of the people" (I 3:5) whom Judas faced, there may well have been Pietists. After the end of the persecution upon Lysias' withdrawal early in 164 (II 11:13–21, 27–38; I 4:35), Pietists on occasion may have made common cause with the garrison of the Akra in the effort to suppress the "wicked rebels" against the legitimate king (I 6:18–21).

Judas' victories may have brought most of the Pietists to side with him, but the seer at Dan 12:7 still predicted his defeat. Alcimus may have believed that the words of the prophets condemned rebellion and for that reason may have opposed the Hasmonaeans as soon as the persecution was over.[18] At I 7:12–13 we find an open admission that scribes and Ḥasidim supported Alcimus despite Hasmonaean rejection of him. Alcimus received the blame for the execution of sixty Pietists who had trusted him and thus alienated many, but some of the "troublers of the people" who remained loyal to him against the Hasmonaeans (I 7:22) surely were Pietists. Jason of Cyrene, who is eager to conceal any trace of Pietist opposition to Judas (compare II 14:3, 6–10 with I 7:12–13), nevertheless admits that those who accepted Alcimus as high priest were pious Jews, including the temple priests (II 14:34–36), Razis (II 14:37–46), and even Nicanor's guides (II 15:2–4).

Those who deserted Judas "out of fear" (I 9:6) may have been Pietists who did not believe that God would henceforth support Judas' cause against the legitimate high priest and king. Judas' death temporarily proved their belief to be true, and the author of First Maccabees tries to explain away the adherence of the majority to the anti-Hasmonaean side (I 9:23–27).

The sudden death of Alcimus gave considerable vindication to the Hasmonaean claims, and even more vindication came from Bacchides' desertion of the anti-Hasmonaean cause (I 9:69–72). Nevertheless, there may have been Pietists among the "subversives" who gathered before Alexander Balas at Ptolemais to accuse Jonathan (I 10:61) and even among those "haters of their people" (our author pointedly does not say they were "men of the Akra") who denounced Jonathan to Demetrius II for laying siege to the Akra (I 11:21).

Immediately after relating the climax of Jonathan's fortunes ca. 145 B.C.E. on the basis of I 12:1–18, Josephus suddenly introduces a note (*AJ* xiii 5.9.171–73) that at this time there were three sects, Pharisees,

---

cf. 8:8–12). Alcimus in destroying the wall of the temple court, an act condemned by the pro-Hasmonaean writer at I 9:54, may have been acting according to the interpretation of pietists who condemned "the builders of the wall" (CD 4:19; 8:12, 18).

[18] See NOTES on I 7:5–7; II 1:7, 14:3; and I 6:18–24.

Sadducees, and Essenes. The note as it stands is a digression from Josephus' narrative, in which at this point none of the sects plays a role. However, Josephus, the descendant of Jonathan who nevertheless admired the Essenes, may have wished to pass over in silence a report in a source lost to us of violent conflict between his ancestor and the Essenes. The issue which led to such a violent break could have been Jonathan's desertion of Demetrius II, to whom he had sworn loyalty,[19] or it could have arisen from differences over Sabbath observance. Probably, however, the conflict arose from far-reaching differences of opinion in Jewish law, particularly over the Jewish calendar, and Jonathan would then be the Wicked Priest of the Qumran texts.[20] In a Pietist anti-Hasmonaean narrative, Josephus' note on the sects could have been an integral part. Jason's unabridged work may have contained such a hostile account of Jonathan's career.

Simon, too, faced an opposition of "wicked" (I 14:14, cf. 14:44–45), who need not all have been apostates. The Roman consul Lucius in his letters on behalf of Simon and the Jews to states of the eastern Mediterranean world, including Ptolemaic Egypt, Seleucid Syria, and Arsacid Parthia, asks that fugitive subversives be sent back to Simon (I 15:16–24). Probably among these émigrés there were members of the Oniad party as well as Pietists. According to an Essene document, the repentant of Israel, apparently at some time after 207 B.C.E., left Judaea and went to Damascus or to Syria, the "land of Damascus." They may well have done so under Jonathan, whom they probably called "the wicked priest," or under Simon, whom they called a "cursed man of Belial."[21]

---

[19] See NOTE on II 1:7, *Jason . . . Kingdom.*

[20] On Jonathan and the Sabbath, see p. 75. The Wicked Priest is said to have come to attack the Teacher of Righteousness on the sect's Day of Atonement (1QpHab 11:2–8); see below, n. 21.

[21] CD 7:13–20; 3:19 – 4:4; 6:2–11; 8:21–24; cf. Enoch ciii 13. The apparent date is derived from CD 1:5–14, assuming that the author of CD took his 390 years from Ezek 4:5, 9, and measured from the exile of Jehoiachin in 597. I cannot deal here in detail with the problems of these obscure texts. Despite the doubts of Cross, ALQ, pp. 81–93, n. 46, one probably should take "Damascus" literally. Damascus or Syria may have been the temporary seat of the mission of the Expounder of the Torah just as the wilderness of Sinai was the seat of Moses'; both teachers taught laws not for their place of mission but for the Promised Land. The entire early Christian community, too, temporarily took refuge in Pella (Eusebius *Historia ecclesiastica* iii 5.2–3). The author plainly states that those who went to Damascus left the land of Judah (CD 4:3; 6:5; cf. 7:19–21); hence, "Damascus" can hardly be a name for Qumran in the land of Judah. See also S. Iwry, "Was there a Migration to Damascus?" EI 9 (1969), 80–88.

Wicked priest: 1QpHab 1:13, 8:8–13, 8:16 – 9:2, 9:9–12, 9:16 – 10:5, 11:2–8, 11:12–15, 12:2–6, 12:7–10, and perhaps also in 4QpPs37, published by J. M. Allegro, "Further Light on the History of the Qumran Sect," JBL 75 (1956), 89–95. Cursed man of Belial: 4Q175 (Testimonia), lines 21–30. See Cross, ALQ, pp. 134–60; however, Cross seems unjustified in trying to identify the wicked priest with the cursed man when the sources never do. Since the cursed man is most likely Simon, the wicked priest is most likely Jonathan.

The author of First Maccabees is most unwilling to concede that a clear-seeing pious Jew could oppose his heroes. Jason of Cyrene has a similar view concerning opposition to Judas. Josephus and rabbinic tradition share this unwillingness with respect to Judas and his brothers and record opposition of pious Jews to the dynasty first under John Hyrcanus, even though Josephus unreservedly approves of him.

Neither Josephus nor some rabbinic authorities were quite sure of the date of the split between the upholders of their Pietist tradition and the later Hasmonaeans. Some passages in the sources date it under John Hyrcanus, others under Alexander Jannaeus. Several factors led to this state of affairs. First, there were the principles of *damnatio memoriae* (wiping out all memory of a person) for great Jewish sinners[22] and of general anonymity in polemic literature. First Maccabees does not name Jason or Menelaus, and the Qumran texts never give the names either of the Teacher of Righteousness and his supporters or of the Wicked Priest.

Second, even in factual narratives the king involved might be hard to identify. Later traditions, whether pro or con, frequently named the Hasmonaean dynasty wholesale, without specifying which member accomplished which deed. There was also great opportunity for confusion in the names of the Hasmonaeans. "Yoḥanan" (John) was miswritten as "Yonatan" (Jonathan) even in the text of the Bible (Neh 12:11; cf. Neh 12:22–23, Ezra 10:6). There was even more possibility of confusing the Hasmonaean high priests since they were known in common speech by short nicknames (hypocoristics). "Yannay" (the Hebrew original of "Jannaeus," equivalent to English "Jonny" or "Johnny") could designate not only the high priest Jonathan son of Mattathias and King Jonathan (Alexander Jannaeus) but also John Hyrcanus.[23] Hence, with

---

[22] The names of the wicked are to be obliterated: Deut 29:19; Jer 11:19; Pss 9:6, 59:29, 109:13 and 15; Prov 10:7; TB *Yoma* 38b. Compare the contemporary and near-contemporary practice in Ptolemaic Egypt, Hans Volkmann, "Ptolemaios," PW, XXIII[II] (1959), 1720–21, 1746; Walter Otto and Hermann Bengtson, *Zur Geschichte des Niederganges des Ptolemäerreiches*, ABAW, N.S., vol. XVII, 136–44.

[23] Wholesale mention of the Hasmonaean dynasty: see for the present NOTE on I 13:52.

Joseph Derenbourg, *Essai sur l'histoire et la géographie de la Palestine* (Paris: Imprimerie impériale, 1868), p. 95, n. 1, demonstrates how hypocoristics were regularly formed from the first two consonants of a Hebrew name plus -ay, and notes that on this principle the hypocoristic of "Yoḥanan" should be "Yoḥay." However, he wrongly assumed that "Yannay" could not also represent "Yoḥanan." The language of the dispute between Abaye and Raba at TB *Berakot* 29a indeed suggests that it could: Abaye says, "Yannay and Yoḥanan are the same person," and Raba says, "Yannay is one person and Yoḥanan another." Derenbourg attempts to dismiss this evidence by suggesting (p. 80, n. 1 and p. 95, n. 1) that for Abaye and other sages "Yannay" was a name for all Hasmonaean high priests. Proof is lacking for such an assertion, though the tradition concerning a high priest Yoḥanan who held office for eighty years (TB *Berakot* 29a, *Yoma* 9a) is an instance of confusing John Hyrcanus and Alexander Jannaeus as if the two were one man. See pp. 68–70.

at least part of the written tradition not naming names and the oral tradition vulnerable to confusion, it is not surprising to find Josephus and the rabbis puzzled.

Since even Judas and his brothers faced Pietist opposition and since the Essenes of Qumran probably remembered Simon as the Cursed Man, Pietists surely opposed John Hyrcanus as well.[24] If the Essenes named John Hyrcanus at all in their dialect, in which laryngeals and pharyngeals were not pronounced, they probably called him "Yannay," and Josephus in his study of the Essenes could have learned their traditions. At *BJ* i 2.8.67–68 he forbears to name the great John's "envious" opponents, perhaps as a result both of his pro-Hasmonaean bias and of his veneration for the Essenes.

Much as Josephus respected the Essenes, when he wrote his *Antiquities* he was a convinced Pharisee. Pharisaic tradition, too, knew of a wicked King Yannay; Pharisees told of a King Yannay who turned against their sect because one Pharisee had dared to suggest that the king was disqualified from the high priesthood inasmuch as his mother had been a captive. There was no doubt that Alexander Jannaeus massacred Pharisees. We now know that the Essenes thought Jannaeus was right to execute them, though perhaps they disapproved of his extreme cruelty.[25] Hence, to the Essenes, "Wicked King Yannay" may have been John Hyrcanus at the same time as to the Pharisees "Wicked King Yannay" may have been Alexander Jannaeus. Josephus may not have been able to penetrate the ambiguities in his sources, but he had to decide when the feud between the Hasmonaeans and the Pietist sects began. In Josephus' *War* the Pharisees are not said to have opposed John Hyrcanus but enter political controversy only after the death of Alexander Jannaeus (i 5.2–3. 110–14). However, by the time Josephus wrote his *Antiquities* he decided that King Yannay of the famous tradition was John Hyrcanus (xiii 10.5–6.288–98; 16:2.408), despite the difficulty of harmonizing the identification with his own strong endorsement of John at *AJ* xiii 10.7.299–300.

The truth is that in the Babylonia of Abaye and Raba as at Qumran and anywhere else where the laryngeal and pharyngeal consonants were no longer pronounced, "Yo-anan" could become "Yannai" as easily as "Yonatan" could. An instance may occur in Josephus, where "Iannaios" of *Vita* 26.131 is "Annaios (*Ḥanay=Yoḥanan*)" at *BJ* ii 21.3.597. The tendency in Hebrew names of *Yo-* to become *Ya-* can be observed in the manuscripts both of the Greek Bible (Iada at I Chron 8:36; Yatham at Judg 9:5; Iareib at I Chron 24:7; Ias at II [IV] Kings 14:8) and of Josephus (see *Flavii Iosephi Opera*, ed. Benedictus Niese, 7 vols. [Berlin: Weidmann, 1887–95], VII [Index], s.vv. *Iaddous, Iasos*).

24 Cf. Cross, ALQ, pp. 58, 122, 155–56.

25 Josephus and the Pharisees: see Part III, n. 3, and cf. Morton Smith, "Palestinian Judaism in the First Century," in *Israel: Its Role in Civilization*, ed. Moshe Davis (New York: Harper, 1956). King Yannay and the Pharisees: see below. Essene opinion: Y. Yadin, "Pesher Nahum (4QpNahum) Reconsidered," IEJ 21 (1971), 1–12; Joseph M. Baumgarten, "Does *tlh* in the Temple Scroll Refer to Crucifixion?" JBL 91 (1972), 472–81.

Perhaps he was unwilling to accept the notion that Pharisees had yielded on a matter of principle where Essenes had persevered against John Hyrcanus. However, Josephus did know an interpretation which attached the story to Alexander Jannaeus, for at *AJ* xiii 13.5.372 he reports how the high priest Alexander Jannaeus was reviled as the offspring of a captive.[26]

The same kind of confusion appears in two texts transmitted by rabbis of the third and fourth centuries of the Christian era. The identical short nickname of Jonathan, John Hyrcanus, and Alexander Jannaeus and the brief, forgotten reign of Judah Aristobulus I allowed a tradition to grow up of a high priest Yoḥanan whose pontificate in round numbers lasted eighty years.[27] Jonathan son of Mattathias became high priest on the festival of Tabernacles, 152 B.C.E., and Alexander Jannaeus died in 76 B.C.E., over seventy-five years later, eighty years in round numbers. Since this same tradition says that the long-lived high priest became a Sadducee at the *end* of his life, it, too, really proves that Alexander Jannaeus was the Hasmonaean who broke with the Pharisees. Though this one tradition does show the rabbis confusing John Hyrcanus with Alexander Jannaeus, rabbinic tradition elsewhere never in any way equates Yoḥanan the high priest with King Yannay. In historical fact, John Hyrcanus was never king, and Alexander Jannaeus never bore the name Yoḥanan. The tradition of the eighty-year pontificate is not attributed to the earlier authorities (*tannaim*) but is late. In other rabbinic texts, especially in authentic texts of *tannaim*, "Yoḥanan the high priest" and "King Yannay" would seem to be unambiguous. Yoḥanan the high priest in these texts is always a person of authority and is never accused of heresy.[28] King Yannay in these texts is the contemporary of Queen Salome Alexandra and her brother Simon ben Sheṭaḥ[29]; his domains were productive.[30] Most important, it is he who breaks with the Pharisees after the challenge to his fitness for the high priesthood[31] and intimidates

---

[26] In their editions of the text of Josephus, Niese, Naber, and Marcus all adopt a harmonizing reading with the plural, *aichmalôtôn*, but P and F, two of the best manuscripts, along with V have *aichmalôton*, which is a slight corruption of the singular *aichmalôtou*, and the Latin has "de captiva." See Alon, I, 33, n. 22 (in Hebrew). Alon there also infers from *AJ* iii 8.9.218 that the era of wickedness (i.e. of wicked priests) began after the death of John Hyrcanus.

[27] TB *Berakot* 29a, *Yoma* 9a.

[28] M. *Ma'aser Sheni* 5:15 and TP *Ma'aser Sheni* 5:5, p. 56d; M. *Soṭah* 9:10 and TP *Soṭah* 9:10, p. 24a–b, TB *Soṭah* 47b–48a, To. *Soṭah* 13:5, 10, and see Saul Lieberman, *Hellenism in Jewish Palestine* (New York: Jewish Theological Seminary of America, 1950), pp. 139–46; M. *Parah* 3:5; Targum J. to Deut 33:11. Cf. J. *BJ* v 6.2.259, 7.3.304; vi 2.10.169.

[29] *Bereshit Rabbah* 91:3; *Qohelet Rabbah* to Eccles 7:12; TP *Nazir* 5:3, p. 54b; TP *Berakot* 7:2, p. 11b; TB *Berakot* 48a, *Soṭah* 22b, *Sukkah* 48b, *Keritot* 28b; *Schol. Megillat Ta'anit* 2 Shebaṭ.

[30] TB *Berakot* 44a.

[31] TB *Qiddushin* 66a.

the sages of the court in the presence of Simon ben Sheṭaḥ[32] and massacres them.[33]

Only one of these texts (TB *Sanhedrin* 107b) has any positive indication that "King Yannay" might mean John Hyrcanus. Joshua ben Peraḥiah is there said to have fled into exile from King Yannay and to have been summoned to return by an eloquent letter from Simon ben Sheṭaḥ when it was safe, presumably on the king's death. Joshua was a pupil of Yosi ben Yo'ezer of Ṣeredah.[34] Rabbinic texts have been interpreted to mean that Yosi ben Yo'ezer was executed just before the death of his nephew, Alcimus, in 159 B.C.E.[35] If so, Joshua would have been a centenarian when Alexander Jannaeus died in 76, and TB *Sanhedrin* 107b would have to refer to the reign of John Hyrcanus. However, the interpretation that Yosi ben Yo'ezer was dead by 159 is probably wrong.[36] We have not yet excluded the possibility that Simon ben Sheṭaḥ was prominent under John Hyrcanus and that Joshua ben Peraḥiah went into exile then.[37] There is another reason to believe TB *Sanhedrin* 107b is unhistorical. The Palestinian Talmud knows nothing of Joshua's exile but has another story of sojourn in Egypt ended by an almost identical elegant letter, but the story is of Simon ben Sheṭaḥ's colleague Judah ben Ṭabbay, and not Simon ben Sheṭaḥ but the "men of Jerusalem" send the letter.[38] The tradition at TB *Sanhedrin* 107b could well be a reconstruction based upon a confused mixture of Alexander Jannaeus' massacres, Judah ben Ṭabbay's sojourn in Egypt, and Simon ben Sheṭaḥ's known associations. Then TB *Sanhedrin* 107b would not have a tradition confusing King Yannay with John Hyrcanus but only one confusing Judah ben Ṭabbay with Joshua ben Peraḥiah.

Hence, we may conclude that with the isolated exception of the late tradition about the eighty-year pontificate rabbinic tradition was not confused by the similar names of Hasmonaean high priests, unlike Josephus. There are other reasons to reject Josephus' identification of John Hyrcanus as the king who broke with the Pharisees. Josephus says that on breaking with the Pharisees the prince went over to the Sadducees, abrogating the oral law (*AJ* xiii 10.6.296–98). In the tradition of *tannaim* at TB *Qiddushin* 66a, the Sadducees are not mentioned, but the king accepts the notion that he may attack the sages since the written Torah is on de-

---

[32] TB *Sanhedrin* 19a; here King Yannay, not Yoḥanan, is confused with Herod (see J. *AJ* xiv 9.2–3.159–76).

[33] TB *Soṭah* 47a, *Sanhedrin* 107b; *Schol. Megillat Ta'anit* 2 Shebaṭ, 17 Adar.

[34] *M. Abot* 1:5–6.

[35] See NOTE on I 7:16–17.

[36] See NOTE on I 7:16–17.

[37] The tradition at TB *Sanhedrin* 107b could also be correct about Joshua's exile under Yannay-John Hyrcanus but wrong about connecting it with the massacre of sages perpetrated by Yannay-Alexander Jannaeus.

[38] *Ḥagigah* 2:2, p. 77d.

posit for anyone to consult. Hence, there, too, the king shows himself to be a Sadducee. The name "Sadducee" has puzzled scholars. Etymologically it can only mean an adherent of Ṣadduq=Ṣadoq=Zadok. The name "Zadok" is important in the period of the second temple only as the name of the priestly line to which the Oniad high priests but not the Hasmonaeans belonged.[39] The Oniads and their partisans, like the Essenes, must have been bitter opponents of John Hyrcanus throughout his reign.[40] Oniads and their partisans first became reconciled with the Hasmonaeans early in the reign of Alexander Jannaeus.[41] Hence, the first Hasmonaean prince able both to break with the Pharisees and join the Sadducees probably was Alexander Jannaeus.[42]

Both Josephus and the rabbis testify to the importance of the charge, that Alexander Jannaeus was unfit by birth to be high priest, in the propaganda against him. Later, Herod, who had neither Davidic nor priestly lineage, was able to rule, but only through Roman backing. Alexander Jannaeus himself for a time renounced the royal title.[43] Both he and his enemies may well have believed that loss of his high-priestly authority would mean the loss of his civil authority. For centuries in Jerusalem the highest native political authority had been the high priest. Political legitimacy without high priestly authority might be difficult for the prince to maintain in the face of pretenders to Davidic descent. Even the upstart Herod wrested royal power from Jannaeus' descendants. Jannaeus had, therefore, to reply to any propaganda challenging his legitimacy whether as high priest or as civil ruler.

The situation became easier after his death. In the reign of Salome Alexandra (76–67) neither Pharisees nor Sadducees questioned Hasmonaean legitimacy, though the Sadducees suffered from the queen's policies (J. BJ i 6.1–4.107–19; AJ xiii 16.1–6.405–32). Nor was Hasmonaean legitimacy at issue for either Pharisees or Sadducees in the struggles which immediately followed her death. The question was only whether Hyrcanus or Aristobulus should rule (BJ i 6.1–4.120–32; AJ xiv 1.2.4 – 3.2.40).[44] In this period Josephus' first report of opposition to the dynasty comes at AJ xiv 3.2.41,[45] in the famous scene before Pompey in 63 B.C.E., where both Hyrcanus and Aristobulus appeal for Pompey's aid and a delegation from "the nation" asks for an end to

[39] See J. AJ viii 1.3.11–12; x 8.6.152–53; xx 10.2.234. At least we never hear of Hasmonaeans claiming descent from Zadok.

[40] Essenes: Note the importance of Zadokite priests in the literature of the Qumran sect. Oniads: see Part III, pp. 57–61, and Appendix III.

[41] See Appendix III, end.

[42] On relations between the Pharisees and the Hasmonaeans, see Alon, I, 15–39 (in Hebrew).

[43] See NOTE on I 8:14.

[44] See Alon, I, 33–34 (in Hebrew).

[45] Cf. Diodorus xl 2.

the monarchy, since both brothers were seeking to reduce the nation to slavery. Even the delegation of "the nation" appears not to have questioned the original legitimacy of the Hasmonaean heirs. The delegation only claimed that the brothers, as tyrants, had forfeited legitimacy. The principle that tyrants forfeited legitimacy was widely recognized in Hellenistic political theory[46] and could be derived from Jewish texts as well.[47] In the version at Diodorus xl 2 the anti-Hasmonaean delegation consisted of two hundred leading men.[48] Josephus does not specify what national body sent the delegation. His vagueness may reflect the truth. The civil strife could well have split the national council or have prevented it from meeting.[49] The crisis likely prompted a wide spectrum of opponents of the dynasty to unite in a self-constituted delegation to plead before Pompey.[50]

Since neither First Maccabees nor the work of Jason can have been written after 63 B.C.E., we need not follow further the decline of the Hasmonaean dynasty. Clearly Essene opposition to the dynasty began early, but the Essenes withdrew into exile or into closed settlements and rarely if ever took to open warfare, waiting for God to act. It is almost certain that the first serious violent challenge to Hasmonaean legitimacy came under Alexander Jannaeus. Pietist challenges ended with his death, unless some continued to come from the quiet Essenes. All politically important factions agreed that the dynasty had been legitimate. Propaganda for the royal legitimacy of Hyrcanus or Aristobulus would have to prove that they personally were not tyrants, not that they were descended from God's favored heroes. Hence, if First Maccabees is propaganda showing the divinely ordered legitimacy of the Hasmonaean line through John Hyrcanus, it can have been written only in the reign of Alexander Jannaeus.

Our first examination of First Maccabees showed it to be propaganda for the Hasmonaean dynasty.[51] Our subsequent discoveries allow us now to say more. The very beginning of First Maccabees serves the purposes of Alexander Jannaeus. From the adverse description of Alexander the Great and his successors (I 1:1–10), a reader living under the victorious Hasmonaean kings, Judah Aristobulus I and Alexander Jannaeus, could infer that the Jewish victors had at least as much right to the royal title as Alexander the Great and his successors. Alexander won kingship over

[46] See Polybius vi 3.9–10, 4.2, 6, 8, 7.6 – 8.2; Livy i 49, 59.6–11; Cicero De re publica ii 25.45 – 27.49.

[47] Deut 17:20; II Sam 12:1–12; I Kings 12:1–24; II Kings 9–10; II Chronicles 10; Jer 22:13–20; Ezek 45:7–10, 46:16–18.

[48] Greek: epiphanestatoi.

[49] But see Alon, I, 34–38 (in Hebrew).

[50] Cf. Eduard Meyer, Ursprung und Anfänge des Christentums, 3 vols. (Stuttgart and Berlin: Cotta, 1921–23), II, 315–19; Eissfeldt, pp. 610–13.

[51] See Part I, pp. 4–26.

the Near East only through overthrowing the Persian king, the king whose legitimacy was proclaimed by the prophets of the God of the Jews. The successors of Alexander owed their titles to his conquests. This purpose of denying legitimacy to the Hellenistic kings goes far to explain the absence from First Maccabees (astounding in a Jewish historical work) of any effort to explain why God allowed those kings to rule. In common with the patriotic propagandists of the other subject peoples our author sees the Greek-speaking exploiters as evil usurpers.[52]

We can read First Maccabees as then turning to assert the illegitimacy of the philhellenic or near-idolatrous Oniad high priests and Menelaus (cf. Hosea 4:6). Their sin and the sin of their apostate followers incurred as punishment the dreadful vistations which came upon Judaea and Jerusalem (I 1:64).[53] Certainly the names of the Oniad high priests and Menelaus are conspicuous by their absence from First Maccabees. Onias III was not involved in the persecutions of Antiochus IV, and his virtues were ignored or denied in later Hasmonaean tradition.[54] Indeed, our author could easily condemn Onias III for his closeness to the wicked Tobiad publican, Hyrcanus; for his long stay at sinful Antioch; for taking asylum at a pagan shrine; and perhaps even for having the esteem of the gentiles (II 3:11, 4:5, 33–37). Jason and Menelaus are certainly included among the wicked of I 1:11–15. Their names do not occur because our author observes the principle of *damnatio memoriae* for wicked Jews.[55]

It was natural to compare the zealous priest Mattathias to Phineas, but the comparison we have noted to the lone courage of Joshua and Caleb was presumptuous; many Pietists refused to obey the king. It was natural to imply that Mattathias in the wilderness acted as David had, but only a propagandist could imply that the Pietist martyrs were comparable to the priests of Nob.[56] The setting of Mattathias' death requires only exhortations to courage and hope in victory over the wicked enemy as at I 2:50, 61–64. The exhortations to look for glory like that of Phineas, David, and Elijah go beyond what is necessary and can hardly be anything but propaganda after the facts of John Hyrcanus' prophesy and Alexander Jannaeus' high priesthood and kingship. Josephus, writing after the fall of the dynasty, may have deliberately re-

---

[52] I 1:1–9; cf. J. *AJ* xiii 11.1.301, 12.1.320–32; *BJ* i 3.1.70, 4.1.85; Strabo xvi 2.40. Legitimacy of Persian king: Isa 44:28, 45:1; Ezra 1:2. Propaganda of the subject peoples against their Greek-speaking rulers: Samuel K. Eddy, *The King Is Dead* (University of Nebraska Press, 1961). See also NOTE on 1:1–9.

[53] Though Aristobulus I is reported to have been philhellenic (*AJ* xiii 11.3.318), Alexander Jannaeus certainly was not.

[54] See Part III, pp. 57–61.

[55] Correct accordingly Geiger, *Urschrift*, pp. 215, 220. Alcimus was a sinner but not an idolater or near-idolater. Moreover, our author wished explicitly to refute Alcimus' claims to high priestly legitimacy and even to being a Pietist and therefore had to mention Alcimus by name.

[56] See Part I, p. 7.

moved such grandiose hints from his version of the speech (*AJ* xii 6.3. 279–84).

The dying Mattathias also calls for obedience to Simon's wise counsel: he is to be viewed as the "father" (I 2:65; J. *AJ* xii 6.3.283). Since there is nothing in the subsequent narrative to indicate so preeminent a position for Simon in the lifetimes of Judas and Jonathan, this dying admonition is probably propaganda to prove the legitimacy of the "father's" descendants as priests and rulers, in particular the legitimacy of Alexander Jannaeus' high priesthood and kingship.

Though our scrupulous author never exaggerates Simon's role under his brothers' hegemonies, he takes advantage of his opportunities to stress that Simon was the brother of the two "saviors" (brother: I 2:65, 5:17, 55, 9:19, 33, 37, 65, 10:74, 11:59, 64, 13:3–5, 8, 14, 25, 14:17–18, 29, 16:2–3; saviors: I 9:21, 12:53).

The Hasmonaeans probably searched the scriptures for prophesies signifying their divine election as rulers of the nation. They could well have found what they wanted at II Chron 6:41–42 and Ps 132:16–18. Both texts could be extremely useful, for in them David and Solomon themselves could be seen to have prophesied victory and rule to anointed priests.[57]

We find a probable echo of some such scriptural exegesis at I 5:62. The costly defeat suffered by Joseph and Azariah is explained first by their failure to obey not only Judas but also his brothers, and second by the fact that the unsuccessful commanders "did not belong to that family of men to whom it had been granted to be the agents of Israel's deliverance." The word "deliverance" may well be derived from Ps 132:16 or from II Chron 6:41. If so, the author unobtrusively presses the view that Judas' brothers were God's agents as much as was Judas: the dynasty was divinely elected. Again, characteristically, Josephus, after the fall of the dynasty, removes even such subtly planted hints from his narrative. The costly reverse was due to failure to follow Judas' wise orders; the brothers are not mentioned (*AJ* xii 8.6.352).

Our author goes out of his way to stress that men of *Israel* joined the delegation from the besieged Akra which pleaded for aid from Antiochus V (I 6:20–22). Since elsewhere our author does not concede that the Hellenizers in the Akra are worthy of the name "Israel,"[58] perhaps the traitorous Israelites, whom he calls "impious," were in fact Pietists who objected to the Hasmonaean rebellion against the legitimate king.[59] Our author portrays the venerated leaders of the Pietists as fools for trusting the promises of Alcimus (I 7:8–18). Again Josephus,

[57] Cf. Test Reuben vi 7–12, where vs. 8 probably alludes to Ps 132:16–18 and perhaps also to Lev 4:3–16; see also Test Levi xviii.
[58] See NOTE on I 1:34.
[59] See NOTE on II 1:7, *Jason . . . Kingdom*.

an admirer of Pietists who had read Jason's work and knew of later Hasmonaean fallibility, obscures the strident propaganda by calling the supporters of Alcimus not Pietist leaders but only "some of the people" (*AJ* xii 10.1.395).

Judas' victories were sufficient proof of his divine election, a proof twice ratified by the nation through the establishment of the Feast of Dedication and the Day of Nicanor as annual observances (I 4:59, 7:48–49). Judas died, not because God had deserted him, but because of the cowardice of men (Pietists?) who deserted him and because of his own heroic obstinacy in the face of good advice (surely from his brothers, though our author refrains from saying so), to withdraw and live to fight another day.[60]

With Judas' death, our author had to prove the legitimacy of Jonathan's succession and does so with great care.[61] Anti-Hasmonaean Pietists might claim that Jonathan, unlike Judas, was a wicked violator of the Sabbath and therefore had forfeited divine favor. Our author takes pains to tell how Jonathan, long before the time of his prosperity, violated the Sabbath in self-defense, fighting and swimming across the Jordan (I 9: 43–49). Far from displeasing God, Jonathan's escape was the beginning of his long series of successes. It was a feat worthy to be compared to the deeds of Joshua and David.[62]

Even before Judas' death, the Hasmonaeans had to face Alcimus' rival claims to authority which our author endeavors to discredit: at every phase of his tenure of the high priesthood, Alcimus was unfit (I 7:5–25, 9:1, 23–27, 54–57). Hasmonaeans, being of the stock of Phineas, probably had as much right to the high priesthood as Alcimus. The high priesthood had long been hereditary in the Zadokite-Oniad line. The Hasmonaeans did not belong to it, but neither did Alcimus (J. *AJ* xii 9.7. 387; xx 10.3.235). There was another important factor for high priestly legitimacy: since the time of David the ultimate designation as to whom among those eligible was to be high priest rested with the royal authority governing the Jews.[63] The Seleucids still ruled the Jews. The belief that

---

[60] See NOTE on I 9:7–10.

[61] See Part I, p. 10.

[62] See NOTE on I 9:34–53.

[63] See Liver, RQum 6 (1967), 3–30. On the high priesthood in the first temple, see de Vaux, *Ancient Israel*, pp. 372–77. On the high priesthood in the second temple, see J. *AJ* xi 7.1.298, where the king's agent can promise it to the incumbent's brother; however, the promise may have been illegal. At *AJ* xi 8.2.311 and 4.324, Josephus does not question Darius' and Alexander's power to confer the high priesthood. At *AJ* xii 4.2.161, he implies that the Ptolemies had the power to do so. The pious Jason of Cyrene does not question the right of the Seleucids to appoint the high priest (II 4:7–10, 24–25; 14:3–13). Alcimus perhaps received his designation first from Antiochus V and then certainly from Demetrius I (II 14:3–13; I 7:5–9). See also Alon, I, 62–64, 71–72, 74–75 (in Hebrew). Hence J. *AJ* xv 3.1.40–41 is to be disregarded.

prophetic revelation forbade rebellion against the ruling king was probably still strong. Even on Jewish grounds, then, high priestly legitimacy required designation by the Seleucid king. Hence, Jonathan and the author of First Maccabees preserved not only the letter of Alexander Balas constituting him high priest (I 10:20) but also the notice that Demetrius II "confirmed" him in the post (I 11:27) and the letter of Antiochus VI reconfirming him (I 11:57). Both rival Seleucid lines of Jonathan's time thus recognized him as legitimate high priest.

Our author is interested not only in priestly authority. The incumbent high priest might be wicked or incompetent, and the reigning sovereign might be an evil violator of his pledged word. Israelite history offered the heroes of the book of Judges as precedents for a man chosen by faithful Israelites to secure deliverance. Hence, our author earlier portrayed Jonathan as a leader accepted by his people, of the same kind as Joshua and the Judges. Now, on receiving designation as high priest from the Seleucid king, Jonathan held legitimate power, both priestly and political.

Pietist enemies might insist that Jonathan forfeited divine favor and legitimacy by deserting his sovereign, Demetrius II, for Antiochus VI. Our author is quick to refute such suspicions. On the contrary, Demetrius violated his pledges to Jonathan (I 11:53); and Jonathan and Simon, after changing sovereigns, enjoyed spectacular good fortune which could only be the result of divine favor (I 11:60 – 12:38).[64] Indeed, when Jonathan fell, it was partly because of his inflexible fealty to Antiochus VI (I 12:40).

Upon Jonathan's fall, even before his death, there was doubt as to who was his successor. Jonathan had both male and female offspring (I 13:16; J. AJ xiii 6.5.204; Vita 1.1.4). On the other hand, Simon in his own right was a high official of Antiochus VI (I 11:59). Our author first carefully tells how Simon received political authority from the Jewish people, as leader to defend them against the perfidious Tryphon and their hostile neighbors (I 13:1–9). Then, in case remoter descendants of Jonathan might dispute the succession, our author shields Simon from blame in the surrender of Jonathan's sons to Tryphon and does not even report their ultimate fate.[65]

As for the high priesthood, Demetrius no longer ruled over the Jews (I 11:54–60), and Antiochus VI, helpless in the hands of Tryphon,

---

[64] Note especially Jonathan's victory against huge odds, I 11:70–74, and the author's remark at the head of I 12:1 and Josephus' version of it stressing divine intervention, AJ xiii 5.8.163.

[65] The reading of La^V at I 13:23, "Occidit Ionathan et filios eius," is completely isolated and probably is a conclusion jumped to by a scribe who saw before him "occidit Ionathan et," even if there was no lacuna in the rest of the verse. Jonathan's descendant, Josephus, goes even further in shielding Simon from blame (AJ xiii 6.5–6.204–10).

could not confer it on Simon. De facto, the organs of the Jewish people may have made Simon high priest (see I 14:35), but our author refrains from asserting that the Jews took the step of full rebellion which might have entitled them to invest Simon themselves. The death of Antiochus VI solved the problem. Tryphon could now be viewed as a usurper, and Demetrius II as the legitimate king. Hence, Simon and our author carefully preserved the letter in which Demetrius II recognized the surviving Hasmonaean as high priest and in effect conferred independence on the Jews (I 13:36–42). They preserved even the letter in which Antiochus VII recognized him as high priest (I 15:2–9), though Antiochus VII later did not carry out his promises. They preserved it even though Antiochus VII at the time of the letter could hardly be said to be sovereign over the Jews. Whatever Seleucid line was the legitimate one, our author had proved that the Hasmonaean high priests had legitimate royal designation.

With the removal of Seleucid rule, sovereignty rested with the national organs of the Jews. In a document quoted in full by our author, those national organs, the assembly of the priests and the people, took note of Simon's earlier legitimacy (I 14:35–43) and conferred upon him as his due reward the political leadership and the priesthood "in perpetuity," that is, to be inherited by his heirs (I 14:41; cf. 49).[66]

There could still be some question even after this national grant of authority. Did Simon do anything to make it void? And who was his legitimate heir? Our author makes it clear that far from becoming unworthy, Simon gained still more prestige. Already in his lifetime, Simon treated John as his successor, with Judas as the next in line (I 13:53, 16:1–3). Hence Simon's son-in-law and murderer could be only a usurper. The sole legitimate heir was John. Alexander Jannaeus after his accession was indisputably the legitimate heir of John (J. *AJ* iii 12.1.320–23). Hence our author ends his work of propaganda to prove the legitimacy of Alexander Jannaeus' monarchy and priesthood with the accession of John and with a brief notice implying that John is dead and stating that his reign is chronicled elsewhere.

So eager was our author to prove the divinely ordered legitimacy of the Hasmonaean dynasty that he cast his book in the impressive Hebrew diction of the books of Samuel.[67] Just as the books of Samuel proved the legitimacy of the Davidic dynasty and became scripture, so our author hoped First Maccabees would serve to prove Hasmonaean legitimacy. As far as we know, contemporary prose writers made no such efforts to write in Biblical Hebrew. Even the poetry of Ben Sira and the Qumran writers is hardly Biblical, much less their prose. Just as clearly

---

[66] See Alon, I, pp. 74–75 (in Hebrew).
[67] Cf. Bickerman, PW, XIV, 791.

"non-Biblical" is the Hebrew of Daniel 8–12, of the original of the document translated at I 14:27–49, and of the fragment of a Pharisaic historical work at TB *Qiddushin* 66a, despite its instances of the *waw*-consecutive. Thus, First Maccabees is both a presumptuous work and a stylistic tour de force. Only pressing needs could have stimulated the labors of the pious talented author to produce it. As we have seen, such pressure existed only in the reign of Alexander Jannaeus.

Written propaganda in Hebrew probably accompanied the oral charges against the legitimacy of the priest-king Alexander Jannaeus. A translation of later Hebrew anti-dynastic propaganda survives in the Psalms of Solomon,[68] and a fragment of a Hebrew original survives at TB *Qiddushin* 66a. However, not only Alexander Jannaeus but also his Hasmonaean and even his Herodian successors (whose royal claims partly stemmed from those of the Hasmonaeans) would do their best to suppress Hebrew propaganda against the legitimacy of the dynasty. Hence, it is not surprising that there is no trace of any history composed in Hebrew to refute First Maccabees. The Hasmonaeans and Herodians, however, could not suppress works circulated in the diaspora, where few Jews read Hebrew, but all who were literate read Greek. Second Maccabees survives as an abridgment of Jason of Cyrene's Greek refutation of First Maccabees. We now proceed to argue that Jason's target was indeed First Maccabees.

We have already discovered many places where the two books contradict each other,[69] enough to lead one to guess that Jason of Cyrene contradicted First Maccabees wherever possible. The very beginning of Second Maccabees sharply contradicts the condemnation of Hellenistic kings and non-military covenants with them at I 1:1–12: covenants with the Seleucids had brought great benefits under Seleucus IV and his predecessor (II 3:2–3), and even under Antiochus IV at first it was sinful Jews who impaired but did not shut off the benefits the Jews received from the Seleucid kings (II 4:11), for Antiochus IV was friendly (II 4:22) and more than three years later acted in the Jews' true interests (II 4:23, 36–38) and was not personally at fault in miscarriages of justice (II 4:43–50). Only the sins of Jason the Oniad, Menelaus, and their followers after years turned Antiochus into the "rod of God's anger."

Jason makes it clear that their deadly sin was not greed or civil strife but neglect of the Torah in their uncontrolled mania for Hellenism. Indeed, the pious peoples of the conquered Near East took it for granted that unlimited greed and civil strife were themselves Greek traits.[70] Jason of

[68] See above, n. 50.

[69] See Part I, pp. 12, 28–34, Part II, pp. 44–54.

[70] Cf. Joel 4:2–3 and the description of Hellenistic armies as locust plagues in Joel 1–2. I shall treat this topic in a study of Joel and in a study of non-Greek peoples under Greek domination. Hence, correct PW, XIV, 795–96, where Bickerman

Cyrene's piety was quite different from that of the author of First Maccabees. To Jason of Cyrene the wicked priests Jason and Menelaus are not to be treated with *damnatio memoriae,* and the high priestly line of Simon II and Onias III deserves the veneration given it by Ben Sira and later by Onias IV, by Pharisaic tradition, and perhaps even by Essene tradition.[71] Jason of Cyrene indignantly rejects the insinuations in First Maccabees that the Pietist martyrs were deluded by their faith into useless martyrdom and that the God who let them die remained angry even after their deaths (I 1:63–64) and favored them less than he favored the Hasmonaeans to whom he gave victory.[72] For Jason, on the contrary, the dead have power: Onias III and the martyrs stand with Judas as the heroes of the story, for their merit purchased from God the aid which won Judas his victories. Jason takes care to show that Judas gave due credit to Onias III and to the martyrs.[73]

Judas observed the Sabbath no less strictly than had the martyrs (II 8:26–28, 12:38, 15:1–5). The martyrs perished on the Sabbath because Philip's attack upon them came in the time of God's wrath. Divine providence somehow saved Judas from a like fate because Nicanor's attack came in the time of God's mercy (see II 8:27–29). Judas' Sabbath observance in fact may have been stricter that that of his father and his brothers, though First Maccabees does not say so and Daniel draws no such distinctions. On the other hand, Mattathias in Jason's view must have been a heinous violator of the Sabbath. Jason would have found it embarrassing to associate the heroic Judas with such a sinner. Hence, the omission of all mention of him in the abridged history is not the result of abridgment: Jason himself inflicted *damnatio memoriae* on Mattathias.[74]

Jason could not fail to resent any insinuations in Hasmonaean propaganda against the martyrs and Pietists. It was not enough to defend them and show how Judas recognized his debt to them. Jason counterattacks where he thinks the Hasmonaeans vulnerable. The author of First Maccabees carefully explains that the incompetent and unsuccessful leaders Azariah and Joseph son of Zechariah were not of Hasmonaean

---

did not appreciate Jason's religious position and had Jason ascribing the cause of the persecution to greed and civil strife, as if Jason drew on a pagan source.

[71] See Sirach 50, esp. vs. 24; *M. Abot* 1:2; Part II, pp. 49–50; Part III, pp. 58–61.

[72] See Part I, pp. 5, 7; Part IV, pp. 72–73.

[73] Glorification of Onias III and the martyrs: II 4:4–6, 33, 37, 6:10 – 7:42, 14:37–46. Judas acknowledges that martyrdom buys victory: II 8:28 in the light of I Sam 30:22–26; Num 31:25–47. See also II 7:6, 38, in conjunction with II 8:27; II 8:2–4; and see NOTE on I 2:29–37. Judas on Onias III: II 15:12–14. Perhaps Jason presented even Jonathan as a respecter of the power of the martyrs, for at II 8:30 we learn that the families of the martyrs received a share of the spoils taken from *Bacchides.* Only Jonathan won a victory over the Bacchides known to us, so as to have been able to have taken spoils from him (I 9:68). See, however, NOTE on II 8:30.

[74] See above, n. 22.

stock[75]; Jason of Cyrene takes care to say (II 8:22) that Joseph was a brother of the heroic Judas. Though Greek scribes seem to have tried to conceal the fact, there is good textual evidence that Jason also made Azariah ("Esdras" or "Esdris" or "Esdrias") a brother of Judas, perhaps identifying him with Eleazar of First Maccabees.[76] "Esdris" appears at II 12:36–40 in a context which may suggest Azariah's incompetence and associates him with sinners even as it contradicts First Maccabees. In First Maccabees Azariah ventures a headstrong foolish campaign only to be routed by Gorgias (I 5:55–60), whereas Jason here has him bravely but ineffectually fighting Gorgias until Judas comes to his aid. Perhaps Jason condemned "Esdris" only for allowing his men to lose divine favor through sin (II 12:39–40). In any case, Jason refuses to give Eleazar credit for his heroic death (II 13:15) and does his utmost to discredit Simon by mentioning his name in contexts involving treason and incompetence (II 10:19–22, 14:17). Furthermore, Jason probably turns Zechariah, who in First Maccabees is the father of Joseph, into yet another incompetent traitor from the Hasmonaean family (II 10:19).[77]

Jason's narrative of the death of Judas, omitted by the abridger,[78] may well have declared it to be punishment for Hasmonaean presumption.

First Maccabees makes it clear that not Judas but Jonathan and especially Simon won lasting freedom for Jerusalem (I 9:23–27, 10:1–47, 11:20–37, 41–43, 13:36–52). Jason, regarding Hasmonaean claims after Judas' death as illegitimate, probably spoke of Judas as the "liberator of Jerusalem" and regarded Jerusalem as free even while Alcimus was high priest.[79] In First Maccabees, Demetrius I is a persecutor of Jews (I 7:9–19, 26, 8:31–32, 9:1–2,[80] 10:5, 46); Jason omitted him from the list of persecuting kings (II 2:20)[81] and portrays Demetrius only as the dupe of Alcimus, who sends Nicanor not against the Jews but only against Judas and his men, though Jason grants that destruction of Judas' band would be a misfortune for the Jews (II 14:3–15, 26–27).

Striking is the fact that the two books claiming to narrate the liberation of the Jews present not a single document in common. Every document presented in First Maccabees can be used to prove Hasmonaean achievement and Hasmonaean priestly or dynastic legitimacy. No document presented by Jason can be so used. What is the nature of the collection

---

[75] I 5:18, 56–62, and cf. vs. 67; note the care with which Judas' blood brothers are identified as such: I 5:17, 24, 55, 61, 63, 65.

[76] See Hanhart's text and apparatus at II 8:23 and 12:36, and de Bruyne, p. x. "Azariah" and "Eleazar" are identical in meaning.

[77] "Zacchaeus" is a nickname for "Zechariah." See above, n. 23.

[78] See Part I, pp. 27, 33.

[79] See NOTES on II 2:22, 15:37.

[80] See commentary.

[81] See commentary.

of letters used by Jason? The letters in II 11 represent concessions to the Jews which twice brought an end to their troubles even though Lysias' forces had not been decisively defeated. As such they were treasured by Jews who believed that rescue would come "not by might and not by power but through the spirit of God" (cf. Zech 4:6). On the other hand, the author of First Maccabees refused to include these documents, which probably were available to him. They could not be used to glorify the Hasmonaeans, for the terms of the conditions for amnesty in the letter at II 11:27–33 were hardly flattering, and the letter at II 11:22–26 followed upon a series of battles in which Judas' armies were badly worsted (I 6:31–54),[82] and even after peace was made Antiochus V was able to violate his word with impunity (I 6:62).

A Pietist work may have contained all four of the documents of II 11. In any case, Jason of Cyrene probably found three of them in a single collection.[83] The other, the letter of Antiochus V to Lysias (II 11:22–26), lacked a date, for the Jews received not the original but a copy, and in the documentary practice of the time dates were omitted from copies.[84] But Lysias' letter to the Jewish people (II 11:17–21) spoke of what the Jewish ambassadors had "requested" (*êxioun*) and what the king had "granted" (*synechôrêsen*). The king's letter to Lysias, speaking of what the Jews "request as a grant" (*axioun synchôrêthênai*), at first glance[85] looked so much like the king's response to the approach which Lysias claimed in his own letter to have made (II 11:18), that Jason even felt it unnecessary to supply the missing date. His readers, many of whom knew Hellenistic documentary practice, could have assumed it was dateless because it was a copy subjoined to Lysias' letter (II 11:17–21) even though unmentioned in it. In actual fact, the dateless letter was of 162 B.C.E.[86] and the others, of 164. To Jason, however, it "obviously" belonged with the rest. Just as obviously, all the letters were to be connected with an expedition of Lysias, chief minister of the child king, Antiochus V. The date, 148 Sel., did not allow the letters to be connected with Lysias' second expedition against the Jews, which Jason knew occurred in 149 Sel. (II 13:1). Jason thus had something to be treasured: a set of documents of 148 Sel. which "proved" (1) that Antiochus IV was dead by 148 Sel. (II 11:23) against the date, 149 Sel., at I 6:16;

[82] On the true date of II 11:22–26, in 162 B.C.E., see commentary. Though defeats are passed over in silence at II 13:9–23, decisive victories are not claimed.

[83] See p. 98.

[84] Bikerman, "Un document relatif à la persécution d'Antiochos IV Épiphane," RHR 115 (1937), 192–96.

[85] A *careful* study of the two shows serious discrepancies between them; see Kolbe, *Beiträge*, pp. 81–82. For example, the king does not mention the Jewish embassy and its petitions or Lysias' previous concessions or even Lysias' "previous" letter.

[86] See commentary on II 11:23–26.

and (2) that Lysias' first expedition occurred after, not before the death of Antiochus IV was known at Antioch, against the narrative of I 4:26–35, 6:6. Jason's account thus doubly discredits the account in First Maccabees.[87]

Jason jumped eagerly to wrong conclusions because for him chronological data were not an indispensable part of a historical work but rather a weapon for discrediting First Maccabees or vindicating Daniel. Like documents, dates are few in Second Maccabees and except at 14:4 appear only where they can be used for one of these two purposes. Since for the most part the dates in First Maccabees come either from official Seleucid records or from reliable Jewish tradition,[88] Jason had few opportunities to prove his rival's chronology false. To do so, he had to draw on sources not used for First Maccabees or catch his rival in a simple mistake. Jason exploited his opportunities to the full. We should study his procedure in detail.

Jason first took the length of the Oniad Jason's high priesthood from the priestly records or from Onias IV's book and used it so as to discredit the statement in First Maccabees, that Antiochus IV was wicked from the beginning (I 1:10).[89] In the next instance suggesting chronological controversy with his pro-Hasmonaean rival, Jason used ambiguity to make the best of a bad business by asserting, without dates, that Antiochus made two visits to Jerusalem, each after attending to affairs concerning Egypt, and that thus Antiochus violated the temple at the end of his "second" expedition to Egypt.[90] This effort of Jason's ever since has been a source of great perplexity to historians.[91]

In his account of the rededication of the temple, Jason does not appear to have felt that he had to stoop to ambiguity: he had documentary "proof." According to II 10:3, 5, the temple cult was restored on 25 Kislev after a lapse of "two years." The two-year lapse is too firmly attested in the manuscript tradition to be rejected as a false reading.[92] Ancient scribes and interpreters were indeed shocked by the interval. To them it clashed not only with the three years implied at I 1:54 and 4:52 but also with the three and a half years implied by Dan 7:25, 9:27, and 12:7, as well as the 1150 days implied by Dan 8:14. Hence, "correctors" labored at the text.[93] Their labor was in vain. Daniel took no note of

---

[87] This origin for the strange chronology of II was earlier suggested by Meyer, *Ursprung*, II, 459–60.

[88] See Bickermann, *Gott*, 155–57.

[89] See p. 91.

[90] See pp. 60–61.

[91] See Walter Otto, *Zur Geschichte der Zeit des 6. Ptolemäers*, p. 40, esp. n. 2.

[92] It is the reading of A V La⁻ᴾ Syr.

[93] Lucian corrected the text to read "three years and six months" in agreement with Dan 7:25, 9:27, and 12:7 and with Josephus *BJ* i. *Prooem.* 7.19 and 1.1.32. Josephus here followed Daniel, as did Porphyry *apud* Jerome *Commentarii in Dan-*

the Feast of Dedication,[94] and Jason was delighted to contradict First Maccabees.

Jason derived his two-year interval from his collection of documents. How did he proceed? The news of the death of Antiochus IV did reach Jerusalem long after the Feast of Dedication.[95] As far as the Jews knew, the king could have received reports of the rededication of the temple before he died. In fact, for religious-minded historians, both pagan and Jewish, the repentance of the temple-robber Antiochus IV on his deathbed became a fixture.[96] Hence, in both First and Second Maccabees Antiochus IV dies after hearing how the God of the Jews has been vindicated by the restoration of His temple. In such axiomatic thinking, the Feast of Dedication could only precede the king's death.[97] Accordingly, Jason's date for the Feast of Dedication had to precede his date for the letter of Antiochus V to Lysias around Xanthicus, 148 Sel. Mac. =February–March, 164 B.C.E.[98] He knew that the desecration occurred in 167 and that it must have endured through more than one year.[99] Thus, for Jason, the Feast of Dedication fell in December 165, two years after the desecration.

Even though a Feast of Dedication on December 24, 165, would seem to leave little time for the news to reach Antiochus IV just before his death and for the campaigns which preceded the letters of II 11, Jason could still have viewed the chronology as possible. He may have endeavored to have it appear more probable by stressing the rapidity of Lysias' reaction to the victories of Judas (II 11:1).

The letters of Lysias and Antiochus V also showed Jason that Lysias' first expedition came after the death of Antiochus IV and after the Feast of Dedication and ended in February–March, 164 B.C.E. It could not have followed close upon the defeat of Gorgias and Nicanor, for that

---

ielem xii 7. La^P omitted the notice of the interval entirely. A minuscule of the mixed class (771) reads "three years" to agree with the interval implied by First Maccabees and given at J. *AJ* xii 7.6.320, where Josephus follows First Maccabees.

[94] See p. 37.

[95] See Appendix III and p. 34.

[96] I 6:5–13; II 9:12–27; J. *AJ* xii 9.1.357–59; Jerome *Commentarii in Danielem* on 11:44–45; Polybius xxxi 9.

[97] Antiochus' death probably did follow the Feast of Dedication. See p. 43, and Appendices I and III, and NOTE on I 4:36–54.

[98] The month of the date in II 11:21 was probably the month which immediately preceded Xanthicus, renamed whether because of the whims of Antiochus IV or because it was intercalary; however, we cannot be sure when the month fell. Hence, to get an approximate Julian equivalent for Jason's date of the letter at II 11:22–26, we must use the date in Xanthicus at II 11:33, of a letter which Jason considered almost simultaneous with that at II 11:22–26.

[99] All Daniel's predictions imply a time of troubles longer than one year. Jason's own account at least suggests the same; see II 6:5–6 (more than one Jewish festival omitted; monthly and annual pagan observances celebrated); II 7:37–38, where the words imply that the persecutions stretched over a considerable time.

preceded the Feast of Dedication. Hence, Jason had to find another occasion and a later date for it. For this purpose, he could only consult his
sources. The sources which Jason thought reliable, as we shall see, were
ambiguous.[100] He used the best logic he could. On Jason's chronology,
Antiochus IV's withdrawal from "Persis" in the course of which he died
began "about the same time" as the Feast of Dedication (II 9:1). The
time immediately following the king's death was one in which the chief
minister had to consolidate his power in Antioch (II 10:11–13), and
even after his rivals had been removed, Lysias would be unlikely to
leave Antioch unless for grave cause. According to Jason's account, Lysias had not even avenged the defeat of Nicanor and Gorgias.

Judas' first victories after the Feast of Dedication were not over Seleucid forces but over Idumaeans (II 10:15–23). Such local feuds by themselves could hardly have provoked the intervention of Lysias. However,
Judas' added victory over Timotheus of Ammon and a large force of
Seleucid troops (II 10:24–38)[101] could well have perturbed the chief
minister of an insecure regime. Jason, proceeding like a modern "critical"
historian thus found the "true" sequence of events, again contradicting
First Maccabees. Lysias' first expedition thus occurred for Jason after the
death of Antiochus IV and over a year after the Feast of Dedication.

Jason did find real errors of First Maccabees to expose. At I 6:20,
Judas' siege of the Akra is given the erroneous date 150 Sel.[102] Whether
from Daniel or some other source, Jason knew the correct date of the expedition in 149 Sel. Mac. So eager is he to contradict the chronology of
First Maccabees that he wrote his own narrative of the campaign of
Lysias and Antiochus V when he found the story absent from one of his
favorite sources and at the head of it flaunted the correct date, not realizing that thereby he disturbed the chonological coherence of his own
work![103] Moreover, this correction of an error in First Maccabees is the
first absolute date in the narrative of the abridged history and one of
only two to appear, for the dates in II 11 are all in the quoted documents.
Jason exposed what were almost certainly other errors of his rival when
he carefully distinguished between two Timothei and between two Philippi.[104]

We have shown that First Maccabees, taken as a whole, meets the
propaganda needs of Alexander Jannaeus and only those needs. It is
more difficult to show that Jason's work so unequivocally aimed to re-

[100] Pages 99–102.
[101] See on II 10:24–38 and on I 5:6–8.
[102] See commentary.
[103] See pp. 90–101.
[104] Since First Maccabees neither identifies nor distinguishes the two Timothei, a
defender of the book could say that there was no error, but Josephus insists that the
two were identical. See on I 5:6–8; II 8:30–32, 10:24–37. On the two Philippi, see on
II 13:23.

fute the claims of Alexander Jannaeus. There is nothing to show that Jason went far into the career of Jonathan. His work may have ended with Judas' death.[105] We can judge only by the abridgment, which ends with the defeat of Nicanor. We can hardly expect to find explicit attacks on the later Hasmonaean claims to priestly and royal legitimacy. Nevertheless, we do find a strong effort to discredit Simon, the real founder of the dynasty from which Alexander Jannaeus sprang.[106] Conspicuous by its absence from the abridged history is any reference to the fact that Judas and his brothers were priests. Elsewhere in the polemic literature the enemies of the dynasty do not hesitate to call them priests.[107] Hence, the silence in the abridged history may well reflect a deliberate effort of Jason's to deny the high priestly legitimacy of Alexander Jannaeus.

There is reason to believe that Mattathias and his early descendants all permitted defensive warfare on the Sabbath and were hostile to the belief in the resurrection.[108] Alexander Jannaeus, however, in becoming a Sadducee, may have been the first to join a sect for which denial of the resurrection was a loudly proclaimed tenet. If so, Jason's efforts, to prove that Judas was uncompromising in his Sabbath observance and believed in the resurrection,[109] may be an effort to discredit Alexander Jannaeus as a degenerate collateral descendant of the great Judas.

A further strong indication that Jason's work was aimed against the claims of Alexander Jannaeus is the fact that it was still unpublished in 103 B.C.E. A polemic work of this sort is not written to be hidden in the author's papers but to be published. If Jason had written his attacks on Simon only to refute the claims of Simon or John Hyrcanus, his book would have been known long before Ep. 2 was written. After the death of Alexander Jannaeus, as we have seen, the question of the legitimacy of the dynastic claims of Simon and his descendants was no longer an issue in Jewish sectarian propaganda. Hence Jason of Cyrene wrote before Jannaeus' death.[110]

Up to this point, although we have written as if we had proved that Jason wrote with First Maccabees before him, we have really proved no

---

[105] See pp. 26, 33, 80.

[106] See p. 80.

[107] On the "wicked priest" in the Qumran texts, see Cross, ALQ, pp. 141–58; other hostile references conceding that the Hasmonaeans are priests: the later interpolation (see p. 39), Test Moses vi 1–2; Psalms of Solomon viii 12; TB Qiddushin 66a; cf. TP Sheqalim 6:1, p. 49d, "Kings who are priests are not to be anointed." Theodorus of Mopsuestia (Commentarius in Zachariae xii 4–5, vol. LXVI, col. 581 Migne) says that the "Maccabees who conducted the war" were from the tribe of Judah.

[108] Pages 5, 10, 12, 75.

[109] Tenet of the Sadducees: J. BJ ii 8.14.165; AJ xviii 1.4.16; M. Sanhedrin 10:1, TB Sanhedrin 90b. Jason's efforts: see pp. 31, 33, 79.

[110] Pages 71–72.

more than that Jason prominently displays the points at issue between him and the author of First Maccabees. Propaganda for and against Alexander Jannaeus surely circulated before either book was written. Could not Jason's work be a reply to the earlier propaganda, and First Maccabees a reply to Jason? A strong indication of the priority of First Maccabees is the chronological polemic. Religious sects and political parties can hardly be discredited by mere matters of chronology, except insofar as their prophets and leaders and official historians can be so discredited. To give dates was well within the tradition of the biblical histories and prophetic books. Mere statement of dates, as in First Maccabees, sufficed to expose the falsity of Daniel. The author does no more than that; he does not even call attention to the fact that the Feast of Dedication fell on the anniversary of the desecration, nor does he spell out the three-year interval between the two.[111] That kind of tendentious chronology appears only in Jason's work (II 9:3, 5). The one false date in First Maccabees (I 6:20) is probably a mere slip. Jason's false chronology for the death of Antiochus IV and Lysias' first expedition is probably a piece of deliberate and elaborate research carried out to prove a point.

Indeed, it is significant that Jason, not his rival, presents documentary evidence for his chronology, a chronology which happens to be erroneous. The litigant who does not present evidence is in all probability the one who spoke first.

In order to get dates absent from the tradition of the Hasmonaeans and their partisans, the author of First Maccabees went straight to Seleucid sources wherever he knew they had no reason to falsify. Jason had no reason to duplicate dates upon which he could not improve and every reason to suppress or to obscure dates embarrassing for the veracity of Daniel.[112] Hence, the paucity of dates in Second Maccabees does not argue for Jason's priority. Indeed, if Jason had published first, his rival, who was unhampered by belief in the veracity of Daniel, could easily have exposed the errors of Jason's tendentiously obscure narrative by giving a few more details.

The author of the first work in a series of polemical exchanges can be silent on many points which will prove to be controversial. He can do so either because he is unaware of them or because he considers them better left in silence. The author of First Maccabees admits that his account of Judas' career leaves out much (I 9:22). One who refutes a previous work must be specific on the points at issue. On this basis one should be able to decide the question of priority between First Maccabees and Jason's work. However, the matter is complicated by several

[111] Cf. Esther 9:1.
[112] Pages 48–54.

factors. First Maccabees had to reply to early attacks on the Hasmonaeans, at least in exposing the errors of the book of Daniel. Such replies to early attacks need not be distinguishable from possible replies to Jason. The effort of the author of First Maccabees to appear objective makes it all the more difficult to assert positively that he could not have been replying also to Jason's attacks on the Hasmonaeans and defenses of Daniel.

However, one who would maintain the priority of Jason has more to do than compile a list of instances where Jason is silent on a polemical point pressed in First Maccabees. Such evidence is inconclusive if Jason could have believed that the best reply to his opponent was silence or obscurity. Moreover, the abridger may have omitted matters important for the polemical exchange.[113] Let us therefore examine closely instances of silence in our two authors which might be used to suggest the priority of Jason's work:

1) I 1:11–15 versus II 3:1–5:10, 14:12–16. In First Maccabees the wicked are not named nor are details of their activity given.[114] Jason of Cyrene, however, must name Jason the Oniad and Menelaus to distinguish from them his hero Onias III. A pro-Hasmonaean propagandist confronted by this portrayal of Onias III would probably have felt driven to refute it, as did Josephus.

2) I 1:16–59 versus II 5:1–6:9. Jason had good reason to be silent on aspects of Antiochus' expeditions against Egypt and on events in Jerusalem down to the beginning of the persecution.[115] Even so, his account is in so many respects fuller than that of First Maccabees that it conveys no impression of priority.

3) Jason had good reason to be silent on the building of the Akra (I 1:33–37).[116]

4) Jason's defense of the glory of the martyrs is far more detailed than First Maccabees' dismissal of them as brave but deluded.[117]

5) Jason's efforts to show that Judas observed the Sabbath rigorously (II 8:25–28, 12:38, 15:1–5; cf. 12:31–32) are at least as massive as the effort in First Maccabees to justify Mattathias' decision to permit warfare on the Sabbath (I 2:39–41; cf. 9:43–49).

6) Jason had good reason to pass over Mattathias' career (I 2) in silence.[118]

7) The battles with Apollonius and Seron (I 3:1–26) are probably included in the summary reference at II 8:1–7, even if the unabridged

---

[113] Just before II 12:10 some or all of the material at I 5:9–13, 16, 17b and 20b has been omitted by the abridger.

[114] Pages 67, 73, n. 22, and see NOTE on 4:54.

[115] Pages 49–52.

[116] See on II 5:24–27.

[117] Pages 7, 12, 30, 33.

[118] Page 79.

work did not treat them. Moreover, it is hard to see how they could be matters of controversy.

8) In First Maccabees there is a detailed description of the role of Gorgias in the campaign of Nicanor (I 4:1–23), whereas Gorgias is only mentioned at II 8:9. However, "Nicanor" is the name of the arch-persecutor (II 8:14, 15:3), and Jason probably employs here his literary license to focus attention upon the principal villain.

9) The abridged history is silent about the eastward expedition of Antiochus IV (I 3:27–37). The abridger may have omitted Jason's reference to it (cf. IV 18:5), but Jason had good reason to pass it over in silence.[119]

10) The abridged history has no reference to Judas' fortification of Mount Zion and Beth-Zur (I 4:60–61). The abridger may be responsible for the omission, since Jason reports that Beth-Zur was a fortress of the Jews (II 11:3, 13:18). On the other hand, Jason's notes that Beth-Zur was a fortress would have been unnecessary if he had reported the fortification earlier. He could well have omitted such mundane affairs as reports of fortification. By omitting the fortification of Mount Zion, he was free to omit the embarrassing fact of the destruction of the walls by Antiochus V.[120]

11) The successful campaign of Simon in Galilee (I 5:14, 17a, 20a, 21–23) for an anti-Hasmonaean writer was best omitted.

12) Jason naturally did not include the Hasmonaean propaganda about the unsuccessful non-Hasmonaean commanders (I 5:18–19, 55–64). Elsewhere, however, Jason seems to have tried to show that they, too, were Hasmonaeans, and he may have said so in his own parallel to I 5 in a section omitted by the abridger.[121]

13) The abridger may have omitted a reference to the attack on Azotus (I 5:68), or Jason himself may have omitted it as trivial or as offensive to a Greek audience.

14) Jason had good reason to pass over in silence the siege of the Akra (I 6:18–30).[122]

15) Jason had good reason to omit the story of the foolish Pietists who deserted Judas to support Alcimus and suffer death on his orders (I 7:8–19). Jason presented "evidence" to make the story impossible (II 14:6). Hence, Jason does not mention Bacchides, who installed Alcimus and probably executed the Pietists, although here, too, Jason may have used his literary license to focus attention upon Nicanor.

Instances (1), (4), and (5) can be used to suggest the priority of First Maccabees. Not one instance need indicate the priority of Jason's

---

[119] Pages 47, 52.
[120] Page 54.
[121] Pages 79–80.
[122] See on II 5:24–26 and 13:1–9.

work. Also significant is the fact that after the publication of Jason's work partisans of the Hasmonaeans could not leave First Maccabees to stand unaided on its own merits. "Super-Hasmonaean" Josephus labored hard to present a revised version of First Maccabees which would not be vulnerable to Jason's attacks.[123] We have thus found strong evidence for the priority of First Maccabees and only inconclusive suggestions that Jason might have written first. Hence, Jason must have written to refute First Maccabees.

[123] Pages 57–61.

V. SOURCES OF FIRST AND SECOND MACCABEES NO LONGER EXTANT

Now that we know when and how First and Second Maccabees were written, let us try to find the sources which lay before the two historians. The work of Onias IV,[1] composed between 131 and 129, could have been used by both. The author of First Maccabees, however, could have regarded it only with hostility. His policy of *damnatio memoriae* for the Oniads[2] has brought it about that we cannot expect to find direct traces of Onias IV's account in First Maccabees. On the other hand, the reason for our author's strong hostility to Ptolemy VI Philometor may be the fact that Philometor was the patron of Onias IV.[3]

We have found clear traces of Onias IV's influence on Jason of Cyrene.[4] There are more such clues. In the abridged history we learn that even after Onias III lost the high priesthood to his usurping brother, he continued to work in the interests of the Jews until he was wickedly murdered (II 4:1–7, 33–35). Jason of Cyrene probably took this information, congenial to his purpose but in no way necessary for his narrative, from Onias IV, for whom the story of Onias III's last efforts for the Jews was of vital interest. Again, though Jason of Cyrene had no reason to mitigate the guilt of Jason the Oniad, he departs from the view of Epp. 0 and 1, that the rebellion of Jason the Oniad in 169 B.C.E. caused the persecution. Rather, we learn that Jason the Oniad was a sinful usurper of the high priesthood, but the sins of all the extreme Hellenizers and, most immediately, the sins of Menelaus brought on the persecution (II 3:7 – 5:20, 23, 13:4). Oniad propaganda would tend to mitigate Oniad guilt, so here, too, Jason's source was probably Onias IV.

A major difference between the views of Jason of Cyrene and those of Onias IV was Onias' denial of the sanctity of the temple at Jerusalem. We have argued that Onias IV was one of the sources for Jason of Cyrene's account of how divine power prevented Heliodorus from seizing money deposited in the temple. One can show, however, that the story of the repulse of Heliodorus is a composite drawn from two sources, one of

---

[1] See Part III, pp. 57–61.
[2] See Part IV, pp. 67, 73.
[3] I 11:1–12; contrast Josephus' favorable account, probably drawn from Onias IV, *AJ* xiii 4.5–8.103–15.
[4] See Part III, pp. 58–61.

which strongly asserts the sanctity of the temple of Jerusalem and is used by Jason in subsequent parts of his narrative.[5]

There is another place in the abridged history where one can deduce that Jason used more than one source. An irreconcilable contradiction exists at II 13:1 combined with II 14:1 and 4. II 13:1 dates the expedition of Lysias and Antiochus V in 149 Sel. Mac. (164/3 B.C.E.); II 14:4 dates Alcimus' conversation with the new king Demetrius I in 151 Sel. Mac. (162/1 B.C.E.); but II 14:1 says that (not two but) three years elapsed between (the reader is entitled to assume) Antiochus V's withdrawal from Jerusalem (II 13:24–26) and the accession of Demetrius I. In reality, Antiochus V and Lysias were still in the midst of a vigorous campaign on June 17, 163.[6] Even on Jason's own chronology, the campaign probably ended in February, 163.[7] In either case, Demetrius became king less than two years later, in the autumn of 151 Sel. Mac.= 162 B.C.E., sometime after October 1.[8] Hence, if Jason is measuring intervals of lapsed time, the number "three" is inappropriate whether one reckons "inclusively," as with ordinal numbers ("in the third year"), or one reckons a fraction of a year as a whole year. 149, 150, and 151 Sel. constitute three calendar years. Jason, however, can hardly have reckoned time here by calendar years. He uses not the bare cardinal or ordinal number, but the compound *trietês*, "three-year." Neither here nor anywhere else in ancient Greek, to my knowledge, does a compound of the form *x-etês* mean anything but a measure of duration: "of at least x-1 year-long periods plus a fraction." This is certainly true of Jason's usage elsewhere (II 4:23, 10:3).[9]

At II 4:23, the three-year interval is measured from the beginning of the high priesthood of Jason the Oniad, mentioned in II 4:7–10. There, however, the intervening narrative is much shorter, and the mention of payment of taxes in II 4:23 immediately leads the reader to the correct conclusion that this is the third such payment after Jason's appointment. Here, nothing directs the reader to measure the interval from an event of 148 Sel. Mac. A careful reader could only conclude that the author had blundered!

Jason himself gives the absolute date, 151 Sel., of Alcimus' meeting with Demetrius I. Hence, he cannot have had a different chronology for Demetrius' accession. It is difficult to see how an author giving both absolute and relative dates could make such an error. However, there is a hypothesis which would account for it. From Lysias' withdrawal in the

---

[5] Belief in sanctity: II 3:30; source analysis: see in AB vol. 41A commentary on II 3:24–39.

[6] See Part II, pp. 43–44.

[7] See Part II, pp. 52–53.

[8] Bickermann, PW XIV, 783.

[9] See NOTES *ad loca*. On the types of reckoning and modes of expression used by ancient writers in their chronological notes, see Appendix VII (in AB vol. 41A).

spring of 164 B.C.E., after his first expedition, to the accession of Demetrius in the autumn of 162, there is a lapse of something more than
two and a half years, which would be counted as three. We can account
for the strange chronological error if we suppose that Jason incorporated
an earlier source without change into his work. The chronological note at
II 14:1 of a lapse of three years comes from that earlier work and takes
no account of chapter 13 but measures the interval of time from some
event in chapter 12. Since all the events in chapter 12 followed closely
upon Lysias' withdrawal in 164 and were over shortly after Pentecost of
148 Sel. Mac. (II 12:31–43), or probably by mid-June, 163 B.C.E., even
the interval between II 12:45 and Demetrius' accession could be given
as "three years."

Chapter 13 is certainly not the work of the abridger, who claims to
have added nothing (II 2:28–31). Jason himself must have included
the chapter; it serves his purposes of contradicting First Maccabees and
bearing out Daniel and shows clear signs of having been abridged from
a longer original.[10] Jason claimed, however, to be writing a history of
Judas' career, including his wars against Antiochus V (II 2:19–20). No
work claiming to be a history of Judas' wars could omit the expedition
of Lysias and Antiochus V. Hence, our hypothetical source for II 14:1,
in which the matter of II 14 followed immediately upon matter of II 12,
could not claim to be a history of Judas. Other genres of historiography
were used by Jews and Christians in antiquity. In II 12 and 14 Jason
could have been drawing on a work similar to the famous *On the Deaths
of the Persecutors* (*De Mortibus Persecutorum*) by the Church Father
Lactantius, written between 316 and 321 of the Christian era.[11] The
genre which tells the history of persecutions and the deaths of the persecutors goes back to Exod 1:1 – 14:21 and includes Judg 3:12–30, 4:1 –
5:31, etc.; II Kings 18:13 – 19:37; Esther; and Judith. Let us assume
that Jason drew on such a work. Let us refer to the hypothetical work
by an abbreviation of Lactantius' title: *DMP*. What follows from the assumption that Jason drew on a book, *DMP?*

Such a book certainly would have included II 14:1–3, where the
deaths of the persecutors Lysias and Antiochus V[12] are reported. On
the other hand, the author of such a work could have omitted II 13, for
in II 11 the narrative tells of the end, in 164, of royal Seleucid persecution of the Jews.[13] According to those Pietists who did not accept the
arguments of the Hasmonaeans, there were no persecutions in the period

---

[10] Bearing out Daniel: see Part II, p. 52. Signs of abridgement of II 13: the extreme concision with asyndeton of II 13:18–26.

[11] On Lactantius' work, which drew on Second Maccabees, see the introduction
and edition of J. Moreau, *Lactance: De la mort des persécuteurs*, 2 vols, Sources
chrétiennes, no. 39 (Paris: Éditions du Cerf, 1954).

[12] II 10:10–13; 11:1–2, 24–25, 29–31.

[13] Cf. *Megillat Ta'anit* 28 Adar.

covered by II 13 and by the parallel I 6:18–63. Judas and his men were the aggressors in besieging the Akra, despite the Hasmonaean claim at I 6:18. So far from persecuting Jews then, Lysias and Antiochus V even allowed hungry rebels to return home unmolested, as the Hasmonaean propagandist admits (I 6:49, 54). One persecutor, Menelaus (see II 4:25, 5:22–23; J. AJ xii 9.7.385), perished in the course of the campaign (II 13:3–8), and his death may have been the only event of the period described in DMP.[14] Because the historical background of Menelaus' death was not given, Jason could place it at the beginning of the campaign and Josephus (AJ xii 9.7.383–85) could place it after the end. Either date is possible, and so is one in between: Lysias and Antiochus V, seeking to subdue rebels but determined to avoid the appearance of persecutors, would be willing to use Menelaus as a scapegoat; equally, on withdrawing to fight Philip, they would gladly sacrifice Menelaus so as to be surer of quiet in Judaea.

The author of our hypothetical DMP must have disapproved of Judas' siege of the Akra without condemning Judas as altogether wicked. If he had approved of the siege, he would have told of it as a first step in the right direction and (like Jason and First Maccabees) would have told of Judas' surprising escape from the threat of crushing defeat. If he had condemned Judas, he would probably have told of the major defeats which ended Judas' string of victories and brought death to his brother and near disaster to him. The author of a work on the deaths of the persecutors would be pious. One who opposed attacking the Akra would probably be a Pietist of the type we have described.[15] The Seleucid garrison in the Akra in itself was no more intolerable to Pietists than the Roman officials and soldiers in Antonia and elsewhere in Jerusalem were later to be to the Pharisees (J. AJ xv 9.4.403–6, 409; xviii 4.3.90–95; xx 1.1.6, 8.1.192).

Our hypothetical author included the story of the victory over Nicanor, II 14–15. Nicanor's great sin was to threaten the holy temple (II 14:31–36, 15:17–18, 24, 32–34). Hence, our hypothetical author believed in the sanctity of the temple of Jerusalem. For Jason of Cyrene, the proof of the sanctity of the second temple was the miracle which balked Heliodorus. We have seen that Onias IV, who did not believe in the sanctity of the second temple, was one of Jason's two sources for the story. The other source believed in the sanctity of the temple of Jerusalem. Are the two sources asserting the sanctity of the temple really one and the same?

The story of the repulse of Heliodorus can be analyzed into Version A (II 3:24–25, 29–30), which asserts the sanctity of the temple, and Ver-

---

[14] On the possibility that the letter at II 11:22–26 appeared in DMP, see below, pp. 98–99.

[15] See Part I, p. 7.

sion B (II 3:26–28, 31–36), which does not.[16] Jason's account of God's victory over Nicanor in II 14 and 15, drawn from the hypothetical DMP, seems closely to echo Version A, whereas the account in II 13 conspicuously lacks such echoes, although it reports battles which involved furious charges, horses, discomfited enemies, and manifestations of God's saving power.[17] One may therefore assume that the authors of Version A and of *DMP* were indeed one and the same. Up to this point, for us the hypothesis of a source, *DMP,* has been a device to explain the chronological contradiction in II 13:1 and 14:1 and 4. The contradiction could be removed by simply emending the text at 14:1 to read "two years later." Now, however, we have literary clues to the reality of *DMP,* and we no longer need call it a "hypothetical" source.

Version B of the repulse of Heliodorus belongs to Onias IV, who denied the sanctity of the temple of Jerusalem. Onias' version also included II 3:1–3 and 11, which display his point of view.[18] If his narrative was to make sense, it must also have possessed the essential content of vss. 4–10 and 12. The essential content of II 3:15–22 also appeared in Onias' version, as is indicated by the fact that the verses are imitated in III 1:16–2:20.[19] The continuation of the story of Onias III in II 4:1–4 may draw either on Onias IV or on *DMP.*[20] Onias IV was naturally interested in his father; the author of *DMP* might be interested in Onias III as a victim of the persecutors Seleucus IV and Menelaus and probably wanted to go on to report the death of Seleucus IV. However,

---

[16] See on II 3:24–39.

[17] God is the "Lord of spirits" at II 3:24 and 14:46, and nowhere else in II. "Spirit" occurs elsewhere in II only at 7:22–23, which may also be from *DMP;* see p. 103 and nn. 34, 52. God is called *dynastês* ("Lord") in II only at 3:24, 12:15, 28; and 15:3, 4, 23, 29. His manifestation of power in victory is called *epiphaneia* in the narrative of II only at 3:24, 12:22, 14:15, and 15:27, and the cognate verb *epiphainein* is used only at II 3:30, 12:9, 22, and 15:13. The verb *kataplêssesthai* is used of the "terror-stricken" enemies of God only at II 3:24 and 15:24; cf., however, II 8:16, where it is used of the Israelites. The verb *enseiein* ("attack," "brandish") occurs only at 3:25, 12:15, 37, 14:46. *Panoplia* ("full armor") occurs only at II 3:25, 10:30, 11:8, and 15:28. *Chara* ("joy") occurs only at II 3:30 and 15:28.

The following words occur in parts of II which could have been derived from *DMP;* the words could well have been used in the narrative of II 13 but are absent from it: *eulogein* ("bless," "praise": 3:30, 8:27, 10:38, 11:9, 12:41, 15:29, 34); *pantokratôr* ("almighty": 3:22, 30, 5:20, 6:26, 7:35, 38, 8:11, 18, 24, 15:8, 32); *pheromenos* ("charging," "tumbling": 3:25, 9:7, 12:22, 14:45).

[18] See Part III, pp. 57–58.

[19] I shall deal elsewhere with Third Maccabees. Only the references to "the place" (*ton topon*) at II 3:2, 12, 18 might be out of character for Onias IV; see Part III, p. 58. The references are in character for *DMP,* for Jason of Cyrene, and for the author of III 2:9–10, 14. Jason on his own initiative could have put the references into the narrative he derived from Onias, or he could have drawn them from the parallel in *DMP.* Similarly, the author of III 2:9–10, 14, writing a refutation of Onias IV's work, could have introduced the references himself into his counterpart of Onias' narrative.

[20] See commentary on II 3:24–39.

the narrative of Jason of Cyrene takes pains to excuse Onias III for seeking the aid of the Seleucid king and simply reports Seleucus' death without describing it (II 4:5–7). The failure to report details may be due to the abridger, but the effort to excuse Onias III certainly suggests the hand of the anti-Seleucid Onias IV, at least in 4:5–7. On the other hand, if our guess is correct that Onias IV tried to mitigate the guilt of his uncle Jason the Oniad, Jason of Cyrene may have drawn the violent attacks on the Oniad (4:11–20, 5:6–10) from *DMP*. II 4:21–22 sound pro-Seleucid, so they, too probably come from *DMP*, not from Onias IV.[21]

These inferences show that *DMP* began at the same point as Jason and the abridger—with the punishment of Heliodorus, the first miracle of the new age of miracles—and that *DMP* continued at least as far as the abridger did—through the defeat of Nicanor.

Jason's account of the defeat of Nicanor may not be drawn solely from *DMP*. At II 15:12–14 Onias III reappears in Judas' dream as a venerated figure and plays a role in Judas' victory. One cannot see why any Jew writing generations after Onias III's death would have thought of bringing him into the story there. Hence, not Jason of Cyrene but one or more of his sources did so. The author of *DMP* venerated the memory of the "anointed one" of Dan 9:26, the man through whose merit the honor of the temple had been miraculously preserved from Heliodorus. The author of *DMP* and, indeed, Judas himself could have spoken of the man of the miracle before the wondrous victory which preserved the temple from Nicanor. Still more, however, would it have been to the interest of Onias IV to press the claims of his family to divine favor. Onias IV left Judaea for Egypt when Demetrius I confirmed Alcimus in the high priesthood, but some partisans of the Zadokite-Oniad line probably stayed behind. When the Hasmonaeans not only refused to recognize Alcimus but also turned to resist Alcimus' Seleucid protectors, Onias IV surely approved, and his partisans probably joined forces with Judas to fight in the battle against Nicanor. Thus, the story of Judas' dream could well have originated with Onias IV or his partisans.[22] Indeed, suggestions from Onias IV or his partisans could have influenced Judas' mind on the eve of the battle, if Judas in fact did report such a dream.

---

[21] On Onias IV's treatment of his uncle Jason, see my article in *Studies Smith*, Part III, pp. 108–9, 121–22. II 4:23 refers back to II 4:9 as if 4:10–22 did not intervene. See NOTE on II 4:7–38. II 4:21–22 can be ascribed to *DMP* also because the probable purpose of the passage is to prove the veracity of Daniel. See Part II, pp. 49–50, Part V, p. 97.

[22] On Onias in Egypt, see Part III, pp. 57–58. The report of the dream in II 15:12–14 resembles Onias IV's version of the repulse of Heliodorus rather than *DMP's*. Thus, the expression "Holy City" for "Jerusalem" occurs in Second Maccabees only at 3:1, 9:14, 15:14, 17. Prayer with hands stretched out occurs there only 3:20, 14:34, 15:12, 21. Interest in the countenance of persons occurs at 3:16, 26, and at 15:12–13, but not at 3:25.

Pietists probably saw in the stories of Heliodorus and Nicanor the fulfillment of prophesies of Zechariah and Enoch. Zechariah prophesied
that at some time after the conquest of Syria and Palestine, presumably
by Alexander (9:1–7), God would protect His temple from all foreign
armies and tax collectors (9:8). Heliodorus and Lysias (II 11:3) could
be viewed as the repelled tax collectors. Nicanor's defeat, too, could be
seen in the prophesy, especially in the subsequent words of Zechariah.
According to the prophet, God will cause "the one who told of the Second" (*maggīd mishneh*) to return (9:12). A Pietist would know how
Jeremiah foretold the second Jewish commonwealth so as to deserve
being called "the one who told of the Second."[23] Zechariah's prophesy
goes on to promise that Zion's children and Judah and Ephraim will serve
as God's sword against the Greeks (9:13), and in a closely following
utterance (10:3–7) the prophet declares that though the shepherds in
charge of the Jews, God's flock, have been remiss, the "sheep" will become mighty men and rout the enemy who so prided himself on his cavalry. Both "the house of Judah" and "the house of Joseph" will be among
the victors. Interpretations regarding Judas' victories as the fulfillment of
Zech 9:1 – 10:8 were still current among Jews at the time of Jerome.[24]

The author of Enoch lxxxix 59 – xc 42 drew on Zechariah's portrayals
of remiss shepherds (Zech 10:2–3, 11:3–17, 13:7), interpreting them as
angels in charge of Israel's fate who will be punished for their misconduct
after Judas Maccabaeus proves to be invincible. Of the three apocalypses,
only Enoch's could be interpreted as predicting Judas' victory over Nicanor. After Enoch has seen Judas prove invincible over all enemies round
about (sc. over Antiochus IV and V and over the hostile neighboring
peoples), he says, "I saw till a great sword was given to the sheep [cf.
Zech 9:13], and the sheep proceeded against all the beasts of the field
to slay them, and all the beasts and the birds of the heaven fled before
their face" (Enoch xc 19).

Jason's account of the victory over Nicanor has Judas operating in Samaria, the territory of the house of Joseph (II 15:1), though the parallel
in First Maccabees (7:39–40) makes no mention of Samaria. Jason's account goes on to tell how the Jews' spirits were roused by the recitation
of prophesies (including those of Zech 9 – 10?), so that they became
mighty men (II 15:8–11). Their invincible power came partly from
Jeremiah and the heavenly sword (II 15:13–18). The enemy cavalry
(II 15:21) proved to be of no avail as God defended His temple. The
Jews routed and slaughtered their enemies (II 15:27). The parallels of

[23] Note the use of the verb "tell" at Jer 42:3–12. On the role of Jeremiah at
II 15:14–16, see commentary on II 15:10–17. On "mishneh" as the restored Jewish
commonwealth, see Isa 61:7. Compare also Zech 9:11 with Jer 38:6.
[24] See Jerome, *Commentarii in Zachariam* on 9:3 – 10:8, vol. XXV, cols. 1486–94
Migne; see also ibid. on chaps. 7–8, col. 1467.

Jason's narrative to the prophesies of Zechariah and Enoch are indeed striking.

Hence, the passages of the abridged history in which we can see the influence of *DMP* also show interest in tracing the fulfillment of prophesies. Such an interest is characteristic of the genre of histories of the deaths of persecutors.[25]

A Pietist author who approved of Judas' career, but with some reservations, need not have restricted his interest in fulfilled prophesies to Zechariah and Enoch. Daniel, too, predicted the mission of Heliodorus and the rise of the "little help"; the seer of the Testament of Moses prophesied of the persecution and the martyrs. Indeed, we have traced the efforts of Jason to vindicate the veracity of all three apocalypses. *DMP* is a probable source for these efforts, especially where Jason gives the names of persecutors and traitors of less than first rank, which might have been forgotten with the lapse of time. If vagueness is characteristic of apocalyptic prophesies, minute specificity is the goal, not always attainable, of historical works which attempt to parade the fulfillment of prophesy (cf. I Kings 13:2). The author of a work on the deaths of persecutors, moreover, will try hard to give the name and rank even of minor officials, if they can be shown to have been persecutors who suffered the miraculous vengeance of God.

No more than Jason of Cyrene need the author of *DMP* have shared the opinions of the apocalypses on the causes of the persecutions, nor need he have been consistent. At one place he could ascribe the visitations to the sin of Hellenization, at another to Jason's rebellion, at another to the sins of Menelaus and his followers.

We can now suggest a probable date for *DMP*. It must have been written after the defeat of Nicanor. On the other hand, even Hasmonaean propaganda did not claim that miracles occurred during the careers of Jonathan and Simon. Nor, except for the farewell address of Mattathias, did any prophesy foretell the mighty deeds of Judas' first two successors. Pietists increasingly opposed them, though their opposition may have grown slowly at first. There is no evidence that Pietists saw in the victories of Jonathan and Simon fulfillments of prophesy. Judas' career saw the great fulfillments. A Pietist interested in tracing fulfilled prophesies would not have waited far into Jonathan's and Simon's periods of leadership to write his book. On the contrary, the sufferings of the pious under the regime of Alcimus belied all the prophesies, especially the prediction that a glorious deliverance would follow the death of Judas.[26] At such a time of bitter disappointment, one who viewed Judas' career as a fulfillment of true prophesies could not remain silent. He would have to

---

[25] Cf. Judg 4:1 – 5:31; II Kings 18:13 – 19:37; and see Moreau, I, 48–49.
[26] I 9:23–27; see Part II, p. 48.

speak out in defense of the prophesies and explain their partial non-fulfillment.

Only a short time later, the death of Alcimus brought first peace (I 9:57, 73) and then the rise of Jonathan; that is, it brought first a lessening of the urgency to defend the prophesies and then events entirely unforeseen by them. Hence, *DMP* if it really existed as a source of Jason's work was probably written between Judas' death in spring 160 B.C.E. and the death of Alcimus in spring 159 (I 9:54–56). If the work had such an origin and date, it was probably written in Hebrew or Aramaic, not in Greek. *DMP*, then, was written by a contemporary of the persecution who must have been well informed on the events. Indeed, *DMP* would be the earliest identifiable written history of the period. The author may even have preserved the documents of II 11:16–20, 27–38, which marked the end of the persecution.

The documents would have interested him as much as the "edicts" of toleration interested Lactantius. Even the letter of Antiochus V to Lysias (II 11:22–26), restoring the temple to the Jews, may have been preserved by this enthusiastic advocate of the sanctity of the temple. However, as a contemporary of the events, the author of *DMP* cannot have made the errors by which Jason constructed his elaborate but false chronology. If the letter at II 11:22–26 appeared in *DMP*, it appeared without any indication as to its date and setting, perhaps in an appendix, separated from the other letters of II 11.[27]

Indeed, peculiarities of Jason's narrative show that he found the other three letters of II 11 embedded in a history, presumably *DMP*, and added II 11:22–26. Thus, at II 11:16 the writer says that the text of letters *to* the Jews will follow and does not mention a letter to Lysias *about* the Jews. At II 11:22 the writer says that a letter of the king will follow, and one would expect a letter to the Jews, not one to Lysias. The words at II 11:27a, "The king's letter to the nation," may not have stood in the original text. At II 11:34, "The Romans, too, sent *them* a letter," there is a masculine plural pronoun, which one would expect after "the Jews" of II 11:16, whereas "the nation" (*to ethnos*) of II 11:27a is neuter. However, such use of masculine plural pronouns to refer to neuter collectives is common in Greek. Even so, the wording is strange enough to suggest that Jason interpolated the letter of Antiochus V to Lysias here into the text of *DMP* and added II 11:27a to connect his interpolation with the document which followed, not realizing that his choice of words made it certain that the suture would leave a scar.[28]

---

[27] On Jason's chronology, see Part IV, pp. 81–84. For an example of documents in an appendix, see the appendix to Pseudo-Plutarch *Vitae decem oratorum* 850f–852e.

[28] Cf. Laqueur, *Historische Zeitschrift* 136 (1927), 234–35. Plural forms to refer to collectives: Friedrich Blass, *Grammatik des neutestamentlichen Griechisch*, 12th ed., rev. by Albert Debrunner (Göttingen: Vandenhoeck & Rupprecht, 1965), p. 89.

Even if the letter at II 11:22–26 stood in an appendix to *DMP,* the Seleucid campaign reported in II 13, of which II 11:22–26 marked the end, cannot have been taken by Jason from that source.[29] Jason composed II 13 himself on the basis of other sources, perhaps even drawing on First Maccabees. He was subtle enough to make his own hints of fulfilled prophesies. However, elsewhere in the abridged history, when the narrative tells of persecution, martyrdom, and the deaths of persecutors, and especially where there is a hint of fulfilled prophesy, Jason may have been drawing on *DMP.*

If so, we can deduce that important information did not appear in *DMP,* for if Jason was able to contradict First Maccabees by constructing an elaborate false chronology,[30] *DMP* must not have belied Jason's fabrication. Could *DMP* have been so ambiguous? Close to the events as he was, the author of *DMP* could have given dates as accurate as those in First Maccabees. However, an author who was a forerunner of Jason in trying to prove the veracity of overprecise apocalypses would have been glad, like Jason, to avoid giving many of the important absolute dates. As for relative dates, *DMP* probably offered no obstacle to Jason's dating of the Feast of Dedication before the first expedition of Lysias. If the author of *DMP* was trying to show the veracity of prophesies, he may have gladly omitted all reference to the Feast of Dedication, for the seers utterly failed to predict it.[31] Also, it marked neither the end of a persecution nor the death of a persecutor.

We must, however, reconstruct a text of *DMP* ambiguous enough to allow Jason to give a false date for Lysias' first expedition, an event which occurred in the midst of persecutions and deaths of persecutors. We can do so on the basis of what is known of the techniques of ancient Jewish writers of history. In general, Jewish historians were not bound by the rules of the annalistic scheme of history used by Thucydides. That is to say, they were not bound by a rule to give all the events of one year before proceeding to tell the events of the next. Biblical historians did not write annalistically. They did not always write even in consistent chronological order. For example, at II Sam 8:1–14, especially in verse 12, there is surely no consistent list of David's campaigns in chronological order. The Jewish writers had to write with a general chronological framework, but they did not care to give every event a precise date. Like Herodotus, Plutarch, and Suetonius, they frequently organized their narratives topically, not chronologically. We need only suppose that (1) in the narrative of *DMP,* as in First Maccabees, Lysias' first expedition followed upon the defeat of Gorgias and Nicanor; (2) in the topical organization of *DMP* first came the story of the battles with the forces of the

---

[29] See pp. 91–93.
[30] See Part IV, pp. 81–84.
[31] See Part II, p. 47 and Note I 4:36–54.

Seleucid government and then, separately, the story of the wars with hostile neighbors; and (3) *DMP* had no chronological indication for Lysias' first expedition or only "within the next twelve months" (*en tôi echomenôi eniautôi*) as at I 4:28. This vague date would allow up to a year to elapse between the defeat of Gorgias and Nicanor and Lysias' first expedition, which ended by spring, 148 Sel. Mac.=164 B.C.E. Spring or summer 165 B.C.E. is indeed a likely date for the expedition of Gorgias and Nicanor.[32] To judge by the wording at II 11:1, Jason's source may well have narrated Lysias' first campaign immediately after Nicanor's defeat, but he did not explicitly connect the two, writing only that soon after Lysias grew very angry over "the turn of events" (*tois gegonosi*). A "turn of events" in a non-annalistic history did not have to be the one mentioned in the immediately preceding narrative. For Jason, documentary evidence "proved" that it was not, and he proceeded to find his "better interpretation."[33]

If *DMP* was a Hebrew or Aramaic work largely sympathetic to Judas written by spring, 159, it could have been a source for First Maccabees, too. Indeed, we find such close verbal parallels between First Maccabees and the abridged history as to suggest strongly that one drew upon the other or that both drew on a common written source. These vivid parallels occur only in those sections which could have had parallels in *DMP*. They do not occur in the stories of the Feast of Dedication and the expedition of Lysias and Antiochus V.[34] Although Jason could have drawn

---

[32] Adopted by both Bickermann, *Gott,* p. 13 and Abel, p. 47.

[33] See Part IV, p. 84.

[34] The most conclusive examples are the following:

1) I 1:24; II 5:21: Antiochus IV "carries off" the spoils of the temple and "returns home" with "arrogance" (*hyperêphania*).

2) I 1:29 (Hebrew original); II 5:24: Antiochus "sent the Mysarch" (*śar hammusim, Mysarchês*). Neither author had to give the official his title, so both may have taken it from *DMP*.

3) I 1:44; II 6:1: The king's decree surely called for a *return* to the pristine Canaanite and "Jewish" cult of the Lord of Heaven (see Part VI, pp. 140–57. Hence, it may be significant that in both I and II the decree is distorted to mean a departure from the native laws inherited from the forefathers. For a Jew, a return to the abominations of the Canaanites would be just as heinous as a departure from the ancestral religion.

4) I 1:62–64; II 6:18 – 7:41: both texts first speak of martyrs who die rather than sin by eating forbidden food, then mention God's anger (*orgê*) as the cause of their suffering.

5) I 3:3–9; II 8:5–7: *systemati* ("band of partisans") at II 8:5 appears to echo *synestêsato* ("he waged") at I 3:3; Judas' invincibility at II 8:5 appears to reflect I 3:3–5; the Lord's anger (*orgê*) appears both at I 3:8 and at II 8:5; burning appears both at I 3:5 and at II 8:6; towns and villages are found at I 3:8 and at II 8:6; the lion simile at I 3:8 may have suggested the nocturnal raids of II 8:7; the spread of Judas' fame occurs both at 3:3, 9, and at II 8:7. Since I 3:3–9 is poetic, it may be a poem contemporary with the events, incorporated both by I and by *DMP*, or composed by *DMP* and drawn on by both I and II.

Compare also I 1:46 with II 6:2; I 1:50 with II 6:9; I 1:60–61 with II 6:10; I 3:38–45, 55–60, with II 8:8–17, 21–22; I 4:27 with II 11:1; I 4:30 (*eulogêtos*)

on First Maccabees as well as on *DMP,* his strong hostility to Hasmonaean propaganda would have made direct borrowings few. Sometimes, indeed, Jason gives what appears to be a fuller version of the common source than the version in First Maccabees.[35] Hence, we may conclude that the author of First Maccabees, too, drew on *DMP,* at least in those portions which show vivid similarities to corresponding passages of the abridged history.

It is also more than likely that *DMP* was a source for I 5. Though the most striking parallels between First Maccabees and the abridged history do not occur in that chapter, it does contain many passages with suggestive parallels. Moreover, difficulties in the narrative of First Maccabees can be solved if we assume that the author mistook the topical order of *DMP* for chronological order. From the sequence of our author's narrative, a reader would assume that the campaigns narrated in I 5 came after the Feast of Dedication and before the death of Antiochus IV (I 6:1–17). The Feast of Dedication fell 25 Kislev on the Jewish calendar, certainly well along in the autumn. Yet a cuneiform document proves that the news of Antiochus IV's death had reached Babylon by December 18, 164 B.C.E., and Dan 8:13–14, 23–25, probably implies that the news had reached Jerusalem by January 28, 163. Even without these accurate dates, scholars have noted the difficulty of squeezing the events of I 5 into the interval implied by our author.

In fact, the events of I 5 can be accommodated in the interval between the Feast of Dedication and the siege of the Akra (I 6:19–20),[36] but the author of First Maccabees was probably mistaken as to the sequence of the death of Antiochus IV and the campaigns of I 5. In arranging his narrative, our author seems again to have been unaware of the difference between his two sets of dates: the date given by his Jewish source for the Feast of Dedication was 148 Sel. *Bab.,* whereas the date given by his non-Jewish source for the death of Antiochus IV was 149 Sel. *Mac.* Accordingly, our author assumed that considerable time intervened between the two events. If his suspicions were not aroused by inconsistencies in his sources, perhaps he found the same order, victories of I 3–4–campaigns of I 5—death of Antiochus, in non-annalistic *DMP.* It is also possible, though much less likely, that our author did not intend his note of the death of Antiochus IV to be taken as later than the campaigns of I 5 but as roughly contemporaneous with them, for there is no reason to

---

with I 11:9 (*eulogêsan*); I 4:35 with II 11:13; I 5:2 with II 12:39; I 5:4–5 with II 10:15, 18, 23; I 5:6–8 with II 10:24, 29a, 31–32, 36; I 5:43b–44 with II 12:21–26; I 5:46–51 with II 12:27–28; I 5:52 with II 12:29; I 5:53–54 with II 12:31; I 5:65–68 with II 12:32–45.

[35] Especially I 1:62–64 as against II 16:18 – 7:41.

[36] Date of the Feast of Dedication: see NOTE on I 4:36–54 cuneiform document: see introductory NOTE to I 3:27–37; Daniel 8: see Part II, p. 43; scholars noting chronological difficulty: see Kolbe, *Beiträge,* pp. 127–34, and Bickermann, PW XIV, 788, and *Gott,* p. 149; accommodation of events: see introductory NOTE on I 5.

suppose that he felt bound by the rules of annalistic history. In that case, there is no serious chronological difficulty in I 5, but the parallels may still suggest that *DMP* was a source.

To sum up, the sources of First Maccabees probably consisted of (1) documents and oral traditions handed down in the Hasmonaean family; (2) a gentile history of the Seleucids from which the Macedonian Seleucid dates were drawn[37]; and (3) *DMP*. Although the author knew the work of Onias IV well enough to attempt to refute it, there are no passages in First Maccabees which were necessarily drawn from it.

Jason's sources present a far more complicated picture. Our studies have not exhausted the possibilities. He may have used other sources than the ones we have discussed. From our study of the abridged history, we can draw up the following TABLE OF SOURCES for each passage:

3:1–23, 26–28, 31–36 — Onias IV[38]	5:1 — Jason[46]
24–25, 29–30—*DMP*[39]	2–10 — *DMP*[41]
37–39 — Jason himself[39]	11–14 — Onias IV and/or *DMP*
40 — Jason or the abridger	15–20 — *DMP*[47]
4:1–4 — Onias IV and/or *DMP*[40]	21 — *DMP*[48]
5–7 — Onias IV[40]	22 — *DMP*[49]
8–10 — Onias IV and/or *DMP*[41]	5:23 — *DMP*[49] and/or Onias IV[50]
11–20 — *DMP*[41]	24–26 — *DMP*[48]
21–22 — Seleucid historian or	27 — *DMP;* the reference to
Onias IV; Jason[42]	"defilement" may be Jason's
23–29 — Onias IV and/or *DMP*[43]	own[51]
30–38 — Onias IV[44]	6:1 — *DMP*[48]
39–42 — Onias IV and/or *DMP*	2 — An interpreter of Dan
43–49 — Onias IV[45]	11:31–32, probably *DMP*[50]

[37] See Part I, pp. 22–24.

[38] See Part III, pp. 58–61; Part V, p. 94, and introductory NOTE on II 3:24–39. On the references to "the Place" in 3:2, 12, 18, see n. 19.

[39] See on II 3:24–39.

[40] See pp. 94–95.

[41] See my article in *Studies Smith,* Part III, 108–9, and above, Part III, pp. 58, Part V, p. 95.

[42] See Part II, pp. 49–50; Onias IV just might have taken the trouble to mention the name of Apollonius son of Menestheus. Otherwise, Jason, interested in authenticating two visits to Jerusalem by Antiochus IV, each after activity concerning Egypt, probably went to a non-Jewish historian for the facts.

[43] Hostility to Menelaus; persecutors named.

[44] The Hellenized Onias IV, not the pious author of *DMP*, would show interest in Greek cities (4:30), have no objection to a Jew's seeking refuge in a pagan place of asylum (4:33), and take pleasure in showing how pagans sympathized with a righteous Jew (4:35–38).

[45] The corruption of the Seleucid dynasty and the sympathy of pagans for Jews are favorite themes of Onias IV.

[46] See Part II, pp. 49–50.

[47] Not Onias IV, for the sanctity of the temple is assumed.

[48] See above, n. 34.

[49] The persecutors are named.

[50] Interest in Samaritans; see Part III, p. 58. But interpreters of Dan 11:31–32 probably also were interested in them; see commentary on II 6:2.

[51] See Part II, pp. 50–51.

3–11 — *DMP*
12–17 — Jason
6:18 – 7:41 — *DMP*[52]
8:1–17 — *DMP*[53]
18–20 — ?[54]
21–26 — *DMP*[53]
27–32 — *DMP?* — the passage owes much to Jason's own interests[55]
33 — *DMP*
34–36 — Jason[56]
9:1–3 — *DMP*[57]
4–18 — research in biblical prophesies by author of *DMP* and/or Jason[58]
19–27 — Lysias or his agents; preserved in *DMP?*[59]
9:28 — Jason
29 — Onias IV or pagan historian[60]
10:1–2 — ?
3 — Ep. 1; chronology by Jason
4 — Jason[61]

5 — oral tradition?
6–8 — Ep. 1 and Jason
9–10 — Jason
11–13 — pagan historian of Seleucid empire?
14–18 — *DMP*
19–22 — *DMP?* The passage owes much to Jason's own interests[62]
23 — *DMP*
24–38 — *DMP;* Did Jason have a pagan source to distinguish one Timotheus from the other?[63]
11:1–38 — *DMP*, the quoted documents, and Jason[64]
12:1–45 — *DMP*
13:1 — pagan historian? Daniel?[65]
13:2, 9–26 — ? Did Jason use a pagan source to distinguish one Philippus from the other?[66]
3–8 — *DMP?*[67]
14:1 – 15:36 — *DMP*
15:37–39 — abridger

[52] See above, n. 34, note also the prophesy of the death of Antiochus IV at 7:17, 19, 35–37, fulfilled in II 9, and the prophesy of the death of Antiochus V at 7:17, fulfilled at 14:2.

[53] See above, n. 34.

[54] The interest in Hellenistic history would suggest Onias IV, but did he write in detail of Judas?

[55] It was Jason who labored hard to prove that Judas was a strict Sabbath observer and that he believed in the efficacy of martrydom to turn the Lord from anger to mercy. Jason was the one who took pains to expose the error in First Maccabees of identifying the two Timothei.

[56] Compare the similar piece of amplification at II 3:37–39.

[57] See above, n. 34.

[58] See commentary ad loc.

[59] See commentary ad loc.

[60] Information about Ptolemy VI probably came from Onias IV; see Part III, p. 58. Jason exposed the error in First Maccabees of identifying the two Philippi; see Part IV, p. 84.

[61] Cf. II 6:12–16.

[62] The passage has a strong anti-Simonid tendency. See Part IV, pp. 80, 85.

[63] Exposure of error in First Maccabees; see commentary ad loc. and Part IV, p. 84.

[64] See above, n. 34, and Part IV, pp. 81–84, and commentary ad loc.

[65] See Part II, pp. 52–53.

[66] See Part IV, n. 104.

[67] See pp. 92–93.

VI. WHAT REALLY HAPPENED: THE CIVIC AND RELIGIOUS POLICIES OF ANTIOCHUS IV

The eruption of Roman power shook the earth under the inhabitants of the whole Mediterranean world in the time of Antiochus IV Epiphanes. Like the historian Polybius, Antiochus Epiphanes was personally able to observe the invincible military machine crush the mightiest powers of the Greek-speaking world. In particular, Antiochus saw the empire of his father, Antiochus the Great, go down to crushing defeat at the battle of Magnesia in 190. Again, like the historian Polybius, Antiochus Epiphanes was personally able to observe the remarkable civic institutions which underlay the military might, for he spent the years from perhaps 189 to 175 and at least from 188 to 176 as a hostage in Rome.[1] Rome impressed the future king at least as much as it impressed the historian.

Indeed, whereas the historian was interested primarily in portraying the Roman institutions as they were, the proud and ambitious Seleucid prince was anxious to learn from and outdo his victorious enemy, especially by use of the most advanced Roman ideas, ideas too radical to have been put to use by the conservative politicians then ruling at Rome. No subtle study is needed to show that Antiochus learned lessons in Rome.

He learned to avoid provoking Roman anger. Striking is the way in which the temperamental and ambitious monarch avoided conflict and attempted to please Roman ambassadors at every turn.[2] Moreover, after his accession to the kingdom, he strangely went around the streets of Antioch, his capital, dressed in a toga, asking his subjects to elect him aedile or tribune. Stranger still, on election he seriously carried out his functions as magistrate. Perhaps easier for his subjects to understand were his introduction of gladiatorial shows at Antioch, his erection there of a splendid temple to Jupiter Capitolinus, and his establishment of an army unit of five thousand equipped and presumably drilled in the Roman manner. Nevertheless, the puzzled Greeks could not understand his Roman-style election campaigns; they decided that King Epiphanes was mad and called him *epimanes* the "madman." There was method in

---

[1] Mørkholm, pp. 22–23, 35–36, 38, 40.
[2] Polybius xxviii 1, 22.3, xxix 27, xxx 27.

his madness. His effort to imitate Rome was far-reaching as he strove to gain for his own realm and surpass the institutional might of the Romans.[3]

Antiochus' reign is famous among historians for the puzzles it poses. I believe that the key to solving them lies in understanding his effort to ape the Romans. Since our evidence is so largely contained in the puzzling texts of First and Second Maccabees, we must organize our own discussion around those texts. Two unsolved problems beset the study of First and Second Maccabees:

1) Early in his reign Antiochus IV *encouraged* Jews to follow Greek ways. What was the nature of Antiochus' policy of voluntary civic Hellenization, which began in Judaea when Jason the Oniad usurped the high priesthood and gained the mysterious privilege of "drawing up the list of Antiochene citizens in Jerusalem" (*tous en Hierosolymois Antiocheis anagrapsai,* II 4:9)?

2) What was the nature of Antiochus' policy of *forced* religious "Hellenization," which began in Judaea with the decrees and persecution of 167 B.C.E.?

Scholars have fruitlessly tried to set Antiochus' civic policy and his religious persecution in the context of Greek institutions. Antiochus followed Roman, not Greek precedents. The years which Antiochus spent at Rome were epoch-making in the history of the development of Roman civic and religious institutions. Let us see first what Antiochus could have learned of Roman civic institutions, and see how well it explains his civic policy; and then let us turn to what he could have learned of Roman religious policy, and see how well it explains the persecutions.

At Livy xlii 6.9, an ambassador of Antiochus IV alludes on the king's behalf to the courteous and friendly relations with the Senate and with youthful members of the aristocracy which he enjoyed at Rome.[4] A house was built for Antiochus in Rome at public expense. Who were the Roman aristocrats who showed such friendship to Antiochus while he was a hostage?

At Rome the great conquering generals as a rule became patrons of those conquered by them. One can hardly go wrong in assuming that in Rome Antiochus IV enjoyed the patronage of Publius Cornelius Scipio Africanus and his brother, Lucius Cornelius Scipio Asiaticus, who had conquered Antiochus III. A Roman philhellene and emulator of Alexander the Great and of Dionysius I and Agathocles, the conquering Greek tyrants of Sicily, Scipio Africanus was an outstanding example of a Ro-

---

[3] Polybius xxvi 1, xxx 25.3, 6, and 26.1; Livy xli 20.1–4, 9–13; Mørkholm, pp. 39–40. Granius Licinianus (xxviii, p. 4 Flemisch) may well be correct in reporting that only the Roman victory at Pydna in 168 over the kingdom of Macedonia put an end to Antiochus' hopes of winning a war against Rome.

[4] Asconius *In Pisonem* 12; Mørkholm, p. 39.

man who successfully adapted Greek ideas to Roman ends. There are reports that Scipio attempted to be looked upon as more than human and that he claimed to have a special relationship to Jupiter Capitolinus.[5]

As Scipio won greatness by studying and imitating his enemy Hannibal, so Antiochus may have thought to do the same with his enemy Scipio. As Scipio had gone through the *cursus honorum,* the Roman sequence of political offices, so did Antiochus go through an imitative sequence of political offices at Antioch.[6] As Scipio may have claimed to be under the special care of Jupiter Capitolinus, so Antiochus built a temple to Jupiter Capitolinus at Antioch and took great interest in Zeus Olympius, the Greek counterpart of the great Roman deity.[7] Scipio may have claimed to be more than human; any such claim by Scipio had to be carefully veiled at Rome. As a Hellenistic king, Antiochus could go much further; he styled himself *theos epiphanês,* "god manifest."[8]

The information on these tendencies in Scipio comes from questionable sources, and no one can prove that Antiochus IV took him for a model or even was on friendly terms with him. We do, however, know that Antiochus enjoyed ties of friendship with Gaius Popillius Laenas[9] and hence, probably, with Gaius' entire family, who were a vigorous factor in the politics of the time. We may also infer that Antiochus was a friend of Tiberius Sempronius Gracchus from the account of Gracchus' embassy to him.[10] Gracchus had been in the retinue of the Scipios in the war against Antiochus III.[11] His later opposition to the Scipios in politics did not prevent him from interceding as tribune in 184 to bar the imprisonment of Lucius Scipio.[12] He was to marry the daughter of Scipio Africanus, probably after becoming censor in 169.[13]

The Popillii, too, may have been friendly to Gracchus. Marcus Popillius Laenas as praetor of Sardinia asked to be excused from taking over his province in order to let Gracchus complete the pacification of the island.[14] Closely allied to the Popillii were the Postumii Albini.[15] Lucius

---

[5] Generals as patrons of the conquered: see E. Badian, *Foreign Clientelae,* pp. 6–7, 154–67. Scipio Africanus: see Howard H. Scullard, *Scipio Africanus: Soldier and Politician* (Cornell University Press, 1970), esp. pp. 18–32, 108, 175–77, 203, 235–38; F. W. Walbank, "The Scipionic Legend," *Proceedings of the Cambridge Philological Society,* CXCIII (1967), 54–69.

[6] Polybius xxvi 1.5–6; Athenaeus x 439; Livy xli 20.1.

[7] Zeus Olympius: Mørkholm, pp. 58, 62, 113, 122, 130–31; cf. II 6:2; Jupiter Capitolinus: Livy xli 20.9.

[8] See Mørkholm, *Studies,* pp. 68–74.

[9] Polybius xxix 27.2–3, 6; Diodorus xxxi 2; Justin xxxiv 3.1–4.

[10] Polybius xxx 27, 30.7–8. Cf. Gracchus' other acts of friendliness to Hellenistic republics and monarchs, Polybius xxx 31.19–20, xxxi 3, 33; Cicero *Brutus* 20.79.

[11] Livy xxxvii 7.10.

[12] F. Münzer, "Sempronius 53," PW, IIA (1923), col. 1404.

[13] Ibid., 1407–8.

[14] Livy xli 15.

[15] Münzer, "Postumius 41," PW, XXIII¹ (1953), 917—inference from the elections of 173 and 172.

Postumius Albinus, consul with M. Popillius Laenas in 173 B.C.E., was praetor of Farther Spain in 180–179, when Tiberius Gracchus was praetor in Hither Spain. Both Postumius and Gracchus distinguished themselves and evidently were rivals,[16] but perhaps friendly rivals. Lucius' first cousin, Spurius Postumius Albinus, was consul with Quintus Marcius Philippus in 186. Quintus Marcius Philippus was also friendly with the Popillii, for M. Popillius Laenas was to serve on his staff during the Third Macedonian War.[17] Marcius Philippus had ties of friendship with the Antigonids of Macedonia and may have shown favor also to the Seleucid dynasty.[18]

All these men were important in the civic and religious history of Rome. Gracchus was a severe censor, who must have striven to restore old Roman ways.[19] His inflexible Roman piety was to cost him and his family dear in politics.[20] In conversation with Antiochus and others Gracchus may already have been touching upon the desirability of extending Roman citizenship as proposed later by his son Gaius. Antiochus was able to watch the consuls Spurius Postumius Albinus and Quintus Marcius Philippus in 186 as they suppressed the Bacchanalia with the same sort of rigor that he was to use against Judaism.[21] Probably when L. Postumius Albinus was consul in 173 with M. Popillius Laenas, the Romans expelled two Epicurean philosophers, although many scholars prefer to date the expulsion in the consulship of Lucius, the son of Spurius Postumius Albinus (154 B.C.E.).[22] In any case, hostility to philosophers could have been a topic of family conversation long before. Extension of citizenship and suppression of philosophies and of religions with a Dionysiac tendency are all matters of interest for the later policies of Antiochus IV.

Antiochus did not have to learn of Rome from his Roman friends. He could observe her institutions for himself. Let us trace first his observation and adaptations of Rome's civic institutions and pass then to his observation and adaptation of Rome's religious policy.

Antiochus, like Polybius, could see that Rome's military power was based on the ties of alliance she had formed, first with her Latin neighbors, then with the non-Latin peoples of Italy. By the time Antiochus was at Rome, many towns of Latium and even of Italy had been granted full Roman citizenship, and yet these towns retained their identity and possessed organs of local government.[23] In 188 Antiochus could himself

[16] Ibid., 916–17.
[17] Volkmann, "Popillius 24," PW, XXIII[I] (1953), 621.
[18] Münzer, "Marcius 79," PW, XIV (1930), 1574. Ambassadors from Antiochus IV evidently trusted him to act in their interest (Polybius xxviii 1.9).
[19] Plutarch Tiberius Gracchus 14.3.
[20] Münzer, PW, II[A] (1923), 1408.
[21] See pp. 131–59.
[22] See below, n. 140.
[23] A. N. Sherwin-White, The Roman Citizenship, pp. 55–69. See also below, n. 43.

observe the bestowal of full citizenship, by vote of the plebs, on the Latin towns of Formiae and Fundi and on the Italian town of Arpinum.[24] Many other towns in Roman Italy possessed the lesser but still considerable civic statuses of Latin rights or of *civitas sine suffragio,* while retaining their identity and organs of local government[25]; some even were still striking coins.[26] In many cases the citizens of Latin and Italian towns preferred to be without Roman citizenship, whether for fear of diluting their local identity or for fear of the cultic and political burdens imposed on Roman citizens. In some cases, Roman religious obligations may have conflicted with the local religion.[27]

Antiochus could have witnessed the decision to found Aquileia in 183 as a "Latin colony," a new Latin town with organs of self-government.[28] In 184 he could have witnessed another type of extension of membership in the Roman system, as the citizen colonies of Potentia and Pisaurum were founded. Down to this time, citizen colonies were still small units with rudimentary local government, usually garrisons, the members of which did not lose Roman citizenship if they possessed it before joining the colony (as they would if they joined a Latin colony). Potentia and Pisaurum may have been the first citizen colonies to have a larger population and full organs of local government.[29] Another practice is first attested with these two colonies. Hitherto, Latins could be accepted in a citizen colony but did not thereby become Roman citizens.[30] In 184, if not before, the Roman people conferred upon the founders of citizen colonies the right to give Roman citizenship to some of the settlers who had not possessed it. Thereupon, in the earliest instance of the practice known to us, Q. Fulvius Nobilior, one of the founders of Potentia and Pisaurum, made the poet Ennius a citizen.[31]

If the status of Potentia and Pisaurum as the first large citizen colonies is doubtful, still the principle of large citizen colonies was certainly being

[24] Livy xxxviii 36.7–9.

[25] Sherwin-White, pp. 1–55.

[26] See Harold Mattingly, *Roman Coins,* 2d ed. (Chicago: Quadrangle Books, 1960), pp. 91–92; E. T. Salmon, *Roman Colonization under the Republic,* pp. 85 and 182, n. 136, to be corrected by M. H. Crawford, review of Salmon, *Classical Review* 85 (1971), 251.

[27] See Sherwin-White, pp. 39, 46–47, 57–58, 128, 130; cf. Theodor Mommsen, *Römisches Staatsrecht,* III (Leipzig: S. Hirzel, 1887), 133–34, and *Gesammelte Schriften,* III (Berlin: Weidmann, 1907), 390, 399–411.

[28] Livy xxxix 55.5–6; on the previous history of the institutions of colonization in Roman Italy, see Salmon, pp. 13–102, with Crawford's review, *Classical Review* 85 (1971), 251–53.

[29] Livy xxxix 44.10–11; Kornemann, "Colonia," PW, IV (1901), 521; Salmon, pp. 104–5, 186–87, n. 182. Earlier citizen colonies: Salmon, pp. 70–81, 95–99.

[30] Sherwin-White, p. 73.

[31] Cicero *Brutus* 20.79; Mommsen, *Römisches Staatsrecht,* III, 135. See also Salmon, pp. 98–99 and 184–85, n. 165, with Crawford's review, *Classical Review* 85 (1971), 251–52.

discussed the next year, as the senate debated in 183 whether the large colony projected for Aquileia should be a colony of citizens or of Latins.[32] Aquileia was founded as a Latin colony, but the new principle of large citizen colonies thereafter became the rule.[33] Thus, in 180 Antiochus' probable friends P. and M. Popillius Laenas were two of the triumviri appointed to found a Latin colony at Pisae,[34] but apparently no Latin colony was founded. Rather, in 177 Luna was established near Pisae as a citizen colony of the type contemplated in the debate over Aquileia, large enough to have its own local government.[35] The subsequent colonies established by the republic followed the new pattern.[36]

Antiochus could also observe citizen colonies being used to subdue a stubbornly rebellious population, as Rome had done long before against the Samnites.[37] By Antiochus' times, the Boii of Cisalpine Gaul had been fighting the Romans for almost a century. Around 200 B.C.E., with the help of allies, the Boii destroyed the Latin colony of Placentia. However, in 191 the consul P. Cornelius Scipio Nasica, first cousin of Scipio Africanus, inflicted the final defeat upon the Boii and required them to surrender half their land for Roman colonies.[38] It would appear that many of the vanquished fled over the Alps and that the rest were submerged in the flood of colonies[39] and even of unorganized settlers.[40] The surviving settlers of Cremona and Placentia probably pressed for this flood of colonists. Indeed, the survivors of Placentia were long afraid to rebuild their ruined city. Even the enrollment of new colonists with Latin rights in 190 B.C.E.[41] may not have quieted their fears; they may have felt insecure until they were surrounded by Roman citizen colonies and linked to a network of military roads.[42]

Thus Antiochus could learn how his enemy, the Roman republic, extended Roman citizenship to self-governing non-Roman towns and also founded new self-governing towns, all bound by strong political and patriotic ties to support the mighty Roman state.[43]

[32] Livy xxxix 55.5; Sherwin-White, p. 74.
[33] Kornemann, PW, IV, 516–17; Salmon, pp. 103–8.
[34] Livy xl 43.1.
[35] Livy xli 13.4; Sherwin-White, p. 74.
[36] Sherwin-White, pp. 72–90.
[37] See Kornemann, PW, IV, 515, 560–61.
[38] Livy xxxvi 38.5 – 39.3; Ruge, "Boii 1," PW, III (1899), 630.
[39] Strabo v 1.6.213 and 10.216; colonies: Livy xxxvii 47.2 and 57; xxxix 55.6.
[40] Livy xlii 4.4; Tenney Frank in *Cambridge Ancient History*, VIII (1930), 327; but cf. E. T. Salmon, "Roman Colonisation from the Second Punic War to the Gracchi," JRS 26 (1936), 54–55.
[41] Livy xxxvii 47.2.
[42] See Rudolf Hanslik, "Placentia," PW, XXII (1950), 1902–3.
[43] Already in 214, Philip V of Macedonia was holding up the Roman policies on citizenship and colonization as an example to be followed. See Syll.³ 543, lines 31–34, translated in Naphtali Lewis and Meyer Reinhold, *Roman Civilization*, I (Columbia University Press, 1951), 387.

Greek cities had shared their citizenship wholesale only with other Greek cities, notably in the Achaean league. Greek states had also granted citizenship to individuals. The Romans had made grants of citizenship to individuals, too, from an early date, but not on a large scale. Though we lack evidence, it is possible that in the time of Antiochus bodies of Roman citizens constituted significant minorities in some of the non-citizen towns of Italy and the provinces as they did later in Cyrene under Augustus. After the Romans retook rebellious Capua in 211, large numbers of Roman citizens settled on land confiscated from the city, and from that year there may have been an organized body of Roman citizens there.[44]

Already in the Second Punic War, however, there were traces of weakness in the Roman system because one class of considerable power and importance lacked full Roman citizenship: the local political leaders of the Latin and Italian towns. Failure to share political rights with the leaders in the important region of Campania may have led to Hannibal's initial successes in central Italy,[45] and loyalty of the leadership in other parts of Italy surely was a major factor in the eventual defeat of the Carthaginians. Unless rewarded, that loyalty could be lost. Roman conservatism was slow to take note of these factors. Thus, the disaster at Cannae in 216 left huge gaps in the ranks of the Roman aristocracy. Yet, when Spurius Carvilius, a man who had been consul, suggested at that critical time that Roman citizenship be granted to two members of the local senate in each of the Latin states, the Senate suppressed all mention of the suggestion, viewing it as monstrous.[46] For a long time the local aristocracies continued to be without Roman citizenship. Our sources do not tell us when in the second century B.C.E. persons who reached the high local magistracies in Latin towns began to receive citizenship automatically. This principle, of citizenship *"per magistratum,"* is taken for granted in the provisions of a Roman law of 123/2 (the Lex Acilia),[47]

[44] Roman citizens in non-Roman communities: Sherwin-White, pp. 54, 76, 210–14; Alan J. N. Wilson, *Emigration from Italy in the Republican Age of Rome* (New York: Barnes & Noble, 1966), pp. 13–27. *Conventus civium Romanorum* at Capua: Kornemann, "Conventus," PW, IV (1901), 1183. One cannot, however, infer what conditions were in the autonomous towns of Roman Italy on the basis of institutions found at Capua after 211. Capua was penalized in 211 by the loss of her status as a city and of all her *de jure* autonomous institutions. Even so, *de facto* autonomous civic institutions were quick to spring up, and Roman citizens settling in Capua then may have formed their own organization partly in order to uphold their own interests as against those of the *de facto* local government. See M. W. Frederiksen, "Republican Capua: A Social and Economic Study," *Papers of the British School at Rome,* XXVII (1959), 82–94, 117–22. There is another difficulty in drawing inferences from the *conventus* at Capua: there is evidence suggesting that it was not the same sort of thing as the later *conventus* of Roman citizens residing in the provinces. See Frederiksen, ibid., pp. 82, 85, 93, but see also Wilson, p. 91.

[45] Livy xxiii 6.8.

[46] Livy xxiii 22.4–9.

[47] CIL I 198, line 78.

so it must be earlier, perhaps considerably earlier. If it was not in force when Antiochus was in Rome, it may have been matter for discussion among his Roman acquaintances. The *Lex Acilia* was part of the legislative program of the party of Gaius Gracchus. Gaius and his ally Fulvius Flaccus strove to enfranchise Rome's Latin and Italian allies. In this political action of the 120s B.C.E. Gaius Gracchus may have been carrying out ideas of his family which went back to his father Tiberius, the contemporary of Antiochus IV. We have no evidence to prove or disprove the supposition.

Such were the civic institutions and theories which might have impressed Antiochus during his stay at Rome. His future kingdom already had features resembling the Roman system. Within the Seleucid empire were cities and peoples with considerable autonomy. Imperial authorities spoke of the union formed by these privileged communities under the king as the "alliance" (*symmachia*). In Syria and Palestine the Seleucids continued to make use of the structure of urban and rural colonies of Greeks and Macedonians by which the Ptolemies provided for domestic tranquillity and security against foreign enemies.[48] Elsewhere in the Seleucid realm were somewhat different urban and rural settlements which the early Seleucids themselves had established for the same purposes.[49] Subject peoples thinking to disobey the king's orders could be cowed by a threat to establish a military colony on their territory.[50] In the same way that Rome limited or violated the autonomy of her allies, the Seleucids limited or violated the autonomy of members of the *symmachia*.[51] Down to the time of Antiochus IV, however, there had been no idea of an imperial citizenship. Let us now turn to the puzzling traces in our sources of what may have been the civic policy of Antiochus IV.

We read in Second Maccabees 4:7–9 that at the beginning of the reign of Antiochus IV, Jason the Oniad, brother of the Jewish high priest Onias III, sought to usurp the high priesthood and did so successfully by offering to bring Antiochus in revenue 360 talents plus 80 talents from an unspecified source, making a sum which was a great increase over the tribute the Seleucids had been receiving from Judaea, plus another 150 talents for two privileges: first, the honor of being the founder of a gymnasium and of ephebic institutions in Jerusalem; and second, the prerogative of being the one "to draw up the list of Antiochenes-in-Jerusalem" (*tous en Hierosolymois Antiocheis anagrapsai*).

A whole literature has sprung up in the effort to explain the quoted words.[52] Without being oversubtle, let us try to see what these words

---

[48] See V. A. Tcherikover, *Hellenistic Civilization and the Jews*, pp. 92–107.
[49] Bikerman, *Institutions*, pp. 80–88, 157–63.
[50] J. *AJ* xii 4.1.159.
[51] Bikerman, *Institutions*, pp. 141–69.
[52] See Bickermann, *Gott*, pp. 59–65, esp. p. 59, n. 1, and Tcherikover, *Hellenistic Civilization*, pp. 161, 404–9.

should mean in simple Greek, and then face the ensuing difficulties. Only if the simplest interpretation is untenable should we desert it for more subtle ones. Jason of Cyrene, the author of the original of which Second Maccabees is an abridgment, wrote to impress; he was pompous and wordy but not deliberately obscure. His abridger insisted he was making the book still easier for the reader (II 2:24–31).

The simplest way to construe "the Antiochenes-in-Jerusalem" (*tous en Hierosolymois Antiocheis*) is as "the Antiochene citizens in Jerusalem." The readers of Jason of Cyrene would have interpreted the words thus as readily as readers of the letter at Second Maccabees 1:1 would have understood *hoi en Hierosolymois Ioudaioi* to be "the Jews in Jerusalem," or as readily as readers of an inscription on Cyprus would have understood *hoi en Paphôi Rômaioi* to be "the Roman citizens in Paphos."[53] Surely it appears strange to have Antiochene citizens in Jerusalem, but let us not abandon the simple unless we have to. What privilege did Jason the usurper seek with reference to these strange Antiochenes? The answer lies in the last Greek word of the passage, *anagrapsai*. It means "to draw up a list" or "to enter in a list." Official lists of citizens are known from many places in the Hellenistic world, and we hear in ancient documents of functionaries empowered "to draw them up" (*anagrapsai*). In some cities the official citizen list was kept by the same scribes who kept the other city records. In others, however, the citizen lists were kept by religious and clan organizations, and in inscriptions of these cities an act of the government conferring citizenship is always accompanied by an order that the new citizen's name be entered in the official list of an organization.[54] In cities where the official citizen list was kept by the same scribes who kept the records of proceedings of the legislative and administrative bodies, the act conferring citizenship usually contains no such order. However, a document from Seleucia in Pieria of 186 records a grant of citizenship and an order to the city scribe to enter the new citizen's name in the official lists.[55]

Could the Jewish high priest draw up an official list of "Antiochene citizens in Jerusalem?" He could, if privileged Jerusalemites were now to be called "Antiochenes," just as only privileged graduates of the ephebic institutions of Alexandria were called "Alexandrines."[56] Still, if

---

[53] ILS, 7208.

[54] At Athens and Aegina "to be entered" on the citizen list is *grapsasthai;* see G. Busolt and H. Swoboda, *Griechische Staatskunde,* pp. 946, 947, n. 2, and OGIS 329. Elsewhere, various compounds of the same verb are used. At Samos and Seleucia in Pieria, as at II 4:9, the verb was *anagrapsai;* see Syll.² 162, and C. B. Welles, *Royal Correspondence in the Hellenistic Period,* p. 187.

[55] Published in Welles, ibid., and in M. Holleaux, *Bulletin de correspondence hellénique* 56 (1933), 6–67.

[56] See Victor A. Tcherikover and Alexander Fuks, CPJ, II (Harvard University Press, 1960), nos. 151 and 153, lines 53–57.

Jerusalemites were now to be called "Antiochenes," one would expect their city to be renamed "Antioch." This is a procedure quite common in the Hellenistic kingdoms,[57] but there is no other evidence whatever that Jerusalem was renamed. Indeed, the abridged history first speaks of "drawing up the list of Antiochene citizens in Jerusalem" (II 4:9) and then gives as the official designation of persons on that list "Antiochenes from Jerusalem" (II 4:19). Neither of these formulas is the normal way in Greek to refer to citizens of a renamed city. On coins of ca. 64 B.C.E. of renamed cities we read of "Seleucian Abilenes" and of "Antiochene Hippenes"; from the time of Nero (54–68 C.E.), of "Nysaeans alias Scythopolites"; on coins from the reign of Marcus Aurelius (161–180 C.E.) we read of "Antiochenes by the Chrysorhoa, the former Gerasenes."[58] If one needed to distinguish a renamed Jerusalem from other Antiochs, there were established formulas. "Antioch in Judaea" would be normal, following the contemporary pattern of "Seleucia in Pieria"[59] or "Antioch in Mygdonia."[60]

There are, indeed, parallels for the strange expressions at II 4:9, 19. Coins of Ptolemais beginning under Antiochus IV bear the Greek legend "Antiochenes in Ptolemais."[61] Coins of Gaza bearing dates from 148/7 to 103/2 bear the Greek legend "Seleuceians in Gaza."[62] Coins of Susa of 31/0–27/6 bear the Greek legend "Phraatans in Susa."[63] Josephus indicates that one could speak of "Antioch in Nisibis."[64] How are these formulas to be explained? One might note how in the very same context Josephus lets us know that Nisibis was the name of a region as well as of a city, as is often true of Greek place names ending in -is. Similarly, Ptolemais may have been the name of a region as well as of a city.[65] But the formula cannot be so explained in the cases of Gaza, Susa, and Jerusalem. Alternatively, one might note that Susa had two parts, the inner, called "Susa the Fortress," and the outer, called "Susa the City."[66] If the inner part was made into a city Phraata, it would be proper to call

[57] See Tcherikover, Hellenistic Civilization, pp. 22, 30, 35, 91–92, etc.

[58] See Head, pp. 785–87 (Leucas, Caesareia Panias, Abila, Antiochia ad Hippum, Canata, Gadara, Gerasa); 803 (Nysa Scythopolis). On Gerasa, see also Tcherikover, Hellenistic Civilization, pp. 100, 449, n. 78.

[59] Welles, Royal Correspondence, 45.1, 71.4, 72.1.

[60] Head, p. 815.

[61] See below, n. 74.

[62] G. F. Hill, Catalogue of the Greek Coins of Palestine, pp. lxix–lxx, 143–44. See also pp. 187–88.

[63] G. Le Rider, Suse sous les Séleucides et les Parthes, pp. 111–13, 409–17.

[64] AJ xx 3.3.68.

[65] See Tcherikover, Hellenistic Civilization, p. 444, n. 12; M. Avi-Yonah, The Holy Land, pp. 130–33.

[66] The Fortress: Esther 1:2, 5, 2:3, 5, 8, 9:11–12; the City: Esther 3:15, 4:8, 8:15, 9:13–14, 18; cf. Supplementum Epigraphicum Graecum, VII, 13 (of the first or second Christian century), and see Bickerman, Four Strange Books, pp. 202–3, 208.

its citizens "Phraatans in Susa." Similarly, Ptolemais had two parts, the inner town or citadel, which had been the prehellenistic town of Akko, and the new town of Ptolemais.[67] Ancient sources likewise mention two Gazas, the "old" and the "new."[68] Again, however, the "Antiochenes in Jerusalem" cannot be so explained. Though our sources speak of the temple area and the citadel (e.g. II 4:12, 5:5), there is no hint of a division of the *city* of Jerusalem into areas of different civic status in the Hellenistic period until the building of the Akra (I 1:31–35), long after Jason had ceased to be high priest. Hence, in view of normal Greek usage and the enigmatic character even of the parallels to our strange formula, it would be rash to take the "Antiochenes in Jerusalem" as deriving their name from a renaming of Jerusalem as Antioch.[69]

Furthermore, both the puzzling "Antiochenes in Jerusalem" and many of the parallels fit into a larger series of puzzling phenomena. Consider the following problems.

1) In the letter probably forged as propaganda for Lysias,[70] Antiochus IV addresses "the good Jews, the citizens [*politai*]," calling himself their "king and praetor [*stratêgos*]."

2) A Babylonian priestly scribe, writing in cuneiform in August or September, 169, noted—probably with disapproval—that the *politai* had made images and works in the Greek manner. He transcribed the Greek word for "citizens" phonetically, showing that no Akkadian equivalent was available.[71]

3) In a Greek inscription from Babylon dated in 147 Sel., Antiochus IV is called "Savior of Asia" and "Founder of the City." In another Greek inscription from Babylon of about the same date, the "city" (*polis*) honors Demokrates son of Byttakos, the *stratêgos* and *epistatês* of the city.[72] *Stratêgos* and *epistatês* were typical titles of elective offices in Greek city-states.

---

[67] Tcherikover, *Hellenistic Civilization*, p. 92.

[68] Ibid., p. 96; F.-M. Abel, *Géographie de la Palestine*, II, 403.

[69] Cf. Bickermann, *Gott*, pp. 59–64; Tcherikover, *Hellenistic Civilization*, pp. 404–9, 539, n. 53; Abel, p. 332; Le Rider, *Suse*, pp. 410–11.

[70] See in AB vol. 41A NOTE on II 9:18–27.

[71] Partially published in Theophilus G. Pinches, *The Old Testament in the Light of the Historical Records of Assyria and Babylonia*, 2d ed. (London: Society for Promoting Christian Knowledge, 1903), pp. 480–81, 553; see also A. T. Olmstead, "Intertestamental Studies," *JAOS* 56 (1936), 247. The full document will be published by A. J. Sachs.

[72] OGIS 253, revised by M. Zambelli, "L'ascesa al trono di Antioco IV Epifane di Siria," *Rivista di filologia* 88 (1960), 374–78, and reprinted by Mørkholm, p. 100, n. 48; OGIS 254.

How should the date in OGIS 253, 147 Sel., be interpreted? The inscription is in Greek and speaks of thank offerings, which could coincide with Antiochus' festival at Daphne in the late summer of 166, and then the date would be Sel. Mac., 166/5 B.C.E.; cf. Mørkholm, p. 100. But perhaps even in a Greek inscription at Babylon one should expect a Sel. Bab. date, which would be 165/4.

4) A unit of Antiochus IV's cavalry, three thousand strong, was called the "citizen" horse (*politikoi*).[73]

5) Ptolemais has a strangely privileged status in the 160s. Her citizens put through an anti-Jewish decree which becomes binding on the gentile cities neighboring Judaea (II 6:8), and Lysias has to justify royal policy to the citizens of Ptolemais, who apparently had some real power to object to his treaty with the Jews (II 13:25–26).

We return to the phenomena we considered before, this time studying them more closely:

6) Coins of Ptolemais issued under Antiochus IV bear the legend "Antiochenes in Ptolemais." These coins probably began to be minted in 169/8.[74]

7) In the reign of Antiochus IV at least nineteen cities of the Seleucid empire were suddenly allowed to coin their own bronze small change. Some of these coins bear dates. The earliest examples, from Antioch, Tyre, and Ascalon, are of 144 Sel. Mac.=169/8 B.C.E.[75] On these coins some, but not all, of these cities call their citizens "Antiochenes." There is such a proliferation of cities inhabited by Antiochenes that the citizens of the great Seleucid capital on the Orontes have to be designated as "Antiochenes by Daphne"; at no other time did they have to be so designated.[76]

8) Although other cities allowed to coin by Antiochus show native motifs on the reverse face of their issues, the cities inhabited by Antiochenes show only the standing Zeus clad in a himation and the seated Zeus Nikephoros, both used on the royal bronze coinage.[77] The obverse types of the coins from "Antiochene" cities are also noteworthy. Although obverses from some of the other coining towns (Apameia and Laodiceia in Seleucid Syria; Aegae and Mopsus in Cilicia) show Antiochus wearing the diadem, the "Antiochene" cities all show him wearing the radiate crown.[78]

What sort of communities are these aggregations of "citizens" or "Antiochenes"? All these strange phenomena can be explained if we assume

---

[73] Polybius xxx 25.6; cf. Bikerman, *Institutions*, p. 72.

[74] Bikerman, *Institutions*, pp. 231–35; Leo Kadman, *The Coins of Akko Ptolemais, Corpus Nummorum Palaestinensium*, I Series, vol. IV (Jerusalem: Schocken, 1961), pp. 51, 92–96.

[75] See O. Mørkholm, "The Municipal Coinages with Portrait of Antiochus IV of Syria," in *Congresso internazionale di numismatica, Roma, 1961*, Vol. II (Roma: Instituto italiano di numismatica, 1965), pp. 63–64.

[76] Antiochenes in Ptolemais: above, n. 74; by the Cydnos (Tarsus): Head, p. 732; by the Saros (in Cilicia): Head, p. 715; by Callirhoe (Edessa): Head, p. 814, Stephanus Byzantius s.v. *Antiocheia*, and Pliny *Historia Naturalis* v 21.86; in Mygdonia (Nisibis): Head, p. 815, Strabo xvi 1.23.747, Plutarch *Lucullus* 11.32, and Polybius v 51.1; by Daphne: Percy Gardner, *Catalogue of Greek Coins: The Seleucid Kings of Syria* (Bologna: Arnaldo Forni, 1963), p. 40.

[77] Gardner, pp. 37 (nos. 31–32) and 39–42; Mørkholm, p. 127 and n. 41.

[78] Mørkholm, *Congresso, 1961*, II, 64–65.

that Antiochus in his zeal to ape the Romans turned his capital into an analogue of Rome.[79] If there was to be an Antiochene republic analogous to the Roman, she should have her own citizen communities of Antiochenes throughout Seleucid territory, just as Rome had citizen communities of Romans throughout Italy. Just as with Roman Italy, some town could be composed entirely of Antiochene citizens and other, noncitizen towns could have substantial bodies of Antiochene citizens among their residents.[80] Antiochus may have conferred Antiochene citizenship on all the inhabitants of Nisibis or Ptolemais, while granting it at Jerusalem only to those selected by Jason. The authorization of Jason to draw up the list of those to receive the privilege of citizenship is in accord with both Roman and Hellenistic practice, to allow the founder of a community to do so.[81]

If our interpretation of Jason's privileges is correct, Antiochus began to develop his institutions of Antiochene citizenship early in his reign, long before the earliest dated municipal coins of 169/8 B.C.E. Undated municipal coins may be earlier. In 170/69 Antiochus accomplished a feat worthy of Rome: he conquered Egypt. Thereupon he could well have expanded his Roman-style system of citizenship and alliance and could well have publicized the new institutions through the municipal coinages from 169/8 on.

We cannot tell whether Antiochus allowed the original Antiochenes of the city on the Orontes to vote on these extensions of citizenship as Romans would have[82] or whether he simply used his prerogatives as royal "founder" to found his own wider Antiochene citizenship, to which he admitted the Antiochenes of the city on the Orontes as a matter of course, as "Antiochenes by Daphne."

The Romans may already have instituted citizenship *per magistratum* before Antiochus left Rome; if they had not, he may have heard the idea discussed in the more progressive political circles.[83] Republican institutions could not be introduced everywhere in an empire like that of the Ptolemies or the Seleucids. However, Hellenistic monarchs had long since

---

[79] See p. 104.

[80] See above, nn. 23 and 44.

[81] Roman: above, n. 31, and Kornemann, "Civitas" PW, Suppl. I (1903), 308; Hellenistic: J. *AJ* xii 3.1.120, 125, and *Ap.* ii 4.35, 38–39.

The important function of drawing up the original list of citizens was not one to entrust to minor functionaries. Indeed, the subsequent responsibility for the list of citizens, the census roll, also belonged to a high official, though the addition of single names to the roll might on occasion be assigned to a minor functionary. At Rome, the censors ranked as the highest magistrates, and the census of the Roman citizens of Italy was to be the function of the highest local magistrates (CIL I² 593, lines 142–56; see also Sherwin-White, p. 86). Cf. Bickermann, *Gott*, p. 59, n. 1, and Tcherikover, *Hellenistic Civilization*, pp. 405–6.

[82] Kornemann, PW, Suppl. I, 309.

[83] See pp. 110–11.

realized that most Greeks would demand some form of republican organization in their civic life. Sometimes it was possible to found Greek cities with fairly autonomous local government. The Ptolemies, however, were determined to keep Egypt under strong central control, and elsewhere the native population might view with distaste the prospect of being ruled through Greek-style republican institutions. Under such circumstances, republican institutions could still exist in Greek social and cultural affairs, especially in the corporations around the gymnasium and the ephebate.[84] The standard ephebic education and the republican administration of the corporations around the gymnasium probably appeared to Antiochus as at least as good a preparation for citizenship as political life in a Latin town.[85] Hence, he well might have used the ephebic education as the Romans were to use the municipal magistracy, as the avenue for the recruitment of new citizens. If so, the original Antiochenes at Jerusalem were selected by Jason. Thereafter, the citizen body would grow and replenish itself through the gymnasium and the ephebic institutions.

If this reconstruction is correct, Antiochus founded an Antiochene citizenship analogous to the Roman. The town-names of Babylon, Ptolemais, and Jerusalem could remain, just as the Latin and Italian towns kept their names on receiving Roman citizenship. If the entire town of Ptolemais became Antiochene, "Antiochenes in Ptolemais" would be the proper style of designation for citizens of such a privileged community and would appear on their coins. One may compare their coins with those struck in the third century B.C.E. for use in the Roman citizen towns of Italy, which bore the legend "of the Romans" (*Romano*).[86] Just as Roman citizens were known as *"cives"* or *"Quirites"* and were so addressed by their officials,[87] so Antiochus' privileged subjects could be called *politai* and be so addressed by him. Just as wealthy Roman citizens served in the cavalry as *equites Romani,* so wealthy "Antiochene" citizens could serve as *politikoi hippeis.*[88]

---

[84] See Rostovtzeff, SEHHW, pp. 1057–61; M. P. Nilsson, *Die hellenistische Schule* (München: C. H. Beck, 1955), pp. 83–92.

[85] See Nilsson, ibid., pp. 80–81.

[86] Mattingly, *Roman Coins* pp. 5–12. Cf. CIL I² 593 (45 B.C.E.), line 145: *"Omnium municipium colonorum suorum queique eius praefecturae erunt, quei cives Romanei erunt."*

Once the formula "Antiochenes in Ptolemais" was established, the people of the city tended to retain it. Long after Antiochus' civic scheme had ceased to exist, the legend continues to appear on the coins of Ptolemais, down to 109 B.C.E.; see Kadman, *Coins of Akko Ptolemais,* pp. 43–45, 92–104. In the reign of Claudius (41–54 C.E.), the citizens of Ptolemais use the same pattern on their coins as they call themselves the "Germanicans in Ptolemais" (ibid., pp. 45, 108).

[87] "Quirites" is too common to require examples. Roman citizens addressed as "cives": Livy ii 55.7; Tacitus *Annals* i 42. "*Politai*": see above, n. 71, and II 9:19.

[88] Above, n. 73; for the expression in Greek, cf. Diodorus xviii 12.2, xix 106.2.

Rome extended lesser privileges to Latin and Italian towns which were not admitted to full Roman citizenship or for some reason, perhaps connected with local religion, did not desire it, and these towns were still issuing bronze coinage in the second century.[89] Just so, Antiochus allowed cities like Tyre and Sidon and Byblos to strike bronze coins bearing local motifs as reverse types,[90] though there may have been minorities of "Antiochenes" at all three.

If the heavily Hellenized citizens of Sidon and Tyre, who had long competed in Greek games and presented their own,[91] did not desire Antiochene citizenship for their cities, much less could Jerusalem, with its large population of Jews loyal to the Torah. Hence, the Antiochenes at Jerusalem could not issue coins, any more than could the Antiochenes at Tyre or Roman citizens residing in Latin or Italian towns. Only some of the Jerusalemites became Antiochene citizens. Jerusalem had a gymnasium but long lacked the political institutions typical of a Greek city. Until the establishment of the Akra in 167 B.C.E., Judaea and Jerusalem retained their old political institutions, including the high priest and the council of elders (gerousia; see II 4:44, and cf. II 14:37 and J. AJ xii 3.3.138, 142).[92] The native institutions at Babylon also may have impeded the full development of Antiochene civic institutions there, but they appear to have been less of an obstacle than those at Jerusalem. At Babylon there was a gymnasium as well as a Greek theater, and the politai called their community "the polis" and, like many Greek cities, had local officials bearing such titles as stratêgos and epistatês,[93] but even all this did not win them the privilege of striking their own coins.

As Rome must have seen to it that Roman citizens were allowed to fulfill their Roman religious obligations even where these conflicted with the laws of subject communities, so Antiochus must have seen to it that Antiochenes at Babylon and Jerusalem could follow Greek ways. Jason's entry into Antiochus' program of Antiochene citizenship did set aside those provisions of the Torah that would have required punishment for Jews who became apostates to fulfill their obligations as Antiochenes (II 4:11; cf. I 1:13). But Jewish law still stood against any Jew who became, not an Antiochene citizen, but a worshiper of Bel or Cybele. Just so, the priestly scribe at Babylon writes disapprovingly of the new-fangled

---

[89] Above, nn. 26–27.

[90] Gardner, Catalogue of Greek Coins: The Seleucid Kings of Syria, pp. 39–42; Mørkholm, pp. 125–30; Bikerman, Institutions, pp. 231–33. Cf. Meyer, Ursprung, II, 140–42, to be corrected by Mørkholm, pp. 116–18.

[91] See Bikerman, "Sur une inscription grecque de Sidon," Mélanges syriens offerts à M. René Dussaud, I 91–99; II 4:18.

[92] Cf. Tcherikover, Hellenistic Civilization, pp. 443–44, n. 12, 447, n. 51. Polis at II 4:22 as at II 2:22, 3:1, etc. means "city" but not in the technical Greek sense of "city-state."

[93] Above, n. 72. Theater and gymnasium (=palaestra): Robert Koldewey, The Excavations at Babylon, tr. Agnes S. Johns (London: Macmillan, 1914), pp. 300–7.

Greek idols of the *politai* but does not complain that Babylonian ritual law has been completely overthrown.

A chronicler who lived in Antioch in the sixth Christian Century, John Malalas, presents many ancient traditions of his own city and may have preserved information on the governmental organs of Antiochus IV's Antiochene republic. He reports that Antiochus built "in Great Antioch, *outside* the city, the building called the *Bouleutêrion* for the convocation there of all his senators [*synklêtikoi*] along with the magistrates and all the property-holders of the state [*polis*], to consider what should be done about current issues and then refer [*anapherein*] to him their proposals for the common interest."[94] The passage has a strongly Roman flavor, which would fit Antiochus' mania for imitating things Roman. The senators are his, not those of Antioch-on-the-Orontes; they are called by the Greek word for Roman senators, not by the normal Greek word for "council members" (*bouleutai*). Like the Roman *comitia centuriata,* his deliberative body has a property qualification and meets outside the walls of his capital. As the Romans "referred" legislative proposals for passage to the Senate or the People,[95] so Antiochus had proposals of his citizens "referred" to him, for the republican institutions did not override his royal authority.

The privileges of the Antiochenes of Ptolemais can also cast light on the constitution of this Antiochene republic. In the Roman system, towns could not propose legislation to the Roman assemblies and Senate except insofar as persons from a town were elected to magistracies or sat in the Senate. Perhaps there were citizens of Ptolemais among the Antiochene magistrates and in the Antiochene Senate. Or Antiochus here may have followed the example of the Achaean League, where the member cities were represented in the federal councils in proportion to population.[96] If the Antiochenes of Ptolemais were represented in such federal organs, they could indeed have proposed an anti-Jewish decree and could have tried to prevent the ratification of a treaty with the Jews.

The hypothesis of such an Antiochene republic and citizenship gives meaning to the puzzling information at I 1:41–43: "The king wrote to all his kingdom, for all to become one people and for each to abandon

---

[94] P. 205 Bonn, vol. XCVII, col. 321 Migne: "*Antiochos ho legomenos Epiphanês ektise prôton en Antiocheiai têi megalêi exô tês poleôs to legomenon bouleutêrion eis to ekeise synagesthai pantas tous synklêtikous autou meta tôn politeuomenôn kai tês poleôs pantôn tôn ktêtorôn kai bouleuesthai ti dei ginesthai peri tôn anakyptontôn kai tote anapherein epi auton ta sympheronta.*"

"*Politeuomenoi*" as "magistrates": Polybius xv 2.2, xxiv 9.6, xxv 5.1, etc.

"*Polis*" here could mean the city of Antioch, but it could even include communities with the "Antiochene" equivalent of Latin rights, for Latins could cast votes in one of the tribes of the *Comitia Tributa*. See Sherwin-White, pp. 33, 106–7.

[95] *Referre ad senatum* or *ad populum;* cf. Polybius xv 8.13, xxi 30.6.

[96] See Jakob A. O. Larsen, *Greek Federal States* (Oxford: Clarendon Press, 1968), pp. 223–31.

his own customs. All the gentiles agreed to the terms of the king's proclamation. Many Israelites, too, accepted his religion and sacrificed to idols and violated the Sabbath."[97] Though our author in this passage clearly was influenced by Daniel 3, nothing compelled him falsely to apply a story of Nebuchadnezzar to the time of Antiochus. The reverse types of the coins of the "non-Antiochene" towns of the Seleucid empire and the description of the "images of all the gods" carried in Antiochus' famous parade of 166 B.C.E. give eloquent testimony to the fact that Antiochus allowed many if not all peoples to continue to worship as their forefathers had.[98] Apart from being apparently in conflict with the facts, I 1:41–43 in context is strangely repetitious. The author has already told of voluntary Jewish apostasy (I 1:11–15). To tell of Jewish apostasy in response to the king's proclamation (I 1:43) would appear to be superfluous. If the author had omitted I 1:41–43, no one would have missed the verses.[99]

Hence, we might well construe I 1:41–43 rather as a parenthesis in the narrative, with verbs to be rendered as pluperfects[100]: "The king had written to all his kingdom, inviting all to become one people and inviting each to abandon his own customs. All the gentiles. . . ." If Antiochus on becoming king had issued a proclamation inviting native communities to adopt Greek ways, including the institutions of the gymnasium and the *ephebeia,* in return for the privileges of his new Antiochene citizenship, our author could well have reported the act in the words used here.[101] If once-Phoenician Ptolemais, once-Assyro-Babylonian Nisibis and Edessa, and once-Cilician Tarsus and Adana fully accepted the king's proposals and other cities like Tyre and Sidon partially accepted them, our author could well have written, "All the gentiles accepted the terms of the king's proclamation."

Indeed, for our author, I 1:41–43 would have been out of place at I 1:11–15, where he wishes to stress the spontaneously willful wickedness of the Jewish Hellenizers. But as a parenthesis before I 1:44 the verses are very much in place as a means of making the persecution intelligible: Antiochus had taken milder steps against religion before, and now he turns to worse atrocities.

---

[97] Cf. Meyer, *Ursprung,* II, 140–44; Franz Hampl, Review of *Beiträge zur Beurteilung des Königs Antiochos Epiphanes,* by Fritz Reuter, *Gnomon* 15 (1939), 622.

[98] Bickermann, *Gott,* pp. 47–48; Polybius xxx 25.13.

[99] Scholars who would try to ignore I 1:41–43 as an unhistorical insertion by the author or a redactor will have to explain why such an insertion would have been necessary or even possible, when readers knew the facts about Greek religious attitudes and even Josephus altered the verses presumably because he found them incredible. See e.g. A. D. Nock, "The Roman Army and the Roman Religious Year," HTR 45 (1952), 209–11.

[100] G. Bergsträsser, *Hebräische Grammatik,* II, 26–27; GKC, § 106 f.

For *graphein* as "invite" or "request," see J. *BJ* i 23.4.456.

[101] Compare Antiochus V's letter of 162 B.C.E. (II 11:24–25); see in AB vol. 41A commentary ad loc., and in present volume pp. 131, 137.

If I 1:41 really does report a proclamation issued at the beginning of Antiochus' reign, we can understand how Jason the Oniad and his "wicked" associates could have thought of making their proposals to Antiochus (I 1:13; II 4:9): they came in response to the king's own invitation.

If such was Antiochus' experiment with citizenship, it was never repeated on so comprehensive a scale. Nevertheless, there probably were some later reverberations. Demetrius I also had been a hostage in Rome and was a friend of Tiberius Sempronius Gracchus.[102] No traces of experiments with Roman institutions appear during the troubled reign of Demetrius I. Under his son, Demetrius II, however, Gaza suddenly begins to issue bronze coins with the legend "Seleuceians in Gaza."[103] Demetrius II, if he had any notions of imperial citizenship, might well reject the name "Antiochenes," which now recalled the name of the rival Seleucid line. Moreover, the line of Demetrius I was not at all successful in holding the loyalty of Antioch, the capital; and when driven out of Antioch, Demetrius II took refuge at Seleuceia in Pieria, a city which proved extraordinarily loyal to the line of Demetrius.[104] Hence, well might Demetrius II have chosen the name "Seleuceians" if he wished to create a counterpart of Antiochus IV's experiments in citizenship. Demetrius II may have had good reason to reward Gaza with such a grant of citizenship, for he may have had an important base of support there.[105] The earliest dated coins of the Seleuceians in Gaza are of 166 or 165 Sel., the same date as that of the earliest dated coin of the Seleuceians in Pieria. The obverse type of the coins of the Seleuceians of Gaza, the *Tyche* of the city, turns up only after 104 B.C.E. on the coins of Seleuceia in Pieria[106] but appears on coins of Seleuceia's sister-city of Apameia already in 163 Sel. as well as on second-century coins of Laodiceia and Epiphaneia.[107] Hence, perhaps Demetrius II tried to create a "Seleuceian" citizenship based upon the loyal cities of Seleucid Syria, to which he admitted Gaza.

Roman citizens were to find life among non-citizens in Roman provinces and client states hazardous, as we learn from the massacres in Numidia under Jugurtha in 112 and in Asia under Mithradates in 88.[108] The An-

---

[102] Appian xi 45; Polybius xxxi 11–12, 33.

[103] Above, n. 62.

[104] I 11:44–51; J. *AJ* xiii 4.7.111, 5.3.135–41; Justin xxxv 1.3, 2.3; Diodorus xxxii 9c, xxxiii 4; Livy *Periocha* lii; Bevan, II, 227, 237, 241, and cf. p. 301, Appendix N.

[105] I 10:69–85, 11:61–62; J. *AJ* xiii 5.5.149–51. Where did Apollonius raise the army he brought to Jamnia? In Gaza?

[106] Hill, *Greek Coins of Palestine*, pp. lxix–lxx; Warwick Wroth, *Catalogue of the Greek Coins of Galatia, Cappadocia, and Syria* (Bologna: Arnaldo Forni, 1964), p. 270.

[107] Wroth, pp. 233, 242, 247; sister cities: Ruge, "Seleukeia 2," PW IIᴬ (1921), 1188.

[108] Sallust *Bellum Iugurthinum* 26 and Diodorus xxxiv 31; Appian xii 4.22–23 and Münzer, "Mithridates 12," PW, XV (1932), 217ʊ.

tiochene citizens of Babylon appear to have evoked hostility from the natives.[109] In Judaea the Torah had long been the law of the land. The people remembered the harsh history of the kingdoms of Israel and Judah and knew that the dire threats of the Torah against adopting the ways of the gentiles were no empty rhetoric. There just might have been a case for asserting that the civic rituals of the Antiochene republic and of the gymnasium did not involve idolatry, but many Pietists were bound to interpret Exod 34:15–16 and Deut 7:2–4 as forbidding Jews to become citizens of the republic. The Antiochene rituals in fact had so strong a taint of idolatry that many Pietists sought to massacre Jews who became citizens of the republic; they did so out of obedience to Exod 22:19 and Deut 13:7–18.[110] The Antiochenes were still more vulnerable: they were neither a blameless nor a harmonious community. The very establishment of the Antiochene community at Jerusalem was tainted with bribery and intrigue; the Hellenizers were rent into at least two factions around the rival high priests, Jason and Menelaus; and Menelaus, who prevailed, bore the stains not only of bribery but also of temple robbery and of suborned murder.

Riots broke out in Jerusalem against Menelaus and were suppressed by royal force and royal judicial decisions (II 4). When civil war broke out among the Hellenizers upon the false report of the death of Antiochus IV, the pious "non-citizen" Jews appear to have struck against both Hellenizing parties, repulsing Jason's attempt to seize Jerusalem and driving Menelaus to take refuge in the old citadel (II 5:1–7).[111] The pious militants may have felt themselves still loyal to Antiochus when he proved to be alive. When Antiochus approached the walls of Jerusalem, pious Jews may even have been the ones who opened the gates of the city to him.[112] Antiochus, however, stood by his agent Menelaus and by Menelaus' "Antiochene" supporters and hence suppressed the militant Pietists. Menelaus repaid his protector by surrendering to him the temple treasures, as once Ahaz had surrendered them to Tiglath Pileser.[113]

Indeed, there had been a sinful rebellion, by Jason, against Antiochus IV, the sovereign chosen by God to rule over the chosen people.[114] The sin could well require as expiation the surrender of the temple treasures as before when Rehoboam had surrendered them to Shishak.[115] We hear

[109] See pp. 114–15.

[110] Jubilees xxiii 20. I shall show elsewhere, in a lecture, "Jewish Parties of the Time of the Hasmonean Uprising," which will be published by the Association for Jewish Studies, that this passage reflects the time of the civic innovations of Antiochus IV.

[111] See Tcherikover, *Hellenistic Civilization*, pp. 187–89; on the factions in Jerusalem, see commentary to II 4:8, 5:5–16.

[112] See on I 1:20.

[113] II Kings 16:8, 14–18.

[114] See Part I, p. 5.

[115] II Chron 12:5–9.

nothing of events in Jerusalem between Antiochus' sack of the temple in 169 and the expedition of Apollonius the Mysarch "two years later" (I 1:29), in 167. However, Jason of Cyrene lets us know that the Jews in the months between suffered harsh repression under the king's appointed official, Philip the Phrygian, and under Menelaus. At the same time, the Samaritans, still regarded as Jews, suffered under Andronicus (II 5:22–23; cf. J. *AJ* xii 5.5.258–64). One need not assume that this repression fell upon an altogether unresisting population. Even if all Jews piously refrained from rebellion against the foreign king whom God had placed over them, they had no such inhibitions against attacking the apostate "Antiochenes" of Jerusalem, who in the years before had more than once needed the king's protection. Pious Jews probably did strike from underground against these "wicked," and Antiochus may well have countered by giving his "Antiochenes" stronger protection.

In any case, as Antiochus passed through Judaea after his withdrawal from Egypt in 168, he "spoke in anger" against the turbulent Jews and on his "return" to Antioch gave a "sympathetic hearing" to the insecure Antiochenes of Jerusalem who had "deserted the Holy Covenant."[116] Antiochus' response was the expedition of Apollonius the Mysarch, in 167.[117] We read that first the Mysarch taught the Pietists of Jerusalem a harsh lesson (I 1:29–32; II 5:24–26). According to Jason of Cyrene, Apollonius struck on the Sabbath (II 5:25); Sabbath observers may have been his special target. In much the same manner, Scipio Nasica fell upon the Boii in 191.[118] Just as Scipio Nasica dispossessed the Boii so that their survivors were swamped by a flood of settlers in Latin and Roman colonies, so Apollonius now established for the first time an Antiochene city at Jerusalem, the "Akra," dispossessing the "non-citizen" Jews and turning their property over to "Antiochenes" (I 1:33–40; Dan 11:39). The bulk of the population of the Akra consisted of a "sinful nation, lawless men" (I 1:34), the "people of a foreign god" (Dan 11:39).[119]

---

[116] Dan 11:30; for *w'šh* read *w'br*, "and he passed on," with Ginsberg, p. 49. The order of events in Dan 11:31–39 is confused, probably because the seer died before he could edit his notes. Dan 11:39 should come between 11:30 and 11:31. Josephus' account at BJ i 1.1.32 probably reflects these events but confuses the sack of Jerusalem in 169 with the expedition of Apollonius and the persecution of 167. Josephus was led astray by his faith in Daniel and by his other sources. See Part II, p. 52, and Appendix V, and commentary on II 5:23–24, *Disposed . . . slaves.*

[117] Not the persecution, which is referred to in Dan 11:31; on the disorder of Daniel 11, see Part II, pp. 43–44.

[118] Livy xxxvi 38.5–7: Scipio Nasica captured 247 *carpenta*, civilian vehicles often used by women. He was also credited with killing 28,000 Boii and capturing 3,400 and 1,230 horses. Livy says the figures may be exaggerated, but surely they are no more so than those at II 5:14. Livy sees no reason to doubt that the massacre was unprecedented in magnitude.

[119] Read *wy'br*, "he shall transfer," for *w'šh* at Dan 11:39, with the Syriac and with Ginsberg, p. 49; and read *'am*, "the people of," for *'im*, "with," as do Ginsberg, p. 43, and J. A. Montgomery, *A Critical and Exegetical Commentary on the Book of Daniel*, pp. 463–64.

All these epithets are peculiar. "Sinful nation" occurs in the Hebrew Bible only at Isa 1:4, where it refers to Israel, hard hit for its sin of deserting the Lord, but still obdurate (cf. Dan. 9:5). Though one might collect examples where biblical authors speak of the sin of non-Jewish nations,[120] a cursory glance at a concordance under the word "sin" (*ḥēṭ'*) will show that "sinful nation" to our author and his audience would immediately suggest apostate Jews. So, too, "lawless men" (="sons of Belial") in the Bible usually refers to wicked Israelites.[121] Similarly, the normal expression used by Jews for "foreigners" was simply "foreigners" or "gentiles."[122] There was no need to specify that they worshiped a strange god. If a biblical writer specifies worship of strange gods, the worshipers are probably Israelites.[123] In the rhetoric of Daniel, wicked Israelites become members of another nation, as do Jason's supporters at Dan 9:26. Hence, Dan 11:39, too, probably means that in 167 the people of the Akra were heterodox Jews, consisting partly, if not entirely, of the hard-pressed Antiochenes.[124] Even at the beginning of the reign of Demetrius II in 145, renegade Jews were still an important and perhaps preponderant element in the Akra (I 11:20–21). However, just as new citizen colonies bolstered the insecure settlers of Cisalpine Gaul,[125] so in order to protect his Antiochenes at Jerusalem the king now surely sent into the Akra new military settlers, at least some of whom were gentiles, and gave them allotments from the land confiscated from the pious Jewish rebels. If Antiochus was following the Roman pattern, the new soldier-settlers surely received Antiochene citizenship. The renegade Jews and their new protectors would be equally foreign to the dispossessed loyal Jews, so Jerusalem became a "colony of foreigners" (I 1: 38, 2:10, 3:45). By the time the long-beleaguered Akra fell to Simon in 141, the bulk of the civilian population of Hellenized Jews must have perished or fled, so that the surviving inhabitants may have been mostly soldiers of foreign origin; nevertheless, the author writes that "a great enemy was beaten *out of Israel*."[126]

---

[120] Ps 9:18; Gen 13:13, 20:9; Exod 9:27; Zech 14:19. When the author of Jubilees wishes to speak of the wicked gentiles who perpetrated the sack of Jerusalem in 169 and set up the Akra in 167, he appears to avoid the language of Isa 1:4. He calls them not "sinful gentiles" (*gōyīm ḥōṭe'īm*) but "the sinners of the gentiles" (*ḥōṭe'ēy haggōyīm;* xxiii 23) and "the sinners, the gentiles" (*haḥōṭe'īm haggōyīm;* xxiii 24). Cf. Jubilees xxiv 8. On the book of Jubilees, see Part II, n. 4.

[121] Exceptions: Nahum 1:11, 2:1; cf. Job 34:18.

[122] See Greek Sir 32:2=Hebrew Sir 36:3.

[123] See Gen 35:2, 4; Deut 31:16; Josh 24:20, 23; Judg 10:16; I Sam 7:3; Jer 5:19, 8:19 Ps 81:10; II Chron 33:15. But cf. Ezek 44:7, 9; Mal 2:11.

[124] See also I 4:1, where the "people of the Akra" are native Jews and I 6:18, where the people of the Akra are not said to be gentiles but "an aid to the gentiles," and see below, n. 236.

[125] See p. 109.

[126] I 8:51; cf. Exod 7:15; Num 19:13; Deut 17:12, 22:22, etc. See also NOTE on I 13:49–50.

Hence, Antiochus' policy toward the Jews down through the establishment of the Akra in 167 can be explained as an effort to use the patterns of Roman civic institutions to cope with the problems of the Seleucid empire.

The fact of such an extension of Antiochene citizenship by Antiochus IV can also explain the anti-Ptolemaic propaganda at Third Maccabees 2:30 and 3:21.[127] The writer holds that the Seleucids were not the only ones to try to drive the Jews to apostasy through the bribe of citizenship and the threat of persecution; Ptolemy IV, he holds, had anticipated Antiochus IV.

We turn now to the puzzle of Antiochus' persecution of the Jews. Can it be that here, too, he was copying Roman methods? Like Polybius, Antiochus appears to have admired not only the civic institutions of Rome but the religious ones as well.[128] Antiochus was in Rome at an important time for observing the religious policies of the Roman republic.

The war with Hannibal had strained not only the civic institutions of Rome. It had also put pressure on her religious institutions.[129] Foreign rites had long been forbidden to Roman citizens, but the terrors of the war drove citizens to seek new sources of divine aid, and refugees from the countryside brought into the city their own superstitions. In 213 the lower magistrates were ordered by the Senate to suppress the public observance of foreign rites. Resistance proved to be too strong for the lower magistrates. Finally a praetor had to undertake the tasks of suppressing the public rites and collecting for destruction the books of prophesies and prayers and rituals.[130] Even so, the authorities of the Republic were driven in 205 to bring in as a new Roman deity the stone fetish of the Great Mother of Phrygia, though thereafter they drastically regulated her orgiastic cult with its rites of self-castration and forbade active participation to Romans.[131]

All this Antiochus may well have heard of while at Rome. He himself could observe the suppression of the Bacchanalia in 186 under consuls who very likely were his friends, Spurius Postumius Albinus and Quintus Marcius Philippus.[132] He could also observe the severe censorship of Marcus Porcius Cato in 184[133] and the burning of the Pythagorean "books of Numa" in 181 by the praetor Quintus Petillius Spurinus, a man allied to Cato in politics.[134] Later, in 139 B.C.E., Gnaeus Cornelius Scipio

---

[127] III 3:12–29 may be based on proclamations of Antiochus IV, as I shall show elsewhere.

[128] Polybius vi 56.6–15; cf. iii 112.8–9; Livy xli 20.9.

[129] See Latte, pp. 253–63, 269.

[130] Livy xxv 1. 6–12; cf. iv 30.9–11, and see Latte, pp. 268–69.

[131] Latte, pp. 258–62.

[132] For details, see pp. 132–40, 158–59.

[133] See Gelzer, "Porcius 9," PW, XXII[I] (1953), 126–30.

[134] Latte, pp. 268–70; F. Münzer, "Petillius 4" and "Petillius 11," PW, XIX[I] (1937), 1136–38, 1150–52.

Hispalus would expel Jews from Rome as teachers of foreign religion.[135] The father of this Scipio was Gnaeus Cornelius Scipio Hispallus, *praetor peregrinus* in 179 and consul in 176, brother of the Nasica who conquered the Boii, and first cousin of Scipio Africanus.[136] One of the consuls in 139, the year of the expulsion, was Marcus Popillius Laenas, son of the Marcus who had deferred to Tiberius Sempronius Gracchus.[137]

Throughout his stay in Rome, Antiochus could have heard of Cato's condemnation of all Greek philosophy,[138] even if he could not be admitted to the circle of that stern hater of Greeks and enemy of the Scipios. Tiberius Sempronius Gracchus yielded little to Cato in severity[139] and may have been just as hostile to the Epicureans and even to the Stoics in a period when Panaetius had not yet redesigned Stoicism to fit the patriotic sentiments of Roman aristocrats. Antiochus' probable friends Lucius Postumius Albinus and Marcus Popillius Laenas during their consulship in 173 are likely to have expelled two Epicurean philosophers from Rome; if the expulsion was not in their consulship, it occurred in 154 under the consul Lucius Postumius Albinus, who was the son of Antiochus' probable friend, Spurius.[140]

To the Romans who suppressed them, the philosophers were corrupters of society, if not revolutionaries, and the devotees of the Bacchanalia were revolutionary conspirators.[141] Antiochus IV probably acted on his suspicions against philosophers and against Dionysiac cults long before he turned against the Jews. An ancient letter against all philosophers addressed by a King Antiochus to an official survives but has wrongly been considered spurious.[142] The content of the letter is as follows:

---

[135] Valerius Maximus i 3.3; see Schürer, III, 58–59.

[136] Münzer, "Cornelius 346, 347," PW, IV (1901), 1492–93. The divergent spellings are found in the sources, and father and son often did have identical names in Rome.

[137] See pp. 106–7; Volkmann, "Popillius 22, 24, PW, XXII (1953), 60–62.

[138] See Plutarch *Cato Major* 22.1 – 23.3; Gelzer and R. Helm, PW, XXII (1953), 117–18, 130, 145–46.

[139] Above, n. 19.

[140] Athenaeus xii 547a; friendships: p. 107. Athenaeus gives only one consul's name, and that as Lucius Sabinus. Scholars have preferred the later date in order to place the expulsion of the Epicureans in the time of the indignation roused by the conduct of the Athenian philosopher-ambassadors of 155; see Plutarch *Cato Major* 22; von Arnim, "Karneades 1," PW, X (1919), 1965; Münzer, PW, XXII (1953), 918. However, Roman hostility to Epicureans is attested as early as 278 B.C.E. (Valerius Maximus iv 3.6; Plutarch *Pyrrhus* 20.3–4). Epicureans could never be welcome to the old Roman aristocracy. Men of Cato's type sought to keep out all Greek philosophers and rhetoricians and made their own influence felt in 161, well before the Athenian embassy of 155 (Gellius xv 11.1; Suetonius *De rhetoribus* 1).

[141] Livy xxxix 8.1, 14.4, 15.10–11, 16.3–6, 13, 17.6. See H. Jeanmaire, *Dionysos* pp. 457–58.

[142] Athenaeus xii 547a–b; L. Radermacher, *"Basileus Antiochos Phaniai," Rheinisches Museum* 56 (1901), 202–14. Cf. Bickermann, "Ritualmord und Eselskult," MGWJ 72 (1927), 183. In a forthcoming study I shall argue for the probable authenticity of the piece as a letter of Antiochus IV.

"King Antiochus to Phanias. We wrote you before, ordering that no philosopher should be allowed in the city and in the territory. Now we learn that there is a considerable number of them and that they are corrupting the young because you have carried out none of the orders concerning them which we wrote you. Upon receipt of this letter, see to it that a proclamation is issued that all philosophers are to leave the country forthwith and that any young men caught frequenting them are to be strung up [for corporal punishment] and their fathers charged as having committed a crime of the utmost gravity. Let there be no departure from these orders."[143]

If the king is indeed Antiochus IV, his orders had some effect, for a papyrus fragment reports that the courtier Philonides, who was an Epicurean, appealed to the king and won him over. The badly mutilated papyrus seems to suggest that he did so through writing no fewer than 125 works on the subject.[144] No other Seleucid had the sort of opinions which could have produced the letter. Scholars have tried to suggest that Jews forged the document to discredit Antiochus IV in the eyes of Greek intellectuals, but who could have forged it? Only a person who had an audience ready to believe that Antiochus IV could have conflicts with Greek philosophers. Later Jews never suspected that Antiochus had occasion to suppress Greek religions or philosophies; they knew of the friendly relations between Antiochus and Athens (the "capital city" of philosophy) and perhaps could recognize the Epicurean allusions in writings attributed to Antiochus. All other Greek testimony shows Antiochus IV to be an enthusiast for Greek culture and religion, and the Roman Tacitus agrees. Indeed, the preserver of the letter was Poseidonius of Apameia, a well-educated Greek from the heart of the Seleucid empire, who had little love for the Jews.[145] It would be astounding if such a man

---

143 "Hanging" (*kremasthai*) was both a form of corporal punishment (Homer *Iliad* xv 16–21; Pollux iii 79; Athenaeus x 459a) and a method of execution (e.g. Aristotle *Politics* v 1311ᵇ39). Here probably corporal punishment is meant. The Romans who expelled the Epicurean teachers surely intended to proceed as severely against young pupils and their parents as did this King Antiochus. Compare the Roman procedure against the initiates of the Bacchanalia (pp. 137–40, 158) and the procedure of the Greeks of Messenia, Cretan Lyktos, and Thessalian Phalanna against the Epicureans (Aelianus fragment 39; Wilhelm Crönert, *Kolotes und Menedemos*, Studien zur Palaeographie und Papyruskunde, ed. C. Wessely [Leipzig: Avenarius, 1906], p. 24, n. 136).

144 Wilhelm Crönert, "Der Epikureer Philonides," *Sitzungsberichte der Königlich preussischen Akademie der Wissenschaften zu Berlin*, 1900, p. 953, fr. 30.

145 Later Jews on Antiochus IV: see I 1:42, 6:11; II 4:15–16, 6:1–2 and 8, 9:15. Epicurean allusions: see commentary on II 9:19. Greek testimony: see Mørkholm, pp. 40, 55–64. Tacitus: *Histories* v 8. Poseidonius: see Crönert, "Die Epikureer in Syrien," *Jahreshefte des Österreichischen archäologischen Instituts*, X (1907), 151; *Kolotes*, p. 177; K. Reinhardt, "Poseidonios 3," PW, XXIIᴵ (1953), 563–64, 639–41; FGH 87, F 109=Diodorus xxxiv 1; J. *Ap.* ii 7.79. A friend and pupil of Poseidonius may have been a descendant of the recipient of the letter; see G. Lippold, "Phanias 5," PW, XIXᴵᴵ (1938), 1774–75.

would have been deceived by forged Jewish propaganda. Poseidonius was the pupil of pro-Roman Panaetius and was himself the friend of Pompey, so that he cannot be suspected of having forged a letter bearing out the prejudice of some Romans against all philosophers. Hence it is best to conclude that the letter is authentic and bears witness to an attempt of Antiochus IV to suppress philosophy.

Antiochus IV seems also to have sought to regulate the worship of those gods in his empire whose cults resembled that of Dionysus (=Bacchus). At Babylon such was the cult of Nergal, also called Ne-uru-gal or Uru-gal.[146] According to a cuneiform tablet in the British Museum,[147] in Ab of 143 Sel. Bab.=August 18–September 16, 169, while Antiochus was marching victorious through Egypt, persons referred to by the Greek word for "citizens" (*politai*)[148] made Greek-style idols(?) and shrines. On the eighth day of the month an "unsuitable" or "untimely" image of the god Uru-gal was dedicated, but "thieves" stripped the image, were captured, and burned to death.

The text is mutilated and obscure, but this much is certain: in a time of "Hellenization" someone tampered with the cult of the "Dionysiac"

[146] Worship of Nergal in Seleucid Babylonia: A. Jeremias, "Nergal," in *Ausführliches Lexikon der griechischen und römischen Mythologie*, ed. W. H. Roscher III¹ (1897–1902), col. 253, and "Nebo," ibid., col. 52; names of Nergal: ibid., cols. 252, 258.
Dionysius and Nergal shared the following traits:
1) Both were lord and judge of the dead (Martin P. Nilsson, *The Dionysiac Mysteries of the Hellenistic and Roman Age* [Lund: Gleerup, 1957], pp. 118–22; Jeremias in Roscher, III, col. 258).
2) Both were identified with the war god (Macrobius i 19.1–4 and Kern, "Dionyses," PW, V [1905], 1038–41; Jeremias in Roscher, III, 256–58).
3) Both were identified with the sun god (Macrobius i 18 and A. Bruhl, *Liber Pater*, BEFAR, vol. CLXV, pp. 262–66; Alfred Jeremias, *Handbuch der altorientalischen Geisteskultur* [Berlin und Leipzig: De Gruyter, 1929], p. 379).
4) Both were terror-inspiring (W. K. C. Guthrie, *The Greeks and Their Gods* [London: Methuen, 1950], pp. 165–73, and Nilsson, *Dionysiac Mysteries*, pp. 122–30; Jeremias in Roscher, III, 256–58).
5) Both were associated with lions (Kern, PW, V, 1038–39, 1041; Jeremias in Roscher, III, 254–55).
6) Both were bringers of plague or insanity (Guthrie, pp. 165–73; Jeremias in Roscher, III, 255–56).
7) Both were worshiped with processions which included shouting and revelry (Jules Girard, "Dionysia," DAGR, II¹ [1892], 230–43, 246; Jeremias in Roscher, III, 252).
8) Both were patrons of hunting (Georges Lafaye, "Venatio," DAGR, V [1919], 681b; Jeremias in Roscher, III, 252, 257).
9) Both were conquerors of powers of evil (Dionysus of the Titans: PW, V, 1038–41; Nergal of Ereshkigal: ANET², pp. 103–4; cf. Morris Jastrow, *The Religion of Babylonia and Assyria*, pp. 584–88).
[147] Pinches, *Old Testament*, pp. 480, 553; Olmstead, JAOS 56 (1936), 247; see above, n. 71. Pinches believed the word rendered "idols" (*puppē*) to be Greek.
[148] They were presumably the "Antiochenes at Babylon"; see pp. 114–15, 117–18.

god Uru-gal. The "thieves" might be pietist Babylonian rebels.[149] There is reason to think that more than sacrilege was involved. In Hammurapi's Babylonian laws of the second millennium B.C.E. some cases of sacrilege are punished by death, but none are punished by burning.[150] On the other hand, the very same Semitic root (*qly*) is used to speak of burning as the Babylonian penalty for high treason at Jer 29:22.[151]

Hence, there is considerable evidence that Antiochus learned from his experience in Rome to beware of subversive philosophies and subversive Dionysiac movements. In the Hellenistic world before the reign of Antiochus IV the Jews had been famous for their lack of revolutionary tendencies,[152] but Greeks had long noted the resemblance of the Jews to philosophers, even to Epicureans,[153] and probably also their resemblance to the worshippers of Dionysus.[154] If the Jews should ever look to be

[149] Cf. Eddy, *The King Is Dead*, pp. 135–36; cf. also Dan 11:14 and the rabbinic use of *biryōnā* for Jewish rebels (TB *Giṭṭin* 56a) and Josephus' terminology (*AJ* xx 8.10.185–88).

[150] Sections 6 and 8; Pritchard, ANET², p. 166.

[151] Seleucid use of Persian and Assyro-Babylonian punishments for treason: Bikerman, *Institutions*, p. 208.

[152] See on II 1:7 *Jason . . . Kingdom*.

[153] Jews as philosophers in Greek sources earlier than Antiochus IV's persecutions: Clearchus of Soli *apud* J. *Ap.* i 22.177–79; Megasthenes *apud* Clement of Alexandria *Stromateis* i 15; Hecataeus of Abdera *apud* Diodorus xl 3 portrays Moses as a Platonic philosopher; Theophrastus *apud* Porphyry *De abstinentia* ii 26; Hermippus *apud* J. *Ap.* i 22.164–65. For the time after the persecutions texts abound. At least from the time of Aristobulus, the "tutor of Ptolemy VI" (II 1:10), the Jews claimed to be philosophers; see Schürer, III, 512–14.

Jews analogous to Epicureans: they were called atheists by Apollonius Molon *apud* J. *Ap.* ii 14.148 (cf. Ap. ii 7.79 and [of Christians] Lucian *Alexander* 38). Sabbaths and the sabbatical year were regarded as self-indulgent idleness; see Tacitus *Histories* v 4.3 and Juvenal 14.105–6. The Sadducees could be compared to the Epicureans; see J. *BJ* ii 8.14.164–65; *AJ* xiii 5.9.173 and *Vita* 2.12.

Epicureans were accused of effeminacy and homosexuality; see Cleomedes *De motu circulari* ii 1, p. 158 Ziegler, and Aelianus fragment 39, vol. II, pp. 201–2 Hercher. Circumcision might cause the Jews to be likened to a sect of effeminate philosophers; cf. Hadrian's prohibition of circumcision (see Schürer, I, 677–78).

[154] Jews and Dionysus: Tacitus *Histories* v 5.5; Plutarch *Quaestiones convivales* iv 6, pp. 671c–672c; Johannes Lydus *De mensibus* iv 53. There are no early Greek sources connecting Jews with worshipers of Dionysus, though one might infer something of the sort from Herodotus ii 49, 104. All the pagan texts in our possession on Jews and Dionysus may well emanate from the propaganda of Antiochus IV. To be credible, however, that propaganda had to have some previous basis in fact. Such a basis can be found in the ritual of sanctification (*qiddūš*) over wine (Test Levi viii 4–5; cf. 1QS 6:2–6). For the date of the original material in the Testaments of the Twelve Patriarchs, see Bickerman, JBL 69 (1950), 249–53; Eissfeldt, p. 635.

More similarities of Jews to Dionysiacs could be found in the ritual of the "rejoicing of the place of drawing water" (*M. Sukkah* 5:1–5; To. *Sukkah* 4:1–10), and perhaps also from Antiochus IV's own experience of the torchlight procession which brought him into Jerusalem during Jason's pontificate (II 4:22); see commentary ad loc., and cf. Nilsson, *Dionysiac Mysteries*, p. 57, and Livy xxxix 13.12.

Phoenician and Syrian cults were widely identified with Dionysiac rites. See Wolf

philosophic corrupters or Dionysiac revolutionary conspirators, one could expect a man like Antiochus IV to use the appropriate Roman methods of repression.

By the time the Akra was established there was abundant evidence that the Jews were religiously motivated conspiratorial rebels.[155] Indeed, from the time of an abortive revolt under Ptolemy IV[156] Jewish "philosophers" (i.e. apocalyptic visionaries) had on occasion corrupted the people and incited them to violence. The establishment of the Akra must have provoked still more violent resistance, all the more conspiratorial for having been driven underground.[157]

Did Antiochus view the Jews as he had once viewed the philosophers? The parallels between the persecution of the philosophers and the persecution of the Jews are striking when one takes note of the peculiar nature of Jewish "philosophy." Philosophers who taught were few and could be expelled, but all Jewish fathers were required to teach Jewish "philosophy" to their sons.[158] Jewish "philosophy" was taught orally, but always with a copy of the Torah.[159] Hence, if Antiochus proceeded to treat the Jews as he had intended to treat the philosophers, he would indeed have pro-

---

Wilhelm Graf Baudissin, *Adonis und Esmun* (Leipzig: Hinrichs, 1911), pp. 231–41; H. Seyrig, *Antiquités syriennes,* V. 99–107, 115–16, and "La triade héliopolitaine," *Syria* 10 (1929), 314–56; René Dussaud, "Temples et cultes de la triade héliopolitaine à Ba'albeck," *Syria* 23 (1942–43), 33–77. Like Adonis, the God of the Jews was called "Adonay" (Lord") by his worshipers; see below, n. 306. Adonis was identified with Dionysus; see Plutarch *Quaestiones conviviales* iv 5.3; Dussaud, *Syria* 23 (1942–43), 68–69.

Already the Jewish philosopher Aristobulus, a contemporary of Antiochus IV, was quoting Orphic hymns (Schürer, III, 599–602). Hence, the Orphic poem and some of the other material at Macrobius i 18.18–21 and 23.22 may also have antedated Antiochus IV's persecution, in particular the oracle from Claros, Macrobius i 18.19–21, which identified the God of the Jews with Zeus, Hades, Helios, and Dionysus. Indeed, the oracle of Claros was functioning long before (Adler, "Klarios 1," PW, XI [1922], 549–51); the cave where the priest at Claros drank from a spring before prophesying was mentioned by a poet of the third or second century B.C.E. (W. Kroll, "Nikandros," PW, XXVII[I] [1936], 250–52. The Seleucids had ties to Colophon and Claros, for Antiochus IV's older brother, Antiochus, was honored there; see Jeanne and Louis Robert, "Bulletin épigraphique," REG 78 (1965), 153, no. 339.

An interpretation of circumcision as deliberate effeminacy (see above, n. 153) might have led pagans to identify Jews with worshipers of Dionysus; cf. Livy xxxix 15.9.

Dionysiacs, like Jews, claimed to be prophets; see Livy xxxix 13.12. Jewish prophesy in this period is seen not only in apocalyptic works like Daniel but also in the book of Joel and in the claims of the Essenes (J. *BJ* ii 8.12.159). I shall deal with the book of Joel in a future study.

155 See pp. 121–23.
156 Reflected by Dan 11:14.
157 Cf. I 1:35–40; Tcherikover, *Hellenistic Civilization*, pp. 194–98.
158 Deut 6:7; J. *Ap.* ii 17.174–75, 25.204; II 7:27; To. *Qiddushin* 1:11, TB *Qiddushin* 29b.
159 TB *Giṭṭin* 60b.

ceeded as described in First and Second Maccabees. He would first destroy the copies of the Torah and make possession of them a capital crime.[160] Then he would try to force the most famous teachers to violate their "philosophy."[161] He would punish the young severely for adhering to the forbidden teachings and punish parents for the very grave offense of allowing their children to associate with the forbidden teachers.[162]

Still more vivid are the parallels between the Roman suppression of the subversion Dionysiac Bacchanalia and Antiochus' suppression of the subversive "Dionysiac" Jewish religion; so much so, as to suggest that Antiochus was again applying Roman methods, to solve the problem of religious rebellion in his empire.

The author of First Maccabees, who so highly praised Rome in chapter 8, could have known little if anything of the Roman origins of Antiochus' civic and religious policy. To Antiochus, the institution of Antiochene citizenship was a benevolent grant, not an arbitrary imposition; and the persecution of the Jews was punishment of a subversive cult. To pious Jews, however, Antiochus' exemption of Antiochenes from the provisions of Jewish law was an arbitrary attempt to abrogate God's law. To our author, Antiochus' civic policy was an arbitrary imposition of foreign religion on the peoples of the Seleucid empire (I 2:18–19), and Antiochus' religious policy of persecuting the Jews was a direct outgrowth of the civic policy (I 1:41–64). For our author, both the civic and the religious policy were unprovoked attacks on Judaism. Our author was aware that the imposed cult as he himself described it bore no resemblance to Greek religion, but he could find only one explanation for the king's behavior: Antiochus must in some sense have been zealously propagating his own religion (I 1:43). Though modern scholars join Josephus (AJ xii 5.4.253) in repeating our author's honest mistake, the eyewitness testimony of Daniel (11:37–38) and careful examination of the character of the imposed cult suffice to prove them wrong.[163] Let us proceed to study in detail the sources on the imposed cult and their Roman parallels.

---

[160] I 1:57; J. AJ xii 5.4.256, end; cf. Diodorus xxxiv 1.4.

[161] II 6:18; cf. I 1:48–50.

[162] I 1:60–61; II 6:10, 7; J. AJ xii 5.4. 256. See NOTE on I 1:60–61 and above, n. 143.

[163] See, however, Martin Hengel, Judentum und Hellenismus, Wissenschaftlich Untersuchungen zum Neuen Testament, vol. X (Tübingen: Mohr [Siebeck], 1969), 486–564. See also M. Stern, Review of Hengel, Kirjath Sepher 46 (1970), 97 (in Hebrew), and Bickermann, Gott, pp. 90–139. Cf. Tacitus Histories v 8.

On Dan 11:37–38, see below, n. 225.

On II 11:24, see commentary ad loc. At II 6:9 we may have "Antiochene" communities imposing their Greek rules on Jews, but perhaps metabainein epi ta Hellenika ("come over to Greek ways") is to be interpreted, not as complete participation in pagan worship, but only as abandonment of Jewish "misanthropy" to the extent of tolerating the idolatry of apostates and eating the meat of pagan sacrifices. See p. 137.

An obstacle to our project is the skepticism of scholars toward Livy's account of the suppression of the Bacchanalia.[164] This is not the place for a thorough treatment of the question. Other scholars have argued well for rejecting very little of Livy's account.[165] Indeed, Antiochus lived at Rome when the Bacchanalia were suppressed. Insofar as we can show that Antiochus was imitating the Roman procedures described by Livy, we shall have confirmed the veracity of Livy's account.

Pious Jews had taken to violence on avowedly religious grounds long before Antiochus outlawed their religion. The Romans moved against the Bacchanalia before there had been any violent action whatever against the Roman state. Quite apart from any offense against Roman religion, the Romans saw in the nocturnal meetings of the cult, unsanctioned by government authority, the earmarks of a revolutionary conspiracy.[166] Especially conspiratorial seemed the oath of cult-loyalty, taken at meetings by the initiates, who recited it after the priest read it from the sacred text. Indeed, Greeks and Romans seem to have had a particularly extreme fear of subversive conspiracies in cases where the members were believed to have bound themselves to the conspiracy by oath. Greeks and Romans would use extraordinary means, even torture, to dissolve what they believed to be the oath of a subversive conspiracy.[167] Restless elements of the population appear to have played a large role in the Bacchanalia.[168] Antiochus knew that Jews, too, worshiped at night,[169] came together in congregations,[170] took upon themselves

---

[164] xxxix 8–19; skepticism: Matthias Gelzer, "Die Unterdrückung der Bacchanalien bei Livius," *Hermes* 71 (1936), 275–87, still strongly endorsed by H. Bengtson, *Römische Geschichte;* cf. Latte, pp. 270–72, and see also P. V. Cova, "Livio e la repressione dei Baccanali," *Athenaeum*, N.S., 52 (1974), 82–109.

[165] See Münzer, "Postumius 44," PW, XXIII¹ (1953), 921–23; A.-J. Festugière, "Ce que Tite-Live nous apprend sur les mystères de Dionysos," *École française de Rome: Mélanges d'archéologie et d'histoire* 66 (1954), 79–99; Bruhl, pp. 87–107. One should bear in mind that any fictions in Livy's account may well have arisen from the official Roman propaganda of the time of the suppression of the Bacchanalia. The Roman consuls had to solve the embarrassing problem of how to prove the existence of a diabolical conspiracy when knowledge of the conspiracy would in itself besmirch the witness. How could they present their witnesses as innocent of the sins of the Bacchanalia? The romantic tale of Aebutius and his mistress, if not true, may well have been concocted by the consuls or their assistants.

[166] Livy xxxix 8.4–5, 12.4, 13.9–10, 14.4, 6–10, 15.6, 9–12; 16.3, 10.

[167] Oath of the Bacchanalia: Livy xxxix 15.13–14; 18.3; Festugière, *École française de Rome: Mélanges* 66 (1954), 96–98.
Extreme fear: see Seidl, "*Synômosia*," PW, IV^A (1932), 1450. Seidl presents examples of how governments tried to dissolve such oaths (ibid., 1446–48).
Torture to induce "conspirators" to violate their oaths: the Romans certainly did so with the Essenes (J. *BJ* ii 8.10.150–53) and with the Christians (Pliny *Epistles* x 96–97). The topic deserves further treatment.

[168] Bruhl, pp. 107–10.

[169] Pss 88:2, 92:3, 99:55, 62, 134:1. Cf. Pss 77:7, 55:18; Dan 6:11; Judith 9:1; Greek Esther 4:16–5:1; J. *AJ* iv 8.13.212; H. Albeck, *Shishah sidre Mishnah, Zera'im*, pp. 7–9 (in Hebrew); 1QS 66–8, 10:11.

[170] Ps 74:8; see NOTE on I 7:16, and cf. Esther 4:16.

the solemn loyalty-formulas of the *Shema'* (Deut 6:4–9) and the Ten Commandments (if not the oaths of the Essenes), reciting them after a leader read them from the Torah.[171] The Jewish loyalty-formulas warned the believer to bear in mind the very laws in obedience to which pious Jews punished and killed Jewish "Antiochenes." Antiochus probably knew other Jewish parallels to Dionysiac worshipers[172] and had ample evidence of Jewish rebellion.

In Livy's account, after the consul Postumius' investigations had convinced him of the "conspiracy," he brought the matter of the Bacchanalia to the attention of the Senate,[173] who ordered that the cult be suppressed. However, before overt action was taken, strong propaganda was used to turn public opinion in favor of suppression. Livy transmits this propaganda in his version of the speech which one of the consuls delivered to the people, as well as elsewhere in his account. It is not surprising that it should coincide in so many points with Antiochus' charges against the Jews. Propaganda against "heinous conspirators" tends to run to stereotypes: the propagandist simply accuses the "conspirators" of the most heinous crimes.

The sexual associations of the cult of Dionysus were a commonplace of conversation and the comic theater.[174] Hence, Roman propaganda against the cult concentrated upon sexual violations (*stupra*)[175] and upon conspiracy to overthrow the state[176] but did not neglect to suggest ritual murder[177] and lesser crimes against humanity.[178] The Jews were as much known for their sexual puritanism as were the old Romans, so charges of sexual violations might not have been credible.[179] But the Jews had openly taken to violence, so Antiochus concentrated his charges

---

[171] *Shema':* J. *AJ* iv 8.13.212–13; Schürer, II, 537–38; and see commentary to II 6:6. *Shema'* and Decalogue in daily ritual: M. *Tamid* 5:1. The *Shema'* was regarded as an oath of loyalty. Thus, Josephus (loc. cit.) calls the recitation of it "bearing witness" (*martyrein*); to the rabbis it constituted acceptance of God's kingship just as the Roman soldier's oath (*sacramentum*) constituted acceptance of the emperor's rule. See M. *Berakot* 2:2, Albeck, *Mishnah, Zera'im*, p. 328; *Midrash Tehillim* to Ps 5:6; and Louis Finkelstein, "The Meaning of the Word *prs* in the Expressions *pōrēs 'al šēma'* . . . ," JQR 32 (1941–42), 387–400. Hence, the *sacramentum* by which the early Christians of Bithynia bound themselves (Pliny *Epistles* x 96.9) may well have been the *Shema'* plus the Decalogue. Cf. Casper J. Kraemer, Jr., "Pliny and the Early Church Service," *Classical Philology* 29 (1934), 293–300.

Essene oaths: J. *BJ* ii 8.7.139–42; CD 15:1–9; 1QH 14:17–18. Worshipers recite after leader reads from Torah-scroll: Finkelstein, JQR 32 (1941–42), 387–400, where one should note that *prs* (literally, "unroll and spread") means "promulgate" probably because the herald unrolled the text of the proclamation before reading it.

[172] See above, n. 154.

[173] Livy xxxix 14.3.

[174] See Festugière, *École française de Rome: Mélanges* 66 (1954), 85–86.

[175] Livy xxxix 8.4–8, 9.4, 10.4–9, 11.7, 13.10–14, 14.8, 15.9, 12–14, 16.1–2, 18.3–4; see Festugière, p. 88.

[176] Livy xxxix 14.4, 16.3.

[177] Livy xxxix 8.8, 13.11, 13, 18.4; and cf. 13.5.

[178] Livy xxxix 8.8, 16.3–5, 18.4.

[179] J. *Ap.* ii 30.215 and 31.220; see, however, Tacitus *Histories* v 5.2.

on ritual murder and on the Jews' evil designs against the members of the human race, whom they were supposed to hate.[180]

The Jews' neighbors knew well the Jewish refusal to mingle with heathens. Antiochus had only to mention it. Human sacrifice, however, was a Phoenician rite which had passed out of fashion in Phoenicia not so long before and was still practiced in the Phoenician colony of Carthage. At such a time Syrians and Greeks could have thought of human sacrifice as a Phoenician but hardly as a Jewish rite. To convict the Jews of human sacrifice required proof. Against the Bacchanalia, which many Romans thought unobjectionable,[181] the Roman consul took care to present the testimony of Aebutius and Faecenia.[182] Similarly, as proof against the Jews, Antiochus supplied his own "eye-witness" testimony and probably produced also the "victim" he claimed to have discovered in the course of his sack of the temple. The "victim" supposedly said he was being fattened to be sacrificed in a forest by the Jews, who would partake of his flesh, swear hostility to Greeks, and cast the remains of the victim into a pit. In part the charge consists of ancient stereotypes of propaganda used against conspiracies,[183] but the similarity to the charges against the Bacchanalia looks too striking to be coincidence. In the Bacchanalia, too, propaganda had it that human beings disappeared to be sacrificed and their remains were hidden away never to be found.[184] In the Dionysiac rite of the Charila at Delphi, once every eight years the female leader of the cult would take the doll representing Charila and carry it to a place full of ravines where it was buried.[185] A fragment of Seleucid anti-Jewish propaganda holds that Jews sacrificed a gentile once every seven years.[186]

Antiochus apparently went still further in his effort to portray the Jews as similar to the followers of the Bacchanalia. Each of the important deities of Syria and Phoenicia was associated with his own animal and on occasion was represented by it. Each such deity was commonly portrayed sitting on a throne, or standing on a platform, of which the supports were a pair of his animals. Similarly, at Jerusalem the God of the Israelites was supposed to be present over the cherubim, and at Dan and Bethel He was supposed to be present over calves. Heads of a deity's

---

[180] Diodorus xxxiv 1=Poseidonius, FGH 87, F 109; J. *Ap.* ii 8. 91–96; on ancient propaganda against conspiracies in general and on Antiochus IV as the author of such propaganda against the Jews, see Bickermann, "Ritualmord und Eselskult," MGWJ 72 (1927), 171–87. The account of Poseidonius at Diodorus xxxiv 1 probably goes back to this propaganda.

[181] Livy xxxix 15.6–7.

[182] Livy xxxix 12.3 – 14.6, 19.3–7.

[183] J. *Ap.* ii 8.91–96; Bickermann, MGWJ 72 (1927), 173–78.

[184] Livy xxxix 8.8, 13.11, 13; however, on 13.13, see the alternative interpretation of Festugière, *École française de Rome: Mélanges* 66 (1954), 94–96.

[185] Plutarch *Quaestiones Graecae* 12, p. 293e; Nilsson, *Dionysiac Mysteries*, p. 4.

[186] *Apud Suda* s.v. *Damokritos.*

animal might appear in the decoration of his temple and as ornaments on his cult-image. Since in Syria and Phoenicia gods tended to be grouped in father-mother-son triads, heads of the animal of the spouse or parent or child might appear in such decorations.[187]

In the Greek and Roman world, the ass was the beast of Dionysus, and the head of an ass appears as the figurehead of the ship of Dionysus and on Dionysiac thrones and couches.[188] Even before Antiochus' embroilment with the Jews, mocking calumnies had circulated among the Idumaeans, that in the mysterious Holy of Holies in Jerusalem there was an image of an ass with a golden head. In the course of a long war between the Idumaeans and the Jews, it was said, a clever Idumaean was able to penetrate the Jewish temple and make off with the golden head.[189] Even if no "long war" between Judaea and Idumaea took place under Ptolemaic and Seleucid rule, contemporary incidents probably led to the spirited verbal battles between Jews and Idumaeans that suddenly break out at the end of the third century, over two hundred years after Malachi attacked the Edomites (Mal 1:1–4).[190] We do not know the occasion which evoked these polemics. In any case, in order to reply in kind to mockery from Jews, a Hellenized Idumaean would have ascribed to them the use of Dionysiac cult-imagery as readily as Plutarch was later to see them as Dionysiacs.[191]

[187] See Baudissin, *Adonis und Esmun*, pp. 37–38; Dussaud, *Syria* 23 (1942–43), 43, 46–49, 54, n. 3; Seyrig, *Syria* 10 (1929), 328–32, and *Antiquités syriennes*, V, 101–3. Families of three gods: Baudissin, pp. 15–17; Du Mesnil, *Études*, pp. xii–xiii; Seyrig, *Antiquités syriennes*, V, 105–7.
Cherubim: Exod 25:22; Num 7:89; II Kings 19:15.
Dan and Bethel: I Kings 7:28–29.

[188] See Michael Tierney, *"Onos agôn mystêria," Mélanges offerts à M. Octave Navarre* (Toulouse: Privat, 1935), pp. 395–403; Olck, "Esel," PW, VI (1909), 652–53, 669–76. Ship: M. P. Nilsson, "Dionysos im Schiff," ARW 11 (1908), 399–400 (on a late Attic black-figured vase). Asses' heads as masks on worshipers or on deities: Tierney, *Mélanges Navarre*, 399–402; on thrones and elsewhere: Olck, PW VI (1909), 669–70, 673 (many instances from Rome and Italy), 675.

[189] Mnaseas of Patara *apud* J. *Ap.* ii 9.112–14. Mnaseas was probably a pupil of Eratosthenes, and Eratosthenes died between 196 and 194 B.C.E.; see *Suda* s.v. *Eratosthenes* and *The Oxyrhynchus Papyri* (London: Egypt Exploration Fund, 1898–), vol. XIII, 130–31. Hence, Mnaseas probably wrote in the first half of the second century B.C.E., if not earlier. On the interpretation of the fragment, see Bickermann, MGWJ 72 (1927) 261–64.
Under the Babylonian, Persian, and Hellenistic kings there could hardly be a "long war" between Jews and Idumaeans, and none is reported. Nevertheless, there were the usual frictions between neighboring peoples with a long history of hostility. The Idumaean's mocking tale is the counterpart of such grand and belliocose Jewish tales as Jubilees xxxvii 1 – xxxviii 14, where Jacob and his sons meet the aggression of Esau and his sons. Jacob slays Esau, who is buried in Adora, and Jacob's sons defeat the sons of Esau and reduce them to servitude. It is perhaps no accident that Mnaseas' clever Idumaean was said to be from Adora, the city of Esau's grave.

[190] Literary attacks on Edom: Jubilees xxxvii – xxxviii (see above, n. 189); Hebrew Sir 50:26; I Esd 4:45, 50.

[191] See above, n. 154.

This propaganda was so fresh that Antiochus could have drawn directly upon it, with or without the help of the Greek writer who preserved the report for us. Antiochus spread the story that he, too, had discovered an image of an ass or an ass's head in the Holy of Holies. There is good evidence that Antiochus came to believe the God of the Jews had a son, "Dionysus."[192] Whether he took the ass as representing the great God of the Jews or as representing His "son," the story helped Antiochus clinch his portrayal of the Jews as a degenerate sect similar to the devotees of the Bacchanalia in Italy.[193]

To the Romans the Bacchanalia were not only degenerate; they were foreign. Roman propagandists tried to prove they were a recent import to Italy, though the consul himself had to admit that the cult of Bacchus had long existed there.[194] The contradiction could be resolved: there was the legitimate cult of Bacchus on the Aventine hill in Rome,[195] as opposed to the impious Bacchanalia. Antiochus, too, appears to have claimed that there was a legitimate Jewish cult of the God of Heaven, as opposed to the impious, subversive, degenerate, and possibly foreign accretions which had turned the religion of Moses into a religion of rebels. Indeed, the Jews themselves said their religion had come from outside the Promised Land and called their God the "God of Heaven" and even "Heaven" (*Ouranos*).

Josephus has preserved a contemporary reflection of Antiochus' propaganda, in the petition of the Samaritans to Antiochus and in the king's reply, both of 167/6 B.C.E.[196] The Samaritans take it for granted that the Jews are being punished for "their wickedness."[197] We may assume that the "wickedness" included Pietist attacks on Hellenizing "Antiochene" Jews. Indeed, the king grants the Samaritans' petition for exemption from the persecutions on the ground that they are so "innocent of the charges brought against the Jews" that they agree to live "according to Greek practices."[198]

What could living "according to Greek practices" mean here? Though the Samaritans accepted the use of a Greek appellation for their God,[199]

[192] See pp. 151–57.

[193] Antiochus' own propaganda probably spoke of an ass's head. Poseidonius' report of an image of Moses riding on an ass may also go back to Antiochus. Greeks knew both of images representing the gods and of statues of cult founders. Moses would ride the special animal of the God of the Jews just as devotees of Dionysus rode the ass of their god.

[194] Livy xxxix 8.3–4, 13.9, 15.2, 16.6–10; native Roman and Italian founders of the cult: 17.6–7; consul's admission: 15.6–7. On the cult of Bacchus in Italy and at Rome, see Bruhl, pp. 13–45.

[195] Bruhl, pp. 30–45.

[196] *AJ* xii 5.5.258–64; Bikerman, RHR 115 (1937), 188–223.

[197] J. *AJ* xii 5.5.260.

[198] Ibid., § 263.

[199] See commentary to II 6:2.

this would not have been enough to clear them of the charge of "wickedness" brought against the Jews. Pious Jews did not reject all Greek divine names. Jason of Cyrene used the Greek appellation *Hypsistos* ("Most High"; II 3:31) as did the translator of the book of Ben Sira, and the pious translator of First Maccabees calls the God of the Jews "Ouranos" (="Uranus") throughout, though the Greek word for "Heaven" was the name of a deity prominent in Greek myth.[200] Indeed, the Samaritans made it clear that they intended to observe the Sabbath and go on offering the sacrifices prescribed by the Torah to their God of Mount Gerizim. Hence, agreement to live "according to Greek practices" must mean chiefly agreement to leave other cults and probably also Hellenizing Samaritans unmolested, in contrast to the militant Pietists of Jerusalem. In the Greek world, in truth, the cult of the nameless god of Tyre or of Mount Gerizim could coexist, side by side with the cult of Greek Zeus and Athena. Such coexistence is known earlier among the Samaritans.[201]

Our interpretation of "living according to Greek practices" in Antiochus IV's letter concerning the Samaritans also will fit Antiochus V's letter of 162 (II 11:24–25). There, Antiochus IV's exemption of "Antiochenes" from Jewish law is called "the changeover to Greek practices" (*têi . . . epi ta Hellênika metathesei*).

The Roman government first spread its propaganda against the nefarious foreign superstition, and then the Senate's decisions on the suppression of the Bacchanalia were published throughout Italy, and the consuls issued edicts to carry out the will of the Senate.[202] Similarly, Antiochus published his propaganda and between April and December, 167, issued his decrees outlawing Judaism.[203]

Generally, the Roman government took action against foreign rites only when there was danger that Roman citizens might participate.[204] In the case of the Bacchanalia, however, the government extirpated the rites from all Italy, presumably because they were felt to be a menace to Romans. Similarly, Antiochus might claim in the first instance that he was protecting his Antiochene citizens from subversive foreign influences. Indeed, Hellenized Antiochenes of Jerusalem, the followers of Jason, had rebelled far more openly than had their pious enemies. Jason of Cyrene noted with pleasure that the Hellenized Jews were the first to suffer Antiochus' "corrective" action (II 4:16–17). To purge "Antiochenes" of the "foreign cult" of rebellion required extirpating it not only from

---

[200] See Cumont, *"Hypsistos,"* PW, IX (1916), 444–50; Ernst Wüst, "Uranos," PW, IXᴬ (1961), 969–80.

[201] II Kings 17:24–41.

[202] Livy xxxix 17.1–4.

[203] I shall demonstrate the date in a future study of Daniel 7.

[204] Theodor Mommsen, "Der Religionsfrevel nach römischem Recht," *Historische Zeitschrift* 64 (1890), 390, 401–16.

Judaea, but also from the entire territory of the "Antiochenes," a measure which was proposed by the delegates of Ptolemais to the deliberative body of the "republic" and passed (II 6:8–9). It is likely that Jews who had not rebelled were not molested if they resided elsewhere in the Seleucid realm, outside Judaea and bordering areas and outside the "Antiochene" citizen communities.[205] There is no evidence that the large Jewish communities in Mesopotamia were molested.

The decree of the Roman Senate has been preserved in an inscription as well as in Livy's paraphrase, so that we can compare its clauses with the decrees of Antiochus IV and the Antiochene republic as preserved in First and Second Maccabees.

The first provision of the Senate's decree required the demolition of all the places of worship of the cult, though one could appeal to the Senate to preserve a place of worship, and a later clause exempted from immediate destruction shrines containing long-recognized sacred objects.[206] Antiochus' decrees probably contained a similar clause. In Judaea there was only one place of worship which contained long-recognized sacred objects—the temple. The preservation of the Jewish temple was guaranteed by naming it for a native deity long recognized by Greeks, Syro-Phoenicians, and Jews: Zeus Olympius, the God of Heaven; the Samaritan temple was similarly preserved.[207] Synagogues could be destroyed and probably were,[208] but synagogues were often mere rooms in private homes and had no special sanctity under Jewish law.[209] Hence, it is not surprising to find no mention of their destruction in the books of Maccabees. Not the closing of synagogues violated the Torah, but the defilement and desecration of the temple and the building of altars and shrines outside the temple as required by Antiochus for the "legitimate" cult of Zeus Olympius, the God of Heaven.[210]

A priestess carried out initiations into the Dionysiac mysteries. The next clause of the Senate's decree forbade any male to approach a female initiate (Baca); i.e. it forbade initiation of males, though again one could appeal to the Senate for special permission.[211] The cult of Bacchus for women was old and legitimate in the Mediterranean world

---

[205] See NOTE on I 1:51. Were Jews persecuted at the Seleucid capital, Antioch, pursuant to the decree proposed by the Antiochenes of Ptolemais? For the ambiguous evidence suggesting that they were, see commentary on II 7:1. If Antiochus IV viewed the Jewish community at Antioch as loyal, he could have exempted them as he did the Samaritans.

[206] ILS 18.3–6; Livy xxxix 18.7.

[207] II 6:2; J. AJ xii 5.5.257–64; Bickermann, Gott, pp. 96–104.

[208] Ps 74:8; see NOTE on I 7:16–17.

[209] See Schürer, II, 498–526.

[210] See I 1:46–47; II 6:2–5, 10:2.

[211] ILS 18.7–9; Livy xxxix 18.8; cf. Festugière, École française de Rome: Mélanges 66 (1954), 92–93.

and in Roman Italy.[212] Jewish males were "initiated" through circumcision, and in the time of Antiochus IV seeing to the circumcision of babies appears to have been the responsibility of the mother, even though she did not perform the operation herself.[213] Antiochus' proclamation prohibiting circumcision may have kept so close to his Roman model as to have spoken of the role of women in the initiation of males.[214]

The next clauses of the Senate's decree prohibited men from being priests and men and women from holding any other sacerdotal or administrative cult office. The worshipers were to have no communal treasury.[215] Antiochus found that the "legitimate" cult of the God of Heaven had a hereditary male priesthood which could not be abolished. Only a limited number of priests were needed for the cult itself, so perhaps Antiochus declared the numerous other priests to be priests no longer. He may also have abolished synagogue magistracies.[216] We have no evidence for either step. Many of the commandments of the Torah, however, invited or required contributions to communal stores or to a communal treasury: votive offerings, tithes, heave-offerings, first fruits, etc. and the Jews felt keenly the impact of Antiochus' prohibition of these.[217]

The next clauses of the Roman decree forbade all observance, public or private, of the rituals peculiar to the Bacchanalia, unless the Senate, on appeal, should allow an exception.[218] Antiochus' proclamation certainly forbade all the characteristic rituals and abstinences of Judaism.[219]

As the Senate prescribed, "Whoever acts contrary to this decree . . . shall be guilty of a capital crime," so did Antiochus.[220] The Senate allowed the local authorities in the Italian towns ten days for destroying the places of worship, from the time they received the text of the decree. Antiochus may even have copied the Senate's ten days in implementing his decrees at Jerusalem.[221]

Dionysus and the God of Heaven were both gods worthy of worship who must not be slighted. They must, however, be worshiped by time-honored native ritual, not by subversive foreign rites (sacra externa). The Romans surely had little trouble seeing to it that Bacchus was worshiped in the usual way after the Bacchanalia were suppressed.[222] An-

---

[212] See Bruhl, pp. 1–81.
[213] Kaufmann Kohler, "Circumcision," JE, IV (1903), 95; Exod 4:24–26; I 1: 60–61; II 6:10.
[214] I 1:60 and II 6:10; contrast J. AJ xii 5.4.256.
[215] ILS 18.10–12; Livy xxxix 18.9.
[216] See Schürer, II, 502–16.
[217] I 1:46 – see NOTE on 3:49–51.
[218] ILS 18.13–18; Livy xxxix 14.8, 18.8–9.
[219] I 1:45–60.
[220] ILS 18.24–25; I 1:50.
[221] ILS 18.28–30; I 1:54, 59.
[222] Livy xxxix 16.8–11.

tiochus, however, provoked war to the death when he tried to induce
the Jews to abandon their own "foreign rites" and worship their God of
Heaven according to what he held to be the original Jewish patterns,
which he had inferred through the theories of Greek "anthropologists,"
perhaps with the help of heterodox Jewish informants.[223] Antiochus told
the Jews that in obeying him they would still be worshiping their own
deity. The Jews could not believe the king, and their seer wrote of
Antiochus, "He shall say things past belief concerning the God of
gods."[224]

Antiochus may have been notorious for somehow neglecting Seleucid
dynastic cults, or perhaps the seer was ironic in suggesting that the king's
zeal in imposing a cult on the Jews was such that the king's own gods
were being neglected. In any case, pious Jews could not understand why
Antiochus was so zealous in imposing upon the Jews pagan patterns like
those prevailing among the Phoenicians and Syrians.[225]

Indeed, even a pagan would have had difficulty understanding Antiochus IV's policy if his aim had been to force the Jews to abandon
their own religion and adopt a Greek or Syro-Phoenician cult.[226] Pagans
readily conceded that the God of the Jews was a god. Persian kings were
eager for His blessings, just as they were for those of Babylonian Bel and
Nabu and of Persian Ahuramazda.[227] The Seleucids continually sought
the favor of the gods of their subject peoples.[228] Ptolemy VI was concerned not to offend the God of the Jews by any breach of the laws
relating to His cult.[229] Pagans, especially the Romans, viewed with dis-
favor and fear any infractions of time-honored religious practices.[230]

If a pagan king was to impose upon the Jews a sweeping religious
change, that change had to be portrayed, like Josiah's and Ezra's reforms,
as a *return* to an old way of life which had been corrupted. Antiochus
found Josiah and Ezra and the Prophets who came after Moses to be
corrupters who had turned the religion of Moses into a cult of rebels! Indeed, Greek intellectuals like Poseidonius believed Moses taught the
Jews that the encompassing heavenly sphere was God and that no cult
images in animal or human form were to be used in His worship.

---

[223] See below, n. 336.

[224] Dan 11:36; cf. Dan 7:25. *dabbēr ʿal* does not mean "speak against" but "say
concerning." Cf. Gen 18:19; Deut 13:6; Josh 23:14; I Sam 25:30. *lᵉṣad* at Dan 7:25
also means "concerning," not "against." See J. Levy, *Chaldäisches Wörterbuch*
(Köln: J. Melzer, 1959), s.v. *ṣyd;* C. Brockelmann, *Lexicon Syriacum* (Berlin:
Reuter & Reichard, 1895), s.v. *ṣyd.*

[225] Dan 11:37–38, as translated earlier, Part II, p. 46.
On the Phoenician and Syrian patterns, see pp. 142–51.

[226] Cf. Stern, *Kirjath Sepher* 46 (1970), 98 in Hebrew.

[227] Ezra 6:10; Pritchard, ANET², p. 316.

[228] Bikerman, *Institutions*, pp. 250–51.

[229] J. *AJ* xiii 3.2.70–71.

[230] See II Kings 17:24–41; Bickermann, *Gott*, pp. 90–96 Latte, pp. 39–41; Pierre
de Labriolle, *La réaction païenne* (Paris: L'artisan du livre, 1940), pp. 44–45.

Throughout, these Greek intellectuals held, Moses taught a rational religion of which they approved. They strongly disapproved of "abuses"
introduced by later successors of Moses, such as Jewish "tyranny" (i.e.
intolerance of pagan practices on Jewish soil) and dietary laws and circumcision.[231]

Poseidonius was born three decades after Antiochus' persecution of the
Jews, but his attitudes may well represent those of Antiochus. Already
in the late fourth or early third century B.C.E. Theophrastus disapproved
of the Jewish practice of daily burnt offerings.[232] Hecataeus of Abdera
gave the same account of Moses' views on God as Poseidonius did and
condemned Jewish aversion to idolaters as inhumane and spoke of how
Jewish institutions had changed in later generations.[233]

Greek intellectual theorists thus observed and condemned in the Jews
the same trait which disturbed Antiochus: the "tyrannous" intolerance
which had led to rioting against the Antiochenes of Jerusalem and seem-
ingly also to rebellion. According to the Greek theorists, such traits were
later corruptions of an originally admirable religion. If later corruptions
had turned the Jews into a subversive sect, Antiochus had good reason
to go beyond the Roman procedure, which merely suppressed the new
corrupt manifestations. At Rome an uncorrupt cult of Bacchus existed on
the Aventine hill. Antiochus appears to have believed that he would have
to impose a restored uncorrupt cult of the God of the Jews upon the
Chosen People. In so doing, not only might he restore order; he might
also win the favor of the true deity or deities of the Jews!

Where could Antiochus find information on the "original" Jewish religion? The Greek theorists wrote as if they knew. Theophrastus was head
of the school of Aristotle at Athens; Athens and the school may well
have been the center of comparative religious studies of the Hellenistic
age. When Ptolemy I wished to revitalize the cult of Sarapis in Egypt,
he used an expert from Athens.[234] Antiochus IV appears to have done
the same in "purifying" the religion of the Jews: he imported an Athenian
expert.[235] Antiochus, however, did not have to follow blindly the traditions represented by his Athenian expert or by Hecataeus, Theophastus,
and Poseidonius. Evidence in the ancient accounts suggests that he also
drew on Jewish sources, perhaps Greek versions of the Scriptures, to reconstruct the uncorrupted Religion of Israel. There were even passages in
the Torah which seemed to confirm the Greek theories on the original religion of the Jews; the parts of the Torah which conflicted with the theories
could be viewed as spurious accretions. Some groups of heterodox Jews
probably still survived with traditions going back to the cults condemned

---

[231] Poseidonius, FGH 87, F 70=Strabo xvi 2.35–37.
[232] *Apud* Porphyry *De abstinentia* ii 26.
[233] Hecataeus, FGH 264, F 6=Diodorus xl 3.5, 8. See NOTE on I 3:48.
[234] See M. P. Nilsson, *Geschichte der griechischen Religion,* II, 156–58.
[235] See II 6:1 and I 1:45 and commentary ad loca.

by the prophets and the Torah. Antiochus is likely to have received information from such Jews, either directly or from observations of them made by Greek "anthropologists."[236] The ancient accounts of the cult imposed on the Jews by Antiochus are difficult to interpret, and we must study them closely.

There is little difficulty in understanding the Greek name given to the God of the Jews. If a non-Greek people worshiped a God of Heaven, Greeks would automatically name him "Zeus." Greek-speaking Jews themselves would do so if there was no danger of taking "Zeus" to be the name of an idol.[237] Even the pious translator of First Maccabees called his God by the Greek word for "heaven," *Ouranos,* the name of a pagan deity. Hence, though Antiochus seems to have been impressed with the Dionysiac traits of Judaism, he did not rename the great Jewish God as "Dionysus" but as "Zeus Olympius."[238] Though some Jews were scandalized, the conferring of the Greek name was hardly significant: Hebrew- and Aramaic-speaking Jews could have gone on calling their God "the LORD God of Heaven."

Although Poseidonius[239] and other Greek theorists approved of the absolutely monotheistic Jewish worship and its prohibition of images, Antiochus apparently did not share their opinions. Did not Romans have images of their gods? Antiochus did not, indeed, require the use of an-

---

[236] Passages in the Torah: see NOTE on I 3:48. The close parallels between the imposed cult and observances condemned by Jeremiah and Ezekiel as well as observances known from the Jewish community of Elephantine (see pp. 148–57) strongly suggest that a small community of such "syncretistic Jews" still existed and served Antiochus IV as informants. See now Morton Smith, *Palestinian Parties and Politics that Shaped the Old Testament* (Columbia University Press, 1971), pp. 82–98. The subject of the continued existence of heterodox Jews from the time of Jeremiah on deserves further treatment.

A small community of syncretistic Jews could have passed unnoticed by Greek travelers such as Hecataeus of Abdera. Even as Antiochus' informants such a community could conceivably have been ignored by the monotheistic Jews who suffered under Antiochus. Nevertheless, no ancient observer mentions the role of such informants in the imposed cult. Since monotheistic Jews were never reluctant to voice loud condemnation of "sinners," this silence suggests that the syncretistic Jewish informants were so insignificant in number that they verged on non-existence. The only possible contemporary references to such informants are the "deserters of the Holy Covenant" at Dan 11:30 and the "people of a foreign god" at Dan 11:39, but both are connected with the expedition of the Mysarch and the establishment of the Akra, not with the proclamation of the imposed cult; see Part II, pp. 45–46, 49–51; Part VI, pp. 123–24. On the passages in the Books of Maccabees relevant to the problem, see below, n. 336.

[237] See *Letter of Aristeas* 16; Aristobulus *apud* Eusebius *Praeparatio evangelica* xiii 12.7–8; J. *AJ* xii 2.2.22.

[238] II 6:2; cf. J. *AJ* xii 5.4.253. Greek Zeus himself on occasion had Dionysiac traits or could be identified with Dionysus. See Arthur B. Cook, *Zeus* (Cambridge: University Press, 1914–40), I, 104–13, II, 274–91, III, 1126. Against Hengel, *Judentum und Hellenismus,* pp. 546–47, see Stern, *Kirjath Sepher* 46 (1970), 99 (in Hebrew).

[239] FGH 87, F 70=Strabo xvi 2.35.

thropomorphic images, but he found other means equally heinous to pious Jews, who were to view as Antiochus' worst infamy his desecration of the temple altar by affixing to it some kind of idolatrous equipment. The prophesies of Daniel are the works of contemporaries. The unintelligible and ungrammatical character of the extant text may be the result of mistaken vowels which were added to the Hebrew text centuries after the prophesies were written. We shall see that good sense can be made of the original consonantal text.

In Daniel, the idolatrous equipment is called *ṣābā* ("host"; 8:12, 13, 10:1), *šiqqūṣīm mšwmm* ("abominations from desolation" [?]; 9:27), *haššiqqūṣ mšmm* ("the abomination from desolation" [?]; 11:31), *šiqqūṣ šwmm* ("abomination of desolation [?]; 12:11),[240] and *šmm* ("desolation" [?]; 9:27, end). From Dan 11:37 we may learn that Antiochus in imposing his cultic regulations on Jerusalem slighted *ḥemdat nāšīm* ("the Delight of Women") and other deities and honored *ĕlōah māʿuzzīm* ("the God of fortresses" [?]), a god unknown to his ancestors.

Though the author of the Testament of Moses had an ambiguous attitude toward the second temple,[241] he revered it enough to resent bitterly the desecration. From the obscure and mutilated text of his prophesy (viii 4–5) we may perhaps learn that Jews were forced to carry heavy idols and affix(?) them to the altar.[242]

---

[240] Hebrew grammar forbids rendering the phrases at Dan 9:27 and 11:31 as "abomination(s) of desolation" or "abomination(s) that make desolate." The usage of *mšmm* at 11:31 frustrates the attempt in the Revised Standard Version to construe *mšwmm* at 9:27 as subject of the clause and render, "Upon the wing of abominations shall come one who makes desolate." The only acceptable alternative is to revocalize the Hebrew as *miššōmēm*, as in our suggested translation. The author of a variant to the Greek version of Theodotion also took the *mem* of *mšwmm* as meaning "from," rendering *apo aphanismou*.

Josephus, too, may well have taken the *mem* as meaning "from." To judge by *AJ* xii 7.6.322, he took "desolation" in Daniel to be a noun of action, meaning "the act of desolating." He seems there to paraphrase it by the verb "they devastate" (*katalyousin*). He may well have read Dan 11:31 as meaning, "they shall make an abomination while devastating," and Dan 9:27 as meaning, "on a wing [?] [there shall be] abominations during the devastation," and Dan 12:11 as meaning, "after the making of abomination and devastation." For *ntn* as "make" in such contexts, see Jer 9:10. For *m-* with the participle as meaning "while" or "during," see Kutscher, *Tarbiz* 22 (5711=1950–51), 190–92, and 23 (5712=1951–52), 36–37 (in Hebrew). But an interpretation of Dan 9:26 (see Appendix V, n. 32) could also have been Josephus' source for a prediction in Daniel that Antiochus would devastate the temple.

[241] See Part II, p. 40.

[242] "*Nam illi in eis punientur in tormentis et igne et ferro, et cogentur palam baiulare idola eorum, inquinata quomodo sunt pariter continentibus ea. Et a torquentibus illos pariter cogentur intrare in abditum locum eorum, et cogentur stimulis blasfemare uerbum contumeliose, nouissime post haec et leges quod haberent supra altarium suum.*" The words following the last comma are ungrammatical, for a neuter singular relative pronoun has as its apparent antecedent a feminine plural noun, and a verb in the imperfect subjunctive follows a main verb in the future indicative. Perhaps we may ascribe the irregular sequence of tenses to the inelegant

As for First Maccabees, at I 1:54 we learn that Antiochus IV had an "abomination of desolation" (*bdêlygma erêmôseôs*) constructed upon the sacrificial altar of the temple. At I 1:59 we learn that sacrifices were offered upon the "pagan altar" (*bômos*) which stood upon the Jewish sacrificial altar.[243] At I 4:43 we learn that the priests who purified the sanctuary first removed to an unclean place "the stones of loathsomeness" or "the stones of the loathsome structure."[244] These stones are sharply distinguished from the defiled stones of the Jewish altar itself, which were reverently hidden away (I 4:44–46). The verb used to speak of the stones of the altar as "defiled" usually means "made unclean." Rabbinic traditions on the stones are more clearly expressed; they speak of the "stones of the altar which the Greeks made abominable for the purpose of idolatry." Hence we may learn that the "uncleanness" was the uncleanness of "abomination," i.e. of idolatry.[245]

The abridged history says nothing of structures upon the altar but speaks of the defilement of the temple in Jerusalem, of how it was renamed the temple of Zeus Olympius, how prostitution was practiced in the temple precincts, how idolatrous objects were brought in,[246] and how the Jews were forced to make processions in honor of Dionysus on Dionysus' festivals (II 6:2–7).

Finally, the sixth-century Christian writer, John Malalas of Antioch, perhaps drawing on traditions and records of his home city, says that Antiochus turned the Jewish temple into a temple of Zeus Olympius and Athene.[247]

From these sources we can learn the following: an idolatrous structure was built upon the sacrificial altar of the Jewish temple. From one point

---

Latin translator. The long sequence of verbs listing the dreadful acts which Jews will be compelled to perform suggests that yet another verb should stand where *leges* ("laws") does, perhaps *locare* or *ligare* ("place," "affix"). If so, we may translate the passage, "For therein they shall be punished with tortures and fire and sword and shall be forced publicly to haul their idols, polluted as they are like those who hold them. By their torturers they shall be compelled to enter their secret place [sc. the Holy of Holies], and by whips they shall be compelled to blaspheme the Word with abusive language, and finally, after these atrocities, even to place over their altar that which they were holding." Antiochus' act of desecration was all the more heinous because he made Jews haul the idolatrous objects and fasten them to the temple altar. See TB '*Abodah zarah* 42a (statement of Raba) and *M. 'Abodah zarah* 3:5.

[243] Cf. J. *AJ* xii 5.4.253, where Josephus appears to have identified the "abomination" with the *bômos*.

[244] *tous lithous tou miasmou.* "*miasmou*" at I 4:43 is not "uncleanness," since in the same verse "*akatharton*" renders "unclean." The related word *miasma* renders *šiqquṣ* ("abomination") at Jer 32 (Greek 33):34. My use of the word "loathsomeness" is an effort to have a synonym for "abomination."

[245] See *M. Middot* 1:6, '*Abodah zarah* 3:6; TB '*Abodah zarah* 52b; *Midrash Haggadol* to Exod 20:24, p. 443 Margulies; *Mekilta de-Rabbi Šim'on bar Yoḥay* to Exod 20:24, p. 156 Epstein-Melamed, commentary to line 3.

[246] See commentary to II 6:4.

[247] *Chronographia* viii, vol. XCVII, p. 321 Migne, p. 207 Dindorf.

of view it was a single "abomination," and perhaps it was a pagan altar, but from other points of view it was multiple: "abominations," "stones," or a "host." The "abominations" were associated with something which could be called "desolation." Nowhere in this connection is a statue mentioned in any source earlier than Porphyry,[248] who wrote late in the third Christian century. Thus, the cult imposed by Antiochus as the "true" Judaism most probably did not involve the use of idols in human or animal form. It was not monotheistic, contrary to the theories of Poseidonius and his predecessors on the original Jewish religion: in addition to the Jews' great "God of Heaven," now called in Greek Zeus Olympius, at least "Dionysus" and perhaps also "Athene" and even "the Delight of Women" were involved. All these clues may well be correct. They fit into a coherent pattern. Let us examine them more closely.

Probably least understood by interpreters ancient and modern is the evidence of Daniel 8. Consider the following new interpretation of Dan 8:8–12. According to the seer, from the Seleucid kingdom, one of the four Hellenistic monarchies which inherited parts of Alexander's empire (Dan 8:8), shall come a king (the "little horn") so arrogant that he will expand his kingdom southward and bring his armies into Egypt (the Kingdom of the South) and into the Holy Land. More, he will presume to lord it over the stars, the Host of Heaven (Dan 8:9–11a); i.e. he shall presume to give prescriptions about the cults of celestial deities. Worse yet, he will claim to have in his control fallen stars (Dan 8:10b), i.e. meteorites.[249]

The traditional vowels of the Hebrew text of Dan 8:11–12 give rise to an ungrammatical text extremely difficult to interpret.[250] A different vocalization results in good grammar and excellent sense[251] and can be rendered as follows:

---

[248] *Apud* Jerome *Commentarii in Danielem* to 11:31: *Qui ab Antiocho missi sunt, post biennium quam templum exspoliaverat, ut tributa exigerent a Iudaeis et auferrent cultum Dei et in templo Hierusalem Iovis Olympii simulacrum et Antiochi statuas ponerent, quas nunc 'abominationem desolationis' vocat, quando ablatum est holocaustum et iuge sacrificium.* See also Jerome to Dan 8:9, 13–14, and cf. Hengel, *Judentum und Hellenismus,* pp. 537–38 and n. 220.

[249] On knowledge of meteors and meteorites in antiquity and on their cultic use, See Gundel, "Sternschnuppen," PW, III^A (1929), 2439–49.

[250] In vs. 11 *higdīl* suddenly introduces a masculine verb into a context where the subject (the "little horn") has been feminine. *hrym,* in defiance of the vowel-letter, is vocalized *hūram.* "The place of his [or "its"] sanctuary was overthrown" is contrary to historical fact. Nowhere else in the contemporary apocalypses or in First and Second Maccabees do we hear that Antiochus destroyed any structure in the temple courts; rather, he built additions onto the existing structures.

In vs. 12 the verbs suddenly become feminine again, though the apparent subject, "host," is masculine.

[251] Hebrew Dan 8:11. *wᵉ‘ad śar haṣṣābā hagdēl ūmimmennū; hārēm hattāmīd wᵉhašlēk mikkan miqdāšō.* 12. *wᵉṣābā tintēn ‘al hattāmīd happeša‘* [or *bᵉpeša‘*]. Since the seer used the infinitive, no emendation of the verbs beginning with *he* is necessary; cf. Ginsberg, p. 50. On such use of the infinitive, especially in the later books

Dan 8:11. It [the "little horn"=Antiochus IV] grew, until it equaled the Prince of the Host, and beyond; it removed the Continual Offering and cast it from its holy base [the altar]. 12. It shall place a Host upon [the altar of] the Continual Offering because of the sin.[252]

If "the Continual Offering" in vs. 12 cannot be taken as a metonymy for the altar, render instead,

Dan 8:12. It shall place a Host as a despite to[253] the Continual Offering because of the sin.

Who is the "Prince of the Host," with whom Antiochus IV vied in his arrogance and passed beyond? Interpreters have been accustomed to take the words as referring to the God of the Jews. This interpretation can hardly be correct. Could the pious Jewish seer have spoken of a presumptuous king "growing to equal the Lord and even beyond"? Even if the seer could have done so, there is evidence that he did not, for, when he turns to speak of his own God, he calls him not "Prince" but "Prince of Princes" (Dan 8:25) and says, not that the presumptuous king will grow to equal Him, but that he will "attack" or "rebel against" the Prince of Princes.

The Host in this context is the Host of Heaven; hence, the "Prince" or "Commander" of the Host is most naturally taken to be the sun.[254] Antiochus IV was the first Seleucid king to have regularly issued coins portraying his own head with the crown of rays, which was the normal attribute of Helios, the sun god, well-known from the abundant coins of Rhodes.[255]

Accordingly, the passage is easily interpreted to mean that Antiochus ordered meteorites to be affixed to the temple altar as objects to be worshiped. The meteorites, being a "host," could be referred to as a collective singular "abomination" (especially if they were all contained in one framework) or as plural "abominations" or "stones."

What of the passages connecting the meteorites with "desolation"? In an article published in 1884, E. Nestle recognized in *šmm* in Daniel a contemptuous deformation of the Phoenician word for "heaven" (*šā-*

---

of the Bible, see GKC, §§ 113y–z, p. 345; on the *plene* spelling of the infinitive absolute, see GKC, § 53k, p. 146. On *kan* (or *kēn*, as it is vocalized at Isa 33:23), see Ginsberg, pp. 44 and 80, n. 15b, and cf. Dan 11:7, 20–21. On the unassimilated *nun* of *tintēn*, cf. *tnšny* at Isa 44:21 and *mī yinten* in the version of Deut 5:26 at 4QTest, line 3, published by John Allegro, "Messianic References in Qumran Literature," JBL 75 (1956), 182; *leḥanṣīlām* at CD 14:2; *nintenū* at 1QH 2:37 (printed as line 38 in Licht's edition); and *tnkh,* probably for *tgh* at DJD, I (1955), no. 28b, col. 5, line 27. Hence, though the non-assimilation probably reflects Aramaic influence, it does not prove that Daniel 8 was translated from Aramaic. Cf. Ginsberg, p. 50. Even the wretched Hebrew of Daniel 11, which surely was translated from Aramaic, regularly assimilates the letter *nun;* see Dan 11:11, 17.

[252] Or "because of sin"; cf. Micah 1:5.

[253] For *'al* meaning "as a despite to," cf. Job 10:7, 34:6; Prov 17:26; Ezek 5:8.

[254] Cf. Gen 1:16, 37:9; Ps 19:5–7; Isa 24:21–23, and the numerous references in the Bible to the Host of Heaven (Deut 4:19, etc.).

[255] See Mørkholm, *Studies,* pp. 14, 20–23, and p. 115.

mēm). He assumed that Daniel's "abomination of heaven" referred to the Phoenician deity Baʻalšāmēm, the "Lord of Heaven," who was identified with the Greek Zeus.[256] However, there is no reason to assume that Antiochus was imposing a specifically Phoenician cult on the Jews. Nowhere in the sources on the persecution does the name "Baʻalšāmēm" occur, nor does "Phoenician" or "Canaanite." In contemptuous references to idolatry by Israelites, *šiqqūṣ* ("abomination") is always used as a predicate, never as a substitute for the name of a pagan god.[257] Jews might deform the name of a pagan god, but they did not substitute *šiqqūṣ* for it. To the Jews, Deut 7:26 did not mean "Change its name to 'abomination,'" but "Treat it as an abomination." Except for the avoidance of the name "Baal" in Hosea[258] and II Samuel,[259] biblical writers do not hesitate to give the real names of pagan gods.

In the seer's time, the Hebrew word for "heaven," *šāmayim*, could have been pronounced exactly the same as "desolation," *šōmēm*, by the many Jews whose pronunciation was substandard.[260] Pious Jews, like the author of First Maccabees, used the word "Heaven" to refer to their own God. Those who used purist pronunciation seem to have been glad to use the vulgar pronunciation, *šōmēm*, to refer contemptuously to the origin of Antiochus' meteorites and express their revulsion. If so, we may see through the disguise imposed on the facts by the language chosen by pious Jews, and we can recognize in the "abominations from desolation" abominations from the sky, meteorites to be used as idolatrous objects of worship. The singular "abomination from desolation" or "abomination of desolation" was the entire structure upon the altar which included the abominations from the sky.

If we read *'al kannām* ("on their base," i.e. on the altar on which the daily sacrifices and meal offerings were brought) instead of the enigmatic *'al keⁿap* ("on the wing of"),[261] Dan 9:27 joins 8:12 in saying that abominable things from the sky were placed upon the altar of the Continual Offering. At Dan 9:27, end, the word "abominations of " (*šikkūṣē*) may have fallen out, or, more likely, the word "host of" (*ṣebā*), since

---

[256] E. Nestle, "Zu Daniel," ZAW 4 (1884), 248; Philo Byblius, FGH 790, F 2= Eusebius *Praeparatio evangelica* i 10.7.

[257] See I Kings 11:5, 7; II Kings 23:13.

[258] Hosea 2:18–19; cf. Hosea 10:10.

[259] In the names "Yerubbesheth" (II Sam 11:21), "Ishbosheth" (2:8 – 4:12), and "Mephibosheth" (4:4, etc.; 31:8). On rabbinic practice with regard to the names of pagan deities, see Lieberman, *Hellenism*, pp. 111–12.

[260] See Kutscher, *Language and Linguistic Background*, pp. 496–98; Montgomery, *Commentary on Daniel*, p. 388. In papyri from Dura-Europos the Aramaic name which means "Son of Baʻalšāmēn" is spelled both "Barbaesamen" and "Barbaesomen." See the indices to C. B. Welles, R. O. Fink, and J. F. Gilliam, *The Parchments and Papyri* (Yale University Press, 1959). Note also the pun at Jer 2:12, *šmw šmym*.

[261] With Ginsberg, pp. 44 and 80, n. 15b. For the possibility of confusing *mem* and *pe* in this period, see the letter forms at Frank M. Cross, "The Development of the Jewish Scripts," in BANE, p. 176, fig. 2, line 1.

we find *ṣābā* wrongly inserted below at Dan 10:1 between "and" (*w-*) and "great" (*gādōl*). If so, here, too, the original text spoke of abominations or a host from the sky, and the seer predicted their eventual destruction. The data at I 1:54, 59, and 4:43 are completely in harmony with this interpretation.

In setting up such a structure of meteorites to be worshiped, Antiochus would not have been an innovator. Indeed, such stones as representations of a deity or containers of his presence are abundantly attested in the Bible and in Phoenician and Syrian cults.[262] Jacob's "Bethel" (="house of God") is not said to have been a meteorite but appears to have been just such a stone containing the presence of the Deity; Jacob set it up as a cultic upright stone or pillar (*maṣṣēbāh*).[263]

This pattern of worship was found widely among Canaanites, Syrians, and those Jews whom the biblical writers viewed as heterodox. Thus, in the periods of Persian and early Hellenistic rule, many Canaanites (or, as they were called by the Greeks, Phoenicians), avoided representing their gods in human or animal form. Instead, these Canaanites would represent a female deity by a tree, which eventually died and was kept as a trunk or a stump (the "asherah" of the Bible); and they would represent any deity by a cult-stone.[264] The biblical accounts on the whole confirm this picture for the pre-exilic period, too. There was no statue of Baal on Mount Carmel, but only an altar.[265] This does not mean that no Canaanites used images; certainly the Philistines did.[266] Still, most of the biblical reports of removals of foreign cults mention no statues but only cult-stones (*maṣṣēbōt*) and asherahs and altars.[267] At Exod 23:24 *maṣṣēbōt* are the only objects of idol-worship mentioned.

---

[262] It is remarkable that Bickermann (*Gott*, pp. 90–109) derived almost the same picture of the cult imposed by Antiochus and did so solely from the study of Phoenician and Syrian parallels, without interpreting Daniel. On the use of stones in ancient Near Eastern religions see Carl F. Graesser, "Standing Stones in Ancient Palestine," BA 35 (1972), 34–63.

[263] Gen 28:16–18, 22, 31:13, 36:7. Note the language at Gen 31:13, *ānōkī hā'ēl bēyt ēl*, "I am the God Bethel. . . ." See Stanley A. Cook, *The Religion of Ancient Palestine in the Light of Archaeology* (London: Oxford University Press, 1930), pp. 26–27. See also Hosea 12:5 with H. L. Ginsberg, "Hosea's Ephraim, More Fool than Knave," JBL 80 (1961), 339–47, and Bezalel Porten, *Archives from Elephantine*, pp. 165–76.

[264] Asherah: Du Mesnil, *Études*, pp. 32, 58–59; cult-stones: see below.

Masculine deities represented by trees and feminine by stones: Jer 2:27. See also R. Du Mesnil, "Origine et évolution du panthéon de Tyr," RHR 164 (1963), 136, n. 5; *Études*, pp. 109–10, 127.

[265] I Kings 18:26; cf. Tacitus *Histories* ii 78.

[266] I Sam 5:4, 31:9.

[267] Asa's reform (II Chron 14:2; cf. I Kings 15:11–13); the destruction of the Baal cult in Israel (II Kings 3:2, 10:26–27); Josiah's removal of the vestiges of Solomon's toleration of idolatry (II Kings 23:14; II Chron 31:1). The account of the eradication of the Baal cult in Judah (II Kings 11:18; II Chron 23:17) and the story of the colonists from the east in Samaria (non-Canaanites!—II Kings 17:41) both mention cult-statues, not *maṣṣēbōt*.

The same pattern prevails in the reports of illicit apparatus used by Israelites to worship their own God.[268] Where the biblical authors mention statues, there is usually reason to assume influence from Mesopotamia on the peoples of Syria and Palestine.[269]

Jacob's *maṣṣēbāh* was an uncut stone; on Canaanite religious monuments and coins appear both uncut stones and cut stones, especially narrow slabs. The Phoenicians had several words for such stones, including *maṣṣēbāh* and *nāṣīb*, a word from the same root. There is evidence that they also called such a stone a "Bethel," or, as we have it in Greek transliteration, a *baityl*.[270] There are also indications that some of these *baityls* were meteorites. The Phoenician writer Philo of Byblos wrote early in the second Christian century but drew on older sources. According to him, the god Baitylos has as his father Ouranos (Heaven) and as his mother Gê (Earth), and Heaven and Earth are both children of 'Elyūn, the Highest; elsewhere Philo says that the god Ouranos created *baitylia*, which he explains as "animate stones."[271] Single or multiple stones or pillars, standing on an altar or a throne, are known as objects of worship among the Canaanites before the time of Alexander.[272] Such stones and pillars are well attested in Phoenician and especially in Punic remains and on Phoenician coins.[273] Quite common are such stones and pillars in groups of three or multiples of three.[274]

---

268 II Kings 17:10, 18:4; note that in II Kings 16 Ahaz is *not* reported to have introduced the worship of foreign gods. The statues used in the later reign of Joash of Judah may well have been for illicit worship of the God of Israel (II Chron 24:18). All references to statues in Hosea probably refer to the "calves" of the northern Israelite cult, not to Canaanite idols (Hosea 4:17, 8:4, 13:2, 14:9); so may Micah 1:7. The calves themselves were probably not objects of worship but platforms for the presence of the deity, analogous to the cherubim in the temple of Jerusalem.

269 The statues mentioned at Amos 5:26 appear to belong to Mesopotamian astral cults. See below, n. 325. Micah 5:12 may reflect Ahaz's aping of Aramaean or Assyrian patterns (II Kings 16:10-15). To judge by the political situation and by the importance given to astral cults, the use of statues under Manasseh and his successors followed Assyrian models (II Kings 21:3-7; II Chron 33:3-7, 19, 22; 34:3-7), so that references to statues in Ezekiel need have no relevance to Canaanite or illicit native Israelite cults. Ps 16:36-38 is probably derived from Ezek 16:16-21. The references to statues in Isaiah 40-46 and at Zech 13:2 are even later and may have less to do with Canaanite or illicit native Israelite cults.

270 See Wolfgang Fauth, "Baitylia," Der kleine Pauly, I (1964), 806-8.

271 FGH 790, F 2=Eusebius Praeparatio evangelica i 10.15-16, 23; F 6=Stephanus Byzantius s.v. Nisibis. The animate quality was magnetism, very common in meteorites. See Th. Hopfner, "Lithika," PW, XIII (1927), 756-57.

272 Sabatino Moscati, The World of the Phoenicians (New York: Praeger, 1968), p. 54 and plate xxvi; cf. Donald Harden, The Phoenicians (London: Thames & Hudson, 1962), p. 94. The horns on the Jewish altar *may* have had such an origin; see Kurt Galling, Der Altar in den Kulturen des alten Orients (Berlin: Curtius, 1925), pp. 59, 67.

273 Moscati, pp. 152-60, 203; Harden, pp. 201-2. Coins: Moscati, p. 48; S. A. Cook, pp. 160-61, 165-66, and plate xxxiii, nos. 5-10; Galling, Der Altar, pp. 61-63, 67-68.

274 Moscati, pp. 153, 156, 224, and plate xxiv; S. A. Cook, p. 24; Gilbert C. Picard, Les religions de l'Afrique antique (Paris: Plon, 1954), pp. 74-76.

We derive more information from the texts and surviving cult objects from Syria. Damascius, a Syrian Greek writing around the beginning of the sixth Christian century calls a meteorite *baitylos,* speaks of it as being "of" the god Gennaios (using the genitive case), and says that other *baityls* "belong to" (*anakeisthai* with the dative) "Kronos, Zeus, Helios, and other gods."[275] Meteorites were worshiped at Seleuceia in Pieria, Diocaesareia in Cilicia, and Emesa.[276] Cult-stones on altars are also known from neo-Babylonian seals. Single or multiple pillars standing on platforms or on a common base are known from Nabataea.[277]

"Bethel" and its equivalent, "Baityl,"[278] as well as *maṣṣēbāh*[279] and even the Greek and Aramaic words for "altar" (*bômos, madbachos* [Aramaic in Greek transliteration])[280] are used in Syria in the early centuries of the Christian era as divine names. Their use presumably reflects the fact that the object in some sense constituted the presence of the deity. Since the trend was in the direction of Greek-style cult-statues and away from the old Semitic cult-stones, the late date of much of this evidence may be disregarded. Thus, Phoenicia and Syria offer abundant parallels for the use of the sacrificial altar of the Jewish temple as a platform on which cult-stones were placed and a pagan altar was built.

Throughout the Hebrew Bible, the writers take it for granted that cult-statues (*pᵉsīlīm, 'aṣabbīm ṣᵉlāmīm, massēkāh*) and asherahs were always forbidden, though the prohibition may have been violated. However, both the biblical writers and rabbinic literature recognize that cult-stones and altars outside the temple were permitted at least to the patriarchs.[281] Thereafter, however, the Pentateuchal codes and the historical and prophetic books condemn *maṣṣēbōt,* often grouping them with statues and asherahs and idolatrous altars[282]; and Deuteronomy and the later histories

[275] Damascius *Vita Isidori* 94, 203; Hopfner, PW, XIII, 757–58. Damascius treats "Gennaios" as a proper noun, but see J. and L. Robert, "Bulletin épigraphique," REG 85 (1972), 507, no. 565.

[276] Hopfner, PW, XIII, 757; S. A. Cook, pp. 157, 159; Herodian v 3.

[277] S. A. Cook, pp. 24–25, 156; cf. Galling, *Der Altar,* pp. 62–63, 67–68.

[278] Above, n. 263, and below, n. 280.

[279] Du Mesnil, *Études,* p. 122, and *Les tessères et les monnaies de Palmyre* (Paris: E. de Boccard, 1962), pp. 724–27.

[280] Zeus Bômos: *American Archaeological Expedition to Syria in 1899–1900* (New York: Century, 1903–14), Part II, *Architecture and Other Arts* (1903), by Howard Crosby Butler, pp. 67–69, and Part III, *Greek and Latin Inscriptions* (1908), by William K. Prentice, pp. 67–70. Zeus Betylos and Zeus Madbachos: M. Seyrig, "Altar Dedicated to Zeus Betylos," *The Excavations at Dura Europos, Preliminary Report, IV* (Yale University Press, 1933), pp. 68–71. See also Bickermann, *Gott,* pp. 106–9; Porten, pp. 167–73.

[281] Gen 38:18; *Sifre Debarim* 146, to Deut 16:22.

[282] Passages forbidding or condemning Israelite *maṣṣēbōt:* Lev 26:1; Deut 12:3, 16:21–22; I Kings 14:23; II Kings 17:10; Hosea 3:4, 10:1–2; Micah 5:12. Passages on *maṣṣēbōt* to foreign gods: Exod 23:24, 34:13–14; Deut 7:5. Isa 19:19 permits a *maṣṣēbāh* and altar to non-Israelites who worship the God of the Israelites.

and prophetic writings forbid Israelites to offer sacrifices on altars outside the temple.

Rabbinic sources contain laws on stones and altars used as objects of worship. The formulation of these laws may go back to the time of Antiochus' persecutions or before, since the rabbis themselves knew that the problems were a burning issue then.[283] The *tannaim* and early *amoraim* call such stones *maṣṣēbōt* and also speak of them by the Greek word for altar, *bômos,* evidently because some cult-stones were shaped like altars. According to the rabbis, a worshiped stone in the shape of an altar differed from a sacrificial altar (*mizbēaḥ*) in being a monolith, whereas a sacrificial altar was a structure of several stones.[284] The pagan altar (*bômos*) mentioned at I 1:59, however, is explicitly said to be an altar upon which sacrifices were offered. It was not itself a cult-stone in altar shape, though the cult-stones were probably placed upon it.

We may suppose that to Antiochus and to Greek intellectuals the prohibitions of cult-stones and of sacrifice outside the temple were late and unwholesome additions to the religion of Moses, like the practice of daily burnt offerings.[285] Hence, Antiochus forbade daily burnt offerings and required sacrifice outside the temple[286] and the worship of cult-stones.

It is clear from the sources on the persecution that the cult-stones were plural, and from the pagan parallels we learn that each meteorite could

[283] See n. 245, above.

[284] Why did rabbis use a Greek word when native Hebrew and Aramaic words were available? Perhaps they did so because *maṣṣēbāh* is an ambiguous term, meaning both an ordinary stone marker and a cult-stone. This is not the place for a detailed elucidation of the rabbinic sources: M. 'Abodah zarah 3:7; To. 'Abodah zarah 5(6):6, 8, p. 468, lines 26–31 and p. 469, lines 3–4 Zuckermandel, and 6(7):10, p. 470, lines 14–15; TB 'Abodah zarah 53b–54a; TP 'Abodah zarah 3:8, p. 43b, and 4:4, pp. 43d–44a; see also Sifra Qedoshim, section 1, 11, p. 87a Weiss; and cf. Maimonides, Mada', Hilkot 'abodah zarah 8:4. The problem is complicated by the ambiguity of *bômos* in rabbinic sources. Sometimes it clearly means cult-stone; sometimes, pagan altar; and sometimes one cannot be sure what it means. Note also the use of *bwms ṣlm* on a Nabataean inscription cited by S. A. Cook, p. 22, n. 3.

Moreover, the rabbis could use *bômos* for "cult-stone" because the Greeks themselves on occasion worshiped their altars, treating them like cult-stones; see L. Ziehen, "Altar I (griechisch-römisch)," RAC 1 (1950), 327–28, and Reisch, "Altar," PW, I (1894), 1642. On the other hand, in the Bible (at Deut 7:5, 12:3, etc.) *maṣṣēbāh* appears frequently in association with *mizbēaḥ* ("altar"), and there is some evidence to suggest that in early times monolithic altars were simultaneously *maṣṣēbōt;* see Hosea 3:4; Gen 25:14; S. A. Cook, p. 17; Galling, Der Altar, pp. 55–59.

For the rabbinic statements distinguishing a *bômos,* meaning "cult-stone," from an altar (*mizbēaḥ*) by the fact that a cult-stone was a monolith, see TP 'Abodah zarah 4:4, p. 44a; TB 'Abodah zarah 53b, end. From the fifth century B.C.E. onward, Greek altars were most commonly monoliths. See Constantine G. Yavis, Greek Altars (St. Louis University Press, 1949), p. 140. The same was true of Syrian and Phoenician altars in the Hellenistic and Roman periods; see Galling, Der Altar, p. 64.

[285] See NOTE on I 1:45.

[286] See NOTE on I 1:47.

represent a different god.[287] At least three gods, Zeus, Athene, and Dionysus, are mentioned in the sources.[288] There is good reason to believe that these are all the gods of the imposed "Jewish" cult. There was a strong tendency among the Phoenicians to worship gods in families of three, consisting of a father god, a mother goddess, and their son[289]; correspondingly, Phoenician cult-stones often appear standing upon altars in groups of three.[290] Here, too, Antiochus may have intended to restore illicit Jewish rites condemned by the prophets, rites which he believed to have been part of the original religion of Moses.

In the Syrian and Phoenician triads, the father god was always a god of the rainstorm, like Aliyan-Ba'al at Ugarit and like the God of the Jews, both of whom "ride the clouds."[291] According to the Byzantine historian John Malalas (d. 578 c.e.), the consort goddess in the imposed cult was "Athene." "Athene" was the Greek name of the Phoenician goddess 'Anath. In Ugaritic texts 'Anath is the sister and probably the consort of Aliyan-Ba'al and is called "Mistress of lofty heaven" (b'lt smm rmm). In Egyptian texts 'Anath is called "Lady of Heaven" (nbt pt).[292] At Tyre around 676 b.c.e. 'Anath was the consort of Ba'al-Ṣaphon (=Aliyan-Ba'al).[293] Pious Israelites gave to their own deity the attributes of Aliyan-Ba'al.[294] Jeremiah angrily censured Israelites who appear to have also given 'Anath to their God as consort, under the name "Queen of Heaven."[295]

[287] See pp. 149–50.

[288] See p. 144.

[289] See above, n. 187. Compare Father, Mother, and Son as they appear in gnostic writings; see Jean Doresse, *The Secret Books of the Egyptian Gnostics* (New York: Viking, 1960), pp. 178, 201, 330.

[290] See above, n. 274.

[291] See Seyrig, *Antiquités syriennes*, V, 112; Du Mesnil, "El et ses épouses vus par Philon de Byblos," *Mélanges d'archéologie, d'épigraphie et d'histoire offerts à Jérôme Carcopino* (Paris: Hachette, 1966), p. 272; Ps 68:5; Cyrus Gordon, *Ugaritic Textbook*, 4th ed. (Rome: Pontifical Biblical Institute, 1965), p. 484, no. 2331. By "father god" here I mean only the father god of the triad, not the father god of the pantheon. At Ugarit, not Aliyan-Ba'al but El bore the *title* "father." One should also note that the tendency to group important deities in familial triads in *not* found at Ugarit.

[292] Du Mesnil, *Études*, pp. 59–60, 119, 136–37; RHR 164 (1963), 146; *Mélanges Carcopino*, p. 283, n. 6; Porten, pp. 165, 171; Gordon, *Ugaritic Textbook*, p. 422, No. 1291a.

[293] Du Mesnil, RHR 164 (1963), 144–48; *Mélanges Carcopino*, p. 283, n. 6.

[294] Above, n. 291.

[295] Jer 7:18, 44:17–25; Jeremiah insists that the "heterodox" Israelites are worshiping "foreign gods" (ĕlōhīm ăḥērim: 7:18 and 44:8); but Jeremiah names, and his opponents admit worshiping, only the Queen of Heaven, whom his opponents regard as a legitimate object of worship. Jews at Elephantine in Egypt mention the divine beings 'Anathbethel and 'Anathyahu, that is, 'Anath of Bethel and 'Anath of YHWH, the God of the Jews! Hence, the Queen of Heaven mentioned in Jeremiah is probably 'Anath. See also Porten, pp. 154–58, 163–64, 171–79; W. F. Albright, YGC, pp. 134–35.

Since many Jews at the time of the persecution called their God "Heaven," among them the author of First Maccabees, "Queen of Heaven" would be an appropriate name for His consort. One might then look to have the God of the Jews called "King of Heaven," but he is not so called in the Hebrew Bible.[296] Among heterodox Jews and Samaritans the teachings about Athene or "Wisdom," the consort of God, may have survived down to the rise of the Simonian gnostics, early in the Christian era.[297] Though among the Phoenicians 'Anath was known only as "*Lady* of the lofty Heaven" and *Asherath* was the Queen of Heaven,[298] the cult imposed on the Jews was theoretically a purified Judaism, not an import from Phoenicia. The one Israelite adult male deity, the LORD, absorbed almost all the powers and epithets of the Phoenician adult male deities, El and 'Elyūn and the Lord of Heaven and Ba'al, rider of the clouds. Just so, Jeremiah's contemporaries may have believed in only one adult female deity, consort of their male God, ascribing to her the powers of all the Phoenician female deities. This tendency to fuse the adult gods of each sex into a single deity is visible in Phoenicia itself.[299]

The third god of the imposed cult was "Dionysus." In Hellenistic and Roman times there was a strong tendency for the young god of a Syro-Phoenician triad to be identified with Dionysus or to take on the traits of Dionysus, even when he bore the name of another Greek god, as did the Hermes of Ba'albek-Heliopolis. Dionysus was a young god who died a violent death and returned to life.[300] The tendencies which would link youthful Syro-Phoenician "third gods" to Dionysus and to Antiochus' meteorites existed long before.

Already in a text of the second millennium B.C.E. from Ugarit, 'Anath is associated with a god who, like Dionysus, perishes by being torn to

[296] See, however, Jer 10:1–16; Mal 1:14; Pss 10:16, 24:7–10, 29:1–10; Matt 3:2, 4:17, and 5:3, 10, 19:20, etc.; and the rabbinic expression *malkūt šāmayim* (*M. Berakot* 22, etc.).

[297] Simon, the "First God," had as his consort Athene or "First Thought" (*Ennoia*)="Wisdom" (*Sophia*); see Irenaeus *Contra haereses* i 23, vol. VII, cols. 670–73 Migne. Simon's own name may have been taken as a play on the Hebrew and Aramaic words for "heaven." See Robert M. Grant, *Gnosticism and Early Christianity*, rev. ed. (New York: Harper & Row, 1966), pp. 73–85.

[298] Du Mesnil, *Études*, pp. 126–27; cf. Albright, YGC, p. 130.

[299] Fusion of adult male gods appears quite early at Tyre; see Du Mesnil, RHR 164 (1963), 140–41. In late sources Athene-'Anath and Europe-Asherath at Tyre and other consorts of major Syrian and Phoenician male deities are confused or identified; see Du Mesnil, ibid., pp. 149–50; Lucian *De Dea Syria* 32; Seyrig, *Antiquités syriennes*, V, 112–13; Albright, YGC, p. 133.

[300] Strong tendency: H. Seyrig, "Bêl de Palmyre," *Syria* 48 (1971), 105–9. Hermes of Ba'albek: H. Seyrig, *Antiquités syriennes*, V, 90–91, 104–5. Though most of the sources on the death and resurrection of young Dionysus are late, the belief was well established long before the time of Antiochus IV. See H. Jeanmaire, *Dionysos*, pp. 372–416.

pieces and eaten. The text appears to mean that 'Anath herself thus tore her own beloved brother Aliyan Ba'al to pieces.[301] We have no trace of any later Canaanite source which has 'Anath herself as the killer, but a suggestive parallel does exist elsewhere.

The Phrygians of Asia Minor told of the young god Attis, beloved by the mother-goddess, who died after castrating himself. The same story was told of the young Phoenician god Eshmun. Both Attis and Eshmun were identified with Dionysus.[302] The parallel to the Ugaritic myth is in the teaching of the Naasene gnostics presented by Hippolytus, who wrote in the third century of the Christian era. The Naasenes, who traced their origins back to the first Christian century, drew on Phrygian and Syrian teachings as well as on heterodox Judaism. The Naasenes spoke of the mother of the gods herself as castrating her beloved Attis. All other versions of the Attis and Eshmun myths have the goddess as the innocent mourner of the torn dead god.[303]

At Tyre the typical Phoenician triad of gods consisted of Ba'alšāmēm and Ašērat and their son Melqart; Ba'alšāmēm and Melqart were represented by cult-stones and Ašērat by an asherah.[304] Melqart was an agricultural deity who disappeared (died?) in the winter, to reappear with the emerging plants in the month of Shebat (ca. February); he was identified with Greek Heracles, a hero who dies and rises as a god.[305] In Phoenicia another famous young god who seasonally dies and returns to life is Adonis, whose very name (Adon=Lord) was used by pious Jews to refer to their God.[306] There is evidence that Adonis was the son of El (Greek "Theias") and a mother goddess.[307] "El," too, was a name Jews used for their God. Adonis was later worshiped at Antioch[308] and may well have been in Antiochus' time. Adonis was identi-

---

[301] See Michael Astour, "Un texte d'Ugarit récemment découvert et ses rapports avec l'origine des cultes bachiques grecs," RHR 164 (1963), 1–15, and *Hellenosemitica* (Leiden: Brill, 1965), pp. 178–81.

[302] Attis myth: Rapp, "Attis," in Roscher, I[1] (1884–90), 715–20. Identification of Attis with Dionysus and Adonis: Hippolytus *Refutatio omnium haeresium* v 7 and 9, vol. XVI[III], cols. 3130, 3155 Migne; oracle *apud* Socrates *Historia ecclesiastica* iii 23; Rapp, in Roscher, I[1], pp. 717–18, 720.
Eshmun: Damascius *Vita Isidori* § 302 (the best edition is now *Damascii Vitae Isidori reliquiae* ed. Clemens Zintzen [Hildesheim: Olms, 1967], where § 302 is on pp. 307–8); Baudissin, pp. 339–44. Identification of Eshmun with Dionysus: ibid., pp. 199, 213–41.

[303] Naasene teaching: Hippolytus *Refutatio* v 7, vol. XVI[III], cols. 3130–31 Migne; Naasene origins: ibid., cols. 3126–27.

[304] Du Mesnil, RHR 164 (1963), 133–42, and cf. p. 149.

[305] Ibid., pp. 154–57; J. *AJ* viii 5.3.146; Albright, YGC, p. 127.

[306] See Du Mesnil, *Études*, p. 106; Otto Eissfeldt, *Adonis und Adonaj*, Sitzungs-berichte der Sächsischen Akademie der Wissenschaften zu Leipzig, Philologisch-historische Klasse, Band 115, Heft 4, Berlin: Akademie-Verlag, 1970; W. Fauth, "Adonis," Der kleine Pauly, I (1964), 70–71; H. Seyrig, "Antiquités syriennes," Syria 49 (1972), 97–104.

[307] Du Mesnil, *Études*, pp. 58–59, 107.

[308] Ammianus Marcellinus xxii 9.5 (autumn, 362 C.E.).

fied with Mesopotamian Tammuz, the dying young son and lover of the mother goddess.[309] Tammuz, too, may well have been known to Antiochus at Antioch, since his cult is later attested there. Adonis was also identified with Dionysus.[310] Just as Jeremiah's rebukes let us know that Israelites worshiped the Queen of Heaven, so Ezekiel's denunciations let us know that Israelites worshiped Tammuz.[311] Again, the "Jewish" deity corresponding to Adonis-Eshmun-Tammuz did not have to be identical in all respects to his Phoenician, Syrian, or Mesopotamian counterparts.

The rites of the Phoenician Adonis occurred in summer; they may have included a procession to "bring him into the air."[312] We have no explicit record of summer rites imposed upon the Jews. Perhaps Antiochus regarded the festival of Tabernacles, which in Greek eyes so resembled Dionysiac rites, as the festival of the Jewish Adonis-Tammuz-Dionysus.[313]

The date of the desecration of the temple in the month just before the winter solstice (Kislev) may have coincided with a festival of Dionysus. Antiochus IV's Athenian expert may have suggested imposing on the Jews the "rustic Dionysia," which in Athens were celebrated in the month of Posideon=Kislev[314]; indeed, the author at I 1:54–55 stresses that the rites were observed in the country towns.[315]

---

[309] Jerome's commentary to Ezek 8:14: *Quem nos Adonidem interpretati sumus et Hebraeus et Syrus sermo Thamuz vocat.* See Alfred Jeremias, "Tamuz," in Roscher, V (1916–24), 49–50; Preisendanz, "Tammuz," PW, IV^A (1932), 2145–48; Albright, YGC, pp. 147–48; Eissfeldt, *Adonis*, pp. 19–23.

[310] Baudissin, pp. 199–200, 231–41.

[311] Ezek 8:14; Isa 17:10, too, may refer to the worship of Adonis-Tammuz. See Albright, YGC, pp. 186–87; Eissfeldt, *Adonis*, pp. 19–20.

[312] Dümmler, "Adonis 2," PW, I (1894), 385–87; Baudissin, pp. 121–37.

[313] See Tacitus *Histories* v 5; Plutarch *Quaestiones conviviales* iv 6, pp. 671c–672c; at p. 671c Plutarch suggests that both Dionysus and Adonis are identical with the God of the Jews.

[314] Kern, "Dionysos 2," PW, V (1905), 1021. These local observances in Attica probably took place on different days of the month at different places. Only for one Attic deme do we have the day of the month, the nineteenth (Kern, ibid., col. 1022).

[315] Some authors have suggested that Antiochus imposed the patterns of the cult of Dusares, god of the Nabataeans, who lived south and east of Judaea; Dusares had a festival around the time of the winter solstice. See Cumont, "Dusares," PW, V (1905), 1866–67; Bickermann, *Gott*, pp. 112–14; Julius Wellhausen, "Ueber den geschichtlichen Wert des zweiten Makkabäerbuchs," *Nachrichten von der Königlichen Gesellschaft der Wissenschaften zu Göttingen, Philologisch-historische Klasse,* 1905, p. 131. However, the Nabataeans were probably independent of the Seleucid empire in Antiochus' time; see II 5:8; Schürer, I, 729–31; René Dussaud, *La pénétration des Arabes en Syrie avant l'Islam,* pp. 51–55. There was no reason for a Seleucid king to impose a Nabataean cult on the Jews. Moreover, the desecration of the temple, whether on 15 or 25 Kislev, occurred before the solstice. Our only source for the date of the festival of Dusares gives it as January 6 (Epiphanius *Adversus LXXX haereses* 51.22 in the edition of K. Holl [Die griechischen christlichen Schriftsteller der ersten drei Jahrhunderte, XXXI (Leipzig and Berlin: Hinrichs, 1922)]). Cumont does place the festival of Dusares on the twenty-fifth of December (PW, V, 1867), but only by using a Greek inscription in which Dusares is called *anikêtos* to identify Dusares with Sol Invictus, a hazardous procedure.

The Athenian expert may have suggested a few details borrowed from Athenian cults, but the basic patterns of the imposed cult were not Greek. How would Jews view Antiochus' transportation of "divine meteorites" into Jerusalem for worship by a "criminal rebellious nation"? Knowing the ways of pious pagans, Jews may well have thought Antiochus' procedure insulting even to the "idols." At the very least, Antiochus was exposing the idols to hatred and contempt from pious Jews. This appears to be the meaning of Dan 8:10 and 11:36–37. The "Delight of Women" in Dan 11:37 may be the Queen of Heaven, worshiped largely by women, to judge by Jeremiah's denunciations. More probably, however, the epithet refers to a Jewish version of Adonis-Tammuz, whose cult was largely observed by women, as we know both from Ezek 8:14 and from Greek sources.[316]

There is evidence that the cult alluded to in Dan 11:37 long survived in heterodox circles. "Delight" translates the Hebrew ḥmdt. The word comes from the Hebrew root ḥmd ("long for," "desire"), which the Greek translator Symmachus rendered by the Greek verb pothein at Psalm 67[68H]:17; more commonly, the verb is rendered by the Greek root epithymein, as in the Greek versions of Dan 11:37.[317] The Naasenes spoke of the loving goddess as "desiring" (epithymei) Adonis, and from a Phrygian hymn used by the Naasenes we learn that the Syrians called Adonis "thrice-longed-for" (tripothêtos).[318]

The imposition of cult-prostitutes mentioned at II 6:4 confirms our theory that Antiochus installed the worship of the Queen of Heaven and of a counterpart of Adonis. Cultic prostitution was usually a part of the worship of female, not male deities.[319] However, prostitution was a part of the worship of Adonis.[320] Here, too, Antiochus could have believed he was restoring rites which the prophets had "wrongly" eliminated. Certainly, the patriarch Judah himself did not hesitate to use a cult-prostitute (qᵉdēšāh),[321] and the prohibition of cult-prostitutes occurs only in Deuteronomy (23:18).

The use of meteorites as cult-stones may imply the identification of the worshiped deities with heavenly bodies but need not. In Jewish lore the Divine resided in the heavens; if the Phoenicians brought their deities

---

[316] See Baudissin, pp. 120, 126, 134–35, 189, 352; Nicole Weill, "La fête d'Adonis dans la 'Samienne' de Ménandre," Bulletin de correspondence hellénique 94 (1970), 591–93.

[317] See also Exod 20:17, etc; Dan LXX 10:3, 11:43; Dan Th. 9:23, 10:3, 11, 19, 11:8.

[318] Hippolytus Refutatio v 7, 9, vol. XVI[III], cols. 3130, 3155 Migne.

[319] See W. von Soden, "Prostitution: I, Kultische," Die Religion in Geschichte und Gegenwart, V (1961), 642–43; George A. Barton, "Hierodouloi," Encyclopaedia of Religion and Ethics, ed. James Hastings, VI (1914), 673a–675a.

[320] Lucian De Dea Syria 6; see also Schol. Megillat Ta'anit 23 Ḥeshvan.

[321] Gen 38:21; cf. Hosea 4:14.

more down to earth, they, too, still connected them with the heavens.[322] It is possible that in the imposed cult the God of the Jews was identified with the planet Jupiter,[323] the Queen of Heaven with the planet Venus,[324] and the young god with the planet Mercury or Saturn[325] or with a constellation.[326]

Throughout, Antiochus claimed he was honoring the God of the Jews, a God unknown to his ancestors; along with "restoring His consort and child" the king probably embellished His temple with rich gifts (Dan 11:38). First Maccabees 3:48 probably means Antiochus' agents tried to convince the Jews that texts proving the imposed cult was indeed the original religion of Israel were to be found in the Torah itself.[327]

The imposed cult, if adopted by the Jews, would leave them with a religion much like that of their Syrian and Phoenician neighbors. If the Jews should no longer be unique and monotheistic, it was reasonable to assume that they might have much less tendency to be "tyrannously" intolerant and rebellious. Thus, even if Antiochus did not happen to be convinced by the theories of "anthropologists" and theologians which underlay the imposed cult, he could still have seen practical reasons for imposing it on the Jews.

The picture we have drawn of the imposed cult fits the most important evidence, especially the words of the seer in Daniel, a contemporary witness. Neither Jews nor Greeks had reason to preserve the theological details of Antiochus' hypothetical restoration of the "original" Jewish religion, especially after his failure to impose it on the Jews. Enough clues are left for us to understand it, even though Josephus could not.

One difficulty remains: Why did Antiochus try to force the Jews to eat and offer up pigs? So far as we know, among the Greeks pigs as a rule

---

[322] Deut 33:26; Judg 5:20; Isa 14:12, 24:21–23, 33:5, 57:15, 66:1; Ezek 1:1; Ps 102:20; Job 16:19, 22:12–14, 25:2–3, etc. Phoenicians: Du Mesnil, *Études,* p. xiv. Phoenician deities were described as "starred" or as "wearing stars" in the time of Cicero; see Du Mesnil, RHR 164 (1963), 138, 156.

[323] Jupiter as the star of Zeus: Plato *Epinomis* 987c; Aristotle *Meteorologica* 343b30; *Placita philosophorum* ii 32.1: Cleomedes 2.7. Jupiter as the star of Bel-Marduk, the Babylonian counterpart of the God of the Jews: Morris Jastrow, *Religion of Babylonia and Assyria,* p. 459.

[324] Du Mesnil, *Études,* pp. xiv, 16–19, 60–61, 126–27; Morris Jastrow, pp. 205–6, 459.

[325] Saturn as Ninurta (=Ninib), god of hunting, firstborn of Bel: Morris Jastrow, pp. 216–17, 459. Amos 5:26 may then allude to such a cult of the Queen of Heaven and the young god, identified respectively with the planets Venus and Saturn; see Terry Leonard Fenton, "*Sikkūt,*" Enc. Bib., V (1968), 1037, and "*Sukkōt bᵉnōt,*" ibid., col. 1043 (in Hebrew).

Mercury: see p. 153 (the young god of Ba'albek identified with Hermes=Mercury). At Babylon the planet Mercury was identified with Nabu, son of Bel-Marduk; see Morris Jastrow, pp. 127, 240, 459.

[326] See Franz Boll and Carl Bezold, *Sternglaube und Sterndeutung* (Leipzig: Teubner, 1926), p. 12.

[327] See commentary ad loc.

were offered only to infernal ("chthonic") deities and used in magical rites. In Egypt and among the Semitic peoples except the Babylonians, the pig was an unclean animal, eaten, if at all, only on exceptional occasions.[328] How would forcing the Jews to sacrifice and eat swine remove dangerous later accretions from an "originally legitimate native cult?"

Two facts can explain Antiochus' strange policy. First, the pig was a favored sacrificial animal of Dionysus.[329] Antiochus could feel himself to be "restoring" the proper Dionysiac ritual of the "God of Heaven." Second, according to the anthropological theories reflected by Poseidonius and preserved by Strabo,[330] the dietary laws and circumcision were indeed later unwholesome accretions upon the praiseworthy teachings of the Jewish religion. Though such "later accretions" existed in the religions of other Semitic stocks, those other stocks, like the Samaritans and unlike the Jews, had not used their religion as a pretext for disturbing public order.[331] Hence, Antiochus proceeded to "purify" only the religion of the Jews by attacking the "unreasonable" prejudice against pork and forbidding circumcision.

Antiochus may well have allowed individual Jews to petition for special permission to observe the forbidden rites, just as the Roman Senate allowed individual worshipers of the Bacchanalia to do so. Certainly the Samaritans sent Antiochus such a petition and received a favorable reply.[332] Despite allowing for exceptions, the Senate sought to exterminate the menace. Throughout Italy, even in remote and desolate regions, Roman officials hunted down the devotees of the Bacchanalia. Two years and even five years later, worshipers in the mountains of southern Italy were not allowed to escape.[333] Antiochus had his officials proceed with equal rigor for more than two years, and the persecution was halted in his absence.[334]

The Senate succeeded in suppressing the Bacchanalia in Italy at the cost of thousands of lives.[335] In the Seleucid kingdom, the results of this mechanical application of Roman procedures were disastrous. The policy of Antiochene citizenship was intended to strengthen the realm. Now the Antiochenes at Jerusalem were hard hit, for many of them prob-

[328] See R. de Vaux, "Les sacrifices de porcs en Palestine et dans l'Ancien Orient," Von Ugarit nach Qumran: Festschrift für Otto Eissfeldt, Beihefte zur ZAW 77 (Berlin: Töpelmann, 1958), pp. 250–65.

[329] See Paul Stengel, Die griechischen Kultusaltertümer, 3d ed. (München: C. H. Beck, 1920), p. 122; Nilsson, Geschichte der griechischen Religion, 3d ed. (1967), 663.

[330] FGH 87, F 70; Strabo xvi 2.35–37.

[331] Cf. de Vaux in Von Ugarit nach Qumran, p. 261; Bickermann, Gott, pp. 130–31, 134–35.

[332] See above, n. 196.

[333] Livy xxxix 14.7–10, 16.11–13, 17.1–18.6, 41.6–7, xl 19.9–10.

[334] I 1:44–4:35; II 6:1–8:36, 11:1–21, 27–38.

[335] Livy xxxix 17.5–6, 41.6–7.

ably still felt bound by some, if not all, of the commandments of the Torah (II 4:16–17). Even the author of First Maccabees stresses that *all* Jews, not merely those untainted by Hellenism, suffered from the persecution (I 1:28, 64). As the first victims of the king's decrees against Judaism, the Hellenizing Antiochene Jews could hardly have welcomed them, much less instigated them.[336] It may be significant that Jason of Cyrene never called Menelaus an idolater, but only cruel (II 4:25, 5:23), a temple robber (II 4:32, 39, 47, 13:6), a briber (4:34, 45), and a sinner against the altar, apparently through violation of the laws of ritual purity (13:8). Lysias blamed Menelaus for "all the evils" (13:4), but that does not necessarily mean that Menelaus was an idolater. Menelaus sufficiently earned the blame by supplanting Jason and by robbing the temple.[337] Menelaus may well have been appalled at the king's decrees (cf. II 4:16–17). Perhaps, like the Samaritans, he survived through a successful petition to be exempted from the persecution. Indeed, at the opportune moment Menelaus sought successfully to get the royal government to end the persecution (II 11:29). Menelaus somehow survived without rebelling; non-violent Pietists were massacred; and the Hasmonaeans successfully rebelled. The Seleucid empire was never able to repair the damage caused by this disastrous policy.

The Roman origin of Antiochus' policy may have been known to Jason of Cyrene and the author of First Maccabees. Our author need not have mentioned at I 1:10 the fact that Antiochus IV had been a hostage in Rome. Jason of Cyrene noted at II 4:11 that Jason the Oniad's accept-

---

[336] Hence Bickermann's theory (*Gott,* pp. 117–39), that the Hellenizing Jews urged Antiochus to undertake the persecution, cannot be correct. One might read Dan 11:30, "And he [Antiochus] shall return and give a sympathetic hearing to those who deserted the Holy Covenant," as showing that the seer ascribed the imposed cult to suggestions of heterodox Jews. Josephus (*AJ* xii 5.1.240–41) appears so to have interpreted Dan 11:30, but Dan 11:30 refers to events of 168, the year of the Roman ultimatum to Antiochus to withdraw from Egypt, not, as Josephus would have it, to the introduction of Antiochene civic institutions at Jerusalem, which occurred long before the sack of 169. Porphyry (*apud* Jerome *Commentarii in Danielem* to 11:30) made the same error as Josephus. In fact, however, the verse is connected neither with the introduction of the Hellenizing "Antiochene" institutions nor with the proclamation of the imposed cult, but rather with the expedition of the Mysarch; see above, n. 236.

Antiochus may indeed have used the advice of heterodox Jews, but the author of First Maccabees and Jason of Cyrene readily speak of Jewish sinners. Why do they not ascribe the imposed cult to the suggestions of heterodox Jews? Why does Jason of Cyrene instead mention only Antiochus' Athenian expert (II 6:1)? Clearly because the Hellenizers, too, were victims! See also Tcherikover, *Hellenistic Civilization,* pp. 183–85.

From the words of the men of the Akra and their supporters at I 6:23 one can deduce only that the speakers obeyed Antiochus' decrees, not that they suggested the decrees or even welcomed them.

[337] Since II 13:4 says nothing about Menelaus as instigator of the imposed cult, Josephus' paraphrase of that passage or of *DMP* at *AJ* xii 9.7.384–85 represents his own misinterpretation.

ance of the program of Antiochene citizenship at Jerusalem annulled Jewish privileges gained by the ambassador John; he need not have mentioned in the same verse that John's son Eupolemus was the ambassador who made the first treaty of the Jews with the Romans. Judas Maccabaeus may have first heard of Rome through Antiochus IV's own propaganda (I 8:1).[338] The human origins of Antiochus' policy, however, were of small interest to theologians. The theologians sought to answer the agonizing question: Why did God allow His people to suffer? The theologians sought proof that the Age of Wrath had ended and believed they had found it. Even Josephus may have known something of Antiochus' "Romanism." However, writing for a Roman audience, he did not wish to evoke Roman sympathy for Antiochus. If so, it was not from failure to comprehend that Josephus suppressed all reference to the civic decrees of Antiochus, but rather from deliberate choice.[339]

[338] See commentary ad loc.
[339] See above, n. 99.

VII. WHAT REALLY HAPPENED: CHRONOLOGICAL TABLE

Though the authors of both books of Maccabees believed they were writing truth, both made mistakes, took literary license, and passed over embarrassing facts in silence. The reader of only a translation and commentary might find it hard to determine the outline of the true course of events. To reduce the difficulty, I have prepared the following table. In the first column appears the approximate Julian date B.C.E. where it can be determined. In the second column appears a brief summary of the events so dated. In the third column appear the sources in our two books for the events. Only if our two books fail to give important information included in the summary is a reference given to a source outside them. Courses of events are listed in the order of the dates at which they began, with longer courses of events listed before shorter ones. Events which are given no dates probably occurred between the nearest dated events above and below them in the table. The footnotes* tell the reader where to find arguments for the dates and facts listed, except when such arguments are easy to find in my commentary to the sources.

Dates (B.C.E.)	Events	Sources
From 189 or 188 to 176 or 175	Antiochus (the future Antiochus IV) serves as hostage in Rome for the Seleucid empire, vanquished by Rome in 190.	I 1:10
July, 187 – September, 175[1]	Seleucus IV reigns over the Seleucid empire. The royal minister Heliodorus comes to confiscate money on deposit in the temple in Jerusalem but fails to do so. Some Jews believe God miraculously prevented him.	II 3:4 – 4:1; Dan 11:20
	The high priest Onias III, under suspicion because of Heliodorus' misadventures and under political pressure from opponents, goes to Antioch to appeal to the king, but Seleucus IV dies or is murdered in September.	II 4:1–7
Later in 175[2]	Antiochus IV, brother of Seleucus IV, seizes power over Seleucid empire.	I 1:10; II 4:7
	In an effort to strengthen the Seleucid empire by copying institutions and ideas he had learned	I 1:41–43; II 4:9

* These "footnotes" follow the table as notes on pp. 173–74.

Dates (B.C.E.)	Events	Sources
	at Rome, Antiochus proclaims an Antiochene republic, analogous to the Roman republic, and invites individuals and communities subject to him to accept Antiochene citizenship.[3]	
Later in 175 or early in 174[4]	Jason, brother of Onias III, purchases the favor of Antiochus by offering him increased revenue and by bidding high for the privilege of being the founder of the Antiochene community at Jerusalem. Antiochus appoints Jason high priest in place of Onias and allows Jason to found an Antiochene citizen-community at Jerusalem with gymnasium and ephebic institutions, exempt from Jewish law.[5]	I 1:11–15; II 4:7–20
Before Jason's replacement as high priest by Menelaus[6]	Young Ptolemy VI celebrates his *Protoklisia*. Apollonius son of Menestheus, representing Antiochus IV at the celebration, discovers that the Ptolemaic empire is plotting a war against the Seleucid realm. On receiving this information, Antiochus takes defensive measures in the direction of the Ptolemaic border. At the end of these maneuvers, he passes through Joppe and then goes to Jerusalem, where he gets a splendid reception from Jason and the Jerusalemites.	II 4:21–22
172, probably after September 20[7]	Menelaus offers Antiochus IV still more revenue and thus wins appointment as high priest in place of Jason. Jason takes refuge in the Ammanitis.	II 4:23–26
	Unable to produce the promised revenue, Menelaus in his trouble uses temple vessels to bribe a royal minister, Andronikos, while Antiochus IV is away from the capital. Onias III from the sacred place of asylum at Daphne reproaches Menelaus.	II 4:27–33
After 1 Tishri (September 28), 170[8]	Andronikos entices Onias to leave his place of asylum and kills him. On returning to the capital, Antiochus, indignant, executes Andronikos.	II 4:34–38
	Depredations of temple property by Menelaus and his brother Lysimachus rouse the wrath of pious Jews. Menelaus and Lysimachus were leaders of the Antiochene Jews of Jerusalem. Pious Jews already believed that the Torah required them to punish the Antiochenes.[9] A bloody riot ensues. Members of the Jewish Council of Elders press charges against Menelaus, but again by bribing a royal official Menelaus escapes punishment.	II 4:39–50
November, 170 – Summer, 169	Antiochus IV vigorously repels Ptolemaic aggression, invades Egypt, and overruns all but Alexandria.	I 1:16–20; cf. II 5:51

Dates (B.C.E.)	Events	Sources
Late summer or early autumn, 169[10]	Jason and his followers, upon a false rumor of Antiochus' death, try to capture Jerusalem. Pious Jews rise against both Jason and Menelaus. Antiochus regards all but Menelaus' faction as rebels, punishes the city, plunders the temple, and attempts to re-establish order, confirming Menelaus in power over the Jews.[11]	I 1:20–28; II 5:1–23; cf. II 1:7–8
July, 168[12]	Antiochus IV, almost successful in his second attempt to conquer Egypt, withdraws completely from the Ptolemaic empire upon receiving a Roman ultimatum. On his way back to Antioch, he utters threats against the turbulent Jews, and on his return he hears the complaints of Menelaus and the Antiochenes of Jerusalem, under attack by pious Jews.[13]	Dan 11:29–30
Nisan (between April 1 and April 29), 167[14]	Antiochus IV, in response to complaints of Antiochenes of Jerusalem, sends a punitive expedition under Apollonius the Mysarch. Pious Jews of Jerusalem are massacred. Privileges of Jerusalem and Judaea are revoked and punitive taxes imposed. Troops fortify and help man Akra (the citadel) north of the temple to preserve order and protect the Antiochenes.	I 1:29–40; II 5:23–27
Between Nisan (April) and Kislev (December), 167[15]	Antiochus IV decrees that on penalty of death the turbulent Jews, including all those in Judaea, must cease observing the Torah and follow an imposed polytheistic cult, said to be a "purified Judaism," free of the tendencies which had turned the Jews into "rebels."	I 1:44–51
	Enforcement of the decrees is at first probably sporadic, as even Antiochene Jews fear to anger their God,[16] though some Jews obey the king. Royal officials begin to persecute pious Jews.	I 1:51–53
15 Kislev (December 6), 167	Antiochus IV takes drastic measures to enforce the imposed cult. "Abomination of Desolation," a framework containing three meteorites representing the three gods of the imposed cult, is placed upon the sacrificial altar of the temple.	I 1:54
	An Athenian expert helps direct the practices of the imposed cult. The practices in the temple include monthly sacrifices on the twenty-fifth,[17] sacred prostitution, and violation of the laws of ritual purity. Outside the temple, too, force is exerted throughout Jerusalem and Judaea to compel Jews to violate the Torah. The Samaritans petition successfully to be exempted from the decrees,[18] but many pious Jews suffer martyrdom. Cities of the Antiochene republic rigorously compel their Jews to follow the imposed cult.[19]	I 1:54–64; II 6–7; J. AJ xii 5.5.257–64 II 6–7

Dates (B.C.E.)	Events	Sources
Very late 167 or some time in 166	Mattathias' zeal leads him to rebel against a king who forces Jews to violate the Torah. He and his family, the Hasmonaeans,[20] attract followers and wage guerrilla warfare against the royal government and against Jews who violated the Torah. Some Pietist Jews still believe that God forbids violent rebellion and trust, in vain, the prophesies that God will protect Sabbath-observers. Believing that God forbade them to flee or defend themselves on the Sabbath, they are massacred by royal troops. Mattathias decides that God must have intended to permit Jews to *defend* themselves on the Sabbath. Many Pietists agree and join forces with the Hasmonaean party.	I 2:1–48; II 6:11
Between April 20, 166, and April 4, 165	Mattathias dies. Judas takes command.	I 2:70–3:2; cf. II 8:1–5
	Judas' force defeats expeditions of Apollonius and Seron.	I 3:10–24; cf. II 8:5–7
	Philip, royal commander at Jerusalem, unable to cope, appeals to the royal government for help.[21]	II 8:8; cf. I 3:25–26
165, probably between May 20 and June 18	Antiochus IV marches off with half the royal army to tax (and loot) the eastern regions claimed by the Seleucids. He appoints his little son Antiochus coregent king over the western part of the empire, with Lysias as his guardian and as chief minister over that same area. Lysias receives half the royal army, with the task of maintaining order in the western part of the empire.	I 3:27–37; FGH 260, F 32
	The governor of Coele-Syria and Phoenicia, Ptolemy son of Dorymenes, perhaps on orders from Lysias,[22] responds to Philip's appeal by sending a strong force under Nicanor and Gorgias. From their base at Ammaus, Nicanor and Gorgias fail to crush Judas' band and instead are routed by them.	I 3:38–4:27; II 8:8–29, 34–36
Some months later, surely not long before March, 164[23]	Lysias himself undertakes to stop the Jewish rebels. After careful preparation, he approaches Judaea from the south and fights a bloody battle with Judas' army at Beth-Zur. Menelaus and other Jews outside the Hasmonaean party, appalled at the prospect of being caught between the royal troops and Judas' men, beg Lysias for a negotiated settlement. Lysias, impressed by his heavy losses in battle, consents to refer their case to the "judgment" of the little coregent king.	I 4:28–35; II 11:1–21. 29
15 Xanthikos (March 12), 164[24]	Roman ambassadors in a letter to the Jews offer to support the Jewish case before the coregent king, at Antioch.	II 11:34–38

Dates (B.C.E.)	Events	Sources
	A letter in the name of the coregent offers Jews an end to the imposed cult, permission to observe the Torah and amnesty if they will cease fighting and return to their homes by 30 Xanthikos (March 27).	II 11:27–33
28 Adar (March 25), 164	The majority of Jews accept the coregent's offer by this date and observe it annually as the anniversary of the end of the persecution. The Hasmonaean party ignored the coregent's offer, to judge by the failure of our author to mention it.	Megillat Ta'anit 28 Adar; contrast I 4:35
March 25 – October 13, 164	Pious Jews wait through the festivals of Tabernacles and the Eighth Day of Solemn Assembly for prophesied miracles to occur— in vain.[25]	
1 or 10 Tishri on defective calendar[26] (July 25 or August 3), 164	Sabbatical year begins, according to the defective calendar. Pious Jews dare to deny the high priest Menelaus the right to control the temple.[27] Pious priests purify the temple and destroy the Abomination of Desolation.[26]	I 4:42–46; II 10:3; Dan 9:27, 11:24, end
Tishri-Marḥeshvan on defective calendar (between July 25 and September 18)[26]	Jews build and prepare a new sacrificial altar and temple vessels.	I 4:47–48; II 10:3
23 Marḥeshvan on defective calendar (September 14), 164[26]	Judas' men remove from the temple court the lattice which had served as apparatus for sacred prostitution.	Megillat Ta'anit 23 Marḥeshvan
27 Marḥeshvan on defective calendar (September 18), 164[26]	Jewish priests resume sacrifice of meal offerings in the temple, upon the new altar.	Ibid., 27 Marḥeshvan
3 Kislev on defective calendar (September 24), 164[26]	Jews destroy the idols which stood by private dwellings in Jerusalem.	Ibid., 3 Kislev
25 Kislev on defective calendar=25 Tishri on fully intercalated calendar (October 16), 164[26]	Judas, following biblical precedents, prolongs the doubtful festival of Tabernacles for a celebration of the dedication of the new sacrificial altar along with the new candelabrum, incense altar, and table. The dedication occurs on 25 Kislev, with the celebration continuing for a total of eight days.[26]	I 4:49–58; II 1:8–9, 10:3–7

Dates (B.C.E.)	Events	Sources
Late 164 or 163	The Jews decide to make the eight-day celebration an annual observance, at first under the name "Festival of Tabernacles in the month of Kislev," later under the name "Feast of Dedication."	I 4:59; II 10:8; cf. II 1:8–9, 2:16
November or early December, 164	Antiochus IV dies in the course of his campaign in Iran. On his deathbed he appoints the courtier Philip to replace Lysias as guardian of his little son and heir, Antiochus.	I 6:1–16; cf. II 9
From soon after Feast of Dedication (perhaps before the death of Antiochus IV), 164, to some time in April, 163[28]	The Jews under the leadership of Judas and his brothers Simon and Jonathan win victories over hostile neighboring peoples and Seleucid officials. The insubordinate Jewish commanders, Joseph and Azariah suffer a bloody defeat at Jamnia.	I 5:1–62; II 10:14–38, 12:1–31
Late 164 or early 163	Judas sees to it that the temple mount and Beth-Zur are fortified.	I 4:60–61
Late 164 or early 163	News of Antiochus IV's death reaches Antioch.[29] Lysias becomes chief power in the regime of little Antiochus V and is probably responsible for the forgery and publication of the letter at II 9:19–27. Philip, Antiochus IV's choice to replace Lysias, fails to win control and flees to Ptolemaic Egypt.[30]	I 6:17; II 9:29, 10:11
12 Adar on the defective calendar (January 28), 163	News of the death of Antiochus IV reaches Jerusalem, 1150 days after desecration of 15 Kislev, 167. Jews thereafter celebrate the day annually as the Day of the Tyrant.[31]	Megillat Ta'anit 12 Adar; Dan 8:14
Probably early 163	Ptolemy Makron, a high courtier under Antiochus V, advocates a just policy toward the Jews but falls from favor and commits suicide.	II 10:12–13
Just after Pentecost on the defective calendar (late April or May), 163	Judas conducts successful campaign against Idumaea and Azotus.	I 5:65–68; II 12:32–45
Late spring, 163[33]	Judas assembles a Jewish army and besieges the Akra.	I 6:18–20
Before June 27, 163[33]	Antiochus V and Lysias march on Judaea with a large force by way of Idumaea and besiege Beth-Zur. Judas lifts the siege of the Akra to go to relieve Beth-Zur, but at the battle of Beth-Zechariah the Jews are defeated, and Judas' brother Eleazar is killed. Jewish diehards, hoping for a miracle, are besieged in the temple. The Hasmonaean family probably hid in the mountains.	I 6:21–48; II 13:1–19

Dates (B.C.E.)	Events	Sources
Some weeks after the battle of Beth-Zechariah	The Seleucid besiegers allow the Jews in Beth-Zur, hard-pressed by siege and by the food shortage of a sabbatical year, to make peace and withdraw. Beth-Zur is garrisoned by Seleucid troops.	I 6:49–50; II 13:20–22
By June 27, 163[33]	Jews besieged in the temple are similarly hard-pressed. The seer in Daniel 12:7 predicts they will be crushed.[34]	I 6:48–54; cf. II 13:22
1 or 10 Tishri on the defective calendar (August 12), 163, 1335 days after the desecration of 15 Kislev, 167[35]	The sabbatical year ends and the date goes by for the miraculous consummation of history predicted by the seer in Daniel.	Dan 12:12
Late in 163 but probably not far from the end of the sabbatical year	Antiochus V deposes Menelaus from the high priesthood and sends him to Beroea in Syria for execution.[36]	II 13:3–8; J. AJ xii 9.7.383–85; Dan 11:24
After the deposition of Menelaus in 163 and no later than the peace of Antiochus V (January 5 or March 5, 162)	Antiochus V appoints the pious Alcimus as the new high priest, thus winning some pious Jews away from the rebellion. The neglected Oniad heir to the high priesthood then or soon after leaves Judaea for Ptolemaic Egypt, where some years later he establishes a Jewish temple at Leontopolis.	J. AJ xii 9.7.386–88; cf. II 14:3
28 Shebaṭ, 162 (January 5, if by the defective calendar, or March 5, if by the fully intercalated calendar)[37]	Lysias and Antiochus V withdraw with their army from Jerusalem in order to crush the rebel regime of the minister Philip at Antioch.[38] Antiochus V makes full peace with the Jews. The Hasmonaean party appears to have held aloof from the agreements. Before departing, Antiochus sees to the demolition of the wall around the temple mount.	I 6:55–63; II 11:22–26; 13:23–26
Early autumn, 162	Demetrius, son of Seleucus IV, having escaped from Rome where he had been serving as a hostage, lands at Tripolis and claims to be king. The troops at Antioch rally to Demetrius and kill Lysias and Antiochus V.	I 7:1–4; II 14:1–2
Shortly afterward	Demetrius I confirms Alcimus as high priest and in response to a petition presented by him sends Bacchides with an army to Judaea to stop the fighting among the Jews. (Alcimus has the support of many Pietists and of some Hellenizers, but the Hasmonaean party and others violently oppose him.) To restore order, Bacchides executes some troublemakers from both the pious and the apostate factions; he leaves Alcimus troops to protect him. The Hasmonaean party refuses to deal with Bacchides.	I 7:5–20; II 14:3–4

Dates (B.C.E.)	*Events*	*Sources*
	Judas leads violent opposition in countryside of Judaea to Alcimus' regime. Alcimus appeals to Demetrius I for additional help. Demetrius sends an army under Nicanor.	I 7:21–26; II 14:5–14
	After an indecisive skirmish at Dessa, Nicanor for a while has friendly relations with Judas, but Alcimus protests to the king, and Nicanor is ordered to capture Judas. Frustrated by what he viewed as non-cooperation by pious Jews, Nicanor threatens to destroy the temple after his coming victory over Judas. Horrified, the Jews pray.	I 7:27–38; II 14:15–36
	Faced with the prospect of being arrested by Nicanor's troops, the pious elder of Jerusalem, Razis, gives an inspiring example of courage and faith through his theatrical suicide.	II 14:37–46
13 Adar (March 8), 161[39]	Judas' army routs Nicanor's force in the battle of Adasa. Villagers of Judaea join in destroying the fugitives. The severed head and right hand of Nicanor are exposed within sight of the temple.	I 7:39–49; II 15:6–36
From some time after March 10 probably to some time before November 11, 161[40]	The national organs of the Jews, with the agreement of the Hasmonaean party, send an embassy to Rome which succeeds in establishing friendly relations, making a treaty of alliance, and having Rome warn Demetrius I not to oppress the Jews.	I 8; II 4:11
	Demetrius I sends a punitive expedition under Bacchides against the Jewish rebels. The troops massacre Jews at Messaloth-in-Arbela in Galilee.	I 9:1–2
Nisan (April 13 – May 11), 160	Bacchides' army reaches Jerusalem.	I 9:3
Shortly thereafter	Bacchides crushingly defeats the demoralized and shrunken Hasmonaean force at Elasa. Judas, brave to the end, falls. The surviving Hasmonaeans probably agree to cease resisting in return for the rights to take up and bury the dead and to go home in peace.	I 9:4–21
	(As narrated in source) >	I 9:23–53
Second month (May 2–30), 159	Alcimus tries to modify architecture of the temple court, an act regarded as impious by the Hasmonaean party. Before he can carry his project through, he dies of a stroke.	I 9:54–56
May, 159 – October, 152	The Seleucid government avoids provoking the anger of Jewish factions: it leaves the office of high priest vacant for seven years.[41]	I 9:57, 10:21 J. *AJ* xx 10.3.237
May, 159 – ca. May, 157	Bacchides leaves Judaea. Two years of quiet follow.	I 9:57

Dates (B.C.E.)	Events	Sources
	(As narrated in source) >	I 9:58–73
152, before October	Alexander Balas lays claim to Seleucid empire, in Ptolemais.	I 10:1
	(As narrated in source) >	I 10:2–20
October 23–30, 152	Jonathan becomes high priest, at festival of Tabernacles.	I 10:21
	Demetrius I tries unsuccessfully to win the Jews away from Jonathan and Alexander Balas by offering great privileges and concessions.	I 10:22–47
150, ca. midsummer	Demetrius I is killed in battle against Alexander Balas. Alexander reigns as sole Seleucid king.	I 10:48–50
150, ca. late summer	Alexander Balas marries Cleopatra Thea, daughter of Ptolemy VI, at Ptolemais. Jonathan at the festivities is treated with honor and is made governor of Judaea, to the dismay of his Jewish opponents.	I 10:51–66
147, probably after March 10	Demetrius II lands in Cilicia as pretender to the Seleucid throne.	I 10:67
145, probably in the spring[42]	(As narrated in source) >	I 10:68–89
145, probably late spring[42]	Ptolemy VI uses war of Alexander Balas and Demetrius II as a reason to send troops into his son-in-law's kingdom, perhaps at Alexander's request.[43] Jonathan as a completely loyal subject of Alexander respectfully escorts Ptolemy as far as the Eleutheros river and returns to Jerusalem.	I 11:1–7
	Ptolemy at Seleuceia-by-the-Sea chooses to back Demetrius II, for whatever reason. With Alexander away in Cilicia fighting Demetrius' partisans, Ptolemy is able to take Cleopatra Thea and give her in marriage to Demetrius. Ptolemy enters Antioch and is proclaimed king of the Seleucid empire. He makes Demetrius "vassal king" of the Seleucid realm.	
Midsummer, 145	Ptolemy VI defeats Alexander Balas in battle at the banks of the Oinoparas. Alexander flees to Arabs but is murdered. Ptolemy dies of wounds received in the battle. Demetrius II becomes sole Seleucid king and has the Ptolemaic garrisons massacred.	I 11:15–19
145, shortly after Demetrius II's accession as sole king	Jonathan besieges the Akra.	I 11:20
145, shortly after accession of Demetrius II as sole king	Anti-Hasmonaean Jews report Jonathan's siege of the Akra to Demetrius II. He summons Jonathan to Ptolemais. Jonathan displays his political strength by bringing with him	I 11:21–37

Dates (B.C.E.)	*Events*	*Sources*
	important Jews. In return for the lifting of the siege[44] and a promised payment of three hundred talents, Demetrius confirms Jonathan as high priest and governor and gives to Judaea three neighboring districts and also large reductions in taxation.	
145, soon thereafter	(As narrated in source) >	I 11:38–43
	Jonathan sends Demetrius II, hard-pressed in Antioch, a Jewish force of three thousand which plays a vital role in the king's victory over rebel soldiers and civilians there. Far from showing gratitude, Demetrius tries to curb so dangerously powerful a subject.	I 11:44–53
September, 145	The rebel officer Tryphon secures custody of Alexander Balas' little son, Antiochus VI, and proclaims him king of the Seleucid empire.	I 11:54–56
	Antiochus VI confirms Jonathan's powers and increases them, probably making him governor of Coele-Syria without Phoenicia.[45] Antiochus also adds another district to Judaea and makes Simon *stratêgos* of the coast from the Ladder of Tyre to the Egyptian border.	I 11:57–59
	(As narrated in source) >	I 11:60–66
	As commander for Antiochus VI, Jonathan astonishingly wins a nearly lost battle at Kedes against Demetrius' generals. The turning point comes when Jonathan prays.	I 11:67–74
143, probably summer[46]	Believing that God is with them, Jonathan and the Jews send an embassy to renew the friendly ties with Rome and Sparta.	I 12:1–23
	(As narrated in source) >	I 12:24–38
	Tryphon plots to eliminate the dangerously powerful Jonathan and lures him to come to Ptolemais with an inadequate bodyguard. There, the bodyguard is massacred and Jonathan is taken prisoner.	I 12:39–48
	(As narrated in source) >	I 12:49–53
	Simon rallies the Jews, who fear the hostility of Tryphon and their neighbors. Simon is accepted as commander in Jonathan's place. Simon raises army, finishes fortification projects, and sends a force which seizes Joppe and expels the inhabitants.	I 13:1–11
	(As narrated in source) >	I 13:12–20
143, late enough to allow a snowfall in Judaea	Tryphon attempts to relieve and reprovision the besieged Akra but is foiled by a snowstorm. He withdraws through the Galaaditis.	I 13:21–22
	Tryphon puts Jonathan to death at Baskama in the Galaaditis.	I 13:23

Dates (B.C.E.)	Events	Sources
November, 143	The Jews desert the regime headed by the tyrannical Tryphon and recognize Demetrius II as king over them.[47]	II 1:7
Late 143 or early 142, before some of the Jews recognize Simon as high priest[48]	Simon besieges and captures Gazara.	I 13:43–48; 14:7, 34
Late November or early December, 143	Jewish authorities of Jerusalem and Judaea send a letter to the Jews of Egypt asking them to observe the Feast of Dedication.	II 1:1, 7–9
Late 143 or before mid-142[49]	Simon's supporters proclaim him high priest, though some Jews refuse him recognition because the king has not ratified his appointment.[50]	I 14:35
142, before the consul's letter in response to Numenius' embassy (see next event)[51]	Antiochus VI dies, probably killed on orders of Tryphon. Tryphon claims to be king of the Seleucid empire.	I 13:31–32
142, after March 10[51]	Simon sends Numenius as ambassador to Rome to renew the ties of alliance. Numenius succeeds and receives a letter written by the consul Lucius Caecilius Metellus to all kingdoms and republics involved with the Jews, strongly supporting Simon's Judaea and asking them to extradite Jewish fugitives to Simon.[52]	I 14:24a–24k, 40
3 Tishri (?) (October 20), 142[53]	Demetrius II confirms Simon as high priest and grants Judaea virtual independence, including exemption from taxes. The Jews begin counting an era of their freedom.	I 13:34–42, 14:38–40
23 Second Month (June 3), 141	The inhabitants of the Akra ask for a truce and are expelled from Jerusalem. After ritual purification of the citadel, the Jews enter it in triumph.	I 13:49–52; 14:36
	Simon incorporates the Akra into the fortifications of the temple mount and resides there himself with his retinue.	I 13:52, 14:37
Between some time in 142 and late 141	The Parthian empire of Mithradates I captures Media and much of Babylonia.	(54)
Between October 6, 141, and September 25, 140	Demetrius II marches eastward to repel the Parthians.	I 14:1
18 Elul (September 13), 140	The Jews pass a decree honoring Simon and giving him and his heirs princely and high priestly power.	I 14:25–47

Dates (B.C.E.)	Events	Sources
Between September 25, 140, and October 14, 139[55]	The Parthians capture Demetrius II.	I 14:2–3
	The future Antiochus VII as pretender to the Seleucid throne sends Simon a letter offering honors and concessions.	I 15:1–9
Between October 15, 139, and October 4, 138	Antiochus VII lands at Seleucia and is proclaimed king.	I 15:10
	Tryphon flees to Dora, where Antiochus VII besieges him. Victorious Antiochus feels strong enough there to show hostility to Simon and sends Athenobius to demand satisfaction for the Jews' "aggression" against the Seleucid empire. Simon gives a firm reply and offers only a token payment.	I 15:10–36
	Tryphon escapes from Dora through Ptolemais and Orthosia only to be besieged in Apameia, where he perishes.	I 15:37–39
	Antiochus VII, while fighting Tryphon, sends Kendebaios to punish "rebellious" Judaea. Simon, old but still vigorous, organizes the counteroffensive but no longer takes command in combat. His sons, John and Judas, decisively defeat Kendebaios in battle.	I 15:38 – 16:10
Between January 27 and February 25, 134	Ptolemy, Simon's ambitious son-in-law, murders him and two of his sons at Jericho and sends assassins who fail to kill Simon's heir, John (Hyrcanus), at Gazara.	I 16:11–22
February, 134, to 104	John Hyrcanus reigns as prince and high priest of the Jews.	I 16:23–24; J. AJ xx 10.3.240
November or early December, 124	Jewish authorities of Jerusalem and Judaea send a letter to the Jews of Egypt, implicitly condemning the Oniad temple of Leontopolis and asking those Jews to observe the Feast of Dedication.[56]	II 1:1–9
103 to 76	Alexander Jannaeus reigns as high priest and king of the Jews. For part of his reign he relinquishes the title "king" for the more modest "prince."[57]	J. AJ xx 10.3–4.241–42 and coins
Probably November or early December, 103[58]	An Egyptian Jew opposed to the Oniad temple at Leontopolis forges and publishes a letter from the Jews of Jerusalem and Judaea, from the Council of Elders, and from Judas. The letter demonstrates the sanctity of the Jerusalem temple and its priesthood and the legitimacy of the Hasmonaean dynasty.	II 1:10 – 2:18

Dates (B.C.E.)	Events
In the reign of Alexander Jannaeus, while he renounced the title of king, and before 90[59]	First Maccabees is written and published as propaganda to justify the dynastic claims of Alexander Jannaeus.
Shortly thereafter	Jason of Cyrene publishes his history as a refutation of the dynastic propaganda, while respecting Judas Maccabaeus.[60]
By ca. 76[61]	The abridged history is published and Epistles 1 and 2 are attached to it.

[1] Parker and Dubberstein, p. 23.

[2] See commentary, NOTE on I 1:10.

[3] Pages 104–21.

[4] The date is derived from II 4:23, 13:1–8, and J. *AJ* xii 9.7.384–85 (see Appendix VI and, in AB vol. 41A, NOTE on II 4:7–38) and supported by the considerations in the introductory NOTE to I 1:16–19. See also below, n. 36.

[5] See pp. 111–21.

[6] Cf. Mørkholm, p. 68.

[7] See in AB vol. 41A NOTE on II 4:7–38 and above, n. 4.

[8] I shall demonstrate in my commentary on II 4:34 in AB vol. 41A how this date can be derived from Dan 9:26.

[9] See pp. 121–22.

[10] See NOTE on I 1:20. In my commentary on Daniel (to be published by Brill), I shall show in detail how Dan 9:26 supports this date.

[11] See pp. 122–23.

[12] See Mørkholm, pp. 93–94.

[13] See Part II, pp. 50–52, and see NOTE on I 1:29–40.

[14] See NOTE on I 1:29–40.

[15] See p. 42.

[16] See pp. 158–59.

[17] The first *act* of idolatry in the temple probably coincided with the first of these monthly sacrifices, on 25 Kislev (December 16), 167. See NOTE on I 1:54–59.

[18] See pp. 136–37.

[19] See p. 138.

[20] See Part I, pp. 17–19.

[21] There is a possibility that Philip's appeal came after the next event in our table, Antiochus IV's march eastward. Our author is probably mistaken in thinking that the financial strain of the Jewish revolt drove Antiochus to undertake the expedition (see introductory NOTE to I 3:27–37). Either order of events is compatible with II 8:8–9, 9:1–2.

[22] See NOTE on I 3:38.

[23] The chief minister would avoid a protracted campaign against stubborn rebels. He surely had political rivals who were dangerous to leave behind in Antioch. Hence the next event in our table, the negotiated peace, probably came not long after Lysias marched on Judaea. In his second expedition (I 6:28–54; II 13:1–22), Lysias could more easily afford a prolonged campaign, for with Lysias was the little king, far from the clutches of his political rivals. Because we cannot identify the month named at II 11:21, we cannot date the negotiations more narrowly.

[24] In our manuscripts the letter of the Romans (II 11:34–38) bears the same date as the letter of the coregent king (II 11:27–33). The coincidence need not be a scribal error. The Romans may indeed have been too late to help the Jews.

25 See NOTE on I 4:36–54.

26 See ibid.

27 I shall show in my commentary on II 10:1 that this is the probable meaning of Dan 11:24, end.

28 See introductory NOTE to I 5.

29 See NOTE on I 6:1–16.

30 See Part IV, p. 84.

31 For the present, see Part II, p. 43.

32 See introductory NOTE to I 5.

33 See NOTE on I 6:20.

34 See Part II, pp. 43–44.

35 See Part II, pp. 43–44. On Josephus' interpretation of references in Daniel and Jason of Cyrene to this time, see in AB vol. 41A commentary on II 13:3–8.

36 The sources are vague on the dates of Jason's and Menelaus' appointments to the high priesthood and of Menelaus' deposition. Nevertheless, Jason certainly became high priest after Antiochus IV's accession late in 175 B.C.E.; while in office Jason sent the annual taxes of Judaea to the royal treasury three times, at the earliest in 174, 173, and 172, probably in the autumn; and upon the last delivery of these taxes Menelaus became high priest. See II 4:23–24 and in AB vol. 41A NOTE on II 4:7–38. According to the largely reliable list of high priests (see Appendix VI), Menelaus served as high priest for at least nine years plus a fractional year (see Appendix VII). Thus, at the very earliest he was deposed in late autumn, 163. He certainly was deposed in the course of the campaign of Lysias and Antiochus V, which ended early in 162. The seer at Dan 11:24 predicted that the beginning or the end of the sabbatical year would bring Menelaus' deposition. See Part II, n. 28.

37 See NOTE on I 6:63.

38 Not the same man as the guardian appointed by Antiochus IV (I 6:14–15). See Part IV, p. 84.

39 See NOTE on I 7:43.

40 See on I 8:17–20. There is no way of being sure that the ambassadors succeeded in returning home before the stormy season.

41 See Appendix VI.

42 See NOTE on I 11:1–11, end.

43 See on I 11:1–11.

44 See on I 11:22–29.

45 See on I 11:59–62.

46 See on I 12:1–38, end.

47 See on I 13:34–42.

48 See on I 14:34–35.

49 Certainly before the fall of the Akra on June 3; see I 14:35–36.

50 See NOTE on I 13:34–42.

51 See on I 13:41 and 34–42.

52 See introductory NOTE to I 14:16–24k.

53 See NOTE on I 13:41.

54 See introductory NOTE to I 14:1–3.

55 See NOTE on I 12:39–40.

56 See Part I, p. 35.

57 See NOTE on I 8:14.

58 See Appendix III.

59 See Part IV, pp. 62–64.

60 See Part IV.

61 See Appendix IV.

VIII. THE WITNESSES TO THE TEXT

My translation of First Maccabees is based on the edition of Kappler,[1] and my translation of Second Maccabees is based on the edition of Hanhart.[2] All departures from the text of those editions are explained in the commentary. The editors in their introductions give good summaries of the problems[3] and of the symbols used to display the witnesses to the text. Since in the commentary I frequently discuss those problems and use those symbols, I must give a brief explanation here.

In the ancient world, where printing was unknown, every published book was copied by hand from an earlier copy. Even a good scribe made errors, and with multiple copying they became more abundant than modern typographical errors. Readers and publishers who cared would make the scribes or special correctors check a new copy against the earlier copy.

There were other threats to a correct transmission of our books, sometimes more dangerous than mere scribal blunders. Words as time went on changed in meaning, and the old shape of human institutions came to be forgotten. Thus, parts of the story became unintelligible to the scribes. Instead of faithfully copying what lay in front of him, a scribe who fancied himself intelligent might make lesser or greater changes in a misguided effort to make his text more intelligible.

The thrilling books of Maccabees were popular. From an early date there were many copies in circulation, widely varying in their readings. Pious and conscientious collectors often would have their own copies corrected on the basis of more than one earlier specimen. In the process errors might be eliminated, but errors and misguided changes might also be added from manuscript to manuscript. Thus the lines of the transmission of the text become very complicated.

---

[1] *Maccabaeorum liber I,* Septuaginta: Vetus Testamentum Graecum Auctoritate Societatis Litterarum Gottingensis, vol. IX, fasc. ɪ (Göttingen: Vandenhoeck & Ruprecht, 1936), ed. Werner Kappler.

[2] *Maccabaeorum liber II,* Septuaginta: Vetus Testamentum Graecum Auctoritate Societatis Litterarum Gottingensis, vol. IX, fasc. ɪɪ (Göttingen: Vandenhoeck & Ruprecht, 1959), ed. Robert Hanhart.

[3] See also Vernerus Kappler, *De memoria alterius libri Maccabaeorum,* Diss. Academia Georgia Augusta (Göttingen: Dieterich, 1929), and *Les anciennes traductions latines des Machabées,* Anecdota Maredsolana, vol. IV (Abbaye de Maredsous, 1932), ed. Donatien de Bruyne, Introduction.

Not even fragments have survived of the Hebrew original of First Maccabees.[4] All surviving witnesses to the text are based upon a Greek translation of the Hebrew, though Josephus[5] and the translator of the old Latin version[6] may have consulted a Hebrew text for a few good readings.

Even the author and his secretary could miswrite. Though there are many exceptions to the rule, in general the earlier the witness to the text, the freer from errors it is likely to be. Josephus used our books in the late first century c.e., long before our oldest surviving manuscripts were written. His allusions to Second Maccabees are few, but he followed the Greek text of First Maccabees very closely in writing his *Antiquities*. However, he was not a scribe but a historian, who sought to make sense of what seemed incomprehensible and sought to impress his readers by use of Greek more elegant than that in his source. Josephus was also a Jew writing to give a pagan audience a favorable impression of his nation. Accordingly, he paraphrases and alters, and can be used as a witness to the text only when good reasons support taking his version as faithful to the original.

There are a few quotations from our books in the works of Christian authors who wrote before the copying of our earliest surviving manuscripts. The quotations serve only to prove that the principal types of texts known from the manuscripts were known already to early Christian writers.[7]

The most important witnesses to the text are therefore the manuscripts of the Greek and the manuscripts of the early translations of the Greek into Latin, Syriac, and Armenian.

Down through the first half of the ninth century c.e., Greek literary manuscripts were written in the uncial script, a style resembling large capital letters. In the ninth century a new style of writing, the minuscule, emerges, using smaller and more varied letter forms. In the course of the tenth century the minuscule becomes and thereafter remains the prevalent style for literary manuscripts. The custom now is to designate uncials by letters of the alphabet and minuscules by Arabic numerals. An important group of minuscules may also be designated by a letter of the alphabet.

The uncials of our two books have no monopoly on the good or interesting readings. A special problem for our books (as for others in the Bible) is posed by the Lucianic recension, represented imperfectly but

---

[4] See Part I, pp. 15–16.

[5] See Part I, p. 14.

[6] See commentary, NOTE on I 11:39.

[7] See Kappler, pp. 12–13, 15, 21–22; Hanhart, pp. 11, 38, 44; de Bruyne, pp. xlix–lvii.

in its purest surviving form by the group of minuscules L (64 236 381 534 728) and still more imperfectly by the group l (19 62 93 542). Lucian, who was martyred in 311 or 312 C.E.[8] had access to a rather good text of our books, in First Maccabees one very close to the text which lay before Josephus. But Lucian was that dangerous kind of text transmitter who did not merely copy what he read but used his intelligence wrongly to "improve" on material he thought unintelligible or infelicitously expressed. A reader of a Lucianic text without some other aid has no way of telling what is a valuable old reading and what is a mere guess of Lucian's.[9]

Even the oldest Greek uncials of our books are young enough to have been influenced by Lucian's work, although there is no proof that they actually were. Even the oldest uncials are so far removed from the time of the authors that they are naturally full of scribal errors.

The following are the uncials:

A. The fifth-century *Codex Alexandrinus* of the Greek Bible, now in the British Museum.

S. The fourth-century *Codex Sinaiticus* containing parts of the Greek Bible, now in the British Museum. The text has been corrected by several hands. There is no proof that Lucian's "improvements" influenced the original reading in the manuscript (where S has an original reading in the presence of corrections, the original reading is indicated as S*). However, at least one of the correctors (the one designated as S[ca]) shows the influence of Lucian. Second Maccabees is lacking in S.

V. The eighth-century *Codex Venetus* of the Greek Old Testament. Though some scholars believe it shows Lucianic influence,[10] Kappler[11] and especially Hanhart[12] value it as an independent witness to the text of our books.

q. This symbol designates the one other important group of minuscules (29 71 74 98 107 120 130 134 243 731). Its origin is unknown, but it is free from Lucianic influence and may on occasion be the lone preserver of the correct text.

There are several ancient translations made from the Greek. Of these, the Latin (La) is most important, preserved in a series of manuscripts progressively conforming more and more to Lucianic and other extant Greek texts. However, the best Latin manuscripts, La[L] and La[X] and often also La[G] and even the so-called "Vulgate" La[V] show an interesting

---

[8] See Sidney Jellicoe, *The Septuagint and Modern Study* (Oxford: Clarendon Press, 1968), pp. 157–58.

[9] See Kappler, *De memoria*, pp. 33–54; Hanhart, pp. 18–23; and cf. Jellicoe, pp. 158–60, 168–71.

[10] See Jellicoe, p. 167.

[11] Page 30.

[12] Pages 16–17.

independence of our Greek manuscripts, the more interesting since quotations in Cyprian show that the old Latin as reflected by La^L and La^X existed already when he was writing, around 200 C.E.[13] There is evidence that the Latin translators may have consulted the Hebrew text and thus could have been Jews.[14] Even the best of the Latin manuscripts contains many scribal errors and mistakes in translation. Nevertheless, the Latin translation existed before the work of Lucian. It may be impossible to prove that the best Latin manuscripts are utterly free from Lucianic influence. Nevertheless, a case of agreement between L or l or both and the best Latin manuscripts often proves to give the most likely original meaning intended by our author, so often as to suggest that La^L and La^X are indeed practically free from Lucianic influence and can serve as a key for discerning between the good readings of the text which lay before Lucian and Lucian's misguided "improvements."[15]

The Syriac version (Sy) is represented by de Lagarde's edition (SyI),[16] by Ceriani's photographic reproduction of a manuscript (SyII)[17] not used by de Lagarde, and by the text of the London polyglot Bible of 1657.[18] It was made from a Lucianic text. Its chief value lies in showing how the speaker of a Semitic language would have expressed the thought and how he recognized the proper names, thus leading us sometimes to a reconstruction of the original Hebrew.

The Armenian (Arm) has been insufficiently studied by scholars writing in languages accessible to me. Hanhart, who appears to have used it thoroughly for Second Maccabees, reports[19] that, though very free, it is usually close to the Latin and has value chiefly in confirming La, and particularly in cases where the best Latin manuscripts agree with the Lucianic recension.

With so complicated a situation, the historian and the textual editor cannot lay down rules to be followed mechanically. He must weigh the evidence of the witnesses according to the above principles and then consider historical probability, always bearing in mind that only our ignorance leads us to consider many possibilities as improbable.

---

[13] See de Bruyne, pp. xii–li.

[14] See NOTE on I 11:39.

[15] So Hanhart, pp. 27–29.

[16] *Libri Veteris Testamenti Apocryphi Syriace,* ed. Paul A. de Lagarde, Lipsiae: Brockhaus, 1861.

[17] *Translatio Pescitto Veteris Testamenti,* ed. A. M. Ceriani, 2 vols., Mediolani: Pogliani, 1876–83.

[18] *Biblia sacra polyglotta,* ed. Brian Walton, 6 vols., London, 1655–57.

[19] Page 31.

Signs and Abbreviations Used in Giving the Witnesses to the Text of First Maccabees

Uncials:

> A S V
> S*:   Original reading of S, later corrected (rightly or wrongly)
> S^c: Reading of a corrector of S
> S^{ca}:   One of the correctors of S; see Kappler's edition, p. 7

Minuscules:

> 19 29 46 52 55 56 58
> 62 64 68 71 74 93 98
> 106 107 120 130 134 236 243
> 311 340 379 381 534 542 671
> 728 731 771

Groups of minuscules:

> q: 29 71 74 98 107 120 130 134 243
> L: 64 236 381 534 728
> l: 19 62 93 542
> L'=L+l

Ancient translations:

> La: Old Latin, with the letters used by de Bruyne to designate the manuscripts written as superscripts to the right (La^L, La^X, etc.)
> Sy: Syriac
> SyI: Syriac text in *Libri Veteris Testamenti Apocryphi Syriace,* ed. Paul Anton de Lagarde
> SyII: Syriac text in *Translatio Syra Pescitto Veteris Testamenti,* ed. A. M. Ceriani
> SyIII: Syriac text in *Biblia sacra polyglotta,* ed. Brian Walton

Quotations in early Christian authors:

> Lucifer: Quotations from First Maccabees in the works of Lucifer of Cagliari as presented by Donatien de Bruyne in his edition of *Les anciennes traductions latines des Machabées,* pp. li–lii.

L^{-64} or q^{-29}, etc.: The entire group L except for 64, or the entire group q except for 29, etc.

(   ): Parentheses surround a witness which possibly but not certainly supports the reading under discussion.

SELECTED BIBLIOGRAPHY

No attempt has been made to present a comprehensive bibliography. The following is a selected list of works frequently cited or used by the author.

A. THE GREEK TEXT AND THE ANCIENT VERSIONS OF FIRST AND SECOND MACCABEES

See notes to Introduction, Part VIII.

B. COMMENTARIES AND TRANSLATIONS

Abel, F.-M. *Les livres des Maccabées.* Paris: Gabalda, 1949.

―――― and Jean Starcky. *Les Livres des Maccabées.* Paris: Éditions du Cerf, 1961.

Grimm, Carl L. W. *Das erste Buch der Maccabäer,* Dritte Lieferung of *Kurzgefasstes exegetisches Handbuch zu den Apokryphen des Alten Testaments,* ed. O. F. Fritsche. Leipzig: S. Hirzel, 1853.

Kahana, Abraham. *Ha-sefarim ha-ḥitzonim,* vol. II. Tel-Aviv: Hozaath M'qoroth, 1936–37. Pages 72–231.

The New English Bible: The Apocrypha. Oxford University Press and Cambridge University Press, 1970.

C. OTHER WORKS

Abel, F.-M. *Géographie de la Palestine.* Paris: Gabalda, 1933–38.

―――― *Grammaire du grec biblique.* Paris: Gabalda, 1927.

―――― "Topographie des campagnes machabéennes (Suite)," RB 33 (1924), 201—17, 371–87; 34 (1925), 194–216; 35 (1926), 206–22, 510–34.

Accame, Silvio. *Il dominio romano in Grecia dalla guerra acaica ad Augusto.* Roma: Angelo Signorelli, 1946.

Adcock, F. E. *The Greek and Macedonian Art of War.* University of California Press, 1967.

Albeck, Hanoch, ed. *Shishah sidre Mishnah.* Jerusalem and Tel-Aviv: Bialik Institute and Dvir, 1952–59.

Albright, William Foxwell. *Yahweh and the Gods of Canaan.* Garden City, N.Y.: Doubleday, 1968. *Cited as* YGC.

Alon, Gedaliahu. *Meḥqarim be-toledot Yisrael.* Tel-Aviv: Hakibutz Hameuchad, 1957–58.

Aquila. *See* Origenes.

Avi-Yonah, Michael. *The Holy Land.* Grand Rapids, Mich.: Baker Book House, 1966.

Badian, E. *Foreign Clientelae.* Oxford: Clarendon Press, 1958.

Baron, Salo W. *A Social and Religious History of the Jews,* 2d ed., rev. and enl. Columbia University Press, 1952– .

Baudissin, Wolf Wilhelm Graf. *Adonis und Esmun.* Leipzig: Hinrichs, 1911.

Bauer, Walter. *Wörterbuch zum Neuen Testament.* 5th ed. Berlin: Töpelmann, 1958.

Bengtson, Hermann. *Griechische Geschichte.* 4th ed. München: Beck, 1969.

―――― *Römische Geschichte.* München: Beck, 1967.

—————— *Die Strategie in der hellenistischen Zeit.* München: Beck, 1937–52.

Bergsträsser, Gotthelf. *Herbräische Grammatik.* Leipzig: Hinrichs, 1918–29.

Bevan, Edwyn Robert. *The House of Seleucus.* London: Arnold, 1902.

Bickerman, Elias J. *Chronology of the Ancient World.* Cornell University Press, 1968.

—————— "Un document relatif à la persécution d'Antiochos IV Épiphane," RHR 115 (1937), 188–223.

—————— *Four Strange Books of the Bible.* New York: Schocken, 1967.

—————— *Der Gott der Makkabäer.* Berlin: Schocken, 1937.

—————— "Héliodore au temple de Jérusalem," AIPHOS 7 (1939–44), 5–40.

—————— *Institutions de Séleucides.* Paris: Geuthner, 1938.

—————— "Ein jüdischer Festbrief vom Jahre 124 v. Chr.," ZNW 32 (1933), 233–54.

—————— "Makkabäerbücher, PW, XIV (1930), 779–800.

—————— "Une question d'authenticité: Les privilèges juifs," AIPHOS 13 (1953), 11–34.

—————— "Ritualmord und Eselskult," MGWJ 72 (1927), 171–264.

—————— "Sur une inscription grecque de Sidon," *Mélanges syriens offerts à M. René Dussaud,* vol. I. Paris: Geuthner, 1939. Pages 91–99.

Broughton, T. R. S. *The Magistrates of the Roman Republic.* New York: American Philological Association, 1951–52.

Bruhl, Adrien. *Liber Pater,* BEFAR, vol. CLXV. Paris: É. de Boccard, 1953.

Busolt, G. and H. Swoboda. *Griechische Staatskunde.* München: Beck, 1920–26.

Charles, R. H., ed. *The Apocrypha and Pseudepigrapha of the Old Testament.* Oxford: Clarendon Press, 1913. *Cited as* APOT.

Cook, Stanley A. *The Religion of Ancient Palestine in the Light of Archaeology.* London: Oxford University Press, 1930.

Corpus Papyrorum Judaicarum. Eds. Victor A. Tcherikover and Alexander Fuks. Harvard University Press, 1957–64.

Cowley, Abraham. *Aramaic Papyri of the Fifth Century B.C.* Oxford: Clarendon Press, 1923.

Cross, Frank Moore. *The Ancient Library of Qumran.* Garden City, N.Y.: Doubleday, 1961. *Cited as* ALQ.

Dictionnaire de la Bible. Eds. F. Vigouroux et al. Paris: Letouzey, 1912– .

Diodorus Siculus, vols. X–XII. Edited with an English translation by Russel M. Geer and F. R. Walton. The Loeb Classical Library. Harvard University Press, 1954–67.

Du Mesnil du Buisson, Robert. *Études sur les dieux phéniciennes hérités par l'Empire romain.* Leiden: Brill, 1970.

—————— "Origine et évolution du panthéon de Tyr," RHR 164 (1963), 133–63.

Dussaud, René. *La pénétration des Arabes en Syrie avant l'Islam.* Paris: Geuthner, 1955.

Eddy, Samuel K. *The King Is Dead.* University of Nebraska Press, 1961.

Eissfeldt, Otto. *The Old Testament: An Introduction.* New York and Evanston: Harper & Row, 1965.

Encyclopaedia of Archaeological Excavations in the Holy Land. Jerusalem: Israel Exploration Society and Massada, 1970 (in Hebrew).

Enoch=I Enoch. See Charles, APOT.

Ettelson, Harry W. "The Integrity of I Maccabees," TCAAS 27 (1925), 249–384.

Festugière, André-Jean. "Ce que Tite-Live nous apprend sur les mystères de Dionysos," École française de Rome: Mélanges d'archéologie et d'histoire 65 (1954), 79–99.

Fischer, Thomas. Untersuchungen zum Partherkrieg Antiochos' VII. Diss. Tübingen. Order from author, Tübingen-Derendingen, Heinlenstrasse 28. 1970.

——— "Zu Tryphon," Chiron 2 (München, 1972), 201–13.

Galling, Kurt. Der Altar in den Kulturen des alten Orients. Berlin: Curtius, 1925.

Gardner, Percy. Catalogue of Greek Coins: The Seleucid Kings of Syria. Bologna: Forni, 1963.

Geiger, Abraham. Urschrift und Übersetzungen der Bibel, 2d ed. Frankfurt am Main: Verlag Madda, 1928.

Gesenius' Hebrew Grammar. Edited and revised by E. Kautzsch. Second English edition, revised by A. E. Cowley. Oxford: Clarendon Press, 1910. Cited as GKC.

Ginsberg, H. Louis. Studies in Daniel. New York: Jewish Theological Seminary of America, 1948.

Ginzberg, Louis. The Legends of the Jews. Philadelphia: Jewish Publication Society of America, 1909–38.

Goldstein, Jonathan A. "The Tales of the Tobiads," Studies Smith, Part III, pp. 85–123.

——— "The Testament of Moses: Its Content, Its Origin, and Its Attestation in Josephus," Studies on the Testament of Moses, ed. George W. E. Nickelsburg, Jr. Septuagint and Cognate Studies, No. 4. Cambridge, Mass.: Society of Biblical Literature, 1973. Pages 44–52.

Hanhart, Robert. Untersuchungen. See Jepsen.

Hatch, Edwin, and Henry A. Redpath. A Concordance to the Septuagint and the Other Greek Versions of the Old Testament (Including the Apocryphal Books). Graz: Akademische Druck- u. Verlagsanstalt, 1954.

Head, Barclay V. Historia Numorum. Chicago: Argonaut, 1967.

Hengel, Martin. Judentum und Hellenismus. Tübingen: Mohr (Siebeck), 1969.

Heuss, Alfred. "Abschluss und Beurkundung des griechischen und römischen Staatsvertrages," Klio 27 (1934), 14–53, 218–57.

——— Die völkerrechtlichen Grundlagen der römischen Aussenpolitik in republikanischer Zeit. Klio, Beiheft XXXI. Leipzig: Dieterich, 1933.

Hill, George F. Catalogue of the Greek Coins of Palestine. Bologna: Forni, 1965.

Holleaux, Maurice. Études d'épigraphie et d'histoire grecques, vol. III. Paris: E. de Boccard, 1942.

Jastrow, Marcus. A Dictionary of the Targumim, the Talmud Babli and Yerushalmi, and the Midrashic Literature. New York: Putnam, 1903.

Jastrow, Morris. *The Religion of Babylonia and Assyria.* Boston: Athenaeum Press, 1898.

Jeanmaire, Henri. *Dionysos.* Paris: Payot, 1951.

Jepsen, Alfred, and Robert Hanhart. *Untersuchungen zur israelitisch-jüdischen Chronologie.* BZAW, vol. 88. Berlin: Töpelman, 1964.

Jones, A. H. M. *Sparta.* Harvard University Press, 1967.

Josephus. *Flavii Iosephi Opera.* Ed. Benedictus Niese. Berlin: Weidmann, 1887–95.

———— Josephus, vols. I–IX. Edited with an English translation by H. St. John Thackeray, Ralph Marcus, Allen Wikgren, and Louis H. Feldman. The Loeb Classical Library. Harvard University Press, 1926–65.

Kadman, Leo. *The Coins of Akko Ptolemais.* Corpus Nummorum Palaestinensium, I Series, vol. IV. Jerusalem: Schocken, 1961.

Kenyon, Kathleen. *Jerusalem.* New York: McGraw-Hill, 1967.

kleine Pauly, Der. Eds. Konrat Ziegler and Walther Sontheimer. Stuttgart: Druckenmüller, 1964– .

Klose, Peter. *Die völkerrechtliche Ordnung der hellenistischen Staatenwelt in der Zeit von 280 bis 168 v. Chr.* München: Beck, 1972.

Kolbe, Walther. *Beiträge zur syrischen und jüdischen Geschichte.* Beiträge zur Wissenschaft vom Alten Testament, ed. Rudolf Kittel, N.S., vol. X. Stuttgart: W. Kohlhammer, 1926.

Kromayer, Johannes, and Georg Veith. *Heerwesen und Kriegführung der Griechen und Römer.* München: Beck, 1928.

Kutscher, Eduard Yehezkel. *The Language and Linguistic Background of the Isaiah Scroll.* Leiden: Brill, 1974.

Laqueur, R. "Griechische Urkunden in der jüdisch-hellenistischen Literatur," *Historische Zeitschrift* 136 (1927), 229–52.

Latte, Kurt. *Römische Religionsgeschichte.* München: Beck, 1960.

Launey, Marcel. *Recherches sur les armées hellénistiques.* Paris: E. de Boccard, 1950.

Le Rider, Georges. *Suse sous les Séleucides et les Parthes.* Mémoires de la Mission archéologique en Iran," tome XXXVIII. Paris: Geuthner, 1965.

Lichtenstein, Hans. "Die Fastenrolle," HUCA 8–9 (1931–32), 257–351.

Lieberman, Saul. *Hellenism in Jewish Palestine.* New York: The Jewish Theological Seminary of America, 1950.

———— Ed. *The Tosefta. See Tosefta.*

———— *Tosefta Ki-fshuṭah.* New York: Jewish Theological Seminary of America, 1955– .

Lurie, Ben-Zion. *Megillath Ta'anith.* Jerusalem: Bialik Institute, 1964.

Magie, David. *Roman Rule in Asia Minor.* Princeton University Press, 1950.

Marcus, Ralph. *See* Josephus.

Mayser, Edwin. *Grammatik der griechischen Papyri aus der Ptolemäerzeit.* Berlin and Leipzig: de Gruyter, 1938–70.

Megillat Ta'anit. See Lichtenstein.

Meshorer, Ya'akov. *Jewish Coins of the Second Temple Period.* Chicago: Argonaut, 1967.

Meyer, Eduard. *Ursprung und Anfänge des Christentums.* Stuttgart and Berlin: Cotta, 1921–23.

Mishnah. *See* Albeck.

Montgomery, James A. *A Critical and Exegetical Commentary on the Book of Daniel.* New York: Scribner, 1927.

Moreau, J., ed. *Lactance: De la mort des persécuteurs,* Sources chrétiennes, no. 39, 2 vols. Paris: Éditions du Cerf, 1954.

Mørkholm, Otto. *Antiochus IV of Syria.* ("Classica et Mediaevalia, Dissertationes," VIII.) København: Gyldendalske Boghandel, 1966.

―――― *Studies in the Coinage of Antiochus IV of Syria.* Historisk-filosofiske Meddelelser udgivet af Det Kongelige Danske Videnskabernes Selskab, Bind 40, nr. 3, 1963.

Moscati, Sabatino. *The World of the Phoenicians.* New York: Praeger, 1968.

Musil, Alois. *Arabia Petraea, III: Ethnologischer Reisebericht.* Wien: Kaiserliche Akademie der Wissenschaften, 1908.

Nickelsburg, George. *Resurrection, Immortality, and Eternal Life in Intertestamental Judaism.* HTS, XXVI. Harvard University Press, 1972.

Niese, Benedictus. *Kritik der beiden Makkabäerbücher.* Berlin: Weidmann, 1900. (=*Hermes* 35 [1900], 268–307, 453–527.)

Nilsson, Martin P. *The Dionysiac Mysteries of the Hellenistic and Roman Age.* Lund: Gleerup, 1957.

―――― *Geschichte der griechischen Religion,* II, 2d ed. München: Beck, 1961.

Origenes. *Origenis Hexaplorum quae supersunt.* Ed. Fridericus Field. Hildesheim: Olms, 1964.

Otto, Walter. *Zur Geschichte der Zeit des 6. Ptolemäers.* Abhandlungen der Bayerischen Akademie der Wissenschaften, Philosophische philologische und historische Klasse. N.F., Heft XI. München: Beck, 1934.

―――― and H. Bengtson. *Zur Geschichte des Niederganges des Ptolemäerreiches.* ABAW (see preceding entry), N.F., Heft XVII. München: Beck, 1938.

Oxford Classical Dictionary. Eds. N. G. L. Hammond and H. H. Scullard. 2d ed. Oxford: Clarendon Press, 1970.

Parker, R. A. and W. H. Dubberstein. *Babylonian Chronology, 626 B.C.– A.D. 75.* Brown University Press, 1956.

Polybius. *Polybii Historiae.* Ed. Theodorus Büttner-Wobst. Leipzig: Teubner, 1882–1904.

―――― *The Histories.* Edited with an English translation by W. R. Paton. The Loeb Classical Library. New York: Putnam, 1922–27.

Porten, Bezalel. *Archives from Elephantine.* University of California Press, 1968.

Préaux, Claire. *L'économie royale des Lagides.* Bruxelles: Fondation égyptologique Reine Élisabeth, 1939.

Pritchard, James B. *Ancient Near Eastern Texts.* 2d ed. Princeton University Press, 1955. *Cited as* ANET².

Roscher, W. H., ed. *Ausführliches Lexikon der griechischen und römischen Mythologie.* Leipzig: Teubner, 1897–1937.

Rostovtzeff, M. I. *The Social And Economic History of the Hellenistic World.* 2d ed. Oxford: Clarendon Press, 1952. *Cited as* SEHHW.

Sachs, A. J., and D. J. Wiseman. "A Babylonian King List of the Hellenistic Period," *Iraq* 16 (1954), 202–12.

Salmon, Edward T. *Roman Colonization under the Republic.* London: Thames & Hudson, 1969.

Samuel, Alan E. *Ptolemaic Chronology.* München: Beck, 1962.

Schaumberger, J. "Die neue Seleukiden-Liste BM 35603 und die makkabäische Chronologie," *Biblica* 36 (1955), 423–28.

Scholia to Megillat Ta'anit. See Lichtenstein.

Schürer, Emil. *Geschichte des jüdischen Volkes im Zeitalter Jesu Christi.* 4th ed. Leipzig: Hinrichs, 1901–11.

——— *The History of the Jewish People in the Age of Jesus Christ.* New English version, revised and edited by Geza Vermes and Fergus Millar. Edinburgh: T. & T. Clark, 1973– .

Seder 'olam rabbah=Midrash seder 'olam. Ed. Ber Ratner. New York: Talmudical Research Institute, 1966.

Sepher Yerushalayim. Ed. M. Avi-Yonah. Tel-Aviv: Bialik Institute, 1956.

Seyrig, Henri. *Antiquités syriennes,* vol. V. Paris: Geuthner, 1958.

——— *Notes on Syrian Coins.* Numismatic Notes and Monographs, no. 119. New York: American Numismatic Society, 1950.

Sherk, Robert K. *Roman Documents from the Greek East.* Johns Hopkins University Press, 1969.

Sherwin-White, Adrian N. *The Roman Citizenship.* Oxford: Clarendon Press, 1939.

Sordi, Marta. "Il valore politica del trattato fra i Romani e i Giudei nel 161 a.C.," *Acme,* vol. V (1950), fasc. III, pp. 509–19.

Stern, Menahem. *The Documents on the History of the Hasmonaean Revolt.* Tel-Aviv: Hakibbutz Hameuchad, 1965 (in Hebrew).

——— "The Relations between Judea and Rome during the Rule of John Hyrcanus," *Zion* 26 (1961), 1–22 (in Hebrew).

Symmachus. *See* Origenes.

Täubler, Eugen. *Imperium Romanum.* Leipzig and Berlin: Teubner, 1913.

Tcherikover, Victor A. *Hellenistic Civilization and the Jews.* Philadelphia: Jewish Publication Society, 1959.

Testament of Moses=Assumption of Moses. *See* Charles, APOT.

Thackeray, Henry St. John. *A Grammar of the Old Testament in Greek.* Cambridge: at the University Press, 1909.

——— *Josephus: The Man and the Historian.* New York: Jewish Institute of Religion Press, 1929.

Theodotion. *See* Origenes.

Tosefta, The. Ed. Saul Lieberman. New York: Jewish Theological Seminary, 1955– .

——— *=Tosephta.* Ed. M. S. Zuckermandel, 2d ed. Jerusalem: Bamberger & Wahrmann, 1937.

Vincent, L. Hugues, and M. A. Steve. *Jérusalem de l'Ancien testament.* Paris: Gabalda, 1954–56.

Volkmann, Hans. "Demetrios I. und Alexander I. von Syrien," *Klio* 19 (1925), 373–412.

Welles, C. Bradford. *Royal Correspondence in the Hellenistic Period.* Yale University Press, 1934.

Will, Édouard. *Histoire du monde hellénistique.* Nancy: Faculté des lettres et des sciences humaines, 1966–67.

Wright, G. Ernest, ed. *The Bible and the Ancient Near East: Essays in Honor of William Foxwell Albright.* Garden City, N.Y.: Doubleday, 1961. *Cited as* BANE.

TRANSLATION
and
NOTES

I. THE HELLENISTIC EMPIRE FROM ALEXANDER TO ANTIOCHUS IV
(1:1–10)

1 [1] [This is a history of events which began in the era of the Hellenistic dynasty. The dynasty had its origins][a] in the time of Alexander son of Philip, the Macedonian. This Alexander marched out from the land of Chetiim, smote . . .[b] and smote Darius, king of the Persians and the Medes, and became king in his place and thus the first to rule over the Hellenistic empire. [2] Thereupon he waged many campaigns, conquering strongholds and slaying kings of the earth [3] until he reached the farthest point of the earth. He despoiled many nations, until the world lay quiet under his rule. Becoming proud and haughty, [4] he raised a very strong army and with it ruled over provinces, nations, and dynasts, all of whom paid him tribute. [5] Then, falling ill, he recognized that he was dying. [6] He summoned his high officers, men who had been raised with him from early childhood, and divided his kingdom among them while he was still alive. [7] So died Alexander after a reign of twelve years. [8] His officers then took power, each in his own territory. [9] They all assumed royal diadems after his death, and their descendants continued to succeed them for many years and brought much evil upon the world.

[10] A wicked shoot sprouted from this stock, Antiochus Epiphanes, son of King Antiochus. This Antiochus Epiphanes, after having been a hostage in Rome, became king in the year 137 of the Hellenistic dynasty.

[a] See introductory NOTE on vss. 1–10.
[b] Same as [a], above.

NOTES

1:1–10, introductory NOTE. On the propagandistic purpose of this passage, see Introduction, Part IV, pp. 72–73.

1:1–10 is an outstandingly long example of a scene-setting sentence, a construction found at the beginning of a work and also at important points of transition in biblical and apocryphal books that were written in Hebrew. Into a scene-setting sentence a Hebrew author sought to pack all the information needed to make the opening stages of his narrative or discourse understandable. The packing of information here and elsewhere can make the sentence look overloaded. A scene-setting sentence can introduce important characters, as I Sam 1:1–3 introduces Elkanah and his wives and Gen 5:1–2 introduces Adam or Man. The sentence may give the occasion for a discourse or set of discourses, as do Jer 1:1–3 and 34:8–11. The sentence may explain the location and the significance of the place of the events or utterances; such was the probable meaning of the original text of Deut 1:1–4, setting the scene "on the other side of the Jordan" at the important spot of Israel's last encampment there, after the defeat of Sihon and Og and before entering the promised land. On the problems of the extant text of Deut 1:1–4, see Gerhard von Rad, *Deuteronomy: A Commentary* (Philadelphia: Westminster Press, 1966), pp. 36–37. Furthermore, a scene-setting sentence can fix the time or occasion of events, rendering precise which king's reign or which era or time sequence is being used to date the opening events, as we find at Esther 1:1; Judith 1:1–4, and here (and perhaps at II Sam 1:1–2).

Nothing prevents a scene-setting sentence from fulfilling several of these functions simultaneously. The overloading characteristic of a long rambling scene-setting sentence can make it difficult for the reader to grasp the point. The Hebrew stylists had a device to get around the difficulty. In the first sentence of the narrative or discourse proper, after the end of the scene-setting sentence, they would repeat, either directly or by use of pronominal expressions, the persons, things, places, times which were the main points of the scene-setting sentence. Thus, in Gen 5:3, "Adam" echoes the name in Gen 5:1; and in I Sam 1:4, "Elkanah" echoes I Sam 1:1; in Deut 1:5, "on the other side of the Jordan" echoes Deut 1:1; in Esther 1:2 and Judith 1:5 and here in 1:11, "in those days" echoes the dating formulas given in Esther 1:1, Judith 1:1–4, and here in 1:1–10.

In 1:11, the first sentence of the narrative proper, the only element repeated from the scene-setting sentence 1:1–10 is the time, "in those days." Hence, the main point of 1:1–10 must be to make clear the dating formula, just as the parallels in Esther and Judith make clear which king it is whose regnal years give the date. Apart from length, our passage differs from those in Esther and Judith only in using a dynastic era instead of regnal years.

In Hebrew there are at least two formulas for beginning a scene-setting sentence. The sentence may begin, as it does here and at Esther 1:1; I Sam 1:1; Ezek 1:1, and perhaps in the Hebrew original of Judith 1:1, with "And it came to pass" (*wayhī*). Alternatively, the sentence may begin with a demonstrative expression, "This is . . ." or "These are . . . ," as at Deut 1:1; Gen 5:1, 25:19. Sometimes the demonstrative pronoun is omitted as superfluous, as at Hosea 1:1 and Jer 1:1, "[These are] the words. . . ." The use of one formula rather than the other was probably a matter of taste. The book of Jeremiah begins with one, the book of Ezekiel with the other. But Jeremiah could as easily have begun, "And it came to pass in the days of Josiah . . . that the word of the Lord came to Jeremiah son of Hilkiah, etc.," and Ezekiel could as easily have begun, "The word [or "The vision"] of the Lord which came to Ezekiel."

In our long scene-setting sentence, the "after" of 1:1 governs all the verbs through "became king" in 1:10. A literal translation would be extremely cumbersome and would not show that the passage is explaining the date formula of 1:11 in addition to setting the scene. We would have, "And it came to pass, after Alexander . . . smote Darius . . . and then, falling ill, he recognized he was dying . . . and his officers took power . . . and their descendants continued to succeed them for many years . . . and . . . Antiochus Epiphanes . . . became king in the year 137 of the Hellenistic dynasty." A key to a clearer translation lies in the alternative Hebrew formula for a scene-setting sentence. Esther 1:1 in this manner would become, "This is the history of events which occurred in the reign of Ahasuerus. This Ahasuerus reigned over. . . ." Our translation of 1:1–10 proceeds in the same manner.

1–9. "Marched out from the land of Chetiim" and "brought much evil upon the world" may be allusions to Num 24:24. Our author then would have seen Alexander and his successors as fulfilling the prophesy of Balaam in that verse (but see Introduction, pp. 72–73). If so, our author's care to identify Alexander the Great as "son of Philip, the Macedonian" may be a hint that another Alexander, Jannaeus the Hasmonaean, is going to fulfill Balaam's prophesy of the star from Jacob who is destined to smash all children of Seth (Num 24:17) by establishing an Israelite empire; see Introduction, Part IV. This prophesy of Balaam may be reflected in the star-anchor coins of Alexander Jannaeus (Meshorer, *Jewish Coins,* p. 18, nos. 8–11). Since Balaam does not call the star a king, our author could make such audacious claims for Jannaeus even during the period when Jannaeus renounced the royal title (see NOTE on 8:14).

1. [*This . . . origins*]. See introductory NOTE on vss. 1–10. On "Hellenistic dynasty," see vs. 10, and the following NOTES here on *Alexander . . . Chetiim* and *and thus . . . empire.*

Alexander . . . Chetiim. Alexander set out from his capital at Pella, Macedonia, on his great adventure of conquest in the spring of 334 B.C.E. Originally the name *Chetiim* or *Kittim* referred to Kition on Cyprus or to the whole island of Cyprus, but by 165, the time of the seer of Dan 11:30 (see Introduction, p. 42), it referred to the islands and most of the coastlands of the Mediterranean and could be used to designate Rome; see J. *AJ* i 6.1.128 and S. Loewenstamm, *"Kittim,"* Enc. Bib., IV (1962), 394–95 (in

Hebrew). The extension of the meaning may well have resulted from efforts such as Dan 11:30 to interpret the obscure prophesy at Num 24:24, but Jeremiah (2:10) already uses *Kittim* as a word for the distant west.

The normal word in Hebrew for Greece, including Macedonia, was *Yawan,* but our author and his contemporaries, except in contexts where no confusion was possible, had to seek other Hebrew names for "Greek" or "Macedonian," because for them *Yawan* was the Seleucid empire (e.g. vss. 1 and 10 here; Dan 8:21, 10:20; 4Q169, in *Qumran Cave 4,* ed. John M. Allegro, with A. A. Anderson, DJD, V (1968), 38; CD 8:11; *M. Giṭṭin* 8:5; and probably also Zech 9:13). See C. C. Torrey, "'*Yāwān'* and '*Hellas'* as Designations of the Seleucid Empire," JAOS 25 (1904), 302–11.

The plural *"Chetiim"* was a good alternative name for "Greeks" and was so used by the Essenes of Qumran (1QM 1:2, 4, 6, 9, 12; 16:2, 6, 8, 9, etc.; 1QpHab *passim*). This is not the place to discuss the vexed problems of the use of the name in Qumran texts. See Loewenstamm, Enc. Bib., IV (1962), 396–98. Our author knew enough to distinguish Macedonians from Greeks. He could even use the foreign word "Macedonian" to describe Alexander, but he preferred to use words naturalized in Hebrew. Hence, at 8:5–9, where he averts confusion by calling the Seleucid realm "Asia," so that he can call Hellenic Greece *Yawan,* he uses *Kittiim* for "Macedonians." Perhaps for him *Kittiim* had only that meaning.

smote . . . place. It is not surprising to find a gap in the text after the first "smote." Ancient books were written on scrolls, the beginnings and ends of which suffered severely from pulling and friction. The few missing words probably referred to the armed forces of the Persian empire. In late spring 334 Alexander defeated an army commanded by satraps at the Granicus and in autumn 333 one commanded by King Darius III himself at Issus (NW and SE Asia Minor, respectively). Darius escaped and still had great military resources, but in the immediate aftermath of the battle Alexander claimed to be king of Asia. Thereafter, he took Tyre in the summer of 332, after an arduous siege, and Gaza in the autumn, after a siege of two months, before overrunning Egypt unopposed. In early autumn 331, Alexander defeated at Gaugamela (N Iraq) the last army of the united Persian empire, which again was under Darius' command. Darius fled, though he had not been wounded; indeed, he was to suffer no wounds at the hands of Alexander and his army. Darius' own subordinates slew him in the summer of 330.

To avoid the assumption of a gap in the text after the first "smote," some scholars have suggested that the author intended the object of the verb to be "Darius," but he perceived that the reader might be led astray by the many words which in his text intervened between the verb and its object (in the Greek text there are eleven, which in our translation are the words "Alexander son of . . . Chetiim"). Accordingly, they suggest, the author repeated "smote," just as the verb "flee" is repeated in Deut 4:42. The cases are not parallel. At Deut 4:42 the first "flee" is complete with its adverb, "there," and the sentence is complete without the explanatory clause, "and that he might flee to one of these cities and save his life." Here a transitive verb is left without its object, and the sentence is a fragment until the clause containing the second "smote."

The Hebrew "smite" is ambiguous. It can mean "slay," as at I Kings 16:16, but it can also mean "defeat" or "attack." To report the murder of a king, the Hebrew Bible everywhere except at I Kings 16:16 and II Kings 19:37 has two verbs, "smote and killed," as does the Syriac here, for one can "smite" a king and leave him alive, as at II Sam 8:3-13 and I Chron 18:3-9. Since Alexander did not kill Darius III and since our author is otherwise surprisingly well informed, the translation should be the ambiguous "smite," if not simply "defeat."

In referring to the Persian and Parthian (14:2) kings, our author calls them "kings of Persia and Media." In this he follows, not the usual style of those dynasties, but the traditions found also in the book of Esther and in legal documents written in Babylon during the years 486–482 B.C.E.; see George G. Cameron, "Darius and Xerxes in Babylonia," AJSL 58 (1941), 323–24.

and thus . . . empire. I here translate the (correct) text of V l 106 LA^G ^{V}. The text was difficult for most Greek readers to understand, since they could hardly know that Hellada, which normally means "Greece," here translates Yawan, the Hebrew name for the empire of Alexander and the Seleucids (see above, on Chetiim). Puzzled Greek scribes therefore probably altered the correct proteros to proteron to make the text mean "first over [sc. Ionian] Greece." The phrase, however, would then be pointless; after his defeat of Darius at Issus, Alexander was king of far more than Ionian Greece. Cf. Dan 8:21 and Torrey, JAOS 25 (1904), 307–9.

Since the nineteenth century, historians have been accustomed to use the adjective "Hellenistic" to refer to the empires and times of Alexander and his successors, though such use rests on a misconception (see Hermann Bengtson, Griechische Geschichte, pp. 299–300). By coincidence, "Hellenistic empire" makes an excellent English equivalent for our author's use of the Hebrew Yawan.

2. After Alexander defeated Darius at Gaugamela, he carried out long and arduous campaigns in Iran, Afghanistan, Central Asia, and the Indus valley, 331–325. Just what our author means by "kings of the earth" is not clear. They could be minor potentates subject to the Persian king; cf. Pss 2:2, 76:13, 89:27, 102:16, 138:4, 148:11, and the title, "King of Kings," borne by the kings of Babylon and Persia (Ezek 26:7; Ezra 7:12).

Josephus reports (AJ xi 8.5.332) that "the kings of Syria" were in Alexander's retinue when he visited Jerusalem. However, nowhere in the sources is Alexander or his army reported to have slain such a minor potentate, and in vs. 4 below our author calls such rulers not "kings" but "dynasts" (tyrannoi).

A key to our author's meaning may lie in the verb "slay" (sphazô) used by the translator. Usually it renders the Hebrew words for slaughtering animals. It is used of human sacrifice (Gen 22:10; Ezek 16:21) and of the slaughter of Zedekiah's sons (IV [II] Kings 5:7). Most important, it is used at I Sam 15:33, where Samuel slays King Agag by hewing him to pieces. Alexander carried out no human sacrifices or mass slaughters of kings, but he did have Artaxerxes IV Bessus, the last pretender to the Persian throne, mutilated before having him put to death (Arrian iv 7.3). Our author may well have used the language of I Sam 15:33 to allude to the execution of

Bessus. If so, the plural, "kings," is probably rhetorical exaggeration; cf. Jer 25:22, 25.

3. earth . . . rule. Cf. II Chron 14:4; Ps 76:9.

proud. The Jews viewed the Hellenistic rulers as arrogant; cf. vs. 21; II 5:21, 9:7; Dan 8:4, 10, 25, etc. Their pride would be brought low (Isa 2:2–17).

4. Far from being illogical or inaccurate (cf. Abel, p. 3), the account here may rest on good information. Alexander's conquests were remarkable because of the small size of his army. In his last months he enlarged his regular forces probably to their greatest size (Arrian vii 6, 23.1–2; cf. Helmut Berve, Das Alexanderreich, I [München: C. H. Beck, 1926], 176–85). He also modified in his last two years his hitherto makeshift arrangements for administration and taxation (see Berve, I, 224–90, 302–18).

provinces . . . dynasts. Like our translation, the original Hebrew probably lacked an "and" between "provinces" and "nations," and so did the original of the Greek version, preserved in S. The Latin manuscripts and SyII reflect this original Greek text, but they misconstrued it to mean "provinces [regiones] of nations and dynasts." The political theory of the Hellenistic age classified what we would call autonomous or semiautonomous states into nations (ethnê), city-states (poleis), territories ruled by dynasts, and empires (basileiai); see Polybius ix 1.4, v 88.4 – 90.5, vii 9.5, 9, 16; OGIS 229.11, 441.130–36; Frank W. Walbank, Polybius (University of California Press, 1972), p. 56, n. 145. The great empires themselves, in addition to the royal domains, might contain semiautonomous nations, city-states, and territories ruled by dynasts; see NOTES on nations and dynasts, below. One who was familiar with these facts of the Hellenistic age and with the occasional omission of "and" in biblical Hebrew would not have misunderstood the original Hebrew and Greek texts. On the omission of "and" in Hebrew, see GKC § 154, p. 484, n. 1. "And" was often omitted in the official Aramaic style used by the empires. See Ezra 4:9, 13, 5:6, 7:24; Dan 3:4, 7, 31, 5:19, 6:26, 7:14.

The classification "city-states" is missing from our author's list, though he may well have been aware of Hellenistic political theory. He could easily omit it, since all the city-states of the Seleucid empire could be considered foundations of Alexander and his successors.

provinces. The Greek word, chôra, translates the Hebrew and Aramaic mᵉdīnāh throughout Esther, Ezra, and Nehemiah. In the Bible and in Aramaic papyri from the time of the Persian empire, mᵉdīnāh, like the Latin regio and the Persian dahyâush, can mean either a whole satrapy or a subdivision of one (J. Liver, "Medinah," Enc. Bib., IV [1962], 693–94 [in Hebrew]). The territory of a medinah was directly administered and taxed by royal officials. Under the Persian empire, at least down to the end of the fifth century, Judaea was a medinah directly subject to a royal official, although at least once the official was a Jew, Nehemiah; see Ezra 5:8; Neh 1:3 and 11:3; Cowley, Aramaic Papyri of the Fifth Century B.C., nos. 30–31; and J. AJ xi 7.1.297–301. Similarly, under the Seleucid empire, the territory directly administered and taxed by royal officials was probably called "the royal [basilikê] chôra." See Bikerman, Institutions, pp. 169–85.

nations. In Hellenistic Greek, the word, ethnos, means an autonomous nation or one with local autonomy though subject to an empire; see Polybius ix 1.4, v 90.5; vii 9.5, 9, 16; and Bikerman, *Institutions,* pp. 164–66. An *ethnos* subject to an empire was not directly administered and taxed by royal officials but by its own communal organs and officials. To be recognized as an *ethnos* was a privileged status, like that of a city-state (on city-states in an empire, see H. Bengtson, *Die Strategie in der hellenistischen Zeit,* II, 141–42). A source quoted by Strabo (xvi 2.2.749) probably means that there were only four peoples with such status in the Seleucid province of Coele-Syria: Jews, Idumaeans, Gazaeans, and Azotians.

If correct, Strabo's source is datable within a short period under the late Seleucids. Sidon and Tyre are conspicuous by their absence, though Antiochus IV gave them such a privileged status (see Introduction, p. 118) and though Sidonians and Tyrians on ancient documents speak of themselves as belonging to an *ethnos* ('*m; Corpus Inscriptionum Semiticarum* I 7 [132 B.C.E.] and *Répertoire de l'épigraphie sémitique* 1215 [96 B.C.E.]). Sidon and Tyre were in Phoenicia. Protarchus in 163 B.C.E. was appointed as governor of Coele-Syria and Phoenicia (II 12:32), and Bacchides in 162 is called "governor of the Trans-Euphrates province," an expression which probably means that he still governed both Coele-Syria and Phoenicia (see NOTE on 7:8). Thereafter, Phoenicia in our sources ceases to be connected with Coele-Syria. Subsequent governors of Coele-Syria never have Phoenicia within their province (I 10:69, 11:59, 15:38). See Bengtson, *Strategie,* II, 176–81, to be corrected by my NOTES on I 7:8, 10:69, and II 13:24. Strabo's source is also right to omit Ptolemais. Ptolemais was originally the Phoenician city of Akko and had been refounded as a Greek city by Ptolemy II (see M. Avi-Yonah, *The Holy Land,* p. 39) and then had received even more privileges as an "Antiochene" city under Antiochus IV (see Introduction, p. 117).

Idumaea was still under a Seleucid governor in 163 (II 12:32). Gaza as the metropolis of the Philistines (cf. I 3:23) may have had the status of an *ethnos* from early Hellenistic times, but from 148/7 Gaza was issuing coins as if it, like Ptolemais, had the status of a *polis.* Hence, one might date Strabo's source between 163 and 148/7. However, if Strabo's authority was not impressed by the civic experiments of Demetrius II, he may have regarded Gaza as still an *ethnos* after 148/7. On the status and coins of Gaza, see Introduction, p. 121.

We now would have to seek a terminus after 148/7 for Strabo's authority. He includes both the Jews and the Idumaeans as having the status of *ethnos.* The Jews became self-governing and free of tribute in 142 but were still an *ethnos* at least nominally subject to the Seleucid empire, as is attested even in Demetrius II's letter of 142 (I 13:36, 40). Antiochus VII still asserted his sovereignty over Simon and John Hyrcanus (I 15:2–9, 27–35, 16:18; J. *AJ* xiii 8.3 – 4.245–53). Josephus describes Judaea under Simon as being "free and immune from tribute" (*AJ* xiii 6.7.213), a technical expression, which in Josephus' time described privileged territories *subject* to the Roman empire. Though Josephus says John Hyrcanus "revolted from the Macedonians" after the death of Antiochus VII, Josephus' own narrative shows that the act was *de facto,* not *de jure:* John Hyrcanus gave no aid to any of the contending pretenders to the Seleucid throne (*AJ* xiii 10.1.273–74). In fact, until one pretender should clearly have established himself as legitimate king, John Hyrcanus had a good legal case for obeying none of them. Nevertheless, he refrained from assuming the title "king." If he coined money at all in his own name, he coined only in bronze; see Ya'akov Meshorer, *Jewish Coins of the Second Temple Period*, pp. 41–52, and Arye Ben-David, "When Did the Maccabees Begin to Strike Their First Coins?" PEQ 104 (1972), 96 (par. 3)–103 (there are errors in the earlier pages of Ben-David's article). Assumption of the royal title and coinage of silver in one's own name were the two acts which would have constituted a *de jure* assertion of independence (Bikerman, *Institutions*, pp. 10–11, 14, 211–12, 219–20, 225, 235).

By the time Judah Aristobulus succeeded John Hyrcanus, the Seleucid empire had been reduced to an ordinary state in Syria and had no claims to being the sort of world empire to which God would subject His people. Ascalon and Gaza were independent from about 104 and began to issue independent coinage; see Bikerman, *Institutions*, p. 235; G. Hill, *Catalogue of the Greek Coins of Palestine*, pp. xlviii–xlix, lxix–lxx; Meshorer, p. 51. Accordingly, Judah Aristobulus assumed the royal title and may have coined bronze in his own name; Alexander Jannaeus both held the royal title and coined in his own name, though still only in bronze. See Meshorer, pp. 53–59. After 104, even a pro-Seleucid writer would not state that the Jews were an *ethnos* subject to the Seleucid empire and living within the province of Coele-Syria. Strabo's source also says that the Idumaeans were an *ethnos*. John Hyrcanus put an end to the Idumaeans as an *ethnos* in the region around 126 (J. *AJ* xiii 9.1. 257). Accordingly, Strabo's authority would be datable between 163 and approximately 126.

There is no clear evidence that the Jews were recognized as such an *ethnos* under the later Persian kings or under the Hellenistic empires before 200. The concept of an *ethnos* may be purely Greek; see Victor Ehrenberg, *The Greek State* (New York: Norton, 1960), pp. 24–27, 29, 114, 121–25, 200. The question of when the Jews became a privileged *ethnos* is made more difficult by the non-technical use of *ethnos* for any ethnic group. It may not be a coincidence, however, that *ethnos* is not used of Jews in the Greek of Ezra and Nehemiah. The use in the Greek Esther and Judith may reflect the later date of the translations of those books. The Ptolemies sold the collection of the taxes of Judaea to the highest bidder (J. *AJ* xii 4.4.175). Hence, we may infer that under the Ptolemies, the Jews did not pay their taxes to the king through their own local organs. Moreover, a Ptolemy could threaten to give the land of the Jews to military colonists, as if they had no more privileges than tenants on the royal domain (J. *AJ* xii 4.1.159). Hence, though Polybius spoke of Scopas' conquest of the *ethnos* of the Jews in narrating the events of 201/0 (*apud* J. *AJ* xii 3.3.135), he may not have meant *ethnos* in the technical privileged sense. Antiochus III may have been the first to confer the special status of *ethnos* upon the Jews. The term appears prominently in his grant of privileges to them (J. *AJ* xii 3.3.141–42); see also Bikerman, "La charte séleucide de Jérusalem," REG 100 (1935), 25–28, 32–34; *Gott*, pp. 53–58; and introductory NOTE to I 1:29–40 and NOTE at II 3:5–8.

dynasts. These were local monarchs who had control of their own territories. Within the Seleucid empire they were subject to the king and would bring him gifts and might be required to provide troops and money. See Bikerman, *Institutions*, pp. 166–69.

5–7. Alexander died at Babylon, the evening of June 10, 323 (Plutarch *Alexander* 75.4; A. E. Samuel, *Ptolemaic Chronology*, p. 47). He left *no* instructions on the succession to his empire. The Babylonian historian Berossus made an error similar to our author's, of regarding the Seleucids as immediate and rightful heirs of Alexander. The errors reflect the propaganda of the Seleucids who sought to legitimize their claims by tracing them to Alexander's conquests. See Bikerman, *Institutions*, p. 5. Alexander began to reign in late summer, 336, so that he was king for about twelve years and nine months. The words describing Alexander's high officials in vs. 6 are taken from II Chron 10:8, but may also reflect the honorary Hellenistic court title, "Schoolfellow of the King" (*syntrophos*); see Bikerman, *Institutions*, pp. 42–43.

8–9. Alexander's most powerful officers at first took their provinces as nominal subjects of Philip III Arrhidaeus, Alexander's feeble-minded half-brother, and of Alexander IV, Alexander's posthumous son. Ptolemy became satrap of Egypt, and Seleucus satrap of Babylon. The struggles of the rival strong men and their armies were extremely complicated and resulted in the dismemberment of the empire and in the death of both powerless kings. Nevertheless, the surviving successors long refrained from assuming the diadem themselves as kings. From the time of Alexander, the diadem, a white band of cloth with decorated edges, worn around the head, was the emblem of kingship (L. A. Moritz, OCD², s.v. "Diadem"). In 306 Antigonus and his son Demetrius, who ruled jointly over much of Greece, Asia Minor, and Syria, assumed the diadem. In 305, Ptolemy and Seleucus took the royal title, establishing the lasting dynasties which were of interest to the Jews. Our author, however, seems to believe that the strong men assumed the royal title at the beginning of the Seleucid era in 312/11. See Introduction, pp. 21–25. Indeed, vss. 1–9 for our author serve to define the Seleucid era, which he calls "the era of the Hellenistic dynasty." On his negative assessment of the Hellenistic dynasties, see p. 50. "Much evil" may reflect the prophesy of retribution at Joel 4:13.

10. Antiochus IV Epiphanes was the youngest son of Antiochus III, "the Great." At the end of 190 or the beginning of 189 a Roman army crushingly defeated Antiochus III at the battle of Magnesia (NE of Smyrna), and in 189 the future Antiochus IV was delivered over as a hostage to the victors at Ephesus. He was to spend twelve or thirteen years at Rome (Appian xi 7.38–39; Polybius xxi 17.8–11; O. Mørkholm, *Antiochus IV of Syria*, pp. 22–23, 35–36, 38–40). Mørkholm conveniently assembles most of the sources on Antiochus Epiphanes, but his analysis of Antiochus' dealings with the Jews must be rejected.

Antiochus III died in 187 and was succeeded by Antiochus Epiphanes' older brother, Seleucus IV. The Romans may well have come to think that a younger brother was a poor hostage for Seleucus IV's good behavior. Probably in 176 or early in 175 Antiochus Epiphanes was released in exchange for Seleucus IV's son Demetrius. Antiochus thereupon spent time at Athens. On September 3, 175, Seleucus IV died. According to some reports, he was murdered by his minister Heliodorus; see NOTE on II 4:7. Heliodorus seized power, setting up as figurehead king little Antiochus, the son of Seleucus IV. Thereupon, Antiochus Epiphanes gained the valuable help of the royal house of the neighboring kingdom of Pergamum. By them he was transported to the border of the Seleucid empire, provided with men and supplies, and crowned with a diadem. On entering the Seleucid realm, Antiochus Epiphanes was victorious. Heliodorus disappears from history. Antiochus Epiphanes adopted the helpless child-king and eventually had him put to death in 170. The intrigue required for Antiochus to assemble forces, march into the Seleucid realm, and supplant the regime around the child heir could hardly have occurred in the short time between the death of Seleucus IV, September 3, 175, and the end of the royal Macedonian Seleucid year 137 on September 22 (see Introduction, pp. 21–25). The date of the accession of Antiochus IV probably reflects his own propaganda, which sought to present him as the immediate successor of Seleucus IV by suppressing mention of the few months of the regime around the child heir. A cuneiform king-list from Babylon similarly presents Antiochus IV as the immediate successor of Seleucus IV, in September, 175. See Mørkholm, pp. 32–50.

Antiochus IV may have been known as Antiochus Epiphanes from his accession; cf. Appian Syriakê 45. Mørkholm has made a thorough study of the epithet "epiphanes" as used with reference to Antiochus IV; see his Studies, pp. 11–43, 47–56, 68–74. As he notes, the epithet has a very wide meaning, ranging from "famous" or "illustrious" in a purely human sphere to the god "appearing" to his worshipers. The Ptolemies officially styled themselves as gods, and Ptolemy V, who died in 180, had styled himself Theos Epiphanes (God Manifest) long before Antiochus became king. From the way in which Appian and Polybius (xxvi 1) refer to Antiochus, it would appear that outside the Seleucid realm the king was called King Antiochus Epiphanes, as he is here. On the other hand, within his kingdom, on coins beginning perhaps in 173/2, in an inscription from Babylon of 166/5 or 165/4, and in a letter of the Samaritans of 167/6 (J. AJ xii 5.258, 264), he is styled King Antiochus Theos Epiphanes.

On the translation, "Hellenistic dynasty," see above on vs. 1.

II. THE JEWISH HELLENIZERS
(1:11–15)

1 ¹¹ At that time, lawless men arose in Israel and seduced many with their plea, "Come, let us make a covenant with the gentiles around us, because ever since we have kept ourselves separated from them we have suffered many evils." ¹² The plea got so favorable a reception ¹³ that some of the people took it upon themselves to apply to the king, who granted them liberty to follow the practices of the gentiles. ¹⁴ Thereupon they built a gymnasium in Jerusalem according to the customs of the gentiles ¹⁵ and underwent operations to disguise their circumcision, rebelling against the sacred covenant. They joined themselves to the gentiles and became willing slaves to evildoing.

NOTES

1:11–15, introductory NOTE. With the scene set (see on vss. 1–10), the author begins his narrative here. On his purposes in these verses, see Introduction, pp. 11 and 73. On Antiochus' policy, see p. 11–21.

Our author does not say much about the sins of the Hellenizers, believing that the wicked are to be relegated to oblivion. For details, we must turn to the fragments of the work of Onias IV in Josephus and to II 3–5. Our author scrupulously refrains at this point from accusing the leading Hellenizers of idolatry. Idolatry might have incurred, not more persecution, but destruction and exile (Deut 4:25–28). Nevertheless, he views the Hellenizers as guilty of heinous sin. A "covenant" allowing free intercourse with the surrounding gentiles would be the entering wedge for worshiping their gods (Exod 34:15–16; Deut 7:2–4). The Torah did command Israel to keep rigidly separate from the seven nations native to the Promised Land (Exod 23:32, 34:12–16; Deut 7:1–4). These nations were long extinct by the time of the second temple, but Ezra and Nehemiah (Ezra 9:1–2, 10:11; Neh 9:2, 10:31, 13:1–3) construed "the inhabitant(s) of the land" as referring also to the pagan inhabitants of their own time. Hecataeus of Abdera, writing near the end of the fourth century, noted (*apud* Diodorus xl 3.4) the rigidity of Jewish separation from pagans, ascribing it to Moses' legislation. On our author's attitude toward gentiles distant from the Promised Land, see introductory NOTE to I:18–19.

The language in vs. 11 is a deliberate imitation of Deut 13:7–8 and 31:17; the author intends to show how close those who propose violation of the separation required by Deut 7:2 are to those who propose idol worship. Similarly, the "practices" and "customs" of the gentiles in vss. 14 and 15 echo Lev 18:3 and II Kings 17:8, to show that when the Hellenizers accept the institutions of the Greeks, their sin is as grave as idolatry, incest, adultery, and perversion. Not all Jews kept rigidly separate or totally rejected the Greek ways of life. The Tobiads were noteworthy for their readiness to enter the Hellenistic world (J. *AJ* xii 4.1–11.154–236). Those who did keep rigidly separate could hardly avoid incurring the hostility of gentiles.

Mass violation by Jews of the law of separation was forbidden by royal as well as by Jewish law. In the time of Ezra, King Artaxerxes had made the Torah as interpreted by Ezra binding on all Jews residing in the Trans-Euphrates province, which included Judaea. Alexander probably confirmed the existing state of affairs; cf. J. *AJ* xi 8.5.338. Antiochus III again made the Torah the law of the land for the Jews (J. *AJ* xii 3.3.142; cf. II 4:11). Hence, to carry out their program, the Hellenizers had first to get license from the king.

13. *took it upon themselves.* The Greek word usually means "became eager"; it translates the Hebrew word for "volunteer" at II Chron 17:16, cf. I Chron 24:5, 6, 9, 14, 17.

14. The gymnasium was a hallmark of Greek civilization in the Hellenistic world. It was the center for not only physical education and recreation but also civic and literary education. For further details, see in AB vol. 41A commentary on II 4:9–15 and in present volume, Introduction, p. 117.

15. In a Greek gymnasium all the physical exercises and sports were performed in complete nudity. Greek acceptance of nudity was in striking contrast to the attitude of most of the non-Greek peoples, including the Jews (cf. Thucydides i 6; Gen 3:7–11). On the other hand, many peoples of the Near East besides the Jews practiced circumcision, but Greeks tended to view it as an unseemly mutilation. Hence, some of the Hellenized Jewish youths who had to strip in the gymnasium were willing to submit to painful operations to disguise the fact that they had been circumcised; see E. Schürer, *The History of the Jewish People in the Age of Jesus Christ*, I, 149, n. 28. On circumcision as the covenant of Abraham and his descendants with God see Gen 17:9–14.

However, the majority of the Hellenizing Jews were not complete apostates (see above, NOTE on vss. 11–15), and probably few among them underwent the operation to reverse their circumcision. Indeed, the contemporary apocalypses at Jubilees xxx; Enoch xc 6–9; and Test Moses v 1–6 make no such accusation. Nor do the apocalypses in Daniel 7–12; I shall treat Dan 11:32 in my commentary on Daniel. It is significant that the Testament of Moses probably mentioned the operation only at 8:3; and there the text appears to mean that in the time of the persecution, after spring, 167, Antiochus' agents will impose the operation by force (*et filii eorum pueri secabantur a medicis pueri inducere acrosisam* [read *acrobystiam*] *illis*).

"Sacred covenant" here and at vs. 63 probably reflects an original Hebrew text *berīt qōdeš* as at Dan 11:28, 30. If so, in all these instances *qōdeš*, "the Holy," may be a substitute for the name of God.

"Joined themselves" reflects Num 25:3, and here as there the writer probably means sexual association.

became willing slaves to. The literal meaning of the Greek and the original Hebrew is "sold themselves [as slaves] to"; cf. Deut 28:68; I Kings 21:20, 25; II Kings 17:17.

III. THE VICTORIES OF ANTIOCHUS IV IN EGYPT (169 B.C.E.)
(1:16–19)

1 [16] As soon as the kingdom was firmly in Antiochus' hands, he began to think of becoming king over the land of Egypt so as to rule over both empires. [17] He invaded Egypt with a strong army, with chariotry and elephants, and with a large fleet, [18] and waged war against Ptolemy, king of Egypt. Routed by Antiochus, Ptolemy fled, and many of his troops fell slain. [19] The fortified cities of Egypt were captured, and Antiochus took the spoils of the land of Egypt.

NOTES

1:16–19, introductory NOTE. One might have thought that Antiochus IV early in his reign, in 175 or 174, was already firmly in control. The seer in Dan 11:21–22 reports the rapid collapse of the opposition within the Seleucid kingdom (cf. Appian *Syriakê* 45), and Jason the Oniad regarded Antiochus IV as firmly enough in power to warrant the investment of large sums of money which would have been lost if another king came to rule (II 4:7–9). However, Antiochus IV could still have been viewed as an insecure usurper. Two direct heirs of Seleucus IV were still alive: the child Antiochus, whom Antiochus IV had adopted and recognized as coregent, and an elder son, the future Demetrius I, now a hostage at Rome. Externally, the Seleucid kingdom faced the threat of a war by Ptolemaic Egypt to reconquer the provinces of Syria and Palestine which had been lost to Antiochus III in 200. Young King Ptolemy VI might even challenge Antiochus IV's right to be the Seleucid king, for Ptolemy VI was himself the son of the sister of both Antiochus IV and Seleucus IV.

By 170, however, Antiochus IV had had ample opportunity to use his talents to consolidate his rule. By then he had done away with the little Antiochus and had established such good relations with Rome that he was probably confident that Rome would do nothing to favor the claims of the hostage Demetrius. Our author is therefore probably correct in saying that Antiochus IV was securely in power on the eve of his war with Ptolemaic Egypt. See Mørkholm, pp. 38–50, 64–66.

Our author sees treachery as characteristic of Seleucids. Without having to draw on the pro-Ptolemaic work of Onias IV (see Introduction, pp. 57–59, 90), he could call Antiochus the aggressor in his war with the Ptolemaic empire. The truth is that this, the Sixth Syrian War, began with a Ptolemaic effort to reconquer the lost provinces of Syria and Palestine. The ministers of Ptolemy VI, who was still very young, began plotting in the 170s. Inasmuch as Polybius' account survives only in fragments, it is difficult to trace the course of the preparations and the war. See in AB vol. 41A commentary on II 4:21 and 5:1 and Mørkholm, pp. 64–101. Mørkholm's treatment of Antiochus' coronation at Memphis (pp. 80–83) must be rejected. The fundamental study is still Walter Otto, *Zur Geschichte der Zeit des 6. Ptolemäers,* ABAW, N.F., Heft XI (1934), I shall deal with the problems elsewhere.

Following Mørkholm, we can outline the first events as follows:

176. The death of the mother of Ptolemy VI, Cleopatra Syra, sister of Antiochus IV, removes a probable pro-Seleucid influence from the Ptolemaic court.

October–November, 170. The Ptolemaic regime declares Ptolemy VI Philometor to be of age. The young king's sister Cleopatra II and his brother, the younger Ptolemy (the future Ptolemy VIII Euergetes II), are associated on the throne with Ptolemy VI. The purpose of this joint regime was presumably to unify all court factions so as to achieve maximum internal strength for the coming war.

Early November, 170. The Ptolemaic army under the royal ministers, Eulaeus and Lenaeus, sets out from Alexandria to invade the Seleucid empire.

Late November, 170. Antiochus, moving rapidly against the threat, stops the Egyptian army by routing it at Mount Casius, well inside Ptolemaic soil, on the Mediterranean coast of the Sinai Peninsula, and grants an armistice.

By December 9. No longer associated with his sister and brother, Ptolemy VI alone remains on throne of Ptolemaic empire.

?. The armistice expires. Antiochus seizes the important fortress of Pelusium, gateway to the Nile Delta, and overruns much of the delta, approaching Alexandria.

By April 17, 169. Ptolemy VI resides in the camp of the Seleucid army, obviously in the power of Antiochus.

We may correct Mørkholm's account by adding the following, probably after, though perhaps before April 17:

Antiochus IV has himself crowned king of Egypt at Memphis but grants the rule of Egypt to Ptolemy VI. A relatively small Seleucid army overruns the rest of Egypt except Alexandria.

Spring or summer, 169. The Ptolemaic authorities in Alexandria fight on. They establish a new regime under the joint rule of Cleopatra II and the younger Ptolemy and seek Roman aid. Antiochus besieges Alexandria but fails to take it.

Late summer or early autumn, 169. Antiochus raises the siege of Alexandria and withdraws from Egypt with huge spoils, probably trusting his "vassal," Ptolemy VI, to remain loyal.

On the confused chronology in other Jewish sources, see Introduction, pp. 46, 49–50, 57.

17. After "elephants" all witnesses to the text except L La$^{L X G B}$ add "and with cavalry." Antiochus probably had a strong force of cavalry; see Diodorus xxx 14 and II 5:1–3. However, our author's "strong army" (*'am kābēd*) may well include cavalry; cf. vss. 20 and 29 and Num 20:20.

IV. ANTIOCHUS IV PUNISHES
THE JEWS
(1:20–64)

1   20 While returning from his conquest of Egypt in the year 143, Antiochus marched against (Israel and) Jerusalem with a strong army. . . . 21 Arrogantly entering the temple, he took the golden altar and the candelabrum with all its furnishings 22 and the table for the showbread and the libation jars and the bowls and the golden ladles and the curtain. He stripped off all the cornices and the ornamentation of gold from the front of the temple 23 and took the silver and the gold coin and the precious articles, whatever he found of the treasures on deposit. 24 With all this loot he returned to his own country, having polluted himself with massacres and uttered words of great arrogance.

25 Great sorrow came upon Israel,
   wherever they lived.
26 Nobles and elders broke out in wailing,
   maidens and young men lost their vigor,
   and the women's beauty was marred.
27 Every bridegroom took up the dirge
   while his bride sitting in the bedchamber turned to mourn.
28 Indeed, the earth had quaked against its inhabitants,
   and the entire house of Jacob was clothed in shame.

29 Two years later, the king sent a Mysarch against the towns of Judah, and he came against Jerusalem with a strong army. 30 Treacherously he addressed the people in peaceful terms, so that they trusted him, and then he hit the city hard with a surprise attack, killing many Israelites. 31 He plundered the city, set fire to it, and destroyed its buildings and the walls around it. 32 He and his army took the women and the children captive and took possession of the cattle. 33 Thereupon they fortified the City of David with a high strong wall and strong towers so as to have a citadel, the Akra. 34 They stationed in it a breed of sinners, wicked men, who grew strong there. 35 The garrison was provided with a store of arms and

provisions and kept there under their hands the spoils of Jerusalem, which they had collected, and became a dangerous menace.

36 It was an ambush against the temple,
and continually a wicked adversary against Israel.
37 They shed innocent blood around the sanctuary
and defiled the temple.
38 The rightful inhabitants of Jerusalem were put to flight by them,
and she became a colony of foreigners;
she became foreign to her own offspring,
for her children abandoned her.
39 Her temple was deserted like a desert;
her festivals were turned into mourning,
her Sabbaths into cause for mockery,
her glory into cause for contempt.
40 Her humiliation matched her former splendor,
and her pride was turned into mourning.

41 The king wrote to all his kingdom, for all to become one people 42 and for each to abandon his own customs. All the gentiles agreed to the terms of the king's proclamation. 43 Many Israelites, too, accepted his religion and sacrificed to idols and violated the Sabbath.

44 The king sent letters by messengers to Jerusalem and the towns of Judah containing orders to follow customs foreign to the land, 45 to put a stop to burnt offerings and meal offering and libation in the temple, to violate Sabbaths and festivals, 46 to defile temple and holy things, 47 to build illicit altars and illicit temples and idolatrous shrines, to sacrifice swine and ritually unfit animals, 48 to leave their sons uncircumcised, and to draw abomination upon themselves by means of all kinds of uncleanness and profanation, 49 so as to forget the Torah and violate all the commandments. 50 Whoever disobeyed the word of the king was to be put to death. 51 Letters to the same effect he wrote to all his kingdom, and he appointed officers to watch over all the people and sent orders to the towns of Judah to offer sacrifices in every town. 52 Many from among the people gathered around the officers, every forsaker of the Torah, and they committed wicked acts in the land 53 and drove Israel into hiding places in all their places of refuge.

54 On the fifteenth day of Kislev in the year 145 the king had an abomination of desolation built upon the altar, and in the outlying towns of Judah they built illicit altars, 55 and at the doors of the houses and in the squares they offered illicit sacrifices. 56 Whatever

scrolls of the Torah they found, they tore up and burned; 57 and whoever was found with a scroll of the Covenant in his possession or showed his love for the Torah, the king's decree put him to death. 58 Through their strength they acted against the Israelites who were found in the towns each month, 59 as on the twenty-fifth day of the month they would offer sacrifices on the illicit altar which was upon the temple altar. 60 The women who had had their sons circumcised they put to death according to the decree, 61 hanging the babes from their mother's necks and executing also their husbands and the men who had performed the circumcisions. 62 Many Israelites strongly and steadfastly refused to eat forbidden food. 63 They chose death in order to escape defilement by foods and in order to keep from violating the Holy Covenant, and they were put to death. 64 Indeed, very great Wrath had struck Israel.

NOTES

1:20–63, introductory NOTE. A very important parallel version of the text here is given by Josephus at *AJ* xii 5.3–4.246–56. Partly out of his religious convictions, partly for rhetorical reasons, Josephus emended and recast the text. See Appendix V.

20. *in the year 143.* The phrase in the Greek here unambiguously dates events of Seleucid history, Antiochus' conquest of Egypt and/or his withdrawal, not his attack on Jerusalem. Hence, it is to be taken as a date on the Macedonian form of the Seleucid era (see Introduction, pp. 21–25). The year 144 Sel. Mac. began October 16, 169 B.C.E. A cuneiform tablet from Babylon dated between August 18 and September 16, 169, still reports Antiochus' victories in Egypt as the news of the day; see Introduction, Part VI, n. 71. Hence, the sack of Jerusalem probably occurred in September or early October.

It is significant that Jason of Cyrene, too, dated Antiochus' sack of the temple by an event of Seleucid history (II 5:1). We may infer that in the time of our writers the only Jewish records of the date were relative dates tying the sack to Antiochus' campaigns in Egypt, like those at Dan 11:28 and 30. See Introduction, pp. 45, 49–51.

Our author presents the attack on Jerusalem as unprovoked, not in order to blacken the character of Antiochus IV, but rather because he here regards Antiochus as "the rod of God's anger," inflicting punishment for the sins of the Hellenizers (see vs. 28 and cf. II 4:16–17). For Antiochus' reasons, see 5:5–16 and commentary in AB vol. 41A. To Jews outside the feuding aristocratic factions, the attack could indeed appear unprovoked. Cf. J. *Ap.* ii 7.83–84.

(Israel and) Jerusalem. In ancient manuscripts, where the scribe knew of more than one reading, he would place the alternative reading in the margin. A later scribe might become confused and in his copy bring the word from

the margin into the text, so that both readings would stand side by side in a "doublet" text. "Israel" here is just such a marginal reading mistakenly brought into the text. Josephus' paraphrase (*AJ* xii 5.3.246) omits the words in parentheses. The peculiar readings of the Latin manuscripts show clearly that the Latin translation was made from a doublet text: La^G has *ascendit ad Israhel in Hierosolima*, "He marched on Israel against Jerusalem," with no "and"; La^{X V} have *ascendit ad Israhel et ascendit in Hierosolima*, "He marched on Israel, and he marched against Jerusalem."

The origin of the doublet can still be seen. In ancient Greek manuscripts "Jerusalem" would be abbreviated *Ilêm* and "Israel," *Iêl*. The reading of V here has the correct *Ilêm*. The reading of S is a scribal error, *Iêlm*, from which the efforts of a uncomprehending scribe could easily have given rise to the variant *Iêl*. Indeeed, "Israel and Jerusalem" is a very rare combination in the Hebrew Bible (Ps 147:2; the special character of the context explains its presence at Isa 8:14; Zeph 3:14; and Zech 2:2). The normal combination in the Hebrew Bible and in First Maccabees (3:34) is "Judah and Jerusalem." For our author, "Israel" means the people, not the land. The doublet here was first noticed by E. Z. Melamed, "Josephus and Maccabees I: A Comparison," EI 1 (1951), 123. Note, however, I 3:35, where "the strength of Israel and the remnant of Jerusalem" occurs, and no textual evidence attests a doublet.

with a strong army. . . . There must be a gap in the text beween the end of vs. 20 and the beginning of vs. 21. In the Hebrew Bible and in First Maccabees, when an army is reported to have attacked a city and then to have had the fallen city at its mercy, the writer always mentions explicitly the defeat of the defenders or the capture or surrender of the city. Cf. Num 21:32; Deut 2:32–34; Josh 6:20–21, 10:31–32, 15:16–17, 19:47; Judg 1:8, 12–13, 9:45, 50–52; II Sam 12:29–30; I Kings 9:16; II Kings 12:18; Isa 20:1; Neh 9:24–25; II Chron 28:18, etc. For our author's usage, cf. I 1:30, 5:3, 7, 28, 44, 50, 6:63, 9:2, 12:33, 13:43. I 5:5 is an apparent exception. Perhaps there, too, the text is defective, or perhaps no need was felt to mention the capture since the ban (*ḥērem*) was irrevocable, once pronounced (Lev 27:29) The verb "ban" occurs also at Jer 25:9 and 50:21 with no mention of defeat of defenders or of capture. At I Sam 15:18 the ban is mentioned even before the waging of war; on the connection of I Sam 15:18 with I 5:4–5, see below ad loc.

The content of the missing words is probably preserved in Josephus' paraphrase (*AJ* xii 5.3–4.246b–247a, 249). If we label the missing verse as 20a, we can reconstruct the Greek as follows:

kai ênoixan autôi hoi ek tês poleôs tas pylas^a *kai eisêlthen eis tên polin*^b *kai katelabeto autên*^c *kai apôlese laon polyn ek Israêl.*^d "The people in the city opened the gates to him, and he entered the city and took it, killing many Israelites."

---

^a Cf. I 10:76, 11:2; Deut 20:11. I have not tried to reflect Josephus' "the men of his party." It looks like a typical piece of his restyling.
^b At *AJ* xii 5.2.243 Josephus renders *eisêlthen* of I 1:17 by *genomenos en*.
^c Cf. 5:28, 35; for "enter and take," cf. Josh 8:19.
^d Compare the way Josephus renders vs. 30 at *AJ* xii 5.4.251. The end of *AJ* xii

It is easy to see how such a passage could have dropped out. In the long sequence of clauses all beginning with *kai*, "and," the eye of the scribe could have jumped from the end of vs. 20 to vs. 21. Vs. 20a was also near enough to the beginning of the scroll to be vulnerable to friction and pulling and may have thus been torn out.

If we have restored the text correctly, I 1:20a joins II 5:11-14 in reporting that massacres accompanied Antiochus' pillage of the temple; cf. vs. 24. See also commentary to II 5:11. Since the seer(s) of the Daniel apocalypses lived through the events, one would expect to find in Daniel some reflection of the events. Since many saints were slaughtered in the long persecutions, there is no way of telling whether Dan 7:21, 25 or 8:24-25 or 9:26 allude to the killing which accompanied the sack of 169. Only Dan 11:28 alludes unambiguously to our events, but it says nothing directly of killing. Let us try, however, to determine the meaning of the obscure verbless phrase there, "his heart against the Sacred Covenant." A similar phrase occurs at Dan 11:25, "his heart against the King of the South," but "his heart" has usually been taken as a second object of the preceding verb, "He shall stir up his power and his heart. . . ." There is no reason why "stir up" at Dan 11:25 should have two nearly synonymous objects. Elsewhere in the Bible, the verb takes only a single object, even in similar contexts (Isa 42:13; Jer 51:1; Hag 1:14; Ps 78:38; Dan 11:2; I Chron 5:26; II Chron 21:6). Hence there should probably be a comma after "his power." "His heart against" means "his greed being directed at," and Dan 11:25 should be rendered, "And he shall stir up his power, turning his greed against the King of the South." "Heart" frequently means "desire" or "greed"; cf. Ps 78:18; I Kings 10:2; Jer 22:17. The "greed" of Dan 11:25 is "wreaked" through war on the Ptolemaic empire and taking its spoils. Similarly, then, the "greed" of Dan 11:28, which Antiochus is there said to have "wreaked" (*wₑ'āśāh*, "he shall work his will") upon the Sacred Covenant, can easily mean greed wreaked through war on Jerusalem and through taking the spoils of the temple. If the seer felt he had alluded to war, he would feel no further need to allude to killing (cf. Dan 7:21).

21-24. On the reasons for the cruel sack, in fact and as seen by the ancient sources, see Introduction, p. 122, and in AB vol. 41A commentary on II 5:14.

The Greek word and the Hebrew underlying it are best translated "ladle," not "censer," though the Greek word is used for "censer" at I Kings 7:50. At Exod 25:29, 37:16, the vessel is part of the furnishings of the table for the showbread, not of the incense apparatus. We find it used for holding incense without burning it at Num 7:14, *M. Tamid* 5:4, 6:3.

curtain. To judge by the context, which mentions the furniture which stood

---

5.3.247 represents our vs. 24. *AJ* xii 5.4.248 is part of Josephus' effort to harmonize First Maccabees with Daniel by emending the text of First Maccabees; see Appendix V. The first words of *AJ* xii 5.4.249, "He spared not even those who let him in," are probably to be combined with "He killed many of the party opposed to him," in 247, as Josephus' expansion of "many Israelites." The author of First Maccabees says nothing of political factions in Jerusalem at this time. The rest of *AJ* xii 5.4.249 is probably Josephus' rhetorical amplification of the "arrogance" mentioned in vs. 21.

inside the sanctuary, this is probably the curtain in front of the Holy of Holies (Exod 26:31–35; II Chron 3:14); it might, however, be that at the entrance to the sanctuary (Exod 26:36–37; *Letter of Aristeas* 86), but not the one at the gate of the temple court (Exod 27:16); cf. J. *AJ* iii 6.4.124–33 and viii 3.3.72.

He stripped . . . temple. The cornices and the ornamentation are to be taken as objects of "stripped," not of "took," as is shown by I 4:57. Greek *stephanos,* "crown," "wreath," renders the Hebrew '*ăṭārāh,* which besides "crown" or "wreath" means an ornamental cornice or molding; see *M. Middot* 3:8 and *M. Oholot* 14:1. Gold-leaf ornamentation on the structure of the sanctuary: I Kings 6:20–22, 30–32; II Chron 3:4–9, 4:22.

21. *Arrogantly.* Our author probably has Isa 10:5–27 in mind. For him as for the seer at Dan 11:10 (cf. Isa 8:8), Isaiah's prophesies of the advances of Assyria were applicable to the campaigns of the Seleucid kings. Indeed, the Seleucids were called kings of Syria=Assyria; see Bikerman, *Institutions,* pp. 4–5, and Th. Nöldeke, "*Assyrios Syrios Syros,*" *Hermes* 5 (1871), 443–68, and cf. the use of *Aššūr* in 1QM 1:2, 6, 2:12, 11:11, 18:2, 19:10. Here Antiochus has come as the "rod of God's anger," and in his "arrogance" has gone beyond his function of chastisement, to crime. Therefore, as Isaiah predicted, Antiochus will be punished.

entering the temple. Jews regarded the entry of a pagan even into the inner courts of the temple as a heinous sin; see Bickerman, "The Warning Inscription of Herod's Temple," *JQR* 37 (1946–47), 387–405, and cf. II 5:15–21 and Lam 1:10; Ezek 44:7–9. Antiochus went farther, for in order to seize the sacred vessels he had to enter the sanctuary.

golden altar. The altar for incense; see Exod 30:1–10, 39:38, 40:5, 26; I Kings 7:48.

candelabrum with all its furnishings. See Exod 25:31–40, 26:35, 30:27, 31:8, 37:17–24, 40:24.

22. *table.* Exod 25:23–30, 26:35, 40:22–24.

libation jars. Exod 25:29, 27:16.

bowls. Exod 27:3, 38:3.

golden ladles. Exod 25:29, 27:16; since the bowls were made of copper, "golden" applies only to the ladles.

23. *on deposit.* Literally, "hidden." The Hebrew was probably *ṭmwnym* (cf. Isa 45:3) or *gnwzym* (see M. Jastrow, *A Dictionary of the Targumim, the Talmud Babli and Yerushalmi, and the Midrashic Literature,* p. 258, and G. R. Driver, *Aramaic Documents* [Oxford: Clarendon Press, 1954], note to Letter X, line 5). In the ancient world there were few safe places to keep money. People would most often hide it or bury it (cf. Sir 29:10). Hence, even when they could take advantage of the sanctity of a temple to deposit their money, it was natural to use the same verb, "hide." See commentary on II 3:6–14.

24. See Introduction, p. 46, and NOTE on vs. 21, *Arrogantly.* On the echoes here of Isa 32:6, see introductory NOTE to I 2:28–38.

polluted himself with massacres. The Greek *phonoktonia* and the related verb *phonoktoneô,* properly used, refer only to the pollution of bloodguilt (Num 35:33; Ps 105 [106H]:38). The use of the words by Aquila, Symmachus, and Theodotion in contexts not involving bloodguilt (Jer 3:1, 2, 9; Isa 24:5) is a result of Aquila's determination to use the same Greek root at every occurrence of the Hebrew root ḥnp. Josephus' narrative of these events is greatly distorted, for he combines the story of the Mysarch's expedition with the story of Antiochus' sack of Jerusalem; see Appendix V. Josephus draws from the story of the Mysarch's expedition (I 1:30) his report that Antiochus penetrated Jerusalem by hypocritically pretending to have peaceful intentions (*AJ* xii 5.4.248–49). Nevertheless, he may have found support for his drastic rearrangement of the text in the words of vs. 24. The Hebrew ḥnp also carries the meanings of "hypocrisy" and "deceit," as at Isa 32:6. Josephus may have understood the Hebrew text here (*wy'š ḥnp*) to mean "he acted deceitfully." If so, we would have a good proof that Josephus had access to the Hebrew text.

On the probable common source of I 1:24 and II 5:21, see Introduction, pp. 100–1, and Part V, n. 34.

25–28. Whether it is a dirge contemporary with the events or the author's composition, the poem represents accurately the reaction of pious Jews to Antiochus' sack of Jerusalem. They would indeed take adversity as punishment for sin and hence would feel more shame than indignation. The poet may have believed that the events were a fulfillment of Joel 2:6, 10–17, and perhaps also of Amos 8:13, both of which may have served him as models.

25. Cf. Esther 4:3.

26. Cf. Lam 2:10; Amos 8:13; Dan 7:28.

27. Cf. Joel 2:16.

29–40. The campaign mentioned here is certainly the same as the campaign of Apollonius the Mysarch narrated, with some additional important details, at II 5:24–26; see p. 123. A Mysarch was a commander of mercenary soldiers from Mysia in Asia Minor; see Otto Schulthess, "Mysarches," PW, XVI (1935), 1187. Instead of "Mysarch," the Greek here has "a tax-gathering official" (*archonta phorologias;* Hebrew: *śar missîm,* which would have been spelled *śr msym* or *śr mysym*). "Mysarch" in Hebrew would have been *śar misîm* (spelled *śr msym* or *śr mysym*) or *śar musîm* (spelled *śr msym* or *śr mwsym*). Even if spelled *śr mwsym,* the Hebrew for "Mysarch" could have been read as "tax-gathering official," because *y* and *w* are indistinguishable in the Hebrew letter forms used by Jewish scribes from pre-Hasmonaean times until long after Josephus was dead. See Frank M. Cross, "The Development of the Jewish Scripts," in BANE, p. 175, lines 5–7, and pp. 176–77, lines 1, 3–10; N. Avigad, "The Palaeography of the Dead Sea Scrolls and Related Documents," *Scripta Hierosolymitana* 4 (1958), 83. Hence, the translator here may have misread the Hebrew, as Julius Wellhausen suggested ("Ueber den geschichtlichen Wert des zweiten Makkabäerbuchs, im Verhältnis zum ersten," *Nachrichten von der Königlichen Gesellschaft der Wissenschaften zu Göttingen, Philologisch-historische Klasse,* 1905, p. 161). However, *śr msym* occurs only at Exod 1:11, where the Greek renders it by "taskmasters" (*epistatas tôn ergôn*), not "tax gatherers." The usual word in Hebrew for both "taskmaster" and "tax gatherer" was *nōgēś* (Exod 5:14; Zech 9:8, 10:4; Dan 11:20). Our author may have intended to give a punning designation to the royal official: though his title was "Mysarch," his function was as tyrannical as that of Pharaoh's overseers in Exod 1:11; see A. Mitt-woch, "Tribute and Land Tax in Seleucid Judaea," *Biblica* 36 (1955), 356.

Indeed, Apollonius' expedition may have had the purpose of taking Judaea, a privileged territory of a nation (*ethnos*) which had a walled capital and paid taxes through its own officials, and reducing it to royal land (*chôra basilikê*) with only unwalled villages, taxed directly by the king; see Bikerman, *Institutions*, pp. 169–85. Then, the title "tax gatherer" would be an appropriate designation for Apollonius. See NOTE on 1:4, *provinces . . . dynasts*. The Seleucid government probably began at this time to levy on Judaea the punitively heavy tax of one third of the grain and one half of the fruit (I 10:30; cf. 11:34). See also Mittwoch, *Biblica* 36 (1955), 352–61, but note that Jerusalem before Apollonius' expedition was not a "city" in the sense of having the privileges of a Greek *polis;* rather it was the main urban center of a privileged people (*ethnos*). See V. A. Tcherikover, "Was Jerusalem a 'Polis'?" IEJ 14 (1964), 61–78.

Significantly, Antiochus V in his letter of 164 (II 11:27–33) still refrains from calling the Jews an *ethnos,* although the Roman ambassadors who at that time addressed a letter to the people (*dêmos*) of the Jews may have granted such recognition (II 11:34). Only in his letter of 162 does Antiochus V call the Jews an *ethnos* (II 11:25), a status which thereafter they appear to have retained (I 8:23–27; 10:20, 25; 11:30, 33, 42; 12:3, 6, etc.).

The expression "Two years later" means that the interval between the events was at least one year plus a fraction. See in AB vol. 41A Appendix VII. This chronology is consistent with the other data in First Maccabees, and no non-Jewish source contradicts it. Difficulties arise only when we compare First Maccabees with Daniel, Second Maccabees, and Josephus. The text of Daniel is the source of the difficulties. Jason of Cyrene and Josephus contradict our author only because they believe in the inspiration of Daniel. See Introduction, pp. 43–46, and Appendix V. However, both Jason and Josephus were wrong in interpreting Dan 11:28 to contradict I 1:20; see NOTE on vs. 20, *with a strong army*. They were probably also wrong in interpreting Dan 11:30 as contradicting I 1:29. Dan 11:30 does seem to have Antiochus himself attack Jerusalem for the second time immediately after his withdrawal from Egypt in 168. However, even Jason of Cyrene knew that Jewish tradition recorded only one attack on the holy city by Antiochus himself (see Introduction, p. 45).

Another interpretation of the text of Daniel, with the help of a plausible emendation, makes the seer speak the truth, as a contemporary witness should, and leaves him agreeing with I 1:29. All the third-person singular pronouns in Dan 11:30 must refer directly to Antiochus. They cannot refer to his agents, because in the immediate context where the seer wishes to refer to royal agents, he does so explicitly (Dan 11:31, 39; cf. the "exactor of tribute upon the glory of the kingdom" at 11:20). Hence 11:30 cannot refer to the expedition of the Mysarch, though some have so construed it (see Bickermann, *Gott,* pp. 161–62, 170).

"He shall be enraged" (*wz'm*) at 11:30 need refer only to Antiochus' thoughts and words without implying any physical violence before the king returned to Antioch. The verb *z'm* refers to attitudes of anger and verbal, not physical, actions at Num 23:7–8 and perhaps at Mal 1:4. At Isa 66:14 it can well refer to God's inner anger, realized externally in 66:15. Zech 1:12 refers to mental attitudes of mercy and anger, for 1:11 says the world is quiet; hence, no expressions of God's anger are present, but only the results of His anger of seventy years before.

As for "he shall take action" (*w'śh*) at Dan 11:30, which implies that the king did act violently, the Hebrew probably represents a misreading *w'bd* ("he shall take action") for *w'br* ("he shall pass through") of the seer's original Aramaic notes, for in this context the seer draws on the contexts of "passing through" and "rage" at Isa 8:8 (as at Dan 11:10, 40) and Isa 26:20 (as at Dan 11:36); see Ginsberg, p. 49. The misreading was all the easier since the similar context of the original Aramaic at Dan 11:28 probably did have "he shall take action." If so, the original Aramaic of Dan 11:30 meant, "He shall return and utter words of rage against the Holy Covenant but shall pass on, returning [to Syria], where he shall give a sympathetic hearing to apostates from the Holy Covenant." The text of Daniel would thus support the account here. The author of First Maccabees, indeed, says nothing of promptings by apostates—with good reason. At this point he prefers to view Antiochus as the "rod of God's anger." The Antiochene apostates at Jerusalem had been harried by pious Jews, whom Antiochus could view as rebels. The complaints of Antiochenes from Jerusalem probably did lead the king to send the Mysarch on his punitive mission; see AB vol. 41A, NOTE on II 5:23–24, *Disposed . . . slaves*. Apollonius' measures followed the usual Greek and Roman practices against rebels. See Introduction, pp. 109, 111, 122–25.

In the disordered text of Daniel 11, the Mysarch's expedition appears at vs. 39; vs. 31 can hardly refer to a defilement of the temple by Apollonius (cf. Jerome on Dan 11:31), for our author and even Jason of Cyrene mention none; see Introduction, p. 45. Dan 11:31 refers to the desecration and persecution which began late in 167.

The seer's scheme of history and the datability of his oracles make it possible to give a more accurate date for the Mysarch's expedition. Our author lets us know that at least one year plus a fraction elapsed between the sack of Jerusalem in September or October, 169, and the expedition. On the other hand, the seer at Dan 7:25 measured his three and a half years from the expedition of the Mysarch to the beginning of the sabbatical year in early autumn, 164. Hence, the Mysarch's expedition probably occurred in April, 167. In my commentary on Daniel I shall give a detailed argument for my interpretation of Dan 7:25.

30. *peaceful terms*. See Appendix IV, pp. 551–52.

31. To destroy the walls completely would have been an unnecessary and arduous task. Surely the Mysarch only made large breaches in them, since portions of the walls standing in his time still exist. See below, NOTE on vss. 33–40.

32. The measures against the civilian population were usual against an enemy city taken in war which had not surrendered. See commentary on II 5:11, *treating . . . war*.

33–40. This passage is the chief source for the establishment of the Akra in Jerusalem and for its effect on pious Jews; see Introduction, pp. 109, 123–24. On the failure of Jason of Cyrene to mention the Akra at this point, see commentary on II 5:24–27.

Misunderstanding of our passage and of texts in Josephus has given rise to the most vexed of the controversies over the topography of Hellenistic Jerusalem: Where was the Akra?

The Greek word *akra* is a synonym of "acropolis." See Xenophon *Anabasis* vii 1.20; J. *AJ* xii 9.3.365 and xiii 2.1.39–40 have "acropolis" where their parallels, I 6:26 and 10:7–9, have *akra*. The word means "a citadel built on a steep hill dominating a town." The subsequent narrative of our author makes clear how dominating the position of the Akra was in Jerusalem (4:41, 6:18–20, 11:20, 12:36, 13:49–52, 14:36–37), though never mentioning its altitude. Josephus repeatedly implies that the Akra stood higher even than the temple (*AJ* xii 5.4.252, 10.5.406, xiii 6.7.215). Difficulty arises because our passage here states that the Akra was located in the "City of David," and our author is not alone in doing so; an official document of the Jews, of late summer 139, does the same (I 14:36). As described in biblical texts (I Kings 8:1 and Neh 3:15) and as known from archaeology (K. Kenyon, *Jerusalem*, pp. 19–62) the City of David lay directly south of the temple, and on lower ground. Indeed, the slope of the hill to the south of the temple is such that no hill could ever have existed there to dominate the temple area. Both the temple and the City of David lay on the eastern of the two hills on which old Jerusalem is built. Only north of the temple area is there ground on the eastern hill dominating it. The only ground in Jerusalem higher than the temple area which lies to the south is southwest of it, across the *"Tyropoiôn"* valley, on the western hill, an area which was part of Jerusalem by the time of Herod and still lies within the walls of the old city. The valley has been much obscured by centuries of accumulated debris. See Map 1, p. 528.

Most modern writers have held that the Akra stood on the western hill, which somehow had been named "City of David" by the time of our author. See L. H. Vincent, "Jérusalem," *Dictionnaire de la Bible,* Suppl. IV (1949), 954–57; M. Avi-Yonah, "Archaeology and Topography," *Sepher Yerushalayim,* ed. M. Avi-Yonah, I (Jerusalem and Tel-Aviv: Bialik Institute, 1956), 316–18 (in Hebrew); Kenyon, *Jerusalem,* pp. 113–14, 135, 142. Some scholars have indeed proposed what we shall show (see Map 1) to be the correct solution, that the Akra stood at the north end of the eastern hill. See George Adam Smith, *Jerusalem* (London: Hodder & Stoughton, 1907–8), I, 158, and II, 446, n. 4; A. Legendre, "Jérusalem," *Dictionnaire de la Bible,* III 2 (1912), 1368–70; and Ben-Zion Lurie, *Megillath Ta'anith,* pp. 111–13 (in Hebrew).

The proposed location on the western hill is not only unnecessary. It is most improbable. Josephus explicitly contradicts it, but his words have puzzled scholars, and we shall treat the correct interpretation of them later. Even our author, however, gives no support to the proposed location on the western hill, for he had no reason to call the western hill "City of David." He knew scripture, and he knew Jerusalem. Writing before the great building projects of Herod, he could still see portions of the walls built by Nehemiah and by Hasmonaeans earlier than John Hyrcanus. Today the traces of those walls nowhere touch the western hill. See Kenyon, *Jerusalem,* pp. 105–37, and

W. A. Shotwell, "The Problem of the Syrian Akra," BASOR 176 (1964),
10–19. We now know that a wall of pre-exilic Jerusalem did extend onto
the western hill, but it was built about 700 B.C.E. Even if it was visible to our
author, there was no reason why he should call the area it enclosed "the City
of David." Moreover, the scarcity and poverty of the Hellenistic and early
Hasmonaean remains found on the western hill suggests that there were no
significant post-exilic structures in that area before the time of John Hyrcanus.
For the recent discoveries on the western hill, see N. Avigad, "Excavations
in the Jewish Quarter of the Old City of Jerusalem, 1970 (Second Preliminary
Report)," IEJ 20 (1970), 129–40, and "Excavations in the Jewish Quarter of
the Old City of Jerusalem, 1971 (Third Preliminary Report)," IEJ 22
(1972), 193–200, Y. Tsafrir, "The Location of the Seleucid Akra in Jerusalem,"
Qadmoniot 5 (1972), 125 (in Hebrew). Against early post-exilic occupation
of the western hill, see also the arguments of M. Avi-Yonah, "The Newly-
Found Wall of Jerusalem and Its Topographical Significance," IEJ 21 (1971),
168–69. Only the monumental Hellenistic column-base lying in fill beneath
an early Herodian level (Avigad, IEJ 20 [1970], 136–37) might indicate otherwise. Jews before the rise of the Hasmonaean dynasty are unlikely to have
produced such structures. If Antiochus IV had done any monumental building
at Jerusalem other than the extension of the fortifications of the Akra, our
authorities would have mentioned it, and all the more if he had begun a temple
for Olympian Zeus, as suggested by Avi-Yonah (IEJ 21 [1971], 169).
Indeed, if Antiochus IV had built a monumental temple to Olympian Zeus
at Jerusalem, he would have done so by replacing or enlarging the Jewish
temple; see II 6:2. Avigad, who excavated the column base, sees no reason
to date it so early ("Excavations in the Jewish Quarter of the Old City,"
Qadmoniot 5 [1972], 100 [in Hebrew]). Hence, the monumental base
would come from a time later than the fortification of the Akra, probably
from the reign of John Hyrcanus or a later Hasmonaean. Similarly, nothing
as yet indicates a date earlier than the time of John Hyrcanus for the Hellenistic remains reported by Ruth Amiran and A. Eitan, "Excavations in the
Courtyard of the Citadel, Jerusalem, 1968–69 (Preliminary Report)," IEJ
20 (1970), 11.

The northern part of the western hill was indeed inside the city walls before
the time of Herod; see C. N. Johns, "Recent Excavations at the Citadel,"
QDAP 14 (1950), 121–90, and the articles of Avigad and Amiran and Eitan,
IEJ 20 (1970), 11, 17, 137–39. According to Johns, pottery finds show
that the pre-Herodian wall around part of the western hill was built in the
Hellenistic period. Coins of Alexander Jannaeus and of John Hyrcanus II
(John Hyrcanus I issued no coins) have been found in connection with ancient
repairs on that wall. Thus we know that it was repaired on or shortly after
the reign of John Hyrcanus II.

The early Hasmonaean princes from Simon on had the power to extend the
limits of the city and its walls (I 14:42). First Maccabees at its very end
speaks of John Hyrcanus' "construction of the walls" (16:23); those walls
could well have enclosed the northern part of the western hill. A tradition
which is very old, since it is quoted by the editor of a Mishnah as an indis-
putable justification of his own ruling, can also be used to prove that the

incorporation of the northern part of the western hill into the city took place in the reign of John Hyrcanus: "Additions to the city and to the temple courts may be made only with the concurrence of a king, a prophet, the Urim and Thummim, and the Sanhedrin of seventy-one members" (Shebu'ot 2:2). Though John Hyrcanus did not have the title "king," he had all the powers of one as the heir of his father, Simon (I 14:41–49), including the power to extend the area of the walled city. However the chronology accepted by the sages of the Mishnah was reckoned, it included the reign of John Hyrcanus in the 103 years it assigned to the "kingdom of the Hasmonaean dynasty" (Seder 'olam rabbah 30, p. 142 Ratner), so that the Mishnah could easily regard him as a king. John Hyrcanus also claimed prophetic power (see Introduction, Part I, n. 8), and according to Josephus had the use of the Urim and Thummim. (See AJ iii 8.9.218 along with xx 12.1.267; two hundred years before 93/4 of the Christian era is 106/5, near the end of John Hyrcanus' reign. Josephus probably intended to refer in round numbers to the year of the Hasmonaean prince's death.) Josephus' tradition is not necessarily contradicted by M. Soṭah 9:12, which in its context need only mean that the Urim and Thummim ceased to function after "the death of the earlier prophets," presumably the death of Jeremiah; cf. To. Soṭah 13:2; TB Soṭah 48b, and TP Soṭah 9:13, p. 24b. It need not mean that the Urim and Thummim no longer existed and were never used in the time of the second temple. Indeed, M. Yoma 7:5 suggests both that they existed and that they could have been used, especially at a time when prophesy for a while was believed to have returned. The tradition at TB Yoma 21b does state that there were no Urim and Thummim in the time of the second temple, but it is the tradition of a Babylonian amora, and Maimonides did not accept it (Mishneh Torah, 'Abodah, Hilkot bet-habbeḥirah, 4:1), surely following other authoritative texts. See Rashi to TB Baba batra 133b s.v. lgzbr and Lieberman, Tosefta Ki-fshuṭah, Zera'im, p. 800, n. 45. Hence, the old Mishnah at Shebu'ot 2:2 may have intended to say that all future religiously binding extensions of the area of the holy city must follow the precedent set by John Hyrcanus.

Accordingly, our author could well have called the western hill the "City of John Hyrcanus." He could never have called it the "City of David." Hence, the Akra must have stood on the eastern hill.

Scholars have been led astray since they assumed that our author could use the name "City of David" only for the area of the eastern hill to the south of the temple. Biblical texts, however, use "City of David" to refer not only to the original city to the south of the temple but also to the entire area within the walls on the eastern hill, as at I Kings 11:27 and Isa 22:9 and Greek III Kings 2:35, 9:15 (Alexandrinus), 10:22a (Vaticanus), 12:24 (Vaticanus); it is used for the millō at II Chron 32:5. On the other hand, "City of David" could mean the citadel (mᵉṣūdāh) alone, as at II Sam 5:9.

Moreover, in view of the strongly fortified position of old Jerusalem on the eastern hill, it, too, was occasionally called citadel (mᵉṣūdāh or bīrāh). It may be for this reason that the Greek translator at Isa 22:9 rendered the Hebrew "City of David" by "akra of David." Certainly later Jewish authors call the city on the eastern hill "citadel"; see J. BJ i 1.4.39, v 6.1.252–53, and

TP *Pesahim* 7:8, p. 35a. Jason of Cyrene, too, probably referred to the temple mount as "acropolis," a synonym of *"akra,"* for he is scandalized that the gymnasium was built just below the acropolis (II 4:12). There would be small point in stressing the fact if the gymnasium stood just below a fort occupied by heathen soldiers (II 4:18) separated from the temple area by the *"Tyropoiôn"* ravine.

"Citadel" and "City of David" are thus ambiguous terms, the interpretation of which depends on the context. In our passage, the Akra, the fortified City of David, could easily mean a citadel to the north of the temple area. The evidence for a citadel there is abundant from the time of David on.

The eastern hill was protected by steep slopes and ravines along its lower reaches. There was relatively easy access only from the north near the highest peak of the hill, where the ravines grew shallower. Farther north lay still higher hills. A citadel on the northern peak of the eastern hill would both dominate the city and protect it at the weakest point in the terrain; cf. To. *Sanhedrin* 3:4=TP *Sanhedrin* 1:3, p. 19b, though not the version at TB *Shebu'ot* 16a. The Hebrew Bible does not give the direction of Solomon's fortification, the *millō,* but by indicating that it closed up the "weak point" (*pereṣ*) of the City of David, I Kings 11:27 reveals that the structure lay at the north end of the eastern hill. Some scholars have been misled by the derivation of *millō* from the Hebrew root *ml',* "be full," so as to believe that the *millō* must have involved filled ground, whereas there would have been no need for fill at the high north end of the eastern hill. However, the use of the word *millō* does not necessarily imply the filling of a depression, for the Akkadian cognate *mīlū* is used of an artificial earthwork, terrace, or embankment and even of a wall; see John Gray, *I & II Kings: A Commentary,* 2d ed. rev. (London: SCM Press, 1970), p. 243.

The Greek translators of the books of Samuel and Kings are more explicit. They call both David's and Solomon's fortifications *"akra"* and say that Solomon's fortifications blocked the easiest access to the City of David (Greek II Sam 5:9, I Kings 2:35f–g, 9:15 [Alexandrinus], 10:22a [Vaticanus], 11:27, 12:24 [Vaticanus]). Josephus, too, understood that David's *akra* lay on higher ground than the rest of the "lower city" (*AJ* vii 3.1.62–65), that is, to the north.

In post-exilic Jerusalem, a citadel (Hebrew *birah;* Greek *baris*) near the temple is attested already in the time of Nehemiah (Neh 2:8, 7:2). There is no reason to assume that the citadel used under Ptolemaic rule (J. *AJ* xii 3.3.133, 138; *Letter of Aristeas* 100–4) was different from the one used under Persian rule. The Seleucids probably continued to use the same citadel after Antiochus III captured Jerusalem in 200 (II 4:12, 28, 5:5). Though Jason of Cyrene calls this citadel *akropolis* rather than *akra,* the Greek words are synonyms, and the author of Fourth Maccabees in a passage (4:20) derived from II 4:12 calls the building *akra.* In the official Seleucid document of Antiochus III at J. *AJ* xii 3.3.138 the citadel is simply called "the Akra in Jerusalem." It was only natural for the Jews to give it the same name, especially since there was a Semitic equivalent with almost the same sound (*ḥaqra; Megillat Ta'anit* 23 Iyyar). The Jews probably also continued to call it by the names used in the Persian period (*birah, baris*), since the names reappear in a later period.

Nothing indicates that the citadel which dominated Jerusalem in the days of Antiochus IV was a totally different structure in a different place. An official Seleucid document (I 10:32), a Seleucid ambassador (I 15:28), the Hellenized Jews who lived behind the walls of the citadel (I 6:26), and pious Jewish authors (I 1:33, 3:45, 14:36, etc.; II 15:31–35) all call it "the Akra in Jerusalem." Since portions of the wall of Nehemiah still survive (Kenyon, *Jerusalem*, pp. 111–12 and plates LIV–LV), Apollonius in breaching the walls (I 1:31) did not demolish the entire circuit around the eastern hill. Even if he had, the terrain of the eastern hill made it such a stronghold that Antiochus would not have left it ungarrisoned by forces loyal to him. With the western hill still unwalled and perhaps unoccupied, Antiochus had no reason to pick a site on the western hill for his citadel in Jerusalem.

Apollonius the Mysarch put an end to the privileged status of Jewish Jerusalem and made it an unwalled village subject to the "foreigners" and "sinners" residing in the Akra; see above, NOTE on vss. 29–40. At first this "colony of foreigners" (I 1:38, 3:45) may have had pretensions to being a city-state. The evidence for such a status lies not in the vocabulary used by First and Second Maccabees; both use *polis* in the non-technical sense of "town," and "colony" (*katoikia*) in First Maccabees is far from proving that the Akra was a city-state. See below, on vss. 38–39. Rather, Antiochus' use of Roman patterns would suggest that the Akra was indeed a *polis,* a colony of Antiochene citizens. See Introduction, pp. 123–24. If so, since the citizens were called "Antiochenes," it would have been most natural to call the Akra "Antiocheia," "City of Antiochus," a name which pious Jews would have resented bitterly. It was probably resented the more as being a departure from Seleucid practice, which was to leave undisturbed the names of cities if the cities were named for kings. Even conquered cities bearing the dynastic names of defeated rivals kept their names: Antigoneia (John Malalas viii, pp. 199–200 Bonn, vol. XCVII, cols. 312–13 Migne; Dio Cassius xl 29.1; Glanville Downey, *A History of Antioch in Syria* [Princeton University Press, 1961], pp. 56–68, 150); Ptolemais (I 5:15, 22, 55, etc., II 13:24–25, etc.); Philadelphia (Ernst Honigmann, "Philadelpheia 3," PW, XIX[II] [1938], 2094–95); and Philoteria (Ernst Honigmann, "Philoteria," PW, XX[I] [1941], 181–82).

Jews had long been accustomed to name their citadel and city after King David. The natural retort to the Seleucid foundation of a Hellenistic Antiocheia in the Akra with Jerusalem as its subject territory was to insist that the citadel and city still were the "City of David." Thus, our author in vs. 33 is asserting the legitimacy of Jewish claims to Jerusalem, not misapplying archaic terminology. For him the City of David was still on the eastern hill and the Akra was the citadel on its northern peak. The scholiast to *Megillat Ta'anit* elsewhere shows no acquaintance with First Maccabees, yet he, too, connects the Akra with David's citadel (Schol. to *Megillat Ta'anit* 23 Iyyar).

Proper interpretation of the statements of Josephus confirms this identification of the Akra, giving us also the subsequent history of the stronghold at the north end of the eastern hill. Moreover, proper interpretation shows how truthful an eyewitness and how competent an interpreter of conflicting sources was this much maligned Jewish historian. I shall give elsewhere a full treatment of the texts in Josephus bearing on the Akra.

As a believer in the veracity of the prophesies of Daniel (*AJ* x 11.7.267–81; xii 7.6.322), Josephus had to disagree with First Maccabees on the date of the building of the Akra; see Introduction, pp. 46–47, 50–51. He produced two solutions to the problem, one in the *War* and one in the *Antiquities*. Both solutions indicate that Josephus never considered the possibility that the Seleucid Akra in the time of the persecution stood on the western hill.

When Josephus wrote the *War*, he had no copy of First Maccabees before him but only a general recollection of its content; see Introduction, pp. 60–61. The account of the Akra at *BJ* i 1.4.39 is probably derived from Dan 11:39. In Dan 11:34 Josephus read of Mattathias' revolt, the "small help," and thereafter of the persecutions and impieties perpetrated by Antiochus (Dan 11:35–38). Josephus then appears to have read the Hebrew text of Dan 11:39 to mean, "He [the small help, now identified with Judas] shall compel the people of a strange god, whom [the wicked King of the North] recognized and honored greatly and placed as rulers over the Many [i.e. over the pious Jews] and allotted land for a price, to become citadel builders [*m^ebaṣṣ^erēy mā'uzzīm*]." For '*śh l-* as "turn into," "compel to become," cf. Gen 12:2; Ezek 35:6, 37:22. If Antiochus' garrison of foreigners had not previously built a citadel, they must have occupied some other strong point before being dislodged by Judas. Josephus guessed that they had occupied the western hill, the "upper city" (see *BJ* v 4.1.137). Even so, when he turns to report that the foreigners when dislodged built a citadel, he firmly locates it in the lower city, on the eastern hill (*BJ* i 1.4.39).

As a matter of fact, the western hill was probably not occupied at the time of the persecution (see pp. 214–16), and Josephus may well have become aware of the truth when he wrote his *Antiquities*. In writing his later work he also had before him a text of First Maccabees which showed his account of the Akra in the *War* to be chronologically impossible. In order to preserve the veracity of Daniel, he took the reference at Dan 11:32 to Antiochus "flattery" of the "evil-doers of the Covenant" to mean that Antiochus protected them by building the Akra. From a later verse Josephus learned that subsequently Antiochus strengthened the Akra by stationing there a Macedonian garrison (Dan 11:39: "He shall provide, for the protection of those who built the fortresses, the nation of a strange god . . ."). Accordingly, he paraphrased Dan 11:39 at *AJ* xii 5.4.252 end. Again, however, Josephus located this Akra, built by Antiochus IV, in the lower city (ibid., beginning). In order to hold to the veracity of Daniel, Josephus found himself forced also to emend the text of First Maccabees; see Appendix V.

On Josephus' account of the later history of the Akra, see NOTE on I 13:52.

33. Cf. II Chron 8:5, 14:6.

34. The Mysarch and his army are the subject of the verb here, as in vss. 32 and 33. Hence, the "breed of sinners" stationed in the Akra must be distinct from the Mysarch's army. In fact the garrison consisted at least

partly of apostate Jews. See Introduction, pp. 123–24 and cf. J. *AJ* xii 5.4.252, 7.4.305.

37. Since the men of the Akra included apostate Jews and perhaps even apostate priests (see II 4:14–15, 5:5), the author of the dirge may be drawing on Lam 4:13. The gentiles and apostates of the Akra received from Antiochus the full privileges of citizens at Jerusalem; see Introduction, pp. 123–24. Therefore, they were entitled by royal law to enter the local temple (cf. V. A. Tcherikover, *Hellenistic Civilization and the Jews,* pp. 194–95). Pious Jews, however, knew that divine law forbade entry to the inner court of the temple to all but Jews in a state of ritual purity. Hence the poet complains that the men of the Akra defiled the temple. Cf. II 5:27.

The Mishnah reports (*Middot* 2:3) that the "kings of Greece" made thirteen breaches in the latticework barring gentiles from approaching the courts of the temple; see NOTE on I 9:54. "Kings of Greece" would be Seleucid kings (see NOTE on 1:1, *and thus . . . empire*), so that the Mishnah, if taken literally, can refer only to breaches made under Antiochus IV. The thirteen breaches could well have opened upon thirteen gates in the structures surrounding the temple courts; cf. *M. Middot* 2:6; *Sheqalim* 6:3; J. *AJ* xv 11.5.418. Perhaps the esthetic value of the latticework preserved it from being entirely demolished when it was no longer to serve to bar gentiles. It is a mistake to hold that the breaches were made later, by the Jewish high priest Alcimus (see I 9:54 and Abel, ad loc.). Even if the author of the tradition in the Mishnah might have wished to conceal Alcimus' role by vaguely blaming the "kings of Greece," our author would have been quick to condemn Alcimus explicitly for the heinous sin of seeking to let gentiles into the temple courts. Indeed, Alcimus was pious and could never have done so, and the structure he sought to demolish was not the latticework, but a barrier in the inner court of the temple. See Introduction, p. 75, and NOTE on vs. 21, above, and on 7:16–17 and 9:54. Since not the breach of the lattice but the entry of gentiles was heinous, both our author and Jason could easily leave it unmentioned.

38–39. Cf. Lam 5:1, 2, 18; I 4:38. On Lamentations 5 taken as a prophesy of Antiochus IV's persecutions, see NOTE on II 7:1.

rightful inhabitants . . . colony. Greek: *katoikoi . . . katoikia.* The Hebrew was surely *yōšᵉbēy . . . mōšab.* Although the Hebrew root *yšb* is vague and can mean simply residence (Gen 24:3; Exod 10:23, etc.), in contexts like ours it means residence and use of the land by right, conferred by a deity (Num 33:53–54; Deut 11:31, 12:29, 19:1, 26:1, etc.) or a king (II Kings 17:24; II Chron 8:2), and the construct plural of the participle (*yōšᵉbēy-*) followed by a geographical name usually means "rightful inhabitants of . . ." in this sense (Exod 23:31; Jer 1:14, etc.). The Greek translator used a Greek technical term, the meaning of which in many Hellenistic texts is hard to ascertain. Nevertheless, *katoikoi* in the Seleucid and Ptolemaic empires appear generally to have been settlers in colonies (*katoikiai*), on land granted to them by the king. See Bikerman, *Institutions,* pp. 100–5, and Rostovtzeff, SEHHW, pp. 477, 482, 491–93, 500–1, 729, 887, 890–91, 1522, n. 77; 1545, n. 164. Thus, the Greek, too, implies that the Jews were the rightful inhabitants.

festivals . . . mourning. Cf. Amos 8:10.

Sabbaths. The Mysarch attacked Jerusalem on the Sabbath. See II 5:25 and below, NOTE on I 2:28–38.

40. Cf. Ezek 24:21–24; Bar 4:34.

41–43. I have left all the verbs in the simple past tense in accordance with the Greek. However, since the verses surely refer to events which occurred shortly after Antiochus' accession and long before the Mysarch's expedition, pluperfect verbs would more accurately reflect historical reality. The author, too, may have known the date of the events, but he was writing in Hebrew, which has no pluperfect tense. See Introduction, pp. 119–20, 131.

44–53. Our author, writing with extreme brevity and using the broadest generalizations, here implies that the Hellenizers worshiped idols, but the relatively detailed account in Second Maccabees exposes the inaccuracy of the insinuation. Jason of Cyrene had no reason to minimize the sin of the Hellenizers, but in his account even Jason the Oniad is not accused of idolatry. See AB vol. 41A, commentary on II 4:18–20. On the nature of Antiochus' decree as an attempt to force a "purified" version of their own religion upon the Jews, see pp. 136–58, and below on vss. 54–64. On the date, see pp. 42–43.

44–51. From the way our author quotes the address and paraphrases the content of the letters, it is clear that he envisioned them as giving *direct* orders to the Jews of Jerusalem and Judah to violate the Torah; he did not envision them as orders to *royal officials* to compel the Jews to apostatize.

44. Josephus' paraphrase (*AJ* xii 5.4.253) has "[The king] compelled them to give up the service of their own God and to worship the gods in whom he believed." Josephus did not realize that his interpretation is excluded by the obscure words of Dan 11:37–38. For the true character of the religion imposed on the Jews by Antiochus, see above, Introduction, pp. 136–57. Like the seer at Dan 11:37–38, our author flatly contradicts Antiochus' claim to be purifying the native cult from degenerate accretions.

45. The first clauses of the king's decree sought to put an end to Jewish practices long condemned by Greeks. The decree as paraphrased says nothing about "peace offerings" and sin offerings. Only burnt offering, meal offering, and libation are forbidden. The three forbidden offerings together constituted the continual daily offering (*Tamid*); see Num 28:3–8; Dan 8:11–13, 7:31, 12:11; I 1:56; II 1:8; J. *AJ* xii 5.4.251; *BJ* i 1.1.32. On the *Tamid* see *M. Tamid.* Greeks did not offer daily burnt offerings, and Theophrastus (*apud* Porphyry *De Abstinentia* ii 26) found the idea monstrous; see Arthur Darby Nock, "The Cult of Heroes," HTR 37 (1944), 162, 174. On the pagan attitude to the Sabbath, see, Introduction, Part VI, n. 153.

46. *holy things.* All the Greek manuscripts have "saints" (*hagious*); "holy things" is found only in the best Latin manuscripts (La$^{L\,X\,G}$: *sancta*). "Saints" meaning "pious Jews" is found at Dan 7:21–22, 25, 27, and 8:24. The usage is derivable from Lev 18 – 19:2, 20:1–27, where the Holy People is commanded not to defile itself with the abominable practices of the gentiles. Note especially the mention of defiling the sanctuary at Lev 20:3 and of the dietary laws at Lev 20:25. If "saints" is the correct reading here, another source text for our author could have been Jer 2:3 (see NOTE on I 2:29–38).

The "holy things" of the Latin manuscripts, however, probably is the correct version. Nowhere in the books of Maccabees are pious Israelites called "the saints." Even at III 6:9 "saints" is an erroneous variant of A and its descendants. With the reading "saints" this verse would be the first to mention the atrocity of the forcible defilement of pious Jews, yet Josephus did not bother to paraphrase our verse at *AJ* xii 5.4.253. Indeed, forcible defilement of pious Jews is mentioned below in vs. 48. That verse is the proper context, for it deals with violations of the commands imposed on the body of the individual Jew, whereas vss. 45–47 deal with the temple service, communal rites, and cult structures. Finally, rabbinic sources speak frequently of the heinous sin of *ṭwm't mqdš wqdšyw*, "the defilement of the temple and its holy things." See especially To. *Shebu'ot* 1:3–5. The Latin translators show little or no knowledge of Hebrew. Their rendition must reflect the Greek which lay before them, an earlier text than our Greek manuscripts. Later Greek scribes knew Daniel and did not know Jewish law and may even have known that in Hebrew there is no distinction between a masculine and a neuter. They could well have changed the neuter *hagia* to the masculine *hagious* in order to get a reference to Daniel's "saints."

Even with the interruption of the daily offerings (*Tamid*), there were still "holy things" which could be defiled, including the meat of "peace offerings" and sin offerings, as well as the vegetable heave-offering (Lev 7:20–21; Num 18:8–19). Jews who partook of these "sacred things" while in a state of ritual impurity would defile them. The complicated Jewish laws concerning ritual impurity struck pagans as strange, if not repulsive. See E. Bikerman, "Une proclamation séleucide relative au temple de Jérusalem," *Syria* 25 (1946–48), 69–82. Antiochus here requires the Jews to violate them. The defilement of the temple and the holy things would make it impossible for pious Jews to offer the sacrifices still permitted to them. The altar itself was not defiled until later (vss. 54, 59).

47. *to build . . . shrines.* The king's intent here was to force the Jews to violate the laws of Deuteronomy which allowed sacrificial altars only in the temple and permitted only one temple (Deut 12:5–29). Josephus understood this in his paraphrase (*AJ* xii 5.4.253) and to make the meaning clear added to his version of our verse the words "in every city and village," which he drew from I 1:51. The Greek *bômos* can mean an idolatrous altar (Exod 34:13, etc.) but here probably means only an illicit one (as at Hosea 10:8; Amos 7:9; Jer 7:31–32 and 39[32H]:35), in accordance with Antiochus' declared intent to "restore" the cult of the Lord. Similarly, the Greek *temenos* here means an illicit temple, as at Hosea 8:14; note the adjacent mention of illicit altars at Hosea 8:11. The "idolatrous shrines" (*eidôlia*) were probably temples to the wife and child which Antiochus' "purged version" of Judaism provided for the Lord; see Introduction, pp. 145–57. To pious Jews the consort and child could only be "other gods," "idols." Josephus probably did not realize the distinction between the illicit temples (*temenê*) to the Lord and the idolatrous shrines (*eidôlia*) to the consort and child. Hence, in his paraphrase he omitted the idolatrous shrines as redundant (*AJ* xii 5.4.253).

sacrifice swine. See pp. 157–58.

ritually unfit animals. Greek *ktênê koina*, literally "ordinary animals," those which had not passed the stringent requirements required for Jewish sacrifices, which were much stricter than those for pagans; see Lev 22:19–24, Deut 15:21 and 17:1, and S. Lieberman, *Hellenism in Jewish Palestine*, pp. 153–56.

48. *uncircumcised.* See Introduction, pp. 139, 141, 158.

draw . . . profanation. Cf. Lev 11:43, 20:25, 21:4, and see NOTE on II 6:4.

49. Cf. Hosea 4:6; Ps 119:61, 109; Isa 24:5.

51. *Letters . . . to all his kingdom.* The reading with "all" is firmly established in the manuscript tradition (SV La^L X B). However, one important Greek manuscript (A) omits "all." Josephus appears to bear witness against the entire clause. He quotes a letter of Antiochus exempting the Samaritans from the persecution (*AJ* xii 5.5.257–64). Since Josephus liked to contrast the Samaritans with the Jews, one would expect him to mention immediately after *AJ* xii 5.5.264 any royal messages requiring persecution of Jews outside Judaea, yet he refrains from paraphrasing our passage. Indeed, in cities of Palestine outside Judaea attacks on Jews began only after Judas' rededication of the temple (I 5; II 12; see Bickermann, *Gott,* pp. 121–22). What messages, then, did Antiochus send "to all his kingdom"?

The key is probably to be found in the petition of the Samaritans to Antiochus, preserved by Josephus. In it the Samaritans write, "Now you have dealt with the Jews as their wickedness deserves, but the royal agents, believing that it is by reason of kinship that we follow the same practices as they, hold us to be implicated in the same sort of guilt." The Samaritans deny any kinship with the Jews and go on to ask the king to order the royal officials "not to molest us in any way by holding us to be implicated in the guilt of the Jews" (J. *AJ* xii 5.5.260–61). From the Samaritans' reflection of the content of the king's decree against the Jews, we may infer that it contained a motivating clause, "since you Jews have been guilty of rebellion." Cf. Welles, *Royal Correspondence in the Hellenistic Period,* nos. 15, line 21, and 73, line 3. On the use of the second person, see above on vss. 44–51. Jews were found widely over the Seleucid empire. In accordance with standard practice, the king may well have had copies made of his letters to Jerusalem and Judah to be sent to his officials throughout his empire, with a note to each official that the subjoined copy illustrated royal policy toward rebellious Jews. Cf. Bikerman, RHR 115 (1937), 191–96. The overzealous officials who had charge of the Samaritans immediately proceeded to apply like measures to them. Elsewhere in the Seleucid empire, officials may well have concluded that the Jews under their jurisdiction were not rebellious, at least for the time being. In speaking of messages to "all" the kingdom, our author may also have had in mind the enactment passed by the "Antiochene republic," on the proposal of the citizens of Ptolemais, against Jews in "Antiochene" communities. "Antiochene" communities were widely scattered over the Seleucid empire. See Introduction, pp. 117–27, 137–38.

51–53. *and he appointed . . . refuge.* The direct orders to the Jews might be disobeyed. Hence, Antiochus appointed officials (Greek *episkopoi,* surely from Hebrew *p^eqîdîm*) over the Jews to see to the implementation, and he specified the towns as the places where sacrifices were to be offered.

The wording of the passage may well be modeled on II Chron 19:4–20:31; Antiochus' impious arrangements are contrasted with Jehoshaphat's righteous ones. Jehoshaphat's reforms apply to every fortified town of Judah (II Chron 19:5); Jews "gather" from everywhere to seek the LORD (II Chron 20:4) and, far from hiding, boldly go out to sing psalms in the presence of an armed enemy (II Chron 20:20–21).

One of Antiochus' supervisory officials was an Athenian; see NOTE on II 6:1. It is likely that Antiochus did not trust Jews to suppress their fellows and appointed exclusively non-Jews to these posts. On Dan 11:30, see Introduction, Part VI, n. 336. Our author believes that Antiochus was acting as the "rod of God's anger," punishing Israel for tolerating the sins even of moderate Hellenizers; see NOTES on vss. 11–15, 20. Our author refrains from ascribing Antiochus' measures to the suggestions of apostates: Antiochus' policy was his own. *After* his decrees the out-and-out apostates gathered around his officials in support; cf. I 6:23. Antiochus, his officers, and their apostate supporters would in turn suffer retribution.

52–64. It is characteristic of the narrative style of the Hebrew Bible to describe how a commandment or a covenant was executed; e.g. II Kings 23:1–3 (covenant) and 4–24 (execution); II Sam 24:2–4a (order) and 4b–9 (execution); and the accounts of the tabernacle in Exodus. Here our vss. 44–51 are a paraphrase of Antiochus' decrees, vss. 52–53 describe voluntary compliance by some Jews, and vss. 54–64 describe the forcible implementation. Josephus, writing in Greek style, which assumes that a powerful king's orders are carried out, intentionally combined and condensed our vss. 44–51 and 52–64 at *AJ* xii 5.4.251–56; and down to 253 he spoke of the king's actions, not of his orders. Indeed, for Josephus, Antiochus' "second" sack of Jerusalem, the decrees against Judaism, the desecration of the temple, and the persecution were almost simultaneous. See Appendix V. Hence, he did not hesitate to telescope the several passages of First Maccabees into a fused narrative.

52. *forsaker of the Torah.* Cf. Ps 119:53; Prov 28:4; Dan 11:30; J. *AJ* xii 5.1.240.

they committed . . . land. They practiced idolatry. Cf. Jer. 44:9 in the context of Jer 44:7–10.

53. Cf. Isa 26:20 and Ezek 33:27, where Symmachus rendered "strongholds" as "hiding places." The pious Jewish victims may well have taken Isa 26:20 as an instruction for their own times. Our author may thus reflect a source contemporary with the events. See Introduction, Part V.

54–59. The "abomination of desolation" probably consisted of three meteorite cult-stones (*maṣṣēbōt*), which represented the God of the Jews; his female divine consort, the Queen of Heaven; and his divine son, "Dionysus." See Introduction, pp. 143–57.

The manuscript tradition is almost unanimous in giving 15 Kislev (December 6, 167 B.C.E.) as the date of the erection of the "abomination of desolation." One of the Syriac versions (SyII) is alone in reading "twenty-fifth" instead of "fifteenth." The oracles in Daniel, properly interpreted, measure the period of the descecration from the fifteenth, as I shall show in my commentary on Daniel. The obvious date for a later writer to give would be the twenty-fifth, the date of the Feast of Dedication; cf. II 10:5 and J. *AJ* xii 5.4.248. No later writer or scribe would be likely to substitute the fifteenth for the twenty-fifth. Hence, our author's account is correct against those of Jason of Cyrene and Josephus and the reading of SyII. The first desecration of the temple altar occurred on the fifteenth, not on the twenty-fifth, and consisted of the erection of the "abomination of desolation." Our author does not single out 25 Kislev as a date of desecration here, and probably never did so. The words indicating that he did, at I 4:54 (cf. I 4:59), are probably an interpolation; see ad loc.

It may have been the Syrian pagan festival calendar which led Antiochus to pick the month of Kislev; see Introduction, pp. 155–56, and introductory NOTE to 4:36–54, end. Jewish or Greek practices may have led him to pick the fifteenth day. The dedication of Solomon's temple began on the great festival in the seventh month (II Chron 5:3); that festival begins on the fifteenth of the month (Lev 23:34, 39). For Greeks, the time of the full moon around the fifteenth was an auspicious one for making beginnings; see Martin P. Nilsson, *Die Entstehung und religiöse Bedeutung des griechischen Kalenders* (Lunds Universitets Årsskrift, N.F., Avd. 1, Bd. 14, Nr. 21 [1918]), p. 37, and *Geschichte der griechischen Religion*, I 624.

As for the twenty-fifth day of the month, it may have been the birthday of Antiochus IV. See NOTE on II 6:7. It is probably by deliberate choice that our author here makes no special mention of 25 Kislev and speaks of observances that occurred on the twenty-fifth of every month.

54–55. *in the outlying towns . . . sacrifices.* See above on vs. 47. "Offer illicit sacrifices" is literally "make to smoke" (*thymian*) and translates the Hebrew *qtr*, the verb used in the Bible for illicit sacrifice. The effort to secure participation in a religious rite by all inhabitants through requiring sacrifices at the doors of houses is known from Greek cities of the second century B.C.E.; see Syll.[3] 695=Franciszek Sokolowski, *Lois sacrées de l'Asie mineure* (Paris: E. de Boccard, 1955), no. 33, lines 7–10, and cf. lines 43–45, 54–55; see also Nilsson, *Geschichte der griechischen Religion*, II, 87–88, and Bickermann, *Gott*, p. 119. The sacrifices at the doors and in the squares may also have been intended as deliberate violations of Deuteronomy and of prophetic teaching. Cf. Deut 12:5–18, where the single legitimate place for sacrifice is contrasted with "thy gates." Ezekiel (16:25, 31) may have condemned illicit shrines ("lofty places") in town squares. According to Jeremiah (7:17), the cult of the Queen of Heaven was practiced "in the towns of Judah and in the streets of Jerusalem."

56–57. The commandments of the Torah had driven pious Jews to attack the "Antiochenes" and rebel against the king; see Introduction, pp. 121–22. Hence, Antiochus viewed the Torah as a subversive book. To possess a copy of the Torah or to obey whatever of its provisions the king had defined as subversive was in itself an act of rebellion and was punished accordingly. Such procedure was surely common in the ancient world against writings deemed subversive to the government. See Jeremiah 36; and cf. Plato *Republic* iii 386a–403b, x 595a–608b, and Herodotus v 67.2. Nevertheless,

Antiochus could again have learned from Roman precedents. See Livy xxxix 16.8 and Introduction, pp. 125–26, 130–31.

57–64. Our author's silence here on the tortures suffered by the martyrs is eloquent, compared to II 6:7 – 7:42. In fact, our author had considerable contempt for the martyrs. For Josephus such an attitude toward the martyrs was inconceivable, and at *AJ* xii 5.4.255–56 he supplemented the account here with material probably drawn from the account of Jason of Cyrene. See commentary to II 6:12 – 7:42 and Introduction, pp. 7, 73.

58–59. Though our author may be drawing on Isa 10:13 and Dan 8:24, the expression, "Through their strength they acted," is unparalleled in the Hebrew Bible. So is the verbal construction: narrative which begins with a finite verb in vs. 58 but appears to be continued by "and" followed by a participle (*thysiazontes*=Hebrew *mᵉzabbᵉḥīm* or *mᵉqaṭṭᵉrīm*), literally, "and . . . offering sacrifices on the illicit altar. . . ." See GKC §§ 111–12 (pp. 326–39) and 116*m–x* (pp. 359–61); Abel, *Grammaire du grec biblique*, p. 330. The difficulty was felt by a few of the Greek scribes, who made the verb of vs. 59 finite.

It looks as if our author was deliberately straining the Hebrew language. Indeed, he could have modeled his expression on two other texts. The third-person plural pronouns in our context refer to the apostates, as is clear from vs. 52. "Through their strength they acted" may be a derisive borrowing of the language of the description of the courage of the martyrs at Dan 11:32b, "but the people who know their God shall be strong and act." For our author, not the Pietist martyrs, but the apostates had strength and acted.

As for the syntactical problem, one other verse in the Hebrew Bible, II Chron 30:21, has the identical grammatical structure. Where I 1:58 has the circumstantial prepositional phrase, "through their strength," II Chron 30:21 has "with great gladness"; where I 1:58 has the finite verb, "they acted" (*epoioun*, Hebrew *'āśū*), II Chron 30:21 has "they kept" (*epoiêsan*, Hebrew *wayya'ăśū*); both verses then speak of the Israelites who were found (=present); then, where I 1:58 has the expression of time, "each month," II Chron 30:21 has "seven days." After the clause with the finite verb, II Chron 30:21 has a circumstantial participial phrase, coordinate with the circumstantial prepositional phrase, as follows: "with great gladness and [with] the Levites and the priests praising the LORD. . . ." Hence, we may take the participle of I 1:59 as coordinate with the circumstantial prepositional phrase, "Through their strength and in offering sacrifices"; our translation of vs. 59, "as . . . they would offer sacrifices," follows this understanding of the syntax, while substituting idiomatic English and preserving the original word order. Where I 1:59 has, within the participial phrase, the expression of time, "on the twenty-fifth of the month," II Chron 30:21 has "day by day."

II Chron 30:21 describes King Hezekiah's reinstitution of the complete observance of the Feast of Unleavened Bread in the sole legitimate sanctuary, at Jerusalem. Our author appears to have been pleased to imitate II Chron 30:21 in telling of King Antiochus' institution of pagan festival rites in the illicit town-shrines and on the idolatrous altar in the temple at Jerusalem. Cf. above, NOTE on vss. 51–53.

58. *in the towns each month.* In the mention of the towns here, see above on vss. 54–55. On the monthly observance of the king's birthday, see on II 6:7. The only possible reflection of the monthly celebration in Josephus is the phrase "each day" (*kath' hêmeran*) at *AJ* xii 5.4.253. Josephus may have misunderstood the reference, or he may have deliberately refrained from an accurate rendering. Since he surely observed the anniversaries of his patrons, the Flavian emperors, he would not have wished to suggest that it was a violation of Jewish law to celebrate a royal birthday.

60–61. See vss. 48–50 and Introduction, pp. 138–39, and cf. II 6:10. "Hanging" (*kremasai*) was also the punishment for pupils of forbidden philosophers; see Introduction, Part VI, n. 143. Verse 61b ("and . . . circumcisions") in the best witnesses to the text (A S La^X; on the reading of La^L G see de Bruyne's apparatus) contains no verb. The difficulty was felt by many Greek scribes so that other witnesses to the text supply various verbs. However, there is no need to assume that a verb has fallen out. Josephus (*AJ* xii 5.4.256) supplied the verb "crucified," perhaps from Test Moses viii 1 or perhaps by seeing a zeugma in the verb "they hanged" of vs. 61a: the babes were suspended, and their parents crucified. It is best, however, to take "they executed" of vs. 60 as the verb governing vs. 61b. Whereas the Greek translator's idiom had only the noncommittal "and," the original Hebrew could have had "and also" (*wᵉgam*), which serves to direct the reader's mind back to the verb of vs. 60. Cf. the use of *wᵉgam* at Gen 14:16; Judg 2:10; I Kings 15:13 (esp.); II Kings 23:15; II Chron 3:32, 36:22. I have translated accordingly, supplying "executing" from "put to death" in vs. 60.

I have translated *oikous* (=Hebrew *bāttīm*) as "husbands." Literally, the word means "houses," and here it could mean "families." Cf. Greek Esther 8:13. To wipe out the entire family in which a circumcision occurred would not be too bloodthirsty a procedure for Antiochus, but it could lead to awkward results: what if a member of such a family was an apostate? Josephus (*AJ* xii 5.4.256) may well have taken the word to mean "spouse," a meaning which it has in rabbinic Hebrew; see *M. Yoma* 1:1, *Miqwaot* viii 4; TP *Niddah* 1:1, p. 48d; TB *Niddah* 5a, etc.

62–63. The Hebrew underlying "strongly and steadfastly" was probably *ḥāzᵉqū wᵉʾāmᵉṣū*, though nowhere else in the Greek Bible is the Hebrew phrase "be strong and steadfast" (Deut 31:7, 23; I Chron 22:13, etc.) rendered by the Greek verbs *krataioô* and *ochyroô*. Our author may have chosen words connoting the utmost in steadfast courage to deny the insinuations at Dan 11:32–35, that only the Pietist elite were steadfast Jews. On the contrary, many Israelites were. They gave up their lives ("they were put to death" at the end of vs. 63 is emphatic) despite the falsity of the Pietist seer's promise (Dan 12:2–3) that they would be resurrected.

For the idiom "strongly refuse" (*ekrataiôthêsan en autois*=*ḥāzᵉqū bᵉnapšōtēhem*), cf. Deut 12:23 and Jer 17:21.

64. "Wrath" (*orgê*) here probably reflects, not the common *qeṣep* (Num 1:53, 18:5; Josh 22:20; II Kings 3:27; Zech 1:2, 7:12; II Chron 24:18, 29:8, etc.) but the rarer *ḥārōn*, found at Ezek 7:12, 14, at Neh 13:18, and (most important) at Num 25:4 in the story of Phineas. Our author here

probably begins to set the scene for the portrayal of Mattathias as a latter-day Phineas; see Introduction, pp. 5, 6, 8.

Our verse also expresses the author's conviction that the persecution and God's failure at first to answer His people's prayers were the result of the sins of the apostates and those who tolerated them; cf. Zech 7:12–14, and see Introduction, p. 73.

V. MATTATHIAS' ACT OF ZEAL
(2:1–26)

2 1 During that time, Mattathias, son of John son of Simeon, a priest of the clan of Joarib, left Jerusalem and settled at Modeïn. 2 Mattathias had five sons: John, nicknamed Gaddi; 3 Simon, called Thassi; 4 Judas, called Maccabaeus; 5 Eleazar, called Auaran; and Jonathan, called Apphus. 6 Seeing the impieties that were being perpetrated in Judah and in Jerusalem, 7 he exclaimed,

> "Woe is me! Why was I born
> to see the ruin of my people
> and the ruin of the holy city?
> The people sat idle there
> as the city fell into the hands of enemies,
> the sanctuary into the hands of foreigners.
> 8 Her people acted like a base coward.
> 9 Her glorious furnishings have gone into captivity.
> Her babes have been killed in her squares,
> her young men by the sword of the enemy.
> 10 What nation has not inherited kingdoms
> and has not seized her spoils?
> 11 All her ornaments have been taken away;
> from a free woman she has become a slave.
> 12 Behold, our sanctuary, our beauty, our glory has been
> laid waste,
> and the gentiles have profaned it.
> 13 Why should we go on living?"

14 Mattathias and his sons rent their garments and put on sackcloth and were overcome by grief.

15 The king's officials in charge of enforcing apostasy came to the town of Modeïn to make them sacrifice. 16 Many Israelites came up to meet them, and Mattathias and his sons were brought into the gathering. 17 The king's officials addressed Mattathias as follows, "You are a respected and distinguished leader in this town, sup-

ported by sons and kinsmen. 18 Now be the first to come forward
and obey the command of the king as all the gentiles have done, as
well as the people of Judah and those who have been allowed to remain in Jerusalem. In return, you and your sons will be raised to the
rank of the Friends of the King, and you and your sons will be honored by grants of silver and gold and many gifts."

19 Mattathias replied in a loud voice, "If all the gentiles under the
king's rule listen to his order to depart from the religion of their fathers and choose to obey his commands, 20 nevertheless, I and my
sons and my kinsmen shall follow the covenant of our fathers. 21 Far
be it from us to desert the Torah and the laws. 22 We shall not listen to the words of the king, that we should transgress against our
religion to the right or to the left."

23 When he had finished uttering these words, a Jewish man came
forward in the sight of all to offer sacrifice upon the altar in Modeïn
in accordance with the king's decree. 24 When Mattathias saw this,
he was filled with zeal and trembled with rage and let his anger rise,
as was fitting; he ran and slew him upon the altar. 25 At the same
time he also killed the king's official in charge of enforcing sacrifices,
and he destroyed the altar. 26 He acted zealously for the sake of the
Torah, as Phineas acted against Zimri the son of Salom.

NOTES

2:1–26, introductory NOTE: On our author's deliberate use of the motifs of
the story of Phineas (Num 25:1–15), see Introduction, Part I, pp. 5–8; on
the counterpart in Second Maccabees, see in AB vol. 41A NOTE to II 6:18–
31.

1–5. Mattathias and his sons had names extremely popular at the time, especially among the priesthood. See the index to *Flavii Iosephi Opera*, ed.
Benedictus Niese, vol. VIII, s.vv. As in Rome, nicknames (*cognomina*) were
used to distinguish one bearer of a common name from another. "Simon" was
so common that Josephus mentions several with cognomina, and in rabbinic
literature several are referred to, not by their names, but by their patro-
nymics. On "Ḥashmonay" as Mattathias' nickname, see Introduction, pp. 17–
19.

Nicknames come from a wide variety of origins. They often are formed by
drastically shortening and distorting names and epithet-phrases; see Martin
Noth, *Die israelitischen Personennamen im Rahmen der gemeinsemitischen
Namengebung* (Stuttgart: Kohlhammer, 1928), pp. 36–41. Here the nick-

names are further distorted by being transliterated from Hebrew or Aramaic into Greek. "Gaddi" and "Thassi" are typical shortened forms. In no case can one be sure of the origins and meanings of the six nicknames.

1. The same pattern of identification, "X, son of Y son of Z, priest," introduces Phineas (Num 25:7, 11). Our author stresses that Mattathias was a priest of distinguished lineage, who had resided at Jerusalem, though he withdrew at the time of the persecution to obscure Modeïn, where the family had long had its seat (I 2:70, 9:19, 12:25). Josephus in his paraphrase (*AJ* xii 6.1.265) seems to wish to avoid suggesting that Mattathias originated in obscure Modeïn: he did reside there, but was a Jerusalemite. On the clan of Joarib (=Yehoyarib), see Introduction, pp. 17–21.

The language "left . . . and settled at . . ." may be derived from the story of the fugitive David at I Sam 23:29 [24:1H].

The town of Modeïn lies in the mountains, northwest of Jerusalem, twelve kilometers east of Lydda; see Map 2, p. 528. Some authors have asserted that Modeïn was outside the political boundaries of Judaea at the time of the persecutions; see Gustav Beyer, "Die Stadtgebiete von Diospolis und Nikopolis im 4. Jahrh. n. Chr. und ihre Grenznachbarn," ZDPV 66 (1933), 234, and Stern, *Kirjath Sepher* 46 (1970), 97 (in Hebrew). The only evidence in favor of their theory is at II 13:13–14, where Judas first decides to engage the Seleucid army before it will have entered Judaea, and then he encamps "near" (*peri*) Modeïn. Since Modeïn was a Hasmonaean stronghold near the main road running through Lydda, Jason of Cyrene or his source could have written in this manner even if Modeïn lay within the territory of Judaea, as it probably did. Furthermore, Jason was probably wrong in placing the battle near Modeïn. See in AB vol. 41A NOTE on II 13:10–17.

2. *Gaddi*. Cf. Num 13:10. If not a shortened or distorted form, it could mean "lucky."

3. *Thassi*. So numerous are the possibilities that speculation is futile as to the origin of the nickname. The best manuscripts at J. *AJ* xii 6.1.266 have "Thatis" or "Thathis."

4. *Maccabaeus*. Hebrew or Aramaic *mqby;* perhaps it means "hammerlike."

5. *Auaran*. The Syriac version has *ḥwrn*. If derived from the root *ḥwr*, the nickname could mean "paleface."

Apphus. The Syriac version has *ḥpws*. Perhaps the nickname is derived from the root *ḥpṣ*, "desire."

6. *impieties*. Greek *blasphêm-* renders Hebrew *n'ṣ* at Isa 52:5 and Ezek 35:12. The original Hebrew here may well have been modeled on Neh 9:18, 26.

7. *sat idle*. Cf. Judg 5:17; Jer 8:14; Hag 1:4. At the very outset of his lament, Mattathias deplores the Pietists' abstention from rebelling against the king who had perpetrated atrocities against God himself; see Introduction, pp. 5–6.

8. The translation "people" follows *laos*, the reading of 93 311 La$^{L X G}$ Lucifer. Other texts have *naos* ("temple"). Greek scribes could easily misread or miswrite lambda as nu. The context demands the reading *laos*. The other reading could be translated only as, "Her temple has become like a man despised." Comparison of a building to a man would be odd. With our reading,

vss. 8–9a become parallel to vs. 7: in both Mattathias complains of pious inaction in the face of outrage.

base coward. The Hebrew original was *'îš niqleh* ("a man disgraced" or "despised"; cf. I Sam 18:23). The root *qlh* expresses the disgrace of cowardice at Jer 46:12; cf. also Nahum 3:13.

9. *Her . . . into captivity.* Cf. Isa 46:1–2.

Her babes . . . enemy. Cf. Lam 2:11, 21.

10. *kingdoms.* Reading *basíleia* with A and numerous minuscules and La^L ^X ^G. The Lucianic reading, *en basileiai,* followed by S, yields very good sense, too: "What nation has not inherited [her] kingdom. . . ." Our reading is attested by more reliable authorities and fits the attitude of our author and his contemporaries and recent ancestors. Israel had been promised rule over many kingdoms by the Torah (Num 24:7–8, 17–19; Deut 3:41, 7:24, 28:25) and by the prophets (Isa 60:12; Obad 19–21; cf. Isa 11:14). After such promises, Jews found it hard to bear that not they but Assyrians, Babylonians, Medes, Persians, and Graeco-Macedonians "inherited" imperial rule over kingdoms. The prophesies in Daniel 2 and 7 and CD 8:56–57 and the conquests of the Hasmonaean princes and kings reflect these longings of the Jews for empire, and so may Mattathias' lament here: not only do other nations get the empire promised to the Jews; they also take the spoils of Judaea.

11. Cf. Exod 33:5–6; Jer 2:32; Lam 5:16.

12. Cf. Isa 64:10; Jer 51:51; Lam 1:10.

15–25. Josephus himself rejected the version of the story which he gave at *BJ* i 1.2–3.35–36; see Introduction, pp. 60–61.

16. An active verb (*prosêlthon*), from which the word "proselyte" is derived, tells how some Israelites "came up to meet" Antiochus' officials voluntarily; a passive verb tells how Mattathias and his sons "were brought into the gathering" (cf. Lev 26:25). The wording of the translator is probably deliberate, and he may well have been reflecting the Hebrew original.

17. *kinsmen.* Literally, "brothers," but the word means "kinsmen" at Gen 29:12, 15, and Num 16:10.

18–19. *as all the gentiles . . . his commands.* See Introduction, pp. 117–20, 131.

18. *those . . . in Jerusalem.* See NOTE on I 1:34.

rank of the Friends of the King. The Friends of the King had the privileges of members of the royal court. They were entitled to wear purple broad-brimmed Macedonian hats and purple robes. See Bikerman, *Institutions,* pp. 40–50.

23. The verse is modeled on Num 25:6.

24. *When . . . zeal.* Cf. Greek Deut 32:19.

trembled with rage. Literally, "his kidneys trembled." For the kidneys used as the seat of the emotions, cf. Prov 23:16.

let his anger rise. For the Hebrew idiom, see Ezek 24:8, 38:18.

as was fitting. Or "in accordance with the law" of Deut 13:7–10, 17:2–7, in contrast to the apostate, who acted "in accordance with the king's decree."

slew him upon the altar. Cf. II Kings 23:20. According to Josephus (*AJ* xii 6.2.270), Mattathias' sons joined him in slaying the apostate, using butchering axes (*kopisin*). Josephus or his source may have assumed that Mattathias and his sons would surely observe the procedure prescribed by Deut 17:6–7, even if the more fainthearted bystanders did nothing. Our author, who equates Mattathias, the lone zealot, with Phineas, the lone zealot, could not have had the sons join in the act of zeal. The axes appear also in the version of the story at *BJ* i 1.2–3.35–36. They, too, may be drawn from oral tradition; as standard equipment for priests, they could have been in the hands of Mattathias and his sons without arousing the suspicions of the royal authorities. Josephus may also have regarded execution by a butchering axe as the punishment prescribed by the Torah. One who sacrificed to idols was to be *ḥērem,* "doomed" (Exod 22:19). In the laws concerning what is redeemable and what is irredeemable, the "doomed" is defined as irredeemable (Lev 27:28–29); if not redeemed, firstborn animals were to be killed by an axe blow in the neck (Exod 13:13, 34:20; To. *Bekorot* 1:17). Josephus or his source may have believed that the law for executing the "doomed" sacrificer was the same.

25. At *BJ* i 1.2–3.35–36, Josephus gives the name of the royal official as Bacchides, but at *AJ* xii 6.2.270 he tacitly corrects his error, changing the name to Apelles. The name of the official could well have been preserved by the author of *DMP* (see Introduction, pp. 92–97), but nothing else indicates that Josephus had in his possession the original text of *DMP*. On the other hand, the name "Apelles" could have been lost by haplography because the word which followed also began *"ape-"* (*Apellēn apekteinen*). If so, in the copy of First Maccabees which lay before Josephus, whether Hebrew or Greek, the name was preserved, even though otherwise it has disappeared from the entire manuscript tradition.

26. *Salom.* The Masoretic Hebrew text at Num 25:14 has "Salu."

VI. MATTATHIAS' GUERRILLA CAMPAIGN
(2:27–48)

2 27 Mattathias cried out throughout the town in a loud voice, "All who are zealous for the sake of the Torah, who uphold the covenant, march out after me!" 28 Thereupon he and his sons fled to the mountains, leaving behind all their possessions in the town.

29 At that time many went down to dwell in the desert, seeking Justice and Vindication, 30 they and their children and their wives and their cattle, hard pressed by the persecutions. 31 A report came to the king's men and to the forces in Jerusalem, the City of David, that men who had violated the command of the king had gone down to the hiding places in the desert. 32 With a large force they pursued them and, on coming upon them, they encamped and formed in battle line against them on the Sabbath day, 33 saying to them, "Come out to us and obey the word of the king, and we shall let you live." 34 They, however, replied, "We shall neither come out nor obey the word of the king to profane the Sabbath day!" 35 Accordingly, they advanced quickly upon them in battle line. 36 But the Jews neither replied to them nor hurled a stone at them nor blocked the entrances to their hiding places, 37 saying, "Let us all die in our innocence. Heaven and earth bear witness over us, that you condemn us unjustly." 38 They attacked them in battle line on the Sabbath. They were killed with their wives, their children, and their cattle, to the number of one thousand human beings.

39 When the news reached Mattathias and his friends, they were deeply grieved over the victims' fate. 40 They said to one another, "If we all do as our brothers have done and do not fight against the gentiles for our lives and our laws, they will now quickly wipe us off the face of the earth." 41 On that day they came to a decision: "If any man comes against us in battle on the Sabbath day, we shall fight against him and not all die as our brothers died in their hiding places."

42 Thereupon, a company of Pietists joined them, mighty war-

riors of Israel, all who volunteered in defense of the Torah. 43 All who were fleeing the persecutions joined them as supporters. 44 As they gained strength, they smote sinners in their anger and lawless men in their wrath, so that the survivors fled to the gentiles for their lives. 45 Mattathias and his friends went around destroying the illicit altars 46 and forcibly circumcising all the uncircumcised babies they found within the boundaries of Israel. 47 They drove out the men of arrogance, and their enterprise prospered. 48 They saved the Torah from the hand of the gentiles and from the hand of the kings and prevented the triumph of the wicked.

NOTES

2:27–48, introductory NOTE. On the parallels to stories of David, see Introduction, p. 7.

27–28. Cf. Exod 32:26; Jer 34:18; I Sam 22:1.

28–38. The author sharply contrasts the Hasmonaeans' David-like realism with the foolish faith of the martyrs in their interpretation of prophesies. The Hasmonaeans flee, unimpeded by property, to the rugged but watered mountains, there to fight successfully. The martyrs flee, encumbered by their flocks, down to the desert, seeking a miracle, only to perish.

Clearly the martyrs believed that armed resistance would be useless if not impious; cf. Zech 4:6 and see in AB vol. 41A NOTE on II 1:7. They held the prophets foretold that God would avenge His people if they went out to the caves in the desert and observed the Sabbath. God would act either by rescuing the martyrs there and then or by being roused to save the survivors should the innocents who went out to the wilderness be slaughtered by the wicked oppressors. Several prophesies allowed such interpretation, especially the obscure Isaiah 32, and the verbal echoes of the passages in the narrative here leave little doubt that they did inspire the actions of the martyrs.

The martyrs "went down to dwell in the desert, seeking Justice and Vindication." They may have called themselves "Seekers of Justice and Vindication," perhaps alluding to Zeph 2:3. See NOTE on 7:12. There is a prediction that Justice and Vindication shall dwell in the desert, at Isa 32:16. The same chapter can be read as predicting that a leader "like a protector from the storm" shall arise, but only a small elite shall hearken to him (vss. 2–3; the elite are called nimhārīm, "quick," an epithet common in Qumran texts, applied to believers; see e.g. 1QS 10:26; 1QH 1:36, 2:9, 5:22). At the same time, a wicked fool (Antiochus) shall speak foolishness and plot wickedness, to do polluting acts (ḥnp) and give voice to error concerning the LORD (literally, Isa 32:6 says, "For the fool speaks folly and his mind plots wickedness, to practice ungodliness [ḥnp], to leave the hungry unsatisfied and deprive the thirsty of drink"). Our author may have drawn upon this sort of interpretation of Isa 32:6 elsewhere, for I 1:24 contains unmistakable echoes of Isa 32:6 in describing the deeds of Antiochus. Perhaps his source was *DMP*.

One can go on reading Isaiah 32 to find that after the persecutions have lasted a year (vs. 10; cf. Dan 11:33) women, cattle, indeed all inhabitants should leave to take refuge in caves (vss. 9–14) in the desert, where God's spirit will bring miraculous rescue and everlasting vindication (vss. 15–18). At Isa 55:6 again one can find "seeking"; at Isa 55:12–13 there is a going out to the desert; and at Isa 56:1–2 Vindication and Justice are near for Sabbath observers. See also Isa 58:11–14 and Jer 2:2–3, 17:19–27.

There is a similar effort to seek miraculous vindication at Testament of Moses ix–x, but there not a multitude but only Taxo and his seven sons go to the cave "in the field" (*in agro*). The "field" of Test Moses ix 6 may be identical to the "desert" here and at Isa 32:14. The desert at Isa 32:14 has wild asses. The desert (*midbār*) at Job 24:5 also has wild asses and is rendered in Greek by the Greek word for "field" (*agrôi*). There are no clear echoes of Isaiah 32 at Test Moses ix–x unless the name "Taxo" itself is a corruption of a Greek *"Stexôn"*="He who Shall Protect"; cf. Isa 32:2. On the other hand, Test Moses x 8 may reflect Isa 58:14, as can be seen from the Greek of Deut 33:29. On the Testament of Moses, see Introduction, pp. 39–40. It is probable that the martyrdom of Taxo and his seven sons and the mass martyrdom described here were separate real incidents. Cf. II 6:11.

28. Modeïn may have been dangerous for the rebels because it was too accessible from the district capital, Lydda. Our author does not tell us in what part of the extensive mountains of Palestine Mattathias and his followers took refuge. Later, Apollonius was to set out from Samaria to make the first expedition of Seleucid forces against the rebels (I 3:10). If the rebels by then had not changed their base, it is likely that Mattathias fled to mountains in or bordering on the district of Samaria; cf. II 15:1. Josephus, too, has Judas later taking refuge in the mountainous terrain of the district of Gophna, bordering on Samaria (*BJ* i 1.5.45). A further indication of the area which served the Hasmonaeans as their base can be found in the sites of Judas Maccabaeus' defensive battles. Most of them occur on the roads running north and west from Jerusalem. See Maps 2, 3, 6, 10, and 11 (pp. 528, 529, 532, and 535). Hence, the base he defended lay in the mountains within the quadrilateral defined by Gophna, Modeïn, Ammaus, and Jerusalem.

29. *many.* Perhaps the word should be capitalized as an epithet for Pietists; see Dan 8:25, 9:27, 11:14 and 44, 12:2 and 10; 1QS 6:1, 7–9, etc.

31. Our author regards the king's men and the Antiochene colony in the Akra as two independent authorities. On the insistence that Jerusalem was still the City of David, see NOTE on 1:33–40. Here and in vss. 36 and 41 our author refrains from using the word "caves," in contrast to II 6:11 and J. *AJ* xii 6.2.272–75. Perhaps he does so to portray the martyrs as following a (to him) correct interpretation of Isa 26:20 rather than an erroneous interpretation of Isa 23:14; see NOTE on 1:53.

33. *Come out to us.* Translators have construed the Greek *heôs tou nyn* as elliptical, "Enough of this!" However, to my knowledge there is no parallel either in Hebrew or in Greek for such an expression. The Greek translator probably misconstrued the Hebrew *'ad hēnāh*, "hither," "to us," taking it to re-

fer to time (as at Ps 71:17 and Eccles 4:2) instead of to space as at II Sam 20:16; II Kings 8:7. Cf. La^B, "*Hactenus progressi.*"

34. According to the martyrs' interpretation of the Torah, they would have violated the Sabbath by coming out of the caves; see Exod 16:29 and CD 10: 20–21, 11:14–15.

37. Cf. Deut 4:26, 30:19, 31:28, and for "unjustly," Ezek 22:29.

38. Josephus (*AJ* xii 6.2.274–75) has the martyrs in the caves dying by fire. Abraham Geiger (*Urschrift und Übersetzungen der Bibel,* 2d ed. [Frankfurt am Main: Verlag Madda, 1928], p. 229) correctly saw Josephus here as showing his dependence on II 6:11. See also introductory NOTE to I 1:57–64. The thousand corpses were probably left in the caves, and the skeletons may yet be discovered by archaeologists.

39. The emphatic "Thereupon" at the head of our verse and the "all" in vs. 43 are special pleading. The Hasmonaean position allowing defensive warfare on the Sabbath was inacceptable to many Pietists; see Introduction, pp. 75, 79. The author of Enoch xc 10, a contemporary of the events, has militant Pietists joining Judas, not Mattathias; see Introduction, Part II, n. 12. Jason of Cyrene and the author of Enoch do not deign to allude to Mattathias. It is likely that our author here only exaggerates but does not lie. Some strict Pietists did join Mattathias. Hence our author can go out of his way to show Mattathias' sympathy for the martyrs. Some Pietists may have identified Mattathias' act of zeal at Modeïn with the act of a nobleman (*nādīb*) they saw predicted at Isa 32:8. Symmachus at Isa 32:8 rendered *nādīb* by *archôn,* the word used of Mattathias at I 2:17. See above, NOTE on vss. 28–38.

41. Cf. J. *AJ* xii 6.2.276–77; *Ap.* i 7.209–11. For the history of Jewish laws concerning warfare on the Sabbath, see Moshe David Herr, "The Problem of War on the Sabbath in the Second Temple and the Talmudic Periods," *Tarbiẓ* 30 (5721=1960–61), 242–56 (in Hebrew, with English summary, pp. vii–ix).

42. *Pietists.* See Introduction, pp. 5–6.

volunteered. The Hebrew had *mitnaddēb,* from the same root as "nobleman" (*nādīb*); see above on vs. 39.

43. *joined them as supporters.* Contrast Dan 11:34.

44. The "sinners" and "lawless" were apostate Jews, as is shown by the author's remark that they were forced to flee for their lives to the *gentiles.*

47. *men of arrogance.* Probably the king's gentile officials, as apostate Jews have already been mentioned in vs. 44.

48. *prevented . . . wicked.* Cf. Ps 75:5.

VII. MATTATHIAS' LAST WORDS
(2:49–70)

2 ⁴⁹When the time drew near for Mattathias to die, he said to his sons,

> "Now arrogance has grown strong, and outrage; it is a time
> of calamity and of fierce anger.
> ⁵⁰Therefore, my children, be zealous for the Torah, and be
> ready to give your lives for the covenant of our fathers.
> ⁵¹Remember the deeds of our ancestors, which they did
> in their generations,
> and win for yourselves great glory and undying renown.
> ⁵²Was not Abraham found to keep his faith under trial,
> and was it not reckoned to his merit?
> ⁵³Joseph in his time of distress kept a commandment
> and became lord of Egypt.
> ⁵⁴Phineas, our ancestor, through his act of zeal received
> a pact of priesthood for all time.
> ⁵⁵Joshua by fulfilling the Word became a Judge in Israel.
> ⁵⁶Caleb by bearing witness before the congregation
> received an inheritance of land.
> ⁵⁷David for his piety received as his heritage a royal
> throne for ages.
> ⁵⁸Elijah for his acts of zeal on behalf of the Torah was
> taken up as if into heaven.
> ⁵⁹Hananiah, Azariah, and Mishael because they maintained
> their faith were preserved from the fire.
> ⁶⁰Daniel through his guiltlessness was saved from the mouth
> of lions.
> ⁶¹In this manner consider the generations past: all who
> place their hopes in Him shall not falter.
> ⁶²Have no fear of the words of a wicked man, for his glory
> is destined for dunghills and worms.

63 He will spring up today, but tomorrow he shall not be found,
> for he shall have turned back into his dust, and his
> plotting shall perish.

64 My children, be valorous and resolute for the Torah,
> because through the Torah will you win glory.

65 Your brother Simeon, I know, is a man of counsel;
> Always listen to him; he shall serve as your father.

66 Judas Maccabaeus has been a mighty warrior
> from his youth.

He shall be commander of your army and shall fight the
> war against the nations.

67 You shall join to yourselves all who observe the Torah,
> and take vengeance for your people.

68 Bring retribution upon the gentiles, and give heed to
> the command of the Torah."

69 Thereupon he blessed them and was gathered to his fathers. 70 He died in the year 146 and was buried in the cemetery of his forefathers at Modeïn. All Israel observed deep mourning for him.

NOTES

2:49–70, introductory NOTE. Our author follows the pattern of the death of Jacob. Jacob, too, uttered hints about the future of his sons (Gen 49:1), and after giving them his charge died (Gen 49:33; cf. vs. 69) and after receiving great mourning rites was buried in the cemetery of his forefathers (Gen 50:10, 13; cf. vss. 69–70).

49–68. On Mattathias' "farewell address," see Introduction, pp. 7–8. On Josephus' version, see NOTE on II 7:1.

49. The verse is modeled on Isa 37:3=II Kings 19:3. As Hezekiah in his time resisted Sennacherib, God's punishing instrument who arrogantly exceeded his mandate (see Isa 10:5–34), so Mattathias and his sons must resist arrogant Antiochus. Greek *elegmos* here probably renders *n^e'āṣāh*, as at Isa 37:3 (though not at II Kings 19:3). For "arrogance has grown strong," cf. Ezek 7:10, especially in the versions of Aquila and Theodotion. For "calamity . . . anger," cf. Job 21:30.

50. *be ready to give your lives.* The Hebrew expression, *msr npš*, does not occur in the Hebrew Bible but is common in rabbinic texts (*Sifre Debarim* 76; TB *Berakot* 32a, *Baba qamma* 61a, etc.). Similar expressions do, however, exist in the Hebrew Bible (Judg 5:18, 9:17; I Sam 28:21; Isa 53:12).

51. Cf. Deut 32:7; Sir 44:1–2.

52. See Gen 15:6, 22:1; Sir 44:20; *M. Abot* 5:3.

53. Joseph refrained from committing adultery (Genesis 39). Joseph in the pseudepigrapha and in rabbinic texts is characteristically called "the righteous"; see L. Ginzberg, *Legends*, V, 324–25, n. 3. The wording here may be drawn from Ps 37:39, by identifying the "righteous" there with Joseph.

54. See Introduction, p. 8.

55. See Numbers 13–14. To my knowledge, only here in Jewish literature is Joshua called a Judge, probably to foreshadow the career of Mattathias' son Jonathan, who paralleled the feats of Joshua and then became a Judge. See Introduction, p. 10. For the wording, cf. Num 32:12; Deut 1:36 and 38. Our author may have added "the Word" to supply an object for the transitive verb "fulfill"; cf. I Kings 2:27 and II Chron 36:21.

56. See Numbers 13–14; Deut 1:36; and Josh 14:6–15. Just as Caleb bore witness that with God's aid the Israelites would prevail over the Canaanites, so Jonathan was to prove that with God's aid the Jews could prevail not only in the mountains of Judaea but also in the plains of Philistia (I 10:69–87). Just as Caleb received Hebron as his heritage, so Jonathan was to receive Ekron (=Akkaron; I 10:89).

57. *piety*. Greek *oleos* regularly renders Hebrew *ḥesed;* cf. Isa 55:3.

for ages. Our author, who writes to prove the legitimacy of the Hasmonaean dynasty, would not wish to assert the eternal right of the dynasty of David to rule over the Chosen People. He appears to have selected his words carefully, and some Christian scribes found them strange enough to emend the text so that it would assert the eternal right of David's descendants.

The Hebrew word *'ōlām*, rendered by the Greek *aiôn*, is ambiguous. Even in the singular it can mean an "age" or "lifetime" (Exod 21:6; *M. Yebamot* 2:1), but in the Bible it usually means "forever." The plural of the Hebrew word and of its Greek equivalent is comparatively rare. It means "ages" and is used in some contexts where it means "forever" (Isa 26:4, 45:17; Dan 9:24; Ps 77:8, 145:13; 1QS 2:3 – 4:22 and 1QM both use the plural as "forever," but 1QS 5:6 – end and other Qumran texts for this sense use the singular almost exclusively). In other contexts, however, the plural means "lifetimes," "the remote past," or "the time since the Creation." Both the author of Kings and the Chronicler knew of the destruction of Solomon's temple and chose not the singular but the plural to express Solomon's hope that God would reside in the temple "for ages" (I Kings 8:13; II Chron 6:2). In contrast, throughout the Hebrew Bible the singular is used in connection with the promises to David of eternal dynastic rule (II Sam 7:13, 16, 25–29; 22:51; 23:5; Isa 9:6; Ps 18:51; 89:4–5, etc.; I Chron 17:12–23; 22:10; 28:4). The Chronicler continued to trace the line of David down to his own time (I Chron 3:17–24) in the firm faith that the dynasty would return to power. Our author's belief is different, but his use of the singular and plural is similar: eternal priesthood is the reward of the line of Phineas (I 2:54), but David's line receives royal rule only "for ages." Ben Sira likewise uses "eternity" in connection with God's covenant with Levi (Sir 45:6), but fails to assert the eternity of the dynasty of David: Sir 47:22c is in the past tense both in Hebrew and in Greek, and 47:11 is ambiguous since only David's "horn," not his dynasty, is there said to be eternal (cf. 49:4–5). I shall deal elsewhere with the complicated problem of Ben Sira's attitude to the dynasty of David.

If they were sensitive to the difference between the singular and the plural of *'olam* and *aiôn*, Christian scribes could hardly tolerate our author's lack of faith in the eternity of the dynasty of David. Indeed, of the witnesses to the text, only S La^L X G V Lucifer (SyII) have the simple plural "ages" (*aiônas, saecula*): La^B has "ages of ages"; A q 56 58 106 La^M have the adjective "eternal" (*aiônias, aeterni*); *L* and some minuscules have the equivalent of the Hebrew *le'ōlām wā'ed*, "forever and ever" (*eis aiôna aiônos*).

The disappearance of the Davidic dynasty after the times of Zerubbabel and Nehemiah created problems for those who believed in the promises that the dynasty would last forever and return to rule. The hope in an ideal Davidic king is conspicuous by its absence from the surviving Jewish literature written after Nehemiah and before the reign of Alexander Jannaeus. See Joseph Klausner, *The Messianic Idea in Israel* (New York: Macmillan, 1955), pp. 248–51; and, on the whole problem of the later history of the dynasty, Jacob Liver, *The House of David from the Fall of the Kingdom of Judah to the Fall of the Second Commonwealth and After* (Jerusalem: Magnes Press, 1959) in Hebrew, with English summary. Some Jews may have continued to hope for fulfillment of the prophesies, as perhaps in Psalm 89. Others may have considered the prophesies already fulfilled in the reign of Hezekiah. See Sir 48: 15–25, especially comparing Sir 48:24 with Isa 11:2 and 36:5: Hezekiah received the gift of "the spirit of might," in the person of Isaiah. Later, long after the destruction of the second temple, Davidic descent was claimed for Hillel and the dynasty of the patriarchs; see Liver, *House of David*, pp. 37–41. Rabbi Hillel was the brother of the patriarch Judah II and was therefore a member of the dynasty of the patriarchs; see Aaron Hyman, *Toldoth tannaim ve'amoraim* (Jerusalem: Boys' Town Jerusalem Publishers, 1964), pp. 373–74 (in Hebrew). No less an authority than Rabbi Hillel held that the messianic prophesies had been fulfilled in the person of Hezekiah. Still other Jews may have viewed the prophesies of a Davidic messiah as voided by sin; see I Kings 2:4; I Chron 28:7, 9; Ps 132:11–12; Sir 49:4–5. This last may have been our author's view. If so, he needed to give no further explanation of why the kingship of the later Hasmonaeans was no usurpation of the rights of the house of David. The house of David no longer had royal rights. Cf. I 14:41, bearing in mind that our author believed John Hyrcanus to have been a prophet; see Introduction, Part I, n. 8.

58. *acts of zeal.* Cf. I Kings 19:10, 14.

taken up as if into heaven. See II Kings 2:1–13. At least from the time of the Greek translation of Kings, there were Jewish authorities who were reluctant to believe that Elijah, a mortal, had been taken up all the way into heaven (cf. Ps 115:16); see Ginzberg, *Legends*, VI, 322–23, n. 32.

59–60. See Daniel 3 and 6 and Introduction, pp. 44–45.

61. As in vs. 51, so here our author probably drew on Deut 32:7; cf. also Ps 34:23.

62–63. Cf. Isa 14:4–22, 51:12–13; Pss 37:35–36, 146:4; Dan 11:19; Sir 10: 8–11; and see commentary to Jason of Cyrene's account of the death of

Antiochus IV (II 9). Our author here probably intends to portray Mattathias as prophesying the death of Antiochus.

64. Cf. Deut 4:6.

65. Only here does the translator use the form *Symeôn* for the name of Mattathias' son. Elsewhere he uses *Simôn* (above, in vs. 1, he uses *Symeôn* for the name of Mattathias' grandfather). The translator probably does so here because he was conscious of the pun, "*šm'wn . . . 'lyw tšm'wn*," ("Simeon . . . listen to him"). The command to listen probably echoes Deut 18:5, 15, in order to suggest that the high priesthood and the gift of prophesy will come to Simeon and his descendants.

he . . . father. Our author may have applied the prophesy at Isa 22:21–25 to Simeon and his descendants.

66. The language may be suggesting comparison of Judas with David; see I Sam 17:33, 18:13, 17; II Sam 25:28.

67–68. Cf. Num 18:2, 31:2; and especially Deut 32:43–46: Mattathias' last words draw on and obey Moses' farewell injunctions.

70. The year 146 Sel. Bab. extended from April 20, 166, to April 7, 165.

VIII. JUDAS' EARLY VICTORIES
(3:1–26)

3 ¹ Judas, called Maccabaeus, his son, succeeded him. ² To his aid rallied all his brothers and all the steadfast followers of his father, and they gladly fought Israel's war.

> ³ He restored the glory of his people, putting on his
> breastplate like a hero,
> and girding on his weapons, he waged war, protecting
> the camp with his sword.
> ⁴ He was like a lion in his deeds and like the king of
> beasts roaring over his prey.
> ⁵ He tracked down and pursued the wicked, and he purged
> the troublers of his people.
> ⁶ The wicked were vanquished by their fear of him, and
> all the workers of iniquity were discomfited, and
> his campaign of deliverance prospered.
> ⁷ By his deeds he brought bitterness to many kings and
> joy to Jacob; forever shall his memory be blessed.
> ⁸ He passed through the town of Judah and wiped out
> the impious therein and turned Wrath away from
> Israel.
> ⁹ His renown spread to the end of the earth, as he
> gathered together those who were astray.

¹⁰ Then Apollonius assembled gentile troops and a large force from Samaria to wage war against Israel. ¹¹ When Judas received the news, he marched out to meet him, defeated him, and killed him; many fell slain, and the rest fled. ¹² When Judas and his men took the spoils, Judas took Apollonius' sword and ever after used it in battle.

¹³ Seron, a commander of the army of Syria, heard that Judas had gathered a band and that a Company of Faithful was waging war under his command. ¹⁴ Seron said, "I shall win renown and glory in the empire by waging war against Judas and his men who despise

the word of the king." [15] He launched a fresh expedition, accompanied by a strong force of impious men who intended to help him wreak vengeance upon the Israelite people. [16] As Seron approached the ascent of Beth-Horon, Judas marched out to meet him with a small force. [17] When the men saw the army marching against them, they said to Judas, "How can our small force fight so numerous and mighty a host, exhausted as we are today for lack of food?" [18] Judas replied, "It is easy for many to be delivered into the hands of few. Heaven sees no difference in gaining victory through many or through a few, [19] because victory in war does not lie in the weight of numbers, but rather strength comes from Heaven. [20] They come against us with the weight of their power for violence and wickedness, intending to destroy us and take our wives and our children as spoil. [21] We, however, are fighting for our lives and our laws. [22] And He will shatter them before us. You, therefore, have no fear!" [23] As soon as he finished speaking, he made a sudden rush upon them, and Seron and his army were shattered before him. [24] Judas and his men pursued him down the descent of Beth-Horon as far as the plain; no fewer than eight hundred of his men fell slain, and the rest fled into the land of the Philistines. [25] Judas and his brothers began to be feared, and the terror of them fell upon the neighboring gentiles. [26] His fame reached the king, and every nation told of Judas' battles.

NOTES

3:1. Cf. Eccles 4:15.

2. Our author stresses that both the Hasmonaean family and the loyal fighters of Israel recognized Judas as the legitimate successor of his father.

3–9. See Introduction, Part 5, n. 34.

3. *He restored the glory.* Literally, "He broadened . . ."; "to broaden glory" is a strange idiom, whether in Hebrew or in Greek. Perhaps our poet is describing Judas as reversing the "thinning" (*yiddal . . . yērāzeh*) of the glory of Jacob predicted at Isa 17:4.

3–4. *putting . . . prey.* The poet probably compares Judas to David. Cf. I Sam 17:34–39, beginning. For "hero" the Greek has "giant," but that is how Greek translators often rendered the Hebrew *gibbor.* Cf. also Gen 49:9; Isa 31:4; and Ps 104:20–22 (with II 8:5–7).

5. *purged.* The Greek has "burned," reflecting an original Hebrew *wayyᵉba'ēr* (cf., for example, Deut 19:13, Judg 20:13), but the translator probably was thinking of I 5:5 and 44.

troublers of his people. Cf. I Kings 18:18 and I Chron 2:7. Context and parallels show our author means apostates. See also I 7:22.

7. *many kings.* Antiochus IV and V, and Demetrius I.

forever . . . blessed. Cf. Ps 112:6; Prov 10:7; Sir 46:11.

8. *turned Wrath away from Israel.* Again a Hasmonaean is compared to Phineas (Num 25:11). See Introduction, pp. 5–8, and Deut 13:13–18.

9. Our poet may have derived his language from Isa 11:12 and 12:5 after reading Isa 11:11–12:6 as a prophesy of Judas' campaigns which are narrated in I 5.

10–24. Neither our author nor Jason of Cyrene gives any indication that Judas' early operations threatened the inhabitants of the Akra. Judas was not yet strong enough to approach Jerusalem or even to block one or more of the main roads. He could only see to it that Jewish law was obeyed in the country towns and villages (I 2:44–48, 3:1–9; II 8:1–7). In marching against Judas, the units of Apollonius and Seron probably responded to no call from the Akra but, as the nearest adequate Seleucid forces to the scene, merely did their routine duty of suppressing a troublemaker. Only after Judas' victory over Seron is Philip, the Seleucid commander at Jerusalem, reported to have called for help (II 8:8).

10. Our author makes no effort to identify Apollonius here, just as he makes none to identify Timotheus at 5:6 and 11 or Apollonius at I 10:69. Since Apollonius here uses troops from Samaria, Josephus (*AJ* xii 7.1.287) had no trouble identifying him with the governor of Samaria (for the titles *merid-archês* and *stratêgos,* cf. I 10:65), known from the document at *AJ* xii 5.5. 259–264. Josephus may well have been correct, and our terse author may well have omitted further identification as superfluous in a context mentioning troops from Samaria. The name, as well as further identification, may have stood in *DMP* and in the unabridged text of Jason of Cyrene, but all we have in the abridged history is the summary statement at II 8:5–7. We lack evidence to decide whether this Apollonius was or was not identical with Apollonius the Mysarch of I 1:29 and II 5:24. The abridger's note at II 8:32–33 probably reflects an effort to include all deaths of persecutors; nevertheless, the abridger includes nothing on the deaths of Gorgias (II 8:9) and Gorgias of Idumaea (II 10:14, 32–37) and Ptolemy son of Dorymenes (II 4:45–46, 8:8; cf. I 3:38) and Alcimus (II 14:3–13, 26). On the other hand, our author does not name all wicked gentiles. The generals of Demetrius (I 12:24) are as anonymous as the Mysarch of I 1:24. Hence, the omission of the Mysarch's name at I 1:29 need not be a textual error and does not prove that our author believed that the Mysarch was distinct from the Apollonius here. Similarly, the omission of the ill-fated campaign of Apollonius from the abridged history does not prove that Jason of Cyrene believed him to be distinct from the Mysarch.

What was the nature of Apollonius' force? Did it contain Samaritans, as the combination "gentile troops and a large force from Samaria" might suggest? From the time of Alexander the Great there were no Samaritans in the pagan Graeco-Macedonian *city* of Samaria; Samaritans lived only in the surrounding *district* of Samaria, especially in Shechem. See F. M. Cross, "The Discovery of the Samaria Papyri," BA 26 (1963), 118–19; G. E. Wright,

"The Samaritans at Shechem," HTR 55 (1962), 263–66; L. H. Vincent, "Le culte d'Hélène à Samarie," RB 45 (1936), 221–32. Persons from the *city* of Samaria are mentioned abroad in inscriptions which leave no doubt that they are pagans; see IG II² 2943. In neither First nor Second Maccabees are the *Samaritans* accused of supporting the Seleucid armies (see esp. II 15:1), and even Josephus (*AJ* xii 5.5.257) accuses them only of denying their kinship with the Jews and in his paraphrase of our passage says only that "Apollonius, the governor of Samaria, took his force" (*ho tês Samareias stratêgos, analabôn tên dynamin*). Hence Apollonius surely raised his force from the surrounding gentile peoples (Arabs, Idumaeans, etc.) and from the Graeco-Macedonians of the city of Samaria. The pagan composition of Apollonius' force made it all the easier for our author to call Judas' party "Israel."

11. No source gives the site of the battle, but see NOTE on 2:28 and Map 2, p. 528.

12. Our author may be denying the traditions which told of a miraculous sword in the hands of Judas; see Introduction, Part II, n. 12, and p. 96.

13. Cf. II Sam 5:17 and I Chron 14:8 (of David). Josephus (*AJ* xii 7.1.288) calls Seron, who is otherwise unknown, "*stratêgos* of Coele-Syria." "Coele-Syria" was sometimes used loosely to refer to the huge province of Coele-Syria and Phoenicia (see NOTE on I 7:8), but Seron cannot have been governor of it, since Ptolemy the son of Dorymenes held that post at the time. See A. Shalit, "*Koilê Syria* from the Mid-Fourth Century to the Beginning of the Third Century B.C.," *Scripta Hierosolymitana*, I (1954), 64–73, middle; II 4:45, 8:8. Bengtson, *Strategie*, II, 159–69, is a useful survey but requires many corrections; see my comments on the texts he cites from Maccabees and Josephus. Apart from Josephus' paraphrase of our passage, nothing suggests that Seron governed a subdivision of Coele-Syria and Phoenicia, one called "Coele-Syria," as Bengtson proposes (*Strategie*, II, 170–72). Josephus probably was using the terminology of his own time (see ibid., p. 171, n. 1). Our author and the translator knew how to say "Coele-Syria" unambiguously (10:69).

It is best to assume that our author meant to say, not that Seron was governor of a province or a district, but that he was commander of an independent tactical unit in the Seleucid army; see Bikerman, *Institutions*, pp. 64–65, and Bengtson, *Strategie*, II, 64–78. His unit surely must have been larger than the force at the disposal of Apollonius. Our author, who is so eager to compare Judas to David, would have mentioned the fact if Seron's base had been in the land of the Philistines. Indeed, Seron's choice of the route through Beth-Horon (vs. 16) shows that he probably came into Judaea from the northwest by way of Lydda and through or near Modeïn; see Map 3, p. 529. The nearest important military base north of Lydda was Dora; see Tcherikover, *Hellenistic Civilization*, p. 92.

a Company . . . command. I follow here the reading of the Lucianic recension and of La^X; the witness of La^X indicates that the reading is not a conjecture of Lucian's, and the Greek text reflects a grammatical Hebrew original (*ūqᵉhal ĕmūnīm 'immō yōṣᵉ'īm baṣṣābā* [or "*laṣṣābā*"]; cf. Num 31:27, 28, 36). The other witnesses to the text, by inserting an "and" after "Faithful," would make our verse mean, ". . . that Judas had gathered a band and a Company of Faithful [was?] with him and of wagers of war," an unnatural expression even if the wagers of war were different from the Company of Faithful, as is hardly likely. Moreover, the barely intelligible Greek text would reflect ungrammatical Hebrew, since the Greek genitives should represent a chain of Hebrew nouns connected with a noun in the construct state (*ūqᵉhal ĕmūnīm 'immō wᵉyōṣᵉ'īm baṣṣābā*), but Hebrew does not tolerate the interruption of such a chain by *'immō*.

Cf. I 2:42; "Company of Faithful" here may have been the name chosen by Judas' band of pious militants to distinguish themselves from the quietist Company of Pietists.

15. *He launched a fresh expedition.* The Hebrew probably had *wayyōsep wayya'al*, with the second verb being in the *hiph'īl;* so renders Josephus (*AJ* xii 7.1.288). The Greek translator misread it as *qal,* so that his rendering has an awkward change of subject, "He made a fresh move, and a strong force of impious men marched with him, intending. . . ." The constructions are good Hebrew; cf. II Sam 2:3; Jer 50:9; Gen 25:1, 38:5; Esther 8:3; Dan 10:18.

impious men . . . vengeance. Apostate Jews had suffered from the attacks of Judas and his men (vss. 5–6) and now gladly joined Seron.

16. *ascent of Beth-Horon.* See Map 3, p. 529. The route between the two villages of Lower and Upper Beth-Horon was famous for its narrowness and difficulty (TB *Sanhedrin* 32b; see A. Legendre, "Béthoron," *Dictionnaire de la Bible,* I 2 [1912], 1699–1705). A small force at Upper Beth-Horon could hold off a much larger force. Perhaps Seron thought he could reach the upper town before Judas, or perhaps he thought he could fight his way through Judas' puny force.

17. Despite the strength of their position, Judas' men were afraid. The Greek here refers to mere lack of food, not to fasting, for which the translator uses another word in 3:47. Cf. II 5:27, 10:6. In fighting "Philistines" Judas would hardly imitate Saul; cf. I Sam 14:24–31.

18–22. In his speech Judas insists that God will aid those who fight for the Torah. Characteristically, Josephus, the admirer of the martyrs, imports into his version of Judas' speech (*AJ* xii 7.1.291) a catch phrase of the quietists, "There is great power in being innocent." For the quietists, so much power was there, one did not need to fight; cf. I 2:37; II 8:4 and 12:42.

18. The speech imitates Jonathan's at I Sam 14:6.

20. The Syriac and Latin translators were misled by the word order into construing the wives and children as objects of "destroy." The usual fate of wives and children as prisoners of war was slavery, not death, and what other property could Judas' band of outlaws have had, to be taken as spoil? The Greek text allows construing the wives and children as objects of "take as spoil," and the construction was probably admissible in Hebrew. Cf. Josh 8:27; Num 14:3; Isa 17:14; Jer 30:16; Ezek 39:10; the texts from Isaiah, Jeremiah, and Ezekiel promise that those who seek to despoil Israel will be themselves despoiled.

23. *shattered.* The Greek word almost always translates the Hebrew root *šbr.* Our author prefers to use *šbr* for "rout" instead of the commoner *ngp;* cf. II Chron 14:11–12. The mannerism could, however, be the translator's,

since his Greek word translates *ngp* at Deut 1:42. The use of *šbr* here may have led Josephus (*AJ* xii 7.1.292) to conclude that Seron was slain; note the use of *šbr* at Isa 14:25 in a context predicting the doom of Assyrian oppressors. Seron as a Seleucid commander was an official of the latter-day Assyria. However, Josephus elsewhere puts no such interpretation on the verb, and *DMP* may have referred to the fall of Seron in this campaign, so that Josephus could have drawn on a live tradition.

24. *Philistines.* See NOTE on 3:41.

25–26. Again our author borrows the language used to describe parallel exploits of David's; see I Chron 14:17. Cf. also Deut 2:25. Judas and his men had in fact defeated forces from the Seleucid army and from surrounding peoples. His power over the hill country of Judaea and over the approaches to Jerusalem now drove the Seleucid commander at Jerusalem to call for help (II 8:8).

IX. THE KING MARCHES EASTWARD
(3:27–37)

3 ²⁷When Antiochus heard of these events, he angrily issued orders to gather all the forces of his empire, a very strong army. ²⁸He opened his treasury and paid out a year's salary to his soldiers and ordered them to be ready for any emergency. ²⁹He perceived that his treasury had run out of money and that the tribute from his territories was small because of the dissension and disorder which he had caused in his land by abrogating the laws which had been in force from the earliest times. ³⁰He was worried lest, as had happened more than once, he might not have enough to cover the expenditures and largesses which hitherto he had been accustomed to give with an extravagance surpassing all earlier kings. ³¹Very much perplexed, he finally decided to go to Persis and gather a large sum of money by collecting the tribute of the territories. ³²He left Lysias, a nobleman who bore the title of Kinsman of the King, in charge of imperial affairs from the Euphrates river to the borders of Egypt. ³³Lysias was also to be the guardian of his son Antiochus until he should return. ³⁴Antiochus handed over to him half of his forces, the king set out from Antioch, his capital city, in the year signs. As for the inhabitants of Judah and Jerusalem, ³⁵he was to send against them a force to wipe out and destroy the strength of Israel and the remnant of Jerusalem and erase their memory from the area, ³⁶settling foreigners throughout their territory and giving out their land in allotments. ³⁷Taking the remaining half of his forces, the king set out from Antioch, his capital city, in the year 147. He crossed the Euphrates river and marched through the inland territories.

NOTES

3:27-37, introductory NOTE. According to Jason of Cyrene (II 8:8), it was Ptolemy son of Dorymenes, *strategos* of Coele-Syria, and not the king himself, who decided upon the measures to suppress Judas. Again Jason exploits his opportunity to contradict our author. However, our author, for whom the rise of the Hasmonaean dynasty was an event of cosmic importance, may be pardoned for making the need to suppress the Jewish revolt into the most important factor influencing Antiochus IV's course of action in 166/5. The full might of the Seleucid empire was far too large to send against Judas, who later was defeated by Lysias and Antiochus V (I 6:33-54) and fell to Bacchides (I 9:1-17). Certainly, however, Antiochus viewed the suppression of Judas' revolt as important. Earlier Hyrcanus the Tobiad, in the far less sensitive area of Transjordan, committed suicide knowing that Antiochus would not tolerate his independent actions there (J. *AJ* xii 4.11.236). Ptolemaic Egypt was hostile in 166/5. Antiochus IV's nephew Demetrius, a hostage in Rome, could always become a dangerous pretender to the throne; a rebellious area near the Mediterranean coast could give Demetrius easy entry to the soil of the kingdom. See II 9:25.

Nevertheless, Judas' force was still small. To suppress it was a task which could be delegated to a subordinate, whereas the task of bringing the rich eastern satrapies back under firm Seleucid rule and collecting their taxes might turn the head of a successful subordinate and provide him with the funds to finance his rebellion, as had happened with the satrap Molon under Antiochus III (see Bevan, I, 301-9). Shortages of funds had continually plagued the Seleucid empire, after Rome stripped it of its provinces in Asia Minor and saddled it with a heavy indemnity under the terms of the Peace of Apameia in 188; see Mørkholm, pp. 25-37, and in AB vol. 41A NOTE on II 8:10. Hence, it is not surprising that Antiochus delegated the suppression of Judas to Lysias and set out himself to restore order and collect tribute in the east.

Centuries later the Roman historian Tacitus was to write (*Histories* v 8), "After the Macedonians became the great power, King Antiochus tried to free [the Jews of] superstition and give them Greek ways, but he was prevented from changing the most loathsome of peoples for the better by his war with the Parthians, for at that time [the Parthian King] Arsaces seceded. Then, when the Macedonians were weak and the Parthians had not yet reached full stature and the Romans were far away, the Jews appointed over themselves kings." The passage might suggest that Antiochus IV's target in the east was rebellious Parthia. However, all other evidence indicates that Parthia was no menace until long after the time of Antiochus IV. The Seleucid who fought the Parthians and whose death brought the period of "Macedonian weakness" and Jewish kings was Antiochus VII; see Mørkholm, pp. 166-80. Since

Antiochus VII never interfered with the Jews' religion (see J. *AJ* xiii 8.2.242–44; Diodorus xxxiv–xxxv 1), Tacitus must have confused Antiochus IV with Antiochus VII.

Antiochus thus probably never thought of himself leading an expedition to suppress Judas. Josephus' statement (*AJ* xii 7.2.293) that Antiochus planned to march against Judaea in the spring of 165 is probably a guess from the fact that spring was the normal campaigning season and from I 3:28, where Antiochus is said to have paid his troops for a full year. Since the chronology of Antiochus' plans and of his eastern expedition is obscure, modern historians have been tempted to take Josephus' guess as evidence that the king marched eastward in the spring; see Mørkholm, pp. 150, 166.

Apart from inferences based on the normal campaigning season, there is only one piece of evidence for deciding when in the year 166/5 Antiochus marched eastward. Eusebius (*Chronicle*, p. 119 Karst=Porphyry, FGH 260, F 32.12–13) says that Antiochus V reigned one year and six months as coregent with his father, Antiochus IV. Antiochus IV's death became known at Babylon between November 20 and December 18, 164; see Sachs and Wiseman, *Iraq* 16 (1954), 204, 208–9. He died at Tabai, near Isfahan, a long way from Babylon. The exact date of his death was probably a matter of indifference to the troubled successor regime governed by Lysias in the name of the child Antiochus V. Lysias may have made no effort to have the reign of Antiochus V as sole king date from the death of his father. Probably Antiochus V was proclaimed king in his own right as of the time when the news reached Antioch (see I 6:17), shortly after it reached Babylon. Antiochus IV probably made Antiochus V coregent at the time of his departure eastward. If so, Antiochus V became coregent and Antiochus IV marched one and a half years before the news of Antiochus IV's death reached Antioch, and we could place Antiochus IV's march slightly after a date between May 20 and June 18, 165 B.C.E. On the problems of the coregency of Antiochus V, see below on vss. 32–33 and NOTE on II 9:25.

27–32. The narrative contains echoes of II Sam 10:15 and I Chron 19:16, again to equate Judas' achievements with David's. In both cases a Syrian (= Aramaean) king issues orders, and forces march from the region of the Euphrates under named commanders.

29–30. Our author here may be following a Greek tradition to portray Antiochus as a tyrant, since for Greeks lawlessness and extravagance were characteristic of tyrants; see e.g. Plato *Republic* viii–ix 566d–580c. Later the Christian writer Lactantius was to use the same technique against persecuting Roman emperors; see *Lactance: De la mort des persécuteurs*, ed. J. Moreau, I, 51–52, 55–57. On Antiochus' extravagance: Polybius xxvi 1, xxviii 20, 25–26; Livy xli 20; Mørkholm, pp. 55–63.

Antiochus' civic and religious policies did indeed provoke reactions in his empire, and not just in Judaea. See Introduction, pp. 114–15, 127–28. However, it is unlikely that outside Judaea the reactions produced any appreciable decline in the royal revenues, and our patriotic Jewish author may be pardoned for thinking so. Everyone knew that Antiochus had a driving need for money. Our author explains it by the fall in tribute. Jason of Cyrene may have been no more correct in explaining it by the need to pay the indemnity to the Romans (II 8:10; see NOTE ad loc.).

The Jews who welcomed Antiochus' civic policy surely shared the opinions of Greek historians of religion, that the "barbaric" features of Judaism were later accretions on the original "philosophy." See Introduction, pp. 140–42. Their opponents made every effort to prove the early origin of every Jewish law attacked by the Hellenists; thus, the book of Jubilees strives to move the origins back into the patriarchal period and earlier. Our vs. 29 may be a faint allusion to the book of Jubilees.

See also NOTE on 6:11.

31. "Persis" properly means the nuclear territory of the Persians, the modern province of Fars in southern Iran. See Map 5, pp. 530–31, and Walther Hinz, "Persis," PW, Suppl. XII (1970), 1036–38. However, Antiochus on his eastern expedition campaigned in Mesene at the head of the Persian Gulf and in Elymaïs before withdrawing to die at Tabai, a town near Isfahan on the edge of Persis; Antiochus probably also campaigned in Armenia; see Mørkholm, pp. 166–71. Hence, "Persis" here, translating a Hebrew Pāras, should have a wider meaning. Our author equates Persis with the inland territories, the eastern satrapies (vs. 37, below; I 6:1, 5), and regards Elymaïs as being inside Persis (I 6:1). Both he and Jason of Cyrene wrote at a time when Jews called the Parthian empire, which then held most of Mesopotamia as well as Iran, by the name "Persia and Media" or simply "Persia," the name they had used for the old Persian empire which Alexander had overthrown. See I 14:2; Dan 8:20; Esther 10:2, etc.; Dan 11:2; II Chron 36:20, etc. Hence here and at I 6:1, 5, and 56 and at II 9:1 our authors were probably using the terminology of their own times. On the other hand, since Antiochus IV did die on the edge of Persis, the letter forged by the regime of Lysias (II 9:21) correctly speaks, though vaguely, of "the regions around Persis."

32–33. Antiochus in fact made his little son, the future Antiochus V, coregent with the title basileus ("king"), with Lysias as his guardian and chief minister. Both coregent and minister held power only west of the Euphrates. This coregency has been a matter of controversy because of gaps in the sources. It is almost as if there had been a conspiracy to hide the fact. The coregency is required to make sense of the documents at II 9:19–27 and 11:16–21, 27–38; see commentary to the passages. However, skeptical scholars have preferred to regard those documents as spurious.

A reference to the coregency of one year and six months survives only in one place, a fragment of Porphyry's Chronicle preserved by Eusebius (FGH 260, F 32.12–13=Eusebius Chronicle, p. 119 Karst). Even in the copy which lay before Eusebius there may have been a gap immediately after the reference to the coregency, for in the context one would expect to have the length and dates of the reign of Antiochus V as sole king, but they are missing. Eusebius himself appears to have misunderstood the obscure reference to the coregency ("Under him his father lived one year and six months"), for he used the "one year and six months" to supply the missing length of Antiochus V's own reign farther on in his Chronicle (p. 153 Karst; John A. Cramer, Anecdota Parisina, II [Oxford, 1839; rep. Hildesheim: Olms, 1967], 129). Georgius Syncellus (Chronographia, vol. I, p. 544 Dindorf) copied from Eusebius the erroneous reign of one and a half years for Antiochus V. So short a reign cannot be reconciled with the evidence that Antiochus IV died before December 18, 164, and that Demetrius I did not supplant Antiochus V before the autumn of 162. See I 7:1; II 14:4; Parker and Dubberstein, *Babylonian Chronology,* p. 23.

Why should the fragment of Porphyry be the sole evidence for the coregency? Cuneiform documents of the Seleucid period are dated by the year in the king's reign, and under a coregency they give the names of both kings in the date; see Bikerman, *Institutions,* pp. 21–22. However, no cuneiform contracts have been published bearing a date between February 15, 165, in the reign of Antiochus IV, and March 9, 163, in the reign of Antiochus V; see André Aymard, "Autour de l'avènement d'Antiochos IV," *Historia* 2 (1953–54), 63, n. 1.

One cuneiform document, indeed, may give evidence of the coregency. An astronomical tablet recording observations of Mars made in 118/7 has on one line, "year 115 [=197/6 B.C.E.] An(tiochus) and An(tiochus) his son, king," thus referring to the coregency of Antiochus III and his son. In the next line "year 147 [=165/4 B.C.E.]" is not followed by a royal name. According to Franz X. Kugler, *Von Moses bis Paulus* (Münster: Aschendorff, 1922), pp. 328–29, the absence of a royal name there serves as a ditto mark: the formula in the second line should be the same as that in the first, so that the second line would refer to a coregency of two kings Antiochus in 165/4. It is somewhat rash, however, to use as proof the absence of words from a document; cf. A. T. Olmstead, "Cuneiform Texts and Hellenistic Chronology," *Classical Philology* 32 (1937), 11–12.

The cuneiform king-list which reports the death of Antiochus IV takes no note of the coregency; see Sachs and Wiseman, *Iraq* 16 (1954), plate LII and pp. 204, 208–9. This fact does not prove there was no coregency. Subjects of the Seleucids paid little attention to, and may not even have understood, the conferring of the title "king" on a child too young to rule by a father still vigorous in power. Even in official documents, the name of Antiochus IV's first coregent, Antiochus the son of Seleucus IV, was often omitted; see Bikerman, *Institutions,* p. 19; Parker and Dubberstein, p. 23.

Even a grown man recognized as coregent would not so appear in Babylonian documents if the terms of his appointment as king restricted his rule to a portion of the empire which did not include Babylon. Thus, Antiochus Hierax was recognized by his brother, Seleucus II, from about 238 B.C.E. as king, but his province was restricted to the territory west of the Taurus mountains. See Justin xxvii 2.6–7; Charles Michel, *Recueil d'inscriptions grecques,* no. 39 (Bruxelles: Lamertin, 1900), lines 7–8; Bevan, I, 191–92; Bikerman, *Institutions,* p. 22; Bengtson, p. 410. The name of Antiochus Hierax appears neither in the cuneiform king-list nor in the dating formulas of Babylonian contracts (Bikerman, *Institutions,* p. 18, n. 2). Bikerman tries to use a document to show that Antiochus Hierax was called "king" at Babylon (ibid.). However, that document (quoted by B. Haussoullier, "Les Séleucides et le temple d'apollon didyméen," *RPh* 25 [1901], 18) does not give Antiochus Hierax the royal title but calls him only the son of Antiochus II and Laodice. Though dated in 236, in the reign of Seleucus II, the document records a grant of Antiochus II, and goes on to say that "Laodice, his [sc. Antiochus II's] wife," and "their sons, Seleucus and Antiochus" have ceded, in writing, their rights to certain property at Babylon and Borsippa. Since, according to the document, Antiochus Hierax held his rights at Babylon as a personal gift to him, even if the document reporting the cession had given him the title "king," it would show no more that he was recognized as co-king of Babylon than the many references to kings in honorific inscriptions at Athens show that those kings ruled over Athens. Since Lysias, Antiochus V's guardian and minister during the coregency, held power only in the western part of the empire, not in Babylonia, we may infer that Antiochus V's position resembled that of Antiochus Hierax, and no note of his coregency need ever have been taken in Babylonian documents.

Antiochus V, unlike Antiochus Hierax, was a child. The limited authority given to the child coregent allowed Lysias to give royal sanction to emergency measures, while still leaving Antiochus IV secure against rebels who might use the helpless boy as a figurehead, for the coregent had no power against the senior king (Bikerman, *Institutions*, pp. 22–23). On the problem of what were the powers of a coregent after the death of the senior king, see NOTE on II 9:25.

Demetrius I saw to it that Antiochus V and Lysias were killed; he and his dynasty probably did their utmost to wipe out the memory of the hated line of Antiochus IV. Our author and Jason of Cyrene, writing long afterward, thus may have known nothing of the coregency. On the other hand, our author may have known of it and yet said nothing of it because Judas refused to recognize it. In First Maccabees, Judas is never reported to have negotiated with Lysias or Antiochus V during the coregency. Jason of Cyrene displaces the first expedition of Lysias into the reign of Antiochus V (see Introduction, pp. 180–82) and has Judas negotiating with Lysias at the end of that expedition, but his assumption that Lysias could negotiate only with the party of the Jews led by Judas brought Jason to misread the good documentary evidence of Lysias' negotiations, from which Judas and his party are conspicuously absent; see NOTE on II 11:13–38.

Judas' refusal to negotiate may not signify his refusal to recognize the coregency but only his correct recognition that Antiochus IV on his return could have overruled any act of the coregent. In that case, too, so far as the Hasmonaeans were concerned, the coregency was an empty form which the historian of the dynasty could leave unmentioned.

This coregency, of Antiochus IV's own son, is not to be confused with the earlier coregency of Antiochus IV's adopted son, also named Antiochus, who was the son of Seleucus IV and had briefly reigned in his own right; see Mørkholm, pp. 42–50, and NOTE on 1:10.

32. *who bore . . . King.* Literally, "of the royal stock." This does not necessarily mean blood relationship to the Seleucid dynasty. "Kinsman of the King" (*syngenês;* cf. II 11:1) was a title given in the Seleucid empire to a high-ranking courtier, who ranked above mere Friends of the King; cf. I 10:89, and see Bikerman, *Institutions*, pp. 42–44.

in charge . . . Egypt. The title of the vizier of the Seleucid empire was "The Man in Charge of Affairs" (*ho epi tôn pragmatôn*); cf. II 3:7, 10:11, 11:1.

Here Antiochus IV restricts the vizier's province to the western part of the empire.

33. In the Seleucid empire a child-king received a guardian. Officially, the guardian was not a regent but the bearer of authority delegated from the child-king. All royal proclamations bore the child-king's name, not the guardian's; cf. II 11:16–36. See Bikerman, *Institutions*, p. 21.

34. *half . . . elephants.* The Greek text here means "half of his forces, as well as the elephants"; i.e. Antiochus entrusted to Lysias all the elephants. Josephus' paraphrase (*AJ* xii 7.2.295) has "a part of his forces and of the elephants." The difference reflects the ambiguity of a Hebrew original, *et ḥăṣī haḥayil wᵉhappīlīm,* and we have preserved the ambiguity in our translation. Josephus' change in his paraphrase is a fairly good indication that he verified his version with the Hebrew text after having his suspicions aroused by the strangeness of a Seleucid king refraining from the use of his elephants in a campaign and leaving them all to his vizier. The translator may have chosen to render the Hebrew as he did because no elephants are mentioned in vs. 37. Had he not been able to check a Hebrew text, Josephus could well have agreed with the translator, despite his own suspicions that the translator had misinterpreted an ambiguous Hebrew original. Cf. Melamed, EI 1 (1951), 127 (in Hebrew).

inhabitants. See NOTE on I 1:38, *rightful inhabitants.*

35. *wipe out . . . the strength of Israel and the remnant of Jerusalem.* "The strength of Israel" is an unparalleled expression, especially in such a context, where one would expect "the name of Israel," as at II Kings 14:27 and Isa 14:22, and in one of the Syriac versions (SyIII) here. Perhaps the translator misread *šm* ("name") as *'wz* or *'ṣm* ("strength").

36. See Introduction, p. 47.

37. For the date, see introductory NOTE above, vss. 27–37.

inland. From Herodotus on, Greek writers use this word to indicate Mesopotamia and Iran, which lay away from the Mediterranean coast; see Herodotus i 95, 177, etc.; Xenophon *Anabasis* vii 1.28; Polybius v 40.7.

X. JUDAS DEFEATS NICANOR AND GORGIAS
(3:38–4:25)

3 ³⁸ Thereupon Lysias commissioned Ptolemy the son of Dorymenes and Nicanor, and Gorgias, influential men who held the rank
of Friends of the King, ³⁹ and sent with them forty thousand infantry and seven thousand cavalry; they were to go to the land of
Judah and lay it waste in accordance with the king's orders. ⁴⁰ Setting out with their entire force, they arrived and encamped near Ammaus in the plateau. ⁴¹ The local merchants, on hearing the news,
took very large sums of silver and gold coin and fetters and came to
the camp intending to buy the Israelites as slaves. The expedition was
also joined by a force from Idumaea and the land of the Philistines.

⁴² Judas and his brothers saw how very dangerous the situation
was, with the enemy forces encamped within their own borders.
Bearing in mind the commands which the king had issued to bring
ruin and extermination upon their people, ⁴³ they said to one another, "Let us rebuild the wreckage of our people, and let us fight
for our people and for the sanctuary." ⁴⁴ The community assembled,
so as to be ready for battle and to pray and ask for Grace and Mercy.

⁴⁵ Jerusalem was uninhabited like a desert; none of
   her offspring went in or out.
The temple was trampled, as foreigners were in the Akra,
   lodging place of the gentiles.
Joy departed from Jacob, and flute and lyre ceased.

⁴⁶ They assembled and marched to Mizpah opposite Jerusalem, because there had earlier been an Israelite place for prayer in Mizpah.
⁴⁷ On that day they fasted and put on sackcloth, and ashes upon their
heads, and they rent their garments. ⁴⁸ They spread open the scroll
of the Torah at the passages where the gentiles sought to find analogies to their idols. ⁴⁹ They took the priestly vestments and the first
fruits and the tithes and assembled the Nazirites who had completed
the periods of their vows. ⁵⁰ Crying aloud toward Heaven, they said,

"What are we to do with these? Whither are we to bring them?
51 Your sanctuary has been trampled and profaned, and Your priests
are in mourning and affliction. 52 The gentiles have gathered against
us to destroy us. You know what they are plotting against us.
53 How shall we be able to withstand them, unless You come to our
aid?" 54 They sounded the trumpets and cried out in a loud voice.

55 Thereupon, Judas appointed officers over the people, commanders of thousands, hundreds, fifties, and tens. 56 He ordered all
who had built houses or betrothed wives or planted vineyards or were
timid to go home as required by the Torah. 57 The army marched
and encamped south of Ammaus. 58 There Judas spoke, "Prepare
yourselves for battle and be brave. Be ready early in the morning
to fight these gentiles who have gathered against us to destroy us
and our sanctuary, 59 for it is better for us to die in battle than to
stand by and watch the outrages against our people and our sanctuary. 60 As He wills in Heaven, so will He do."
4 1 Gorgias took a force of five thousand infantry and one thousand picked cavalry; the detachment set out during the night, 2 intending to fall upon the camp of the Jews and take them by surprise.
The men of the Akra served him as guides. 3 Judas, however,
learned of their plan. He set out himself with his warriors to attack
the king's force at Ammaus 4 while Gorgias' troops were still away
from the camp. 5 Gorgias marched by night to the camp of Judas and
found no one there. He searched the mountains for Judas' men, saying, "They are fleeing from us." 6 At daybreak, Judas appeared in
the plain with three thousand men, though their armor and swords
were not such as they would have wished to have. 7 They saw a
strong camp of gentiles armed with breastplates, surrounded by
outposts of cavalry, and the enemy were veteran soldiers. 8 Judas,
however, said to the men with him, "Have no fear of their numbers
and do not be dismayed at their onslaught. 9 Remember how our
forefathers were saved at the Red Sea, when Pharaoh was pursuing
them with an army. 10 Now, too, let us cry to Heaven. If He grants
us His favor, remembering His covenant with our forefathers, He will
smash this army before us today, 11 so that all the gentiles will know
that there is a Redeemer and Savior of Israel."

12 The foreigners caught sight of Judas and his men advancing
against them. 13 As the foreigners marched out from their camp for
battle, Judas' men sounded their trumpets. 14 When battle was joined,
the gentiles broke and fled toward the plain, 15 the hindmost all being cut down by the sword. They pursued them as far as Gazera and

the plains of Idumaea, Azotus, and Jamnia. No fewer than three thousand of the enemy fell.

16 When Judas and his force returned from pursuing them, 17 he told the people, "Do not be greedy for the spoils, for a battle lies ahead of us. 18 Gorgias and his force are in the mountains near us. Rather, stand to face our enemies and fight them, and afterwards confidently take the spoils." 19 Judas was still completing his speech when a unit of Gorgias' army was seen looking down from the mountains. 20 The men perceived that their comrades had been routed and that the Jews were setting fire to the camp, for the smoke was visible to show what had happened. 21 On seeing this, they were greatly dismayed; on seeing also that Judas' army was in the plain ready for battle, 22 they all fled to the land of the Philistines. 23 Judas returned to take the spoils of the camp. They took large sums of gold and silver coin, and cloth dyed marine blue and purple, and other rich booty. 24 On returning to their base they sang hymns of thanksgiving to Heaven, "For He is good, for His mercy endures forever." 25 A great victory was won for Israel on that day.

Notes

3:38 – 4:25, introductory NOTE. Both here and in II 8:9–36 the two commanders, Nicanor and Gorgias, are mentioned. Here, attention is focused on Gorgias; there, on Nicanor. The difference need not reflect a difference in sources but rather a difference in the authors' interests. Here, we can see the hand of the admirer of Hasmonaean Judas, who out-generaled the wily Gorgias. There, we can see the hand of the literary artist, who organized his narrative in parallel sections around the Feast of Dedication and the Day of Nicanor and probably identified Nicanor here with Nicanor in II 14–15, since he uses the rare epithet "thrice-accursed wretch" (*trisalitêrios*) of both (II 8: 34 and 15:3). Similarly, Jason of Cyrene concentrated on Nicanor in II 14–15 to the exclusion of Bacchides; see in AB vol. 41A NOTE on II 14:12. For the geography of the campaign, see Map 3, p. 529. On the reference to the campaign in Enoch xc 13–14, see Introduction, Part II, n. 12.

3:38. *Ptolemy the son of Dorymenes*. See II 4:45–47, 8:8. He was not the same man as Ptolemy Makron; see NOTE on II 10:12. Our author has Ptolemy as one of the commanders of the expedition, though after vss. 38–39 nothing more is said of him. Jason of Cyrene discovered that Ptolemy the son of Dorymenes, as governor (*stratêgos*) of Coele-Syria and Phoenicia, was the superior of Nicanor and Gorgias and that he, not Lysias, sent the other two against Judas and his men. Characteristically, Jason did not pass up the opportunity to contradict our author's narrative and does so at II 8:8–9.

Nicanor and Gorgias. At II 8:9 Nicanor's father's name is given as Patroclus. There is insufficient evidence to decide whether he was the same as "Nicanor, the royal agent" (*tôi ta basilika prattonti*) mentioned in the Samaritan correspondence quoted at J. *AJ* xii 5.5.261–62, or the same as the one or two Nicanors associated with Demetrius I (I 7:26–47; II 14:12 – 15:37; Polybius xxxi 22.4; J. *AJ* xii 10.4.402). Jason of Cyrene's apparent identification of the Nicanor of II 8 with the one of II 14–15 may be only a literary device (see introductory NOTE above). Josephus' identification of the Nicanor at Polybius xxxi 22.4 with the one at I 7:26–47 may be only a guess. Evidence is lacking, too, to decide whether the Gorgias here is the same as the one at I 5:59, and as the governor (*stratêgos*) of Idumaea at II 10:14–15, 12:32–37.

Since, however, the government would be likely to entrust an expedition into a difficult area to men already familiar with the territory, there is some reason to identify Nicanor here with the agent who had dealt with the Samaritans, and Gorgias here with the governor of Idumaea.

Friends. See NOTE on I 2:18.

39. Like most of the historians of antiquity, our author would have found it very difficult to get accurate figures on the size of armies, especially the armies of the enemy. Like the authors of the biblical histories and like Herodotus and Livy, he has a strong tendency to give an exaggerated estimate of the size of a vanquished enemy force. Jason of Cyrene has the same tendency and estimated the enemy force here at twenty thousand. Both his estimate and our author's are probably drawn from traditions equating Judas' achievements with David's. Forty thousand infantry and seven thousand cavalry appear in the Aramaean (=Syrian) force annihilated by David, I Chron 19:18, and twenty thousand infantry appear in the Aramaean force captured by David, I Chron 17:4. So large a cavalry force would have been useless in rugged Judaea. At his climactic battle at Magnesia against the Romans in 190 Antiochus III had a total of only forty-two thousand infantry, so that forty thousand were far too many to bring against Judas' guerrilla warfare; see Livy xxxvii 40 and Bikerman, *Institutions,* pp. 55–73.

40. *Setting out . . . force.* S and La[L B] have "He set out with their entire force, and. . . ." Their reading reflects an ancient error, perhaps in the original Hebrew. Except in Numbers and Deuteronomy, in the Hebrew Bible "to set out" is usually in the singular (*wys'*), with the commander or the force as the subject. From force of habit, the author or scribe thus may have written the singular. Here, as at I 7:10 and 9:4, there is a compound subject: two or three men are accompanied by the army, so that the verb should be plural.

40–57. *Ammaus . . . south of Ammaus.* The spelling "Emmaus" is more familiar to modern readers. See Map 3, p. 529. From their camp the Seleucid commanders could observe several important routes from Jerusalem into the coastal plain and send detachments to block others. The fertility of the neighborhood made it easy to supply the army there over a long period. Perhaps the first consideration of the Seleucid commanders was to make sure that Judas would not be able to join forces with their rivals in Ptolemaic Egypt. To block

Judas from this course, the Seleucid force had only to close the coastal routes, since the inland routes through Beth-Zur were guarded by the Idumaeans, who had no love for the Jews (I 5:65; II 12:32–37, etc.). Ammaus was a rather good base for a static defense force seeking to close the coastal routes leading from Jerusalem, though the Seleucid campsite was vulnerable to attack by forces moving unseen along the hills to the south (Abel, at vss. 40 and 57).

However, Judas never is reported to have sought Ptolemaic aid, and the large Seleucid force surely intended to take the offensive. Slave traders came in large numbers (cf. II 8:10–11), as if they expected the Seleucid army soon would strike a decisive blow against the Jewish rebels. Judas moved promptly, as if forced to counter an offensive threat. We may guess that the Seleucid force was large enough to move simultaneously on several routes to join forces with their allies in the Akra in Jerusalem, and that Judas' force was too small to block all these roads. By moving to the high ground south of Ammaus, Judas could observe any moves from the Seleucid camp along the northern approaches to Jerusalem as well as any move to use the southern approaches. From his campsite Judas could also, if necessary, withdraw into friendly hill country. Finally, Judas' presence near the Seleucid camp might make Gorgias and Nicanor think twice before dividing their forces and reducing the strength of their main base at Ammaus. If so, Gorgias' rashness was to solve Judas' problems for him, allowing Judas to rout the whole expedition.

40. *plateau*. The Shephelah, the region of low hills between the mountains and the coastal plain.

41. *slaves*. The regular practice in the Hellenistic world was to hold prisoners of war and captives for ransom or sell them as slaves.

Idumaea. All witnesses to the text read "Syria," but the main expeditionary force had just come from Syria. Later, the fiercest opposition to the Hasmonaean armies came from Philistia and Idumaea, and here, too, one would expect a reference to the "Philistines" to be accompanied by one to the Idumaeans. Probably the translator misread Hebrew *'dm* ("Edom") as *'rm* ("Syria").

Philistines. The Greek has the peculiar word for "foreigners" which the translator of the books of Samuel regularly uses for "Philistines." Our author delights in borrowing the language of the books of Samuel to portray Judas as a latter-day David, but Judas' contemporaries in Gaza, Azotus, and Ascalon may well have called themselves Philistines, however few of them were descended from the original Philistine stock. Sidon was destroyed in 677 B.C.E. and repopulated with Assyrian colonists, yet less than a century later the colonists were calling themselves "Sidonians," and no one questioned their right to use the name of the earlier stock; see Honigmann, "Sidon," PW II^A (1921), 2219–20. Indeed, in the Christian era the Romans were to use the name "Palaestina," "Land of the Philistines," for the region which included Judaea and Samaria and the adjoining coast as well as neighboring territories; see A. Legendre, "Palestine," *Dictionnaire de la Bible*, IV 2 (1912), 1975–76. The narrative of the campaign from here on contains several echoes of the reports of David's victories over the Philistines at II Sam 5:17–25 and I Chron 14:8–17. See below, NOTES on 3:43 and 60 and on 4:3, 12, 15, 22.

42. *how very dangerous . . . was*. Literally, "that the evils were multiplied"; cf. Joel 3[4H]:13, "their wickedness is multiplied."

43. *Let us rebuild . . . people*. Cf. Amos 9:11; again our author alludes to a context dealing with David. In Amos the rebuilder is God. It is characteristic of our author to regard the Hasmonaeans as God's instruments in the fulfillment of the prophesies of restoration and glory.

let us fight . . . sanctuary. Cf. David's exhortation at II Sam 10:12 and I Chron 19:13. "Sanctuary" could be an alternative name for Jerusalem; see *Shishah sidre Mishnah, Seder Mo'ed*, ed. Hanoch Albeck (Jerusalem and Tel-Aviv: Bialik Institute and Dvir, 1952), pp. 269, 476, to *Sukkah* 3:12. Hence, our passage is probably a paraphrase of David's exhortation.

44–45. There may be an effort in these verses to suggest the impending fulfillment of the prophesies in Isaiah 24. After a period of apostasy (Isa 24:5), the land and the city shall be laid waste, and all joy shall disappear (ibid., vss. 6–13). Then, the people shall lift up their voices to God (vss. 14–16), and God will bring about a great victory in which there will be panic and traps for the enemy (vss. 17–23). Here, vss. 44–45 may show that the preconditions for the great victory have been fulfilled, and the reader who knew the prophesies could expect the further course of the campaign to bring the great victory.

45. *trampled*. See Isa 63:18 in the context of Isaiah 63–64.

46. Samuel convoked repentant Israel at Mizpah, and his prayer there brought God to win for Israel a great victory over the Philistines, according to I Sam 7:2–14. See also Philip Davies, "A Note on I Macc. III. 46," JTS 23 (1972), 117–21. The location of Mizpah is still a problem. Some would locate it at Tell en-Naṣbeh, thirteen kilometers north of Jerusalem. Though Jerusalem cannot be seen from there, it was as much "opposite Jerusalem" as Beth-Zechariah was "opposite the king's camp" at Beth-Zur (I 6:31–32). Others would locate it at Nebī Samwīl, northwest of Jerusalem (see Map 3, p. 529), from which Jerusalem can be seen and roads from the west surveyed. Nebī Samwīl is closer to Ammaus, but the lay of the land and the poverty of the archaeological finds do not suggest that the important center of Mizpah was at Nebī Samwīl. For the present it is best to admit that we do not know where ancient Mizpah was. See Zechariah Kallay, "*Miṣpah* 2," Enc. Bib., V (1968), 237–42 (in Hebrew); N. Avigad, "New Light on the MṢH Seal Impressions," IEJ 8 (1958), 113–19.

48. Ancient scribes had a hard time understanding this verse. Greek manuscripts of the group q render ". . . where the gentiles sought to inscribe the likenesses." The Syriac version paraphrases, "They spread out the scroll of the Law and mourned before the Holy One over the fact that the pagans were compelling them to follow practices like theirs." For the guesses of modern scholars, see Abel, ad loc.

Our verse, however, is surely patterned after the story of Hezekiah and Sennacherib's message (II Kings 19:14–19; Isa 37:14–21). Whereas Hezekiah used Sennacherib's letter to call attention to the contrast between the God of Israel and the gods of the pagans, Antiochus IV attempted to use the Torah to prove that illicit "pagan" rites and deities belonged in the religion of Israel. The syntax of the Greek words which I have translated "at the passages where" (*peri hôn*) is difficult. Any solution must also have an intelligible Hebrew text underlying the Greek. Our author's idiom probably did strain Hebrew as his translator's idiom strained Greek, but it remained intelligible to an audience which knew the story of Hezekiah. Greek *peri* usually reflects Hebrew *'al*. The Hebrew word commonly means "concerning," "on account of." Both the Hebrew and the Greek preposition are common with verbs of telling and revealing; see M. Johannessohn, "Der Gebrauch der Präpositionen in der Septuaginta," *Nachrichten von der Königlichen Gesellschaft der Wissenschaften zu Göttingen, Philologisch-historische Klasse*, 1925, pp. 219–21; I 12:21, 14: 21; Lam 2:14, 4:22; Esther 6:2. To spread the scroll was also to reveal. Therefore, we may translate either, "They unrolled the scroll of the Torah on account of the efforts of the pagans to find analogies to their idols," or "They unrolled the scroll of the Torah to reveal the texts wherein the pagans sought to find analogies to their idols." The original Hebrew was probably something like *"wayyipreśū et sēper hattōrāh 'al ašer hippeśū* [or *dāreśū*) *haggōyīm et demūyōt elōhēhem."* For *'al ašer,* cf. Exod 3:35; Deut 29:24, etc. For *demūyōt* as "analogies" or "equivalents," cf. Isa 40:18.

Not a few texts in the Torah lent themselves to the purpose of showing that the imposed cult was indeed the original religion of Moses and the patriarchs. Gen 1:26–27 apparently has God consulting other deities and then creating man *in the image of God, male and female.* One could easily infer that both male and female deities had had a hand in the creation. The Torah does not object to Jacob's cult-stone; see Introduction, pp. 147–48, 150. Moses, too, set up cult-stones (*massēbōt*), according to Exod 24:4. The names of the Israelites' God also lent themselves to Antiochus' purposes. They were multiple, as if there were several deities, *YHWH,* Lord, God, etc. "Lord" (*ădōnāy*) looked just like "Adonis"; "God" (*ĕlōhīm*) was plural in form and occasionally was used with a plural verb (Gen 20:13 [Abraham speaking!], 35:7; Exod 22:8, 32:4, 8). Then there were the *three* men who appeared to Abraham in Genesis 18. That all three were male was of no consequence. Athena herself appears in male disguise in the *Iliad* (iv 86, etc.) and *Odyssey.* God appears to be female at Deut 32:18; cf. Isa 42:14; Ps 2:7. In Hebrew the "Spirit" of the Lord is feminine and could be taken as a separate person, just as was the Holy Spirit in Christianity and "Tanit, the Face of Baal" at Carthage; see Gen 1:2; Num 24:2; Isa 63:11, 14 (role of God's "Spirit" in the Exodus); Charles-F. Jean and Jacob Hoftijzer, *Dictionnaire des inscriptions sémitiques de l'ouest* (Leiden: Brill, 1965), p. 229, s.v. *pnh.* Exod 20:24 could be cited to show that sacrifices could be offered elsewhere than on the temple altar. The period of the wandering in the desert was the "honeymoon" period of God and Israel (Jer 2:2); yet circumcision was not then practiced (Josh 5:5). According to Gen 9:2–4 the meat of all types of animals is permitted. Thus, the imposed cult, with its God accompanied by Athena and "Dionysus" and with its violations of Jewish law could be "proved" legitimate by the Jews' own scriptures!

49–54. Pietists before had tried to rouse God's vengeance against the persecuting gentiles by displaying helpless martyrdom, in accordance with Deut 32:36, 42–43. See Introduction, p. 40, and NOTE on 2:28–38. Now the Hasmonaean force makes use of the same texts, but with a different interpretation, supported by many other scriptural texts. Martyrdom was unnecessary, they held; display of mere helplessness by the pious would rouse God to act.

See also Lev 26:40–45; Deut 26:7–8, 30:1–10; Judg 2:15–18; I Sam 7:2–14; II Kings 14:25–27.

49. Non-perishable first fruits and tithes could be kept a long time, but according to rabbinic interpretation of Deut 26:12–13, they must be removed from the owner's premises and taken to Jerusalem by Passover in the third or sixth year of the sabbatical cycle (*Sifre Debarim* 302–3; Rashi to Deut 26: 12–13). Thus we might receive confirmation that the year of the campaign of Gorgias and Nicanor (165/4) was the sixth year of the sabbatical cycle and that 164/3 was a sabbatical year (see NOTE on 6:20). We still would not be able to date the campaign near the time of Passover, because as long as Jerusalem remained closed to them, the pious could remove the produce which had been turned into sacred dues from their own premises but were at a loss as to what to do with it. We do not know, however, what interpretation of Deut 26:12–13 prevailed at this time.

priestly vestments. These were usable only for the rituals at the temple in Jerusalem (Exod 28:40–43, 39:1; *M. Zebaḥim* 14:10; TB *Zebaḥim* 119b).

first fruits. The Greek word might include also the firstborn of clean animals. As obligatory offerings, both could be brought only at the temple (first fruits: Exod 34:22–26; Lev 23:17–20; firstborn: Exod 13:12–15; Num 18:17; Deut 12:6–18, 14:23, 15:19–20; see also *M. Megillah* 1:10–11).

tithes. Likewise obligatory, the tithe of livestock and the "second tithe" could be brought only at the temple (Lev 27:32–33; TB *Bekorot* 53a; Deut 12:6–18, 14:23; *M. Megillah* 1:10–11).

Nazirites . . . vows. Their obligatory burnt offerings and peace and sin offerings could be brought only at the temple (Num 6:13–20; *M. Megillah* 1: 10–11).

50. Since the priestly vestments are analogous to harps, cf. Ps 137:2–4.

51. *trampled*. See above, on vs. 45.

profaned. Cf. Ezek 25:3 in its context.

priests . . . affliction. Cf. Joel 1:9; Lam 1:4.

52. The verse again echoes the story of Hezekiah and Sennacherib. Cf. II Kings 18:25 and Isa 36:10; II Kings 19:27 and Isa 37:28. Cf. also Jer 18:23.

53. Cf. Ps 94:16–17.

54. See Num 10:9.

55–60. Judas acts in accordance with Deut 20:1–9. Cf. Exod 18:21, where Judas or our author understood *anšē ḥayil* as "warriors." However, the scheme of ranks was not only biblical. The same scheme was followed widely in the Hellenistic world. See Marcel Launey, *Recherches sur les armées hellénistiques*, II, Index II, s.vv. *dekadarchês* and *pentêkontarchos*, and Index III, s.vv. *chiliarques* and *hekatontarque*.

57. See above, on vss. 40–57.

59. Cf. Esther 8:6.

60. Again our author has Judas echo David (II Sam 10:12; I Chron 19:13).

4:1. Unlike the figures for the size of the whole expedition (see above on 3:39), the figures here for the size of Gorgias' detachment are reasonable, especially since Judas had a force of three thousand (vs. 6). The prudent Gorgias made sure his force outnumbered his Jewish enemy.

2. *men of the Akra.* These experts on the terrain of Judaea must have been native Jews, not foreign settlers; Josephus' paraphrase (*AJ* xii 7.4.305) says that the guides were "some of the renegade Jews." See Introduction, pp. 123–25. Our author exploits the opportunities to display the treason of the renegades in the Akra.

3. *Judas . . . plan.* Neither here nor in the abridged history (II 8:12–27) is there any claim that Judas got his information through a supernatural source, but the author of Enoch 90:14, a contemporary of the events, apparently so believed; see Introduction, Part II, n. 12. Our author was surely aware that if Judas had had a supernatural source of information, his feat would have equaled David's at I Chron 14:14–16 and II Sam 5:23–25.

plan . . . Ammaus. Josephus in his paraphrase has more than the narrative here. Between "plan" and "He" Josephus (*AJ* xii 7.4.305) adds, "He decided to attack the enemy camp himself." Then comes Josephus' paraphrase of vs. 4, followed by *AJ* xii 7.4.306, "He had his men dine early, and then, after leaving many fires burning in the camp, he marched all night against the enemy at Ammaus." Though Josephus' paraphrase elsewhere in this context is very close, the additions here do not necessarily indicate a gap in the text of First Maccabees, since the stratagem of leaving fires burning to deceive the enemy was a commonplace of Greek war narratives (e.g. Herodotus viii 19; Thucydides vii 80.3, etc.; and cf. I 12:28–29). Josephus may have inserted it to add to the interest of the story, not realizing that thus he impaired our author's effort to portray Judas' feat as parallel to that of David at I Chron 14:14–16 and II Sam 5:23–25. Josephus need not have invented his addition. He could have derived it from another source.

4. *away.* The Greek, *eskorpismenai,* "scattered," probably reflects an original Hebrew *niprādīm,* "separated," as at Neh 4:13 and its Greek version, II Esd 4:13. Cf. "till we have drawn them away" at Josh 8:6.

5. *mountains.* Judas' camp was in the hills; see above on 3:40–57. Gorgias naturally expected his enemy to cling to the security of their own hill country.

They are fleeing from us. Cf. Josh 8:6. Judas' stratagem equals Joshua's.

6. *three thousand men.* See above on 4:1. At II 8:16 Judas is said to have had six thousand men; see commentary ad loc.

though . . . have. Cf. I Sam 13:19–22.

7. Our author contrasts the strength of the Seleucid force with the weakness of Judas' band. Cf. I Sam 17:38–47.

8–11. Our author has Judas encourage his men with the example of the crossing of the Red Sea (Exodus 14). Indeed, they were in danger of being trapped between the forces of Gorgias and of Nicanor and in danger of being enslaved, just as the Israelites at the Red Sea were caught between the sea and Pharaoh's pursuing force. Jason of Cyrene at II 8:16–20 was pleased to portray Judas as encouraging his men not with the example of the crossing of the Red Sea, but with other examples, including the deliverance of Jerusalem from Sennacherib (II Kings 18:13 – 19; Isaiah 36–37). Our author, too, alludes indirectly to the deliverance from Sennacherib, since vs. 11 echoes II Kings 19:19 and Isa 37:20; cf. also Isa 49:24–26. See also I Sam 17:46.

12. *foreigners.* See above on 3:41, *Philistines.*

13. *sounded their trumpets.* They fulfilled the commandment at Num 10:9.

15. *Gazera.* The Greek translator may well have used this alternative form of the name of the town of Gezer=Gazara in imitation of the Greek of II Sam 5:25 and I Chron 14:16; if so, he made all the clearer the author's effort to equate an exploit of Judas' with one of David's.

There may already have been a Seleucid post at Gezer to serve the fugitives as a refuge. See Map 3, p. 529. Only for a later time do we have a literary record of a Seleucid fort at Gezer, at I 9:52, but that verse speaks of Bacchides' fortification of Beth-Zur, Gezer, and the Akra. Since Beth-Zur and the Akra were actually old strongholds which Bacchides *re*fortified (I 1:33; 4:61; 6:7), Gezer, too, may have been a fort before.

Indeed, the most recent excavations at Gezer suggest that any Hellenistic post at Gezer probably reused much earlier Canaanite fortifications which still stood above ground. See D. Ussishkin and G. Ernest Wright, "Gezer," *Encyclopaedia of Archaeological Excavations in the Holy Land* (Jerusalem: Israel Exploration Society and Massada, 1970), p. 117 (in Hebrew); William G. Dever, "Excavations at Gezer," BA 30 (1967), 49; Dever et al., "Further Excavations at Gezer, 1967–71," BA 34 (1971), 108–9.

Traces of such a post may have been found in two areas of the recent excavations. In Field II, two phases of occupation lie in a stratum dated by pottery to ca. 175–150. The later phase may represent Bacchides' refortification; if so, the earlier phase could be a post existing in the time of the defeat of Nicanor and Gorgias. Similarly, in Field III, the vicinity of the great Solomonic gate, there are two Hellenistic phases. The earlier is datable by pottery to the early second century B.C.E., and may represent a post existing in 165. The later is very brief and may represent Bacchides' refortification; it is followed by massive structures attributed to Simon the Hasmonaean. See Dever, BA 30 (1967), 61–62, and Dever et al., BA 34 (1971), 112, 118–19.

the plains of Idumaea, Azotus, and Jamnia. The word order shows that a tongue of Idumaean territory extended northward from Marisa, separating Judaea from the Philistine towns of Azotus and Jamnia. See Map 4, p. 529.

three thousand. The figure should be reliable, since Judas' army later took the spoils (vs. 23).

16–18. See NOTE on II 8:26.

20. Cf. Josh 8:8, 19–20.

22. *Philistines.* See above on 3:41.

23. *marine blue and purple.* The two famous "Tyrian" dyes, made from the marine mollusc Murex brandaris. The word "marine" here distinguishes them from imitations made from other sources. In the Hebrew, the adjective corresponding to "marine" followed both nouns, in accordance with Hebrew word order. The Greek translator wrongly applied it only to the second, "purple."

24. Judas and his men sang hymns beginning with the formula, "Give thanks unto the Lord." See I Chron 16:8–36; II Chron 20:21; Pss 106, 107, 108, 136. All these texts celebrate how God vindicates his sometimes wayward people when they become righteous. On the *Hallel,* see NOTE on 4:55–59. I have rendered *eulogein* here by using the word "thanksgiving." If the Greek transla-

tor had had the usual Hebrew equivalent, *brk* ("bless"), before him, surely he would have treated the verb as transitive. Between verb and object stands the preposition *eis,* suggesting that *eulogein* may indeed reflect the author's use of *hwdh* ("give thanks"), as at Isa 12:1, a context which may have been in our author's mind as he recorded a victory over "Philistines"; see Isa 11:14.

25. Cf. I Sam 19:5; II Sam 23:10, 12; and I Chron 11:14. Again our author echoes narratives of David's victories.

The victory over Gorgias and Nicanor left Judaea free from Seleucid force until Lysias' expedition (4:28–35), since the garrison in the Akra was now still less able to cope with Judas' force (cf. II 8:8). Now even unrebellious pious Jews could feel free again to observe the Torah openly. Hence, the immediate aftermath of the victory over Gorgias and Nicanor may have been the day commemorated in *Megillat Ta'anit* 24 Ab, "On the twenty-fourth of that month we returned to our own Law." The day would hardly commemorate Mattathias' rebellion, for the zealous old priest would not have waited for the winter month of Kislev to the midsummer month of Ab before rebelling.

XI. LYSIAS FAILS TO CRUSH
JUDAS' BAND
(4:26–35)

4 26 The surviving foreign troops came to Lysias and reported all that had happened. 27 On hearing the news, Lysias was perturbed and disheartened, because the outcome for Israel had met neither his own wishes nor the commands he had received from the king. 28 During the year which followed, he mustered sixty thousand first-class troops and five thousand cavalry so as to bring to an end the war with the Jews. 29 They marched into Idumaea and encamped at Beth-Zur. Judas came to meet them with ten thousand men. 30 He saw how strong was the encampment, and prayed, "Blessed are You, Savior of Israel, Who broke the onslaught of the mighty by the hand of your servant David and gave the camp of the Philistines into the hand of Jonathan son of Saul and his armorbearer. 31 Deliver this camp into the hand of your people Israel, and let them be disappointed by their infantry and cavalry. 32 Put cowardice in their hearts, and cause their bold confidence to melt, and let them totter in defeat. 33 Make them fall by the swords of those who love You, and let all who know Your name sing hymns of praise to You." 34 They joined battle, and from the camp of Lysias no fewer than five thousand men fell as they were routed before them. 35 On seeing the severe reverse suffered by his troops and the boldness exhibited by Judas', perceiving that they were prepared either to live or to die nobly, Lysias departed for Antioch and raised a very large mercenary force, intending to invade Judaea again.

NOTES

4:26. *foreign*. Our author uses the Greek word which usually means "Philistines"; Judas, however, had routed a detachment of the royal army, and the surviving royal troops surely were the ones who reported to Lysias.

28–29. The later expedition, of Lysias and Antiochus V (I 6:28–62), also approached Judaea from the south, through Idumaea and the border town of Beth-Zur. Some scholars, noting this fact, have tried to reject the account here of an earlier expedition of Lysias through Idumaea and Beth-Zur, regarding it as an erroneous "doublet" of the later account or even as a fabrication of a fictitious victory at Beth-Zur to balance Judas' heavy defeat there in 163 (I 6:32–47); see Kolbe, *Beiträge,* pp. 79–81, and Mørkholm, pp. 152–55. The theory that the account of Lysias' first expedition is a propagandist's fiction is easily refuted. Judas enjoyed great victories after the heavy defeat of 163. Previous victories do not cancel defeats; only subsequent victories do. If our author had wished to fabricate a victory, he could well have done what Jason of Cyrene did at II 13:19: he could have reported the defeat itself as a victory!

In fact, Lysias' first expedition is well attested. The contemporary apocalypse, Enoch 90:15, alludes to it; see Introduction, Part II, n. 12. Jason of Cyrene's account (II 11) corroborates our author's, when we allow for the propagandistic biases of both men and for Jason's love of rhetorical embellishment. Careful attention to the wording of our verses removes the most serious of Mørkholm's objections to the narrative here.

Our author dates Lysias' preparations for his first expedition "during the year which followed." The Greek translator of First Maccabees throughout observes strictly the distinction between the Greek *etos* ("calendar year") and *eniautos* ("yearlong period of time"). The Hebrew *šnh* can mean either, though "yearlong period" can be unambiguously expressed by *šnt ymym* (Gen 41:1) or by *ymym* alone (Lev 25:29, where the Greek has *eniautos hêmerôn*). Whatever the original Hebrew here, the translator appears to have rendered the author's meaning correctly. The author was intentionally vague: within the yearlong period which followed the defeat of Gorgias and Nicanor, Lysias prepared a new expedition and then marched. Our author was a Hasmonaean propagandist; he did not wish to publicize the awkward interval of months of inaction which elapsed between Lysias' withdrawal and the dedication of the new altar; see NOTE on 4:36–54. The defeat of Gorgias and Nicanor probably came in the summer or autumn of 165, since it followed Antiochus' departure eastward; see introductory NOTE to 3:27–37. Since our author gives no date for Lysias' withdrawal, he was free to let the preparations and the expedition float within the period between summer or autumn, 165, and Kislev, 164, "the year which followed." He thus left the reader free to assume, falsely, that very little time elapsed between Lysias' withdrawal and the Feast of Dedication.

In fact, the Seleucid authorities could not tolerate an increasingly successful revolt near the sensitive Ptolemaic border, especially when Antiochus IV was far away with half the imperial army; see II 9:25. Hence, Lysias was driven to risk an autumn or winter campaign, though Mørkholm (p. 154) found it strange. In fact, as we know from other sources (II 11:11–21, 27–38; *Megillat Ta'anit* 28 Adar), Lysias' expedition *ended* in Adar, 164 (late winter), with a proclamation terminating the persecution and granting amnesty to the Jews. Later, Tryphon was to conduct a winter campaign against the Hasmonaeans (I 13:20–24). Both Lysias and Tryphon approached Jerusalem from the more arid south, perhaps partly in order to avoid as far as possible the winter rains.

Chronological difficulties result if we assume that the translator wrongly rendered the original Hebrew by the Greek *eniautos*. Josephus' paraphrase (*AJ* xii 7.5.313) does have *etos* instead of *eniautos*. If the original Hebrew meant "during the calendar year which followed," and if we are right in dating Antiochus' departure in late spring, our author must have derived his knowledge of Lysias' preparations from a Seleucid source dating them in 148 Sel.-Mac. (October 2, 165–September 21, 164). Since the expedition was against Judaea, one might doubt that our author would have bothered to consult a Seleucid source to date Lysias' preparations. If the date had been our author's own inference, it would have to be a Sel.-Bab. date, but the next Sel.-Bab. year after Antiochus' departure did not begin until the spring of 164, when Lysias' expedition had already ended.

28. *sixty thousand . . . five thousand.* See NOTE on 3:39.

29. *Idumaea . . . Beth-Zur.* See above, on vss. 28–29, and Map 6, p. 532. Although the wish to avoid the winter rains may have contributed, Lysias' main reason for taking the route through Idumaea and Beth-Zur was that it alone allowed him to enter hostile Judaea after already having crossed the crest of the mountains. The disadvantage of giving the enemy the uphill position had ruined Lysias' predecessors. The Idumaeans had long been hostile to the Jews (see Introduction, pp. 134–35) and were even more hostile to the pious Jewish rebels (I 4:61, 5:3, 65–66, 6:31; II 10:15–23, 12:32). The Idumaeans appear to have been loyal subjects of the Seleucids. See NOTE on 1:4, *nations*.

Our author's wording leaves it possible that Beth-Zur lay within Idumaea. Josephus, however, in his paraphrase (*AJ* xii 7.5.313) insists that Beth-Zur was a village of Judaea. Indeed, at this time, the town had long been part of Judaea, and nothing indicates that it fell into the hands of the Idumaeans; see Neh 3:16, and, for a summary of the archaeological discoveries, Robert W. Funk, "Bet-ṣur," *Encyclopaedia of Archaeological Excavations in the Holy Land*, pp. 60–63 (in Hebrew). The town was as yet unfortified. Far from having to besiege it, Lysias used it as his campsite. Hence, there is no foundation for Abel's theory (see ad loc.), that Judas' encroachments on Idumaea, and in particular his capture of Beth-Zur from the Idumaeans, drove Lysias to fight in this theater. Judas dared to invade hostile areas outside Judaea only after Lysias' withdrawal.

Only at II 11:5 does Lysias besiege Beth-Zur, which there appears as a Jewish-held fort. Jason of Cyrene thought he had proof that the purification of the temple (I 4:41–59; II 10:1–6) occurred in the winter of 165; hence, he could date Judas' fortification of the temple mount and of Beth-Zur late in 165 or early in 164, before Lysias' expedition. However, Jason's chronology is wrong; see Introduction, pp. 81–84; cf. R. W. Funk, "The 1957 Campaign at Beth-Zur," BASOR 150 (1958), 16, n. 8. On I 6:7, see ad loc.

Judas had only three thousand men against Gorgias and Nicanor. Here he has ten thousand. His victories had attracted many new adherents.

30. The narrative of Judas' exploits has teemed with tacit allusions to the victories of Jonathan and David over the Philistines. Now Judas' prayer alludes explicitly to those ancient victories. Judas' prayer has the form of a benediction of God ("Blessed are You . . . Who . . ."), a form already used at I Chron 29:10 and at Ps 119:12 and frequently in Tobit (3:11, etc.), and one which subsequently became the favorite form in Jewish prayer. Goliath is called "mighty" at Greek I Sam 17:4, and his "onslaught" is described at vs. 48. Jonathan's victory: I Sam 14:1–15.

31. Cf. Micah 7:16.

32. Cf. Lev 26:36; Deut 28:65; I Sam 10:26; Josh 5:1; Ps 107:26–27.

33. Cf. Ps 9:11–12.

34. The Greek translator used the same word (*epeson*) to render "fell" (Hebrew *wayyippᵉlū*) and "were routed" (Hebrew *wayyinnāgᵉpū*). Josephus' paraphrase has Judas' men engaging only the vanguard (*tois prodromois*) of Lysias' force. He or his Greek assistant may have failed to understand the translator's text, which could be rendered, "From the camp of Lysias no fewer than five thousand men fell; they fell from the front of them [i.e. from the vanguard of the force]." Hence, Josephus' account of the battle is no evidence for toning down our author's claims of a victory. Again, since Judas' force remained in control of the battleground, there is no reason to doubt that they could count the enemy dead, even though five thousand is a large figure. Still larger are the figures at II 11:11–12.

35. Even if he had five thousand dead, Lysias still had a large force, and the reasons for using it to suppress Judas' rebel band were as strong after Judas' victory at Beth-Zur as before; see above on vss. 28–29. Why, then, did Lysias withdraw? Our author may well have known the facts, but, if so, to him they were at best unedifying and at worst embarrassing. He omitted them from his narrative. Jason of Cyrene misunderstood his sources, but he has preserved for us the necessary evidence. The increase in Judas' combat force from three thousand to ten thousand presupposes a much greater increase in the number of his non-combatant supporters, so as to constitute a large percentage of the Jewish population. This wide support came not only because of Judas' victories but also because the badly fragmented groups of pious Jews could unite in viewing victory for Lysias as the final disaster for their nation and religion. So soon as Lysias should no longer be a threat, much of Judas' force would melt away. The Hellenizing high priest, Menelaus, probably perceived this fact early. We have documentary evidence that he approached the royal authorities, urging an end to the persecution (II 11:29–32); see Introduction, pp. 158–59.

Though Jason of Cyrene supposed that the letters preserved at II 11:16–21, 27–38, were to Judas and his party, the prominence in them of Menelaus and the absence of all mention of Judas prove him wrong. Lysias' letter is addressed (II 11:16) to "the people [*tôi plêthei*] of the Jews," a designation which takes note of the fact that from the time of the Mysarch's expedition the Jews were no longer a privileged *ethnos;* see NOTES on I 1:4, *nations,* and on 1:29–40. Lysias may well have viewed himself as addressing the survivors of the aristocracy and commons of the Jewish community which existed as a privileged nation before the Mysarch's expedition and still existed *de facto.* The high priest, Menelaus, was the head of that community, and the ambassadors, John and Absalom (II 11:17), surely represent the same group.

Neither our author nor Jason had any desire to portray Menelaus and his followers as the ones who secured the end of the persecution. Those, however, who viewed the end of the persecution as the proof of God's mercy lovingly preserved the documents so that Jason could later misinterpret them.

We may envision the true course of events as follows: In the opening stages of his expedition Lysias believed he could crush Judas' force and saw no reason to yield to any appeals Menelaus may have made. On being repulsed at Beth-Zur, however, Lysias probably hesitated long enough for Menelaus and his circle to approach him. For them, the prospect of being caught in a war between Judas and Lysias was appalling. Now Lysias himself could see that the campaign would be arduous. Menelaus and his followers probably urged that an end to the persecution would immediately drain support away from the rebellion. Lysias agreed, and all the more readily after the Jewish petitioners received the support of Roman ambassadors. The letters preserved at II 11: 16–21, 27–38 resulted. Jews remembered 28 Adar (=Xanthicus) as the end of the persecution (*Megillat Ta'anit* 28 Adar). These facts serve to date the end of Lysias' expedition in late Adar, 164. The Feast of Dedication did not occur until over half a year had elapsed. The facts of the long delay were embarrassing and constituted one more reason for our author to leave Lysias' withdrawal largely unexplained. See NOTE on 4:36–54.

The negotiations for the amnesty ignored Judas. The terms were unflattering, amounting to an ultimatum that the Jews quickly lay down their arms. Enough Jews accepted them so that Judas' force was reduced to the point that Lysias felt it safe to withdraw without forcing the remainder to lay down their arms. Lysias would return in 163/2, with a stronger army. Under the circumstances, the pro-Hasmonaean historian felt justified in ignoring the amnesty and in speaking only of Lysias' intentions to resume the conflict later. See also end of NOTE on 3:32–33.

raised . . . again. My translation reflects the probable Hebrew original, which was something like wyśkr ḥyl hrbh lhwsyp lb' 'l yhwdh. Cf. II Kings 7:6; Jer 49:14[29:14 Greek]; and I Sam 7:13; and for *hrbh,* see the Greek and Hebrew of Deut 30:5. The Greek scribes were puzzled by the translator's literal and unidiomatic rendering, *exenologei pleonaston genêthenta palin paraginesthai eis tên Ioudaian,* and wrongly tried to improve upon it. Even the old Latin versions reflect such misunderstandings, though they still correctly connect "again" with "invade."

XII. THE RESTORATION OF
THE TEMPLE
(4:36–61)

4 ³⁶ Thereupon, Judas and his brothers said, "Now our enemies
have been defeated. Let us go purify the sanctuary and restore it."
³⁷ The entire army assembled, and they went up to Mount Zion.
³⁸ They saw the temple laid desolate and the altar profaned and the
gates burned and the courts overgrown with plants as "in a thicket"
or like "one of the mountains" and the chambers laid in ruins.
³⁹ They rent their garments and made great lamentation and put on
ashes. ⁴⁰ They prostrated themselves upon the ground and sounded
the signal trumpets and cried out to Heaven. ⁴¹ Then Judas assigned
soldiers the duty of fighting the men in the Akra while he purified
the sanctuary. ⁴² He appointed unblemished priests, lovers of the
Torah, ⁴³ who purified the sanctuary and removed the stones of the
loathsome structure to an unclean place. ⁴⁴ They deliberated over
what they should do with the profaned altar of the burnt offering,
⁴⁵ and they came up with the good idea of dismantling it lest the fact
that the gentiles had defiled it should be held to their disgrace. Accordingly, they dismantled the altar, ⁴⁶ and put its stones away on
the temple mount in a suitable place until a prophet should come to
give an oracle concerning them. ⁴⁷ Taking uncut stones as prescribed
by the Torah, they built a new altar after the pattern of the old.
⁴⁸ They repaired the sanctuary and sanctified the interior of the
house and the courts. ⁴⁹ They also made new sacred vessels, and
they brought the candelabrum and the altar of incense and the table
into the nave. ⁵⁰ They burned incense on the altar and kindled the
lights on the candelabrum so that they illumined the nave. ⁵¹ They
set loaves upon the table and hung the curtains and brought to completion all the work which they had done. ⁵² They rose early on the
morning of the twenty-fifth day of the ninth month (that is, the
month of Kislev), in the year 148, ⁵³ and they brought a sacrifice
according to the Torah upon the new altar of burnt offerings which
they had built. ⁵⁴ At the very time of year and on the very day on

which the gentiles had profaned the altar, it was dedicated to the sound of singing and harps and lyres and cymbals. 55 The entire people prostrated themselves and bowed and gave thanks to Heaven Who had brought them victory. 56 They celebrated the dedication of the altar for eight days, joyfully bringing burnt offerings and sacrificing peace offerings and thank offerings. 57 They decorated the front of the nave with golden cornices and bosses and restored the gates and the chambers and fitted them with doors. 58 The people were overjoyed as the shame inflicted by the gentiles was removed. 59 Judas and his brothers and the entire assembly of Israel decreed that the days of the dedication of the altar should be observed at their time of year annually for eight days, beginning with the twenty-fifth of the month of Kislev, with joy and gladness. 60 At that time they also fortified Mount Zion, surrounding it with a high wall and strong towers to prevent the gentiles from ever coming and trampling it as they had done before. 61 He posted a special force there to guard it, and he fortified . . . Beth-Zur so that the people might have a fortress facing Idumaea.

NOTES

4:36–54. There is a mystery in Judas' long delay in recovering and purifying the temple, though Lysias had withdrawn by early spring, 164. Clearly, he was not waiting for royal permission. Judas did purify the temple in the autumn of 164/3, though Antiochus V officially restored the temple to the Jews only in 162 (II 11:23–26). Even the Abomination of Desolation long continued to stand, until the beginning of the seventh month of the Jewish year; see below. Why did Judas wait so long?

The delay was probably deliberate. The Pietists who believed the prophesies of the apocalyptic seers insisted on waiting for God to fulfill them. Not all the predicted disasters had occurred. Before Antiochus IV's predicted conquest of Egypt and final war to exterminate the pious (Dan 11:40–45a), before the predicted "worst time of troubles" (Dan 12:1), before the predicted earthquake and natural upheavals (Test Moses x 1–6), it would be imprudent to restore the temple in Jerusalem. Indeed, perhaps the age of a man-made temple was past. The end of the persecution would see judgment visited upon Antiochus (Dan 7:11, 22, 26, 11:45b) and punishment upon the gentiles (Test Moses x 7) and wicked Jews (Enoch xc 26–27). The Seleucid empire would come to an end, to be replaced by an eternal empire of the Saints (Dan 7:11–14, 22, 26–27; Enoch xc 30). There would be a resurrection of the dead Jews, to reward the righteous and punish the wicked (Dan 12:2–3; cf. Enoch xc 33). God's own temple would descend from heaven to Jerusalem to replace the desecrated one built by men (Enoch xc 28–29). No prophesy mentioned any human act of restoration. Would it not be presumptuous to restore a temple which God Himself was going to remove and replace? There was a prophesy that God Himself would destroy all idols (Test Moses x 7). Hence, would it not be presumptuous for mere flesh and blood even to destroy the Abomination of Desolation? Even those who disbelieved the prophesies, as the Hasmonaeans probably did, were not averse to waiting for events to prove the prophesies utterly false.

The date at which God Himself would act against Antiochus IV, according to Dan 7:25, was the beginning of the sabbatical year; see Introduction, pp. 42–43. The sabbatical year began in Tishri, the seventh month of the Jewish year, though perhaps Jewish sects disputed whether it began on Rosh ha-shanah (1 Tishri) or on the Day of Atonement (10 Tishri); see Lev 25:8–9 and *M. Rosh ha-shanah* 1:1. However, it was not enough for Judas and his men to wait through the Day of Atonement as it fell on their calendar. There were further uncertainties. The persecution had probably made it impossible to carry out the normal adjustment of the Jewish calendar to keep it in step with the seasons.

We can explain Judas' further delay if we make the following assumptions:

a) In this period the Jewish calendar had no regular cycle of intercalation; see Introduction, p. 23.

b) A supreme Jewish religious authority proclaimed intercalations when observation or calculation showed them necessary.

c) The rules governing such proclamations, which are preserved in tannaitic sources (*M. 'Eduyot* 7:7; *M. Sanhedrin* 1:2; To. *Sanhedrin* 2:1–15; TB *Sanhedrin* 10b–13b; TP *Sanhedrin* 1:2, pp. 18b–19a), were substantially in force in the time of Judas Maccabaeus. These assumptions can be shown to be probable.

Indeed, when only the central religious authority can fix the dates of religious festivals, the central authority by that very fact has a powerful disciplinary hold on all pious worshipers. The existence of a fixed cyclic calendar releases the pious worshipers from this control by the central authority. As soon as a fixed cyclic calendar should become established throughout the far-flung Jewish communities, the central authority would have great difficulty reestablishing its prerogative of regulating intercalations. We hear nothing of any such arduous reestablishment of central authority. Instead, from later sources we have abundant evidence of how tenaciously the supreme Jewish authorities in Palestine clung to this prerogative. See Jacob Neusner, *A History of the Jews in Babylonia*, I, 2d ed. (Leiden: Brill, 1969), 122–30; II (1966), 123, 141–42; Gedaliahu Alon, *Tol^edot ha-y^ehudim b^e-eretz yisrael bit^oqufat ha-mishnah veha-talmud* (Tel-Aviv: Hakibutz Hameuchad, 1952), pp. 66–67, 126, 149–56, 198–99. Hence, our first two assumptions are likely.

As for the third assumption, no direct evidence attests that the relevant rules were in force in our period. On the other hand, nowhere does their content serve the interests of the tannaitic age rather than an earlier period. The authorities at Jerusalem in the early Hasmonaean age were just as much concerned to assert their exclusive prerogative of regulating the Jewish festal calendar, as can be seen from the authentic festal letter at II 1:1–10 and even from the forged one at II 1:10–2:18. If the rules restricting the power to intercalate to Palestinian authorities acting in Palestine had been recent, Hananiah, the nephew of R. Joshua, who tried around 145 C.E. boldly to proclaim intercalations in Babylonia, would have protested against them as recent usurpations and might have been able to cite earlier precedents for his action than R. Aqiba (TB *Berakot* 63a; see Neusner, I, 122–30; Hananiah, living after the cessation of prophesy, did not dare to take the prophets mentioned at TP *Sanhedrin* 1:2, p. 19a, as precedents). Hananiah's attempt and the rulings which relaxed the restrictions and allowed intercalations to be proclaimed from Galilee and even from places outside the Holy Land reflect the disastrous effects on Jewish Palestine, especially Judaea, of the wars with Rome.

On the basis of our assumptions, it is easy to argue that the Jewish calendar missed one and perhaps two intercalations before it could be adjusted after the end of Antiochus IV's persecution. Indeed, we know that 145 and 148 Sel. Bab. (167/6 and 164/3 B.C.E.) were intercalary.

Jewish intercalations were a consequence of the regulations for the Jewish festivals prescribed by the Torah (Exod 34:22; Deut 16:1; To. *Sanhedrin* 2:2 and parallels). Hence, since Jewish intercalations were not an automatic consequence of a fixed cycle, the proclamation of them was an act of observing the Jewish festivals, and as such was surely forbidden by Antiochus' decrees (cf. Dan 7:25). But even if pious Jews dared to disobey a royal prohibition on intercalation, their own laws, which we have assumed to have been in force, would have made it impossible for them to adjust their calendar. The early laws provided that intercalations could be proclaimed only by a specially constituted committee of members of the national court or council, acting with the concurrence of the patriarch (*Mekilta, Pisḥa*, chap. 3, end [to Exod 12:2–3], vol. I, p. 22 Lauterbach; To. *Sanhedrin* 2:5–6 and parallels; M. '*Eduyot* 7:7; TB *Sanhedrin* 10b–11b; TP *Sanhedrin* 1:2, p. 18c). The committee was required to meet in Judaea, not in Galilee or in some refuge outside the Holy Land (To. *Sanhedrin* 2:13, according to the reading of the Vienna manuscript and the early editions; TP, ibid., pp. 18d bottom–19a top; TB, ibid., 11b). In the time of Judas Maccabaeus the national court or council was the Council of Elders and the counterpart of the patriarch was probably the high priest (but note the absence of the high priest's name from the festal letter at II 1:1 and see To. *Sanhedrin* 2:15). Whether apostate or pious, the high priest Menelaus and the members of the Council of Elders were probably in no position to proclaim intercalations. None of them is reported to have been with Judas. The Seleucid authorities probably were quick to take them into custody; see II 6:18 and 14:37–38. Unlike his brothers, Jonathan and Simon, Judas won the approval of Pietists like Jason of Cyrene by never usurping the authority of the high priest.

Even the amnesty of early 164 did not make it possible to bring the Jewish calendar into adjustment. The letter granting the amnesty bears the date 15 Xanthicus. Xanthicus normally coincided with Adar on the Jewish calendar. However, the Seleucid calendar had had an intercalary month in 166 B.C.E. and the Jewish calendar had had no intercalations since the publication in

167 of Antiochus IV's decrees. Hence, on the unintercalated Jewish calendar the month of the amnesty was not Adar but Nisan at the earliest.

We must pause here to deal with a difficulty which otherwise might disprove our theory. According to *Megillat Ta'anit* 28 Adar, Jews observed that date in *Adar*, not a date in Nisan, as the anniversary of the amnesty. However, the commemorative day of rejoicing may have been decreed later, after the Jewish calendar had been adjusted, and the month may have been derived from the letter of Antiochus V, treasured in the archives. As we shall see, the Feast of Dedication was fixed in the month which it occupied in the unintercalated calendar. It is not surprising to find the anniversary of the amnesty, on the contrary, fixed according to the intercalated calendar. Different circles of Jews were responsible for establishing the two observances. The Hasmonaeans had no interest in preserving the memory of the amnesty of 28 Adar.

To return to our argument: after the amnesty, the Jews still could not adjust their calendar. The Jewish regulations forbid declaring an intercalation between the end of Adar and the day afer Rosh ha-shanah (To. *Sanhedrin* 2:7, TB *Sanhedrin* 12a). Indeed, Judas and his contemporaries may have accepted traditions which forbade declaring intercalations even after Purim (14 Adar; M. *'Eduyot* 7:7; To. *Sanhedrin* 2:13; cf. the tradition given by Samuel at TB *Sanhedrin* 12b). This situation was the more unfortunate because the sabbatical year was to begin with Rosh ha-shanah. The Jewish regulations forbade intercalating the sabbatical year and the year after it and recommended intercalating the year before the sabbatical year (To. *Sanhedrin* 2:9 and parallels).

Hence, not only had the Jewish calendar missed an intercalation during the years since Antiochus IV's decrees of 167. The year 165/4, the end of which saw the end of the persecutions, should have been intercalary, too. Circumstances had forced upon God's chosen people an imperfect calendar. Would God himself, in performing his promised miracles, be bound by the imperfect calendar? Or would he follow what normally would have been the correct Jewish calendar? To allow for all possibilities Judas and his men had to wait through two more months.

Important events occurred during the delay. The Jews waited into Tishri, for the beginning of the sabbatical year on their unadjusted calendar. It was midsummer, though normally intercalations kept Tishri as the month of the autumnal equinox. The Jews perceived that no miraculous fulfillment had occurred. As I shall show elsewhere, in my commentary on Daniel, it is possible to deduce from Dan 9:27 that on the festival which began the sabbatical year Judas and his followers took the audacious step of destroying the Abomination of Desolation; cf. vs. 43. There were plenty of other idols in the world for God to destroy. Surely, then, God would not disapprove of the destruction even on a festival, by pious Jews of the Abomination which desecrated His temple. Was not idolatry the worst of all sins, so that the destruction of the Abomination, even on a festival, would be a fulfillment of God's law? Cf. the old tradition at TB *Nedarim* 25a and parallels, "Idolatry is so grave a sin that to reject idolatry is like fulfilling the entire Torah." Since the destruction took place on Rosh ha-shanah or on the Day of Atonement, there was no way later to record the date in *Megillat Ta'anit,* a list of dates on which emergency fasts may not occur. Rosh ha-shanah was a festival which already excluded emergency fasts, and the Day of Atonement was a fast day.

A second step was also possible. If one could destroy the Abomination without offending God, one could also be safe in preparing the way for God to act, by purifying the holy place, beginning with the altar. As we shall be able to deduce from *Megillat Ta'anit* 23 and 27 Marḥeshvan, it was probably at this point, immediately after the festival which began the sabbatical year, that Judas and his followers decided to dismantle the desecrated altar. Respectfully they hid its stones away (vss. 44–46). Since the apocalyptic prophesies might yet be fulfilled, it took yet more boldness for Judas to have a new altar built (vs. 47). Some Pietists may have opposed the step, but Judas could have softened their opposition by promising that the altar would not be dedicated for animal sacrifices until it was certain that no new temple would come down from heaven. The labor could hardly have taken very long. Indeed, the new altar may have been completed before the time of Tabernacles and the Eighth Day of Solemn Assembly (15–22 Tishri), ready for the possible fulfillment of the prophesies of Zechariah 14. In the time of Solomon God had miraculously instituted the sacrificial cult of the temple on the festival of Tabernacles (I Chron 7:1–3). Nothing more happened, however, in the month which was the seventh on the unintercalated calendar.

Accordingly, Judas and his men waited through the twenty-second day of the eighth month on their unintercalated calendar, through "Rosh ha-shanah," the "Day of Atonement," "Tabernacles," and the "Eighth Day of Solemn Assembly." Again no miracle occurred. Full dedication of the new altar, with animal sacrifices, would have to wait at least one more month, but Judas and his followers were ready now to risk meal offerings, which were once permitted even to the Jewish temple at Elephantine in Egypt (see Porten, *Archives from Elephantine,* pp. 291–93). First, however, Judas and his men found it necessary to remove from the temple court the lattice used in the sexual rites of the imposed cult (see Introduction, pp. 156–57). Perhaps at first the lattice had not been viewed as a defilement, since only vessels, not structures, were capable of becoming unclean through contact with semen (see Lev 15:16–18; *M. Kelim* 1:1); but now the discovery of jewels in the lattice structure left room for doubt (see *Schol. Megillat Ta'anit* 23 Marḥeshvan; jewels susceptible of uncleanness: TB *Shabbat* 63b). Or perhaps at first the lattice had been left for God to demolish (cf. Micah 1:7). Josiah, too, proceeded to demolish structures for cult prostitution only after he had removed the idols and the equipment for idolatrous sacrifices (II Kings 23:4–7). Accordingly, on 23 Marḥeshvan the Jews demolished the lattice (*Megillat Ta'anit* 23 Marḥeshvan and *Scholium;* Lichtenstein, "Die Fastenrolle," HUCA 8–9 [1931–32], 273–75). The work of removal and purification may have taken several days. When it was finished, meal offerings could be offered to the LORD upon the new altar, on 27 Marḥeshvan (*Megillat Ta'anit* 27 Marḥeshvan). Our account the new altar is based upon these dates from *Megillat Ta'anit.*

At the insistence of Pietists, idols at the doors of private houses (see I 1:55) may still have been standing, in the hope that God at the "real" beginning of the sabbatical year would destroy them. That may well be implied by

Megillat Ta'anit 3 Kislev, which reports that on that date "The idols were removed from the houses" (*dārātā*=houses; see TB *Baba batra* 67a).

In any case, Judas and the Jews waited through the twenty-second of the month which was the ninth (Kislev) on their unintercalated calendar; that is, through the "Eighth Day of Solemn Assembly." When again no miracle occurred, the prophesies were clearly proved false. The words at vs. 46, "Until a [real] prophet should come," probably preserve the bitterness the Hasmonaeans at the time felt against the false prophesies.

There was no longer any reason to put off the dedication of the altar and the reintroduction of the full sacrificial cult. On the unintercalated calendar, three years had elapsed since the desecration of 15 Kislev. The twenty-fifth, the day of the imposed monthly offering, was now only two days away; see NOTE on 1:54–59. Judas probably was struck by the appropriateness of having the dedication occur on the day of the imposed monthly offering. The two intervening days were enough time to prepare for the great day. He now had to consider the biblical precedents to be followed. Were only certain times of the year suitable for dedicating the altar of God's temple? Solomon dedicated it around the time of the autumn festival (Tabernacles; see I Kings 8:2, 65–66, and II Chron 5:3, 7:8–10). In the time of Zerubbabel the dedication of the altar for obligatory (as opposed to voluntary) offerings coincided with the festival of Tabernacles "as written [in the Torah]" (I Esd 5:50–52; the consonantal text of Ezra 3:4–6 allows the same interpretation; cf. *M. Megillah* 1:10 and see Albeck's comments at *Mishnah, Mo'ed*, pp. 499–500); if so, it lasted eight days, through the seven days of Tabernacles proper plus the Eighth Day of Solemn Assembly. Moses had dedicated the altar of the portable sanctuary for eight days at the beginning of the first month of the Jewish year (Nisan; see Exod 40:2, 17, and Lev 9:1, 17, and J. *AJ* iii 8.4–6.201–207, and in AB vol. 41A, NOTE on II 2:10–11, as against the rabbinic tradition, Ginzberg, *Legends,* III, 176, 179, and VI, 73, n. 373). Hezekiah did not dedicate an altar; nevertheless, his purification of the temple after Ahaz's desecrations offered vivid parallels to the situation facing Judas and his men (see II Chron 28:22 – 30:27). Under Hezekiah, the priests cleansed the temple for eight days, from the first to the eighth of the first month, and sanctified it for eight more, from the ninth to the sixteenth (II Chron 29:17), with a great day of burnt offerings and sin offerings coming on the sixteenth (II Chron 29:17–36). The first month was a long way off, for Judas and his men. Astronomically, however, it was still the season of Tabernacles, and the accounts in Kings and Chronicles might lend themselves to an interpretation allowing the festival of Tabernacles to be prolonged to cover the time at hand. The accounts are difficult and inconsistent. We know that the difficulties arise because the author of Kings follows the laws for the festival of Tabernacles given at Deut 16:13–15 and ignores the provisions of the Priestly Code, which place the beginning of Tabernacles firmly on the fifteenth day of the month and require an Eighth Day of Solemn Assembly (Lev 23:34, 36, 39; Num 29:12, 35), whereas the Chronicler knew the Torah as a unitary consistent revelation and therefore had to give a different account. Our solution was not available to Judas and his contemporaries; they, too, believed that the Torah was consistent and that it must have been known to Solomon. Cf. Jubilees xxxii 27–29.

The plain meaning of I Kings 8:2 and 65 is that Solomon doubled the length of the autumn festival for the sake of the dedication of the temple and the altar. "On the eighth day" in I Kings 8:66 was probably interpreted to mean "on the day which came after the second sequence of seven days." The Greek translator of I Kings 8:65 omits the words "and seven days, fourteen days [in all]," whether because his text was different from the Masoretic text or because he could not accept the suggestion that the dedication ceremonies could prolong the observance of the autumn festival. Certainly the Essenes of Qumran considered anything of the sort forbidden (1QS 1:14–15). The Chronicler, too, found the plain meaning of the text unacceptable, though textual difficulties obscure his solution, if any. There is obvious confusion in the Hebrew text of II Chron 7:8–10. In II Chron 7:8–9 the author speaks of seven days of dedication which began upon the date of the first day of the autumn festival (II Chron 5:3) yet were followed by seven days of the autumn festival plus the Eighth Day of Solemn Assembly. Since the first day of the autumn festival falls on the fifteenth of the month, one would expect Solomon to send the people home on the thirtieth. But the writer responsible for the Masoretic text of II Chronicles himself appears to have found unacceptable the idea that the autumn festival could be prolonged. Against the simplest interpretation of the Masoretic text of II Chron 7:9 and in sharp contradiction of I Kings 8:65, the Masoretic text of II Chron 7:10 has Solomon send the people home on the twenty-third of the month, as if the seven days of dedication preceded the autumn festival, or as if the two sequences of seven days coincided and were followed by the Eighth Day of Solemn Assembly.

As in Kings, so in Chronicles, the Greek version avoids the problems. At II Chron 7:9, where the Hebrew has "seven days and the festival seven days," the Greek has "as a festival for seven days." However, the problems of the Masoretic text are clearly ancient, for Josephus (*AJ* viii 4.1.100, 5.123) has Solomon's dedication ceremonies beginning on the first day of the autumn festival, with a total of fourteen days of festivities. The most natural way to interpret *AJ* viii 4.5.123, *eti de . . . êgagen*, is that the festival of Tabernacles on that occasion was prolonged to last fourteen days. Josephus knew of the Eighth Day of Solemn Assembly (*AJ* iii 10.4.245, 247), but no more than the author of Kings does he say how it was observed in the year of Solomon's dedication of the temple.

We cannot tell what text of II Chron 7:8–10 lay before Judas. Josephus, however, is likely to represent the Hasmonaean tradition as to what Solomon did; see Introduction, pp. 55–57. If so, Judas believed that Solomon prolonged the festival. He could have found another precedent in Chronicles: seven extra days were added to Hezekiah's famous Passover in the second month (II Chron 30:21–23). The Chronicler is careful in his choice of words: the additional seven days are days of "rejoicing," not days of Passover, but Judas may not have perceived the Chronicler's fine distinction. Beyond these precedents, Judas could remind any pious opponents that he was prolonging only a doubtful festival: on their own unintercalated calendar, the month was

Kislev, not Tishri. Indeed, the festival had not even been sanctified by animal sacrifices.

On these interpretations, Judas could feel safe in dedicating the new altar during a prolonged festival of Tabernacles. Accordingly, he took the doubtful festival of Tabernacles in the month of Kislev on the unintercalated calendar and prolonged it through the two days of preparation and the eight (!) days of dedication. Neither the Masoretic nor the Greek text of Kings and Chronicles could serve Judas as a source for an *eight*-day celebration by Solomon of the dedication of the altar. Did Judas (and the author of II 2:12) have a different text of Kings and Chronicles? Perhaps. He could also learn that the dedication should occupy eight days from the above-mentioned precedents set in the times of Moses, Hezekiah, and Zerubbabel. The prolonged festival lasted through eighteen days. However, the first eight, the doubtful days of Tabernacles and the Eighth Day of Solemn Assembly, had been days of disappointment, as no miracle occurred. The two days of preparation, if not days of disappointment, were too insignificant to be remembered. But the final eight days of the prolonged festival were indeed the memorable Feast of Dedication and became an annual rite. The earliest name of the Feast of Dedication was "the Days of Tabernacles in the Month of Kislev" (II 1:9), a title which reflects the complicated developments we have traced.

The long vain wait for prophesies to be fulfilled was embarrassing both for Judas and for the believers in the veracity of the prophesies. Hence, all important parties among the pious Jews had reason to suppress the strange history of the unfulfilled prophesies of 164 B.C.E., and the origin of the strange first designation of the Feast of Dedication as "the Days of Tabernacles in the Month of Kislev" was quickly forgotten. Neither the author of the forged letter of 103 at II 1:10–2:18 (see Appendix III) nor Jason of Cyrene (see II 10:6–7) could properly explain it.

There is evidence to suggest that Judas and the Hasmonaean partisans themselves sought a miracle at the dedication of the altar. The description here and in Josephus of the procedure of Judas and his men suggests that they followed the procedure used by Moses in dedicating the tabernacle and by Solomon in dedicating the temple: first, probably on the eve of 25 Kislev (see J. *AJ* xii 7.6.319), they brought the candelabrum and the incense altar and the table into the inner sanctuary and offered incense and kindled the lights and set forth the showbread. Only later, on the morning of the twenty-fifth, did they bring the prescribed sacrifice to the new altar of burnt offerings. At that point, for Moses and Solomon, miraculous fire had come down from heaven as proof that the Divine Presence (*Šᵉkīnāh*) dwelt in the temple. See Exod 40:22–27 and Leviticus 9; II Chron 4:19–20, 5:1– 7:1. Jewish tradition takes Moses' burnt offering at Exod 40:28 as part of the dedication of the new tabernacle (see Ginzberg, *Legends*, III, 180–81, and VI, 73, n. 374); hence, it was not a precedent for Judas, who was dedicating only an altar. On the absence of the fire from heaven and of the *Šᵉkīnāh* from the second temple, see TB *Yoma* 21b and Appendix III, n. 1.

No miracle, however, occurred for Judas and his men. Accordingly, the officiating priests kindled the fire themselves and offered up the burnt offerings, as is reported here in vs. 53, with no mention of how the fire was kindled.

A trace of the disappointment is probably to be found in the prayer '*Al hannissīm*. Though it is a prayer giving thanks for the events which led to the festival of the Dedication of the Altar, its words do not mention the altar. The prayer treats the Hasmonaean victories as miracles, and its account of the restoration of the sacrificial cult at the temple stops short with the kindling of the lights, as if it would be impolitic to refer to God's failure to send fire down from heaven.

There were other ways to treat the disappointing facts. The pious elders who sent Ep. 0 (II 1:7–8) avoided all suggestion that the victorious Jews put their God to the test (cf. Deut 6:16). Similarly, Jason of Cyrene (II 10:1–4) gives no suggestion of any such temerity on the part of pious Judas. Instead, both sources imply that Judas and his men followed, not the procedure of Moses and Solomon, but rather that of Aaron, who, after his consecration, first offered up the burnt offering to dedicate the altar and then kindled the lights (consecration and burnt offering: Lev 8:1 – 10:20; cf. Numbers 7; lights: Num 8:1–4; see Ginzberg, *Legends,* III, 217–18, and VI, 79, n. 418; the sages who fixed the Torah reading for the Sabbath of the Feast of Dedication seem to have agreed with Jason, choosing Num 7:1 – 8:4; see *Soferim* 20:10). No miracle was sought, Jason seems to say when he insists that the priests struck fire from red-hot stones or flints (II 10:3). Curiously, Yosippon (ch. 20) follows the order of events in Second Maccabees but insists that fire miraculously issued from the stones of the altar.

Judas and the Hasmonaean party probably made much of their kindling of the candelabrum on the eve of 25 Kislev. This was the cultic act which introduced the eight-day festival; it was the act which expressed the hope of a miraculous return of the *S*ᵉ*kīnāh;* and it was an act which, unlike the sacrifice of a burnt offering, could be imitated everywhere outside the sanctuary as a commemorative rite, one symbolic of joy and victory (cf. Esther 8:16 and J. *AJ* xii 7.7.325). Hence Josephus (ibid.) knows the Feast of Dedication by the name "Lights," and the lights are mentioned prominently in '*Al hannissim*. Understandably, the Hasmonaeans did not wish to commemorate their dashed hopes for a miracle. By the time of the forged letter of 103 (Ep. 2) the origin of the ritual lights, too, had been forgotten.

Clearly, Jews who rejoiced over the restoration of the temple cult and accepted the festival commemorating it could differ in how they view the Hasmonaean initiatives. These differences are probably reflected in the names for the festival. Judas and his brothers from the first were probably proud of having found a way out of the dilemmas (vs. 45). Though they did not dare to claim prophetic inspiration (vs. 46), they had no hesitation in considering their dedication of a new altar the most remarkable fact, and for them the name of the festival may always have been the "Feast of the Dedication of the Altar" (vss. 56, 59).

In *Megillat Ta'anit* and the prayer '*Al hannissim* the name of the festival is simply "Dedication" (*ḥ*ᵃ*nukkah*). Since otherwise only the gates were "dedicated" (see below, on vss. 36 and 57), these two sources omit the mention of the altar either by way of abbreviation or, as suggested above, as a matter of tact.

On the other hand, the non-Hasmonaean circle that sent Ep. 1 may have opposed the Hasmonaean initiative or at least the Hasmonaean evaluation of the consecration of the new altar. The biblical historians had used the Hebrew root "dedicate" (ḥnk) to refer to the consecration of a new altar only when the consecration had been confirmed by miraculous fire from heaven, as in the times of Moses and Solomon (contrast Ezra 3:2–6). Those who sent Ep. 1 gave the festival the to them neutral name of the "Days of Tabernacles in the Month of Kislev." The name may have been unacceptable to the Hasmonaeans from the first because of its unfortunate similarity to the name of Jeroboam's "illicit" festival (I Kings 12:32–33). Still less acceptable would it have been to later Hasmonaean princes, whom Pietists would reject as latter-day Jeroboams.

Jason of Cyrene and the author of Ep. 2 admired Judas, but did not accept the Hasmonaean point of view. Both call the festival the "Purification of the Temple" (II 2:16, 10:5), though Jason mentions the building of the new altar without disapproval (II 10:3). Curiously, the abridger may have called the festival both "Purification of the Temple" and "Dedication of the Altar" (II 2:19).

Josephus in his works nowhere uses the Greek word "dedicate" (enkainizein). Even in his paraphrase of our passage he uses only Greek words connoting resumption or restoration or renewal, and he speaks not of the consecration of the new altar but of the resumption of the temple cult and the restoration of the temple, and finally he gives "Lights" as the name of the festival (AJ xii 7.6–7.316–25). It would appear that his abstention from the word "dedication" here is deliberate, whatever the reason for it.

From the first there may have been varying ways of observing the Feast of Lights. The usual way, according to the tradition at TB Shabbat 21b (cf. Schol. Megillat Ta'anit 25 Kislev) was to kindle one light for each household, and punctilious householders lit one per person, and extremely punctilious persons followed either the school of Shammai, lighting eight lights on the first night and so on down to one on the last, or the school of Hillel, lighting one light the first night and so on up to eight on the last. To judge from Ep. 2, in Egypt a petroleum fire may have been lit.

Did the practices of the schools of Hillel and Shammai have a pagan origin? Antiochus IV could well have picked a popular pagan festival for the day of desecration or for the day of the monthly offering. A pagan winter solstice festival could well have had the ritual of lighting one light on its first day with one more light being added to the lights each night to symbolize the resurgent sun, until the end of an eight-day festival. Though the Jews used a lunar calendar and the Romans a solar one, it is tempting to compare the Jewish 25 Kislev with the Roman December 25, known to have been observed later as the birthday of the sun god, Sol Invictus, who was probably imported to Rome from Syria; see Latte, p. 350. There was nothing intrinsically idolatrous in the kindling of lights. If the Jews, to symbolize their victory, had seized upon the pagan light ritual and reinterpreted it to glorify their own God, rigorists like the school of Shammai might still have insisted on deliberately reversing the order of the pagan practice so as to leave no suspicion that Jews were performing a pagan rite. The hypothesis has attracted more than one modern scholar. The trouble is that in the year of desecration (167 B.C.E.) 15 Kislev was December 6, and 25 Kislev was December 16, both dates being too early for a solstice festival. On the unintercalated calendar of 164 B.C.E. Judas' festival was still farther from the solstice, for it began on October 16. There is not even any solid evidence for the existence of a pagan solstice festival in the area at the time. See Introduction, Part VI, n. 315.

A tradition of *tanna'im*, preserved at TB *Shabbat* 21b and *Schol. Megillat Ta'anit* 25 Kislev, tells the following story:

> "When the Greeks entered the temple they made all the oils in the temple unclean, and when the Hasmonaean dynasty prevailed and defeated them, they searched and found only one cruse of oil still in its place bearing the seal of the high priest. It contained only enough to kindle the lights for one day. A miracle occurred with the cruse. From it they kindled the lights for eight days. The next year these days were made a fixed annual festival to be observed by the recitation of the Psalms of Praise and of the Prayer of Thanksgiving."

The legend of the miraculous cruse of oil is probably derived from the old prayer '*Al hannissim* as understood by the rabbis; I shall show elsewhere the early date of the prayer. A rabbinic mind could well be perplexed by '*Al hannissim*, which begins by giving thanks for *miracles* but goes on to mention only Hasmonaean victories in war and normal cultic acts of purification, ending with the kindling of the lights and the establishment of the eight-day festival. At least from the first century of the Christian era and probably before, Jewish festivals were associated with miracles: Passover with the Exodus, Pentecost with the theophany at Sinai (see Ginzberg, *Legends*, V, 161, against S. Zeitlin, "Hanukkah," JQR 29 [1938], 18), and Tabernacles with the miraculous shelters mentioned at Lev 24:43 (Targum ad loc.; *Sifra* ad loc. [*Emor* 17:11]; *Mekilta* to Exod 12:27; TB *Sukkah* 11b; Ginzberg, *Legends*, V, 438, n. 241). As long as the Hasmonaeans looked to be the permanent deliverers of Israel, their victories could appear to be miracles of God, fulfillments of prophesy, achieved through the family which was God's elected instrument (cf. I 5:62). The downfall of the dynasty and the loss of Jewish independence could well have cast doubt on the theory that the Hasmonaean victories were *miracles* justifying a religious festival. One could still rejoice over the memory of the victories, but the miracle would have to be found elsewhere. First Maccabees, now rejected by pious Jews, told only of victories. Though Second Maccabees told of miracles, it, too, if known, could be rejected as a work in Greek and as unreliable because of the author's well-intentioned pious fictions. The prayer '*Al hannissim*, however, was now an accepted part of the liturgy. Surely it would identify the miracles for which its words gave thanks! If the miracles were not the victories, one had only to read beyond the summary of the victories in '*Al hannissim* to find the words, "And then Your children came to the Holy of Holies of Your temple and cleared Your nave and cleansed Your sanctuary and *kindled lights in Your holy courts and established these eight days of Dedication*. . . ." The context suggests that the eight days of the Feast of Dedication are to be connected somehow with the kindling of the lights in the time of Judas. From this point it was a short step for pious Jews to deduce the legend of the cruse of oil which burned for eight days.

36. Again a step taken by Judas is narrated in language reminiscent of the stories of David; cf. II Sam 7:1–2. Our author stresses that the initiative came from Judas and his brothers. Those who believed the apocalyptic prophesies would have waited for God Himself to act.

restore. The Greek word *enkainizein* in these contexts can be translated only by reconstructing the original Hebrew. Usually the Greek word translates the Hebrew *ḥnk* ("dedicate"), but it can also translate the Hebrew *ḥaddēš* ("restore," "renew"). On the other hand, the Greek word *anakainizein,* which usually translates the Hebrew "restore," is used by Josephus to translate the Hebrew "dedicate" (J. *AJ* ix 8.2.161, paraphrasing II Chron 24:4). At II Chron 15:8 the Greek manuscript B renders the Hebrew "restore" by *anakainizein,* while the other manuscripts have *enkainizein.* Since the scribes knew of the Feast of Dedication, they may have had a tendency to misread or alter the text from *anakainizein* to *enkainizein* here, too. Since *enkainizein* has both meanings, however, *anakainizein* may never have been in the Greek translation of I 4–5.

The key to rendering our verse is the fact that in Hebrew one dedicates only a new structure (see Deut 20:5; I Kings 8:63; II Chron 7:5). Only a new altar, not a new temple, was built at this time.

37–38. Our verses may contain echoes of Ps 74:2–7; on Psalm 74 as a document of the persecution, see NOTE on I 7:16.

37. *The entire army.* Our author stresses that even the vast majority of the Pietists followed the Hasmonaean initiative.

Mount Zion. The temple mount (Isa 18:7; Joel 2:1; Ps 74:2, etc.).

38. *desolate.* Cf. 1:39, 3:45. The Seleucid forces and the apostates had driven away the pious Jews, and now, for fear of Judas and his men, the pagans and apostates could not approach the temple.

profaned. By the Abomination of Desolation. Cf. Ps 74:4.

the gates burned. Cf. Ps 74:6–7, and see NOTE on II 8:33.

the courts . . . mountains. This passage probably does not refer to pagan usages such as sacred groves and asherahs which Antiochus IV might have required to be set up in the temple, though Bickermann (*Gott,* pp. 109–11) so interpreted the words. The plants which overgrew the temple area are called *phyta* in Greek, a word which is never used for "tree" or "asherah" in the Greek Bible, and the whole context after mentioning the desecrated altar treats only devastation and neglect, not the imposition of idolatrous practices.

Far from containing an allusion to pagan practices, our passage echoes Jewish texts and legends. We noted above that Psalm 74 (=Greek Psalm 73) may refer to damage inflicted on the temple during the persecution. At Greek Ps 73:6, *drymôi* ("thicket") correctly renders the rare *sbk* of Hebrew Ps 74:5. So rare did the Greek translator of Gen 22:13 find the word, that he rendered it by "a plant, *sbk*" (*phytôi sabek*). Our context thus contains the words "plant" and "thicket" from the Hebrew and Greek of Genesis 22. Hence, "one of the mountains" here is certainly an allusion to "one of the mountains" at Gen 22:2. Our verse would then be the earliest reference to the belief that the temple mount, Mount Moriah, was identical to the mountain in the land of Moriah where the sacrifice of Isaac occurred—unless II Chron 3:1 already reflects that belief. See Ginzberg, *Legends,* V, 253, n. 253.

40. *signal trumpets.* See Num 10:9, 31:6; II Chron 13:12.

41. *the duty of fighting the men in the Akra.* Since the text of the amnesty did not contain permission for the Jews to purify the temple (II 11:29–31; contrast the letter of 162, II 11:24–25), the Seleucid garrison at Jerusalem might well have tried to prevent Judas from acting, especially since Judas and the Hasmonaean party probably did not recognize the agreement with Lysias. This fact prevents us from using our verse to prove that among the apostates in the Akra were zealous partisans of the imposed cult who were ready to fight to preserve it, though that may indeed have been the case.

42. *unblemished priests.* See Lev 21:17–23.

43–44. See Introduction, p. 144 and Introduction, Part VI, nn. 244–45, and cf. II Kings 23:6, 12.

44–46. Because the altar of the Lord had been used for idol worship, the Jews faced a dilemma: according to Deut 12:2–3 Jews were bound to destroy any altar within the Promised Land which had been used for idol worship, but according to Deut 11:4 they were bound not to destroy the altar of the Lord. See *Sifre* Deut 61 (to Deut 12:2–4); To. *'Abodah zarah* 5 (6):7–8 and parallels; and note the late version of the dilemma given at TB *'Abodah zarah* 52b. Judas and his followers, however, appear to have escaped the dilemma by holding that the juxtaposition of Deut 12:4 with Deut 12:2–3 envisioned precisely their case: though the altar of the Lord had been used for idol worship, still it was not to be destroyed. But if the desecrated altar was left standing, Jews were still forbidden to use it (To. *'Abodah zarah* 5 (6):8 and parallels; cf. TB *Makkot* 22a). The unusable altar could serve only as a monument to the Jews' shame, for their sins had incurred the persecution (see NOTE on 1:64).

A "good idea" gave Judas and his men a way out. They probably noticed that Deut 12:4 forbade only treating the Lord's altar in the same way as heathen altars. The desecrated altar could be removed if it was treated differently from a heathen altar. Heathen and illicit altars were to be smashed; see II Kings 23:12 with 21:5, 23:15; II Chron 34:4, 7; To. *'Abodah zarah* 5 (6):7–8; TB *'Abodah zarah* 53b bottom – 54a top. Hence the desecrated altar of the Lord could be dismantled by gently taking it apart and preserving the stones "until a prophet should come" to say what should be done with them.

For the place in the temple where the stones of the desecrated altar were stored, see *M. Middot* 1:6.

47. See Exod 20:25 and Deut 27:6.

48. Since the "interior of the house" is hardly to be distinguished from the "sanctuary," and since the innermost structure of the temple is not reported to have been damaged, we must take "the interior of the house" as object not of "repaired" but of "sanctified." Judas and his men were restoring a desecrated sanctuary, not building a new structure, so that "sanctified" here probably means "purified," as at II Chron 29:5, 17, not "anointed with holy

oil" as at Exod 30:22–29, 40:9, especially since the courts were not to be anointed.

49. It would appear that the vessels had not been replaced after Antiochus IV's sack of the temple in 169. See I 1:21–22 and commentary, and cf. II Chron 29:19.

50–51. Cf. II 1:8, where there is no mention of incense.

50. *kindled . . . nave.* Cf. II Chron 4:20.

52. For the date, see above vss. 36–54; on the false date at II 10:3, see Introduction, pp. 82–83. The labor of the priests at the temple began before dawn; see *M. Tamid* 1:1 – 3:3.

53. See Exod 29:38–42.

54. *At the very time of year and on the very day on which.* The reading of our verse is suspect, because at I 1:59 our author pointedly fails to single out 25 Kislev as a day of desecration, probably contradicting intentionally the tradition followed by Jason of Cyrene at II 10:5. See NOTE on 1:54–59. Indeed, "At the very time of year and on the very day" is an odd expression, especially in Hebrew. One would expect to have only "At the very time of year" (cf. vs. 59 and Esther 9:31); or perhaps "On the very day and at the very time of year" (cf. Joel 4:1; Jer 33:15 and 50:4, 20). Or else one would expect "in the very month and on the very day"; contrast Esther 9:1, 22. Literally, the Greek text of our verse says "At the time of year and on the day on which the gentiles had profaned the altar, on that [sc. day] it was dedicated." The variants in the manuscript tradition may indeed be otherwise explained, but they may also be used to suggest that the words "and on the day" are an interpolation and that the Greek words for "which" and "that" have been altered from an original masculine (*hôi, ekeinôi*), agreeing with "time" (*kairos*), to the feminine (*hêi, ekeinêi*), agreeing with day (*hêmera*). Hence, the original reading of our verse probably was "At the very time of year in which the gentiles had profaned the altar. . . ."

to the sound . . . cymbals. Cf. Neh 12:27; II Chron 5:13.

55–59. Judas and his followers in vss. 55–56 set the precedents for the future observance of the Feast of Dedication (vs. 59). On the word *eulogein* in vs. 55, here translated by "gave thanks," see NOTE on 4:24. Probably the prayers of thanksgiving included both previously existing compositions and new works written for the occasion. Both types henceforth probably became parts of the fixed ritual of the Feast of Dedication. The way our author uses *eulogein* at vs. 24 suggests that for him it may have had the technical meaning of "recite the formula, 'Give thanks to the Lord, for He is good,'" (Ps 118:1=Ps 136:1). According to the earliest versions of the prayer *'Al hannissim* and to the rabbinic account at TB *Shabbat* 21b and *Schol. Megillat Ta'anit* 25 Kislev, Judas and his men made the ritual of the feast include both *Hallel* (Psalms of Praise) and *Hoda'ah* (Prayer of Thanksgiving). Already II Chron 5:13 and 7:3, 6, use *Hallel* as the name for the formula "Give thanks to the Lord for He is good." Rabbinic authorities call Psalms 136 or 134–137 the "Great Hallel" (*M. Ta'anit* 3:9; TB *Pesaḥim* 4b, 118a). But in the liturgy of the Feast of Dedication all our sources make the Hallel consist of Psalms 113–118. Rabbinic literature repeatedly calls these Psalms simply *Hallel* (*M. Pesaḥim* 5:7, 10:7; *M. Sukkah* 4:1; *M. Ta'anit* 4:4; see also TB *Pesaḥim* 118a).

Some of these Psalms may have been written for the occasion. See NOTE on I 7:16–17. Psalms 113–114 probably were not; they were selected because their references to God's supremacy over the nations (Ps 113:4) and over the whole earth (Ps 114:3–8) were appropriate. On the other hand, Psalm 115 begins by begging God for a miraculous theophany to display the difference between Him and the contemptible idols (vss. 1–8). But even without a theophany Israel must trust in the Lord, for the Lord has remembered them by bringing them victory and blessing them from heaven (vss. 9–16). Verse 17 and probably also vs. 16 look like polemic of the sort Hasmonaeans might have written. The author insists that the dead do not rise (see Introduction p. 12) and probably also that the seers of the apocalypses did not tour heaven.

Ps. 116:15 may concede that the death of the martyrs led God to grant the victories. The Psalm as a whole is so general that it, too, probably was selected rather than composed for the occasion, and so was Psalm 117. Psalm 118 may well have been composed for the Feast of Dedication. It contains what again may be polemic against the Pietist martyrs' belief in resurrection or immortality (vss. 17–18), and it contains references to the gates (vss. 19–20) and to the altar (vs. 27), perhaps because they had just been rebuilt.

I shall deal elsewhere with the Prayer of Thanksgiving (*Hoda'ah*) and the possibility that it was composed for the Hasmonaean ritual. I give a translation of the prayer at Introduction, Part I, n. 33.

57. They restored the losses mentioned at 1:22 and 4:38.

restored. See above on vs. 36, *restore*. However, the parallel at Neh 12:27 suggests that here *enkainizein* renders the Hebrew "dedicate," rather than the Hebrew "restore." If so, one should translate, ". . . and dedicated the new gates and the new chambers and fitted them with doors."

58. *shame . . . gentiles.* See above, on vss. 44–46, and cf. Isa 25:8; Ezek 36:15.

59. Cf. Esther 9:21–22. To judge from the text here and at II 10:8 and from *'Al hannissim,* the decree was made shortly after the dedication of the altar. I do not know why the tradition at TB *Shabbat* 21b says that the decree came in the following year. We have no evidence to tell us what sort of political institution existed at this time to pass the decree of "the entire assembly of Israel."

60. For our author, "Mount Zion" probably always means the temple mount. For Josephus, "Mount Zion" was ambiguous; it could mean either the temple mount or Jerusalem. Here he misinterpreted the words to mean the entire city (*AJ* xii 7.7.326); cf. his paraphrase of I 4:37 at *AJ* xii 7.6.316 and his paraphrase of I 10:11 at *AJ* xiii 2.1.41.

trampling it. The Greek has a neuter plural pronoun, probably because the translator was thinking of the "sanctuary," which is a neuter plural word in Greek; see I 3:51.

61. *guard it.* Again, as in vs. 60, the best witnesses to the text have a neuter plural pronoun, referring to the sanctuary.

fortified . . . Beth-Zur. Where my translation shows a gap, the Greek text is probably corrupt, having an inelegantly repetitious "to guard it" (*auto* or *autên* or *auton têrein*), even more inelegant because the sentence ends with another infinitive of purpose, which I have rendered by "so that . . . Idumaea." The gap can be filled from Josephus, who probably possessed a correct text (*AJ* xii 7.7.326); the missing words are "the town" (*tên polin*). Cf. I 6:7 and 9:50, 52; II Chron 8:2, 5. Perhaps in an early copy the words *tên polin* became effaced or only the letters *tê* remained visible. If so, later scribes would try to restore the text by using "to guard it" from the preceding clause.

XIII. WARS WITH HOSTILE
NEIGHBORS
(5:1–68)

5 ¹ When the neighboring nations heard that the altar had been built and the temple restored as it was before, they were furious ² and plotted to wipe out the descendants of Jacob who lived among them. Accordingly, they began to perpetrate murders on our people so as to exterminate them.

³ Therefore, Judas proceeded to wage war against the descendants of Esau in Idumaea of the Akrabattene inasmuch as they were beleaguering Israel, and he inflicted upon them a heavy defeat, routing them and taking their spoils. ⁴ Bearing in mind the wickedness of the Baianites, who had set up traps and roadblocks and were continually ambushing our people, ⁵ Judas drove them to shut themselves up in their forts, surrounded them, ritually doomed them to destruction, and burned their forts together with all who were inside. ⁶ Thereafter, on crossing over against the Ammonites, he found a strong and numerous force under the command of Timotheus. ⁷ In a series of battles he routed and defeated them. ⁸ After capturing Yazer and its suburbs, he returned to Judaea.

⁹ Then the gentiles in Gilead gathered against the Israelites who lived in their territory, intending to exterminate them, but the Israelites fled to the fortress Dathema. ¹⁰ They sent a letter to Judas and his brothers, as follows:

"Our gentile neighbors have gathered against us to exterminate us. ¹¹ They are preparing to come and capture the fortress in which we have taken refuge. Timotheus is in command of their force. ¹² Now, therefore, come and rescue us from their hands, for many of us have fallen. ¹³ All our fellow Jews who were members of Tubias' troop have been killed, and the enemy have taken captive their wives and their children and carried off their property and have almost destroyed there a unit of one thousand men." ¹⁴ The letter was still being read when more messengers came from Galilee, their garments rent, to report that, ¹⁵ "All heathen Galilee and men from Ptolemais and Tyre and Sidon have gathered against us to wipe us out." 16 After Judas and the people had heard these words, a mass meeting was called to consider what they should do for their fellow Jews who were in distress and under enemy attack. 17 Judas said to his brother Simon, "Pick your own men and go to the rescue of your fellow Jews in Galilee. My brother Jonathan and I will go to Gilead." 18 Judas left behind in Judaea Joseph son of Zechariah and Azariah in command of the people, with the rest of the army as a holding force, 19 giving them these orders: "Take charge of our people, but do not join battle with the gentiles until we return." 20 A party of three thousand men went with Simon to Galilee, and one of eight thousand with Judas to Gilead.

21 Simon marched to Galilee, and after a series of battles he routed the gentiles. 22 He pursued them to the gate of Ptolemais, killing no fewer than three thousand of the gentiles and taking their spoils. 23 He took back with him the Jews of Galilee and . . . ,ª along with their wives and their children and all their property and brought them to Judaea with great rejoicing.

24 Meanwhile, Judas Maccabaeus and his brother Jonathan crossed the Jordan and marched a three-days' journey through the wilderness, 25 at the end of which they came upon the Nabataeans, who greeted them peaceably and told them all that had happened to their fellow Jews in Gilead: 26 that many of them were being held captive at Bosora and Bosor-in-Alema, Kaspho, Maked, and Karnain—all large fortified towns; 27 that Jews had come together in other towns of Gilead, but tomorrow the enemy were set to besiege their strongholds and capture and exterminate them all in one day. 28 Thereupon Judas and his army made a sudden turn across the desert to Bosora, captured the town, and put all the males to the sword. He plundered all their property and set fire to the town. 29 From there he made a night march to the Jews' fortress. 30 At dawn they saw before them a vast army, indeed innumerable, raising scaling ladders and siege engines in order to capture the stronghold and battling the defenders. 31 Perceiving that the battle had begun and that the cry of the city and trumpet sound and loud shouting rose heavenward, 32 Judas said to the men of his army, "Now is the time to fight for our fellow Jews!" 33 He had his men march in three columns against the rear of the enemy, sounding their trumpets and crying out in prayer. 34 When the army of Timotheus recognized that it was Maccabaeus, they took

ª See NOTE ad loc., second paragraph.

to flight before him. He inflicted upon them a heavy defeat, killing no fewer than eight thousand of their men on that day. 35 Thereupon he turned off to . . . ,[b] attacked it, captured it, and killed all males within. He plundered the town and set fire to it. 36 From there he marched and captured Kaspho, Maked, and Bosor and the other towns of Gilead.

37 Thereupon, Timotheus raised another army and encamped opposite Raphon, on the other side of the torrent. 38 Judas sent men to spy on the camp, who reported to him, "All the gentiles in our vicinity have joined him, a very large force indeed. 39 He has also hired Arab mercenaries to back them up. They are encamped on the other side of the torrent ready to go into battle against you." Judas marched forth to meet them. 40 As Judas and his army approached the torrent, which was full of water, Timotheus said to the commanders of his force, "If he crosses over against us first, we shall not be able to resist him, because he will surely defeat us. 41 If, however, he is afraid and halts on the other side of the stream, we shall cross over against him and shall defeat him." 42 As Judas approached the torrent of water, he posted officers of the army by the torrent and ordered them, "Allow no man to halt! Let all advance into battle!" 43 Judas was the first to cross over against the enemy, with all the people following him. The gentiles broke before them, threw away their arms, and fled to the pagan temple at Karnain. 44 But Judas and his men captured the town and burned the temple and all within. With the fall of Karnain, the enemy ceased to be able to offer resistance to Judas. 45 Judas assembled all the Israelites of Gilead, from the humble to the great, along with their wives, their children, and their property, a very large host, for the march back to the land of Judah. 46 They marched as far as Ephron, a large heavily fortified town on the road. It was impossible to turn off either to the right or to the left. They had to pass through the town. 47 But the people of the town would not let them through, blocking up their gates with stones. 48 Judas sent them a peaceable message, as follows: "Let us pass through your territory on our way back to our own. No one shall harm you. We shall merely pass through on foot." However, the townspeople refused to open their gates to him. 49 Thereupon Judas ordered the message to be passed throughout the camp, that everyone was to halt where he was. 50 The men of the army halted, and Judas attacked the town throughout that day and throughout the night until

[b] See NOTE ad loc.

it fell to him. 51 He put all males to the sword and razed the town to its foundations and plundered it and marched through the town over the bodies of the slain. 52 They crossed the Jordan into the broad plain by Beth-Shan. 53 Throughout the march Judas gathered up the stragglers and spoke words of encouragement to the people, until he reached the land of Judah. 54 They went up to Mount Zion in gladness and joy and offered burnt offerings because not a man of them had fallen up to the time of their return in peace.

55 While Judas and Jonathan were in Gilead and Judas' brother Simon was in Galilee by Ptolemais, 56 the commanders of the army, Joseph son of Zechariah and Azariah, heard of their heroic exploits in battle. 57 They said, "Let us, too, win fame and go into battle against the neighboring gentiles." 58 They issued orders to the troops under their command and marched against Jamnia. 59 Gorgias and his men sallied forth from the city to meet them in battle. 60 Joseph and Azariah were routed and were pursued as far as the borders of Judaea. No fewer than two thousand men of the people of Israel fell on that day. 61 Thus the people suffered a grave defeat because those men, thinking to play the hero, failed to obey Judas and his brothers. 62 Indeed, they did not belong to that family of men to whom it had been granted to be the agents of Israel's deliverance.

63 The man Judas and his brothers, however, received great respect from all Israel and from all the gentiles who heard of their fame. 64 Crowds gathered around them with joyful shouts of praise. 65 Again Judas and his brothers set out on an expedition, warring against the descendants of Esau in the territory to the south. He attacked Hebron and its suburbs and destroyed its fortifications and burned its circuit of towers. 66 Then Judas marched off to the land of the Philistines. As he was passing through Marisa, 67 some priests fell in battle because they thought to play the hero there by rashly going into battle on their own. 68 Judas turned off to Azotus, to the land of the Philistines. He destroyed their altars and burned the graven images of their gods and plundered the towns and then returned to the land of Judah.

NOTES

5:1–68, introductory NOTE. On the chronological difficulties of ch. 5, on its relationship to the accounts in II 10–12, and on the probable original source, see Introduction, pp. 83–84, 99–102.

In fact, the Feast of Dedication probably began on 25 Kislev of the defective calendar (October 16, 164 B.C.E.) and not on 25 Kislev of the intercalated calendar (December 14, 164), as we showed in the NOTE on 4:36–54; hence, there was ample time for the events mentioned in our chapter. The campaigns against Idumaea of the Akrabattene and the Baianites could have been very brief. The battles against the Ammonites need not have taken more than a few weeks. The campaign in Gilead involved crossing a torrent (4:37–43); hence, it must have come before the dry season, at the latest in April. Indeed, according to II 12:31–32, it was over before the Feast of Weeks=Pentecost (Pharisaic date: 6 Sivan=April 21, 163 B.C.E., on the defective calendar). As soon as Judas devoted all his forces to the siege of the Akra (6:19), there could be no more campaigns against the neighboring peoples. From 6:20 we can learn only that the siege of the Akra began after 1 Nisan=January 28, on the defective calendar; see NOTE on 6:20. However, from Dan 12:11 we can deduce that by June 17, 163 B.C.E., the battle of Beth-Zechariah had occurred and Judas' force was under siege (6:32–48); see Introduction, pp. 43–44. The time from October 16, 164, to sometime in May, 163, is indeed ample to accommodate the events of our chapter.

Pious Jews kept separate from the gentiles to avoid all contact with idolatry; see introductory NOTE to I 1:11–15. Gentiles easily interpreted the Jews' self-segregation as reflecting the Jews' "hatred for the human race" and reacted by hating the Jews in return (Diodorus xxxiv 1=Poseidonius, FGH 87, F 109). This factor, however, is not sufficient to explain why the news of Judas' victory and restoration of the temple led the neighboring nations to try to exterminate the Jews. The decisive factor was surely the Jews' claims to possess the entire area by divine right, claims based upon the Torah and reinforced by prophesies. Judas' victories could only be taken as a sign that God's favor again rested upon the Jews. Now the Jews expected, and the gentiles feared, the fulfillment of the prophesies. Our author still portrays Judas as a second Joshua. Judas' contemporaries, Jewish and gentile, probably did so, too. We can understand how gentiles came to view Jews living on their territory as a "fifth column" preparing the way for the new conquest of the Promised Land. Gentiles so minded would show no mercy to Jews. Psalm 83 may date from the time of this outburst of gentile hatred; see NOTE on I 7:16–17.

1. *restored.* Not "dedicated." See NOTE on 4:36, *restore.* Since our verse

imitates Lam 5:21, "restore our times as they were before," we may be certain
that the Hebrew here had "restore," not "dedicate."

2. *perpetrate murders on.* The Hebrew construction (*hmyt* [?] *b*-) has
parallels at I Sam 6:19; II Sam 24:16–17; and Esther 9:16.

3–5. On the version of these same events at II 10:15–23, see ad loc.

3. *descendants of Esau.* This is an unusual expression for "Edomites" or
"Idumaeans." Probably our author is alluding to Obad 15–21, especially
vss. 18–19, in order to hint that Judas' campaigns may have fulfilled the
prophesies there.

Idumaea of the Akrabattene. All the Greek manuscripts and ancient translations are corrupt here, but Josephus' paraphrase (*AJ* xii 8.1.328) probably
reflects the correct original, which on the basis of the paraphrase may be
reconstructed as *"en têi Idoumaiai têi kata tên Akrabattênên."* This probable
original is the basis of my translation. An early scribe was bewildered by the
accumulation of the letters tau, eta, kappa, and alpha and perhaps also by the
unfamiliar place name and omitted the words *"têi kata"* to produce the ungrammatical text of the best Greek manuscripts. The scribes responsible for
the version of mss. A and 130 knew nothing of any such Idumaea but probably knew that the "Ascent of Akrabin" was a point on the southern boundary
of Judah (Greek Num 34:4; Josh 15:3) and accordingly changed "Idumaea"
to "Judaea."

The Ascent of Akrabbim lay to the southwest of the Dead Sea. Between it
and Judas' bases lay the entire width of the main territory of Idumaea. See
Map 4, p. 529, and George Ernest Wright and Floyd V. Filson, *The Westminster Historical Atlas to the Bible* (Philadelphia: Westminster, 1945), plate
X, F-4. A campaign in which Judas had to march across the whole of hostile
Idumaea would not be described merely as a campaign against the Idumaeans of
the Akrabattene. On the contrary, no ancient source calls the area around the
Ascent of Akrabbim "the Akrabattene," but Josephus repeatedly mentions
a district or "toparchy" by that name (*BJ* ii 12.4.234–35, 20.3.568,
22.2.652, iii 3.4.48, iv 9.3.504, 9.4.511, 9.9.551). It was named after
Akrabatta, its chief town. In Josephus' time the district lay just over the
border from Judaea, inside Samaria, the "Samareitis" (*BJ* iii 3.4.48). In the
time of Judas' campaign it was also surely part of the Samareitis, not of
Judaea, since all the campaigns of ch. 5 take place outside Judaea (see
vss. 1–2), and since the toparchy of 'Ephrayim (*Aphairema*), south of the
Akrabattene, became part of Judaea only during the career of Jonathan
(I 10:30, 11:34). See Map 13, p. 537. Evidently, in Judas' time there was a
considerable settlement of Idumaeans in the Akrabattene, so dense that the
area could be called "Idumaea" and the main territory of Idumaea had to
be distinguished from it by being called "the Idumaea which lay to the
south" (see vs. 65) or "Great Idumaea" (J. *BJ* iv 9.4.511, written many
years after the Idumaean settlement in the Akrabattene had probably ceased
to exist). A village in the Akrabattene continued to be called Eduma (Eusebius
Onomastikon, pp. 86–87 Klostermann) and is still called Dōmeh; see Abel,
p. 42, and Map 7, p. 532.

4–5. Who were the Baianites? Modern scholars have been unable to find a
satisfactory answer; see Abel, pp. 89–90. Our author's language seems to

imitate the biblical passages on the Amalekites, I Sam 15:2–3; Exod 17:14; and Deut 25:17–18. In vs. 3 our author has just treated Edomites, descendants of Esau; Amalek, too, was a descendant of Esau (Gen 36:12). The parallel at II 10:15–23, indeed, calls the enemy besieged in the towers "Idumaeans."

The best manuscripts (L A M W) of Josephus' paraphrase (*AJ* xii 8.1.328) for "Baian" here have *Sabaanou*. Josephus' reading probably reflects the original Hebrew *ṣbʿn*. *Ṣibʿōn* ("Zibeon") at Gen 36:20, 24, and 29 and at I Chron 1:38 and 40 is a descendant of Seir. At Gen 36:2 *Ṣibʿōn* is the name of the grandfather of Esau's second wife. Seir is closely associated with Esau=Edom, if not identical with him; see Hebrew Gen 25:25 and Gen 32:4, 36:21. Even the difference between the reading of Josephus and the reading here strongly suggests that the Hebrew original was *ṣbʿn*. The Hebrew name *Ṣibʿōn* is cognate with the Arabic *dibʿānun*, plural *dabāʿīnu*, "hyena." When Hebrew *ṣ* corresponds to Arabic *d*, the Aramaic cognate has *ʿayin*. The Aramaic name of the "Hyena" tribe would then be *Beney ʿAbʿān*. Another tendency in Hebrew and Aramaic in words which contain the sound *ʿayin* twice is for the first *ʿayin* to become *aleph*. Indeed, "hyena" at Targum I Sam 13:18 and in Syriac is *ʾapʿā*. Then the initial *aleph* could have been lost, just as *ʾElʿāzār* became "Lazarus." So one would get *Beney ʾAbʿān* and then *Beney Bʿān*. The latter was difficult to pronounce, and the common phenomena of the weakening of the laryngeals and the insertion of a *y*-glide could have finally brought about the translator's pronunciation, *Beney Baian;* see E. Y. Kutscher, *Language and Linguistic Background*, pp. 500, 505–11, 515–16, and Theodor Nöldeke, *Compendious Syriac Grammar* (London: Williams & Norgate, 1904), pp. 24–25. In exactly the same manner the Hebrew *Beʿōn* at Num 32:3 came to be rendered *Baian* in the Greek. If this is indeed the phonetic development that took place, we learn that the translator's native language was an Aramaic dialect and that Josephus either had a Hebrew text or was well informed about the Hebrew and Aramaic names of an obscure tribe.

Where the Sabaanites=Baianites lived cannot be determined. Seir was old Edom, in southern Transjordan, but the Seirite tribes, like the Edomites, could have migrated into Cisjordan. For the same reason, nothing can be concluded from the existence in modern times of clans or families called Ḍabāʿīn or Banū Ḍibʿān around Madaba in Transjordan; see Alois Musil, *Arabia Petraea*, III, 107, and cf. p. 122. Josephus believed that Judas marched from the Sabaanites directly against the Ammonites (cf. II 10:19), as is clear from Josephus' use the adverb *ekeithen* ("from there") at *AJ* xii 8.1.329. However, according to II 10:24, the Ammonites took the initiative and had invaded Judaea, so that Judas could have marched directly from the Sabaanites against the Ammonites if the Sabaanites lived anywhere around the borders of Judaea. One cannot even conclude from "crossing over" in vs. 6 that the Jordan lay between the Sabaanites and the Ammonites, for Judas could have crossed a Transjordanian wadi; cf. Judg 11:29, which our author may be imitating.

If our author regarded Seir as distinct from Edom, he may have seen fulfillment of the prophesy at Num 24:18–19 in the events: first Israel crushes Edom, and then Seir.

6–8. Our author may have seen a parallel between Judas' campaign against the Ammonites, and Jephthah's, to judge by the language of "crossing over" here and at Judg 11:29 and 32. See also above, on vss. 4–5, end. The narrative at II 10:24–38 describes the same campaign, since either Jason or his source had "Yazer" (*Iazêr*) where our manuscripts and versions have "Gazara." See ad loc.

The identity of the personages named "Timotheus" in First and Second Maccabees has been a vexed problem. For a list of the various interpretations, see Johannes Regner, "Timotheus 8," PW, VI^A II (1937), 1330–31. However, one reason for the controversy has been the obstinate skepticism of some Protestant scholars against our two books; see Introduction, Part II, n. 2, and Regner, PW, VI^A, 1330.

There is, indeed, a real problem. In First Maccabees (5:6, 11, 34, 37, 40) and in Josephus (*AJ* xii 8.1.329–330, 3–4.337–44) there is no hint that more than one Timotheus figured in the events. In fact, Josephus insists that there was only one Timotheus (*AJ* xii 8.3.339, "When Timotheus and his men recognized that it was Maccabaeus, whose courage and good fortune in war they had already faced once before. . . ."). On the other hand, the abridged history first (II 8:30–32) mentions a Timotheus as having been defeated and speaks also of a phylarch Timotheus (the same man?) as having been killed. Then, at II 9:3 Jason of Cyrene says that Antiochus IV before his death received the news of Timotheus' defeat; at II 10:24–37 a Timotheus, identified apparently as "the one who was earlier defeated by the Jews" (*ho proteron hêttêtheis hypo ton Iudaiôn*), leads a menacing invasion of Judaea with the help of a Seleucid elite cavalry force (see commentary in AB vol. 41A on II 10:24), only to be repulsed, besieged in the fortress of "Gazara" (read "Yazer"; see commentary to II 10:32), and killed. As we have noted, this campaign is identical with the one narrated here. Thereafter, at 12:2 a Timotheus appears as a Seleucid official with the title *stratêgos*. The abridger failed to put in a transitional sentence to cover the awkward gap in the narrative between II 12:9 and 10, but apparently this same Seleucid official is the enemy against whom Judas marches in II 12:10, for that enemy is also a Seleucid official with power and responsibility over a territory (II 12:18). The events of the campaign narrated at II 12:10–31 are clearly from the same campaign as the events narrated at I 5:24–53. Our author reports the defeat of Timotheus in this campaign but says nothing of his fate; Jason of Cyrene reports that by deceit Timotheus escaped with his life (II 12:24–25). If there was only one Timotheus, as Josephus insists, Jason of Cyrene was guilty of incredible stupidity: at II 8:30–32 Timotheus is probably dead; at 9:24–37 he turns up alive, only to be killed; at 12:2–31 he reappears alive and survives defeat.

The keys to solving the problem are as follows:

a) "Phylarch" is the title of a local chief, not one of an imperial Seleucid official. See Fritz Gschnitzer, "Phylarchos 5," PW, Suppl. XI (1968), 1072–73, and Bikerman, *Institutions,* pp. 170–71.

b) A *stratêgos* is a high Seleucid official with considerable power and military resources. See Bengtson, *Strategie,* II, 1–193.

c) There were two Timothei: Timotheus the phylarch was a local chief in the Ammonite territory, an area loosely held, if at all, by the Seleucids, as we learn from the stories of Hyrcanus the Tobiad (J. *AJ* xii 4.9.222, 11.229–36) and Jason the Oniad (II 5:5–7). This Timotheus appears here in I 5:6–8 and in II 10:24–37 (a local chief might on occasion have the use of some elite Seleucid cavalry, as at II 10:24; see ad loc.). Timotheus the *stratêgos* was an important Seleucid official with power over what is now northern Transjordan and southern Syria. We hear of him in I 5:11–44 and in II 12:2, 10–31.

d) II 8:30–33 is a timeless "footnote" in which the author or the abridger gives additional information on the topics of sharing booty with widows and orphans of the martyrs and of slaying enemies of the Jews. As such a footnote, it stands outside the sequence of the chronologically ordered narrative. In our texts it may also be somewhat corrupt; see commentary ad loc. Judas and his men are said to have taken spoils and plural fortresses only in the campaign against Timotheus the *stratêgos* (I 5:28, 35–36, 43–44, 51; II 12:13–16, 19, 26–28), not in that against Timotheus the phylarch (I 5:6–8; II 10:24–37). Hence, in II 8:30 we have Timotheus the *stratêgos*. At II 8:32 the text identifies the Timotheus who was killed as Timotheus the phylarch, distinguishing him from the other.

e) At II 9:3 the mention of Timotheus is a piece of stupidity. Either the abridger or a later scribe took the timeless note at II 8:30–32 as part of the narrative sequence.

f) At II 10:24 "the one who was earlier defeated by the Jews" is not the precise translation of the description of Timotheus (*ho proteron hêttêtheis . . .*) but rather "the first [of the two bearing the name] to be defeated by the Jews." Thus Jason of Cyrene, both at II 8:30–32 and at 10:24, distinguishes the two Timothei.

g) These efforts by Jason of Cyrene to distinguish the two Timothei where First Maccabees does not are examples of Jason's determination to expose every possible error in First Maccabees. See Introduction, pp. 28–34, 45–54, and especially 78–84.

h) Except in the matters of the resurrection and the value of martyrdom, Josephus insists on refuting Jason of Cyrene wherever Jason contradicted First Maccabees; see Introduction, pp. 56–57. For this reason Josephus insists, wrongly, that there was only one Timotheus. The huge scope of Josephus' work serves to excuse Josephus for not perceiving the difficulties involved.

The two Timothei may have been mentioned without any remark to distinguish them in our author's probable source, *DMP;* see Introduction, Part V. Jason of Cyrene probably had some other evidence (Seleucid histories or documents?) which proved that the two were distinct.

8. *After . . . suburbs.* Literally, "He took Yazer and its daughter towns." Our author uses the language of Num 21:32, perhaps to suggest that Judas was God's instrument in beginning a new conquest of Israelite Transjordan. See Map 7, p. 532.

Josephus (*AJ* xii 8.1.329) says that Judas burned the city, which he calls Iazora. Apparently misunderstanding the word "suburbs," literally, "daughters," Josephus' paraphrase also says that Judas took captive the wives and children. Our text of First Maccabees says nothing of burning, which Josephus may have derived from II 10:36. However, the words "and burned it" may have fallen out of the text. Cf. Judg 9:50, 52; Greek III Kings 5:14b, 9:16 (Alexandrinus); and I 5:35, 44.

9–65. Most pious Jews agreed that Judas was God's agent for winning victories, but many opposed Judas' brothers; see Introduction, pp. 64–67. Accordingly, our author makes every effort to associate Judas' brothers with him; see p. 74. Jason of Cyrene, on the contrary, strives to distinguish the wicked or incompetent brothers from the glorious Judas; see pp. 79–80.

The punitive expeditions against Joppe and Jamnia, narrated by Jason of Cyrene at II 12:3–9, probably belong between the expedition against the Ammonites and the expeditions to Galilee and Gilead. See pp. 83–84, 99–102. Our author omits the punitive expeditions, probably because Judas failed to save the Jews of Joppe and Jamnia.

9–54. Our author here might seem to be telling the events in simple language as they occurred. Nevertheless, Jews would perceive the parallels to Joshua's rescue of the Gibeonites, to Jephthah's rescue of Gilead, and the suggestions that the expeditions of Judas and Simon fulfilled prophesies of Isaiah. See below on vss. 10–13, 15, 28, 31, 53–54. A great deliverance on the east bank of the Jordan and in Galilee might be read from the prophesy at Isa 8:23 – 9:6. The abridged history treats the same campaign in Gilead at II 12:10–31.

9. *Gilead.* Jews in this period called the entire territory east of the Jordan, and Abel, p. 91. Our author had no other motive for using the word, since no appropriate prophesy mentions Gilead.

Dathema. The location can be guessed at only from our author's narrative. Map 7, p. 532, shows the guess of Abel, p. 98, but the guess is probably wrong, since it puts Dathema at least eighty kilometers from Bosora and vss. 27–29 would lead one to believe that the distance was smaller.

10–13. The parallelism of vss. 10 and 12 to Josh 10:6 suggests that our author again hints that Judas is a latter-day Joshua. The mention of Gilead and the complaint that even the militant Jews associated with Tubias (Hebrew *Ṭwbyh*) were helpless to resist may have been used by the author to suggest that Judas faced a worse crisis than Jephthah did when Jephthah came from the land of Tob (*Ṭwb*) to rescue the Israelites of Gilead (Judg 11:4–33).

11. *Timotheus.* See NOTE on vss. 6–8.

13. *members of Tubias' troop.* Literally, the Greek has "who were in Tubias' [unspecified masculine or neuter plural noun]." La^L ^X and SyII supply "places" or "region" (="estate") as the missing noun, and they are followed by Abel, p. 93, and by B. Mazar, "The Tobiads," IEJ 7 (1957), 139. The correct solution lies elsewhere. Josephus gives an account covering two generations of a Jewish family which used the name Tubias=Tobias and was prominent in Transjordan (*AJ* xii 4.2.160 – 5.1.241). The family is also known from papyri (CPJ 1, 2, 4, 5) and is mentioned in the Hebrew Bible (see Mazar, IEJ 7 (1957), 137–45, 229–38). The Tubias mentioned here is surely a member of this "Tobiad" family. The location of the territories in which the Tobiads were powerful is known (Mazar, ibid., pp. 139–43). Their chief center was at 'Arāq el-Emīr, which Josephus calls "Tyre," in the area our author would have called the "Land of the Ammonites" (above, vs. 6; cf. CPJ 1, line 13; II 5 7), very near the location of Judas' campaign against the Ammonites, a few kilometers from Yazer, and far removed from

his targets in Gilead. See Map 7, p. 532. Judas' earlier campaign would have saved any Jews around 'Arāq el-Emīr, and in narrating the campaign against Gilead our author says nothing about activity so far south. Jason of Cyrene was aware of the location of 'Arāq el-Emīr and did not balk at the absurdity of having Judas march a three-days' journey (750 stadia=125 kilometers) south from Kaspin (=Kaspho) to the old stronghold of the Tubian Jews and another three-days' journey back to Karnain (II 12:17–26). Indeed, contrary to what the message of the Jews of Gilead in our author's account says, Jason (II 12:17, 35) insists that not all of the Tubian Jews were slain. In so doing, Jason again made his account different from our author's and made Judas' exploits all the more remarkable. I do not know why Jason put the march to the Jews' stronghold after, not before, the march to Kaspin (contrast vss. 29–36).

Neither our author nor Jason nor their contemporaries called the territory south of the Jabbok "Gilead" (see above, on vs. 9). Except for the matter of the survival of some Tubians, with Josephus we may unhesitatingly accept our author's account against Jason's. Hence, the Tubian Jews can no longer have been located in the area called "Tubias' Land" (see CPJ 2d, line 16). The unspecified noun of "in Tubias' . . ." is to be taken as masculine and the phrase, literally rendered, becomes "in Tubias' troop." A unit by that name is known to have existed much earlier (see CPJ 1), and at this time the Tubian Jews of II 12:17, 35, were members of one. After the suicide of Hyrcanus the Tobiad (J. *AJ* xii 4.11.236), the Tubian troop, which had made him for a time independent in the family territory, probably surrendered to Antiochus IV and were resettled somewhere in "Gilead."

The Greek translator was aware that our phrase named a military unit, for in reporting the number of the slain he calls them not just a "thousand" but a "unit of one thousand" (*chiliarchian*), using military terminology; see Launey, *Recherches sur les armées hellénistiques*, pp. 363, 747.

14. Cf. Job 1:16–18.

15. *heathen Galilee*. Cf. Isa 8:23. For some reason the Greek translator rendered the Hebrew *goyim* by the peculiar word for "foreigners" which often renders "Philistines"; see NOTE on 3:41.

16. *mass meeting*. The Greek might be rendered "a great assembly" (*ekklêsia megalê*). In Greek an *ekklêsia* is a duly constituted meeting of all citizens. We do not know whether at this period the Jews had such an institution. Furthermore, Judas and his band were outlaws and were probably regarded as such even by the high priest and the national Council of Elders. Hence it is best not to render the Greek by words which imply the meeting of a legally constituted body.

18–19. Cf. Exod 24:14.

18. *in command of*. The Greek has a singular adjective (*hêgoumenon*), though later scribes tried to "correct" it to the plural. The Greek may reflect a Hebrew "as head of" (*rōš*); the author and the translator may have intended it to mean that both men were left in command, and so Josephus (*AJ* xii 8.2.333) and I have taken it. It is less likely that the author meant that Azariah alone already bore the title "head of the people," for Azariah re-

appears in vs. 56 without a title of his own, sharing the title "commander of the army" with Joseph son of Zechariah.

20. Cf. I Kings 16:21.

21–23. See Map 8, p. 533.

23. The Hasmonaeans were still not strong enough to give permanent protection to the Jews of remote Galilee, so the decision to evacuate them to Judaea was a realistic one. Nevertheless, it probably was also an attempt to follow biblical precedents and fulfill prophesies. See II Chron 15:1–9; Jer 31:6–12; Obad 20–21 (Zarephath lies between Sidon and Tyre; Judas' next campaign was through the Negeb, then held by the Idumaeans); Zech 10:6–8. See also below, on vss. 53–54.

I have left a gap in the translation where all ancient witnesses to the text are probably corrupt. Literally, the Greek means, "He took back with him those from Galilee and those in Arbatta." Arbatta is otherwise unknown, and idiomatic Hebrew probably would not change prepositions; one would have instead ". . . from Galilee and from Arbatta." Cf. II Kings 17:24. Josephus mentions a town Narbata and a Narbatene toparchy, both in the neighborhood of Caesarea (BJ ii 14.5.291, 18.10.509). We may guess that here the Greek translator originally had "from Narbatta" (EKNARBATTA; for his treatment of names ending in -a as indeclinable, cf. Adasa at I 7:40, 45, Elasa at 9:5, Medaba at 9:36, etc.). In Greek hands of the period kappa could resemble nu, and an early scribe left out the kappa, to produce ENARBATTA; a later scribe read the result as *en Arbatta* and "corrected" the "case ending" of the indeclinable noun to produce "in Arbatta" (*en Arbattois*). According to Josephus (BJ iii 3.1.35), the *western* frontiers of Galilee are the territory of Ptolemais and Mount Carmel. Caesarea lies not far to the south of Mount Carmel. Accordingly, Narbatta lay inland, between Mount Carmel and the territory of Caesarea, perhaps as shown on Map 8, p. 533.

24–54. The geography of the campaign has to be guessed from our author's and Jason's narratives and from the survival of place names down to modern times. Such is the basis of Map 7, p. 532. Alema probably should not be shown as a separate point attacked by Judas. See below, on vs. 26, and Map 7. Modern Kerak-Qanata was probably not a point Charax attacked by Judas' men. "Charax" at II 12:17 is a common, not a proper noun ("fortified camp," "stronghold"); see above, on vs. 13.

25. Famous even today for their city of Petra, the Nabataeans were an Arab people who played an important role in the commerce, art, agriculture, and politics of Transjordan and southern Palestine from the fourth century B.C.E. down to the Muslim conquests in the seventh century C.E. See Nelson Glueck, *Deities and Dolphins: the Story of the Nabataeans* (New York: Farrar, Straus, and Giroux, 1965). Our author, followed by Josephus (AJ xii 8.3.335), uses the definite article (*the* Nabataeans), as if his audience knew that Nabataeans could be expected at a point in the wilderness three days' journey from where Judas crossed the Jordan. Indeed, at this period Nabataeans were nomads; see Diodorus xix 94–97; Glueck, *Deities*, pp. 3–4; and II 12:11–12. Our author and Josephus say that the encounter of Judas' party with the Nabataeans began with the exchange of peaceful greetings; see Appendix IV, pp. 551–52. Jason of Cyrene pointedly contradicts our

author's account and says that there was first a violent skirmish with the Arab nomads, who turned friendly only after being decisively defeated (II 12:11–12). Since Alexander Jannaeus had good reason to curry favor with the Nabataeans (J. *AJ* xiii 14.382, 15.2.392), our author, who was Jannaeus' propagandist (see Introduction, pp. 72–77), need not be believed here against Jason, who had no reason to falsify.

26. The change of preposition from "at" (*eis*) to "in" (*en*) suggests that "in Alema" is an attribute of Bosor, not another location at which Jews were held captive. This impression is confirmed if our author did not mention Alema in vss. 35–36 (see on vs. 35). Bosor would need an identifying attribute only at the first mention of it. The manuscripts of First Maccabees and of Josephus *AJ* xii 8.3.340 show great variation with the names Kaspho and Maked. The uncertainty over the first letter of Kaspho (kappa or chi) is easily explained. Our author probably spelled the name *kspw*. Hebrew and Aramaic *k* is regularly represented in Greek by chi, but the inhabitants of Kaspho may well have spoken Arabic or some other Semitic dialect in which the *k*-sound was not aspirated. "Kaspin" at II 12:13 probably names the same place, and shows that the *p*, too, could be unaspirated. The final *w* of *kspw* is characteristic of Arabic names (e.g. the Arab Gashmu at Neh 6:6), and the -*in* of "Kaspin" may be an Arabic *tanwīn*-form. Josephus seems to have consulted a Hebrew text in which he read "Kaspho" and "Maked" as one word, *Kasphomakê* or *Chasphomakê*. The long *ê* and the absence of the *d* suggest that Josephus read the *d* as *y*. However, the Greek translator's text may well be correct. There is nothing strange about the absence of "and" before "Maked"; see GKC, sec. 154*a*, n. 1.

The words used to describe the towns as strong echo Deut 3:5.

27. *had come together.* Almost all witnesses to the text have "were being held captive" (*eisi syneilēmmenoi*), a reading supported by Josephus' paraphrase (*AJ* xii 8.3.336: *apeilēmmenoi*). The reading, however, has probably been contaminated by the "held captive" of vs. 26; the enemy would not have to besiege strongholds and capture the Jews if they were already being held captive. The scribes of two manuscripts (71 and 107) may have perceived the difficulty, for they omit the verb. S^ca has *syneilêgmenoi*, a slight phonetic corruption of *syneilegmenoi*, the probable correct reading, which still appears in one manuscript (311) and is the basis for my translation. Another manuscript (534) has the synonymous *synêgmenoi*. Cf. Esther 9:15, 16, 18.

but tomorrow. The Greek has no conjunction before "tomorrow," reflecting the common Hebrew mannerism which has no conjunction before *māhār* or *lᵉmāhār; cf.* Exod 8:9, 17:9; Num 14:25; II Chron 20:16–17.

were set to besiege. Our author's wording may be patterned after I Sam 23:26 or after Ps 17:11 (see Symmachus' translation of it).

exterminate . . . day. Cf. Esther 3:13, 8:11–12.

28. Though I rendered *erêmôi* in vs. 24 as "wilderness," there the author was telling of territory near the Jordan, which is not desert. Bosora, however, lay at the edge of the Syrian desert, and Judas surely surprised the town by striking from that direction. Hence, here I render *erêmon* as "desert." In the fate of Bosora some may have seen a fulfillment of Isaiah 34, though our Bosora is distinct from the Bozrah in Edom.

29. *the Jews' fortress.* Following Josephus (*AJ* xii 8.3.337), I have taken the liberty of supplying the word "Jews'." Our author certainly means to refer to the fortress Dathema, mentioned in vss. 9 and 11. See above, on vs. 9.

30. Cf. Joel 1:6, 2:7–10.

31. Most witnesses to the text have it as we have presented it. If this is what our author wrote, he borrowed the language of I Sam 4:5–6, 5:12, and of Jer 4:19 and/or Zeph 1:16. The mention of "trumpet sound" (*šōpār*) may continue from vs. 30 the allusion to Joel; see Joel 2:1. On the other hand, the old Latin versions (La$^{X G V}$) have "the cry of battle rose heavenward like a trumpet, and a loud cry from the city." Which reading is the original is hard to say. I Sam 5:12 speaks of the cry of the Philistines' city. Scribes who knew that famous context could have altered a verse resembling the one presented by the old Latin into what we have. Alternatively, the originator of the tradition preserved by the old Latin may have found inappropriate the use of the verse on the Philistines to refer to Jews and may have altered our verse to turn it into an allusion to Isa 66:6.

32. Cf. Neh 4:8.

33. Cf. Judg 7:16, 9:43; I Sam 11:11; II Sam 18:2. Most likely, our author had I Sam 11:11 in mind. On the trumpets, see Num 10:9. The pious Jewish warriors naturally cried out in prayer. Does our author continue to allude to Joel (1:14)?

34. Our author's words do not necessarily imply that Timotheus the *stratêgos* had fought Judas before, though that is the way Josephus interprets our passage. See NOTE on 5:6–8. Our author may have meant only that Judas' reputation intimidated Timotheus and his army. The eight thousand dead are probably an exaggeration. In their haste to relieve the beleaguered Jews, Judas and his men did not stay to take the spoils and count the dead. Jason of Cyrene characteristically insists that Timotheus was not at the battle (II 12:18). See NOTE on 5:6–8. He is probably wrong, having based his statement on his erroneous location of the fortified camp of the Tubian Jews; see above, on vs. 13, and NOTE to II 12:18–26.

35. I have left blank the name of the town because there is no way of establishing which reading is correct. La$^{G B}$ and many good manuscripts at J. *AJ* xii 8.3.340 have *Mella;* La^X has *Mala;* one manuscript of Josephus (W) has *Malla;* cf. SyII *m'l.* On the other hand, S here has *Mapha* and A has *Maapha* and several good manuscripts of Josephus have *Maaphê.* If a name from our author's list in vs. 26 had stood here, no scribe would have altered it to something else. On the other hand, if our author did the unexpected and suddenly introduced here a name not mentioned in vs. 26, scribes would suspect a mistake and try to correct it. Hence the readings *Salema* of the Lucianic recension and *'lym* of SyI and *Alema* of 19 and *Lema* of 93 do not prove that the original reading was the *Alema* of vs. 26.

36. Our author says nothing here of whether Judas succeeded in rescuing the Jews beleaguered "in other towns of Gilead," probably because he succeeded only in rescuing some; see vs. 45.

37. *Timotheus.* See NOTE on 5:6–8.

Raphon. Although two manuscripts of Josephus (*AJ* xii 8.4.341) have this reading, the others have *Romphôn* or *Ramphôn.* Josephus inserts *m* before *p* elsewhere, too, evidently in accordance with his own pronunciation (Ampheka at *AJ* v 11.1.352, from Apheka at I Sam 4:1; Emphron at *AJ* xii 8.5.346, from Ephron at vs. 46 below; etc.).

torrent. Hebrew *naḥal;* a seasonal stream (wadi) which has water in the rainy season. See above, introductory NOTE.

38. As spies Judas naturally used Jews from Gilead, as is reflected in their report ("All the gentiles in *our* vicinity").

39. On the use of Arab mercenaries by the Hellenistic empires, see Launey, *Recherches sur les armées hellénistiques,* pp. 560–62. On Arab penetration into the Seleucid empire, see René Dussaud, *La pénétration des Arabes en Syrie avant l'Islam* (Paris: Geuthner, 1955), p. 148.

40–41. Our author probably intended here to suggest the practical reasoning behind Timotheus' tactics. The spies did report that Timotheus was ready to take the initiative in going into battle. Judas foils him by striking first. Hence, it is unlikely that our author intended to display Timotheus' superstitious effort to see an omen in the acts of his enemy, as suggested by Calmet (quoted at Abel, p. 101).

41. *halts.* The verb *paremballein* (Hebrew *ḥnh*) is regularly translated "encamp," but the context here and at vss. 42 and 49–50 shows that here it means "halt," as it can throughout Num 33:1–49.

42. *officers.* Our author probably used the word *šwṭr* found at Deut 20:5–9, Josh 1:10 and 3:2.

43. *pagan temple at Karnain.* The Greek word for "temple" here is *temenos;* see NOTE on 1:47. For the location of Karnain, see Map 7, p. 532. The site is mentioned in the Bible also as Ashteroth-karnaim (Gen 14:5; cf. Josh 9:10, 12:4; Amos 6:13). The name suggests that Astarte (Ashtoreth) was worshiped there in her aspect of having the horns of a cow. See Abel, p. 102; S. Aḥituv, "'Aštārōt," *Enc. Bib.,* VI (1971), 404–5; B. Mazar, "'Ašterōt qarnayim," ibid., col. 406; and S. E. Loewenstamm, "'Aštōret," ibid., cols. 409 and 411 (identified with the cow-horned Egyptian goddess Hathor; all three articles in Hebrew). See also II 12:21, 26. The fugitives may have thought that the Jews would respect the pagan holy place as an asylum, or they may have hoped that their goddess would miraculously come to their aid. Cf. I 10:83–84.

45. On the evacuation of the Jews of Gilead, cf. above, on vs. 23. The echoes in our verse of Exod 12:37 and 42 and of Gen 50:8–9 (a context which again deals with a mass journey from Transjordan into Cisjordan) are probably intentional. Judas can be compared to Moses and to Joseph. See also commentary at II 12:27–31.

46. *Ephron.* See Map 7, p. 532 and above, on vs. 37. The site fits our author's description. See also II 12:27.

48–51. Judas treats the town in accordance with Deut 20:10–15.

48. *peaceable message.* One which began with the greeting "Peace!" (*šālōm*). See Appendix IV, pp. 551–52.

"Let us pass . . . foot." Cf. Num 20:17–19; Judg 11:17, 19.

49. *halt.* See above, on vs. 41.

52. The Jordan has several fords near Beth-Shan. The broad plain is the Jordan valley. In accordance with his convictions, our author pays no atten-

tion to any friendly contacts with the pagan city of Beth-Shan (=Scythop-olis). Contrast II 12:29–31, and see Introduction, pp. 12, 34.

53–54. Our author's echoes here of prophesies of Isaiah are so audacious that he must be hinting that he saw their fulfillment in Judas' victories. At Isa 35:10 (cf. 51:11) a joyful arrival at Mount Zion follows an exodus of formerly helpless Israelites. Similarly, at Isa 52:11–12, there is a confident exodus of Israelites to Jerusalem, only there the "gatherer of the stragglers" (*episyna-gôn*) is the God of Israel himself. How audacious of our author to use the same word of Judas! "Joy" (*euphrosynê*) translates the Hebrew root *rnn*, found at Isa 52:9 as well as at 35:10. Finally, in the miraculous course of the campaign with no Jewish deaths, our author probably saw fulfillment of Isaiah 25. Isa 25:1–5 could describe the campaign in Gilead. The "fortified city" (*qryh bṣwrh*) of Isa 25:2 could be taken as an allusion to Bosora (*bṣrh*) or Bosor (*bṣr*). Isa 25:6–7 could be taken as describing the impact of Judas' victories on the human race. Thereafter, our author probably read Isa 25:8 as meaning "God has swallowed up death for the sake of victory." The word in Isa 25:8 usually translated "forever" (*lāneṣaḥ*) Aquila and Theodotion ren-dered "for victory" (*eis nikos*). For this meaning of the root in Hebrew, see M. Jastrow, *Dictionary*, p. 928.

55–62. Our author saw the parallel at Num 14:40–45 and used language resembling Num 14:45. He is intent on proving the legitimacy of the Has-monaean dynasty; see Introduction, pp. 6–12, 72–78. Just as the author of the book of Samuel proved that God had chosen David and his dynasty to rule by exhibiting the failure of the house of Saul and the superiority of the house of David over all competitors, so our author proves the divine election of the Hasmonaean dynasty. Our author's thesis was unacceptable to Jason of Cyrene, who insisted that the vanquished Joseph and Azariah themselves be-longed to Judas' family; see Introduction, pp. 79–80, and NOTE on II 7:1.

As usual in a controversy between Jason of Cyrene and our author, Jo-sephus supports the pro-Hasmonaean propaganda and tries to refute Jason. He insists that Joseph was not a Hasmonaean but was the son of Zechariah (*AJ* xii 8.2.333, 6.350) and repeats our author's careful identification of Judas' blood brothers (*AJ* xii 8.2.332, 333; 3.335, 6.353). However, Josephus' sup-port of our author's account is tempered by Josephus' knowledge of the fall of the Hasmonaean dynasty. He does not use the failure of Joseph and Azariah to prove the divine election of the Hasmonaeans but only to demonstrate Judas' wisdom and foresight (*AJ* xii 8.6.352). Elsewhere in Josephus we find Hasmonaean propaganda retaliating for the efforts of anti-Hasmonaean prop-agandists to associate incompetents and traitors with the family of Mattathias. See NOTE on II 4:23, *Menelaus . . . Simon.*

56. See above, on vs. 18.

58. See Map 9, p. 534. Jamnia had been guilty of atrocities against her Jewish residents; see II 12:8–9. At this period Jamnia was the capital of the province of Azotus (Ashdod); see M. Avi-Yonah, *The Holy Land*, pp. 37–38. To reach Jamnia, the Jews had to cross a narrow stretch of Idumaean territory; see NOTE on 4:15.

59. Despite our author's tendency to introduce names abruptly without explanation (see NOTE on 3:10), one would expect Gorgias here to be the same

as the one in 3:38 – 4:25. At this time, according to Jason of Cyrene, the governor (*stratêgos*) of Idumaea bore the name Gorgias (II 12:32). The Gorgias who was in Jamnia may be the same as the governor of Idumaea, though if he was, it is strange to find our author not mentioning the fact. He portrays Judas' subsequent victories as doing more than cancel the defeat, and should have stressed that Judas and his brothers harried the province of the man who routed Joseph and Azariah.

60–62. Our author first borrows the language of I Sam 4:10 and 17, a context which likewise has Israel suffering a grievous defeat in the land of the Philistines because of the sins of two men, the sons of Eli, members of a rejected line of priests. Our author then refers to the Hasmonaeans by the phrase zr' 'nsym ("seed of men"), which I have rendered "family of men." In the Hebrew Bible the phrase is used only in connection with Samuel, the divinely elected successor of Eli (I Sam 1:11). The phrase may have had eschatological connotations in Hasmonaean circles. See Introduction, pp. 79–80, and below, NOTES on vss. 63–88.

63–68. God's chosen agents, Judas and his brothers, cancel the defeat by winning victories which dwarf it. As Joseph and Azariah cut across an undefended strip of Idumaea to attack "Philistine" Jamnia, so Judas and his brothers carve their way across the whole width of greater Idumaea and successfully attack the very shrines of the old Philistine towns. See Map 9, p. 534.

63. *The man Judas.* Our author still plays upon his use of "seed of men" (I Sam 1:11) in vs. 62. However, he probably also knew how the Bible uses "the man . . ." to refer to great heroes. Thus, it is used of Moses at Exod 11:3, 32:1 and 23, and Num 12:3; of Elkanah, father of Samuel, at I Sam 1:21 (on the greatness of Elkanah, see Ginzberg, *Legends,* IV, 57–58, and VI, 215). It is used of Jeroboam before his sin, at I Kings 11:28; of Gabriel at Dan 9:21; of Mordecai at Esther 9:4; and cf. I Kings 2:2 and I Sam 26:15. Only Judg 17:5 offers a contrary example.

64. "Crowds gathered" (*episynêgonto*) literally is "they were gathered" and my rendering "joyful" comes from the Greek *euphêmountes,* which probably renders a Hebrew word derived from the root *rnn* (so Symmachus at Pss 31 [32H]: 11, 32 [33H]:1, etc.). Accordingly, see above, on vss. 53–54.

65. *in the territory to the south.* See above, on vs. 3.

67. Again our author finds divine providence protecting the Hasmonaeans and deserting those Jews who do not subordinate themselves to God's chosen family. Jason of Cyrene, too, found a clear sign of the operation of providence in the course of this expedition, but not one showing the divine election of the Hasmonaeans; see II 12:36–40 and commentary ad loc.

68. *to . . . Philistines.* "Azotus" here refers to the province, not the city, as the apposition with "the land of the Philistines" shows. The province did take in ancient Philistia south of the Yarkon river, except for Ascalon and Gaza; see Avi-Yonah, *The Holy Land,* pp. 26, 37–38.

XIV. THE DEATH OF ANTIOCHUS IV
(6:1–17)

6 1 Meanwhile, as King Antiochus was marching through the inland territories, he heard that in Elymais in Persis there was a city famous for its wealth in gold and silver. 2 The temple there was said to be very rich, containing golden helmets and breastplates and shields left there by King Alexander, son of Philip, the Macedonian, the first to rule over the Hellenistic empire. 3 Antiochus came and tried to take the city and plunder it but failed because his intention became known to the people of the city. 4 When they stood against him for battle, he fled and with great chagrin withdrew to make his way back to Babylonia. 5 A messenger reached him in Persis with the news that his armies which had marched into the land of Judah had been routed; 6 that Lysias had set out at the head of a strong force and had been repulsed by the Jews, who had gained in arms and in wealth and especially through the abundant plunder which they had taken from the armies they had defeated; 7 that the Jews had destroyed the abomination which he had built upon the altar in Jerusalem, and they had surrounded the temple as it was before with high walls, and also their town of Beth-Zur. 8 When the king heard this news, he was thunderstruck and so deeply dismayed that he took to his bed and sank into melancholia because his plots had been foiled. 9 There he lay for many days as his great distress grew worse. Finally, he realized that he was dying. 10 He summoned all his Friends and said to them, "Sleep has fled from my eyes and the weight of anxiety has broken my heart. 11 I have said to myself, 'How deep I have sunk in distress! How great is the tempest which has now come upon me, kind though I was and popular in my realm.' 12 Now, however, I remember the wicked deeds which I perpetrated in Jerusalem which I took all the silver and gold vessels there and for no cause sent orders to exterminate the inhabitants of Judah. 13 I have come to understand that because of these deeds these evils have come upon me as I die in great agony on foreign soil." 14 He summoned Philip, one of his Friends, and gave him power over all his kingdom, 15 handing over to him his diadem, his robe, and his ring, for Philip to bring to his son Antiochus, of whom Philip was to be the guardian until the boy was ready to rule. 16 Thereupon King Antiochus died in the year 149.

17 When Lysias received the news that the king had died, he took the late king's very young son Antiochus, of whom he had been the guardian, and made him king in his place, giving him the name "Eupator."

NOTES

6:1–17, introductory NOTE. A cuneiform document from Babylon (Sachs and Wiseman, *Iraq* 16 [1954], 202–4, 208–9) shows that the news of the death of Antiochus IV reached Babylon in the ninth month (Kislimu=Kislev; November 20 – December 18) of 148 Sel. Bab. (164 B.C.E.). The news probably became known in Jerusalem on January 28, 163; see Introduction, p. 43. Since the Feast of Dedication was probably celebrated according to the Jews' own defective calendar (see NOTE on 4:36–54), Antiochus' death probably did come after the dedication of the new altar. It is unlikely, however, that the news from Jerusalem was urgent enough or could travel fast enough to reach the king before he died. Jews and pagans both delighted in imagining how retribution came upon the royal temple robber; see Introduction, p. 83. If Antiochus on his deathbed was aware only that he had been foiled at a pagan temple in Elymais, nothing would lead him to regret his successful plundering of the temple in Jerusalem and his persecution of the Jews. Our author or his Jewish source would have been embarrassed if only the victory of the idol of Elymais had brought Antiochus to die. Hence, for this Jewish observer, Antiochus IV's death had to have a cause emanating from Jerusalem and Judaea: it *must* have been news of Judas' victories and restoration of the temple. Thus our author or his Jewish source, reasoning a priori, supplied the story of the messenger bringing the news from Judaea.

On the other hand, the rest of the details of our author's account of the death of Antiochus are irrelevant to or embarrassing to the theological interests of a pious Jew. Moreover, our author certainly did draw on a pagan source, since his date for Antiochus' death is according to the Macedonian Seleucid era; see Introduction, pp. 22–25 and Appendix I. Hence, apart from the story of the messenger, no part of our author's account of the king's death need be suspected of being a propagandist's invention. See Maurice Holleaux, "La mort d'Antiochos IV Épiphanès," REA 18 (1916), 97–98=Holleaux, *Études d'épigraphie et d'histoire grecque*, III, 275–76. Holleaux's article is a superb study of the ancient accounts of the king's death. Our author may also have made one or two innocent mistakes. He may have regarded Elymais as a city, though that is probably the error of a later scribe; see below, on vs. 1. He may also have jumped to conclusions about the direction Antiochus took after his repulse from the temple there and about the extent of Antiochus' holdings in the Iranian east; see below, on vss. 4 and 13. Otherwise, our author's account is in harmony with that of the reliable pagan historians Polybius (xxxi 9) and Appian (xi 66).

It is characteristic of our author, and a further guarantee of his veracity, that he gives only the remotest hints that Antiochus' death was a fulfillment of prophesy. Indeed, the manner of Antiochus' death confounded the expectations of all the Jewish seers of the time. See below, on vss. 4, 5, 11, 12. Our author rightly refrained from having the messenger report any of the events of ch. 5.

There were very different ways in which pious Jews could treat the story of Antiochus IV's death. See in AB vol. 41A commentary on II 1:11–17, 9:1–29.

1. *the inland territories.* See NOTE on 3:37.

in Elymais. Elymais was the biblical Elam. It lay in what is now southwestern Iran (Khuzistan). The chief city of Elam was Susa, but Susa was securely held by Antiochus IV as was the surrounding province of Susiana; see Mørkholm, pp. 30, 106, 111. The name Elymais may have been reserved for the part of Elam not effectively controlled by the Seleucids. Cf. Pliny *Naturalis historia* vi 135, and see Hans Treidler, "Elymais," Der kleine Pauly, II (1967), 253–54. The Lucianic recension, the old Latin, and Josephus (*AJ* xii 9.1.354) all have Elymais as the name of the city. Nowhere else is a city by that name mentioned. Though it is conceivable that our author made the error of taking Elymais as the name of a city, the error probably belongs to someone else. My translation is based on the good readings *en Elymais* (q 56 58 106 340) or *en Elymes* (A). These show that the translator treated the noun as indeclinable. However, *Elymais* is the *Greek* name for the area, and after the preposition *en* it should have a normal dative *Elymaidi.* The translator would so treat the word only if he found it spelled out phonetically the same way in the original Hebrew, as *'lwm'ys.* If so, our author was drawing on a Greek source and did not know that Elymais was called Elam (*'ylm*) in Hebrew. Later scribes, confused by the succession INENEL of "there was in Elymais" (ESTINENELYMAIS) could have produced the above-mentioned erroneous Greek text or that of S and V (ESTINENLYMAIS).

a city . . . silver. Evidently the city was not Susa, which would have been mentioned by name both by the Greek source and by our author, who knew Neh 1:1. Polybius (xxxi 9) and Appian (xi 66), too, name no city.

2. An author writing in 103 B.C.E. identifies the temple as the temple of Nanaia (II 1:13–15; see Appendix III). Since the Greeks identified Nanaia with Aphrodite and Artemis (Dietz O. Edzard, "Nanai(a)," Der kleine Pauly, III [1969], 1565); Polybius (xxxi 9: Artemis) and Appian (xi 66: Aphrodite) corroborate this testimony. Strabo (xvi 1.18 [744]) tells how the great wealth of the temple of Artemis in Elymais later attracted another plundering king, Mithradates I of Parthia.

Alexander passed through Susa and may well have dedicated offerings at the temple in Elymais, though no other source says so.

helmets. So La^B and the Syriac render here the vague Greek *kalymmata,* which I translated "armor" at 4:6. The mention of breastplates and shields suggests that this word, too, referred to a specific kind of armor. Elsewhere Hebrew "helmet" (*kwb'* or *qwb'*) is rendered by Greek *perikephalaion,* as at I 6:35.

shields. The vague Greek *hopla* ("arms") often renders the Hebrew "shield" (I Kings 10:17, etc.).

the first . . . empire. See NOTE on 1:1.

3. Ancient observers believed Antiochus IV had no scruples over drawing on the riches of temples within his power (I 1:21–24; Polybius xxx 26.9=Athenaeus v 195; Granius Licinianus xxviii 6). In this he followed the examples of his father Antiochus III (Polybius x 27.12–13; Diodorus xxviii 3, xxix 15) and his brother Seleucus IV (II 3:7). But see AB vol. 41A, NOTES on II 3:6, *These funds . . . confiscate,* and 3:11, *treating . . . war.*

4. *When . . . battle.* The Greek and the Hebrew underlying it (*wayyāqūmū 'ālāw lammilḥāmāh;* cf. Jer 49:14 and Obad 1) easily allow the interpretation that no battle occurred, that the determination of the natives drawn up in line to resist intimidated Antiochus IV, who knew how Antiochus III had been slain in trying to plunder a temple in Elymais (Diodorus xxviii 3, xxix 15). Holleaux (REA 18 [1916], 87 and 279) noted that Polybius' words (xxxi 9: *diapseustheis tês elpidos dia to mê synchorein têi paranomiai tous barbarous*) also imply that Antiochus withdrew without a battle. Even II 9:2 does not imply that a battle took place, for it speaks of the ignominy of Antiochus' retreat, an ignominy which would be all the greater if Antiochus did not fight the natives who poured out ready to defend their temple. Josephus (*AJ* xii 9.1.355) reports a battle, probably by reading into his sources more than was there.

Babylonia. The province of Babylonia lay just to the west of Elymais (Susiana) and was securely held by the Seleucid government at this time; see Mørkholm, pp. 30, 100, 106–7. One would expect the repulsed king to withdraw in that direction. In Hebrew "Babylon" (the city) and "Babylonia" (the region) are both *bbl;* the translator was probably mistaken in writing "Babylon" here.

Nevertheless, to judge by the probable location near Isfahan of Tabai, the place where Antiochus died (Weissbach, "Tabai 4," PW, IV [1932], 1840–41), Antiochus "withdrew" northward or even northeastward, not toward Babylonia. See Mørkholm, pp. 170–71. See also below, on vs. 5, *Persis.*

Jason of Cyrene in his parallel account drew heavily on prophesies of the punishment of Babylon and its king. See NOTE on II 9. Our author is so far from doing so that he mentions Babylon or Babylonia only as the destination where the king would have been safe.

5. *A messenger.* The story of the messenger is probably fictitious (above, introductory NOTE to vss. 1–17). Characteristically, our author did not make the messengers plural, though if he had done so he could have alluded to Jer 51: 31–32.

Persis. Our author probably means that Antiochus did not live to reach Babylonia; indeed, he did not—see above, on vs. 4. However, in our author's time Babylonia was under the Parthian empire, which the Jews called "Persis" (see NOTE on 3:31). Our author's Greek source may have had *Persis* or *Paraitakênê* (the name of the region which contained Tabai). Either one our author could have called "Persis" (*pāras*) in Hebrew—*Paraitakênê* may have been altogether unfamiliar to him. And then he could have made the natural assumption that Antiochus withdrew westward through "Persis" to Babylonia, as above in vs. 4.

armies . . . routed. 3:34–4:22.

6. *Lysias . . . Jews.* 4:28–35.

at the head of. The Greek reflects the same Hebrew idiom as at I Kings 20: 17 and I Chron 11:6 ("first").

wealth. Greek: *dynamei;* so the Greek translator renders Hebrew "wealth" (*hwn*) at Ezek 27:18, 27.

abundant . . . defeated. 3:12, 4:23.

7. See 4:36–61.

their town. Such is the reading of the Lucianic recension, supported by La[B V]. The original scribe of S omitted the words. The other witnesses to the text have "his [*sc.* Antiochus'] town." If "his" had stood in the original text, no one would have changed it, in view of the "confirmation" at 4:29, 6:50, 10:14, 11:65–66, and the similar language at 15:28. However, Beth-Zur was in fact a town of Judaea; see NOTE on 4:29. Moreover, one would expect the messenger to say "They *have captured* and fortified Beth-Zur," if in fact the town was not part of Judaea; similarly, the language at vs. 26 seems to imply that Beth-Zur, like Jerusalem, is Jewish; the Jews' crime is not in possessing it but in fortifying it.

10. *Friends.* See NOTE on 2:18.

Sleep . . . eyes. Cf. Gen 31:40.

broken my heart. The Hebrew idiom is that at I Sam 17:32.

11. In the presence of the friends and in the complaint our author may have been thinking of Job 29–31. There may also be an allusion here to Zech 10: 3–11, parts of which could appear to have been fulfilled by the Hasmonaean exploits and by the Seleucid defeats, though certainly not Zech 10:10. In Zech 10:11 the Masoretic text has "Trouble [*ṣārāh*] shall pass through the sea and strike up waves in the sea." One would expect "A storm [*sa'ar*] shall pass through. . . ." Our author may have known texts with both readings. Antiochus complains of sinking in a sea of "trouble" and of being caught in a "storm" (Greek *klydôn* renders Hebrew *sa'ar* at Jonah 1:4, 11, 12).

kind . . . realm. Antiochus IV was famous for his conviviality and extravagant, if capricious generosity; see I 3:30 and Polybius xxvi 1, xxx 25–26. Our author allows the king his claim and thereby sharply distinguishes Antiochus IV from the atrocious tyrant of Isaiah 14. Jason of Cyrene makes Antiochus' death a fulfillment of Isaiah 14; see NOTE on II 9.

12. Again our author and the translator refuse an opportunity to allude to Isaiah 14, this time to Greek vs. 20.

13. *foreign soil.* Our author did not know that Antiochus still may have held Tabai as his own; in our author's day it was subject to the Parthians.

14–15. By placing Philip in power and making him guardian of the young heir to the throne, Antiochus IV surely intended to depose Lysias from all the offices conferred upon him at 3:32–36. Perhaps the king did have some news of failures of Lysias', including the defeats in Judaea. Philip's power is to be greater than Lysias', for it is to extend over the entire Seleucid empire. The diadem, robe, and ring were the emblems of royal power (Bikerman, *Institutions*, pp. 21, 33).

15. *for Philip to bring to his son Antiochus*. The correct meaning is preserved only in the Lucianic recension and in Josephus, both of which have "his son Antiochus" in the dative case. The other witnesses to the text can be rendered "for Philip to bring up his son Antiochus"; in these "his son Antiochus" is in the accusative case. The Greek *agagein* can mean both "bring" and "bring up," depending on the case of the noun. The Greek scribes were probably led astray by the context. "Be the guardian of" in Greek is *trephein*, literally, "nourish." Another connotation of *trephein* is "to bring up a small child." In contrast to *trephein*, *agagein* can mean the formal training of a school-aged child. Hence, the presence of *trephein* in the context led the scribes to expect *agagein* to mean "educate," so that consciously or unconsciously they altered "his son Antiochus" from the dative to the accusative. The resultant text was illogical in putting the formal training before the bringing up. A decisive argument against the reading of the scribes is the fact that *agagein* never means "bring up" or "educate" in Greek translations from the Hebrew Bible. Moreover, the reading of the scribes is hard to reconcile with what precedes, since it is hard to see how the diadem, robe, and ring would be of use in bringing up the young Antiochus but easy to see how they would serve to legitimize the young Antiochus' succession and the power of his guardian Philip if Philip conveyed them to the young heir.

Josephus and the Lucianic recension may have been aware of the danger of confusion. Instead of *agagein* they use words which unambiguously mean "convey."

16. *the year 149*. The year 149 Sel. Mac. included the months October–December of 164 B.C.E. See above, introductory NOTE to vss. 1–17.

17. With Antiochus IV dead, Lysias refused to yield power to Philip without a fight. Indeed, with the helpless boy king in his power, Lysias was to prevail. According to Appian xi 46 and 66, Antiochus V was nine years old when he became full king in late 164 B.C.E. According to Porphyry, FGH 260, F 32.13, Antiochus V was then twelve years old. However, Antiochus IV's only wife was probably Laodice, the widow of Seleucus IV. If so, Antiochus V could have been born in 174 B.C.E. at the earliest. The tradition reflected by Porphyry may have arisen from confusing the birth date of Antiochus V with that of the other child king Antiochus, the son of Seleucus IV. See NOTE on 1:10, and Mørkholm, pp. 36–50, 62, and esp. p. 48, n. 41. On the guardian of a child king, see NOTE on 3:33.

The epithet conferred on the boy king (*Eupatōr*="born of a noble sire") reflects the popularity of Antiochus IV.

XV. THE EXPEDITION OF
ANTIOCHUS V AND LYSIAS
(6:18–63)

6 18 The men of the Akra had been besetting Israel in the neighborhood of the sanctuary as they continually sought to do evil and
give aid to the gentiles. 19 Accordingly, Judas planned to wipe them
out. He assembled the entire people to put them under siege. 20 The
people gathered and laid siege to the Akra in the year 150, constructing a siege wall and siege engines.

21 Some of the men of the Akra slipped through the siege lines.
Joined by some wicked Israelites, 22 they went to the king and said,
"How long must we wait for you to do justice and avenge our comrades? 23 We were willing to serve your father and follow his instructions and obey his commands. 24 As a result, our own coun-
trymen have become our enemies. Indeed, they have killed as many
of us as they could find and have been plundering our property.
25 Not only against us have they raised their hands but also against
all your domains. 26 And now at this very moment they are holding
the Akra in Jerusalem under siege and mean to take it. They have
also fortified the temple and Beth-Zur. 27 If you do not act promptly
to stop them, they will accomplish even more, and you will not be
able to suppress them."

28 When the king heard this, he was furious. He assembled all his
Friends who were commanders of his army as well as the masters of
the horse. 29 From other kingdoms and from the Mediterranean islands he got mercenary troops. 30 His army numbered one hundred thousand infantry and twenty thousand cavalry and thirty-two
trained war elephants. 31 They marched by way of Idumaea and laid
siege to Beth-Zur, keeping it under attack for many days. When the
Seleucid force constructed siege engines, the besieged made a sortie
and burned them, fighting courageously. 32 Judas withdrew from
the Akra and encamped at Beth-Zechariah, blocking the road ahead
of the camp of the king. 33 The king had his army make an im-
petuous early morning dash down the road to Beth-Zechariah. Drawn

up ready for battle, they sounded their trumpets. 34 They displayed grape and mulberry juice to the elephants to prepare them for battle. 35 The great beasts were distributed among the phalanxes. By each elephant were placed one thousand men wearing coats of chain mail and bronze helmets. A special force of five hundred cavalry also was assigned to each beast. 36 The assigned troops would be wherever the beast was at the moment; wherever it went, they went, too, never leaving it. 37 Each elephant bore an armored and roofed wooden howdah, fastened to it by straps; on each elephant were two warriors who would fight while riding and, in addition, the elephant's mahout. 38 The remainder of the cavalry the commander posted on the two flanks of the army, to intimidate the enemy and protect his own phalanxes. 39 When the sun began to shine upon the golden and silver shields, the mountains began to shine from their reflected light as they flashed like fiery torches. 40 Part of the king's army was deployed over the heights and part over the low ground; they marched forward confidently and in good order. 41 The shouting of the vast army and the din of its advance and the clashing of their arms struck all with fear, for the king's army was indeed very great and powerful. 42 When Judas and his army approached and joined battle, six hundred men from the king's army were slain. 43 Eleazar Auaran caught sight of one of the elephants which was wearing royal armor, one which was taller than all the others. Thinking that the king was riding it, 44 Eleazar gave his life to save his people and win eternal fame. 45 Boldly he dashed into the midst of the phalanx at the elephant, slaying men right and left as he cut the enemy down on both sides of his path. 46 Going in underneath the elephant, he stabbed it to death, whereupon the elephant fell to the ground on top of him, killing him there. 47 Perceiving the power of the empire and the warlike spirit of the imperial army, Judas and his men withdrew.

48 Thereupon, the king's army marched after them to Jerusalem, and the king encamped against Judaea[a] and against Mount Zion. 49 However, he made a truce with the defenders of Beth-Zur, so that they withdrew from the town, inasmuch as they had no store of food there for withstanding a siege because it was the sabbatical year when the land was left fallow. 50 Thereupon the king occupied Beth-Zur and stationed there a garrison to hold it. 51 He besieged the temple for many days, setting up against it a siege wall and siege engines,

---

[a] The translator has probably made a mistake here; by 'al yᵉhūdāh our author probably meant "against Judas," not "against Judaea." See NOTE ad loc.

including launchers of incendiary missiles, catapults for hurling stones, scorpionettes for hurling darts, and slings. 52 The besieged, too, devised engines to counter those of the enemy, so that the siege continued for many days. 53 However, there was no longer food in the bins because it was the seventh year and also because the refugees who had been evacuated to Judaea from among the gentiles had consumed what was left of the stores. 54 Hence a few men were left in the sanctuary because hunger pressed the defenders hard; the rest dispersed, each to his own place.

55 Lysias, however, received word that Philip, whom King Antiochus had appointed before he died to be the guardian of his son Antiochus until he was ready to reign, 56 had returned from Persis and Media accompanied by the late king's expeditionary force and was seeking to take control of the empire. 57 In his dismay, Lysias decided upon withdrawal. To the king and to the army commanders and the soldiers he said, "We grow weaker day by day. We are short of food. The place we are besieging is strong. The affairs of the empire are demanding our attention. 58 Let us therefore now grant a truce to these men and make peace with them and with their entire nation. 59 Let us allow them to follow their own laws as formerly, for our violation of their laws so enraged them that they have done all this." 60 The king and his staff approved. The king sent the besieged a proposal to make peace. They accepted. 61 The king and his staff took oath in their presence. In return, the men came out of their stronghold. 62 Thereupon, the king entered Mount Zion. On seeing how strongly the site was fortified, he went back on the oath which he had sworn; by his orders the wall surrounding it was torn down. 63 Thereafter, the king departed in haste. On his return to Antioch, he found Philip in control of the city. The king and his army attacked Philip and took the city by force.

NOTES

6:18–63, introductory NOTE. The act of besieging the Akra was an act of rebellion against the king; see below, on vs. 26. Some Pietists surely opposed it; see below, on vss. 18–24. Judas and his followers already believed that God permitted them to besiege the Akra; see below, on vss. 55–63.

On the different account of the events given by Jason of Cyrene, see commentary on II 13. Josephus' account at *BJ* i 1.5.41–46 depends on the account here, for like the account at *AJ* xii 9.3–7.362–83, the account in *BJ* misreads the word "phalanxes" as "narrow passes" (*pharangas*) in vss. 35 and 38. See Introduction, pp. 60–61.

18–24. Characteristically, our author gives the apostates in the Akra an ambiguous status. They are no longer of Israel, yet they are not quite gentiles: they only "give aid to the gentiles." See J. *AJ* xii 9.3.362, and NOTE on 1:34 and pp. 123–24. Wicked Israelites (i.e. anti-Hasmonaeans, even Pietists) can make common cause with the garrison in the Akra, since the Seleucid regime after the amnesty no longer sought to outlaw Jewish religion (see Introduction, p. 74, and NOTE on 4:35) but only to maintain its power in Jerusalem. Though anti-Hasmonaean Pietists would feel obliged to punish any apostates that fell into their power (see Introduction, pp. 121–23), they could have tolerated the presence of Seleucid troops. It is probable that a large portion of the garrison of the Akra consisted of gentiles; see Introduction, p. 124. Our author insists that all true Israelites joined the attack on the Akra.

Also characteristic of our author is the attitude that normally it is wicked to give aid to the gentiles; see Introduction, p. 12.

20. *in the year 150.* The date in 150 Sel. can hardly be correct. Judas' siege of the Akra lasted for some time before the rescue expedition of Lysias and Antiochus V. The expedition resulted in the defeat of Judas at Beth Zechariah. From our interpretation of Dan 12:11 we learn that Judas had been defeated by June 27, 163 B.C.E.; see Introduction, pp. 43–44. As a date of local Jewish history, our author's 150 Sel. should be 150 Sel. Bab., a year which ran from spring, 162, to spring, 161 (see Introduction, p. 24). Even 150 Sel. Mac. ran from autumn, 163, to autumn, 162. Furthermore, Jason of Cyrene (II 13:1) dates the rescue expedition in 149 Sel., which would have to be 149 Sel. Mac. if his dates on the Seleucid era are consistent (see Appendix II). Thus, Jason of Cyrene would appear to contradict our author's date. Finally, our author (vss. 49–53) places the time of the sieges of Beth-Zur and Mount Zion in the sabbatical year. The most probable date for the sabbatical year is from autumn, 164, to autumn, 163.

At least two pieces of evidence support our probable date. Every seventh year was sabbatical (Lev 25:1–4). Josephus (*AJ* xiv 16.2.475, 4.487) implies that autumn, 38, to autumn, 37, was a sabbatical year, and an early rabbinic tradition (*Seder 'olam rabbah* 30, p. 147 Ratner; TB *Ta'anit* 29a) states that the second temple was destroyed in the year after a sabbatical year. If so, to determine whether a date B.C.E. falls within a sabbatical year, subtract 3 from the year number if the date lies within the period 1 Tishri-December 31, and otherwise subtract 2 from the year number; if the result is divisible by seven, the year is sabbatical. To determine whether a date C.E. falls within a sabbatical year, add two to the year number if the date falls within the period 1 Tishri-December 31, and otherwise add one; if the result is divisible by seven, the year is sabbatical.

Unfortunately, Josephus did not have time to solve all chronological problems and followed erroneous traditions and interpretations, some of which were incompatible with the evidence we have just cited. On the difficulty presented by J. *AJ* xiii 8.1.230–34, see Appendix I. On the difficulties at *AJ* xiv 16.4.487–

88 and elsewhere which led some scholars to put the events and the sabbatical year in 37/6 B.C.E., see R. Marcus, *Josephus,* VII, LCL, no. 365, pp. 700–1, note *d,* and the literature cited there. The plain meaning of the rabbinic text was challenged by commentators because of the difficulty of fitting it into the wider rabbinic chronological scheme of history; therefore, some commentators assert that the equivalent of 69–70 C.E. was the sabbatical year. See TB *'Abodah zarah* 9b, *Iosafot* s.v. *hay;* and Maimonides, *Mishneh Torah, Zera'im, Hilkot shemiṭah weyobel* 10:3–6, and the commentary *Kesef mishneh,* ibid., 10:4. For us, the very failure of the tradition on the year of the destruction of the second temple to fit into the rabbis' theologically motivated chronology argues that the tradition presents the facts, not later theories. Despite the difficulties, Maimonides (10:6) attests that according to the Geonim and the Palestinian Jewish tradition the cycle of sabbatical years was the one implied by the plain meaning of our rabbinic text. He declares that to be the authoritative cycle.

Heinrich Grätz (*Geschichte der Juden,* III, 5th ed. [Leipzig: Leiner, 1905], 655) combined J. *AJ* xix 5.3.287 with 6.1.292 and *M. Sotah* 7:8 and argued that the sabbatical year fell in 41/2 C.E. However, contrary to Grätz's assertion, Agrippa I easily could have been in Judaea by Tabernacles in 41 C.E., since Claudius very soon after his accession bore the title "consul-elect for the second time" (Gaheis, "Claudius 256," PW, III [1899], 2787). It is also possible that Agrippa at *M. Soṭah* 7:8 is Agrippa II.

Ben Zion Wacholder has done well to assemble the evidence on the sabbatical cycle, but his study ("The Calendar of Sabbatical Cycles During the Second Temple and the Early Rabbinic Period," HUCA 44 [1973], 153–96) is so full of errors that one cannot accept his conclusion, that the sabbatical years fell one year later than the dates we have assumed. Wacholder agrees that most of the evidence is equivocal and unsatisfactory. I present the following in refutation of his arguments that some evidence unequivocally supports his theory:

Wacholder (pp. 163–65) reads I 16:14–17 with J. *BJ* i 2.3.54–60 and *AJ* xiii 7.4.228 – 8.1.235 to imply that Simon the Hasmonaean was killed in 177 Sel. and that 177 Sel. was a sabbatical year. Josephus, however, asserts that the sabbatical year came *after* the murder of Simon. Moreover, only if I 16:14 gave the date of Simon's death as 177 Sel. Mac. could the sabbatical year have fallen where Wacholder places it, between Tishri, 135, and Tishri, 134 B.C.E. A date in First Maccabees on the Macedonian form of the Seleucid era for a local event in Judaea is improbable; see Appendix I.

Wacholder (p. 168) asserts that the year from Tishri, 40 C.E., to Tishri, 41 C.E., could not have been a sabbatical year because Josephus in his account of the momentous events of the reign of the Roman emperor Caligula attests that pious Jews of Judaea sowed their fields in that year (*BJ* ii 10.5.200; *AJ* xviii 7.3–4.271–74). But Philo (*Legatio ad Gaium* 33–34.249–57) puts the same events, not at the time of the autumn sowing, but at the time of the spring harvest. Hard as it may be to explain how Josephus could have been mistaken, it is harder still to explain how Philo could have been in error; see F. H. Colson, *Philo* X, LCL, no. 379 (1962), pp. xxvii–xxxi. The problem is still unsolved (the suggestions of Vermes and Millar in Schürer, *History of the*

Jewish People in the Age of Jesus Christ [New English version] are unsatisfactory, too; Philo and Josephus cannot both be correct). But one certainly cannot take Josephus' chronology of the events of Caligula's reign as a sure basis for a theory of the dates of the sabbatical year.

Wacholder (pp. 169–71) finds strong evidence for his theory in a papyrus from Wadi Murabba'at (*Mur.* 18, published by J. T. Milik in *Les Grottes de Murabba'at*, eds. P. Benoit, J. T. Milik, and R. de Vaux, DJD, II (1961), 100–4. The papyrus is dated in the second year of Nero Caesar, (55–56 C.E.), and line 7 was read by Milik, "*wšnt šmṭh dh*," which Wacholder translates "in this year of release." Thus, the sabbatical year (=year of release) would be 55–56 C.E. However, the papyrus is a scribbled tatter, extremely difficult to read. Whatever the context of line 7 may mean, Milik misread a crucial word, for the papyrus clearly has *wšnt šmṭh hwh*, "and it was [or would be] the year of release." See R. Yaron's review of Milik, in JJS 11 (1960), 158. Since the verb is either in the past tense or conditional, the context does not prove that 55–56 C.E. was a sabbatical year.

Wacholder (pp. 175–76) cites the rule of thumb for sabbatical years given by Rab Huna son of Rab Joshua (fourth century C.E.) at TB '*Abodah zarah* 9b as presented in our printed editions and interpreted by Rashi. However, the text of the rule is hopelessly ambiguous and corrupt. See the comments ad loc. of Rabbenu Ḥanan'el and the *Tosafot* (s.v. *hay*) and the commentary *Kesef mishneh* to Maimonides, *Mishneh Torah, Zera'im, Hilkot shemiṭah weyobel* 10:4, and *Tractate 'Abodah Zarah of the Babylonian Talmud*, ed. Shraga Abramson (New York: Jewish Theological Seminary of America, 1956), pp. 17, 147 (in Hebrew).

Wacholder next (p. 176) exploits information in Josephus. Josephus reports that the forces of Simon son of Gioras in the winter of 68–69 C.E. captured vast supplies of grain in Hebron (*BJ* iv 9.7.529) and that on a march through Idumaea Simon's forces, short of provisions, stripped the vegetation (ibid., §§534–37) and so trampled the ground that the cultivated land became harder than barren soil (ibid., §537). Wacholder argues that therefore 68/9 C.E. could not have been a sabbatical year. But the grain captured in Hebron could have been stored grain. The shortage of supplies which made Simon's troops strip the vegetation may have been due precisely to the sabbatical year. The reported hardening of the trampled ground may be literary hyperbole. In any case, even when left unplowed for a year, a field which has been regularly plowed can remain softer than barren soil. Finally, there is considerable doubt that the sabbatical year was observed in Idumaea. See *M. Shebi'it* 6:1 (the exiles returning from Babylonia did not take possession of Idumaea) and To. *Shebi'it* 4:11 with the commentary of S. Lieberman, *Tosefta Ki-fshuṭah, Zera'im*, II, 534–38.

Finally, Wacholder (pp. 176–79) uses the papyrus documents published as *Mur.* 24 (in DJD, II, 122–34) to argue for his date of the sabbatical year, especially *Mur.* 24E (cf. *Mur.* 24C). *Mur.* 24E is dated in Shebaṭ of the "year two of the Redemption of Israel by Simeon bar Koseba, the prince of Israel," and in lines 8–10 says that there remain five full years of tax payments (and rental payments) to the end of the year just before the sabbatical year (*mn hywm 'd swp 'rb hšmṭh šhm šnym šlmwt šny [m]ksh hmš thkyr*).

The question of how the years of the Era of Redemption were numbered is a vexed one. However, the date of the beginning of bar Koseba's revolt would seem to be established as the first half of 132 c.e.; see Schürer, *History of the Jewish People* (New English version), I, 542, and B. Kanael, "Notes on the Dates Used During the Bar Kokhba Revolt," IEJ 21 (1971), 40. *Mur.* 30, written at Jerusalem, bears a date of 21 Tishri in the year four of the Redemption of Israel. The war continued after the fall of Jerusalem to the Romans and ended in summer, 135 c.e., only after a long siege of Bether (Schürer, I, 550–52). Jerusalem can have been in Jewish hands in the year four, if years were numbered from Tishri (spring–end Elul, 132=year 1; Tishri, 132–end Elul, 133=year 2; Tishri, 133–end Elul, 134=year 3; Tishri, 134, saw the beginning of year 4), but not if years were numbered from the outbreak of the revolt, for then year four would be spring, 135–spring, 136, and Jerusalem would still have been in Jewish hands after the fall of Bether. One cannot escape this difficulty by suggesting that the rebellion began before Nisan and that the years were numbered from the spring month of Nisan. Year one cannot have been a fractional year from late winter or early spring, 132, to 1 Nisan, 132, because the date of Naḥal Ḥever document No. 42, published by Y. Yadin in IEJ 12 (1962), 249, is 1 Iyyar of the year one of the Redemption of Israel. Iyyar is the month which follows Nisan. Indeed, the documents of the revolt nowhere give Simeon bar Koseba the title "king," so that the years of Redemption could easily have been calendar years to be measured from Tishri rather than regnal years of a king to be measured from Nisan (see Introduction, p. 23).

Hence, Wacholder can hardly be right in jumping to the conclusion that the years of Redemption were measured from Nisan. The language of the documents implies that "years of tax payments," like sabbatical years, begin from Tishri. If so, at the time of *Mur.* 24E (20 Shebat), the year of tax payments corresponding to the year two of the Redemption of Israel (Tishri, 132–end Elul, 133) was a fractional year, and the five full years of tax payments were to begin in 133/4 and to end in 137/8, so that 138/9 would be the sabbatical year, not 139/40 as held by Wacholder. See also Yigael Yadin, *Bar-Kokhba* (New York: Random House, 1971), p. 183.

Admittedly, the evidence even for our own theory is somewhat unsatisfactory. Jewish sects may have differed on the date of the sabbatical year (see Jubilees i 4, xxiii 19), and those sectarian differences may be responsible for many of the inconsistencies in our sources. Pharisaic and rabbinic texts do not reproach the Hasmonaean princes or the Sadducees for deviation on the date of the sabbatical year, so that the Hasmonaean date for the sabbatical year probably agreed with the rabbinic date. Here as elsewhere, we must be content with probability. See Introduction, p. 24. Our theory assumes an error in the date in I 6:20.

Following Bickermann (*Gott,* p. 157), we can easily explain how our author could have made the error: he recorded the death of Antiochus IV at vs. 16, taking the date, 149 Sel. Mac., from his pagan source. Knowing that the siege of the Akra came in the Jewish and Babylonian calendar year after the news of the king's death reached Jerusalem, our author added one year to the date of the king's death. Probably he was unaware that his pagan source used a different form of the Seleucid era.

Jason of Cyrene was glad to correct our author's error; see Introduction, pp. 43–44. Josephus felt compelled to oppose Jason by reiterating our author's error (*AJ* xii 9.3.363).

siege wall. Literally, the Greek word (*belostaseis*) means "emplacements for artillery," but the Hebrew here, as at Ezek 17:17 and 21:27 (Greek vs. 22), was probably *dāyēq*, a rare word of uncertain meaning, but its contexts show that it was a kind of siegework and was made by building.

23. The words of the delegation need signify no more than that the men of the Akra passively consented to observe the imposed cult; see NOTE on 4:41.

24. At the head of our verse in many of the ancient witnesses to the text stand the words "And they laid siege to it." The words originally were probably a marginal note to vs. 26, calling the reader's mind back to vs. 20. A scribe mistakenly copied the words from the margin into the text. An uncontaminated text still appears in A 55 La^V and at J. *AJ* xii 9.3.364.

25. *all your domains.* Our author refers to the campaigns of ch. 5. The original Hebrew was probably *kol gᵉbūlekā*, literally, "all your border"; cf. Exod 7:27, 13:7; Deut 16:4, 28:40. Only the oldest Latin versions (La^{L X G} preserve the reading of the original Hebrew, for only Latin, not Greek, shares with Hebrew the idiomatic use of "border" (Latin: *fines*) for "territory." In idiomatic Greek, "borders" means only borders, not territory, and the Hasmonaean forces had passed far beyond mere borders of the king's provinces. Hence, the Greek scribes changed the text of the unidiomatic translation from "your borders" to "their borders": the Jewish rebels had attacked all the neighboring gentile territories.

26. Judas and his men might claim that in attacking the apostates they were merely obeying the law of their God, and in fighting the neighboring gentiles they were merely defending Jews. But the siege of the Akra and the fortification of the temple and of Beth-Zur were acts of rebellion against the empire. See Introduction, pp. 5–6, 123–25, and on 1:33–40 and NOTE on 6:7, *their town.* See also Micah 5:1[10H].

28. The decisions were made by the king's guardian and ministers; see NOTE on 3:33.

masters of the horse. Literally the Greek means "officials in charge of the reins." I have tried to make the translation ambiguous, since the meaning is a matter of controversy. A "master of the horse" could be a chief of the cavalry, as is suggested by the mention of the commanders of the *army* (*dynamis;* the word is often used for "infantry" as opposed to "cavalry"). Or the horses involved could be racehorses, and the title could be that of a non-military high-ranking courtier. An inscription from Delos mentions a high official of Ptolemy IX Soter II (116–81 B.C.E.) as "the man appointed over the reins." See Félix Dürrbach, *Choix d'inscriptions de Délos* (Paris: Leroux, 1921), pp. 205–7; Otto and Bengtson, *Zur Geschichte des Niederganges des Ptolemäerreiches,* p. 12, n. 2, and p. 175, n. 1; Bikerman, *Institutions,* p. 37.

29. After crushingly defeating Antiochus III, the Romans in 188 B.C.E. imposed upon the Seleucid empire the peace of Apameia. A clause in the peace forbade the Seleucids to hire soldiers or accept volunteers from nations under the control of the Roman people (Polybius xxi 42 Paton [43 Buettner-Wobst]. 15; Livy xxxvii 38.10). Hence Seleucid recruitment of foreigners had to be

from the still independent Greek islands and the surviving independent kingdoms of Pergamum, Bithynia, Pontus, and Cappadocia. Hostile Ptolemaic Egypt surely sent no aid to the unsteady Seleucid regime of Lysias.

30. See NOTE on 3:39. The use of one hundred twenty thousand, the number of the Midianites slain by Gideon and his tiny force of three hundred men (Judg 7:7, 8:10), suggests that our author or his source ascribed the failure of Judas' campaign to Judas' use of too large a force: God finally came to the rescue of the tiny force besieged in the Akra (vss. 54–61).

A clause in the peace of Apameia forbade the Seleucids to have elephants (Polybius xxi 42 Paton [43 Buettner-Wobst].12; Livy xxxviii 38.8). The Roman government had not yet taken the trouble to enforce it; see NOTE on 7:1. Elephants marched in Antiochus IV's famous victory parade of 166 B.C.E. (Polybius xxx 25. 11).

31. See NOTES on 4:28–29 and 4:29, *Idumaea . . . Beth-Zur*.

32–47. On Jason of Cyrene's counterpart (II 13:13–17) to the narrative here, see in AB vol. 41A ad loc.

32. The king's vast army could bypass Beth-Zur, and Judas and his men could be trapped in supply-short Jerusalem between the king's army and the garrison of the Akra. Hence Judas had good reason to abandon the siege; see below, on vss. 47–62. The hill of Beth-Zechariah still bears the name. It lies ten kilometers north of Beth-Zur. Since Beth-Zur cannot be seen from there, I have rendered the Greek "opposite" (*apenanti*) by "blocking the road ahead of." The "passes" mentioned at J. *AJ* xii 9.4.370 and *BJ* i 1.5.41 are derived from misreading a word in vss. 35 and 38; see NOTES ad loc.

34–37. Our author may have taken his detailed account here from a Hellenistic work on the tactics to be used with war elephants. The hard-pressed Jewish eyewitnesses could hardly have preserved such minute information, and a Greek historian in giving the details of elephant tactics probably would have chosen a broader context than the mere suppression of a local rebellion. On elephants in warfare at this time, see S. Reinach, "Elephas," DAGR, II^I (1892), 537b–542a.

34. It is unlikely that the elephants were made drunk. Intoxicated, they would have been as dangerous to their own side as to the enemy. Grape- and mulberry-juice were unnecessary if all that was needed was to show red to the beasts; cloth would have done as well. Perhaps the elephants were fond of fruit juice, and rousing their appetites roused their spirit for battle (Abel, pp. 117–18).

The very expression "juice" (literally, "blood"; Gen 49:11 and Deut 32:14) here suggests that we deal with unfermented liquids. The ancients knew how to prevent juice from fermenting, by cooking it; see A. Jardé, "Vinum," DAGR, V, 920b; TB '*Abodah zarah* 29b–30a. Hence our verse cannot be used to date the battle of Beth-Zechariah at the time of the grape and mulberry harvests.

35. "Phalanxes" were infantry formations. For the position of the elephants in the battle line, cf. Livy xxxvii 40. Many ancient scribes as well as Josephus (*BJ* i 1.5.41 and *AJ* xii 9.4.370) misread the word "phalanxes" here and in vs. 38 as "narrow passes" (*pharangas*). Perhaps in our author's Hebrew there was a loanword, *prnks* for "phalanx." Or perhaps the Greek scribe was

conscious of no error because he pronounced "phalanx" as "pharanx"; see Abel, *Grammaire*, p. 19.

Our author used the language of I Sam 17:5 to describe the armor of the soldiers.

Horses had to be specially trained to tolerate the presence of elephants.

36. *at the moment*. Greek *pro kairou* renders Hebrew '*ēt* at Sir 46:19 and Greek Sir 51:30.

37. The extant ancient representations of howdahs do not show them as roofed, but that is what one would guess the Greek *skepazomenoi* ("covered") means on the basis of how it is used in translating the Hebrew Bible. The word "armored" (*ochyroi*) here is sufficient to express any other kind of covering. "Straps" here are literally "devices" (*mêchanais*), but Symmachus and Theodotion use the related word *mêchanôma* for the fastening (*ḥēšeb*) of the ephod at Exod 28:27–28 and Lev 8:7.

The two warriors (*šālīšīm*) on each elephant I derive from the reading "thirty-two" of A V q La^V 62 46 56 58 106 340, by assuming that the translator misread our authors *šlšym* ("warriors") as *š^elōšīm* ("thirty"). The other witnesses to the text have "thirty," a reading which on the same assumption would leave the number on each elephant unspecified. Both thirty and thirty-two are impossible totals for a force riding a single elephant. The term *šālīš* ("third man") for a riding "warrior" occurs several times in the Hebrew Bible for a warrior on a chariot and has a precise cognate in Ugaritic. The expression probably is derived from the fact that the warrior on board a chariot made three with the driver and an armorbearer (Hebrew Exod 14:7 and *Mekilta Bešallaḥ* 2, lines 203–7, vol. I, 202 Lauterbach). Ancient sources vary as to the number of warriors in a war elephant's howdah; an ancient cameo shows a war elephant with two warriors in the howdah and the mahout on the elephant's neck. See Reinach, DAGR, II^I, 540.

The Greek word for "mahout" is "Hindu" (*Indos*), because most of them came from India; see Reinach, ibid., p. 541a.

38. *and . . . phalanxes*. All witnesses to the text have, not the active participle followed by the accusative (*kataphrassontes tas phalangas*), which I have taken as the basis of my translation, but a passive participle followed by a prepositional phrase (*kataphrassomenoi en tais phalanxin*), which would be rendered "while protected within their own phalanxes." However, the phalanxes could hardly protect the cavalry, since our author has just said that the cavalry was posted on the flanks. Indeed, in Greek warfare the cavalry was usually posted to protect the flank of the infantry; see Johannes Kromayer and Georg Veith, *Heerwesen und Kriegführung der Griechen und Römer*, pp. 92–93. Moreover, we know that a very old misreading of the text of our verse had "narrow passes" (*pharang-*) for "phalanxes"; see above, on vs. 35. I suspect that a very early scribe who had the reading *kataphrassontes tas pharangas* perceived that it was nonsense to speak of an aggressively advancing army as "protecting the narrow passes." Thinking that the cavalry could rest its own flanks on the walls of the passes, the scribe picked the wrong way to correct the reading, producing the text followed by all subsequent witnesses, even those who later perceived that the correct reading was not "narrow passes" but "phalanxes."

39–41. Our author's source appears to have seen in the campaign of Antiochus V, "king of Babylon," a fulfillment of Ezek 21:8–23, where a polished sword flashes and intimidates and vanquishes Israel, and the king of Babylon comes against "Judah in fortified Jerusalem" and builds elaborate siegeworks. Our author himself would hardly draw on Ezekiel 21, with its hostility to the Israelites; Ezek 21:25–27 could be taken as a hostile prophesy of Judas' death.

39. It was the shields which "flashed like fiery torches," though the Greek strangely has the mountains doing so. In the original Hebrew the verb "flashed" could have as its subject either the shields or the mountains, and the translator chose the wrong alternative.

40. Our verse may contain a faint echo of Hab 1:6–9.

41. Our author does everything possible to show that Judas lost the battle to overwhelming force, through no fault of his own.

43. *Eleazar Auaran.* See NOTE on 2:5, and Introduction, pp. 79–80.

one . . . others. The elephant may indeed have been the one upon which the king was accustomed to ride, but the boy king certainly did not go into combat.

44. Cf. 2:64, 67–68.

48. *encamped against Judaea and against Mount Zion.* The Greek (*paremballein eis*) can mean merely "encamp at" or "halt at" as in Numbers 33 and here at vs. 32, but in our verse it is used of a hostile army, and this was not the first time the king's army had encamped in Judaea. Beth-Zur, too, was in Judaea; see NOTE on 4:29. Why, then, mention Judaea here? Can it be that the end of our verse should be translated "pressed sieges both against Judaea [i.e. against Beth-Zur] and against Mount Zion?" It is hard to understand why our author would replace the precise "Beth-Zur" with the vague "Judaea."

It is also very strange that the text as we have it fails to mention Judas in vss. 47–62. Did he not participate in the defense of the temple mount? Hence it seems probable that the Greek translator has wrongly rendered our authors *'al yehūdāh* ("against Judas") as "against Judaea." "Encamped against" here then would mean "besieged." For the use of the Hebrew and Greek expressions with a personal object, see Judg 6:4, and cf. Ps 27:3; I 2:32, 5:5. Josephus may well have rejected the strange Greek of our verse and looked at the Hebrew. He takes care to say (*AJ* xii 9.5–7.375–82) that Judas participated in the defense. On the other hand, he may have ignored the textual difficulty and written what seemed obvious to him.

49–62. Judas' name is strangely absent from the rest of our author's account of the campaign. If Judas had been among those "providentially" rescued from the siege of the temple by Lysias' sudden decision to withdraw, our author might well have said so. Hence, Judas himself probably was not among the last few defenders of the temple mount, though Josephus says he was (*AJ* xii 9.7.382). Judas was probably realist enough to see that with its lack of provisions the temple was a trap. We may imagine him hiding in the hill country and perhaps even going home to Modeïn, taking advantage of the Seleucid determination to avoid the posture of persecutors. "Each to his own place" may well mean "homeward," as at Judg 7:7, 9:55. Judas would then have been ready to resume guerrilla warfare when enough food should become available to support a band. Josephus may preserve a correct tradition at *BJ* i 1.5.45, that Judas' refuge was the toparchy of Gophna (see Map 10, p. 536).

On the other hand, Judas probably did nothing to discourage a handful of his pious supporters from trying to withstand a siege in the fortified temple. The "hand of the Holy People" at Dan 12:7 may refer to Judas, to the besieged force, or to both.

Our author's tactful silence serves his purposes admirably. To have stated that Judas did not stay in the besieged temple would have opened Judas to criticism. To have mentioned him in connection with the negotiations with Lysias would probably have been false and would have opened Judas to the charge that he, too, could be deceived by Seleucid promises. After having mentioned in *BJ* Judas' refuge in the toparchy of Gophna, Josephus at *AJ* xii 9.5.375 feels he must insist that Judas was in the besieged temple.

On the date of the siege, see Introduction, pp. 43–44.

49–50. Our author has to concede that the Seleucid regime was willing to grant the rebels their lives, but the regime's intentions were still bad. Beth-Zur with its Seleucid garrison was to become a last refuge of apostate Jews (10:14; 14:33). On the sabbatical year, see Exod 23:10–11; Lev 25:1–7; and Introduction, pp. 42–44. Pietists held that observance of the sabbatical year would bring victory and vindication to the Jews (Lev 26:7–12 in the context of Lev 25:1–7; cf. Lev 26:34, 43 and II Chron 36:21). In addition, the Pietist believers in the apocalyptic prophesies held that God Himself would intervene during this sabbatical year and put an end to Israel's long subjugation to foreign rulers; see Introduction, pp. 39–44.

In a sabbatical year crops were not planted, and even spontaneously growing grain could not be regularly harvested. Although normally stores from preceding years would suffice to feed the Jews until the crop came in from the year after the sabbatical year, the expeditions of Gorgias and Nicanor and of Lysias had probably disrupted agriculture in Judaea. Moreover, believers in the apocalyptic prophesies may well have failed to plant crops. Another cause depleting stores in Judaea was the large number of refugees brought back to Judaea from Galilee and Gilead (vs. 53). Thus, the observance of the sabbatical year made it impossible for Judas to carry on large-scale resistance at the fixed points of Beth-Zur and Jerusalem; pious Jews had to seek food where it grew spontaneously. Correct accordingly R. North, "Maccabean Sabbath Years," *Biblica* 34 (1953), 506–8. Characteristically, our author, though he believes the sabbatical year should be observed, here and in vs. 53 stresses how the observance was an impediment to resistance, whereas Jason of Cyrene has to omit the fact as embarrassing for a pious audience: II 13 does not mention the sabbatical year.

51. *siege wall.* See above, on vs. 20.

scorpionettes. Greek *skorpidia.* They were catapults for hurling darts. See Lammert, "Skorpion," PW, III^A (1929), 584–85.

53. See above, on vss. 49–50.

54. Again our author has to concede that the Seleucid regime would grant the rebels their lives.

55–63. Believers in the apocalyptic prophesies must have been perplexed at the end of the sabbatical year, and all the more after Antiochus V's withdrawal from Jerusalem. The prophesies predicted that by this time the period of Israel's subjugation to foreign rulers would be past, and other great events should also have happened. Dan 11:40–12:3; Enoch xc 20–38; and Test Moses 4–10 remained unfulfilled. Were the Jews now free? Or were they perhaps in the predicted time of trouble (Dan 12:1)? Or were the Seleucids still the rightful rulers over Israel?

Judas' party appears to have believed that the period of divinely imposed Seleucid domination was over: they probably took no part in the negotiations with Lysias and Antiochus V and refused to accept Antiochus V's and Demetrius I's appointment of Alcimus as high priest, and Judas resisted Demetrius I without hesitation (I 7). Some may have believed that the line of Antiochus IV was doomed because of the persecutor's heinous sins (see Isa 14:21 and II 7:17), and Antiochus V's perfidy (vs. 62) might render his rule over the Jews illegitimate. But Judas' party rebelled even against Demetrius I, a legitimate Seleucid with no part in the persecutions, who had personally committed no perfidy. Clearly, then, Judas' party believed the period of subjugation was past. We cannot tell whether Judas at this point believed to some extent in the apocalyptic prophesies or whether he simply relied on the fact of the Jewish victories. Other Jews clearly regarded themselves as still subjects of the Seleucids, negotiating with the government and accepting Alcimus as high priest, or believed that they were now passing through the time of trouble (see NOTE on 7:12). There was good reason to be cautious: Jews had been disastrously wrong before in interpreting prophesies (Dan 11:14).

55–56. Our author is probably wrong in identifying the Philip at Antioch with the guardian Antiochus IV appointed on his deathbed. See NOTES on II 9:29 and 13:23, and Introduction, p. 84.

56. *Persis and Media*. This may be our author's designation for the region occupied in his day by the Parthian empire (cf. Esther 1:3, 14, 18, 19), or it may show geographical knowledge in our author or in his source: to march westward from Tabai where Antiochus IV died, one passed through Media.

57–59. Our author does not have Lysias mention Philip in his speech. Josephus probably had no other evidence than this for his statement that at the prompting of the (boy!) king Lysias thus counseled withdrawal while concealing the true nature of the emergency.

58–59. Our author deliberately ignored Lysias' amnesty of 164 B.C.E., which had ended the persecution; see NOTE on 4:35. In so doing, our author left incongruous the clemency of the Seleucid army here at vss. 49 and 54, but only the most careful reader would have noticed the incongruity. Indeed, the amnesty of 164 was only for those who would lay down their arms. Now, Lysias proposes a peace which can include the militant Hasmonaeans and their followers. See also commentary on II 11:23–26.

60–61. Our author says as little as possible about the negotiations, in which the Hasmonaean brothers probably did not participate. Judas is not mentioned in the king's letter at II 11:23–26. See above, NOTE on vss. 47–62.

61. The Seleucid authorities swore to observe the peace terms, and by coming out of their stronghold the besieged ended their rebellion by placing themselves in the king's power.

62. Our author takes pleasure in recording the act of perfidy. See Intro-

duction, pp. 12, 48. He could also take pleasure in the thought that a very few careful readers would understand that the Hasmonaean brothers were not the ones who made the agreement with the perfidious Seleucids. It is possible that the king did not expressly swear to leave the fortifications intact. See the document at II 11:22–26. On the revocability of Seleucid royal concessions, see Bikerman, *Institutions*, pp. 139–40.

63. According to *Megillat Ta'anit* 28 Shebaṭ, Antiochus V withdrew on that date from Jerusalem. On the defective Jewish calendar, that would be January 5, 162 B.C.E.; on the Babylonian calendar it would be March 5, 162 B.C.E.

Immediately after speaking of the king's withdrawal to Antioch, Josephus (*AJ* xii 9.7.383–85) narrates the execution of Menelaus, on which see Introduction, pp. 92–93, and commentary on II 13:3–8.

Josephus reports (*AJ* xii 9.7.386) that after his victory Antiochus V had Philip executed. Josephus may have derived the fact from the unabridged work of Jason of Cyrene.

Josephus goes on, in *AJ* xii 9.7.387–88, to report that Antiochus V appointed Alcimus high priest to replace Menelaus and that Onias IV at this point took refuge in Egypt, where he enjoyed the favor of Ptolemy VI and built the temple of Leontopolis. These facts Josephus derived from the book of Onias IV. See Introduction, pp. 57–58. Inasmuch as Josephus was following the best-informed of sources on Onias IV, his account is to be trusted. It does not matter that a Jewish courtier Onias may have been the addressee in Egypt of a letter sent September 21, 164 B.C.E. (CPJ 132). Ulrich Wilcken restored the name at a damaged point of the papyrus. Even if the restoration is correct, the Onias of the papyrus need not have been either Onias III or Onias IV. Among the high-ranking courtiers of Ptolemy VI (a king friendly to Jews), there was probably Jews and even members of the high priestly family before Onias IV went to Egypt. See II 1:10 and commentary ad loc., and Appendix III.

Our author does not hesitate to mention Alcimus as high priest in chs. 7 and 9, so that he cannot be accused of relegating all non-Hasmonaean high priests to oblivion. Why, then, is nothing said here of Alcimus' appointment? We may guess that our author reflects the Hasmonaean position that Antiochus V was an illegitimate ruler with no right to appoint a high priest; see NOTE on vss. 55–63.

XVI. THE HIGH PRIEST ALCIMUS AND THE CAMPAIGN OF NICANOR
(7:1–50)

7 ¹In the year 151 Demetrius son of Seleucus left Rome, sailed with a handful of men to one of the coastal cities and there made himself king. ²As he was marching on the Seleucid capital, the soldiers seized Antiochus and Lysias, intending to deliver them up to him. ³When the news reached Demetrius, he said, "Do not let me see their faces." ⁴Accordingly, the soldiers slew them, and Demetrius became undisputed king.

⁵Then all the sinful and wicked men of Israel came before him led by Alcimus, who wanted to be high priest. ⁶They brought charges against their people, telling the king, "Judas and his brothers have killed all your friends, and he has driven us from our land. ⁷Now, therefore, send a man whom you trust and have him go view all the havoc Judas has wreaked upon us and upon the king's domains, and have him punish Judas and his men and all their abetters." ⁸The king chose Bacchides, one of the Friends of the King, governor of the Trans-Euphrates province, a leading man in the kingdom, and one loyal to the king. ⁹He sent him with the wicked Alcimus, whom he confirmed in the high priesthood, with orders to wreak vengeance on the Israelites. ¹⁰They set out on the march with a large force against the land of Judah. Bacchides sent a message to Judas and his brothers, treacherously couched in peaceful terms. ¹¹However, Judas and his brothers paid the messengers no heed, for they saw how large a Seleucid force had come. ¹²Nevertheless, an assembly of men learned in the Torah gathered before Alcimus and Bacchides "to seek justice." ¹³The Pietists took the lead among the Israelites in seeking peace at their hands, ¹⁴saying, "A man who is a priest of the stock of Aaron has come with their force; he will not wrong us." ¹⁵Indeed, Alcimus spoke with them in peaceful terms and swore to them that "We intend no harm to you or to your friends." ¹⁶As soon as he had won their trust, however, he arrested sixty of them and had them executed all in a single day, in accordance with the verse

which he himself wrote, 17 "The bodies and blood of Your saints they have poured out around Jerusalem, and there is no one to bury them." 18 The fear and dread of them seized the entire people, as they said to one another, "There is no truth or justice among them. They have violated their pledge and their sworn oath."

19 Thereafter, Bacchides left Jerusalem and encamped at Beth-Zaith. There he sent out orders and had many of the turncoats who had gone over to him arrested, as well as some of our people; he had all these butchered by the great cistern and their bodies cast into it. 20 After putting the country under the control of Alcimus and leaving with him troops to assist him, Bacchides returned to the king.

21 Alcimus then faced a struggle for the high priesthood, 22 in which, however, all the troublers of their people rallied to him, overran the land of Judah, and inflicted a great defeat upon Israel. 23 Judas saw all the harm that Alcimus and his supporters had done to Israelites, far worse than anything the gentiles were doing. 24 Accordingly, he went around the entire territory of Judaea, punishing the turncoats so that they shrank from going out into the countryside. 25 When Alcimus saw the growing strength of Judas and his men, knowing that he could not cope with them, he went again to the king and accused them of atrocities.

26 Thereupon the king sent Nicanor, one of his high-ranking officers, a hater and a foe of Israel, with orders to exterminate our people. 27 Nicanor entered Jerusalem with a large force and sent a message to Judas and his brothers, treacherously couched in peaceful terms: 28 "Let there be no strife between us. I propose to come with a few men for a peaceful meeting with you." 29 When he came to Judas, though the two men exchanged peaceful greetings, the enemy were making ready to kidnap Judas. 30 Judas, however, got wind of the fact that Nicanor's visit was a treacherous plot against him. Wary of Nicanor, he refused to have any further meetings with him. 31 Nicanor perceived that his plot had been detected; accordingly, he marched out to meet Judas in battle near Chapharsalama. 32 There about five hundred of Nicanor's men fell, and his army fled to the City of David.

33 Some time thereafter, Nicanor went up to Mount Zion. Some priests came out of the sanctuary along with some elders of the people to greet him peacefully and show him the burnt offering which was being sacrificed on behalf of the king. 34 He, however, mocked them, laughing in their faces and rendering them unclean with his spit. Presumptuously he spoke, 35 angrily swearing that "Unless

Judas and his army are delivered over into my hands immediately, upon my victorious return I shall burn this temple." Then he went out, in a hot rage.

36 Thereupon, the priests went in and stood before the altar and the nave. Weeping, they said, 37 "You have chosen this house to bear Your name, to be a house of prayer and entreaty for Your people. 38 Take vengeance upon this man and upon his army, and make them fall by the sword. Remember their blasphemies, and let none of them survive."

39 Nicanor marched out from Jerusalem and encamped at Beth-Horon, where he was joined by a force from Syria. 40 Judas encamped at Adasa with three thousand men. There Judas prayed, 41 "Long ago when a king's emissaries blasphemed, Your angel went forth and slew one hundred eighty-five thousand of the king's men. 42 In the same manner crush this army before us today. Let all other men know that Nicanor has blasphemed against Your sanctuary. Pass judgment on him in accordance with his wickedness."

43 The armies joined battle on the thirteenth of the month Adar, and the army of Nicanor was defeated, he himself being the first to fall in battle. 44 When Nicanor's army saw that he had fallen, they threw away their arms and fled. 45 Judas and his men pursued them as far as the approaches of Gazera, one day's journey from Adasa, and sounded the signal trumpets in the enemy's rear. 46 In response to the signal, men came out of all the neighboring villages of Judaea and struck all along the flanks of the enemy and then wheeled about to meet Judas and his men, so that the enemy all fell by the sword; not even one of them was left. 47 Taking the spoils and the booty, the victors cut off the head of Nicanor and his right hand, which he had so presumptuously raised in oath, and brought and raised them where they could be viewed from Jerusalem. 48 The people were overjoyed, and observed the day as a day of great rejoicing. 49 They decreed that the day, the thirteenth of Adar, should be observed annually. 50 There followed a brief period of peace for the land of Judah.

NOTES

7:1–50. Jason of Cyrene's parallel account to ch. 7 is at II 14–15.

1–11. See NOTE on 6:55–63.

1. Victory over Philip in 162 B.C.E. did not end the troubles of Antiochus V and his guardian Lysias. A Roman embassy led by Gnaeus Octavius came to enforce full compliance with the peace of Apameia, imposed in 188 after the Romans had crushingly defeated the Seleucid empire (Polybius xxi 42 Paton [43 Buettner-Wobst]; Livy xxxviii 38). In particular, the warships and elephants were to be destroyed. So offended were the subjects of the empire at the sight of the destruction that a certain Leptines murdered Octavius, and there were calls to put the rest of the Roman ambassadors to death. When the news reached Rome, a rival to Lysias and Antiochus V thought that their embarrassment might be his opportunity. Demetrius had been a hostage in Rome since 176 or early 175 B.C.E.; see NOTE on 1:10. The historian Polybius was a close friend of Demetrius and tells how Demetrius fruitlessly pleaded with the Senate to release him and recognize him as the legitimate heir to the Seleucid empire. The Romans, however, preferred that the Seleucid empire be under the weak regime of Lysias and Antiochus V rather than in the hands of the vigorous Demetrius. Polybius describes in detail Demetrius' dramatic escape from Rome. See Polybius xxxi 2, 11–15; Appian *Syriakê* 46–47.

In the year 151. In the autumn of 162 B.C.E.; see Bickerman, PW, XIV 783. Antiochus V still appears as king in a Babylonian cuneiform document dated October 17, 162 B.C.E.; see Aymard, *Historia* 2 (1953–54), 62. However, Demetrius seized power by force and was still in Antioch in the autumn of 161 (Polybius xxxi 33; Hans Volkmann, "Demetrios I. und Alexander I. von Syrien," *Klio* 19 [1925], 393). There was nothing to compel the Seleucid authorities in Babylon to recognize him; indeed, the rebel satrap of Media, Timarchus, was to seize control of the area until he was crushed by Demetrius in the winter of 161/0 (Volkmann, ibid.). To accommodate all the events between Demetrius' accession and the day of Nicanor, March 8, 161 (see NOTE on 7:43), the accession has to be set very early, surely within the first month of 151 Sel. Mac. (September 29–October 28, 162 B.C.E.).

one of the coastal cities. Tripolis (II 14:1; J. *AJ* xii 10.1.389), a Phoenician city important enough to have received the privilege of coinage from Antiochus IV (see Mørkholm, pp. 126–38). See Map 12, p. 538.

2. *the Seleucid capital.* Antioch, 283 kilometers from Tripolis. See Map 12; our author expresses "Seleucid capital" by "house of the kingdom of his fathers" (*byt mlkwt 'btyw*).

3. As presented by our author, Demetrius avoided the odium of asking directly for the murder of his nephew and of Lysias.

4. *Demetrius . . . king.* The Hebrew idiom is that at I Kings 2:12. Early in his reign Demetrius decreed that the Jews of Judaea were to be governed by the Torah; see NOTE on 10:36–37.

5. For our author, all opponents of the Hasmonaeans are sinful and wicked. Other pious observers would not have agreed. See Introduction, pp. 64–66. On Alcimus and his associates, see below, on vss. 16–17. The Greek infinitive *hierateuein* can mean either "to be high priest" or "to become high priest." Alcimus had already been appointed high priest by Antiochus V; see NOTE on 6:63. The Hasmonaeans, however, probably regarded the appointment as invalid. In any case Alcimus would have had to seek confirmation as high priest from the new king; see Introduction, pp. 75–76, and in AB vol. 41A NOTE on II 14:3–4.

6–7. For our author, Jews bring charges against their own people and seek the punishment of their own people if they accuse the Hasmonaean brothers and seek the punishment of Judas and his men and all their abetters. The word "friends" here means "all who are friendly to the Seleucid empire," not "holders of the rank of Friend of the King."

We are not told what arrangements, if any, were made by the regime of Lysias and Antiochus V to protect "Antiochene" Jews and others whom the Hasmonaeans and the Pietists viewed as apostates. The Hasmonaeans and the Pietists certainly viewed the full restoration of Jewish law in the king's letter (II 11:25) as permitting them to destroy the apostates; see Introduction, pp. 121–23.

6. *has driven us.* Literally, "has dispersed us." The Hebrew idiom is that at Ezek 46:18.

8–20. Our author takes pains to give the details of Bacchides' expedition, for thus he shows how the Pietists became inept victims whenever they opposed the Hasmonaeans. Cf. Kolbe, *Beiträge*, pp. 146–47, and Geiger, *Urschrift*, pp. 215–16. Jason of Cyrene, on the contrary, tries to portray the Pietists as steadfast allies of Judas. See Introduction, p. 88, and NOTE on II 14:6.

8. The Hebrew or Aramaic terminology underlying the Greek of Bacchides' title, "governor of the Trans-Euphrates province," is unambiguous, though Josephus (*AJ* xii 10.2.393) misunderstood it. Our author gives the huge province the name it had under the Persian empire (Ezra 4:10–11, 17, 20, 5:3, 6, 6:13, etc.). The Ptolemies called the province "Syria and Phoenicia," and the Seleucids called it "Coele-Syria and Phoenicia" (Bengtson, *Strategie*, II, 159–62). The use of the old name suggests that Phoenicia was still attached to Coele-Syria at this time; see NOTES on 1:4, *nations,* and on 3:13 and on 11:59–62.

As Shalit has shown (*Scripta Hierosolymitana*, I, 64–73, middle), "Coele-Syria" originally meant the whole area between the Euphrates and the Mediterranean, from the Taurus mountains (now in Turkey) to the border of Egypt. After the Seleucids founded the privileged area of Greek cities (the *Seleukis*) in northern Syria, northern Syria was no longer reckoned as a part of Coele-Syria.

The hatred of the Syrians and the Phoenicians for each other was proverbial (see E. L. von Leutsch, *Corpus Paroemiographorum Graecorum*, II [Hildesheim: Olms, 1958], 646) and may account for the dual names "Syria and Phoenicia" and "Coele-Syria and Phoenicia," long before Phoenicia was separated from the province. The existence of Hegemonides' province (II 13:24) may have been limited to the reign of Antiochus V, and in any case it probably did not subtract Judaea from the province of Coele-Syria; see ad loc. In view of these facts there is no foundation for Bengtson's denial that Bacchides was governor of Coele-Syria and for Bengtson's suggestion that Bacchides' province was the Seleukis (*Strategie,* II, 181–85).

Demetrius I was to busy himself subduing the rebel satrap of Babylonia down into the winter of 161/0; see Volkmann, *Klio* 19 (1925), 392–94. Only to a high and loyal official could Demetrius entrust the difficult problem of pacifying turbulent Judaea, strategically located near the hostile Ptolemaic border. Bacchides did indeed enjoy wide discretionary powers, to punish all the feuding factions among the Jews (vss. 16, 19; ch. 9) and even to make peace with Jonathan without consulting Demetrius (9:70–72).

Josephus (*AJ* xii 10.2.393) adds that Bacchides had held the title "Friend of the King" under Antiochus IV, a fact which may be true and derived from a reliable source. Demetrius, viewed with hostility by Rome, needed the support of all the able and influential men who would come over to him, and the unpopular regime of Lysias and Antiochus V must have driven many to do so; see Polybius xxxi 8.6 and 12.4.

9. Again our author equates taking vengeance on Judas and his men with taking vengeance on all Israel.

10. Again, the march is not simply "to Judaea" but "against the land of Judah. A message couched in peaceful terms began with the greeting "peace"; see Appendix IV, p. 551.

12. In this verse our author may be mocking the Pietist scholars for regarding Zeph 1 – 2:3 as a prophesy for their own time; the scholars could have read the passage as follows:

The day of wrath has come (Zeph 1:2–3) with the persecutions. The idol worshipers and the Hellenizers and the compromisers have been slain by the Hasmonaeans (vss. 4–6, 8–9), so that the surviving sinners complain loudly and bitterly (vss. 10–11), and those who disbelieved in God's avenging power are defenseless in the face of wrath (vss. 12–13). Now the final day of wrath is at hand (vss. 7, 14–16) in which human blood and flesh will be poured out in abundance (vs. 17) and wealth will be no protection (vs. 18). Therefore "the nation without shame," or, as the Greek translation has it, "the nation without learning" (*apaideuton*) is warned to "assemble" (Greek *synachthête*) before the day of God's wrath and to "seek justice" and to "seek humility" in the hope of being protected on the day of wrath (Zeph 2:1–3).

In our verse we have the "assembling" (*episynêchthêsan*). There is probably irony in the replacement of the "nation without learning" by "men learned in the Torah" (*grammateôn*): though learned in the Torah, they do not learn from experience to distrust Seleucid officials and to follow the Hasmonaeans. The fools believe that Jews to be safe from the coming day of wrath must now "seek humility" and "seek justice" by submitting to Seleucid rule and accepting the high priest appointed by the king. Indeed, they misread the prophesy: their own blood and flesh was to be poured out (below, vs. 17).

The word for "men learned in the Torah" is "scribes," a usage familiar from the New Testament, from Ezra 7:6, 11–12, from II 6:18, as well as from Jewish literature.

13. Every group of pious Jews had "men learned in the Torah," and more than one group may have been victimized by Alcimus and Bacchides. Our author stresses that the sect of Pietists mentioned in 2:29–38, 42, took the lead in being gullible. The Hebrew expression for "took the lead" was probably the one at I Chron 4:42–43 and II Chron 20:27. These Pietists are said to have been "seeking peace"; perhaps they took Ps 34:15 as their text.

14. After their bitter experiences with the Hellenizing high priest Menelaus (II 4:25–50, 5:15, 23), how could the Pietists have put such trust in the mere fact of priestly descent? Some pious Jews did deny that Menelaus was of priestly stock (Test Moses v 4). However, Menelaus, brother of Simon of the clan of Bilgah, probably was of legitimate priestly stock; see NOTE on II 3:4. Our author may have known of Pietists who conceded the fact of Menelaus' priestly descent. If so, we must change the translation of our verse. Literally, the Greek has the Pietists saying, "A man a priest of the stock of Aaron" (*Anthrôpos hiereus ek tou spermatos Aarôn;* Hebrew *îš kōhēn mizzera‘ ahărôn*). In the Hebrew of the time "lord priest" or "lordly priest" appears to have been precisely *îš kōhēn;* cf. the form of address, "my lord high priest" (*îšî kōhēn gādōl*) at M. *Yoma* 1, 4:1; *Tamid* 6:3; *Parah* 3:8. Cf. NOTE on 5:63. Priestly descent was indelible, but by his base conduct Menelaus could have forfeited his right to be called "lordly" by Pietists; only a "lordly priest" like Alcimus deserved trust. If so, our verse should be translated "A lordly priest of the stock of Aaron. . . ."

15. See above, on vs. 10.

16–17. Our verses say, with emphasis, that Alcimus *himself wrote* Ps 79:2–3. Our author loses no love over Alcimus and would not credit him with writing words revered by the pious unless Alcimus was in fact the author of the verses. The verses could hardly have been written in isolation; Alcimus must have written them in a context. Either the words in Psalm 79 are borrowed from Alcimus, or Alcimus borrowed them from Psalm 79, or Alcimus himself wrote Psalm 79. As we shall see, the content of Psalm 79 reflects events of 169 or 167, so that probably the author of Psalm 79 did not merely borrow words from Alcimus; he was Alcimus. Indeed, ancient commentators already regarded Psalm 79 as a prophesy of Antiochus' persecution (see Eusebius *Demostratio evangelica* x 1.12; Athanasius *Expositio in Psalmum* LXXVIII, vol. XXVII, col. 357 Migne); and modern scholars have often suggested that the psalm was written then (see Eissfeldt, p. 450). Since the recognition that Alcimus wrote Psalm 79 leads to much interesting information about the man, this is the place for presenting the available details on him. First, however, we must establish our interpretation of vss. 16 and 17.

Already ancient scribes recognized that vs. 17 is a free quotation of Ps 79: 2–3, for La[G] ascribes vs. 17 to Asaph, the supposed author of Psalm 79, as does Eusebius *Demonstratio evangelica* x 1.12. Our vs. 17 strangely modifies Ps 79:2–3. I believe that both our author and the translator worked from memory, with the influence of Zeph 1:17 in their minds; see above, on vs. 12. Zeph 1:17, like our vs. 17, speaks both of flesh and of blood as being "poured" and lacks the reference to the beasts of the field found in Ps 79:2. Moreover, the original Greek of our vs. 17, unlike the Greek of Ps 79:2, used the word *kreas* for "bodies" or "flesh" (Hebrew *bāśār*). *Kreas* normally means "meat," and occurs only once in the Greek Psalter, with that meaning, at Ps 50 (Greek 49):13. In the sense of "flesh," as here, it is used in the Greek Bible only where synonyms of the Hebrew *bāśār* have preempted the normal Greek word *sarx*. At Zeph 1:17 the Hebrew word *leḥummām* ("their flesh") is rendered by *sarx*, so that with Zeph 1:17 in his mind the translator rendered "flesh" (*bāśār*) at Ps 79:2 by *kreas*. Hence, our author and the translator certainly did think they were quoting Ps 79:2–3.

In fixing the text of the end of vs. 16, modern editors have been correct in taking as most reliable the unidiomatic original text of S, *ton logon hon egrapsen auton*, literally, "the verse which he wrote it." According to Rahlfs, the reading is exhibited by at least one minuscule as well. This reading, however, is impossible Greek unless it is Greek distorted by a translator's intent to be literal. Moreover, this Greek would reflect impossible Hebrew, and our author was a good Hebraist. Idiomatic Hebrew would have had either "in accordance with the verse which he wrote" (*kaddābār ăšer kātab;* cf. Josh 8:32 and II Kings 17:37) or "as is written" (*kakkātūb;* cf. Josh 8:31 and II Kings 14:6). There is no way in which the original reading of S could have arisen unless the Greek translator wrote the text which we have taken as the basis for our translation, *hon egrapsen autos*, reflecting an idiomatic Hebrew original *ăšer hū kātab* (cf. I Sam 22:18). Christian scribes, horrified at the suggestion that someone other than David or Asaph wrote Psalm 79, labored mightily to correct or obscure the text. The original reading of S already has changed the nominative emphatic pronoun *autos* ("himself") to the accusative. Still close to the original are the idiomatic readings of the next most reliable witnesses. V and La^L have "the verse which he wrote" (*ton logon hon egrapsen*) and A and q have "the words which he wrote" (*tous logous hous egrapsen*). The scribes may have felt that our author meant to say that Alcimus quoted Psalm 79 in writing, but the most natural interpretation even of their texts is that Alcimus was the author of the verse. Other scribes were quick to supply "the prophet" or "David" or "Asaph" as the subject of "wrote." Perhaps before their eyes still stood the reading "he himself," and they interpreted it much as a pious Epicurean would take "he himself" to refer to Epicurus.

Alcimus, then, is the author of Psalm 79. What else is known of him?

Josephus (*AJ* xii 9.7.385; xx 10.3.235) reports that Alcimus' Hebrew name was Iakim (variant: Ioakim); the note of the same fact above at vs. 5 in Lucianic manuscripts is probably derived from Josephus. "Jakim" and "Joakim" (as they are usually spelled in English) occur as names of priests in the Hebrew Bible (I Chron 24:12; Neh 12:10, 12, 26; cf. Judith 6:6), as does the equivalent "Eliakim" (Neh 12:41; Greek ms. A at I Chron 24:12), from which Alcimus derived his Greek name (*Alkimos;* literal meaning: "valiant").

If Alcimus wrote Psalm 79, clearly the background was Antiochus IV's sack of Jerusalem in 169 B.C.E. and perhaps also the Mysarch's expedition in 167; the writer complains that the land of Israel has been invaded and the temple defiled and Jerusalem laid in ruins and pious Jews massacred (vss. 1–2, 7), but nothing is said of the imposed cult. Alcimus is a devout Jew. He calls the slain victims *ḥăsīdīm* ("Pietists"); is he using the word as a proper or as a common noun (see Introduction, pp. 5–6)? Alcimus feels deeply hurt as the neighboring nations mock Israel and Israel's God (vss. 3, 10, 12), though he is convinced that Israel suffers because God is angry over Israel's sin (vss. 5, 8, 9). Passionately he borrows the words of Jer 10:25 to call upon God to take pity on Israel and pour His wrath instead upon the wicked gentile kingdoms and nations (vss. 6–7, 12). Though Alcimus feels himself a prisoner and perhaps literally is one (vs. 11), he remains convinced that God's election of Israel is permanent (vs. 13). Nowhere does he call for Jewish resistance. He expects prayer and God's pity and forgiving grace to rouse God Himself to act "for the sake of His Name" (vss. 8–12).

Psalms 73–83 are all ascribed to Asaph, and scholars have often suggested that at least Psalms 74, 79, and 83 date from our period; see Eissfeldt, pp. 450–51. In the absence of direct testimony such as we have for Psalm 79, it is impossible to be certain, but Alcimus may well have written Psalms 73, 74, 82, and 83. The mysterious divine beings reproved in Psalm 82 could be the evil angelic shepherds of Enoch lxxxix 59 – xc 25. All these Psalms fit Alcimus' background and contain no call for human action and express rather faith that ultimately God will act against the wicked. If this is Alcimus' point of view, he resembles the authors of Daniel and the Testament of Moses and the martyrs of I 2:29–38; see Introduction, pp. 5, 39–40, 42–44.

The evidence from the Psalms for associating Alcimus with Pietist groups suggests that there is some truth behind the legend of a certain Yaqim preserved at *Bereshit Rabbah* 65:26, pp. 741–44 Theodor-Albeck; at *Midrash Haggadol* to Gen 27:27, pp. 476–77 Margulies; at *Midrash Tehillim* to Ps 11:7; and at *Yalqut Makhiri* to Ps 11, par. 18. The texts report that Yaqim (or Yoyaqim, according to the Adler Yemenite manuscript of *Bereshit Rabbah* and to *Yalqut Makhiri*) of Ṣerodot (Bereshit Rabbah *ed. princeps* and *ed. Venice* 5305; manuscript commentary to *Bereshit Rabbah*) or Ṣeredah (one manuscript of *Midrash Haggadol*) or Ṣerorot was the stepson (*Midrash Tehillim*) or nephew of Yosi son of Yoʻezer of Ṣeredah. The legend goes on to say that this Yaqim was riding his horse while Yosi son of Yoʻezer was walking ahead of the cross on his way to be crucified. Yaqim said to him, "Look at the horse my master has given me to ride, and look at the horse your Master has given you to ride!" Yosi replied, "If thus He rewards those who anger Him, how much more will He reward those who do His will!" Yaqim replied, "Did any man do His will more than you?" Yosi answered, "If thus He treats those who do His will, how much worse will He treat those who anger Him!" Yosi's retort affected Yaqim like the venom of a snake, so that Yaqim went and inflicted upon himself all four modes of capital punishment: stoning, burning, the sword, and strangling. How did he do it? He procured a beam, fixed it vertically in the ground, tied a rope to it, built a stone wall around it, and built a fire in front of it, in the midst of which he set up a sword. He hanged himself from the beam, the rope broke as he was being strangled, he fell upon the sword, and the wall collapsed over him as he was being burned.

The legend goes on to report that Yosi son of Yoʻezer heard of Yaqim's deed, fainted or fell asleep, and in a trance saw Yaqim's bier flying through the air. Yosi interpreted the vision to mean that Yaqim had entered Paradise.

Modern Jewish scholars long ago identified Yaqim of the legend with Alcimus (see Geiger, *Urschrift*, p. 64). They are probably correct. Yosi (Joseph) son of Yo'ezer of Şeredah was an early head of the Pharisaic order, one of the main links in the Pharisaic chain of tradition (*M. Abot* 1:4; *Ḥagigah* 2:2); chronologically he could have been a contemporary of Alcimus. He was a priest (*M. Ḥagigah* 2:7). Teachings and enactments of his may have been intended to help Jews cope with Antiochus IV's persecutions (*M. Abot* 1:4; '*Eduyot* 8:4; see B.-Z. Lurie, *Megillath Ta'anith*, pp. 41–42 [in Hebrew]). Even if Yaqim was only the nephew, not the stepson, of Yosi, he could well have been strongly influenced by the sage. Yaqim's town is given as Şerodot or Şerorot or Şeredah; even the first two may be variant names or errors for Şeredah or the name of a town close by; see Bustanay 'Oded, "*Şeredah, Şere-rah, Şaretan*," Enc. Bib., VI (1971), 765–68.

Not even Alcimus' enemies accused him of violating a specific Jewish law. Our author can name as a violation only Alcimus' conduct in a disputed matter of temple architecture (I 9:54). The suggestion in some texts of the legend, that Yaqim was riding his horse *on the Sabbath,* is an interpolation; see Theodor's commentary to *Bereshit Rabbah*, p. 742, line 6. On Jason of Cyrene's view of Alcimus, see NOTE on II 14:3. The Psalms, too, attest his fervent piety. Both our author and Jason hold against Alcimus his collaboration with the Seleucids against Judas. On our interpretation of II 14:3, even for Jason such collaboration was a "defilement" from the time Antiochus V appointed Alcimus high priest. For our author, as soon as the regime of Lysias and Antiochus V had revealed its perfidy (I 6:62), no loyal Jew could collaborate with it. If Alcimus during 167–162 B.C.E. held to the non-violence of the Pietist martyrs, the Seleucid government would indeed have viewed him as an ideal high priest to replace Menelaus, and as a man who could turn the turbulent Jews back into loyal subjects.

Josephus notes that Alcimus was not of the Oniad family, which had long held the high priesthood, and that on seeing the appointment of an outsider, Onias IV, the surviving Oniad, left Judaea and took service as a soldier in Ptolemaic Egypt (*AJ* xii 9.7.387–88; xx 10.3.235–36). If Onias was old enough to decide to leave and to take service, the Seleucid authorities did not pass over him because he was too young; see J. *AJ* xv 3.3.51–56, TB *Ḥullin* 24a-b and *Sifra Emor* 3:1 to Lev 21:17. J. *AJ* xii 5.1.237 and 9.7.387 should not be translated so as to mean that Onias IV was an infant when his father died in 170, but only that he was a child who had not reached puberty.

Perhaps Onias IV was inacceptable to the Seleucid authorities because he had already shown militant anti-Seleucid tendencies by supporting the Hasmonaeans or because he had exhibited the pro-Ptolemaic tendencies of his father Onias III, his uncle Jason, and his kinsman Hyrcanus the Tobiad; see Introduction, pp. 57–59, 95. Perhaps he was inacceptable to Pietists on theological grounds: he may have been too Hellenized or, as a proto-Sadducee he may have disbelieved in the apocalyptic prophesies and in other Pietist doctrines; see Introduction, ibid., and esp. Part III, n. 17, and pp. 70–71. If inacceptable to the Pietists, Onias would have been useless to the Seleucids for pacifying Judaea. The Hasmonaeans from the time of the battle of Beth-Zechariah long refused to risk pitched battles with the Seleucid authorities, limiting themselves to guerrilla warfare. Such tactics may have appeared cowardly to Onias IV, who probably expected that through the merit of his family yet another miraculous victory might win him the high priesthood. Hence, during this period Onias IV could have broken also with the Hasmonaean party.

The legend about Yosi and Yaqim can well reflect a break between them over collaboration with the Seleucid king. There was a real theological issue: Were Antiochus V and Demetrius I really to be viewed as kings placed over the chosen people by God? Only a king so placed by God could appoint a legitimate high priest. See Introduction, pp. 5–6, 75–76. On the one hand, the Hasmonaean victories might be taken as proof that the period of Israel's subjugation to foreign kingdoms was over; then Antiochus V and Demetrius I and their appointee Alcimus had no legitimacy over the Jews. Such appears to have been the view of the Hasmonaean party. Pietists, however, who believed in the apocalyptic prophecies, on noting how they were still unfulfilled would tend to hold that Demetrius I was king over Israel by the will of God, though some of them may have refused to recognize the regime of the child king Antiochus V, son of the monstrous persecutor. We do not know how Yosi viewed the militant Hasmonaean resistance to Antiochus IV. He may well have opposed Alcimus' collaboration with Antiochus V. If Alcimus faced the vigorous opposition even of Yosi, a member of his own family, we can understand why he later seized the opportunity to have Pietist leaders whom he viewed as troublemakers executed. The words of the legend in its various versions nowhere state flatly that Yosi was killed. He may have survived crucifixion or he may have been released (that may be the meaning of the word *'tnḥ* which comes immediately before the word "he fainted" in *Midrash Haggadol*); he is reported alive under a Hasmonaean ruler (TB *Baba batra* 133b).

Whereas Jason of Cyrene in II 14 says nothing of the execution of sages and Pietists, Josephus, as a partisan both of the Hasmonaeans and of the Pietist Pharisees (see Introduction, pp. 55–56) cannot solve his problems by mere silence. In *AJ* xii 10.1–2.391–96 he, like Jason, says nothing of a split between the Hasmonaeans and the Pietists. He calls the dupes not "Pietists" or "men learned in the Torah" but only "some of the people." He says nothing of the victims' trust in Alcimus as "a priest of the stock of Aaron" and leaves Alcimus innocent of the executions, ascribing them entirely to Bacchides. For Josephus, only after Bacchides' return to Antioch does Alcimus become thoroughly wicked, as the man supported by apostates and traitors, dependent on royal force, actively hunting down members of the Hasmonaean party (*AJ* xii 10.2–3.297–401).

On the accounts of Alcimus' death and on the possible origin of the legend of Yosi and Yaqim, see NOTE on I 9:55–56.

19. Bacchides' orders were to observe and take measures against the troublemakers not only in the neighborhood of Jerusalem, but also in all of Judaea (vss. 7, 9). Having dealt with the troublesome Pietists of Jerusalem, Bacchides moved southward to the vicinity of the border with Idumaea. His base, Beth-Zaith, lay about six kilometers north of Beth-Zur on the road to Jerusalem (Abel, p. 135; the reading of some manuscripts of J. *AJ* xii 10.2.397, *Bêrzêthô*, is incorrect; see A. Schlatter, "Einige Ergebnisse aus NIESE's Ausgebe des Josephus," ZDPV 19 [1896], 225). The location of Beth-Zaith can thus be estimated from Map 10, p. 535.

There Bacchides found it necessary to deal with several troublesome factions. Apostates probably moved to this region, the more easily to flee to Idumaea or Beth-Zur (see 6:50, 10:14) when pressed by the zeal of pious Jews. There must also have been pious Jews, both adherents of the Hasmonaeans and opponents of them. Since the persecution was long since over, pious Jews could again consider the Seleucid king as ruler over them by the will of God. Collaboration with the Seleucids no longer implied apostasy, but if the period of the subjugation of Israel to foreign rule was over (see NOTE on vss. 16–17), such collaboration was obedience to an illegitimate regime. Hence, our author from now on speaks of Jews who collaborate with Demetrius I as "deserters" or "turncoats" (see also vs. 24 below and 9:24), as opposed to genuine members of the Jewish people. All these Jewish factions were ready to fight one another.

Bacchides' mission was to place Alcimus in power over a pacified Judaea; troublemakers had to be removed, of whatever faction. As in Jerusalem, Bacchides executed some pious Jews, opponents of the regime or of Alcimus. Though apostate Jews had to favor the regime, their only possible protector, they might balk at being made subject to the pious Alcimus. For the sake of internal harmony a Seleucid regime had sacrificed Menelaus (II 13:3–8), and now Bacchides did not hesitate to execute "deserters," whether pious or apostate. Some ancient scribes could not understand how a Seleucid official could so treat "deserters" to the Seleucid side and in their versions wrongly altered the text to read "deserters from his side."

The disposal of the bodies of the slain into the cistern deprived them of proper burial; cf. Jer 41 (Greek 48):7. There are ancient cisterns or traces of them in the vicinity of Beth-Zaith.

21–22. Bacchides' severe measures could not deter Alcimus' opponents from rejecting him as high priest. As always, pious believers, confident that their cause was God's cause, refused to abandon the struggle. Now dependent on the Seleucid regime, Alcimus may even have accepted the support of apostates, despite his piety, but we cannot infer that fact from our author's words, for our author was ready to call any Jewish opponent of the Hasmonaeans a "troubler of his people." With Seleucid backing and a considerable base of support among even pious Jews, Alcimus and his partisans at first prevailed throughout Judaea; undoubtedly they slew many followers of Judas (cf. J. AJ xii 10.3.399).

23. Our author's comparison between the deeds of Alcimus' party and those of the Seleucid authorities applies only to the reign of Demetrius I, not to the atrocious persecutions under Antiochus IV; hence I supply the verb form "were doing" rather than "had done."

24. Too weak to face Alcimus' force in open battle, Judas still had enough support in the countryside to conduct guerrilla warfare against the "turncoats," the partisans of the high priest, so that they no longer dared to leave Jerusalem and the garrisoned fortified towns.

25. To suppress guerrilla warfare in difficult terrain where the population is sympathetic to the rebels requires a force many times larger than the rebel force. See NOTE on II 14:5–10.

26. On Nicanor, see NOTES on I 3:38, and on II 14:12. Our author's propaganda here becomes somewhat clumsy. Even his own subsequent account does

not show Nicanor to be an extreme hater of Jews. If Demetrius I indeed commanded him to "wipe out" the Jewish people, Nicanor, who had a large force, carried out his commission with incredible laxity. Our author "protests too much," in order to hide the fact, revealed to us by Jason of Cyrene, that Judas himself for a time had friendly relations with Nicanor (II 14:18–28).

27–30. Our author does not say that Nicanor faced opposition in his march to Jerusalem. According to Jason of Cyrene, the Jews were dismayed at Nicanor's advance and prayed to God for help, and "the commander" (i.e. Judas) ordered a force to go against Nicanor. Simon, Judas' brother, was in command in the battle which took place at "Dessa" or "Dessau." Nicanor's force won, but Nicanor was so impressed by the Jews' valor that he sent emissaries to offer peace to Judas and the Jews, thus recognizing Judas' party as representatives of the nation. Negotiations led to peace and friendship between Nicanor and Judas. Judas even married and "enjoyed life," until Alcimus' protests brought Demetrius I to order Nicanor to arrest Judas and bring him to Antioch. Only at that point did Nicanor's treacherous intentions lead Judas to refuse to come near him (II 14:15–30; see commentary, ad loc.).

In this case, our author's account is the one strongly colored by bias. Our author never concedes the legitimacy of Demetrius I's rule over the Jews. He condemns the Pietists who trusted Demetrius' official, Bacchides, and passes over in silence Judas' collaboration with Demetrius' official, Nicanor. Our author also has Judas and Simon as his heroes and prefers to pass over their defeats in silence. Jason of Cyrene, too, was reluctant to mention defeats of Judas. On the other hand, he loathed Simon and had no reason to invent a story of how his hero Judas collaborated with Alcimus' protector Nicanor. We may guess that Jason narrated the battle of Dessa only because he could use the fact of Simon's defeat and moral victory to expose the falsity of the account here; see Introduction, pp. 78–84, Jason can tell of the battle the more easily since Simon was acting under Judas' orders, and the valor was not so much Simon's as that of "Judas' men" (II 14:18). Hence, we may accept Jason's account: the battle of Dessa, the negotiations, and the peace did take place, and at least several weeks elapsed before Judas broke with Nicanor.

The story of the interlude of peace is important in the history of the persecutor Nicanor and probably is derived from DMP; see Introduction, pp. 92–97, 103.

Josephus in his paraphrase (AJ xii 10.4.402–5) slightly amplifies our author's account in a way which displays more clearly the treachery of Nicanor. In so doing, Josephus need not have had any other source and may have intended to refute Jason's narrative.

27–29. On "peaceful terms" and "peaceful greetings," see NOTE on vs. 10.

30. On breaking with Nicanor and fleeing to the countryside, Judas was once again a guerrilla chieftain. He probably had a wide base of sympathizers, but he was in no way commander of a national army. For his climactic battle with Nicanor Judas could muster only three thousand men (vs. 40), in contrast to the ten thousand he had when he could count on the support of all pious Jews against the persecuting regime (4:29).

31–32. In accordance with the king's orders to end the guerrilla warfare in Judaea, Nicanor tried to bring the rebels to battle and defeat them. Despite his dismissal of the irregular forces which had joined him (II 14:14, 23), Nicanor probably had an army large enough to march anywhere in the area (see vss. 27 and 39), though Judas' guerrilla bands might try their luck with ambushes. One would expect Judas to have withdrawn to what appears to have been his favorite territory for guerrilla warfare, the mountains of northern Judaea and southern Samaria, at the edge of which lay his home village of Modeïn (see NOTE on 2:28). Indeed, during this period Judas was in the vicinity of Samaria when he somehow escaped a trap set for him by Nicanor (II 15:1–5). Our author reports that Nicanor first marched out to meet Judas in battle near Chapharsalama ("Village of Salama").

We know of more than one village by such a name. An early tradition quoted at TP 'Abodah zarah 5:4, p. 44d, and at TB 'Abodah zarah 31a mentions a gentile village Kᵉpar-šālēm near the Samaritan community of 'Ēyn Kūšīt (location unknown). Here might be a "Capharsalama" within Judas' favorite territory. If, however, it is the same as the Kafar Sallām and Cavar Salim mentioned by medieval writers (see Guy Le Strange, Palestine under the Moslems [London: Palestine Exploration Fund, 1890], pp. 471–72), it is only barely possible as the battle site, for it is said to have been on the main road through the plain from Ramlah to Caesarea, equidistant from Nablus, Ramlah, and Caesarea. That would be south of Narbatta on Map 8 and between twenty and thirty kilometers north of Modeïn. Though Judas there would have been no farther north than he would have been at the city of Samaria (cf. II 15:1), he would have been in the flatland, not in the mountains. Would he have risked battle on such terrain? He would, if circumstances warranted, just as he once ventured to engage a superior force at Ammaus (I 3:39–40, 57, 4:1–21). Abel ("Topographie des campagnes machabéennes," RB 33 [1924], 375) objects that if the battle site had been in or near the flatland, the repulsed troops would have fled to the friendly towns of the coastal plain, not to the "City of David" (i.e. the Akra in Jerusalem; see NOTE on 1:33–40). But the "flight" may be simply our author's interpretation of what was really an orderly retreat. Nicanor may have broken off the costly engagement with the intention of catching Judas some other time in circumstances more favorable to the Seleucid force. Indeed, Nicanor was stratēgos of Judaea (II 14:12) and probably had his seat at Jerusalem; far from shutting himself up as a fugitive in the citadel, he moved freely around in Jerusalem and Judaea after his return (I 7:33 and 39). Hence, Abel's objection is not decisive against this possible location of the battle site.

Abel (p. 139) prefers another possibility. He places Capharsalama about ten kilometers northwest of Jerusalem, just off the road to Beth-Horon, where Eusebius (Onomastikon, p. 153 Klostermann) speaks of a village Salem and a ruined site Khirbet Selma still exists. See Map 11, p. 535. With such an identification, we must suppose that Judas felt secure enough to come so close to Nicanor's superior force in Jerusalem, but then it is difficult to understand how Nicanor later managed to move unopposed from Jerusalem to Beth-Horon, where he was joined by reinforcements (vs. 39). Surely Judas, if he felt strong enough to come near Jerusalem along the very same road, would have tried to engage Nicanor before Nicanor could increase his forces. More plausible is Abel's earlier suggestion (RB 33 [1924], 376), the ruined village Khirbet Erhā or the adjacent ruined monastery Khirbet Deir Sellām, north-northeast of Jerusalem. See Map 11. Though also about ten kilometers from Jerusalem, they are well off the main road. Thus there are arguments against all the known possible identifications of Capharsalama; any or none may have been the battle site.

The text here may be defective, since our author after announcing that one army marched out to meet another always says explicitly that the battle took place and tells which side was victorious; elsewhere, he never leaves those facts to be inferred, as here, from the remarks on the aftermath of the battle. See 3:11, 16 with 23–24; 5:39 with 43–44, 59–60; 9:11–18; 10:2; 16:5–9. A complete text may have lain before Josephus. However, all extant manuscripts of *AJ* xii 10.4.405, as well as Niese's edition, have nonsense, for they say that Nicanor was victorious in the battle and forced *Judas* to flee to the (Seleucid-occupied!) Akra of Jerusalem. Josephus' own secretary may have been responsible for the ancient error. Josephus' intended original text probably was *kai nikêsas anankazei auton Ioudas . . . pheugein,* "and Judas, victorious, drove him to flee. . . ." By omitting the letters "au," the scribe produced first the ungrammatical *ton Ioudas,* which was then corrected into *ton Ioudan,* resulting in the nonsensical "and, victorious, he drove Judas to flee. . . ."

33–49. A Jewish tradition summarizing the events is preserved at TP *Ta'anit* 2:13, p. 66a, and *Megillah* 1:6, p. 70c; TB *Ta'anit* 18b; and *Schol. Megillat Ta'anit* 13 Adar.

33. In our author's stereotyped usage, in approaching the temple one "goes up." Cf. I Kings 8:1 and I 4:37. Aware of the geography of the Akra (see NOTE on 1:33–40), Josephus (*AJ* xii 10.5.406) has Nicanor "coming down from the Akra."

Nicanor, a pagan, could not come all the way into the temple court; see NOTE on 1:21, and G. Alon, *Meḥqarim,* I, 133 (in Hebrew). Hence, the priests and elders came out to him.

From the time of the old Persian empire sacrifices were offered at the temple in Jerusalem on behalf of the reigning king as a token of Jewish loyalty (Ezra 6:10; J. *Ap.* ii 6.77; *BJ* ii 10.4.197, 17.2.409; Philo *Legatio ad Gaium* 23.157).

34–35. Religious tokens of loyalty were not enough for Nicanor. He knew Judas' support lay among pious Jews, and therefore he suspected the pious of being rebels against the king. Only by delivering Judas into his hands could they prove their loyalty. Cf. II 14:31–34.

Literally, the Greek here says only that Nicanor "defiled" the priests and does not mention spit. Since our author places the "defiling" between "laughing" and "speaking," the defilement surely must have been caused by Nicanor's mouth, i.e. by spitting. On the uncleanness caused by the spit of an idolater, see Samuel Krauss, *Talmudische Archäologie* (Leipzig: G. Fock, 1910–12). I, 251, and Lieberman, *Tosefta Ki-fshuṭah,* Part IV (*Mo'ed*), pp. 805–6 (in Hebrew).

35. Cf. Judg 8:9.

36. Only those priests who had not been defiled could go back into the temple court (*M. Kelim* 1:8).

37. The priests' prayer uses I Kings 8:29–30, 43, 9:3.

38. *let . . . survive.* The Hebrew expression was probably that at Jer 40:11.

39. Even before being reinforced, Nicanor was strong enough to move along the road from Jerusalem and occupy the strategic point of Beth-Horon so that Judas could not hope to seize it and obstruct the new forces coming from Syria; see NOTE on 3:16.

40-44. Judas and his guerrilla band of three thousand took their position at or near Adasa (Hebrew *Ḥădāšāh*), convincingly located by Abel at Khirbet 'Adaseh on the road from Jerusalem to Beth-Horon (RB 33 [1924], 377-80). See Map 11, p. 535. The village was on an isolated hill to the north of the road and commanded it. If Judas and his men were able to occupy the hill without Nicanor's knowledge, the advantages of the position plus the factor of surprise would easily explain the victory over a greatly superior force. M. Avi-Yonah notes that the fugitives from Nicanor's army fled toward Gezer, as if the road southward to the much-nearer Jerusalem had been blocked, and suggests that Judas surprised Nicanor from the south of the road, opposite the village of Adasa ("The Battles in the Books of Maccabees," *Sefer Yoḥanan Levi,* eds. M. Schwabe and J. Gutman [Jerusalem: Magnes, 5709=1949], p. 17 [in Hebrew]). However, both our author and Jason of Cyrene write as if Nicanor was not surprised but marched knowingly into battle. Confident of divine aid, Judas may have taken his stand right on the road, to block Nicanor from marching on Jerusalem and fulfilling his oath against the temple. Our author may be right in explaining the rout as the effect of the fall of the commander.

Josephus, writing from memory in Rome, wrongly estimated the distance of Adasa from Beth-Horon as thirty rather than the actual sixty stadia (*AJ* xii 10.5.408). The text there also gives the number of Judas' men as two thousand but that may be a scribal error. At *AJ* xii 10.5.411 Josephus gives the number of Nicanor's men as nine thousand. Perhaps the number stood in his copy of vs. 39 and otherwise has been lost from the entire manuscript tradition.

41-42. So well-known and appropriate was the story of Sennacherib's repulse from Jerusalem, that our author does not have to name the king mentioned in Judas' prayer. Cf. II 15:22-24, and see NOTE on I 3:48 and 4:8-11.

43. Our author does not give the year of the battle, for at vs. 1 he took the date of Demetrius I's accession, 151 Sel. Mac. (autumn, 162 B.C.E.) from his non-Jewish source and apparently did not realize that the date was on a different basis from the next one he gives, the date at 9:4 for the arrival of Bacchides at Jerusalem, the first month of 152 Sel. Bab. (April–May, 160 B.C.E.). See Introduction, pp. 22–25. Taking the Julian equivalents from Parker and Dubberstein, we may ask: Did the battle of Adasa occur on March 8, 161 B.C.E. or on March 27, 160?

If it occurred in 160, there is plenty of time for the events: Alcimus' first approach to Demetrius, Bacchides' expedition, Judas' guerrilla warfare against Alcimus' partisans, Alcimus' second approach to Demetrius, Nicanor's expedition, the truce during which Judas married and "enjoyed life," and Judas' break with Nicanor and renewed guerrilla campaign. Moreover, with this chronology, Bacchides' revenge follows, as one might expect, close upon Nicanor's defeat. However, the Jews could hardly have sent the embassy to

Rome (I 8:17–18) until after the victory over Nicanor, and the embassy occurred in 161 (see introductory NOTE on ch. 8). On the interlude of peace after the victory, see NOTE on vs. 50.

Thus, it seems we must date the victory over Nicanor March 8, 161. The day would fall so late only if the Jewish calendar by then had been brought back into adjustment with the solar and Seleucid years by emergency intercalation. The Jews could hardly have done otherwise with a calendar now almost three months off. How they would have proceeded, we cannot tell. They certainly did not intercalate the sabbatical year during the expedition of Lysias and Antiochus V, and probably not even the emergency induced them to intercalate the post-sabbatical year; see To. *Sanhedrin* 2:9. Following Babylonian procedure, they might have intercalated a Second Elul at the end of the post-sabbatical year 150 Sel. Mac.; but see To. *Sanhedrin* 2:11. Otherwise, the year 151 Sel.-Mac. itself was the first year in which they could have made adjustments. Did they intercalate more than one month into 151 (cf. To. *Sanhedrin* 2:8)? In any case, the time from early October to March 8 will accommodate all our events, though if so their pace must have been rapid. Bacchides' delayed revenge is no problem. Demetrius reserved the bulk of the army for subduing the eastern provinces, and the annihilation of Nicanor's large force left Bacchides for more than a year with insufficient troops to move against dangerous Judaea.

Josephus (*AJ* xii 10.5.409) may have been right in regarding as hyperbole our author's statement that Nicanor was the first to fall. Would so seasoned a commander expose himself to the enemy? Indeed, other Jewish traditions contradict our author (TP *Ta'anit* 2:13, p. 66a, and *Megillah* 1:6, p. 70c; cf. II 15:27–28). To make the narrative more plausible to his audience or to follow these other traditions, Josephus adds a few words so as to indicate that after a hard fought conflict, in which his men were losing, Nicanor boldly entered the battle and fell. On the other hand, commanders occasionally are accidentally killed by the enemy at the beginning of engagements. Why else would Judas' outnumbered band have been able to press hard upon Nicanor's troops?

44. Josephus (*AJ* xii 10.5.410) agrees that the rout was the effect of the commander's death.

45–46. Judas and his men were so confident of having the sympathies of the country population that they pursued the routed enemy as far as Gazera (Gazara); see NOTE on 4:15, and Map 3, p. 529. On the other hand, the Jews of the countryside had some reservations about Judas: only when the rout of Nicanor's army showed that God was with the Hasmonaean party did the pious Jews of the countryside join forces with it in combat.

Our author imitated the parallels at I Sam 14:21–22 (see the Greek text) and Judg 7:21–24. The Greek *hyperekerôn*, which I have rendered "struck all along the flanks of," elsewhere in Greek means "outflank," but Nicanor's routed men no longer presented a front to be outflanked. The Greek word is not used in translations of the Hebrew Bible. Here and at Judith 15:5 it may represent a Hebrew word "to wing" (*aggēp? kannēp?*) analogous to the word *zannēb*, "to tail" (="to cut down in the rear"), at Deut 25:18 and Josh 10:19.

Not one member of Nicanor's force survived, says our author; the prayer in vs. 48 was fulfilled.

47. *right hand . . . oath.* The Greek does not have the words "in oath." The author and the translator could leave the words unexpressed, for Greeks and Jews knew that one who swore raised his hand. See Gen 14:22 and Édouard Cuq, "Jusjurandum," DAGR, III 1 (1899), 751b. Thus, in taking the oath mentioned in vs. 35, Nicanor had presumptuously raised his hand against the temple.

raised . . . Jerusalem. Nicanor's arm and head, being unclean, could not be brought into Jerusalem (Num 19:11–16, 21; *M. Kelim* 1:4, 7, 8). Nicanor suffered precise retribution: the hand he raised against the temple is now raised, powerless in death, within sight of the temple. See also NOTE on II 15:30–33.

49. The day of Nicanor was still being observed in Josephus' time (*AJ* xii 10.5.412) and is listed in *Megillat Ta'anit.* Unlike the Feast of Dedication, it is no longer observed by Jews (TP *Ta'anit* 2:12, p. 66a; TB *Rosh ha-shanah* 18b).

50. Apparently a source available to our author mentioned the interlude of peace between the day of Nicanor in March 161, and the death of Judas in midspring 160. If so, the interval must have been long enough to be worth mentioning. Indeed, within it fell the Jewish embassy to Rome (see introductory NOTE to chap. 8). However, our author seems to have been misled by his ignorance of the difference between dates on the Macedonian and Babylonian forms of the Seleucid era (see NOTE on vs. 43), so that he reduced the interlude to "a few days," from 13 Adar, 151 Sel. Bab. (March 27, 160 B.C.E.) to Nisan, 152 Sel. Bab. (April–May, 160 B.C.E.). "A few days" in Biblical Hebrew should be taken literally (cf. Num 9:20–22) and not interpreted to mean a whole year. On Josephus' chronological distortion, reporting at this point the death of Alcimus (*AJ* xii 10.6.413), see NOTE on 8:17–20.

XVII. THE ALLIANCE WITH ROME
(8:1–32)

8 1 Judas had heard about the Romans: that they were a great power who welcomed all who wished to join them and established ties of friendship with all who approached them. 2 As for their being a great power, Judas' informants told him of the Romans' valor in war: they had fought and conquered the Gauls and imposed tribute upon them. 3 They had fought in the land of Spain, conquering the silver and gold mines there. 4 They had conquered the whole region through their sagacity and perseverance, though it was a large area, far removed from Rome, and thus they had also overcome the kings who had come against them from remote quarters of the earth, defeating them heavily so that the survivors were still paying them annual tribute. 5 They had defeated in battle and conquered King Philip and King Perseus of the Macedonians, who had attacked them. 6 Even Antiochus the Great, King of Asia, was defeated by them when he went to war against them, though he had one hundred and twenty elephants and cavalry and chariotry and a very large infantry force. 7 The Romans captured him alive and decreed that he and his successors on the throne should pay the Romans a heavy tribute and give hostages and be barred 8 from the fairest of their domains.*a* These domains the Romans took from him and gave to King Eumenes. 9 The Greeks of mainland Greece, too, had planned an expedition to destroy the Romans, 10 but when their plot became known to the Romans, they sent a single general against the Greeks and waged war on them, so that many of the Greeks fell slain, and the Romans took captive their wives and children, plundered their property, conquered their land, destroyed their fortresses, and reduced them to servitude down to the present day. 11 As for the remaining kingdoms and the islands, the Romans had reduced to ruin and servitude all who had ever opposed them. 12 With their friends, however, and with those who relied on them, the Romans had maintained

---

a For the words I have omitted see commentary.

their ties of friendship and had conquered the kings both near and far, and all those who heard of the Romans feared them. 13 Those whom they chose to aid to be kings, were kings; those whom they chose to, they deposed. Thus the Romans had risen to great heights of power. 14 Nevertheless, not one of them had sought self-glorification by putting on a diadem or wearing purple. 15 They had instituted a senate for themselves, in which every day three hundred twenty sat to deliberate continually over how to maintain the people's good order. 16 They entrusted their government and the ruling of all their territory to one man each year, everyone obeying him, without any envy or jealousy among themselves.

17 Judas chose Eupolemus son of John of the clan of Hakkoz and Jason son of Eleazar and sent them to Rome so that the Romans might establish ties of friendship and alliance with the Jews 18 and lift from them the yoke, for they saw that the Seleucid empire was imposing slavery upon Israel. 19 They went to Rome, a very long journey, and came before the senate and addressed it as follows: 20 "Judas Maccabaeus and his brothers and the Jewish people have sent us to establish ties of alliance and peace with you and to gain our enrollment as your allies and friends." 21 The senate accepted their proposal. 22 The following is the text of the copy of the letter which the Romans engraved on bronze tablets and sent to Jerusalem for the Jews to keep there as a record of the ties of peace and alliance:

23 Forever may there be peace between the Romans and the nation of the Jews on sea and land! May sword and enmity be far from them! 24 If any aggressor wages war upon the Romans or upon any of their allies throughout their empire, 25 the nation of the Jews shall give aid wholeheartedly, as circumstances indicate, 26 and to those at war with them the Jews shall not give or supply food, arms, money, or ships, as was agreed at Rome. The Jews shall carry out their obligations incorruptibly. 27 In the same manner, if any aggressor wages war upon the nation of the Jews, the Romans shall give aid wholeheartedly, as circumstances indicate, 28 and to those at war with them there shall not be given food, arms, money, or ships, as was agreed at Rome. The Romans shall carry out these obligations without deceit. 29 On the foregoing terms have the Romans made a treaty with the Jewish People. 30 If hereafter both sides shall agree to add or to subtract anything, they shall act according to their decision, and any such addition or subtraction shall be valid.

31 As for the misdeed which King Demetrius is perpetrating against you, we have written him as follows: "Why have you made your yoke weigh heavy upon our friends, our allies, the Jews? 32 If they make any further complaint against you, we shall get justice for them by waging war on you by sea and by land."

NOTES

8:1–32, introductory NOTE. If ch. 8 had been omitted, no modern reader would have missed it. Nevertheless, it is an essential part of our author's narrative. The reference to Demetrius in the letter of the Romans (8:31) firmly places the embassy to seek an alliance with Rome in the reign of Demetrius I. Indeed, there is independent evidence of a Jewish embassy to Rome in 161 B.C.E., in the letter of the consul Gaius Fannius, son of Gaius, asking the officials of the island of Kos to see to the safe conduct of Jewish ambassadors returning home from Rome (J. *AJ* xiv 10.15.233). The only consul Gaius Fannius, son of Gaius, was Gaius Fannius Strabo, consul in 161; see T. R. S. Broughton, *The Magistrates of the Roman Republic*, II (New York: American Philological Association, 1951–52), 564–65, and B. Niese, "Eine Urkunde aus der Makkabäerzeit," *Orientalische Studien Theodor Nöldeke zum siebzigsten Geburtstag . . . gewidmet*, II (Giessen, 1906), 817–29. Even without the evidence of the letter, religious factors would guarantee that our author was not mistaken in placing the embassy at this point.

If material factors had been decisive, Judas would long since have sought Roman aid: Antiochus IV had been balked by Rome (Dan 11:30); Jews had received Roman support before, against the regime of the coregent Antiochus V (II 11:34–38); Rome had humiliated the regime of King Antiochus V (see NOTE on I 7:1); and Demetrius I took power over the opposition of the Romans (see ibid.). Religiously, however, Judas' decision to seek an alliance with Rome was as drastic a step as was Mattathias' rebellion; see Introduction, pp. 5–7. Jewish victories had ended the persecution and, for the time being, had stopped the Seleucid government from imposing upon the Jews an "impious" high priest. Clearly, Jews could now resist royal wickedness. Were they free, however, to deny the king's sovereignty over them and make a foreign alliance against him? God's prophets had strongly condemned such a step before, and punishment had been quick to follow (Ezek 17:11–21; II Chron 36:13–19; cf. Jer 27:1–15). To Judas and his men, the brilliant victory over Nicanor suggested that the Jews were indeed free to seek alliances inasmuch as God was with them.

1–19. Even if Demetrius I no longer ruled the Jews by divine right, Judas and his men still had to convince themselves that God permitted an alliance with the Romans. The Torah forbids alliances with "the people of the land" (Exod 23:32–33, 24:12–15; Deut 7:2) but permits them with distant nations as we learn from the story of the Gibeonites (Josh 9:3–27). Our author describes a Jewish embassy which, unlike the deceitful embassy of the Gibeonites, was straightforward and honest, but his language unmistakably echoes the story of the Gibeonites. He takes particular care to stress that Rome was far from the land of Israel (vs. 19).

Prophets had bitterly condemned Jewish alliances with pagan powers. Judas could seek alliance with Rome only if he was sure that Rome was neither a cruel and wicked power like Assyria and Babylon nor a "broken reed" like Egypt; see Jer 2:18, 36; Ezek 16:28–29, 23:5–7, 12, 16, 19–21, 29:6; Hosea 5:13, 7:11, 8:9, 14:4; Lam 5:6; II Kings 18:21; II Chron 28:16–21. Hence, alliance with Ptolemaic Egypt never entered Judas' mind. Invincible Rome was clearly no broken reed; virtuous Rome (vss. 12–16) was no Assyria or Babylon and had far outstripped those earlier empires (contrast Isa 10:7–14). Hence, in his praise of Rome our author reconstructs the kind of argument which Judas must have had in mind.

Pious searchers of the scriptures could find prophesies of an alliance with Rome in Isa 26:11 (the Hebrew could be rendered ". . . Rome is Thy hand") and 15 (which might refer to the Roman empire) and 55:5, and Mal 1:5–14 (where faithless priests come at a time when the Lord's name is "great among the nations"; Roman "Jove" sounded like the name of the God of Israel; see Schürer, III, 58–59).

1–16. At the time of our author, in the reign of Alexander Jannaeus, the Roman republic was about midway in its conquest of the Mediterranean world. Our chapter is a rare piece of evidence, telling us how Mediterranean peoples viewed the Roman republic at this point. Otherwise the surviving evidence is to be found in the Romans' own writings; in inscriptions set up by non-Romans currying favor with Rome; and in the histories of Polybius, a Greek who had made his peace with Rome. Our chapter, on the contrary, is an assessment of Rome at the beginning of the first century B.C.E. by a member of a people still independent. When our author wrote, Rome was all but ignoring the affairs of Syria, Judaea, and Ptolemaic Egypt; for example, Rome did nothing to act upon the bequest of Ptolemy Apion, who in 96 left to Rome his kingdom of Cyrene, which had long been a part of the Ptolemaic empire. There is no evidence to suggest that Alexander Jannaeus sought the support of Rome. Our author's Hebrew work might never be read by a Roman. Hence the warm praise here of Rome as a righteous and powerful republic is important evidence on the image Rome projected of herself in this period.

Our author wishes to portray the Romans as being very similar to the Jews. Just as the Jews accept all who are willing to become full proselytes as "full citizens," so do the Romans. Just as Jews grant friendship to all who make even a partial approach to the ways of the true God, so the Romans grant friendship to all who seek their alliance. Just as Jews defeated the fierce Galatians (=Gauls; see AB vol. 41A, commentary on II 8:20), so did the Romans (vs. 2). Just as the Jews fought off the Greek kingdom which sought to destroy them, so did the Romans destroy their Greek adversaries (vss.

4–11). Our author also seems to include Roman parallels to later Hasmonaean achievements, to ones which came long after Judas' death. Just as Jonathan, Simon, John Hyrcanus, Judah Aristobulus, and Alexander Jannaeus had reconquered the heritage of David, so the Romans had conquered their part of the world (vss. 2–11) and no part of the land promised to the Jews by divine prophesy. Just as Jews won victories for their allies (see I 10–13), so did the Romans for their (vss. 12–13). Just as Alexander Jannaeus had renounced the royal title, so no Roman presumed to be king (vs. 14). Just as the Jewish elders in the *Gerousia* deliberated for the good order of the Jews, so did the Roman senate for the Romans (vs. 15). Just as each of the "judges" and "princes" of the Hasmonaean dynasty ruled with the "full consent" of his subjects (I 14:4–15, 41–47; see Introduction, pp. 6–12, 73–78, so did the Romans submit to rule by their single (!) consul (vs. 16). For details on these parallels, see below on the individual passages.

The conquered peoples of the Hellenistic empires had no reason to love their Greek-speaking exploiters; consequently, the eulogy of Rome here is full of gloating over the downfall of the Greeks (see below on vss. 4–11). Conspicuous by its absence is any mention of the Roman victories over Carthage. Carthage was a Phoenician (=Canaanite) colony, and as long as Carthage survived, so did the Canaanite religious practices viewed as abominations by the Torah and the prophets; see Moscati, *World of the Phoenicians*, pp. 114–17, 136–44. One might expect Jews to be pleased when Rome defeated the center of such "abominations" in 241 and 201 and then totally destroyed it in 146 B.C.E. Josephus in his paraphrase was quick to supply the missing allusion to the Roman defeats of Carthage (*AJ* xii 10.6.414).

It is hard to see any reason for passing over the defeat and destruction of Carthage in silence, unless our pro-Hasmonaean author was writing in a time when the Hasmonaean ruler was trying to maintain friendly relations with the Phoenician cities and in particular with Tyre, the mother city of Carthage. Phoenicians, whose language was very close to Hebrew, could easily have read any references to the fall of Carthage in our author's work and might have been offended. No such attempts at friendly relations existed in the time of Judas or his early successors (I 5:15, and cf. Ps 83:8; Eissfeldt, "Tyros," PW, VII^A I [1943], 1897). Even while taking over from his source the fact that Sidon and Tyre were hostile to the Jews in the time of Judas (I 5:15), our author carefully avoids saying that Simon during his campaign fought men from Sidon and Tyre (I 5:21–22). Later, with the disintegration of the Seleucid empire, the Phoenician cities, like Judaea, asserted their independence, Tyre in 126/5, Sidon in 111 (Head, pp. 675, 659). We have no information on their relations with Judaea from then until 47 B.C.E. At no time in these years are the aggressive Hasmonaean rulers reported to have attacked either Sidon or Tyre. Their restraint parallels the practice of David and the kings of Israel and Judah and contrasts with Josh 13:6; see L. Fillion, "Sidon" and "Tyr," *Dictionnaire de la Bible*, V (1922), 1706, 2340. Evidently, the Hasmonaean kings sought to be friendly with Sidon and Tyre. Even later, when Julius Caesar in 47 B.C.E. granted privileges to Hyrcanus II and the Jews, he ordered that the Latin and Greek bronze tablets recording the grants be set up at Sidon, Tyre, and Ascalon; Ascalon, too, appears to have maintained good relations with the

Hasmonaeans down through the reigns of Alexander Jannaeus and his sons; see I 10:86, 11:60; J. *AJ* viii 2.8.55, xiii 4.4.101, 5.5.149, 10.180, xiv 1.3.10, 6.4.126; Schürer, II, 121–22; Stern, *Zion* 26 (1961), 20–21 (in Hebrew). It is probable that by 47 B.C.E. Sidon, Tyre, and Ascalon had long had friendly relations with the ruling dynasty of Judaea. Hence, we derive one more indication that First Maccabees dates from after Tyre's assertion of independence in 126/5.

The friendly attitude toward Carthage may have persisted in Jewish tradition. Noteworthy is the sympathetic treatment of Carthage in early rabbinic sources, which stress the merit of the Girgashites for withdrawing from the Promised Land to make room for Israel, in return for which God gave them Africa; see Ginzberg, *Legends*, IV, 9–10, and VI, 177–78, n. 34, and see also the medieval sources summarized ibid., II, 165–66, and V, 373, n. 426. The name of the Girgashites sounded like a phonetic variant of the alternative form of the name of Carthage, *Krkḥdš*. See David Neiman, *"Carchêdôn=*'New City'" JNES 25 (1966), 42–47.

1. Since the Romans had long since made their presence felt in Judas' world (Dan 11:18, 30; II 11:34–38; perhaps Judas even had some inkling of the Roman origins of Antiochus IV's civic policy, insofar as Roman institutions were said to make a state strong), the Greek verb "heard" must be translated by the pluperfect. Our author says nothing of how Roman ambassadors exerted influence on behalf of the Jews in 164, because the Hasmonaeans had no role in those negotiations; see NOTES on 4:35 and on II 11:34–38.

Although our passage introduces the story of how Judas sought an *alliance* with Rome, one must render the Greek *prostithemenois* by the vague "who wished to join them," not by "who sought their alliance." Our author and the translator deliberately use the Jewish vocabulary of conversion, to suggest that the Romans, like the Jews and unlike the Greeks, accept "proselytes." Indeed, while not granting full Roman citizenship to all who sought it, the Romans in our author's time were far more generous in conferring their citizenship than were most other ancient peoples; see Introduction, pp. 107–11. On Jewish "citizenship" as refused to no one who is willing to become a full proselyte, see Harry A. Wolfson, *Philo*, II (Harvard University Press, 1948), 354–57, 361–64, and Philo *De specialibus legibus* i 51.

The verb which we have rendered "who wished to join them" appears in biblical contexts dealing with proselytes. It translates "join" and "cleave" at Isa 14:1 and "join" at Esther 9:27 (cf. also Josh 23:12), and the Greek verb which regularly supplies the perfect passive of our verb renders "join" at Isa 56:3, 6. The verb which we have rendered "welcomed" (*eudokousin*) is not used of proselytes in Greek versions of the Hebrew Bible, but the related noun *eudokia* probably stood for "accepted" in Aquila's version of Isa 56:7; see Joseph Reider, *An Index to Aquila*, VTS, XII (Leiden: Brill, 1966), 99, s.v. *eudokia*. The technical terms of Greek and Roman citizenship are used to define the word "proselyte" by Theodoret to Ps 96:6 (*apud Suda* s.v. *prosêlytoi*) and in the Latin and Greek versions of *Acta Pilati* 2 (=*Evangelium Nicodemi;* see Ignazio Cazzaniga, *Vangelo di Nicodemo*

[Varese-Milano: Istituto editoriale cisalpino, 1966], pp. 87–88, "facti sunt Iudaei," and cf. Sherwin-White, pp. 39, 57).

Our author uses a form of the verb "join" here for "full proselyte" because the verb "approach" (*proselthein*), from which the Greek word *"prosêlytos"* is derived, was an ambiguous term which included the "incomplete" proselyte, the "fearer of the Lord," who accepted some but not all of the beliefs and practices of Judaism. Our author then proceeds to use a form of the verb "approach" for persons who have not received full Roman citizenship but only ties of "friendship." Just as the Romans gave their friendship and alliance to righteous peoples who "approached" them, so the Jews gave firm friendship (*philia, oikeiôsis*) to "fearers of the Lord" (Wolfson, *Philo*, II, 369–74). The translator of the old Latin version of Exod 12:49 may have been aware of such parallels between Jewish and Roman civic institutions, for he renders the Greek *prosêlytos* by *colonus* ("member of a colony"). See Introduction, pp. 108–9. Even if none of Philo's predecessors treated the Jewish institutions of conversion as analogous to Greek and Roman institutions of citizenship, the texts of the Hebrew and Greek Bibles readily lent themselves to such use by our author and his contemporaries; see Exod 12:48–49, 22:20, 23:9; Lev 19:33–34; Num 9:14, 15:14–16; Deut 10:19, etc. "Friendship" (*amicitia*) was an official status in Roman international relations, approximately the equivalent of modern diplomatic recognition. It could exist with or without a formal treaty. The precise content of the term is difficult to establish, probably because the Romans themselves did not use it consistently. See H. H. Scullard, OCD^2, s.v. "Amicitia," A. Donati, "I Romani nell' Egeo. I documenti dell'età repubblicana," *Epigraphica* 27 (1965), 11–12, and NOTE on I 8:19–32.

2. *As for . . . power.* The Greek has a literal repetition of the clause from vs. 1, "that they were a great power." Though the repetition could be a scribal error, I have translated it as an example of a construction common in Hebrew legal texts. A writer can introduce a section with a general statement of its entire content and then go back to give detailed comment on one of the clauses of the general statement. To direct the reader's attention to the clause thus receiving comment, the writer repeats the clause; cf. Lev 23:2 and 4, 28:1 and 29:1–4, and *M. Baba meṣi'a* 2:1–2, and the genealogical context at I Chron 5:27 and 6:1. Cf. also the construction with a scene-setting sentence treated above, NOTE on 1:1–10.

Gauls. Greek *Galatoi* ("Gauls") is used both of the Celts who raided Greece and settled in Asia Minor (the "Galatians") and of the Celts of central and western Europe. Everywhere the Celts were famous as formidable warriors; see T. G. E. Powell, *The Celts* (New York: Praeger, 1958), pp. 20–28, 63. Our author could well have heard of Roman victories over Gauls both east and west: the campaigns in which is today Italy, down to the conquest of Cisalpine Gaul in 222 (Polybius ii 18–35); the crushing of the resurgent tribes of Cisalpine Gaul by the 180s B.C.E. (Livy ix 36.4–15, 43.4, 46.1; Introduction, pp. 108–9); and the pacification of the fierce Galatians of Asia Minor by Gnaeus Manlius Vulso in 189 (Livy xxxviii 12–27, 40.1). The events in Asia Minor may well have been in our author's mind, since he knew how Jews had fought the Galatians; see above, on vss. 1–16. However,

Rome had not yet imposed tribute on the Galatians of Asia Minor nor did she rule them, so that the end of our verse surely refers to the Roman victories in Cisalpine Gaul.

3. Rome first conquered Spain from Carthage in the course of the Second Punic War (218–201). Our author was in no danger of offending Phoenician sensibilities (see above, on vss. 1–16), for Rome had to fight many wars in the second century B.C.E. (and still others down to 19 B.C.E.) before she could impose her rule on the natives. See C. H. V. Sutherland, *The Romans in Spain* (London: Methuen, 1939), pp. 22–151. On the fame of the mines of Spain, see Strabo iii 8, C146, and Sutherland, index, s.vv. "Minerals" and "Mines."

4. *They . . . from Rome.* Our author appears to be contrasting the wise and deliberate Romans, who come from afar and conquer through their own merit, with the "bitter and hasty" Chaldaeans (Hab 1:6), who come from afar (vs. 8) and conquer through their greed (vss. 6–17, 2:5). Perhaps he also contrasts the Roman conquerors with Assyria, the rod of God's anger, who can conquer only because God wishes to punish the nations who have sinned (Isa 10:5–15).

thus. The Greek does not have this word, which I have supplied for the sake of clarity: Roman sagacity and perseverance conquered both Spain and the kings.

they had also . . . tribute. Kappler and Abel wrongly adopt the reading of some Greek manuscripts as well as La^{L X G} SyII, which has "until" (*heôs*) before "they had overcome." The word makes the content difficult and can hardly have stood in the Hebrew original; the Lucianic recension accordingly omits it. It is probably an old scribal error for *hôs*, a Greek particle by means of which the translator indicated that he was still quoting Judas' informants. The correct reading still stands in S and 311.

"King" had a definite meaning for our author. Even if he had not wished to avoid all mention of Carthage, he would never have spoken of a king of the republic of Carthage. Spanish chiefs never "came against" Rome. Our author has in mind kings over vast empires, kings of the kind that God had placed in power over the Jews to punish them, though prophets predicted that a time would come when such kings would serve Israel; see Ezra 9:7; Neh 9:37; Isa 60:10–11; Dan 2:37–45. Roman victories over such kings are listed in vss. 5–11. Since all the Hellenistic empires defeated by Rome could be viewed as parts of Alexander's empire (Dan 2:40–41), our author could see divine purpose operating even in Rome's defeat (vs. 5) of the Antigonid empire of Macedonia, which did not rule over Judaea. The Romans themselves called their victory over the Seleucid empire a victory over kings (Bikerman, *Institutions,* pp. 6–7).

Our author accepts the Romans' dubious claims, that in every case the Hellenistic monarchies were the aggressors. On the case of Philip V and the Second Macedonian War (200–197), see Livy xxx 26.2–4, xxxi 1.9–10, 3.5–8, 18, and Bengtson, *Römische Geschichte,* p. 110. On the case of Antiochus III and his war with the Romans (192–188), see Polybius xviii 50 and E. Badian, "Rome and Antiochus the Great: a Study in Cold War," *Classical Philology* 54 (1959), 81–99. On the case of Perseus and the Third Macedonian

War (171–168), see Livy xlii 29–30, 36–48. Our author is correct in speaking in the same breath of the distance of Spain and the distance of the "aggressor kings" from Rome. The heartland of Antigonid Macedonia is quite as far from Rome as is eastern Spain.

Our author appears to use the word "tribute" imprecisely, so as to cover indemnity payments as well. After defeating Philip V of Macedonia in 197, the Romans imposed upon him the payment of an indemnity of one thousand talents, to be paid within ten years (Polybius xviii 44). In 190, however, the Romans excused him from further payments (Polybius xxi 3; Appian Syriakê 23). After defeating Antiochus III, the Romans in the Peace of Apameia (188) imposed upon him the payment of an indemnity of fifteen thousand talents, a heavy burden for years upon the Seleucid treasury, even if Antiochus IV did manage to finish paying it; see NOTE on II 8:10, and Mørkholm, pp. 22–24, 31–32, 65. The Roman defeat of Perseus in 168 brought the end of the Antigonid dynasty and its kingdom of Macedonia. No tribute was imposed, but by our author's time Macedonia had long been a tributary province (since 146).

5. See on vs. 4. The Greek has kai tous epêrmenous ep' autous, literally, "and those who had attacked them." Our context deals with how the Romans defeated kings who ruled over empires. All such kings down to Judas' time are mentioned by name in vss. 5–6. Who, then, would be the "others" who had attacked the Romans? Though Philip V and Perseus had allies and sympathizers, none ruled over empires or were conspicuous for attacking the Romans. Rather, one would expect in our verse a statement that Philip and Perseus were included among the aggressor kings (cf. vs. 6, where Antiochus III is said to have gone to war against the Romans). My translation is based on either of two ways of dealing with the Greek text. The kai may be a scribal error, or it may reflect a Hebrew explanatory waw (see GKC, p. 484, n. 1).

6. The Seleucid King Antiochus III earned the epithet "the Great" by a conquering march toward India (212–206) similar to Alexander's. He also conquered southern Syria and Palestine from the Ptolemaic empire (202–198), enlarging the Seleucid empire in Asia to its greatest extent. On his war with the Romans, see above, on vs. 4. The Seleucid empire was often called "Asia" (Bikerman, Institutions, p. 5). In his climactic battle with the Romans at Magnesia in 190 or early 189, Antiochus III is reported to have had only fifty-four elephants (Livy xxxvii 39.13), but he brought back one hundred fifty from his conquering march toward India (Polybius xi 34.12) and had 102 at the Battle of Raphia against Ptolemy IV in 217 (Polybius v 79.13). In 191 Antiochus III faced the Romans in Greece with an army of ten thousand infantry and five hundred cavalry (Livy xxxv 43.6), of which he lost all but five hundred men (Livy xxxvi 19.11). At Magnesia he had sixty thousand infantry and more than twelve thousand cavalry (Livy xxxvii 37.9).

7–8. The Romans did not take Antiochus III prisoner (Livy xxxvii 44–45, xxxviii 45.1–2), but he had to accept the terms they imposed on him. Perhaps a folk tale had grown up, of how the Romans took Antiochus III prisoner; or perhaps the fact that the Romans did take Perseus alive (Livy xlv 6.6) led our author, who may have been writing from memory, to think that they also took Antiochus III.

The terms of the treaty of Apameia, which the Romans imposed on Antiochus III in 188, are at Polybius xxi 42 Paton [43 Buettner-Wobst] and Livy xxxviii 38.

Though our author calls it "tribute," what Antiochus III and his heirs had to pay the Romans were installments of an indemnity; see above, on vs. 4.

The treaty required twenty hostages, none younger than eighteen or older than forty-five (Polybius xxi 42 Paton [43 Buettner-Wobst] § 22; Livy xxxviii 38.15). The future Antiochus IV served as a hostage; see NOTE on 1:10.

be barred . . . domains. On the territorial terms of the treaty of Apameia, see A. H. McDonald, "The Treaty of Apamea (188 B.C.)," 57 (1967), 1–8. Our passage has several textual difficulties. My translation "be barred" is based on my own correction of the Greek text to read *diastalênai.* All Greek manuscripts have *diastolên kai* ("separation [?] and") and La$^{L(X)}$ $^{G V}$ have *constitutum et* ("treaty[?] and"), probably reflecting an original Greek *diastalsin kai (diastalsis* is known only from II 13:25) or *diestalmena kai* (cf. II 14:28; Polybius iii 23.5). Since in Greek there is no idiom whereby a vanquished party can be said to "give" a treaty or terms, one would expect not a noun but another infinitive, parallel to "pay" and "give."

Though our context has other difficulties, there is no doubt that it deals with the territory which Antiochus III had to yield. Greek *diastalênai* renders Hebrew *yibbādēl* ("be barred") at Ezra 10:8 (cf. 10:11); as an unfamiliar word it could easily have been misread by an early Greek scribe as *diastolênkai* or *diastalsinkai* (words were not separated in early Greek manuscripts).

8. *from . . . domains.* Before "from" the Greek manuscripts all have the erroneous "and," followed by "Indian land and Media and Lydia"; then just before "from" in some manuscripts comes another "and," but not in S *L'* 311 La$^{L X B V}$ SyI SyII. Antiochus III did not have to abandon claims to India and Media, and there is no reason to single out Lydia. Our author is otherwise very well informed. The error is probably not his, but rather a badly informed person's marginal note which crept into the text early. This is indicated not only by the doubtful last "and," but also by the Latin versions, where the cases fluctuate from the genitive to the accusative, as if a scribe had not fully accommodated the marginal note grammatically into the text. Read "his domains" with the Lucianic recension, the other manuscripts have "their domains."

In fact, Antiochus III had to withdraw from all territory in Asia Minor claimed by him north and west of the Taurus Mountains. See McDonald, JRS 57 (1967), 1–8.

These . . . Eumenes. King Eumenes II of Pergamum got most of the ceded territory, but some was given to Rhodes, and the Greek cities in Antiochus III's domains which had sided with Rome received their freedom (Polybius xxi 45 Paton [46 Buettner-Wobst]; Livy xxxviii 39).

9–10. Our author here falls into anachronism: the war of the Achaean league with Rome came in 146, long after Judas was dead, and our author's description of the fate of the vanquished leaves no doubt as to what war he means. The Achaean league was much too weak to contemplate destroying Rome; but when Rome backed Sparta in a dispute with the Achaean league, the leading politicians rashly induced the Achaeans to brave a war with the Romans (Polybius xxxviii 9–13; Pausanias vii. 12.4 – 14.6). As usual, our author believes that the Greek-speaking enemies of Rome were the aggressors, though the plot he alleges may represent a confused recollection of a boast by a politician of the Aetolian league in 192, that he would answer the requests of the Roman commander when his own camp was pitched on the banks of the Tiber (Livy xxxv 33.10). Rome acted quickly in 146. A Roman army under the consul Lucius Mummius crushed the Achaeans and captured their great city of Corinth with great slaughter, sacking and destroying it and selling the women and children into slavery. The walls of all cities which had made war against Rome were demolished, and much if not all of Greece was made tributary to Rome under the governor of the province of Macedonia (Pausanias vii 15–16; Bengtson, *Griechische Geschichte,* p. 503, n. 1).

I have translated the Greek *hoi ek tês Hellados* ("the people of Hellas") as "the Greeks of mainland Greece." "Hellas" and its Hebrew equivalent were ambiguous terms for our author and the translator; see NOTE on 1:1 end. Here, the context leaves no doubt. The translator followed current Greek usage; see E. Bikerman, "Les préliminaires de la seconde guerre de Macédoine," RPH, 3d series, 9 (1935), 76.

11. *remaining kingdoms.* Our author probably has in mind the Attalid kingdom of Pergamum, willed to Rome by its last king, Attalus III, in 133 B.C.E. The pretender Aristonicus led a formidable struggle against Roman rule until he surrendered in 130; some of his followers continued to resist to 129 or 128. In 129 the former Attalid realm became the Roman province of Asia. See Esther V. Hansen, *The Attalids of Pergamon,* 2d ed., Cornell Studies in Classical Philology, vol. XXXVI (Cornell University Press, 1971), pp. 150–63. Here, too, our author falls into anachronism.

the islands. The Romans won Sicily, Sardinia, Corsica, and the Balearic Islands in the course of their wars with Carthage in the third century. Though our author may be alluding also to those islands, in his time they were not famous for having opposed the Romans. Indeed, in this context our author is gloating over the downfall of Greek-speaking states, and the word "island" in ancient Hebrew and Greek texts generally refers to the Greek islands, especially those of the Aegean; see Gen 10:5; Jer 2:10; Dan 11:18; Esther 10:1; Walther Schwahn, "Nesiotai 4," PW, XVIII[I] (1936), 74–77; Lieberman, *Tosefta Ki-fshuṭah,* Part I (*Zera'im*), p. 316 (in Hebrew). The city of Chalkis on the island of Euboea had suffered severe punishment with the Achaeans for joining them against Rome in 146; see Livy *Periocha* lii; Polybius xxxix 6.5, and Pausanias vii 16.9. The other island cities must have been thoroughly cowed. If our author had the fate of Chalkis in mind, again he was guilty of anachronism.

12. The reference to conquering the kings both near and far is not redundant if the prepositional phrase "with . . . them" is taken with both verbs: by faithfully making common cause with their friends, the Romans overcame the kings. Verses 4–11 deal with a different aspect: how the Romans fought wars in their own defense against kings. Both Greek and Roman writers held

that the Romans entered the Second Macedonian War to protect their allies from Philip V; see E. Bickerman, *"Bellum Philippicum:* Some Roman and Greek Views Concerning the Causes of the Second Macedonian War," *Classical Philology* 40 (1945), 137–48. The Romans made such claims even concerning the Third Macedonian War (Livy xlii 30.10). On such explanations of the origins of the Roman conflict with Antiochus III, see Badian, *Classical Philology* 54 (1959), 81–99. Rome's power to help her friends continued to impress our author in the times that followed Judas' death; see e.g. Stern, *Zion* 26 (1961), 1–22 (in Hebrew).

and all . . . them. The context suggests that in this clause our author still speaks of kings. Perhaps again he implicitly compares the Romans to ancient Israel (cf. Josh 5:1).

13. By Judas' time Rome's power had secured the accession or continued reign of several kings: of Masinissa of Numidia in 203 (H. H. Scullard, OCD², s.v. "Masinissa"); of Ptolemy VI and Ptolemy VIII as kings independent of the Seleucid empire in 168 (Volkmann, PW, XXIII, 1709–11); perhaps of Ptolemy VI in 163 after he had been driven out of Egypt by Ptolemy VIII in 164 (ibid., cols. 1711–12); of Ptolemy VIII as king of Cyrene against plots he feared from 162/1 on (ibid., cols. 1713–15); of Antiochus V from 163 to 162 against the claims of the future Demetrius I (Polybius xxxi 2, 11); and of Timarchus as king of Media in 161 over the opposition of Demetrius I, who claimed Media as Seleucid territory (Diodorus xxxi 27a). Rome had deposed Perseus as king of Macedonia (see above, on vs. 4). Our author knew of more such Roman successes down to his own time. On the other hand, here he passes over in silence Rome's failures to maintain Antiochus V and Timarchus in power (I 7:1–4; Hans Volkmann, *Klio* 19 [1925], 393), and also Rome's own recognition of Demetrius I as king of the Seleucid empire in 160 (Polybius xxxi 33, xxxii 3.13; but see John Briscoe, "Eastern Policy and Senatorial Politics, 168–146 B.C.," *Historia* 18 [1969], 52–53).

14. Our author has more than one reason to praise Rome for being a republic. Eschatological prophesy believed by our author predicted that the Kingdom of the Greeks (the Hellenistic empires beginning with Alexander's) would be followed by a fourth and last world kingdom (Dan 2:44). Jews believed that the fourth kingdom would be their own, but they were also aware of the danger of misinterpreting prophesy (cf. Dan 11:14; J. *BJ* vi 5.4.312–13). Though Rome might fulfill Num 24:24 (cf. Dan 11:30), as a republic it could not be the fourth kingdom. See also above, NOTE on vss. 1–16.

Our verse is at first sight strange in a work attempting to prove the princely legitimacy of the Hasmonaean dynasty, for it appears to condemn the institution and trappings of kingship. On the diadem and the purple as royal prerogatives, see Bikerman, *Institutions,* p. 32. In Rome at this period only victorious generals granted the honor of a parade into Rome (a "triumph") could wear such trappings, and that only during the triumph itself (see Plutarch *Marius* 12.5). Alexander Jannaeus probably used the title "king" at the very beginning of his reign (J. *AJ* xiii 12.1.320; *BJ* i 4.1.85; Strabo xvi 2.40; Meshorer, *Jewish Coins,* pp. 56–58). Like his brother and predecessor, Jannaeus wore a diadem, and diadems appear on his coins (J. *AJ* xiii 11.1.301; *BJ* i 3.1.70; TB *Qiddushin* 66a; Meshorer, p. 118, nos. 5A, 7, 7A, 8, 8A). Like his predecessors since Jonathan and Simon (I 10:20, 62–64, 14:43), Jannaeus wore purple.

However, on many coins of Alexander Jannaeus types with the legend *yhwntn hmlk* ("Jannaeus the King") are overstruck by another type with the legend *yntn hkhn hgdl whbr hyh[dym]*, ("Jannaeus the high priest and the Council[?] of the Jews"), showing unambiguously that Jannaeus for a time abandoned the title "king." None of the coin types with the non-royal legend displays a diadem. See Meshorer, pp. 58–59, 119–21. Jannaeus' temporary willingness to forgo the royal title explains the tenacity with which he held to his legitimacy as high priest (TB *Qiddushin* 66a). Thus, even in our verse, our author remains a propagandist for the priest-prince Alexander Jannaeus. Our passage also helps date First Maccabees to the period after the beginning of Jannaeus' reign during which he was renouncing the royal title.

We can only speculate as to why Jannaeus for a time renounced the kingship. Perhaps it was from modest fear of being overconfident in interpreting prophesies: when God restored kingship to Israel, the king would accomplish great things. The prophesy had been unfulfilled in the brief reign of Judah Aristobulus, however considerable his accomplishments. The spate of aggressive warfare in the later reign of Jannaeus suggests that he was confident God was with him as the predicted great king. Such presumption could have brought upon him the wrath of Pietist Jews.

15. For *bouleutêrion* as the senate itself rather than the building in which it met, cf. Dionysius of Halicarnassus ii 12.3–4. The number of senators was approximately three hundred until Sulla increased it to six hundred in 81 B.C.E. The Roman senate did not, as our verse avers, meet daily, but only when summoned by the presiding magistrates. See Arnaldo Momigliano, OCD^2, s.v. "Senatus." On the senate's function as the guardian of good morals, see Cicero *Oratio de haruspicum responsis* 27.58, *Pro Sestio* 65.137, and *De oratore* i 52.226.

Our author's mistake about the daily sessions of the Roman senate may have arisen from his desire to equate Roman traits and institutions with Jewish; see above, on vss. 1–16. According to To. *Sanhedrin* 7:1 (=TB *Sanhedrin* 88b), the supreme Jewish Sanhedrin met daily. We are but scantily informed of Jewish parallels in Judas' and our author's times to the Roman senate. Before the embassy to Rome we have evidence of a Jewish "council of elders" (*gerousia*) in the document of Antiochus III at J. *AJ* xii 3.3.138, at II 4:44, and in the document of Antiochus V at II 11:27. The "elders" (*presbyteroi*) mentioned at I 1:26, 7:33, and II 13:13, 14:37, may have been members of it. Between Judas' time and our author's there are similar references to the *gerousia* at I 12:6 and II 1:10 (in the spurious letter written in 103 B.C.E., the last datable reference to a Jewish *gerousia*) and to *presbyteroi* at I 11:23, 12:35, 13:36, 14:20 and 28. See also Sir 23:14 and 30:27 (33:19 Rahlfs), where the Jewish council seems to have been an aristocratic body, closed to the sage Ben Sira. Ben Sira apostrophizes the members but tells us nothing of any moral functions of the council; moral teaching he considered to be his own function, as sage. Rabbinic sources may preserve references to moral and legal functions of a court of "sages" in the time of Alexander Jannaeus (TB *Sanhedrin* 19a–b), but the rabbinic tradition appears to have mistakenly transferred the case of Herod in the reign of Hyrcanus II (J. *AJ* xiv 9.3–4.165–76; *BJ* i 10.5–7.204–11) to the reign of Alexander Jannaeus. Our author's Jewish counterpart of the Roman senate may have been the Hasmonaean court referred to at TB *'Abodah zarah* 36b.

16. Our author does not know that the Romans, always wary of trusting power to a single man, elected their officials characteristically in groups of two, one able to countermand the other. Normally the chiefs of state were two consuls. Only in times of emergency would a single dictator be appointed. Our author's belief in a single consul may be derived from the fact that only one magistrate's name appeared in the prescripts to the Roman documents known to him. See I 15:16 and J. *AJ* xiv 10.15.233 (of the time of Judas); ibid., 8.5.145 and xiii 9.2.260 (from the time of John Hyrcanus). Since our author praises Roman concord, he knew nothing of the civil war between Sulla and his rivals. Hence, his single supreme magistrate cannot be based on Sulla's dictatorship (82–79). Had our author known that the Romans had two consuls, he would have passed over the whole matter in silence, rather than have the Romans be a good example in the hands of Jannaeus' opponents, who condemned him for uniting in his person both prince and high priest.

Greeks, too, were struck by the stability and harmony of Roman politics (Polybius vi 11–18), but by our author's time Rome had at least passed through the violence of the period of the Gracchi (133, 123–121) and of the suppression of Saturninus and Glaucia (100), if not the agitation and murder of Marcus Livius Drusus and the War of the Allies (91–87). Local violence in the city of Rome and even a war in Italy may have gone unreported in our author's Judaea. It is possible that our author holds up the example of harmonious Rome to the Jews, restive under Alexander Jannaeus, in the hope that the Jews will work to fulfill Isa 11:13–16 by imitating the Romans.

17–20. If Judas took the initiative in a treaty binding the Jewish nation, one would expect him to have held some legal office. The only title our author gives Judas is "Commander of the Army," and that, through the mouth of Mattathias (I 2:66). Since Mattathias himself was a guerrilla chieftain, Judas did not thereby become a legal national authority. Our author does not even portray Judas with such authority in the struggle against Nicanor, though Jason of Cyrene presents Judas as having negotiated with Lysias (II 11:13–15; see NOTE on I 4:35) and as having consulted the elders in the struggle against Lysias and Antiochus V, as if Judas were chief of state. Our author himself presents later Hasmonaeans as acting with legal titles and in consultation with the elders (11:23, 12:6 and 35, 13:36, 14:20 and 28). Hence, our author's silence in a work to prove Hasmonaean legitimacy is eloquent. Judas had no authority *de jure* to initiate negotiations on behalf of the nation. Either he acted as *de facto* head of state, by virtue of his victory over Nicanor and Alcimus; or else our author jumps to the conclusion that the initiative was Judas', when in fact it belonged to Eupolemus and the duly constituted *gerousia;* cf. II 4:11. The text of the treaty here no more mentions Judas than do the documents at II 11:13–38, where Jason of Cyrene jumped to a similar conclusion. In fact, we shall see below (on vss. 17–18 and vss. 19–32) that both the Hasmonaeans and more hesitant national organs (presumably the *gerousia*) had a share in the initiative. See also Adalberto Giovannini and Helmut Miller, "Die Beziehungen zwischen Rom und den Juden im 2. Jh. v. Chr.," *Museum Helveticum* 28 (1971), 168–70.

In writing his paraphrase here, Josephus (like the source of Diodorus xl 2.2) could not believe that Judas acted as a usurper with only *de facto* authority and never thought of the possibility that the initiative was not Judas'. Josephus thought that only the high priest had the authority to send an embassy; see *AJ* xi 4.8.111 and *Ap.* ii 21.185 and 22.188. The high priest was Alcimus! Disregarding the plain facts at I 9:54–57, Josephus moved the account of Alcimus' death to a point just after the victory over Nicanor (*AJ* xii 10.6.413); thereby he was able to assume that Judas then became high priest (ibid., 414), with power *de jure* to bind the nation. Where our author, refusing to go beyond the facts, still presents Judas and his brothers in vs. 20 with no more titles than they had as guerrilla leaders in 5:10, Josephus (*AJ* xii 10.6.414, 419) assumes that Judas must have been high priest and gives his brother Simon the title *stratêgos,* perhaps by jumping to the conclusion that the situation was already similar to that at I 11:57–59. It is also possible that by *stratêgos* Josephus meant that Simon was the second ranking priest; see A. Büchler, *The Priests and Their Cult in the Last Decade of the Temple in Jerusalem* (Jerusalem: Mossad Harav Kook, 1966), pp. 86–87 (in Hebrew). Josephus may have possessed sources in which Judas was called *kōhēn gādōl* or *archiereus.* Though these expressions are used for "high priest," Josephus knew they could also refer to any distinguished member of the priesthood. See Walter Bauer, *Wörterbuch zum Neuen Testament,* 5th ed. (Berlin: Alfred Töpelmann, 1958), cols. 223–24, and Lieberman, *Tosefta Ki-Fshuṭah,* Part IV (*Mo'ed*), 909, n. 48. In the prayer *'Al hannissīm,* Mattathias is called *kōhēn gādōl.* In any case, Josephus recognized his error of believing that Judas was high priest and tacitly corrected it at *AJ* xx 10.3.235.

Our author gives no date for the embassy to Rome, but we have some clues suggesting when it occurred. The embassy could not have occurred before the victory over Nicanor (see introductory NOTE to I 8). After that defeat, Demetrius I would have been eager to punish the Jews, and the Jews therefore had an interest in seeking Roman aid as soon as possible. At Rome, the senate might receive an embassy at any time of the year, but most came early in the Roman year (von Premerstein, "Legatus," PW, XII [1924], 1137). Embassies may have made efforts to reach Rome in time to deal with the consuls, who usually left Rome as commanders during the military campaigning season (Polybius vi 12.12). Fannius, the consul who did deal with the Jews (see introductory NOTE to I 8), is not reported to have gone on a campaign (Münzer, "Fannius 20," PW, VI [1909], 1194–95), but the Jewish embassy setting out for Rome could not foresee that Fannius would remain at Rome.

On the other hand, ancient sailors were extremely reluctant to brave the winter storms of the Mediterranean, which were not thought to be past until March 10 (Vegetius iv 39). We may thus guess that the Jewish embassy set sail as soon after March 10, 161, as they could find a ship to carry them. They certainly received their favorable hearing in 161, while Gaius Fannius Strabo was still consul, and probably left before the storms again became a menace from November 11 on (ibid.).

17–18. Eupolemus was a member of the priestly clan of Hakkoz (I Chron 24:10), long since recognized as legitimate despite the doubts at Ezra 2:61 and Neh 7:63. His father, John, secured from Antiochus III the privileged status of the Jews as an *ethnos* (II 4:11; see ad loc. and NOTE on I 1:4). Eupolemus may be identical with the author of a historical work in Greek, *On the Kings in Judaea* (Eupolemos FGH 723, F 1–5), written in the reign of Demetrius I (ibid., F 4). The surviving fragments do not present Solomon as contributing a gift to a pagan temple (ibid., F 2, end=Eusebius *Praeparatio evangelica* ix 34.16), but only as sending a golden pillar to the king of Tyre, who placed it in a temple (cf. J. *Ap.* i 18.118; Herodotus ii 44). Hence, there is no reason to question Eupolemus' piety. Many pious Jews, like him, bore Greek names.

Nothing further is know of Jason son of Eleazar. Since "Jason" was a common Greek equivalent of Hebrew "Jesus" or "Joshua," both the man and his father bear names characteristic of the priesthood; see NOTES on 12:16 and II 6:18.

so that . . . they saw. Where I have "the Romans" and "the Jews" the Greek has only "to establish with them ties of friendship." That the subject of "establish" is the Romans and that "them" refers to the Jews is clear from vs. 1 as well as from the fact that obviously in vs. 18 the Romans are the subject of "lift" and "them" refers to the Jews. Construing the pronouns in this manner provides a mention of the Jews in the sentence, so that the Jews can be the subject of the third-person plural verb "saw," as they should. Our author's point, or rather, as we shall see, that of his source, is to show that God permitted the Jews to send the embassy, despite the fact that they were still under Demetrius' "yoke." Indeed, Jeremiah (27:1–15) had warned of dire consequences should the Jews themselves try to cast off the yoke of Nebuchadnezzar, of whom Demetrius was the remote successor. In the struggle which led up to the victory over Nicanor, Jews could see themselves as merely resisting the injustices of Nicanor and Bacchides (see 7:18) and as not yet in full rebellion against Demetrius.

Isaiah (14:3–4, 25) had prophesied that when the land had rest, as now (see I 7:50), the "slavery imposed" by the "Assyrian" king would cease, as would the "tax gatherer"; the "yoke" would be "removed," and the king himself would perish. Another important prophesy of Isaiah (10:17–27) predicted that Israel would inflict great slaughter on the army of "Assyria" (ibid., vss. 17–19), as in the victory over Nicanor. Thereafter, the time would soon come when Israel would no longer have to depend on the punishing power (ibid., vs. 20). God would rouse a "whip" (Rome) to put an end to the "Assyrian" empire, and then the yoke would be removed. Ezekiel, too, predicted

(34:27) the removal from Israel of the "enslavers'" yoke. Jews found more explicit predictions of Rome's might in other prophesies; see NOTE on 8:1–19. The victory over Nicanor had fulfilled part of the prophesies of liberation. Hence, Jews believed that though Israel herself must not attempt to cast off the yoke, the Romans might be God's instrument in the fulfillment of the rest of the prophesies. Cf. 13:41.

"Yoke" and "slavery" probably refer to Demetrius I's effort to maintain Alcimus in power as high priest and probably also to the continuation of punitive rates of taxation, despite Antiochus V's restoration of the status of *ethnos* to the Jews; see NOTE on 1:29–40. The maintenance of such "slavery" was contrary to the prophesies as interpreted above, and hence, even pious Jews who still accepted the legitimacy of Seleucid rule could regard the "slavery" as illegitimate. In fact, the interpretations of the prophesies, alluded to in our passage, proved to be false. Our author is not one to ascribe to a Hasmonaean the misinterpretation of a prophesy. Indeed, the interpretations support a position of avoiding open rebellion against Demetrius. The Hasmonaeans, who rejected the overtures of Alcimus and Bacchides (7:10–11), may have been ready for open rebellion from the time of Demetrius' accession, and the victory over Nicanor surely convinced them that Demetrius' rule over the Jews was no longer by God's decree. Hence, our author quotes here a non-Hasmonaean point of view. Indeed, our verses are awkwardly constructed. At first the subject is Judas, and then suddenly the subject becomes the Jews, though the Jews have been mentioned only by a pronoun. Though the construction is harsh, it could hardly have arisen if it did not represent the original text. Hence, the reading of S and 58, "he [Judas] saw" is to be rejected as a misguided attempt to correct the text. Our author ordinarily wrote well. The harsh construction here probably results from his effort to insert Judas' initiative where his source mentioned only the Jews. We may imagine, however, that Judas, who was already willing to rebel openly, welcomed the idea of an alliance with Rome, and may even have suggested to the more legitimate national organs the kind of scriptural interpretations to justify the step.

On "friendship and alliance," see below, on vss. 19–32.

19–32. According to Roman law, the full procedure for making a treaty was to have the terms fixed and approved by the senate and then passed by a vote of the people and ratified by an oath taken by certain Roman officials; see Polybius vi 13.7 and 14.10–11, and Alfred Heuss, "Abschluss und Beurkundung des griechischen und römischen Staatsvertrages," *Klio* 27 (1934), 14–53. However, in our period the senate by itself, for whatever reason, concluded treaties at least with the small states and peoples of the Greek-speaking East, without a vote of the people and without the oath; see Silvio Accame, *Il dominio romano in Grecia dalla guerra acaica ad Augusto* (Roma: Angelo Signorelli, 1946), pp. 79–101. Hence, the procedures described here for the negotiations and the conclusion of the treaty follow the regular patterns of the time.

In the eyes of most ancient peoples, only expediency, not law, prevented them from treating foreigners as enemies and waging war on them. Individuals might acquire greater security through the institutions of hospitality and through seeking the protection of the foreign government. Collectively, however, the citizens of one political unit enjoyed protection abroad from the citizens of another only if between the two there was a treaty of peace. On Greek practices, see Busolt and Swoboda, *Griechische Staatskunde*, pp. 1240–42. The case of the Israelites can be inferred from the story of the Gibeonites. The Gibeonites approached Joshua with a request for a covenant, and Joshua granted the Gibeonites "peace" and made a covenant, involving an oath by the princes of Israel (Josh 9:6, 15; cf. I Kings 5:26); only then did Israelite law protect the Gibeonites (cf. Deut 20:10–12). Greeks similarly made such treaties of "peace," which among them were usually limited to pacts of mutual non-aggression. The Romans felt themselves under legal obligations to wage only "just" wars; see Heuss, *Grundlagen, Klio,* Beiheft XXXI, 18–25. Nevertheless, Romans, too, needed protection, and without a treaty citizens of another state would be at the mercy of the Romans' own conceptions of what constituted a just war; hence, the early Romans, too, made such treaties of peace (Dionysius of Halicarnassus vi 95.2; Polybius iii 24.6).

By Judas' time, however, the Romans preferred to use the term "friendship" (*amicitia, philia*) rather than "peace" (*pax, eirênê*) to describe their peaceful and amicable relations with another party, and their formal treaties of "friendship" were much more than pacts of mutual non-aggression; see Eugen Täubler, *Imperium Romanum,* I (Leipzig and Berlin: Teubner, 1913), 47, 420–22; Heuss, *Grundlagen,* p. 54, n. 1; and Accame, pp. 48, 54–55. Täubler has shown that Rome in this period made two standard types of treaty with eastern Mediterranean political units: treaties of friendship and treaties of friendship and alliance. The latter type incorporated the clauses of the former with slight modifications which need not concern us. On the basis of Täubler, pp. 47–62, we may reconstruct the standard text of the treaty of friendship and alliance as follows:

Friendship section:

1) Forever may there be peace and friendship and alliance between the Roman people and the people of X, both on land and on sea. Let there be no war.

2) The people of X shall not by their own official decision allow to enemies or opponents of the Roman people passage through their own land or land under their control so as to wage war against the Roman people and the subjects of the Romans. Neither shall they by their own official decision by any deceitful device aid such enemies with arms, money, or ships. The Roman people shall not by their own official decision allow to enemies or opponents of the people of X passage through their own land or land under their control so as to wage war against the people of X and their subjects. Neither shall they by their own official decision by any deceitful device aid such enemies with arms, money, or ships.

Alliance section:

3) If any aggressor wages war upon the people of X, the Roman people will come to the defense of the people of X, as circumstances require. If

any aggressor wages war upon the Roman people, the people of X will come to the defense of the Roman people, as circumstances require.
Provision for alterations:
4) (Similar to vs. 30.)

The Jews who sent the ambassadors would have found it impossible to accept the terms of paragraph 2. Both the Romans and the Jews were making the treaty with a view to the threat posed by the Seleucid empire of Demetrius I. Seleucid forces already occupied Jewish territory, at least in the Akra and Beth-Zur. Pious Jews still felt bound not to oppose the entry of any further Seleucid forces as long as those forces "came in peace" and did not attack them (see 7:10–15); hence, they would feel bound to violate the first sentence of paragraph 2. Moreover, Demetrius was already an "opponent" of the Romans, though no state of war existed (see Diodorus xxxiv 27a). The second sentence of paragraph 2 would require the Jews to cease paying taxes to Demetrius, yet those Jews who believed that they were still "under the yoke" held that God required them to pay those taxes. Indeed, at first pious Jews feared divine punishment for any rebellion against Demetrius unless Demetrius first attacked them; it would appear from vs. 24 that now they came to believe that they might be safe in rebelling also if Demetrius attacked Rome (the "arm of the Lord"? see NOTE on I 8:1–19) or an ally of Rome and thus brought upon himself war with the invincible republic. Hence, the ambassadors do not ask for a treaty of friendship and alliance but for one of alliance and peace, and vs. 22 calls the pact one of peace and alliance. Logically, peace must come before there can be alliance. The ambassadors, however, mention first "alliance" and then "peace." The inversion of the logical order, if it is not fortuitous, probably reflects the ambassadors' desire to mention first the form of treaty usually acceptable to the Romans, and only thereafter the unusual form they themselves desired. Though the treaty desired by the ambassadors would not follow the Roman norm, it could be drafted out of the standard clauses. First, from paragraph 1 one would omit the word "friendship." Then the applicable phrases of paragraphs 2 and 3 would be combined as we find them in vss. 24–28. Ordinarily the alliance section required the other party to come to Rome's aid only if Rome herself was attacked. Since the Jews could not accept the obligations of the friendship section, by way of compensation they undertook to come to Rome's aid also if any of her allies was attacked.

The novel form of such a treaty would rouse the suspicions of ancient statesmen familiar with the Roman norm, who might think the document a forgery. Hence, each departure from the norm is authenticated by the remark "as was agreed at Rome" (vss. 26 and 28). Since the treaty was no longer a stereotype, to mark the point where the operative clauses were at an end so that no forger could insert further clauses, the draftsman inserted the authenticating and limiting remark which is vs. 29. My interpretation of these peculiarities in vss. 26, 28, and 29 is a conjecture on the basis of the obviously unusual character of the treaty. One can hardly expect to find an ancient parallel: Roman treaties were unusual for their stereotyped form; for the great variety of treaty forms elsewhere, see Heuss, *Klio* 27 (1934), 231–35. To find a parallel, one would have to find a kind of ancient contract which was equally stereotyped and then find a surviving example of it wherein the contracting parties found themselves forced to depart from the stereotyped form. The fragmentary Roman treaty in Latin with Callatis may have been just such an example. Departures from stereotyped form may well be responsible for the fact that no one has succeeded in restoring its text. See *Inscriptiones Latinae Liberae Rei Publicae*, ed. Attilio Degrassi, vol. II (Firenze: La nuova Italia, 1963), no. 516. The clause beginning *utei et* ("as also"[?]) may have been analogous to the formulas in vss. 26 and 28. At present one can draw no inferences from the fragmentary text. Compare, however, the procedure prescribed at TB *Baba batra* 161b for the authentication of erasures and for a clause like our vs. 29 at the end of a document. Such formulas have been found in the still unpublished documents of the first and second centuries C.E. from Nahal Hever, drawn up under Roman, Nabataean, and Jewish rule; see Y. Yadin, "Expedition D," IEJ 12 (1962), 237. An erasure is in a sense a departure from stereotyped form. Since the Jewish ambassadors had a share in drafting the treaty (see above, on vs. 22), it is not far-fetched to suggest that they insisted on the inclusion of the formulas. Indeed, a formula similar to our vs. 29 occurs in the Peloponnesian draft of terms for a treaty at Thucydides iv 118.8 and is followed immediately by a provision for modification of the terms analogous to our vs. 30. Hence, our formulas here may follow the usages of diplomacy in the Greek-speaking world, despite our lack of surviving parallels.

The remarks in vss. 26 and 28 do not reflect the Latin *censuere* ("the senate so voted") which regularly appeared in reports of senatorial decrees (*senatus consulta;* see Sherk, pp. 7–10), though scholars have unanimously followed Täubler (*Imperium Romanum*, I, 243, 358) in saying so. Täubler himself recognized that our document does not follow the prescribed form of *senatus consulta* (I, 244; see Sherk, pp. 7–10). Moreover, one would then expect the note of the senate's vote to come at the end of vss. 26 and 28, not in the middle; one would also expect to find such notes at the end of vss. 23 and 30. Cf. Heuss, *Klio* 27 (1934), 47–48, note. Finally, on Täubler's interpretation the notes could only be translated, "so it was voted by Rome," whereas Greek usage, well understood by the Greek translator, would require "so it was voted by the Romans." Täubler also held (I, 242) that vs. 29 was a note inserted by our author, not part of the text of the treaty; but, if so, our author should have inserted it after vs. 30. On the other hand, it is clear that a special terminology and precedure had to be invented when the Jews could not subscribe to the friendship section of the standard Roman treaty. This fact confirms Täubler's thesis, that the friendship section was standard in treaties of friendship in this period, against the doubts of Heuss (*Grundlagen*, pp. 12–18).

Apart from the modifications required by the special circumstances of the Jews, the text of the treaty follows the formulas of a Roman treaty made on an equal basis with a sovereign power (*foedus aequum;* see Sherk, pp. 97–98, and Täubler, I, 2–6, 44–62, 239–54); the senate even recognizes the Jews as an *ethnos* (see below, on vs. 20). Otherwise, all departures from regular Roman formulas are due to errors in translation, for our author turned a

Greek original into Hebrew, and then the Greek translator of his work turned
the Hebrew back into Greek.

Despite their inability to make a treaty of friendship, the Jewish ambassadors go on in vs. 20 to ask that the Jews be enrolled in the official Roman list
of allies and friends (*formula sociorum et amicorum*). They were correct in
doing so, for Rome often conferred the status of "friend" on political units
which had no treaty of friendship with her. See vs. 31 and Heuss, *Grundlagen*, pp. 25–29; Ernst Badian, *Foreign Clientelae*, p. 12; Peter Klose, *Die
völkerrechtliche Ordnung der hellenistischen Staatenwelt in der Zeit von 280
bis 168 v. Chr.*, pp. 140–41.

In vs. 22 our author surprisingly calls the document containing the text of
the treaty a "letter" (*epistolê*). Ancient letters ordinarily began with the name
of the sender, the name of the receiver, and a formula of salutation (see e.g.
I 10:18, 26). As reproduced by our author, the document contains nothing of
the kind. Yet after the text of the treaty, as if they were part of the same document, without any introduction, come instructions from the Romans to the
Jews (vss. 31–32) which could only have stood in a letter. This fact in itself
shows that our author did not just mistake vs. 23 for a salutation (see also below, on vs. 23). In fact, there is at least one parallel to the strange phenomena
here, suggesting that the senate or the authorities appointed by it did com-
municate documents in this manner to those affected, by sending a "letter,"
with only the document at the head, followed abruptly by further instructions. In the inscription of the senate's decree on the Bacchanalia (ILS 18) the
senatus consultum is followed immediately, with no trace of a salutation, by
instructions to the recipients. Hence our author's presentation of the document is correct.

Josephus did not understand that the Jews could not make a standard treaty
of friendship and alliance with the Romans. In his paraphrase (*AJ* xii
10.6.417–18) he revised the text here to conform to the standard treaty. He
supplied the document with a title, as was customary with such documents
(see Heuss, *Klio* 27 (1934), 240–41, 245–50), but the title is "Decree of the
Senate [*dogma synklêtou*] concerning Alliance and Friendship [*eunoias*] with
the Jewish nation." *Dogma synklêtou* is the Greek equivalent of the Latin
senatus consultum (Sherk, p. 15). We have seen that the text of the treaty
here is not in the form of a *senatus consultum*, and ancient Greek archivists
knew how to distinguish the two kinds of documents (Syll.³ 694, lines 23–29).
Josephus may have made the same mistake as Täubler about the formula in
vss. 26 and 28, "as was agreed at Rome," so as to take it as an earmark of a
senatus consultum, but if so, it is strange that he does not reproduce the
formula. Perhaps, then, Josephus' title reflects a loose use of *dogma synklêtou* for any document drawn up pursuant to a vote of the senate; the letter
of the consul Fannius, indeed, may include the text of our treaty among the
synklêtou dogmata it mentions (*AJ* xiv 10.15.233). Since Josephus regarded
our document as a copy drawn up on bronze by the Jews themselves (see below, on vs. 22), he appears to have omitted vs. 23 in the belief that it was a
pious wish added by the Jews, since he could not see how it reflected the language of Roman treaties. Thereafter, however, Josephus' intended text is mu-

tilated in all the manuscripts; perhaps his own secretary is responsible for a blurred and defective text which later scribes were helpless to correct. Of the beginning of the first sentence of paragraph 2 of our standard text, only "shall not allow passage" (*mê diietô*) appears to have been legible, and even it was misread as "no one" (*mêdena*). Of the rest of the first sentence, all that remained was "to wage war" and "the subjects of the Romans." The second sentence of paragraph 2 was legible, but all the rest of the paragraph is missing from the text of Josephus as we have it. The paraphrase of paragraphs 3 and 4, however, is complete.

Hugo Willrich in 1900 believed he had found proof of the falsity of the Jewish claims to have made an alliance with Rome already in the time of Judas: Julius Caesar in the decree quoted at J. *AJ* xiv 10.6.205 says that the Jews possessed Joppe "from an early date, from the time they established ties of friendship with the Romans," yet Joppe did not fall to the Jews until Jonathan took it after Demetrius II's landing in 147 (I 10:76). See Schürer, I, 220, n. 32. Caesar, however, merely uses the language of the Jewish claimants, which was slightly inaccurate; neither they nor he saw any reason to take the trouble to get the precise date. Professional historians and leisured writers in antiquity were guilty of much more blatant errors; see NOTE on 1:8–9, and Bickerman, AIPHOS 13 (1953), 28–29.

Independent testimony to the fact that the Jews made an alliance with Rome in the time of Judas exists in the letter of the consul Gaius Fannius Strabo (see introductory NOTE to this chapter) and also at Justin xxxvi 3.9 and Diodorus xl 2.2, if "Demetrius" there refers to Demetrius I and not to Demetrius II (cf. I 11:52 – 12:4).

19. *a very long journey.* See NOTE on 8:1–19.

20. We saw above (on vss. 17–20) how frank our author is about the status of Judas and his brothers. He may have been equally frank about the status of the segment of the nation backing them. He used not the usual word for "people" (*'am;* Greek *ethnos* or *laos*) but another word which the translator rendered by *plêthos*, presumably *qahal* ("congregation"; cf. Exod 12:6; II Chron 31:18; I Esd 9:4, 10, etc.). Contrast I 12:3. Unlike *ethnos*, *plêthos* had no connotations of privilege; Lysias used it to address the Jews when they were still under the disabilities of the persecution (II 11:16). Though Antiochus V had restored to the Jews at least the title of *ethnos*, the Jewish ambassadors appear to take no note of the fact. Demetrius I may have revoked any privileges conceded by Antiochus V. However, our author in vs. 15 has just used the Hebrew equivalent of *plêthos* to refer to the Roman people, so that we cannot be sure of the reason for his choice of the word.

21. Seleucid claims to sovereignty over Judaea were no obstacle to Roman acceptance of the Jews' proposals. Only a king could claim such sovereignty (Bikerman, *Institutions,* pp. 3–7, 11–24), and the Romans had not yet recognized the only available heir, Demetrius I, as king. Similarly, they recognized the rebel satrap Timarchus as king of Media against the claims of Demetrius (Diodorus xxxi 27a), and in 166 or 165 they had granted autonomy to the Galatians (Polybius xxx 28), despite the claims of King Eumenes II of Pergamum, who had Roman recognition.

22. The Romans kept copies on bronze of treaties and other important resolutions of the senate in the temple of Jupiter Capitolinus (Suetonius *Ves-
pasian* 8; Sherk, p. 98). Josephus in his paraphrase altered vs. 22 to say that a
copy of the senate's decree was sent to Judaea, but the original, engraved on
bronze, was deposited in the temple of Jupiter Capitolinus (*AJ* xii 10.6.416).
Apparently Josephus found it incredible that the copy the Romans sent to the
Jews was engraved on bronze. Since Täubler (I, 362–65, 368, 371), modern
scholars have taken it for granted that the Romans did send the other party
to a treaty a copy on bronze; see Heuss, *Klio* 27 (1934), 249; Accame, pp. 82,
84, 86–87; Sherk, pp. 11–12. However, the ancient texts presented by Täubler
and Heuss show only that bronze tablets bearing copies of a treaty were set up
at Rome and in the territory of the other party and that copies of the treaty
were sent from Rome to the other party. The restoration of the word "tablet" at a point where no words were legible on an inscription (Täubler, I, 364=
Sherk, no. 16, lines 21–22) would even show that such a copy was sent from
Rome on a tablet, but tablets could be of wood (Regenbogen, *"Pinax,"* PW,
XXII [1950], 1410). No ancient text other than our verse says that *the copy
sent from Rome* to the other party was on a *bronze* tablet. Hence, Josephus
may be right. Indeed, it was the Jews for whom it was important to have the
text written on durable material, and they may have copied it onto bronze,
following a practice well attested in Greek cities (Syll.[3] 694; see Heuss,
Klio 27 (1934), XXVII, 246–50).

Greek states were ready to praise their ambassadors even when they gained
a stereotyped treaty of friendship and alliance from the Romans (*Corpus Inscriptionum Graecarum* II 2485=Sherk, no. 16; *Inscriptiones Graecae* IV[2]
1 63); all the more should the Jewish ambassadors receive praise for drafting
an unusual treaty (see Heuss, *Klio* 27 [1934], 28). At Rome, to date the year
one gave the names of the consuls; in most Greek states, similarly, one gave
the name of an official holding a certain office that year. A Greek state in setting up a copy of a treaty might give the names of the Roman consuls, of the
local official(s), and of the ambassadors; see Sherk, no. 16, and Syll.[3] 732.
The names of the consuls did not form part of the text of a treaty, and all
that lay before Josephus was the text of the treaty here. We are able to give an
accurate date of the treaty only because we know the true setting of the document at J. *AJ* xiv 10.15.233 (see NOTE on 7:43 and introductory NOTE to this
chapter). Josephus did not know the true setting, and even if he would take
the trouble to look at the Roman list of consuls, he would hesitate to guess at
the year for fear of being proved wrong. Hence, he does his best to provide
what a Greek audience would expect, in writing (*AJ* xii 10.6.419) that the
treaty "was drafted [*egraphê*] by Eupolemus son of John and by Jason son of
Eleazar, at the time when Judas was high priest of the nation and his brother
Simon was *stratêgos*" (see above, on vss. 17–20). Other communities in the region dated by the names of the priest and the *stratêgos;* see J. A. Goldstein,
"The Syriac Bill of Sale from Dura-Europos," JNES 25 (1966), 9.

23–29. The Romans ignore the claims of Demetrius I and perhaps go beyond the Jews' own requests: they recognize the Jews as an *ethnos*. See above,
on vs. 20 on 1:4, *nations,* and on 1:29–40; and cf. Justin xxxvi. 3.9, Diodorus
xl. 2.2.

23. The Greek text has, "Forever may all be well for the Romans and the nation of the Jews. . . ." The Greek translator was unfamiliar with the formulas of Roman treaties, though he knew Greek very well. The Hebrew *šālōm* is the equivalent both of the Greek *eirênê* ("peace") and of the Greek *kalôs genesthai* ("to be well"); though *šālōm* in extant texts never corresponds to Greek *kalôs genesthai*, it frequently corresponds to the synonymous *chairein* (Isa 48:22, 57:21; Appendix IV, p. 551; NOTE on II 1:1). In retranslating our author's version of the Greek letters of the Seleucid kings, the Greek translator always renders the Hebrew *šālōm* by the idiomatic *chairein* (10:18, etc.). Here, too, he tried to give an idiomatic rendering. Greek wills regularly began, "May I enjoy good health to order my own affairs. But if I suffer the fate of mortals, I leave . . ." (e.g. CPJ 126). The Greek translator took our verse, in the context of vs. 24, as a similar pious wish, "Forever may all be well. . . . But if war should come. . . ." Comparison with other Roman treaties, however, renders it certain that the Greek translator was wrong and that our author's *šālōm* here meant "peace." For the standard text of Roman treaties, see above, on vss. 19–32. On the other hand, it is surprising to see the omission of the words "and alliance" after "peace," especially when the words occur in vs. 22, but they could easily have been lost in the course of the multiple translations and copying.

The Greek text has "foe" where I have "enmity." The standard language of Roman treaties would have at this point "war," a synonym of "sword and enmity." "Foe" may have been substituted by the translator who could have misread *'ybh* ("enmity") as *'yb* ("foe"), or by an early scribe who could have misread *echthos* or *echthra* ("enmity") as *echthros* ("foe").

24. The Greek has "If war should come first upon Rome." However, the standard clause in Roman treaties is "If anyone should move first in bringing war [*proteros epipherêi*] upon the Roman people." This use of "first" (*proteros*) is the Greek idiom for "If any aggressor wages war. . . ." We have here the standard condition of a defensive alliance. See Täubler, I, 5, 55–57, 242–43. In turning the clause into Hebrew, our author probably substituted for the construction with the indefinite pronoun "anyone" the impersonal construction *'im tāqūm milḥāmāh 'al Rōmī*, "If war should come upon Rome." Though the Hebrew construction would then by itself imply that the Romans were being viewed as the victims of aggression (cf. Ps 27:3), our author went on literally to translate *proteros* as *bārīšōnāh* ("first"). The translator then misunderstood the word as referring to Rome, rather than to the aggressor.

Rome did have dependent allies subject to her empire; see A. N. Sherwin-White, OCD², s.v. "Socii." That the Greek *kyria* here means "empire" is proved by *inperio* at the corresponding place in the fragmentary Roman treaty with Callatis (A. Passerini, *Athenaeum*, N.S., 13 (1935), and by *epikrateiai* at the corresponding place in the Roman treaty with Mytilene (*Inscriptiones Graecae* XII 2 35).

25. The expression "wholeheartedly" (*kardiai plêrei*) does not occur in the parallel texts collected at Täubler, I, 55–56, but is equivalent to a stock expression (*panti sthenei*) in Greek treaties; see e.g. Hatto H. Schmitt, *Die Staatsverträge des Altertums, Dritter Band: Die Verträge der griechisch-*

römischen Welt von 338 bis 200 v. Chr. (München: Beck, 1969), no. 551, lines 15 and 66, and no. 552, line 30.

26. Täubler's parallels (I, 50–51) do not have the word "food." It may appear here because of the peculiar position of the Jews, on whom Demetrius levied heavy taxes in produce; see 10:30. Since the Jews at this time had no seacoast, the inclusion of ships here must be the result of a stereotyped requirement.

On the formula "as was agreed at Rome," see above, on vss. 19–32. At the end of the standard clause of a Roman treaty at this point would stand the adverbial phrase "by any deceitful device" (Greek *dolôi ponêrôi;* Latin *dolo malo;* cf. vs. 28, end), but the formula "as was agreed at Rome" interrupts the context, so that the draftsman found it necessary to supply a complete sentence, "The Jews shall carry out their obligations," to support the adverbial expression. I do not know how our author rendered in Hebrew "by any deceitful device" so as to give rise to the Greek translator's *outhen labontes,* literally "having taken nothing," a good equivalent for the original Greek *dolôi ponêrôi* inasmuch as *outhen labontes* is an idiom for "incorruptibly" (see Dinarchus 1.104 and cf. Greek Psalm 14[15H]:5).

27. See above, on vs. 25. Though the translator here expresses "wholeheartedly" by *ek psychês,* the Greek original probably had the same words here as in vs. 25; cf. the Greek translation of II Chron 15:15.

28. Through an extraordinary lapse, the Greek translator has "and to the allies there shall not. . . ." Probably our author here as in vs. 26 rendered the standard Greek *tois polemiois* ("the enemies") by *lannilḥāmīm* ("those at war"), using the same verb stem as he used to express the Romans' giving aid in war in vs. 27 (*yillāḥāmū*), and the translator mechanically used the same Greek verb (*symmachein*) in both places. See above, on vs. 26.

The text of Josephus' paraphrase (*AJ* xii 10.6.417) omits "arms," perhaps only because early scribes found much of this context of the paraphrase illegible. See above, on vss. 19–32.

29. On this verse, see above, on vss. 19–32. I capitalize the word "People" here because it represents the Greek word for the duly constituted assembly of the nation (*dêmos*), in contrast to the word used above in vs. 20; see ad loc. The word renders "nation" (*'am*) in the Greek translations from the Hebrew scriptures only in Daniel and at I 12:6, 14:20, 25. Our Greek translator uses it only in contexts wherein the Jews have received recognition as a nation.

31–32. See above, on vss. 19–32. Our verses are not a forged interpolation (cf. Giovannini and Müller, *Museum Helveticum* 28 [1971], 167). Demetrius I's commander Bacchides may have defeated and killed Judas even before the Jewish ambassadors returned from Rome (9:1–18). In any case, events moved too rapidly for the distant Romans to fulfill the alliance or act on their threats. Indeed, the political situation gave the Romans ample excuse for not acting: they had made a treaty not with Judas but with the Jews, and Bacchides could claim he was supporting the legitimate Jewish authority of Alcimus, who was accepted by the Jewish national organs after Judas' death (9:23–24). Those organs did not protest to Rome against the heavy taxes levied by Demetrius I, the protector of their legitimate high priest. Near contemporaries of the embassy would not have dared to forge our verses, for the Romans would have been quick to expose the forgery. What motive could a later writer have had, in falsely presenting the Romans as uttering threats which Demetrius defied with impunity? Only the motive of discrediting the Romans! But our author and his sources admire the Romans. Hence, our verses have been preserved only because they did stand in the original document.

XVIII. THE DEATH OF JUDAS
(9:1–22)

9 1 When Demetrius heard that Nicanor and his army had fallen in battle, he proceeded again to send Bacchides and Alcimus back against the land of Judah, this time along with the Right Wing of the army. 2 They marched by way of Galilee and laid siege to Messaloth-in-Arbela, captured it, and slaughtered many persons. 3 In the first month of the year 152 they encamped against Jerusalem. 4 However, they broke camp and marched off to Bereth with twenty thousand infantry and two thousand cavalry. 5 Judas had placed his camp at Elasa and had with him three thousand picked men. 6 When they saw how numerous was the army of the enemy, they were terrified. Many melted away from Judas' camp; only eight hundred men remained. 7 When Judas saw how his camp had melted away, the prospect of battle dismayed him. His heart sank, because he had no time to rally them. 8 Though discouraged, he said to his remaining men, "Up! Let us advance against our foes! Perhaps we may be strong enough to fight them!" 9 They tried to dissuade him. "Certainly we shall not be strong enough," they said. "Rather, let us save our own lives now and come back with our brothers and fight them! Now, however, we are too few!" 10 Judas replied, "Far be it from me to do such a thing or to flee from them! If our time has come, let us die bravely for the sake of our brothers and not leave behind a stain upon our glory!"

11 The army marched out from its camp, and they drew up opposite the Jews. The cavalry was divided into two units, and the slingers and archers marched ahead of the infantry, along with all the champions of the vanguard. 12 Bacchides placed himself with the Right Wing. As the phalanx drew near along both ends of the front, they sounded the trumpets, and Judas' men, too, sounded theirs. 13 The earth trembled from the din of the armies, and they were locked in battle from morning till evening. 14 Judas saw that Bacchides and the main strength of his army lay with the men of the Right. Thereupon, all Judas' stouthearted men rallied to him, 15 and

the right flank broke before them, and the Jews pursued them as far as. . . .[a] 16 When the men of the Left Wing perceived that the Right Wing had been routed, they turned about and followed on the heels of Judas and his men, taking them in the rear. 17 In the course of the fierce battle many fell slain on both sides. 18 Finally, Judas fell, and the surviving Jews fled. 19 Jonathan and Simon took up the body of their brother Judas and buried him in the cemetery of his forefathers at Modeïn. 20 They wept for him; indeed, all Israel observed deep mourning for him. Plunged into grief for many days, they said, 21 "How has our hero fallen, the savior of Israel?" 22 There is no written record of the other details of the history of Judas, his battles and his heroic deeds and his personal greatness—there was simply too much to set down.

[a] See NOTE on vss. 4–15.

NOTES

9:1–16. "Right wing" and "left wing" belong to the standard vocabulary used by Greek and Roman historians for describing battle lines. A given military unit could be stationed on either side of the battle line. Here, however, the term "right wing" should be capitalized, since it clearly names a unit of the Seleucid army, probably one half of the phalanx. See Polybius v 53.2–6, and cf. vi 26.9 and 40.4, 6. The phalanx was the massed infantry, the backbone of a Graeco-Macedonian army; according to the figures at Polybius xxx 25.5, Antiochus IV's phalanx of "Macedonians" had twenty thousand men in 166 B.C.E. See Bikerman, *Institutions*, pp. 56, 73–76. From vss. 12–16 one would judge that the elite Right Wing constituted half of Bacchides' infantry. In vs. 4 we learn that Bacchides had a total of twenty thousand infantry, so that one may infer the Macedonian phalanx in 160 had the same number of men as it had in 166. In the winter of 161/60 Demetrius I defeated the rebel Timarchus (see NOTE on 7:1), so that it was now possible to use so important a unit as the Right Wing against Judas.

1–2. The expression "proceeded again" seems to echo *ywsyp . . . šnyt* at Isa 11:11, and "Messaloth" may echo *mᵉsillāh* ("highway") at Isa 11:16. If so, our author is probably mocking those who expected fulfillment of Isaiah 11 after the victory over Nicanor. Indeed, the Lord's great future victory over the enemy is compared at Isa 10:26 to Gideon's victory over Midian; so was Judas' victory over Nicanor, as we can see from the way our author narrated it in language borrowed from Judg 7:21–24. See NOTE on 7:45–46.

Even if several hundred were killed at Messaloth-in-Arbela, one may wonder why our author takes the trouble to mention so insignificant a skirmish, far away from Jerusalem, in which the Hasmonaeans were not involved. Perhaps he wishes to refute a view, held by some Jews, that Demetrius I was not a persecutor but a legitimate sovereign, against whom the Hasmonaeans were rebels; see in AB vol. 41A NOTE on II 2:20. If so, our author here insists that even in the course of an expedition supposedly directed only against the rebellious Hasmonaean party, the army of Demetrius I massacred the innocent Jews of Messaloth-in-Arbela. Probably for the same reason our author in vs. 1 calls Bacchides' objective the "land of Judah," meaning all Palestinian territory inhabited by Jews (see Abel, *Géographie*, I, 314), including Galilee, as Josephus says explicitly (*AJ* xii 11.1.421).

2. *Galilee*. This is the reading of Josephus (*AJ* xii 11.1.421). The manuscript of First Maccabees have Galgala (=Gilgal) or Galaad (=Gilead). There were no Jewish targets left across the Jordan in Gilead (I 5:45), nor was there any other reason to go from Antioch to Jerusalem by way of Gilead. Gilgal played no role in Jewish history after the time of Hosea and Amos; Beth-Haggilgal of Neh 12:29 was an insignificant village near Jerusalem. No Arbela is ever associated with a road to Gilgal. On the other hand, there is an Arbela in Galilee (see Map 14, p. 538), and Greek scribes wrote "Galgala" for "Galilee" at Josh 22:10 and "Galilee" for "Gilgal" at Josh 12:23. By mentioning the route through Galilee, perhaps our author wishes to stress that the route was different from that of the enemy in Isa 10:28–32. See above, on vss. 1–2. In any case, Bacchides marched over an inland route, not through Phoenicia.

Messaloth-in-Arbela. The spelling "*-ess*" is very well attested (A La^G L); the "*-ais-*" of S and V is probably a mere spelling variant. Hebrew *mᵉsillot* means "roads" or perhaps "stairs" (it is rendered by *anabaseis* ["stairs"] at I Chron 26:18 and II Chron 9:11). Josephus (*AJ* xii 11.1.421) says that Bacchides besieged Jews who had taken refuge in caves. In the steep cliffs around Arbela there are plenty of caves, and a considerable village of Jews could have grown up there and been named for the stepped paths leading to it.

3. The first month of 152 Sel. Bab. extended from April 13 through May 11, 160 B.C.E. See NOTE on 7:43.

4–15. As soon as Bacchides and Alcimus knew that the troublemaking Hasmonaean force was not at Jerusalem, they probably saw no reason to terrorize and antagonize the pious Jews in the holy city who might accept Alcimus once Judas was crushed. Our understanding of the subsequent narrative depends on fixing the names of the places mentioned and on identifying them on the map. The manuscript tradition here and in Josephus has variant readings, and the only clues for identifications are the place names used by modern Arabs.

The name of Judas' campsite in manuscripts of First Maccabees is firmly established as *Elasa, Alasa,* or *Eleasa,* reflecting a Hebrew *El'āśā*. One must agree with Abel in preferring for Bacchides' destination the reading *Bereth* derivable from SyIII and La^L G X B (where the endings -*im,* -*in,* and -*em* represent dittography of the following Greek or Latin preposition *en* or *in*). The reading *Berea* of ASVqLa^V and various minuscules could be a grammatical variant of the same name. El-Bireh lies sixteen kilometers north of Jerusalem, by Ramallah, on the road to Nablus; see Map 11, p. 535. The reading *Beêrzath* of the Lucianic recension for Bacchides' destination is suspect. Probably it is derived from a careless reading in Josephus. Josephus (*AJ* xii 11.1.422) strangely gives no special destination for Bacchides' march from Jerusalem, saying only that *Judas* encamped at *Bêrzêthô* (variants: *Barzêthô, Birzêthô, Bêrzêthoi, Zêthô*) and Bacchides marched to meet him. Bēr-Zēthā ("the well of the olive") is Birzeit, about seven kilometers north of El-Bireh on a road off the main road from Jerusalem to Nablus; see Map 11. As long as a campsite was off the main road it could have served Judas' outnumbered guerrilla force. But why, then, did our author call his campsite "Elasa"? And, if our author gave separate campsites for Judas and Bacchides, why did Josephus omit one? Josephus or his secretary may have read in the Greek text lying before them *Berzeth* for *Bereth* and could have read ENTHADE ("there") for ENELASA ("in Elasa"). Hence, it is best to keep the place names as given in First Maccabees.

Off the Jerusalem–Nablus road, by modern Ramallah and across a valley from El-Bireh, lies Khirbet el-ʿAššī, where Judas could well have camped and faced battle (Abel, RB 33 [1924], 384–85); see Map 11. Abel wrongly rejected this possibility later ("Éclaircissement de quelques passages des Maccabées," RB 55 [1948], 187). His later suggestion is much less likely, for Khirbet Ilʿasa lies between Upper and Lower Beth-Horon, more than fifteen kilometers by road from El-Bireh and still farther from Birzeit.

In trying to locate the site of the battle can we find help in the point to which Judas pursued the routed half of Bacchides' army in vs. 15? The manuscripts here have *Azôtou orous,* "a mountain of Azotus." The reading is difficult. Azotus, in the coastal plain, was much too far from any conceivable location of the battle and had no mountain in its territory. Josephus (*AJ* xii 11.2.429) has *Eza orous* or *Aza orous,* "A mountain, Eza [or ʿAza]." Both here and in Josephus the word order and the absence of the definite article are strange. One would expect "the mountain of Azotus" or "the mountain, Eza." No mountain Eza is known. Since the name of the place both here and in Josephus begins *Az-,* it cannot be Mount El-ʿAṣūr (Baʿal Ḥāsōr), eight kilometers east of Birzeit (cf. Abel, RB 33 [1924], 385–87), because the Greek translator would have represented ṣ by sigma, not zeta.

Almost certainly correct is the brilliant conjecture of Johann David Michaelis (*Deutsche Uebersetzung des ersten Buchs der Maccabäer mit Anmerkungen* [Göttingen und Leipzig, 1778]), that someone misread *ʾšdwt* as *ʾšdwd* ("Azotus") from the Hebrew original. Indeed, a similar mistake appears in the Syriac version of Josh 10:40, 12:8, where *ʾšdwt* is rendered *ʾšdwd.* The Greek translator of Joshua merely transliterates it (*Asêdôth*). The word *ʾšdwt* means "watersheds" or "slopes" and occurs those two times in Joshua in association with "mountains," referring to territory conquered by the hero. Our author may have drawn on the contexts to suggest that Judas just missed being as successful as Joshua. Ramallah and El-Bireh stand at the highest point of the road from Jerusalem. The road and its immediate surroundings have almost entirely a downward slope from there until the road crosses Wādi ed-Damm southwest of Khirbet Erhā. Thereafter, the road slopes mostly upward until it passes by Mount Scopus and enters Jerusalem. To the east, west, and north of Ramallah the country is very rugged. Bacchides' routed men could have an easy flight only southward, toward the Akra. Our author may then mean that they fled southward to the lower slope of the rise of which Ramallah is the top, or that they fled southward to the lower slope of the next rise, leading to Jerusalem. As for the absence of the definite article, perhaps the original text was *'ad ašdōt har-* . . . ("as far as the slopes of the mountain of . . ."), and a word has been lost, perhaps "Scopus" or "Jerusalem." Alternatively, the definite article may have been lost somehow, and the original may have had *'ad ašdōt hāhār* ("as far as slopes of the mountain"), "the mountain" meaning "our mountain, the hill of Jerusalem."

Josephus (*BJ* i 1.6.47) has Judas falling at Akedasa. Though he wrote the account in *BJ* from memory, "Akedasa" may be a misreading of *El'asa*. The upper stroke of the *l* could have been neglected because absent or too small, and the large lower hook of the late Herodian and post-Herodian *l* could have been taken as the right-hand curve of a *q*. Indeed, a small upper stroke of a *l* could be taken for the characteristic late Herodian and post-Herodian loop on the upper left corner of a *q*. See F. M. Cross, "The Development of the Jewish Scripts," in BANE, pp. 177 (lines 7–10), 229, and 233. The right downstroke of the ' could have been straight enough to be taken as the vertical left stroke of a *q* and the left stroke of the ', with the late Herodian and post-Herodian thickening of its head, could have been taken as a *d*. See Cross, BANE, pp. 177 (lines 8–10), 227, and 232.

6. Perhaps our author wishes to suggest that had they not been terrified, God would have brought them victory as at II Chron 20:15 and 32:7.

7. *the prospect . . . him.* Cf. Judg 10:9 and I Sam 30:6.

7–10. *His heart sank . . . glory!* According to the prophesy at Enoch xc:9–36, Judas would remain invincible and would live to see the fulfillment of God's glorious promises. Our author seems to borrow the language of Jeremiah's reaction to false prophets (Jer 23:9), "My heart has sunk [literally, 'has broken'] within me." If so, he suggests that even Judas suspected that the prophesies were false. Nevertheless, Judas may have been obstinate in refusing to flee because of his belief in the prophesy of Enoch. Those who advised him not to fight probably included his brothers, who survived. The fate of Judas would then be one more reason for our author's hostility toward those who claimed to have prophetic revelations; see Introduction, pp. 13–14, 44–48. Cf. Neh 6:11–13.

8. *discouraged.* For the expression, cf. Jer 49:24.

9. *dissuade.* The use of the verb here appears to echo Jer 23:22, in the section on false prophets, and confirms our suggestion above, on vss. 7–10, *His heart sank . . . glory!* The dissuaders, if anyone, are the true prophets.

"*Rather . . . few!*" The Greek particle *ê* here may well be the emphatic "surely," accented with a circumflex, rather than "than," accented with a grave. A similar occurrence of the particle occurs at 11:42. "We are [too] few" probably reflects Gen 34:30.

10. Cf. II Sam 23:17; I Chron 11:19.

11. At first sight there is some ambiguity in this sentence, because it is not said of which army are the units who are the subjects of the verbs, and the

Greek has not "the Jews" but only "them." Nevertheless, Josephus (*AJ* xii 11.2.426) was right in taking "them" as "the Jews" and the army units as those of Bacchides. The passage from vs. 6 on stresses the factors intimidating Judas and his band and here goes on to give details on the advancing Seleucid army.

12. On the "Right Wing" see above, on vss. 1–16. Not surprisingly, that unit did occupy the right side of the battle line.

15. See above, on vss. 4–15.

17. Cf. I Sam 31:3; I Chron 10:3; Judg 20:34.

19–21. Surely Bacchides' victorious army controlled the battlefield after they routed Judas' men. How did Jonathan and Simon get Judas' body? And, with their forces completely scattered, how were they able to carry out the lengthy funeral rites at Modeïn unmolested? Josephus (*AJ* xii 11.2.432) says Jonathan and Simon got Judas' body "under a truce" (*hypospondon*), implying that the customary rules of Greek warfare applied, that the defeated could thus get the bodies of the slain; see J. A. O. Larsen, OCD², s.v. "War, Rules of." However, Judas' men were not ordinary enemies, but rebels who had slaughtered the men of Nicanor and mutilated Nicanor's body, so that the customary rules did not apply. Even if they did, why did Bacchides allow the protracted public mourning rites? Hence, Abel's guess is plausible, that Jonathan and Simon in return for a promise to cease resisting Alcimus' regime received the body and permission for the funeral. Our author had no interest in recording the fact that his heroes "collaborated" with the wicked. Pro-Hasmonaean Josephus, too, would have been glad to suppress the details of how the "truce" he reports was won. He may have read a full account of the "truce" in the unabridged work of Jason of Cyrene.

21. Cf. II Sam 1:19, 27.

22. The verse implies that our author based his narrative on written sources. The imitation of a formula of the books of Kings (I Kings 11:41, etc.) befits a dynastic history.

XIX. JONATHAN SUCCEEDS JUDAS
(9:23–31)

9 23 After the death of Judas, "the wicked sprouted" throughout the territory of Israel, "and the evildoers flourished." 24 At the same time occurred a very severe famine, so that the land went over to their side. 25 Bacchides deliberately took the wicked men and placed them in power over the land. 26 Thereupon they began to search and track down Judas' friends and brought them to Bacchides, who inflicted punishment and wanton torment upon them. 27 Grievous trouble came upon Israel such as had not occurred from the time that prophets ceased to appear among them.

28 Then all the friends of Judas assembled and said to Jonathan, 29 "Since the death of your brother Judas there has been no man like him to go forth against our enemies and Bacchides and against the [internal]ᵃ foes of our people. 30 Accordingly, we hereby choose you today to replace him as our commander and chief to carry on our war. 31 On that occasion Jonathan accepted the leadership and took the place of his brother Judas.

ᵃ See NOTE ad loc.

NOTES

9:23–27. On the bitter attack against false prophets here, see Introduction, p. 48. Our author cannot say that the period after Judas' death was a time of renewed Seleucid tyranny, with no Jewish government. Rather, he condemns Alcimus' regime as one of sinners. Though Alcimus is condemned at II 14:3–11, 26–27, the abridger and probably Jason of Cyrene regarded the Jewish local regime after Judas' death as a legitimate and free Jewish government: the holy city was free from the time of the victory over Nicanor (II 2:22, 15:37).

23. Our author clearly parodies Ps 92:8. Does he mean to suggest that the hypocritical wishful thinking of Alcimus and his circle produced this Psalm, too? See NOTE 7:16–17.

24. Our author was aware of the fact we derived above (see on 23–27) from II 2:22 and 15:37, that most Jews readily accepted the local regime

around Alcimus. He has to explain the fact away. On the meaning of "desert" (="go over to their side"), see NOTE on 7:19.

25–31. See NOTES on 7:19–24.

29. At the end of our verse most witnesses to the text have only "the foes of our people." That internal foes are meant is clear from the earlier mention of "enemies and Bacchides." The Lucianic recension and SyI remove the ambiguity by reading "our foes from among our own people."

30. Judas' surviving followers freely choose Jonathan to be "commander" (*śār*) and "chief" (*rōš*); cf. Exod 2:14 and I Sam 15:17. He thus legitimately acquires two of the Hasmonaean titles of political authority. It may or may not be accidental that our author gives Judas only the title "commander" (2:66). Later our Greek texts use the Greek word *stratēgos* of Hasmonaeans bearing the title "commander" because they in fact held the Greek title from the Seleucid king, and later Hasmonaeans continue to bear the title "chief." See I 10:65, 13:8, 42, 53, 14:35, 41, and the coins of John Hyrcanus II. See also Introduction, pp. 10, 75. The echoes of Judg 10:18, 11:8–11, are intentional. Jonathan is to be a latter-day Judge. If Jonathan had promised Bacchides to cease resisting (see above, on vss. 19–21), the atrocities of the regime against members of the Hasmonaean party (vs. 26) were probably a sufficient violation of Bacchides' own promises to make Jonathan feel no longer bound by the agreement.

XX. JONATHAN AS GUERRILLA
CHIEFTAIN
(9:32–73)

9 32 When the news reached Bacchides, he sought to kill Jonathan.
33 When the report reached Jonathan and his brother Simon and all
his men, they fled to the desert of Thekoë and put their camp by the
pool Bor-Asphar. 34ᵃ. . . .ᵃ 35 Jonathan sent his brother in charge of
the non-combatants with a request to his friends, the Nabataeans,
to let him leave with them for safekeeping their cumbersome household goods. 36 But the Jambrites of Medaba marched out, captured
John and all he had, and carried them off. 37 Sometime thereafter,
Jonathan and his brother Simon received a report that the Jambrites
were about to celebrate an important marriage, escorting the bride
(a daughter of one of the great nobles of . . .)ᵇ from Nadabath with
a long procession. 38 Mindful of the blood of their brother John, they
went and hid under the cover of the mountain. 39 As they looked out,
they saw a loud throng with a heavy train of goods. The bridegroom
came out to meet them with his friends and brothers to the sound of
drums and singers and. . . .ᵇ 40 The Jews emerged from ambush and
began to kill them. Many fell slain, and the rest fled to the mountain.
Jonathan and his men took all their goods as spoil. 41 Thus their
marriage celebration was turned into mourning, and the music of
their singers into a dirge. 42 Having avenged their brother's death,
Jonathan and Simon and their men turned back toward the swamps
of the Jordan valley.

43 Bacchides received the news and came on the Sabbath day to
the banks of the Jordan with a large force. 44 Jonathan said to his
men, "Up! Let us fight for our lives! Our plight today is like none
before! 45 Facing us is battle, behind us the water of the Jordan, and
on both sides swamp and thicket! There is no room to draw back!
46 Now, therefore, cry out to Heaven that you may be saved from the
hands of our enemies!" 47 Battle was joined. Jonathan stretched forth

ᵃ. . . .ᵃ Verse 34 is a misplaced gloss. See NOTE on vss. 34–53.
ᵇ See commentary.

his hand to strike down Bacchides, but Bacchides drew back to escape him. 48 Thereupon, Jonathan and his men leaped into the Jordan and plunged across to the other side. The enemy did not cross the Jordan to pursue them. 49 Indeed, Bacchides lost that day about a thousand men.

50 After returning to Jerusalem, Bacchides fortified several towns in Judaea with high walls, gates, and bars: the stronghold in Jericho, Ammaus, Beth-Horon, Bethel, Thamnatha, Pharathon, and Tepho. 51 He stationed garrisions in them to harass Israel. 52 He also strengthened the fortifications of the town of Beth-Zur and Gazara and the Akra and stationed therein troops and stores of food. 53 He took the sons of the leading men of the country as hostages and put them under guard in the Akra in Jerusalem.

54 In the year 153, in the second month, Alcimus issued an order to tear down the wall of the inner court of the sanctuary, thus tearing down the work of the prophets. Alcimus had already begun the work of having it torn down 55 when he suffered a stroke which put an end to his project. Unable to open his mouth and paralyzed, he could no longer speak or issue a will for his family. 56 So died Alcimus in great agony on that occasion. 57 On finding that Alcimus was dead, Bacchides returned to the king. The land of Judah was undisturbed for two years.

58 Then, however, all the wicked formed a plot. They said, "Jonathan and his men now live confident and undisturbed. Let us now have Bacchides come and arrest them all in a single night." 59 They went and presented their plot to Bacchides. 60 Bacchides set out with a strong force, sending secret messages to all his confederates in Judaea to arrest Jonathan and his men, but they failed because their plot became known. 61 Thereupon they seized about fifty of the men of the country who had been ringleaders in the evil plot and put them to death.

62 Jonathan and Simon and Jonathan's men withdrew to Beth-Bassi in the desert. Jonathan had the ruins there rebuilt, and they fortified the place. 63 When the news reached Bacchides, he assembled all his manpower and summoned all his supporters from Judaea. 64 He marched and laid siege to Beth-Bassi. For many days he pressed the attack and constructed siegeworks. 65 Jonathan left his brother Simon in the town and slipped out into the countryside. Accompanied by a few men, he went 66 and . . .ᵉ Odomera and his

---

ᵉ The missing word is probably "summoned." See commentary.

brothers and the Phasironites at their encampment, so that they began to harass and attack Bacchides' troops. 67 Then Simon and his men sallied forth from the city and burned the siegeworks. 68 In battle with Bacchides they defeated him, causing him great chagrin because his strategy and his expedition had been frustrated. 69 Furious at the wicked men who had advised him to come to our country, he put many of them to death and with his men decided to return to his own land. 70 When this news reached Jonathan, he sent an embassy to Bacchides to negotiate with him a treaty of peace and secure the return of their prisoners. 71 Bacchides consented to his proposals and carried them out. He swore to Jonathan that for the rest of his life he would never seek to harm him, 72 and he returned to Jonathan the prisoners he had previously taken from the land of Judah. Then he returned to his own land and no longer marched across their borders. 73 Israel ceased to be at war. Jonathan dwelt at Machmas and began to judge the people and to wipe out the wicked from Israel.

NOTES

9:32. As Bacchides saw it, Jonathan had violated any agreement that had been made between them and was once again a rebel to be killed.

33. Even the territory once dominated by Judas' bands (see NOTE on 2:28) was no longer safe for Jonathan, now viewed as a rebel against a non-persecuting king. Abel has convincingly located the site of his refuge in the desert of Thekoë (=Tekoa), at a point where a pool or cistern provided water. The modern Arabic place names, Khirbet Bîr ez-Za'farān and Šeikh Aḥmad Abu Safar may well be derived from the ancient name of the pool. The Greek translator translated "Bor-" as "pool" (lakkos). I have left it as "Bor-," considering it to be part of the name. See Map 13, p. 537.

34–53. I have omitted from my translation vs. 34: "When the news reached Bacchides on the Sabbath day, he marched with all his army to the other side of the Jordan." Though vs. 34 clearly lay before Josephus (AJ xiii 1.2.9) and caused his entire version of the events to be dislocated, it is a misplaced gloss on vs. 43, for the following reasons:

1) The subject of vs. 35 is clearly Jonathan, as in vs. 33, whereas the subject of vs. 34 is Bacchides. Under such circumstances one would expect to find the subject of vs. 35 clearly expressed, but the text does not indicate the change of subject even by a particle or a demonstrative pronoun.

2) If at that moment Jonathan were being pursued by Bacchides and a large force, he never would have risked sending a slow-moving baggage train to the Nabataeans.

3) Bor-Asphar and the desert of Tekoa are nowhere near the Jordan.

4) Verse 43 leaves it distressingly obscure which bank of the Jordan Bacchides occupied, as can be seen from Josephus' wrong solution of the problem, at *AJ* xiii 1.3.12–14. The Hebrew "banks of the Jordan" (*gᵉdōt hayyardēn;* Greek *tôn krêpidôn tou Iordanou*), from the point of view of one in Jerusalem, allowed of either bank; whereas "the other side of" (Greek *peran;* Hebrew *'ēber*) means only the (correct) east bank. For Hasmonaean propaganda it was important that Jonathan should cross the Jordan westward (like Joshua), not flee eastward out of the Promised Land: see below. Thus a knowing reader, perhaps even the author or the translator, could have felt the need to gloss "banks" by "other side."

5) Verse 34 itself is disordered: no one cared when the news reached Bacchides. The important fact was the possibility of violating the Sabbath if Bacchides should attack the Jewish force on the sacred day. The phrase "on the Sabbath" could be more easily misplaced in the mechanics of scribbling a note in a narrow margin and later copying it into the text. On the other hand, this is not a strong argument that vs. 34 is a gloss, since the writer may have intended to describe Bacchides' prompt action: he received the news on the Sabbath (Friday night) and by a rapid march to the Jordan confronted Jonathan's encampment while it was still the Sabbath.

6) Removal of vs. 34 can be shown to solve the difficulties and leave an intelligible text.

It made good sense for Jonathan to get rid of cumbersome possessions before his refuge came under Seleucid attack. Throughout our verses, Jonathan's bases remain in the wilderness of Judaea, not in Transjordan. Only in Judaea could he have hopes of survival. Though he had some reason to trust the Nabataeans, they might not long back his desperate cause. The baggage train which he wished to entrust to them might have served to bribe them. Once it was lost, that hope was gone. The Nabataeans might even have resented his vengeance on the Arab marauders of Medaba and their allies from Nadabath. In the wilds of Judaea he, like David (cf. I Samuel 22–26), at least had some supporters.

In the framework of Hasmonaean propaganda which is the purpose of First Maccabees, the events of our verses function as proof that Jonathan, far from being a sinful usurper, won God's favor by violating the Sabbath in self-defense and performed feats parallel to those of Joshua and of David's commanders. Thus, vs. 44 contains a deliberate echo of Josh 3:4, and the rest of vss. 44–47 contains allusions to the speech and acts of Joab in war against Israel's enemies across the Jordan (I Chron 19:10–15). Bacchides' fearful closing of the cities of Palestine behind fortifications echoes the fearful measures of the Canaanites after Joshua's crossing (Josh 5:1, 6:1). It is probably no coincidence that Jericho is the first to be mentioned in vs. 50, and that all the places mentioned in that verse but Ammaus and Pharathon are important in the book of Joshua. Hence, strange as it seemed to Josephus, our author portrayed Jonathan in vss. 44–49 as winning his way westbound across the Jordan.

H. Bruppacher ("Textkritisches zu I Macc.," ZAW 49 [1931], 139) argued that vs. 34 was a gloss of vs. 43. He held that it was a note to the Greek translation and could not have been in the Hebrew text which lay before the

Greek translator. Bruppacher in so arguing used our feeble point 5 and the fact that manuscript A here uses the form *Iordanê* as the genitive of "Jordan," rather than the biblical Greek form *Iordanou*. Even if *Iordanê* is the original reading in vs. 34, such genitives are known in biblical Greek; see Henry St. John Thackeray, *A Grammar of the Old Testament in Greek,* I, 163–64. Our translator may have used the strange form himself: this is the first occurrence in First Maccabees of "Jordan" in the genitive, and the translator may have used the unusual but legitimate form here, and in later occurrences he may have remembered the established usage in translation-Greek. Alternatively, the odd form may be the lapse of a later scribe. Hence, Bruppacher's arguments are hardly conclusive.

However, the problem of the origin of the gloss has a bearing on whether the Hebrew text was available to Josephus, for he could have corrected a misplaced gloss of the Greek translation by comparison with the Hebrew text. Josephus was unable to find the true solution. Did the gloss stand in his Hebrew text, or did he lack a Hebrew text?

The gloss may well have stood in his Hebrew text. Above, in our point 4, we have seen how the author himself or his Hasmonaean patron or the translator might have felt the need to gloss vs. 43. Glosses were usually written in the margin, but the margins of Hebrew scrolls could be quite narrow, requiring the scribe to write them sideways, parallel to the column of text; see e.g. The Dead Sea Scrolls of St. Mark's Monastery, ed. Millar Burrows, vol. I: *The Isaiah Manuscript and the Habakkuk Commentary* (New Haven, American Schools of Oriental Research, 1951), plates XXXII–XXXIII. If written sideways, vs. 34 (*wyd' bkydys bywm hšbt wyb' hw' wkl sb'w 'l 'br hyrdn*) could run down a long part of a column, so that a reader could be uncertain to which line of the column it referred. Worse, in a scroll the narrow margin lay between two columns, so that an unwary reader or scribe might connect material in the margin with the wrong column. Such misplaced material would end up usually about one column away from its proper place, but the factor of the uncertainty of finding the proper point of reference of a note written sideways might lead to a larger displacement, of more than one but less than two columns. In the Greek text our gloss is displaced through the 898 letters of vss. 35–42. 898 letters of Greek would correspond to about 480 letters of Hebrew; see Appendix V. On the admittedly shaky basis of the calculations below, the NOTE on I 14:16–24k, a column of the Hebrew archetype which gave rise to the misplaced text there contained about 268 letters, so that the displacement here would indeed be more than one but less than two columns. It is not necessary that the archetype which gave rise to the displacement there be the same as the one which gave rise to the misplaced gloss here, but the possibility is interesting: both may go back to the original edition.

Josephus perceived some of the difficulties brought by the misplaced gloss. Since the Jordan is far from the desert of Tekoa he omitted at *AJ* xiii 1.2.8 the reference to Thekoë. If Bacchides was close upon Jonathan, pursuing him with a large force, it was impossible that Jonathan could have taken vengeance on the Jambrites for the killing of his brother; the vengeance could have occurred only after Bacchides withdrew. Also strange to Josephus was the prospect of Bacchides driving Jonathan and his men to flee into Judaea from Transjordan. Surely fugitives "always" took the opposite direction (cf. II Sam 2:8, 17:22; II 4:26, 5:7–8; J. *AJ* xii 4.11.229–36). Such seems to have been Josephus' reasoning. Not perceiving that the misplaced gloss was at fault, Josephus wrongly assumed that columns of a scroll had been put together in the wrong order. When Josephus attempted to solve difficulties in I 1 by a similar assumption, he operated on the theory that the Greek archetype had about 350 letters per column or that the Hebrew archetype had about 190 letters per column; see Appendix V. Here vss. 37–42 contain 686 Greek letters or 13⅔ lines of Kappler's text. Verses 43–53 contain 20 lines of Kappler's text, 1½ times as much as vss. 37–42. If Josephus used the same theory he employed in I 1, he found that vss. 37–42 occupied two full columns and that vss. 43–53 occupied three full columns. He assumed that the two sets of columns had been transposed. At *AJ* xiii 1.2.7–11 he placed the content of our vss. 34–36, omitting the reference to Thekoë and adding a note at section 11, that he would tell how John was later avenged. Then at xiii 1.3.12–17 he placed the content of vss. 43–53, following his own preconceptions for the direction of Jonathan's crossing of the Jordan. After recording Bacchides' return to the settled centers of Judaea, he would then have Jonathan free to take vengeance. Accordingly, Josephus turned at *AJ* xiii 1.4.18–21 to give the content of vss. 37–42. Josephus' drastic surgery, however, leaves an embarrassing problem: Bacchides advance to the banks of the Jordan would have prevented the despatch of John with the baggage train long before it would have prevented Jonathan's attack on the marauders of Medaba.

Since the book of Jubilees was written long before Jonathan's campaigns and Bacchides' fortifications (Introduction, Part II, n. 4), those events did not inspire the mention of Beth-Horon, Thamna, Pharathon, and Tappuah in Jubilees xxxiv, though Abel thought so ("Topographie des campagnes machabéennes (Suite)," RB 34 [1925], 208–11). Pietist supporters of Alcimus, basing themselves on Jubilees, may have asked that these be the points to be fortified.

35. *his brother.* John (see vs. 36).

his friends, the Nabataeans. See NOTE on 5:25. Always able to maintain a degree of independence against the Hellenistic empires, the Nabataeans in southern Transjordan were now practically free of the Seleucid realm and would resist Seleucid incursions. See II 5:8 and Schürer, III, 731. Our author does not say whether John's destination was the remote and almost impregnable Nabataean stronghold of Petra, some eighty kilometers south of the Dead Sea. The Nabataeans surely controlled land farther north as well. See Map 7, p. 532.

cumbersome household goods. Greek *aposkeuê* renders Hebrew *tp* ("children"), *rkwš* ("property"), and *mqnh* ("property," "cattle"). Below, in vs. 39, it occurs with *throus* ("loud throng"). The Greek *throus* may reflect a Hebrew *hmwn*, for the verb *throein* renders the Hebrew root *hmh* at Song of Songs 5:4. Like vs. 39, Jer 49:32 deals with disaster to Arabs and contains the phrase *hmwn mqnyhm* ("their herds of cattle"). Hence, in vs. 39 the word accompanying *hmwm* is probably *mqnh*, and so also here in vs. 35 *aposkeuê* would reflect *mqnh.* Our author used similar vocabulary in vss. 35 and 39 to stress that the Arab marauders suffered precise retribution.

36. *Jambrites of Medaba.* The Greek gives the name of the tribe as *hyioi Iambri,* reflecting a Hebrew *bny y'mry.* Josephus calls the tribe *Amaraioi,* perhaps reflecting a Semitic *'mry.* Phonetic slurring of a doubled *y* or doubling of a single *y* could easily turn one reading into the other, as could scribal dittography or haplography. The personal name *y'mrw* is attested on the Nabataean inscription, *Corpus Inscriptionum Semiticarum* II 195, of 39 C.E. from Umm-er-Reṣaṣ, sixteen miles southeast of Medaba. Charles Clermont-Ganneau (*Recueil d'archéologie orientale* [Paris, 1888–1924], II, 185) inferred from the inscription that the Jambrites were a Nabataean tribe, though our author gives no such indication. Clermont-Ganneau could indeed be right; our author would avoid calling attention to hostility between the Hasmonaeans and the Nabataeans; see NOTE on 5:25. On the other hand, had our author wished to avoid offending Nabataeans, he could have omitted the name of the tribe. Thus, though the marauders probably were Arabs (see on vs. 37), there is no evidence to show that they must have been Nabataean. There is more than one modern tribe called 'Amārī ('Amārāt); see Alois Musil *Arabia Petraea,* III, index, p. 515, and *Arabia Deserta* (New York: American Geographical Society, 1927), index, p. 589. The road from Jericho and the Jordan valley to the Nabataean stronghold of Petra went through Medaba. See Map 13, p. 537.

37. The names connected with the origin of the bride here were a matter of controversy already in antiquity. "Nadabath" is solidly established by A La^LXV, and the readings of S and V (*Gabadan, Nabadath*) look like corruptions of it. Already Josephus probably knew of no place named "Nadabath" and read instead "Nabatha," presumably an Aramaic form of the name of Nebo near Medaba (Isa 16:2, etc.). However, our author is intent on portraying Jonathan as a hero who performed feats equal to great Israelite victories of old. No earlier victory involved Nebo. If an earlier victory involved "Nadabath," we can be almost certain that our author included the place name in order to allude to it.

At I Chron 5:18–22, the Reubenites, Gadites, and the half-tribe of Manasseh with divine aid won a war against the Hagrites, Jetur, Naphish, and Nodab, *killing many and carrying off vast quantities of cattle (mqnh) as spoil.* Jetur and Naphish were certainly Arab tribes (Gen 25:12–15), and so, probably, were the Hagrites (see S. E. Loewenstamm, *"Hagri,"* Enc. Bib., II [1954], 784–85 [in Hebrew]). For "Nodab" at I Chron 5:19, the Greek has *Nadabaioi.* Arab tribes frequently can be named in two ways, by the gentilic adjective ending in -*y* (Aramaic -*ay*) or by the feminine noun ending in -*ath* (modern Arabic -*a, -e, -eh;* see e.g. Musil, *Arabia Petraea,* III, 40–43).

As the earlier Israelites crushed Arab Hagrites and their Nadabite allies, so Jonathan's band crushed Arab Jambrites and their allies of Nadabath. The allusion to the victory over Hagrites would be all the more pertinent if our author and his audience believed that Psalm 83, with its allusion to Hagrites in vs. 7, was contemporary with the wars of Judas Maccabaeus; see NOTE on 7:16–17.

Strangely, all texts of First Maccabees say that the bride's father was a noble of "Canaan." Our author imitates biblical usage. Accordingly, by writing "Canaan" he would have implied that the bride came from west of the Jordan. Nothing in our narrative makes that origin impossible, though one might then have expected Jonathan to try to capture the bridal procession before it neared Medaba. Josephus, however, describes the bride's father as an *Arab* noble, as one would expect if our author likes to see parallels to I Chron 5:18–22. Greek translators of the Bible more than once misread other names as "Canaan." At Deut 32:49, "Moab" is rendered in Greek by "Canaan." Since Medaba lies in Moab this would be plausible, but it is hard to see how a translator in our context would misread "Moab" as "Canaan." A more likely possibility is illustrated by the way in which Symmachus rendered *M'wn* at Judg 10:12 as "Canaan," apparently by misreading the initial *m* as *kn*. Not only is *Mā'ōn* there the name of an ancient enemy of Israel. Beth-Baal-Meon=Baal-Meon=Beth-Meon (Num 32:38; Josh 13:17; Jer 48:23; Ezek 25:9; I Chron 5:8), modern Mā'īn, lies some seven kilometers southwest of Medaba. See Map 13. Hence, it is likely here that we should fill the blank by "Maon" instead of "Canaan." If so, we may guess that Nadabath, a village named for the Nadabite tribe, lay in the territory of the town of Maon.

39. I have left a blank instead of translating the last two words. Most texts of First Maccabees have here *hoplôn pollôn*, which normally would mean "many weapons" and would hardly fit the context. Greek *hopla* renders Hebrew *kelim* ("instruments") at Jer 21:4 and Ezek 32:24, so perhaps here our author may have meant musical instruments; cf. Gen 31:27. However, both in Jeremiah and in Ezekiel the context deals with instruments of warfare. Our author to dramatize the exactness of the retribution used similar vocabulary in vs. 35 and in vs. 39 (see on vs. 35). This fact would suggest that the original reading here was *ochlôn pollôn*, "a large crowd" (in vs. 35 I have rendered *ochlos* by "non-combatants"). Indeed, that is the reading of Josephus and the Lucianic recension. A scribe familiar with Gen 31:27 could have misread it or corrected it by assuming that *hoplôn* could mean "musical instruments."

40. On the echo of I Chron 5:21–22, see above, on vs. 37.

42. The natives of the neighborhood might try to take vengeance on Jonathan's band, who made for the relative security of the tangled swamps of the Jordan valley.

43. See above, on vss. 34–53. Vigorous Bacchides did not wish to let Jonathan's raid go unpunished and surely jumped at the chance to trap the troublesome force away from its home base and on the Sabbath.

44–47. On the allusions to campaigns of Joshua and Joab, see above, on vss. 34–53.

Bacchides marched to the east bank of the Jordan to trap Jonathan's band. Once that fact is understood, vs. 45 as we have it can be punctuated as in my translation and then makes sense also in Greek and in the hypothetical Hebrew. Hitherto the verse has troubled commentators (e.g. Abel). Despite Josephus' misconceptions, his paraphrase (*AJ* xiii 1.3.13) is correct, though perhaps only because it avoids the difficulties.

Our author uses "draw back" (Greek *ekklinein*) both in vs. 45 and in vs. 47. The Greek word renders Hebrew *ta' arṣu* ("be in dread of") at Deut 20:3

(cf. Hebrew Josh 1:9). Our author's point may well be that despite Jonathan's fight and river crossing on the Sabbath, the punishment promised at Deut 28:7 and 25 falls not upon Jonathan but upon Bacchides. God approves of Jonathan. Since Deut 28:7 and 25 speak of fleeing in seven directions, it may not be accidental that our author names seven places in vs. 50 as towns fortified by Bacchides.

46. Prayer was second nature to the pious warriors. Nevertheless, our author may still have in mind I Chron 5:21–22, where the Chronicler openly speaks of the divine aid which brought the victory. Our author is very cautious of making any such claims directly; see Introduction, pp. 13–14.

48. Did our author know of the legend of Nahshon who boldly plunged into the Red Sea, trusting in God? See Ginzberg, *Legends*, III, 195, and VI, 75–76, n. 388.

50. See above, on vss. 34–53 and 44–47. However heavy the losses Jonathan's band inflicted on Bacchides' troops, the Jewish rebels were a small force, and Bacchides probably felt he could safely concede to them the desert from the Dead Sea to their base at Bor-Asphar. Indeed, they might eventually fall to Idumaeans or Arabs. Our author is anxious to parallel the book of Joshua. To identify Thamnatha, Pharathon, and Tephon we have to rely on help from modern Arabic place names and from the book of Joshua. Those sources lead us to the sites identified by Abel. See his commentary ad loc. and RB 34 (1925), 205–8, and see Map 13, p. 537. All the towns in our verse fortified by Bacchides are strong points lying to the north of Jerusalem, as if Bacchides was trying to deny to Jonathan and like-minded rebels the territory once dominated by Judas; see NOTE on 2:28. Our author describes the sites as lying "in Judaea," though some of them were in the province of Samaria. Our author uses "Judaea" of all Palestinian territory inhabited by Jews; see NOTE on 9:1–2.

Jericho had more than one fortress; see Strabo xvi 2.40.C763. Simon's son-in-law Ptolemy need not have been the first to fortify Dok (I 16:15).

On Ammaus, see NOTE on 3:40–57. On Beth-Horon (Josh 10:10–11, 16:3, 5, etc.) see NOTE on 3:16. At Bethel (Josh 8:9, 12, 17, etc.) Hellenistic remains ascribable to the time of Bacchides' fortification have been found; see J. Kelso, "Bet-El," *Encyclopaedia of Archaeological Excavations in the Holy Land*, I, 37 (in Hebrew).

In the Greek manuscripts all the town names from "Ammaus" to "Tepho" except "Pharathon" are preceded by *kai tēn* ("and"), as if "Pharathon" were part of a compound name, "Thamnatha-Pharathon." However, La[L G B V] SyI SyII and Josephus (*AJ* xiii 1.3.15) treat "Pharathon" as the name of a separate town, as one would expect from Josh 19:50, 24:30 and Judg 12:13, 15. Tepho is Tappuah (Josh 16:8, 17:8); though one might expect a name beginning with Hebrew *t* to have *Th* in Greek, aspiration is often lost in words containing two or more aspirated letters; see Thackeray, *Grammar*, I, 104. The name is much mutilated in the many witnesses to the text. A and S add a final *n*, but the ending in -o, which one would expect (Abel, RB 34 [1925], 207), is attested by VqLa[L V] and many minuscules.

51. Since the menaced regime of Demetrius I could ill afford to tie down valuable soldiers, we may assume that the garrisons consisted mostly of Jews

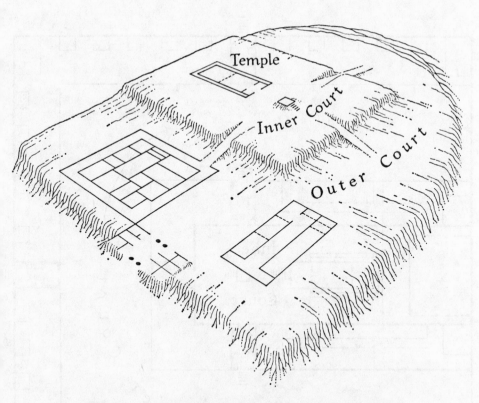

Figure A: The temple and other buildings of Solomon's royal citadel (Adapted from Shemuel Yeivin *"Miqdaš,"* Enc. Bib., V (1968), col. 337)

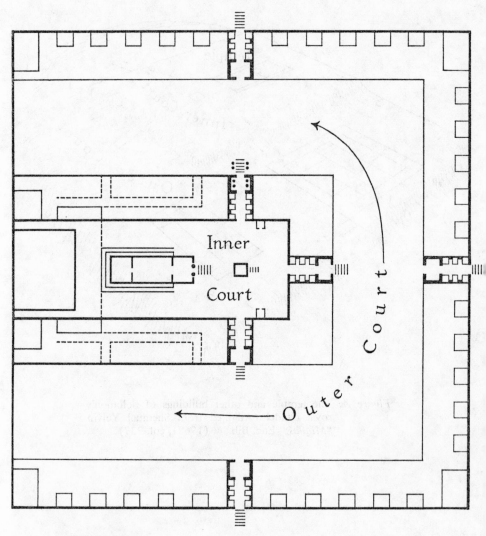

Inner

Court

Outer Court

0   50   100
Scale in cubits

Figure B: The temple and its courts as envisioned by Ezekiel (Adapted from ibid., cols. 347–48)

Figure C: Opposite: The temple and the enclosed areas of the temple mount as known to Josephus and the Mishnah (Adapted from Michael Avi-Yonah, "The Second Temple," in *Sepher Yerushalayim,* ed. M. Avi-Yonah [Jerusalem and Tel-Aviv: Dvir, 1956], I, 415)

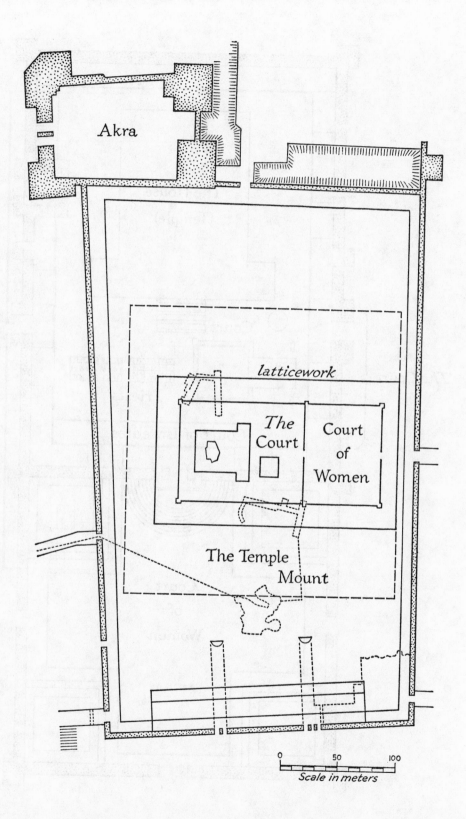

Akra

latticework

The
Court

Court
of
Women

The Temple
Mount

0   50   100

Scale in meters

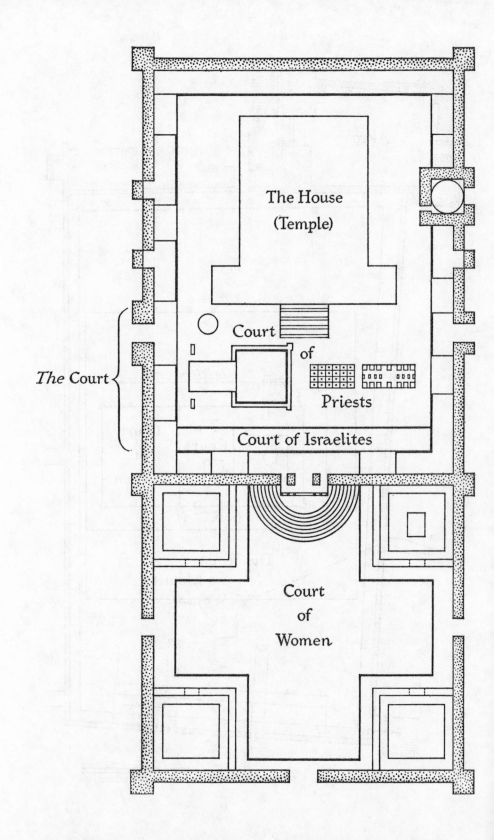

The House
(Temple)

The Court

Court of Priests

Court of Israelites

Court
of
Women

who accepted the regime of Alcimus; see NOTE on 9:23–29, and see 10:12–14 (esp. 14).

52. Beth-Zur, Gazara, and the Akra are mentioned separately here from the points in vs. 50, probably because in their garrisons were regular Seleucid army men; see NOTES on 1:29–40 and 33–40, and on 4:15 and 29, and see 6:50.

54–57. On the displacement in Josephus, see NOTE on 8:17–20.

54. The second month of 153 Sel. Bab. extended from May 2 to May 30, 159 B.C.E. The words of our verse were clear to our author and his audience, but they are difficult for us. What was the "inner court" of the sanctuary, and what wall did Alcimus seek to demolish? What religious issues were involved? "Temple" and "sanctuary" are ambiguous terms. They can refer to the whole complex of sacred buildings and enclosed spaces on the temple mount, or only to the innermost structure, the "house" (*bayit*). In the second temple, "court" was an ambiguous term: it could refer to the court of priests and the narrow part of it open to non-priestly Israelite males (the court of Israel), and it could refer to the court of women, and perhaps even to the outermost enclosed area of the temple mount which is called "the great court" at I Kings 7:9. See *Figures A–D* and S. Yeivin, "*Miqdaš*," Enc. Bib., V (1968), 328–37, 341 (in Hebrew).

Our author seems to agree with Ezekiel and the Mishnah and perhaps with the Chronicler (see II Chron 4:9) in using "court" only of the area around the innermost building (such as *the* court of *Figures C* and *D* and the inner court of *Figure B*), or else of an area like the court of women in *Figures C* and *D* and the outer court in *Figure B*. We may define the latter case as follows: the east wall of the innermost court also constitutes the western boundary of the court in question, and the north and south walls of the court in question continue the line of the north and south walls of the innermost court. In this our author would appear to disagree with the Essenes of Qumran, for according to their Temple Scroll there was to be a vast outer "court" more than large enough to fill the entire temple mount; see for the present Y. Yadin, "The Temple Scroll," BA 30 (1967), 138–39. Josephus, however, like our author uses the Greek word for "court" (*aulê*, reflecting Hebrew *ḥāṣēr* or *'ăzārāh*) only of the enclosure adjacent to the "house" (*BJ* v 5.6.227). The English translations of Josephus are misleading, in using the word "court" for any enclosure.

Accordingly, for our author, "outer court" would have meant the court of women, and the barrier which Alcimus sought to remove could not have been one lying outside the court of women, such as the latticework (Hebrew *sōreg*; Greek *dryphaktos*) which barred gentiles from the structures surrounding the court of women (J. *BJ* v 5.2.193; *M. Middot* 2:3). The latticework was said to have been breached in thirteen places by the "kings of Greece" (*M. Middot* 2:3), surely under Antiochus IV; see NOTE on 1:37.

Therefore, the barrier which Alcimus sought to remove must have belonged to the inner court, "*the* court [par excellence]" (*hā'ăzārāh*) according to the Mishnah, subdivided into the court of priests and the court of Israelites (*M.*

Figure D: Opposite: The temple courts as known to Josephus and the Mishnah (Adapted from ibid., 406)

Middot 2:6; J. *BJ* v 5.6.226–27). Even if Alcimus had not been pious, there could be no issue of introducing gentiles or Greek practices to the inner court. The issue of the "wall of the inner court" must have been an internal Jewish controversy, between Jewish sects. Already Ezekiel in the strongest language presents God as insisting that deviations in matters of temple architecture were dreadful sins; see Ezek 43:8–11, and cf. II Kings 16:10–18 and II Chron 29:7–8. Evidently, the Essenes of Qumran believed so, too, and their Temple Scroll when published will probably cast much light on our passage. We can infer that the issue was one which divided sects admired by Josephus, from the vagueness of his paraphrase here: he does not even say that the barrier belonged to a court, but calls it only "the wall of the holy place" (*AJ* xii 10.6.413).

Ezekiel's complicated arrangement of the inner and outer temple courts was surely intended to keep all but Zadokite priests well away from the inner court, to which only Zadokite priests were to be admitted (Ezek 44:10–16, 46:3 and 9; M. Haran, "*Miqdāš*," Enc. Bib., V, 351–52, 355; cf. Avi-Yonah, *Sepher Yerushalayim*, I, 393 [both in Hebrew]). There is a flagrant difference between the second temple and the temple envisioned by Ezekiel: as we have seen, in the second temple non-priestly male Israelites in a state of ritual purity were allowed to enter at least part of the inner court; see also Neh 8:16 and Haran, Enc. Bib., V, 357.

In this instance, too, Josephus' troubles serve as clues to the existence of Jewish sectarian controversy. Josephus (*BJ* v 5.6.226) uses the word *geision* to refer to the barrier separating the area of the inner court restricted to priests from that open to Israelites. At *AJ* viii 3.9.95 he says that a structure "called *geision* in our native language and *trinchos* ['cornice,' or 'barrier'] in Greek" surrounded the altar and the "house" already in Solomon's temple in order to bar non-priests from the sacred area. At *AJ* xiii 13.5.373, however, Josephus says that Alexander Jannaeus was the one who built "a wooden lattice around the altar and the sanctuary extending up to the *trinchos*" in order to bar non-priests. Was the *geision* a rectangle around the altar and the sanctuary, or a linear barrier just going straight across the inner court? Was there a *geision* in Solomon's temple, or was it a later innovation? Cf. Ralph Marcus, *Josephus*, VII, LCL, 413, note *g*. Josephus appears to have reflected now one, now another Jewish sectarian point of view.

We may guess that some Jews accepted the implication of Ezekiel, that no non-priests were to be allowed anywhere in the inner court. For them, no *geision* was necessary: the structure itself was the result of a dreadful misconception of Jewish law. Others insisted that the practices which the *geision* made possible existed already when the inspired Solomon was building the temple. Our author evidently had no explicit records of prophetic sanction for "the wall of the inner court"; perhaps only the fact that Haggai, Zechariah, and Malachi said nothing against it led to his conviction that the barrier was "the work of the prophets." Cf. Alon, *Meḥqarim*, I, 133, n. 33.

Although Josephus says that *geision* is a word of "our native language" (*tēn epichôrion glôttan*), no one has yet found a satisfactory Hebrew or Aramaic equivalent. Generally Greek gamma reflects Hebrew or Aramaic *g*. On occasion, however, it can also represent Hebrew or Aramaic *ḥ*. Thus, *Gella* (ms. B)=ḥln (Josh 21:15); *Gaber* (ms. B)=ḥbr (I Chron 7:31); *Geththaios* (ms. A) =ḥty (II Chron 1:17); *Ganan* (ms. S)=ḥnn (Neh 7:49); *Gibrôn*= Ḥebrōn (J. *AJ* vii 1.2.7, 3.19, 4.24, 5.31, and often elsewhere in *AJ* vii). Since the word should mean "barrier," *geision* may be the Hebrew word *ḥyṣ* (Ezek 13:10; Greek: *toichon*) or a derivative of the same root. In the context of Ezek 13:10 the "wall" is a physical or metaphorical wall of defense put up by God's erring people and whitewashed by false prophets. In the living language, the associations of *ḥyṣ* were not limited to the context of Ezek 13:10, and it may be the normal word for "barrier," used by those who thought that Israelites should be admitted to a marked-off area of the inner court. The Essene author of CD (4:19, 8:12, 18, 19:25, 31) takes the expression "builders of the wall" from Ezek 13:10 and uses it as a name for a Jewish sect he hates. Did the hated sect get that name because of its theory that Israelites should be admitted to an area of the inner court marked off by a barrier? Some day evidence may be discovered to let us know.

55–56. The Hasmonaean party and our author were quick to take Alcimus' sudden death as proof that God hated him; see J. *AJ* xii 10.6.413. That fact may explain how circles less hostile to Alcimus produced the strange legend of the death of Yaqim; see NOTE on 7:16–17. The wall (*gdr*) which collapses and stones Yaqim may reflect the wall mentioned here.

According to Josephus' paraphrase (*AJ* xii 10.6.413), Alcimus had been high priest for four years. Later (*AJ* xx 10.3.237), Josephus changed the figure to three years. He was probably wrong to change. Alcimus became high priest upon the deposition of Menelaus, which occurred during or immediately after the expedition of Antiochus V and Lysias, and perhaps even at its beginning; see Introduction, pp. 92–93. The expedition came in 149 Sel. Bab. (April 16, 163 – April 4, 162 B.C.E.) and was over by March 5 or perhaps even by January 5. See NOTES on 6:20 and 63. Since Alcimus died in May, 153 Sel. Bab., Josephus' source readily computed his tenure as four years. On that source and on Josephus' problems, see Appendix VI. The easy chronological fit suggests both that Josephus' source for the length of tenure was reliable and that Jason of Cyrene was correct in placing the deposition of Menelaus at the beginning of the expedition (II 12:1–8).

When Josephus tacitly corrected himself at *AJ* xx 10.3.237, he had come to accept our author's date for the death of Alcimus, but he still labored under the burden of accepting our author's erroneous date in 150 Sel. for the events which provoked the expedition of Antiochus V and Lysias. That date was one year too late (see NOTE on 6:20). Josephus felt all the more need to alter the figure of Alcimus' tenure because he placed the deposition of Menelaus at the end of the expedition (*AJ* xii 9.7.383–85). Between the end of an expedition which began in 150 Sel. and a death in the second month of 153 Sel. there could be no more than three years.

57. Evidently the violent Jewish struggles had centered on the issue of whether Alcimus was to be high priest; cf. II 14:3–10. With Alcimus dead, even Jonathan and his men saw little reason to fight, and nothing remained to keep so high ranking a minister as Bacchides in Judaea. Our author, now intent on portraying Jonathan as a latter-day Judge, gladly borrows the language of Judges (3:11, 30, 5:31, 8:28) to refer to the two years of quiet which ensued.

Apparently the Seleucid government could find no satisfactory person to fill the high priesthood and sought to avoid trouble by leaving the position vacant. Did Jonathan's band receive some kind of promise of amnesty? See below, on vss. 58–60. Our author was not interested in reporting Hasmonaean compromises with "wicked" Jews and their Seleucid protectors. He does not even tell us where the band spent the two years of quiet. In vs. 62 we hear of a "withdrawal" by the band to Beth-Bassi. Bor-Asphar was in a remoter part of the desert than Beth-Bassi, so that the "withdrawal" in vs. 62 probably was not from Bor-Asphar, and Jonathan and his band may well have returned to their homes in Judaea.

58–60. Since the "wicked" anti-Hasmonaean Jews surely had ample forces at their disposal (see above, on vs. 51), why did they have to apply to Bacchides? We may guess that either they or the Seleucid government had made promises to Jonathan and his band which could be circumvented or revoked only by calling in Bacchides. The anti-Hasmonaean Jews may also have been afraid that large numbers of Jews would rally to support Jonathan and his band if the anti-Hasmonaeans attempted the arrests alone (whether there had or had not been promises of amnesty). Indeed, Bacchides did not intend to carry out the arrests himself, but sent orders to "his confederates in Judaea" (the anti-Hasmonaean Jews?) to do so while he marched to their aid with a large force.

58. Cf. Ezek 38:11.

61. The Greek text does not identify the subject of the sentence. In view of Bacchides' readiness to sacrifice pro-Seleucid Jews for the sake of peace (see 7:19, 9:69), one might think that the subject is Bacchides' force, as did Josephus (*AJ* xiii 1.5.25). However, one would then expect a word like "again" in vs. 69. Furthermore, the "withdrawal" of Jonathan and his band to Beth-Bassi in vs. 62 would follow well upon their act of violent vengeance here.

62. See above, on vss. 57 and 61. Abel (to our verse and RB 34 [1925], 212–16) correctly identified Beth-Bassi with Khirbet Beit Baṣṣa, some two kilometers southeast of modern Bethlehem; see Map 13, p. 537. Jonathan's choice of Beth-Bassi rather than remote Bor-Asphar shows him to have been much stronger now than he was in vs. 33. We know nothing of the importance of Bethlehem in this period, but it is hard to believe that the town was totally insignificant. It was probably a Jewish town of some importance which Jonathan could threaten and perhaps also view as a potential source of support. Jonathan had his men refortify the ruined site of Beth-Bassi. Had it been one of Uzziah's posts (II Chron 26:10)?

Josephus may have been misled by his topographical and chronological misconceptions (see above, on vss. 34–53) so as to believe that Bacchides left Jonathan free to move in Transjordan and the wilds of the Jordan valley but by fortifying Jericho cut him off from Judaea, including Beth-Bassi. If so, Josephus had to emend "Beth-Bassi" to the name of some strategic point "Beth- . . ." near the lower Jordan. The Greek manuscripts of J. *AJ* xiii 1.5.26 have *Bethalaga*. Abel is probably right in using *Vithagalam*, the reading of a manuscript of the Latin translation of Josephus, to identify Josephus' choice with Deir Ḥajla, six kilometers southeast of Jericho.

63. Bacchides responded immediately to the threat Jonathan's band posed from a fort so close to the heartland of Judaea.

65–66. The word which fills the blank in most witnesses to the text is "smote" (Greek *epataxen*). This reading would make our passage difficult to understand. Though Judas with a large force may have won the aid of the Nabataeans by first defeating them (see NOTE on 5:25), would Jonathan after slipping through siege lines with a tiny force have risked adding to the number of his enemies by "smiting" nomad tribes? Josephus' paraphrase (*AJ* xiii 1.5.28) has "he secretly slipped out into the countryside and gathered a large force from those who sympathized with him." Greek manuscripts V and 340 have *epetaxen*, a word which renders Hebrew *ṣwh* ("command") at Esther 3:2, 12, and *'mr* ("say," "command") at Dan 1:18, 2:2, etc., and occurs elsewhere in First Maccabees (4:41, 5:49, 9:54, 10:81, 12:27 and 43). At 5:49 some scribes actually misread it as *epataxen!* Though elsewhere our translator has it take the dative of the person commanded, Greek usage allows it to take the accusative, as it would here. Perhaps our translator used the accusative when the verb meant "summoned," the sense required here. The language of the last clause of vs. 66 appears to have been taken from Judg 20:31, 39. I have translated the Greek *anebainon en* by the English verb "attack" because the Greek reflects Hebrew *'lh b-*; cf. I Kings 17:5 and II Chron 21:17.

Nothing more is known of the nomad tribes. Their very names are uncertain. Variants of *Odomêra* include *Oidomêra* (S*), *Odoar(r)ên* (L), *Odaren* (La^{X G V}), *'dwr'* (SyI), and *'dwr* (SyII). Variants of *Phasirôn* include *Pharisôn* (V), *Pastron* (La^{X G}), *pšyrwn* (SyI), and *pslwn* (SyII).

The Greek translator by putting the verbs in the imperfect tense implied that Jonathan's nomad allies attacked Bacchides' troops more than once. According to Josephus (*AJ* xiii 1.5.29), however, there was only one such raid, at night, and Simon on perceiving it immediately sallied forth as described in vs. 67. Did Josephus have a family tradition about his ancestor Jonathan?

69. See NOTE on 7:19.

70–72. Twice now Bacchides had acted against the enemies of the Hasmonaeans. Jonathan had reason enough to seek negotiations with him, and for the same reason our author no longer needed to avoid all mention of Hasmonaean compromise with Seleucid officials. Unlike the peace of Lysias (see NOTE on 4:35), the peace of Bacchides could be viewed as a Hasmonaean victory. As guerrilla warriors, Jonathan and his band had few if any living prisoners to exchange with Bacchides. See NOTE on 10:2.

73. The beginning of our verse may be an allusion to Ps 46:10, with our author's characteristic avoidance of naming God.

By moving to Machmas (see Map 13, p. 537), Jonathan and his band had a base at a strong point in the hill country which had been Judas' stronghold. No longer could the fortified towns mentioned in vs. 50 block the band from access to that territory. In days of yore Machmas had been a base for an incipient Israelite kingdom (I Sam 13:2) and had also been the scene of an Israelite victory through the valor of an earlier Jonathan (I Sam 14:5–31).

On Jonathan as Judge, see above, on vs. 30, and Introduction, p. 76. Our author may view Jonathan, the man who wiped out the wicked and purged Israel's dross, as a worthy successor of Josiah (see II Kings 23:24) and as a fulfillment of Isa 1:25–26. Indeed, Isaiah goes on in 1:27–28 to predict the liberation of Jerusalem and the rout of the wicked, exactly as we find them in I 10:7–14.

XXI. ALEXANDER BALAS MAKES JONATHAN HIGH PRIEST

(10:1–21)

10 1 In the year 160 Alexander Epiphanes son of Antiochus landed and captured Ptolemais, where the people accepted him and he was proclaimed king. 2 When the news reached King Demetrius, he assembled a very large army and marched out to meet him in battle. 3 At the same time, Demetrius sent a letter to Jonathan couched in peaceful terms, promising to raise him to high rank. 4 In his mind was the thought, "Let us be the first to act and make peace with him before he makes a pact with Alexander against us. 5 Surely he will remember all the injuries we have perpetrated upon him and upon his brothers and upon his nation." 6 Accordingly, Demetrius conferred upon Jonathan power to raise troops and manufacture arms and made him his ally and also included an order that the hostages in the Akra be turned over to him. 7 Jonathan marched into Jerusalem and had the letter read aloud to all the people and to the men of the Akra. 8 Great was their fear when they heard that the king had granted him power to raise troops. 9 The men of the Akra handed over to Jonathan the hostages, and he restored them to their parents. 10 Jonathan took up residence in Jerusalem and began to rebuild and renovate the city. 11 He ordered those in charge of the enterprise to use squared stone for strength in building the city walls and the circuit around Mount Zion; they did so. 12 The foreigners in the forts built by Bacchides fled. 13 Every one of them deserted his post and returned to his own land. 14 Only in Beth-Zur remained some of those who had deserted the Torah and the commandments; the place served as their refuge.

15 When King Alexander heard of the promises which Demetrius had sent to Jonathan and he was told of the wars and heroic deeds of Jonathan and his brothers and of the hardships they had endured, 16 he exclaimed, "Will we ever find his like? Indeed, let us make him our Friend and Ally right now!" 17 Accordingly he wrote a letter and sent it to Jonathan, as follows:

18 "King Alexander to his brother Jonathan, greeting. 19 We have heard about you, that you are a valorous man and worthy to be our Friend. 20 Accordingly we hereby appoint you today as high priest of your nation and confer upon you the title Friend of the King [Alexander also sent Jonathan a purple robe and a gold crown], so that you may support our cause and maintain friendship toward us."

21 Jonathan put on the sacred vestments in the seventh month of the year 160, on the festival of Tabernacles. He also raised troops and manufactured large quantities of arms.

NOTES

10:1. The year 160 Sel. Mac. ran from September 20, 153, to October 9, 152 B.C.E.

The forceful Demetrius for a while managed to hold and even to strengthen the crumbling Seleucid empire. From the beginning he faced the hostility of the superpower, Rome, for he had become king over the opposition of the senate; see NOTE on 7:1. Demetrius made strenuous diplomatic efforts to win the favor of Rome, and a Roman embassy headed by his friend, Tiberius Gracchus, consented to address him as king (Polybius xxxi 33), probably in 160. Nevertheless, the senate remained basically hostile. They sent him the frigid message that they would accord him kind treatment provided his behavior in his reign proved satisfactory to the senate (Polybius xxxii 3.13).

All the kingdoms of the eastern Mediterranean, however, were overawed by Rome. The fact of Rome's hostility to Demetrius quickly led Ariarathes, king of the nearby kingdom of Cappadocia, to break his engagement to marry Demetrius' sister (probably already in 161; see Diodorus xxxi 28; Justin 1.2). Although Demetrius retaliated by vigorously supporting Orophernes, a pretender to the Cappadocian throne, against Ariarathes, Orophernes eventually proved to be both incompetent and hostile; and Ariarathes, despite only half-hearted support from Rome, became a dangerous enemy. So did Ariarathes' ally, King Attalus II of Pergamum (Diodorus xxxi 32, 32a, 32b, 34; Justin 1.2). Although Demetrius had once had friendly relations with Ptolemy VI (Diodorus xxxi 18), that king, too, turned hostile (Appian *Syriakê* 67), perhaps merely following Rome's example, but also probably having the real grievance of a plot by Demetrius to seize control of the Ptolemaic island of Cyprus (in 156/5, to judge by Polybius xxxiii 5; see Volkmann, PW, XXIII (1959), 1714). We are told that Ariarathes, Attalus, and Ptolemy were all involved in raising Alexander Epiphanes as a pretender against Demetrius (Justin xxxv 1.6; cf. Polybius iii 5.3).

The Hasmonaean party consistently supported the pretender, so that it is not surprising to find our author and Josephus saying nothing to indicate that Alexander's claims to be a son of Antiochus IV were widely doubted, even by some Jews (see NOTE on 13:23). Since our author had ample documents from both branches of the house of Demetrius I to confirm the Simonid Hasmonaean claims (see Introduction, p. 76), he had no need to lie about Alexander, for in so doing he would only validate grants by the extinct Seleucid line of Antiochus IV to the extinct male line of Hasmonaeans descended from Jonathan (cf. Volkmann, *Klio* 19 [1925], 403). Hence, our author simply believed Alexander's claims, as did Strabo (xiii 4.2, C624).

On the other hand, all the other surviving non-Jewish sources (Appian *Syriakê* 67; Livy *Periocha* lii; Justin xxxv 1.6–7; Diodorus xxxi 32a) say that Alexander's claims to be a Seleucid were false. They may all, however, reflect only the propaganda of the ultimately victorious Seleucid line of Demetrius I. Our evidence does not suffice to let us know the truth: Antiochus IV could have had a surviving son, and Demetrius' enemies did not need a real son of Antiochus to set up a pretender; cf. Bevan, II, 300–1.

According to Diodorus xxxi 32a, the young pretender, who resembled Antiochus V, was living at Smyrna shortly after 158 B.C.E., when the king of Pergamum set him up as Seleucid king, sending him to Cilicia, within or just outside Demetrius' borders. According to Justin xxxv 1.6, Alexander's original name was "Balas," but the way in which "Balas" is used as Alexander's epithet in J. *AJ* xiii 4.8.119 and Strabo xvi 2.86, C751, suggests that "Balas" was an epithet given Alexander after he became king. The possible derivation of the epithet from the Syrian and Phoenician divine name "Ba'al" would support this suggestion. In modern works the Alexander of our verse is usually called "Alexander Balas."

In the summer of 153, the rival claimants were pleading their cases before the Roman senate. Young Demetrius, son of Demetrius I, got a merely polite reception and was dismissed homeward. Shortly afterward Alexander himself came before the senate. With him was Laodice, daughter of Antiochus IV. Also at Rome was Herakleides, brother of Timarchus, the late rebel satrap of Media. With Herakleides' help, Alexander gained the consent of the senate, that he and Laodice should receive assistance in their attempt to be restored to their ancestral realm. Thereupon, Herakleides vigorously prepared the means for Alexander to press his claims by war (Polybius xxxiii 18).

Meanwhile, Demetrius I, beset by difficulties domestic and foreign, took to drink (Polybius xxxiii 19) and seclusion in a fortified palace outside Antioch (J. *AJ* xiii 2.1.35–36, perhaps derived from Polybius). According to Josephus (ibid.), Demetrius' resulting unpopularity led the soldiers at Ptolemais to betray the city to Alexander.

By autumn, 152, Alexander had made Jonathan high priest (see on vss. 18–21). The rival bidding for Jonathan's support cannot have lasted more than a few months. Hence, Alexander surely seized Ptolemais by the spring or summer of 152. The earliest known dated coin of Alexander is of 162 Sel. Mac.=September 28, 151 – October 17, 150 B.C.E. (Gardner, *Catalogue of Greek Coins: The Seleucid Kings of Syria*, p. 51, no. 6).

2. Our author is interested in describing in some detail only those events of the conflict which directly concerned the Hasmonaeans: the diplomatic contest (vss. 3–47) and the outcome of the final battle (vss. 48–50). He refers to the early military struggles only in our verse. Demetrius was facing not only

Alexander, but the help sent by the neighboring kings who supported Alexander's claims to the throne; see above, on vs. 1. Ptolemais was an easily defended strongpoint with a harbor, convenient to Ptolemaic Egypt. The pretender there might easily cut Demetrius off from the revenue of all domains to the south, including Judaea. Demetrius probably tried to move promptly against the threat. His unpopularity with his troops may have made it impossible for him to dislodge Alexander from Ptolemais, so that he was all the more forced to try to come to terms with Jonathan.

The story of Demetrius' vigorous resistance at Justin xxxv 1.10–11 is ambiguous: it may refer to a spaced sequence of battles or only to several phases in the final battle which cost Demetrius his life. If Justin's *primo proelio* means "in the first battle" rather than "in the first phase of the [final] battle," we would learn that Demetrius at first inflicted severe defeats on Alexander and his allies. These might explain why we have no traces of coinage by Alexander before 162 Sel. Mac.

3. See Appendix IV, p. 551, and NOTE on 7:10.

4–5. Our author probably reads Demetrius' mind correctly. Nothing tells us how the king reacted to the peace of Bacchides or how Bacchides subsequently fared. To judge by vs. 4 and by 9:71, Bacchides made with Jonathan a personal agreement which was not binding upon Demetrius. Our author is aware that Jonathan at this point was a factional leader, not the recognized head of the whole nation. See below, on vss. 6–9, but cf. NOTE on 10:22–45. Thus we must reject the reading of many witnesses to the text, "to make peace with *them*" (sc. the Jews). Indeed, our reading, "to make peace with *him*," is attested by excellent authority (*L* La^G ^V SyI SyII) as well as by Josephus (*AJ* xiii 2.1.37).

6–9. The letter of Demetrius is not quoted. The Hasmonaean records preserved only the content of permanent interest to the dynasty. By constituting Jonathan the sole local authority empowered to raise and equip an army, and by giving him the prestige of liberator of the hostages, Demetrius assured that Jonathan would become so widely accepted as to become very much the *de facto* head of the nation. Jonathan was quick to move to Jerusalem and take advantage of Demetrius' concessions. Significantly, our author himself admits that not only the men of the Akra but also the *people* were made to hear the text of the letter. The people are sharply distinguished from the "traitors" and foreigners in the Akra, but they, too, can recognize Jonathan as leader only after hearing the king's words. The people may have been as much struck with fear as the "traitors" (vs. 8).

10–11. No power was left to keep Jonathan from residing in Jerusalem and assuming the prerogatives of the head of the nation, including the repair of the city walls and the temple complex; cf. II Sam 5:9; I Kings 6:1, 11:27; II Kings 15:35; Neh 2 – 6:1; Isa 45:13; Zech 6:12–13. "Rebuild and renovate" may echo Isa 61:4.

The Greek text leaves it doubtful whether the squared stone was used both for the city walls and for the temple mount or for the temple mount alone. Josephus, who knew well the fortifications of Jerusalem, at *AJ* xiii 2.1.41 makes it clear that the city walls were rebuilt with squared stone. Josiah, too, used expensive "hewn" or "squared" stone (II Chron 34:11). By fortifying the temple mount, Jonathan worked to make it safe from another Antiochus IV, and from the men of the Akra, and probably also from sectarian Jews opposed to the Hasmonaean interpretations of the Torah.

The most difficult side of the temple mount for wall building was the steep eastern face, and there even Herod may have seen fit to leave the work of Jonathan's men in place. If so, their achievement is still visible, in the fine Hellenistic stonework of the east wall of the Old City, with stones smaller than the Herodian masonry, beginning thirty-two meters from the southeast corner; see Charles Warren and Claude R. Conder, *The Survey of Western Palestine: Jerusalem* (London: Palestine Exploration Fund, 1884), pp. 127, 133, 145–46, 176–77, and Tsafrir, *Qadmoniyot* 5 (1972), 126 (in Hebrew).

12–14. In vss. 12–13 our author writes as if the garrisons of Bacchides' forts were manned entirely by foreigners, but vs. 14 suggests that our author here follows his tendency to call apostates "foreigners," too. See Introduction, pp. 123–24.

The fort and garrison of the Akra were not founded by Bacchides, so that our author, unlike Josephus (*AJ* xiii 2.1.42), feels no necessity to mention that the garrison of the Akra remained at its post. Surrounded by a Jerusalem under Jonathan's control, the Akra could no longer serve as a refuge for apostate Jews, but only Beth-Zur.

16. On the rank of "Friend," see NOTE on 2:18. It is possible that "ally" (*symmachos*) here means more than that Alexander and Jonathan would help each other in war. Privileged regions with some degree of autonomy within the Seleucid empire were said to belong to the "alliance" (*symmachia*). As high priest, Jonathan was head of state and thus could be viewed as privileged dynast over the privileged area of Judaea; see NOTE on 1:4, *nations*, and Introduction, p. 111, and Bikerman, *Institutions*, pp. 141–44. However, the Jews had already been given the title *ethnos* and surely some of the privileges that went with it, and our author's text of Alexander's letter (vss. 18–20) contains nothing about privileges for Judaea but only inducements to Jonathan to support Alexander's cause in war.

18–21. Alexander does his utmost to flatter Jonathan, addressing him as "brother," a Hellenistic title usually reserved for the highest dignitaries of the kingdom; cf. II 11:22 and OGIS 138.2. The use of the title here and at I 11:30 is a mere flattering form. In both cases Jonathan's title remains "Friend," not "Kinsman" (see NOTE on vs. 89, and 11:27). On Jonathan's eligibility for the high priesthood and on Alexander's power to appoint, see Introduction, pp. 8, 75–76. The words in brackets in vs. 20 are a note by our author interrupting the text of the letter.

A purple robe was the uniform of the Friends of the King (Bikerman, *Institutions*, p. 42), but here we have the standard equipment of a priest in the Hellenistic period, a purple robe and a gold crown. See Meyer Reinhold, *History of Purple as a Status Symbol in Antiquity*, Collection Latomus, vol. CXVI (Bruxelles: Latomus, 1970), 35–36.

On the other hand, the vestments of the Jewish high priest included a *blue* robe and a gold "frontlet" (Exod 28:31, 36, 39:22, 30; J. *AJ* iii 7.4.159 and 6.172). The blue dye, indeed, was obtained from the same mollusc as the purple; see NOTE on 4:23. But our author's vocabulary clearly differentiates the purple robe sent by Alexander from the "sacred vestments" (cf. Exod 28:2, 4) donned by Jonathan in vs. 21.

In the year 160 Sel. Bab., the festival of Tabernacles with the Eighth Day of Solemn Assembly fell October 23–30, 152 B.C.E.

Josephus reports erroneously (AJ xiii 2.3.46) that Jonathan became high priest four years after Judas' death. Josephus was drawing on a list of high priests which allotted four years to Alcimus followed by seven years without a high priest; see NOTE on 9:55–56. Josephus appears to have believed that the author of the list had at first been reluctant to recognize Hasmonaean high priests. In correcting this "tendentious reluctance," Josephus subtracted from the seven years without a high priest the three years he himself had allotted to Judas at AJ xii 11.2.434. Since Josephus rejected our author's dates for this period, Josephus had no other way of measuring the interval between Judas' death and Jonathan's investiture. See Appendix VI.

XXII. JONATHAN GROWS IN POWER
(10:22–66)

10 22 When news of these developments reached Demetrius, he was troubled and said, 23 "How did we come to let Alexander get ahead of us in gaining the friendship and support of the Jews? 24 I, too, shall send them a letter offering inducements, promising them honor and rewards, so that they may come to the aid of my cause." 25 He sent them the following message: 26 "King Demetrius to the nation of the Jews, greeting. Since you have kept the terms of your agreements with us and have continued your friendship with us and have not gone over to our enemies, we have rejoiced at the news. 27 Continue now to maintain your loyalty to us, and we shall repay you for your good conduct toward us, 28 with many exemptions and rewards. 29 I hereby release you and exempt all Jews from payments both of the salt price and from the crown dues. 30 *I abandon, from today on, my claim to receive the sums due me, of the value of one third of the sown crops and the value of one half of the fruit of the trees, from the land of Judah, and (. . .) from the three nomes (. . .) from today for all time.* 31 I declare Jerusalem to be sacred and, along with her territory, exempt from tithes and tolls. 32 I also give up my authority over the Akra in Jerusalem and confer it on the high priest, so that he may station there a garrison of whatever men he chooses. 33 All Jewish persons taken prisoner from the Land of Judah to any place in my kingdom I set free without ransom; let all treat them and their cattle as exempt from taxes. 34 All Jewish festivals and Sabbaths and new moons and appointed days, as well as the three days before a festival and the three days after a festival, shall be days of freedom from sales taxes and of exemption, for all Jews in my kingdom, 35 during which no one shall have power to collect money from or harass any of them for any reason. 36 Let up to thirty thousand Jews be enrolled in the royal army; they shall receive the compensation due all members of the royal army. 37 Garrisons drawn from them shall be stationed in the important royal for-

a–a See NOTE ad loc.

tresses, and men drawn from them shall be assigned to positions of trust in my kingdom. Their officers and commanders shall be drawn from their own ranks; they shall follow their own laws, in accordance with the king's decree concerning the Land of Judah. 38 The three nomes, which are to be taken from the territory of Samaria and annexed to Judaea, shall be annexed to Judaea in the sense of complete union, so as to be subject to no other authority than the high priest's. 39 Ptolemais and her possessions I grant as a gift to the sanctuary in Jerusalem to pay for the current expenses of the sanctuary. 40 I also grant annually fifteen thousand shekels of silver from the royal revenue accounts drawn from places in my domains. 41 And if there should be any surplus which the officials in charge shall not have paid out, they shall apply it from now on, as in former years, to the needs of the temple. 42 In addition, our claims to the five thousand shekels which . . .ᵇ temple officials annually used to take from the account are hereby abandoned, inasmuch as the money rightfully belongs to the ministering priests.

43 "Whoever takes refuge at the temple in Jerusalem or anywhere within its precincts, whether owing a debt to the king or to anyone else, shall be free from distraint upon his person and upon any of his property, throughout my kingdom. 44 The expenses of rebuilding and renovating the appurtenances of the sanctuary shall be paid from the royal account. 45 The expenses of rebuilding the walls of Jerusalem and of constructing its circuit of fortifications shall be paid from the royal account, as well as those of building town walls in Judaea."

46 When Jonathan and the people heard these words, they distrusted the proposals and rejected them, because they remembered the great injury he had done to Israel and the harsh oppression he had inflicted upon them. 47 They favored Alexander, because he was the original cause of their opportunity for peaceful discussions. Accordingly, they remained allies of Alexander as long as he lived.

48 King Alexander assembled a large army and encamped opposite Demetrius. 49 When the two kings joined battle, Alexander's army fled. Demetrius pursued him, but Alexander's forces stiffened against his. 50 The battle raged fiercely until sunset, and in the course of the day Demetrius fell.

51 Thereupon, Alexander sent an embassy to Ptolemy, king of Egypt, bearing the following message: 52 "I have returned to my

ᵇ The missing word is probably "the." See NOTE.

kingdom and ascended the throne of my ancestors and have taken power. I have defeated Demetrius and have conquered our territory. 53 Indeed, I joined battle with him, and he and his army were defeated by us, and I have ascended the throne of his kingdom. 54 Therefore, let us now establish ties of friendship between us. Give me now your daughter to wife, and I shall become your son-in-law and give you and her gifts in accordance with your dignity."

55 King Ptolemy replied as follows: "Happy is the day on which you have returned to the land of your ancestors and have ascended the throne of their kingdom. 56 Therefore, I shall now do as you have requested in your letter. Meet me at Ptolemais so that we may see each other face to face, and I shall become your father-in-law as you have proposed."

57 Ptolemy set out from Egypt with his daughter Cleopatra and came to Ptolemais in the year 162. 58 When King Alexander came to meet him, Ptolemy gave him the hand of his daughter Cleopatra and celebrated her marriage in Ptolemais in royal style with great pomp. 59 Alexander wrote to Jonathan, inviting him to come and meet him. 60 Jonathan set out in pomp for Ptolemais, where he met the two kings and gave them and their Friends silver and gold and many other gifts and won their favor. 61 At the same time a group of factious and wicked men of Israel conspired against him, thinking to lodge complaints against him, but the king paid them no heed. 62 Instead, the king gave orders to remove Jonathan's clothing and to dress him in purple, and the orders were carried out. 63 The king had Jonathan sit with him and then said to his officers, "Go with him into the center of the city, and proclaim that no one is to lodge complaints against him for any cause, nor is anyone to harass him for any reason." 64 Accordingly, when those who came to lodge complaints perceived the distinction conferred upon him through the proclamation and saw him wearing purple, they all fled. 65 The king also conferred upon him the distinction of enrolling him in the list of Friends of the First Rank and appointed him *stratêgos* and *meridarchês*. 66 Jonathan returned safe and joyful to Jerusalem.

NOTES

10:22–45. Our author writes in vs. 23 as if by gaining Jonathan's support Alexander had immediately gained the support of the Jews. Apparently Demetrius did not think so. As Grimm already recognized (ad loc.), Demetrius' letter takes no account of Jonathan, being addressed only to the "nation of the Jews." Though the provisions of vss. 32 and 38 involve the high priest, nothing indicates that Demetrius viewed Jonathan as the holder of that office. Indeed, there may have been other aspirants to the post, with support among the Jews, although positive evidence for the fact may no longer survive. Hence, Demetrius was not only bidding for the Jews' support against Alexander. He was probably also trying to win them away from Jonathan. The letter was probably first preserved by anti-Hasmonaean Jews. Our author was unaware of these probabilities. Finding that vss. 32 and 38 were useful for tracing the legitimacy of Hasmonaean power back to a grant by Demetrius I, ancestor of the surviving Seleucid line, he incorporated the letter into his book. The fact that our author misunderstood the text and used a document actually hostile to his own purposes would guarantee that he did not forge it. Josephus perceived the incongruities but never dreamed that our author might be mistaken here. In his paraphrase, Josephus presented the letter as having been addressed both to Jonathan and to the nation of the Jews (*AJ* xiii 2.3.47–48).

The letter is one of our most valuable sources for the fiscal and political structure of the Seleucid empire at this time.

26–28. On the status of a privileged nation (*ethnos*), see NOTE on 1:4, *nation*.

Demetrius opens his letter by praising the Jews for already granting what he seeks: they are already on his side! He goes on to offer them rewards for their present policy, as if there had been no Jewish moves in favor of Alexander's cause. Such an opening maneuver was standard practice in Greek and Roman rhetoric; see e.g. *Rhetorica ad Herennium* i 4.7, 5.8. Nevertheless, Demetrius' maneuver may not have totally ignored the facts. Those Jews who had supported Alcimus, and probably many others outside the Hasmonaean party, had remained loyal to Demetrius. Given some incentive, they might be induced to resist Jonathan's growing armed band. Demetrius offers both exemptions from onerous duties and positive rewards.

29. In the absence of other information on the fiscal institutions of the Seleucid empire, the vocabulary and syntax here are distressingly vague. My translation, indeed, exhibits bad syntax ("both of . . . and from . . ."). Good syntax would require omitting either "both" or "from." Indeed, 62 46 106 SyII omit "from." See also Mayser, II^{II}, 516, lines 1–3. The bad syntax may have arisen from the fact that our document was translated by our author from Greek into Hebrew and then by our Greek translator from Hebrew back into Greek. There is a way of rendering our verse so that it exhibits good syntax. *Phoroi*, the word I have rendered by "payments" can mean "payments

of tribute," and one can translate our passage "from payments of tribute and the salt valuation and from the crown dues." "Tribute" in the Seleucid empire consisted of lump sum payments assessed annually upon communities (cities, temples, nations), not upon individuals. Each community would then make up the sum from the resources of its members; see Rostovtzeff, SEHHW, pp. 464, 469, and 1434, n. 255. It is easy to see how Demetrius could exempt the Jews of Judaea from tribute. It is somewhat harder to see how he could give Jews living in other communities the invidious privilege of not helping to meet community obligations. Moreover, if *phoroi* here are payments of tribute, one would expect the preposition "from" to be repeated before "the salt valuation," but this reading is found only in a few inferior witnesses to the text (311 SyI SyII). Finally, the similar language used earlier by Antiochus III should be decisive: he exempted privileged Jews from "the poll tax and the crown payment and the [payment] concerned with salt" (*hôn hyper tês kephalês telousi kai tou stephanitikou phorou kai tou peri tôn halôn* [J. AJ xii 3.3.142]). Indeed, "payment" (*phoros*) as used by Antiochus III in connection with the salt- and crown-dues certainly has nothing to do with assessed annual payments of tribute (*phoroi*); those are mentioned separately in a later paragraph of Antiochus III's letter (§ 144). I have translated our passage accordingly.

Phoroi here is plural. Whatever the word means, the plural may be conventional and synonymous with the singular (plural *phoroi* translates a singular Hebrew noun at Neh 5:4), or it may refer to payments of tribute over the years or to cases in which an individual Jew belonged to several categories obliged to make payments. Josephus appears to take the plural as indicating exemption from all assessed annual payments (*AJ* xiii 2.3.49).

We have to guess the nature of the salt price payment from its name. It is probably identical with "the [payment] concerned with salt" mentioned in the letter of Antiochus III. Bikerman (*Institutions*, p. 113) guesses that originally the Jews were required to deliver to the king an annual quantity of salt. For this delivery in kind was substituted later the payment of its value in cash, "the salt price payment." However, at the corresponding point of the document at I 11:35, Demetrius II relinquishes his claim to the salt pans, not to a payment substituting for deliveries to him of salt. Perhaps, then, the salt price payment was a compulsory minimum payment that every Jewish household had to make to the royal saltworks, regardless of how much salt it needed.

"Crowns" were originally presents to the king from his subjects, to congratulate him or purchase his favor. They became compulsory exactions, to be delivered to the king upon his accession and whenever else he chose to require them, perhaps even annually (Bikerman, *Institutions*, pp. 111–12).

30. Our verse bristles with difficulties. The Greek, where I have "of the value of . . . and the value of," has what normally would be translated "in return for . . . and in return for. . . ." Since Demetrius here is making sweeping concessions, not requiring afresh a huge portion of the crops, the normal meaning makes no sense. Both here and at I 11:34 we must take Greek *anti* as *to anti*, "the value of." The absence of the word *to* is explainable by the multiple translations underlying our text. Even with the insertion of *to*, I have had to translate somewhat freely to get our verse into clear idiomatic English. A literal rendering of the emended verse would be, "I abandon . . . my claim

to receive the value of one third of the sown crops and the value of one half of the fruit of the trees, which I have the right to receive. . . ." In the Greek, the clause "which I have the right to receive" is a participial phrase which probably modifies both "one third" and "one half." Cf. the parallel at I 11:34, "which the king used to receive."

Also strange, if a regular tax on produce is involved, is the extremely high rate of one third to one half of the crop. The peculiar expressions suggest that Demetrius alludes here to a special exaction laid upon the Jews at the discretion of the king. The high rate suggests that in origin these exactions were a punishment imposed upon the Jews, when they were deprived of their privileges as an *ethnos* and reduced to the position of the lowliest tenants upon the royal domain; see NOTE on I 1:29–40, and Bikerman, *Institutions,* pp. 179–80, and cf. Claire Préaux, *L'économie royale des Lagides,* pp. 182–84. The peculiar language used here and at I 11:34 would be the kings' euphemisms, to avoid reminding the Jews of how the dynasty had punished them. Rostovtzeff's view, that the high rates were usual in Judaea because they recur under Julius Caesar (SEHHW, pp. 468, 1000–1), is probably mistaken; Rostovtzeff himself notes that under Caesar the rate was only one quarter and important concessions were made, such as exempting the sabbatical year; indeed, the source document (J. *AJ* xiv 10.6.203) probably means that one quarter of the crop was to be paid only every second year.

and . . . from . . . time. The Greek text has "and from the three nomes from Samaritis-and-Galilee which are being annexed to the land of Judah, from today for all time." The passage would have several awkward, though not incredible features. The repetition of "from today" in our verse is awkward. If the large portion taken from the value of the crops was a punishment laid upon Judaea (see NOTE on I 1:29), did it also involve three districts of the province of Samaria-and-Galilee? Perhaps. The parenthetic reference to the annexation of the three districts to Judaea here, before the proper place at vs. 38, is also awkward. Josephus' paraphrase, however, has before "from the three" the words "And as for the poll tax which was to be paid me by the inhabitants of Judaea and"; the paraphrase goes on to identify the three districts as "Samaria, Galilee, and Peraea," as if Demetrius dreamed of ceding to the Jews all of Palestine west of the Jordan and part of Transjordan as well! Finally, the paraphrase concludes by having Demetrius say of the poll tax, "I exempt you from it today for all time." Our context here in vs. 30 lacks the reference to the poll tax found in the parallel at J. *AJ* xii 3.3.142.

In these facts we can find clues enough to guess that the original text had "and I exempt from payment of the poll tax those from the land of Judah and from the three nomes, from today for all time." The words "I exempt from the poll tax those from the land of Judah" (APOLYÔAPOTOUYPERTÊ-SKEPHALÊSTOUSAPOGÊSIOUDA) were easily lost from a context so confusing for a scribe (APOGÊSIOUDAKAIAPOLYÔAPOTOUYPERTÊSKEPHALÊSTOUSAPOGÊSIOUDAKAIA-POTÔNTRIÔN). The three names were well known to the recipients of the letter, but Josephus, puzzled, jumped to the conclusion that they were Samaria, Galilee, and Peraea, though at the time of the letter Samaritis and Galilee constituted a single province. An early scribe who was unknown to Josephus correctly explained "the three nomes" with the gloss "from Samaritis-and-Galilee

408   I MACCABEES   § XXII

which are being annexed to the land of Judah." The author of the gloss was very well informed. He knew that the official name of the province was "Samaritis-and-Galilee," not the informal "Samaria" used in vs. 38; see Avi-Yonah, *The Holy Land*, p. 48. As often happened, the gloss was taken up into the text. We can only make guesses about the nature of the Seleucid poll tax. See Bikerman, *Institutions*, p. 111, and Rostovtzeff, SEHHW, pp. 445, 471, 1477.

On the three nomes, see NOTE on vs. 38.

31. The title "sacred" would serve to protect the city from being attacked in time of peace and perhaps also brought some exemptions from taxation. Demetrius would thus renounce his right to attack Jerusalem unless Jerusalem herself should first make war on him. See Bikerman, *Institutions*, pp. 149–56, and Rostovtzeff, SEHHW, pp. 844–47 and 1534, n. 123. According to Josephus (*AJ* xiii 2.3.51), Demetrius promised to make Jerusalem not only "sacred" but "inviolable" (*asylos*). Josephus probably jumped to conclusions, for the privilege of inviolability (*asylia*) would have rendered vs. 43 superfluous. See on vs. 43.

The Greek translator, perhaps failing to understand the Hebrew original, carelessly put "tithes and tolls" in the nominative case, leaving an unintelligible context. Some scribes were able to correct his error, by turning the nominative into an accusative of specification, as we have in our translation. Josephus, too, correctly interpreted the text (*AJ* xiii 2.3.51).

There is little evidence to help us decide what the tithes and tolls were. Demetrius has already dealt with taxes on agricultural produce in vs. 30. Another possibility is more likely. There is evidence that the Seleucid kings levied duties upon all goods entering a city or passing a toll post. If levied as a percentage of the value of the goods, such duties might be called "tithes" even if the rate was other than 10 per cent (Bikerman, *Institutions*, pp. 116–17; cf. Rostovtzeff, SEHHW, pp. 464–70).

32. For subjects to receive control over their own citadel was a great privilege. Normally the Seleucid kings kept garrisons in the citadels of important cities; see Bikerman, *Institutions*, pp. 53–55. Only under the heavy pressure of circumstances did Demetrius consider turning over to a Jewish high priest control of so strong a position in a turbulent area. Earlier, when Jews were famous for being unrebellious (see in AB vol. 41A NOTE on II 1:7, *Jason . . . Kingdom*), Jews may have manned the citadel at Jerusalem (*Letter of Aristeas* 100–4).

Josephus wrongly identifies the high priest as Jonathan (*AJ* xiii 2.3.51); see above, on vss. 22–45.

33. Prisoners of war and captives were regularly sold as slaves. Here Demetrius sets free all Jewish slaves outside Judaea; cf. J. *AJ* xiii 2.3.52.

The end of our verse is obscure and grammatically difficult. Literally it can be translated "Let all abstain from collecting their payments, even of their cattle." Again the difficulty may well be due to the multiple translations lying behind our text. Who are those who would otherwise collect? Which payments (*phoroi*) are meant? Which payments of (or for) cattle? The scribes struggled with the verse, as did the Latin translators, without success. Can it be that Demetrius meant to exempt such Jews from all taxes by way of compensating them for their slavery? Such magnanimity, going far beyond liberating the slaves, would have been unprecedented. Contrast *Letter of Aristeas* 12–27. The guess of Bikerman (*Institutions,* 117) is plausible: Jews taken abroad as slaves with their cattle are to be exempt from paying customs dues and tolls for themselves and their cattle on their way back to Judaea. Cf. OGIS 266, lines 10–11.

Also plausible is Josephus' interpretation, though he appears to ignore the "even" before "of their cattle." Greek *Phoros* renders the Hebrew word *mas,* which means both "tax" and "corvée." The great empires would force corvée duty upon both their subjects and their subjects' beasts of burden, to transport the government mail as well as the persons and baggage of government officials; from the time of the Persian empire on, such duty was called *angareia.* See Kornemann, "Postwesen," PW, XXII¹ (1953), 994–95. Josephus' paraphrase (*AJ* xiii 2.3.52) has, "I command that the Jews' beasts of burden shall not be requisitioned for *angareia.*" If Josephus had made the command say "the Jews and their beasts of burden . . . ," he would have given a thoroughly plausible interpretation of the text here. By serving as slaves, the captives had more than given the equivalent of *angareia.*

34. If "festivals" here reflects an original Hebrew *mō'ădīm,* the festivals are those prescribed in the Torah: Passover, Pentecost, the Day of Remembrance (later to be called Rosh *ha-shanah*), the Day of Atonement, Tabernacles, and the Eighth Day of Solemn Assembly. If "festivals" here reflects an original Hebrew *ḥaggīm,* the festivals are Passover, Pentecost, and Tabernacles with the Eighth Day of Solemn Assembly; the others would then be "appointed days." See Hosea 2:13, Ezek 45:17, and S. Loewenstamm, "*Ḥag, Ḥaggīm ūmō'ădīm,*" Enc. Bib., III (1958), 21–22 (in Hebrew). If so, Demetrius I had his letter drawn up in accordance with the distinctions followed in biblical usage, with the help of Jewish advisers. He could well have done so.

On the other hand, "appointed days" are here called *hêmerai apodedeigmenai,* and nowhere else in the Greek Bible. In Greek, such "appointed days" are annual festivals decreed by the community (see Syll.³ 695, lines 24 and 37–38), like Purim and Hanukkah and the Day of Nicanor. Hence, "festivals" here probably reflects an original Hebrew *mō'ădīm.*

Evidently, there was an established practice to declare freedom from sales taxes and tolls at privileged places during the week surrounding an imperial festival. This practice is probably still reflected by Rabbi Ishmael at *M. 'Abodah zarah* 1:2, but not by his opponents, who regard only the three days preceding a pagan festival as requiring special prohibitions for Jews. However, the authorities of the Talmuds show no knowledge that Rabbi Ishmael's view reflects earlier practice. See *M.'Abodah zarah* 1:1–2, 4; To. *'Abodah zarah* 1:6–9; TB *'Abodah zarah* 11b–12a; TP *'Abodah zarah* 1:4, p. 39c–d; S. Lieberman, "*'Eśer millīn,*" Eshkolot, III (1959), 75–81 (in Hebrew).

"Exemption" probably means "freedom from customs duties and tolls"; see above, on vs. 31.

35. Jews are to be freed from the threat of having to violate the Torah by making payments or appearing in court on a Jewish holy day.

36–37. Demetrius here continues to make concessions, not exactions (but cf. Bikerman, *Institutions,* p. 71). Not every ethnic group was trusted to belong to the regular royal army. For example, Syrians were generally not used; see Launey, *Recherches sur les armées hellénistiques*, I, 536–40. Jews, famous for unrebelliousness, had been favored as soldiers (see NOTE on II 1:7, and Launey, pp. 541–56), and now Demetrius goes beyond restoring to them the favor they had previously enjoyed. Some soldiers served without salary, military duty falling upon them as a condition of their land tenure; see Bikerman, *Institutions*, pp. 68, 78–87. Others were paid by their own local governments (ibid., p. 71). See also Launey, pp. 728–35. Demetrius offers to pay the full salary of his Jewish soldiers; see Bikerman, *Institutions*, pp. 68–70. The word "army" (*dynameis*) here is ambiguous. It might even mean that Jews were to be admitted to the elite massed infantry, the phalanx, customarily manned by Macedonians. Indeed, the unpopular Demetrius' lack of soldiers and the large number of thirty thousand would suggest that Jews were to be admitted to the phalanx; see ibid., pp. 73–74.

The appointment to positions of trust (vs. 37), such as the command of a citadel (as suggested in Josephus' paraphrase) is a further indication that Jews were to be admitted to elite units; see Bikerman, *Institutions*, pp. 54–55. Since the king specifies that even the commanding officers over Jews shall be Jews, we learn that such was not the general practice, even with troops drawn from trusted subject peoples; cf. Launey, pp. 546, 559.

At the end of vs. 37, Demetrius alludes to his own earlier decree, that the Jews of Judaea are to be governed by the rules of the Torah, and extends it to cover any Jews enrolled in the army. Our author regards Demetrius as a wicked persecutor and passed over the decree in silence, just as he did with the decree of Antiochus V (II 11:24–25). The existence of Demetrius' decree on the Torah goes far to explain why pious Jews were so ready to accept Alcimus and to welcome Bacchides (I 7:5–15).

38. The three nomes were so well known to Demetrius' audience that he did not have to specify their names. The names are given in the letter of Demetrius II to Jonathan (I 11:34), as Aphairema (*'ăpārayim;* see Samuel Klein, *Sepher hayyishuv* [Jerusalem: Dvir, 1939–44], I, 112 [in Hebrew]), Lydda, and Ramathaim; see Map 13, p. 537. The three nomes, though not previously part of Judaea, were part of the area that had been Judas' stronghold (see NOTE on 2:28), and may well have been solidly Jewish. They may already have been dominated by Jonathan. Jews may long before have been pressing historical claims to the areas and perhaps to all of Samaria, alleging that the territories had been granted to Judaea by Alexander the Great (J. *Ap.* ii 4.23); see John C. Gager, "Pseudo-Hecataeus Again," ZNW (1969), 135–36.

The wording of our verse is peculiar. The word which I have translated "which are to . . . be annexed" is an aorist (past) participle in Greek. The tense of the participle may not be significant, for the Greek translator worked from our author's Hebrew translation of Demetrius' Greek original, and in biblical Hebrew the participles are tenseless. Still, the use of the participle here may reflect an effort in Demetrius' letter gracefully to recognize either the alleged grant of Alexander the Great or the *fait accompli* of the detachment of the three districts from the province of Samaria; cf. Avi-Yonah, *The Holy Land*, p. 56. Finally, it is also possible that Demetrius here contemplates removing the three nomes from *Jonathan's* control by annexing them to a Judaea ruled by a high priest yet to be named by the king, a Judaea wherein many of the people viewed Jonathan with hatred and fear.

Josephus was led by the provisions in vs. 37 for the observance of the Torah to construe our verse, too, as dealing with religious law rather than with political authority: the Jews of the three nomes from Samaria are to be compelled to recognize the sole legitimacy of the temple in Jerusalem (*AJ* xiii 2.3.54). However, violent Jewish hostility toward the schismatic temple of the Samaritans seems to have erupted only with the reign of John Hyrcanus (J. *AJ* xiii 9.1.255–56), when it appeared to be clear that the temple of Jerusalem was again "the place which the Lord hath chosen" (see Introduction, pp. 40, 58). Thus, Josephus' interpretation, which hardly fits our author's words, may also be anachronistic.

"Nome" (*nomos*) is a Greek word used of districts in Egypt. The use of the word in the letters of Demetrius I and Demetrius II may well be a survival from the time of Ptolemaic rule over the area. Elsewhere (at 11:28) our author, like Josephus (*AJ* xiii 2.3.50), calls the districts "toparchies," which may have been the usual Seleucid term for such areas; see Bikerman, *Institutions*, pp. 198, 203.

39–42. Earlier, Kings Antiochus III and Seleucus IV had made gifts to the temple expressly for the expenses of the sacrificial cult (J. *AJ* xii 3.3.140; II 3:3). The language used at the end of vs. 39 shows that Demetrius here, unlike them, contemplates not donations expressly for sacrifices but general gifts toward the expenses of the temple. Already at this time, Jews may have held that pagans were not to bear the expenses of the regular obligatory sacrificial cult, but only Jewish individuals or the Jewish community. See AB vol. 41A, NOTE on II 3:3, and cf. "*Gōy*," Enṣiqlopediah talmudit, V (1953), 302.

We learn in vs. 41 that part of the money contributed by the king could be used for construction work (*erga*) on the temple and its utensils. For the meaning of *erga* (Hebrew *ml'kh*, '*bwdh*), cf. Exod 36:5; II Kings 12:12–15; I Chron 29:7; II Chron 24:12–13. In vs. 44 the king himself promises to pay for the upkeep of the existing structure and utensils of the temple, so here in vs. 41 Demetrius probably refers to expenditures on new construction. The word *erga* is vague enough to include other expenditures as well. In vs. 41 the king is making a concession: the freer application of royal grants to purposes other than sacrifice was known from earlier times and from now on will again prevail. Clearly the matter had been the subject of a dispute between the temple authorities and the Seleucid government. According to later Jewish law and according to Greek law, money given to pay for sacrifices (*heqdēš mizbēah*, in rabbinic terminology) could be used for no other purpose. See "*Heqdēš*," Enṣiqlopediah talmudit, X (1961), 353, 366, and E. Pottier, "Dedicatio," DAGR, II¹ (1892) 42b, and Th. Homolle, "Donarium," ibid., pp. 367a, 370a, and 380, and AB vol. 41A, NOTE on II 3:6. There is no reason to think that the Jewish law on this point was different at the time of the letter. Thus Demetrius here cannot be referring to money given expressly for sacrifices.

On the other hand, donations to the temple given without specifying that they were for sacrifices could easily lead to disputes, as one can see from debates in rabbinic literature; see Enṣiqlopediah talmudit, X, 356–62. Could such gifts be applied at the discretion of the priests to any temple expense? Since Demetrius' concession reflects previous disputes, we may infer that the letter here was not the first occasion of a gift toward the general expenses of the temple. Greek systems of law regularly provided means for auditing the accounts of temple officials. See Homolle, DAGR, II^I, 370a, 379b–381a. Hence, the king could demand that the Jewish priests similarly render account.

We learn in vs. 42 that not only had temple authorities applied some of the king's gifts to non-sacrificial purposes; the ministering priests had even taken a considerable part for themselves. Again the king could have felt he was entitled to demand an accounting.

The Jewish temple authorities could find reasons to resist the king's demands. There was the precedent of their earlier free application of the surplus of unspecified gifts to non-sacrificial purposes. Furthermore, the Torah gave the priests a generous share of the property flowing into the temple and even portions of many sacrifices (Num 18:8–9; see also II Kings 12:17), and there were Jewish precedents against subjecting the administrators who handled the general temple funds to an accounting (II Kings 12:15, 22:17).

Hence, we may guess that the earlier dispute reflected in vs. 41 arose because the king made a gift to the temple without specifying that it was for sacrifices but assuming that it would so be used, whereas the temple authorities assumed it could be freely applied to construction costs. We may guess that the dispute reflected in vs. 42 arose because the Jewish priests took for themselves more than the royal government thought was their due, though the priests may have been entitled to take it under Jewish law. In both cases, the Jews may have objected to requiring the priests to give an accounting to the king.

Josephus in his paraphrase of vs. 40 (AJ xiii 2.3.55) has the king specifying the terms of his donation: the donation is to pay for sacrifices, but the surplus over the sacrificial needs is for unrestricted use by Jonathan and the Jews. That may have been the practice in Josephus' own time, but our interpretation, unlike his, fits the words of the document here.

Verse 42 has baffled interpreters. As it stands, it looks as if some persons (who?) or Demetrius I himself previously had been taking money from the temple, money which Jews claimed belonged to the ministering priests. Josephus (AJ xiii 2.3.55) has "the kings" as the takers of the money. Although the kings did tax temples, our verse then would be strangely expressed. Again the multiple translations underlying our text may well have led to corruption. A very simple solution is to insert hoi ("the") before apo tôn chreiôn, yielding "the officials in charge," as in vs. 41, and so I have rendered the context by "temple officials," leaving a gap for the missing "the." The financial officials of the temple could easily have taken the annual surpluses and spent them for temple purposes, and the Seleucid government, seeking to recover the sums, could have held them liable. The Greek expression meaning "the officials in charge" was difficult to handle in our author's Hebrew (did he write ăšer 'al haṣṣᵉrākîm?), especially in a sentence which had a closely preceding ăšer ("which"). The second ăšer could easily have been omitted to produce our text. If so, here as in vs. 41, Demetrius concedes to the Jewish authorities the money in dispute.

39. Ptolemais was the base of the rival king, Alexander Balas. At least for the present, Demetrius' gift of the city and its revenues to the temple was an empty gesture to bribe the Jews and punish Ptolemais. Josephus omits the gesture from his paraphrase. Seleucid kings did make such gifts; cf. II 4:30.

40. Having made the empty gift of Ptolemais, the king now makes the real offer to the temple of fifteen thousand shekels of silver annually, to be drawn from his own assured revenues. The word "place" here (*topos*) has the technical meaning of "an unprivileged area in the royal domain"; see Bengtson, *Strategie*, II, 9–12, but his interpretation of *ethnos* is to be rejected for the one in the NOTE on 1:4. The multiple translations and the multiplicity of ancient standards make it impossible to establish what unit of weight in silver Demetrius had in mind. The Seleucid stater weighed about 8.5 grams. The Tyrian shekel, basis of the standard used by the Jews (TB *Baba qamma* 36b), weighed about 7 grams, and the sacred shekel, used for fulfilling biblical requirements, was a double Tyrian shekel of about 14 grams (TB *Bekorot* 50a; cf. J. *AJ* iii 8.2.194: 1 shekel=4 drachmas=2 staters). If Demetrius' standard here was the same as that in the letter of Antiochus III (J. *AJ* xii 3.3.140), and if our author's shekel was a stater, the 15,000 staters here would be half again as much annually in silver as Antiochus III's 20,000 drachmas. Hence, there is no reason to regard the figure as small, though Josephus in his paraphrase has Demetrius offering 150,000 drachmas (*AJ* xiii 2.3.55).

Josephus' larger figure cannot be explained by protracted inflation, since prices, so far as we know, remained quite stable, and some even fell. See Fritz Heichelheim, *Wirtschaftliche Schwankungen der Zeit von Alexander bis Augustus* (Jena: Fischer, 1930), p. 122, and *idem, An Ancient Economic History* (Leyden: Sijthoff, 1958–70), III, 216–17, and cf. AB vol. 41A, NOTE on II 4:19.

43. The Hellenistic kings recognized the Greek institution of the right of asylum at privileged shrines. Even condemned criminals could receive immunity there as long as they remained within the sacred precincts. See E. Caillemer, "Asylia," DAGR I¹ (1877), 507a, and Bikerman, *Institutions*, pp. 149–52. However, Demetrius does not use the word "asylum" or its derivatives. Few refugees if any would be permitted to reside within the sacred precincts of the Jewish temple. And the right of asylum for debtors is a concept foreign to Jewish law. Therefore, it would appear that Demetrius here confers a more limited privilege on the Jewish temple; see Caillemer, DAGR, I¹, 505b– 506a. The verb "shall be free" (*apolelysthôsan*) is vague. I have taken it to mean, not that the debts shall be canceled (which would be contrary to Jewish law), but that the refugee should thereafter be immune from being pressed to pay by distraint upon his person or upon his property.

44–45. Jonathan probably carried out his building projects from the booty taken from the "wicked" by his band and from taxes levied upon the people. Both sources could serve to make Jonathan hated. Demetrius here exploits the situation, offering to shoulder the entire burden and more; cf. Ezra 6:4; Neh 2:8. Later Jewish law would have barred the Jews from accepting his offer (Enṣiqlopediah talmudit, V, 308–9).

46–47. Small wonder that Jonathan distrusted offers probably designed to wean people away from him. Even the people may have been glad to choose the side of Alexander because of the harsh treatment they had previously received from Demetrius. Those Jews who favored Demetrius now must have been too afraid of Jonathan's growing power to do anything.

The end of vs. 47 has proved difficult for translators, since *archêgos* normally means "originator," and by our author's own account Demetrius made overtures to Jonathan and the Jews before Alexander. However, with my translation all is logical: Alexander was indeed the original cause (*archêgos*) of the Jews' opportunity.

Josephus in his paraphrase passes over our verses in silence (*AJ* xiii 2.4.58). Since Alexander Balas had a bad reputation with the Graeco-Roman audience for whom Josephus wrote, Josephus avoided mention of Jewish sympathy for Alexander's cause; see NOTE on I 11:1–11. Furthermore, Josephus may well have been apprehensive over the strange impression created by quoting Demetrius' sweeping concessions only to record that the Jews rejected them.

48. See above, on vs. 2.

49–51. The text of vs. 49 is difficult. Kappler is probably right in adopting the more difficult reading of ASLa^V, "Alexander's army fled. Demetrius pursued him." S^{ca} V L La$^{L G B}$ have "Demetrius' army fled. Alexander pursued him." Most of our author's battle descriptions are straightforward, especially when both armies are pagan. Scribes probably did not expect a report of a seesaw battle and altered the text so as to have Demetrius losing from the outset. Other sources, however, indicate that there was a seesaw battle. Josephus surely had another source for his description of Demetrius' brave death, telling how the king fought on alone to the end after having lost his horse in a swamp; Josephus' account of the beginning of the battle says that the left wing of Demetrius' army routed their opponents, but his right wing, where he was, suffered defeat. See J. *AJ* xiii 2.4.59–61.

If Justin xxxv 1.10–11 describes only the final battle (see NOTE on 10:2), Justin's account, too, largely confirms our version of the one here: Demetrius at first routed the forces of Alexander and the kings allied to him and then vigorously met their counterattack, but finally fell, bravely fighting to the end.

Kappler's text still leaves a difficulty: where I have "Alexander's forces stiffened," the Greek has only a verb in the third person singular (*ischysen*, "was strong"), with no indication of a change of subject. If the forces of Demetrius routed Alexander's men and then Demetrius strongly prevailed, it is hard to see how the battle could have raged throughout the day and cost Demetrius his life. Hence, it is best to accept the reading of La$^{L X G}$, *ischysan* ("they were strong," "they stiffened"). The change from the singular Greek verb "pursued" to the plural "stiffened" is enough to indicate the change of subject. At the same time, the sudden change from singular to plural could well have puzzled an unwary ancient scribe so that he mistakenly corrected the plural "stiffened" to the singular so as to produce the text of our Greek manuscripts.

Demetrius was still recognized as king in Babylon on the third day of some month in 161 Sel. Bab. (that is, between April 6, 151, and March 26, 150; Parker and Dubberstein, *Babylonian Chronology*, p. 23). The latest dated coins of Demetrius and the earliest of Alexander are of 162 Sel. Mac. (September 28, 151 – October 16, 150). Polybius, presumably reckoning by Olympiad years, which began in midsummer, says that his friend Demetrius I reigned twelve years (iii 5.3). Josephus' unknown source (*AJ* xiii 2.4.61) gives him eleven years, reckoning by some other system. Probably, this means that Demetrius I reigned more than eleven years from his accession in the early autumn of 162 B.C.E. but less than twelve full years. Accordingly, Demetrius I fell at a time close enough to midsummer, 150, that Polybius could credit him with a reign of twelve years.

51–58. Why does our author narrate the marriage of Cleopatra and Alexander in such detail? There is also another problem, in the narrative of Jonathan's career. Judas' siege of the Akra failed, and he was killed for his mistaken belief that Israel's subjection was over (9:8–18). Jonathan had long refrained from rash assumptions concerning God's will for Israel. He long raised no challenge to the legitimacy of the rule of Demetrius I and was a loyal subject of Alexander Balas. He will even show loyalty to Demetrius II. How, then, could he besiege the Akra (11:20–29; see NOTE on 11:22–29) and seek to renew the alliance with Rome (12:1–4)?

One fact may give solutions for both problems. Pious Jews, including the Hasmonaean party, accepted Daniel 2 as prophesy (see Introduction, p. 44; I shall treat this subject in detail elsewhere). In Dan 2:43–44, the seer predicts that there will first be a marriage between two dynasties from among the dynasties of the now-divided Graeco-Macedonian empire; one of these dynasties shall be as strong as iron and the other as weak as clay. Shortly thereafter, the whole structure of pagan empires will collapse. Inept Alexander could be called as weak as clay, and so could his inept successor, Demetrius II; before his untimely death, able Ptolemy VI could be called as strong as iron. The Jews had already been disappointed twice, through the failures of the prophesy to be fulfilled by the marriage of Antiochus II and Berenice in 252 and by the marriage of Ptolemy V and Cleopatra Syra in winter 194/3. Nevertheless, many kept their faith and expected fulfillment now, with the marriage of Cleopatra Thea to a Seleucid.

Indeed, the disintegration of the Hellenistic empires soon became obvious: Alexander Balas fell; Ptolemy VI was slain; Ptolemaic Egypt was torn by strife; Demetrius though sole Seleucid ruler was inept and unpopular and soon was challenged by a pretender. Hence, Jonathan must have been sure that the days of pagan kingdoms were numbered. Even in acting with increased boldness, he remained cautious, since God's timetable was not clear. Jonathan took no irrevocable step. He could consent to end his siege of the Akra. He could still serve his pagan sovereign as a valuable and loyal subject. He could even have broken off an alliance should it have proved to have come too early for God's timetable.

Our author, wise with hindsight, probably still accepted the veracity of Daniel 2 but knew that it had not yet been fulfilled. From his sources he took over the details of Cleopatra's marriages to Alexander and to Demetrius II. Prudently he refrained from putting any echo of Daniel 2 into his narrative.

51. Our author appears not to know that Ptolemy VI Philometor had been backing Alexander for months; see NOTE on 10:1.

52–56. Although our author would in any case have turned the Greek letters of the kings into Hebrew idiom, the flavor of the correspondence here is so

Hebraic that the text is probably his own composition. There is, indeed, no reason why the original correspondence of Alexander and Ptolemy VI should have been preserved. The rhythm of our verses may be compared with Ps 68:19, and their general character with the exchange of messages at I Kings 5:16–23. Verse 52 gives a general view of Alexander's achievements; vs. 53 gives details of how they were accomplished. Ptolemy VI may have previously proposed the marriage of his daughter Cleopatra Thea to Alexander. Perhaps already he thought his dynasty might dominate the Seleucid realm through marriage, as once Antiochus III had sought to dominate the Ptolemaic empire by giving his daughter Cleopatra I (mother of Ptolemy VI) in marriage to Ptolemy V; see Walter Otto, *Zur Geschichte der Zeit des 6. Ptolemäers*, pp. 118–24.

Alexander had good reason to seek the marriage even if Ptolemy VI had not previously proposed it. Demetrius I had taken the precaution of sending his sons to safety outside the kingdom (Justin xxxv 2.1), and now their claims could be a rallying point for any elements in the Seleucid realm hostile to the young and inexperienced Alexander. Modern observers have interpreted, as a gesture to curry favor with Ptolemy, Alexander's early royal coinage in Phoenicia, beginning in 162 Sel. Mac., for it is on the Ptolemaic standard and bears on the reverse side the Ptolemaic eagle (Volkmann, RE, XXIII, 1716). The city in the Seleucid realm which bore the dynastic name of the Ptolemies was indeed a good site for so political a wedding.

57. The date here may be either 162 Sel. Mac. or 162 Sel. Bab. Since the events took place at Ptolemais, near Judaea, and involved Jonathan, our author need not have taken the date from a Seleucid history; see Introduction, pp. 22–25. Indeed, Seleucid histories available to our author were probably written for the line of Demetrius I and could well have omitted the date. Josephus finds puzzling our author's dates for events from the last years of Judas and from the career of Jonathan; he includes in his paraphrase only Seleucid dynastic dates which he could verify from other sources. He omits the date here from his paraphrase (*AJ* xiii 4.1.82) as if he could not verify it elsewhere. See Appendix VI. The wedding probably occurred in late summer of 150 B.C.E. at a time when the date was both 162 Sel. Bab. and 162 Sel. Mac.

60–64. It was important for Jonathan to make a powerful impression on Alexander. It was no time for humility! Again his resources must have come from booty taken from the "wicked" or from taxes levied upon the people; cf. 1QpHab 8:8–13, 9:4–5, and see Introduction, pp. 65–66. Inevitably the victims sought to protest. Partisans of the Oniad line of high priests, now influential with Ptolemy VI (see p. 57) also probably came to protest. Power in Judaea, however, rested with Jonathan, and insecure Alexander needed power, so that the protests were fruitless.

On the purple of the King's Friends, see NOTE on 10:18–21. For the king's procedure, cf. Esther 6:4–12, 8:15.

65. The order of the King's Friends had several ranks: simple "Friends," "Honored Friends," "Friends of the First Rank," and probably also, at the top, "Highly Honored Friends of the First Rank"; see Bikerman, *Institutions*, pp. 41–42.

By becoming *stratêgos* and *meridarchês,* Jonathan probably became military and civil governor of the province of Judaea. The civil and military governor of the province of Samaria appears to have borne the same title (J. *AJ* xii 5.5.261, 7.1.287).

66. Contrast Esther 6:12 end, and cf. Isa 55:12.

XXIII. JONATHAN DEFEATS
APOLLONIUS
(10:67–89)

10 67 In the year 165, Demetrius son of Demetrius came from Crete to the land of his ancestors. 68 King Alexander on receiving the news was deeply troubled and returned to Antioch. 69 Demetrius reappointed Apollonius, the incumbent governor, over Coele-Syria. Apollonius assembled a large force and encamped at Jamnia. There he sent the following message to Jonathan the high priest:

70 "Only you rebel against us. Because of you I have become a laughingstock and an object of reproach. Why are you lording it over us in your mountains? 71 If you now have confidence in your troops, come down against us into the plain and let us take the measure of one another there, because on my side is the power of the cities. 72 Ask, and you will learn who I am, and who are the others coming to my aid! They will tell you that your feet cannot stand before us, because twice your ancestors were routed in their land. 73 Now, too, you will not be able to withstand such cavalry and infantry in the plain, where there is neither rock nor pebble nor a place to flee."

74 Stirred on hearing the words of Apollonius, Jonathan took ten thousand picked men and marched out from Jerusalem and was joined by his brother Simon who came with reinforcements. 75 Jonathan encamped by Joppe. The people of the town barred their gates to him because Apollonius had a garrison in Joppe. Accordingly, they attacked the town. 76 Frightened, the townspeople opened their gates and gave Jonathan control over Joppe. 77 On receiving the news, Apollonius took three thousand cavalry and a large force of infantry and marched toward Azotus as if traveling through, at the same time leading on into the plain because of his confidence in his large cavalry force. 78 Jonathan pursued him toward Azotus, where the armies joined battle. 79 Apollonius left a hidden force of one thousand cavalry to the rear of the Jews. 80 Jonathan perceived that there was an ambush to his rear. The enemy had his army surrounded

and shot arrows at his men from morning to evening. 81 The men, however, stood their ground as Jonathan had ordered, and the enemy's horses grew tired. 82 Then Simon drew out his troops and engaged the enemy phalanx. The enemy cavalry was exhausted, so that they broke before him and fled. 83 With their cavalry dispersed over the plain, the enemy fled to Azotus and sought to save themselves by going into Beth-Dagon, the temple of their idol. 84 Jonathan, however, set fire to Azotus and the surrounding towns and plundered them; the temple of Dagon along with those who had taken refuge there he burned. 85 The number of those who fell by the sword plus those who were burned to death reached eight thousand. 86 From there Jonathan withdrew and encamped against Ascalon, but the townspeople came out to welcome him with great pomp. 87 Thereupon, Jonathan and his men returned to Jerusalem loaded with much booty. 88 When King Alexander heard of these events, he conferred even more distinction upon Jonathan. 89 He sent him a gold brooch such as was customarily given to persons with the title "Kinsman of the King" and granted him Akkaron with its entire territory, to be his heritage.

NOTES

10:67–68. The year 165 Sel. Mac. extended from September 25, 148, through October 13, 147 B.C.E. We may guess that Demetrius II landed after March 10, 147. Earlier in the year ancient sailors were reluctant to risk the storms (Vegetius iv.39).

Alexander Balas proved to be an inept and lazy king (Justin xxxv 2.2–3). His own incompetence and the conduct of his subordinates made him unpopular with his subjects (J. *AJ* xiii 4.6.108; Diodorus xxxiii 3; Livy *Periocha* 1), and other evidence may indicate how unsteady was the ruling hand of the king (Volkmann, *Klio* 19 [1925], 406).

Young Demetrius II was just a teenager (Justin xxxv 2.1–2) when he took advantage of Alexander's ineptitude and pressed his own claims to the Seleucid throne. When Demetrius I had sent his two sons for safety to the Greek city of Knidos, he sent with them a large sum in gold. Using the money, young Demetrius secured Cretan mercenaries (ibid.) and landed in the Seleucid border province of Cilicia (J. *AJ* xiii 4.3.86). Alexander Balas had begun as pretender from the same area; see NOTE on 10:1.

Alexander seems hitherto to have stayed away from Antioch, entrusting the administration of the Seleucid capital to subordinates (Diodorus xxxiii 3). Perhaps he had been residing at Ptolemais. By moving to Antioch he was nearer to the trouble zone of Cilicia and forestalled any attempt by Demetrius to seize the capital (so J. *AJ* xiii 4.3.87), where he had supporters (Justin xxxv 2.3).

69–89. As translated by us, our text makes good sense and is supported by all the extant texts of First Maccabees. Josephus, however, either had a bad text or misread ours, for by failing to read "Demetrius" and by joining vs. 69 to vs. 68, Josephus has *Alexander* now appointing Apollonius. Since Apollonius was the incumbent (*ton onta*), Alexander had indeed previously appointed Apollonius. A pagan history or the work of Onias IV may have said so, and with such confirmation Josephus would have felt no need to check the reading of his Greek text with the reading of a Hebrew text.

Josephus' Greek text was probably still more deceptive. Though one good manuscript (F) of Josephus has *ton onta* ("the incumbent"), the others have *ton Taon* or *ton Daon*, as if Apollonius bore the epithet "Taos" or "Daos"; the reading of F may well be a scribe's correction based on our text here. If so, the Greek scribe whose work lay before Josephus failed to understand *ton onta*. Indeed, in Greek the verb "reappointed" also means "appointed," and in such contexts one usually has the name and epithets of the appointee and then the name of his office. For the scribe "the incumbent" appears to have been a totally unexpected expression, so that he emended the text. His result is hardly credible, even given the ineptitude of Alexander: *Alexander's* general Apollonius challenges Jonathan on the king's behalf; Jonathan defeats Apollonius *and* receives the praise of Alexander, who pretends that Apollonius' actions were unauthorized (*AJ* xiii 4.3–4.88–102). It is barely possible that a writer (Onias IV?) to demonstrate the perfidy of Seleucids presented the story in accordance with the version given by Josephus. If so, again Josephus would have felt no reason to consult a Hebrew text and get the correct story.

Our narrative suggests that Apollonius originally was a local grandee of the Philistine cities (see below, on vss. 70–73), to whom Alexander had conceded power just as he conceded power to Jonathan in Judaea. Demetrius II showed favor to Philistine Gaza during his reign; see Introduction, pp. 120–21. Jamnia, too, was a Philistine town (II Chron 26:6). See Map 13, p. 537.

Our passage clearly draws on I Kings 20:23–32. As usual, our author avoids directly mentioning divine intervention. His audience, knowing the story in Kings, would readily jump to such conclusions. Though the story in Kings is of the defeat of Aramaeans, not Philistines, Apollonius was the agent of the pretender to the throne of Syria ("Aram" in Hebrew). Unlike Ahab in Kings, Jonathan did not make the impious mistake of sparing the enemy. Only respectful (and probably uninvolved) Ascalon received his clemency.

The analogy with the story in Kings may have contributed to Josephus' belief that Apollonius was a general of Alexander King of Syria, not a general of Demetrius II Pretender in Cilicia. Thereby, Josephus was also able to see Jonathan, like Ahab, receiving honor from a vanquished king of Syria, but Josephus should have asked himself how our author could have suggested comparing Jonathan with Ahab! On the date of the events, see NOTE on I 11:1–11, end.

70–73. Our author probably had a good tradition as to the content of Apollonius' letter, but the Hebraic flavor again seems to indicate that the wording is our author's own composition, using I Kings 20:23–28.

As governor of Coele-Syria first for Alexander and then for Demetrius II, Apollonius was Jonathan's superior but apparently had been unable to make Jonathan obey orders (vs. 70). In vss. 71–72, Apollonius proudly implies that he and his allies are men of the Philistine cities, descended from those who twice vanquished Jonathan's ancestors in "their" land. Since the whole point is to dare Jonathan to come down into the Philistine plain, the antecedent of "their" must be "the Philistines'," not "the Jews'." If so, Apollonius in his challenge probably alludes not to victories mentioned in the Bible but to victories in the plain remembered in Philistine tradition, whereby the Philistines secured their independence against Israel or Judah at some time after the death of Solomon. Josephus (*AJ* xiii 4.3.90) may have understood. Whether our author understood which victories Apollonius meant, we cannot tell. Our author himself may have identified the victories with the battles of Aphek, in which Philistine forces twice defeated Israelites on Israelite territory (I Sam 4:1–11). Such a misunderstanding was all the easier because the battle at I Kings 20:26–30 also occurred at a place called Aphek.

73. *pebble*. Is this an allusion to the story of David and Goliath (I Sam 17: 40, 49)? Josephus may have thought so (*AJ* xiii 4.3.90). Our verse certainly echoes the exploits of the earlier Jonathan at Greek I Sam 14:14.

74–82. Our author takes care to display the role of Simon in Jonathan's victory.

75–76. See Map 13, p. 537. Jonathan's objective was not to capture Joppe (=Joppa), because he made no attempt to hold it at this time (see vs. 87, 11:6, and 12:33). Rather, he responded to Apollonius' challenge by entering the coastal plain at the point closest to his own strongholds. The territory of Joppe adjoined Jonathan's district of Lydda.

Our author here does not portray Joppe as a town hostile to Jonathan and the Jews (cf. II 12:3–7). In this period Joppe counted as a Phoenician, not as a Philistine town; see Magen Broshi, "Yāfō," Enc. Bib., III (1958), 742 (in Hebrew). The townspeople barred their gates only because Apollonius had a garrison there. Hence, the first Greek verb in vs. 75 means only "encamped," not "besieged."

77–79. Although good witnesses to the text say that Apollonius "assembled a camp of" (*parenebale*) three thousand cavalry, etc., the corresponding Hebrew verb *ḥnh* is intransitive, so that one must read "took" (*parelabe*) with V L and J. *AJ* xiii 4.4.92.

Verse 77 is difficult. To judge by vs. 69, Apollonius was in Jamnia, north of Azotus and south of Joppe. Why, then, did he march south to Azotus "as if traveling through," and whom did he "lead on" into the plain? Though it is not difficult to supply "Jonathan" as the object of "leading on," the absence of an object makes our text look defective. And even if Apollonius feigned cowardice and did march away from Jonathan's challenge at Joppe, how could he be sure that Jonathan would follow him toward an ambush near Azotus? All these difficulties seem to have led Josephus wrongly to reconstruct the text. He probably assumed that a second "he marched to" and the words following it had dropped out because a scribe became confused after the preceding "he marched to." Josephus' reconstructed text, to judge by his paraphrase (*AJ* xiii 4.4.92) had, after "Azotus," "Thence he marched to Joppe, pretending to be traveling through the countryside, and then he pretended to retreat from Jonathan, at the same time leading him on into the plain" (*kai hôs diodeuôn eporeuthê eis Ioppên kai ekeithen hôs anachôrôn apo Iônathan proêgen eis to pedion*).

Josephus, however, failed to solve the problem: Why would Apollonius march south to Azotus on his way to Joppe? It is better to assume that our text is basically sound. Apollonius was confident that after being challenged by the mocking letter, Jonathan would pursue him if he feigned cowardice and retreated from Jamnia. Jonathan could be lured to begin the pursuit by receiving misinformation from pretended deserters. Indeed, our author's words seem to mean that Apollonius pretended that his destination lay even farther south than Azotus. To have confronted Jonathan by marching from Jamnia toward Joppe would have brought Apollonius into somewhat rougher country and into sand dunes much less advantageous for his cavalry than the flatter country near Azotus. With no source available to him other than our text, Josephus was probably guessing when he added that Apollonius posted his cavalry ambush "in a valley" (*AJ* xiii 4.4.94).

80–81. The Greek word for "army" and "men" here is *laos* (Hebrew '*am*, "people"), as often in the Hebrew Bible (I Sam 13:5; Exod 14:6, etc.) and as at I 5:6; hence our author in using it here need have had no special purpose, but he may have meant to indicate that now Jonathan commanded a national army which obeyed him loyally.

82. Again our author stresses the role of Simon.

83–84. Without cavalry of his own, Jonathan could not pursue the dispersed enemy horse. Apollonius' infantry, however, had to flee for their lives. To judge by I 11:4, the temple (*beth*) of Dagon lay outside the walls of Azotus. Our author and his audience knew of Dagon's temple at Azotus (=Ashdod) from I Sam 5:2–5. They would readily view Jonathan as the one who completed the vengeance for the ancient humiliations at Aphek. See above, on vss. 70–73, and NOTE on 5:43.

86. Though Ascalon was a city with Philistine traditions, it consistently maintained polite relations with the Hasmonaeans; see NOTE on 8:1–16.

89. A person with the title "Kinsman" was of still higher rank than the Friends. A Kinsman was entitled to fasten his purple cloak with a golden brooch. See Bikerman, *Institutions*, pp. 42–44. The gift of the old Philistine town of Akkaron (Ekron) made Jonathan now similar to David, who had received Ziklag as his heritage in return for his services to a pagan king (I Sam 27:6).

XXIV. THE FALL OF ALEXANDER
BALAS
(11:1–19)

11 1 Meanwhile, the king of Egypt assembled troops as numerous as the sand on the seashore and many ships. His aim was to conquer Alexander's kingdom by treachery and add it to his own. 2 He set out for Syria professing peaceful intentions. At town after town the people opened their gates and came out to meet him, because King Alexander had issued an order to go out to meet him, inasmuch as Ptolemy was his father-in-law. 3 As Ptolemy marched into each town, he would detach troops to be a garrison there. 4 When he drew near Azotus, they displayed to him the burnt temple of Dagon and the ruined town and suburbs of Azotus, still strewn with the unburied corpses of the slain, and also the bodies of those who had been burned to death by Jonathan in the course of the fighting. The burnt corpses the townspeople had heaped up along Ptolemy's route. 5 They told the king what Jonathan had done, intending to bring the king's censure upon him, but the king said nothing. 6 Jonathan came in pomp to Joppe to meet the king. They exchanged greetings and slept over in the town. 7 Then Jonathan marched with the king as far as the river called Eleutherus and returned to Jerusalem.

8 Thus King Ptolemy became master of the coastal cities as far as Seleuceia-by-the-Sea. All the while, he was devising evil schemes against Alexander. 9 He sent ambassadors to King Demetrius with the following proposal: "Come, let us make a pact. I shall give you my daughter, who was formerly Alexander's wife. You will be king over your father's kingdom, 10 for I now have come to regret having given Alexander my daughter inasmuch as he has plotted to kill me." 11 Ptolemy accused Alexander because he coveted Alexander's kingdom. 12 He took his daughter from Alexander and gave her to Demetrius, breaking off relations with Alexander so that they became open enemies. 13 Ptolemy thereupon marched into Antioch and placed upon his own head the diadem of Asia; thus he wore two diadems around his head, one for Egypt and one for Asia.

14 All this time, King Alexander had been in Cilicia because the people there were in revolt. 15 On receiving the news, Alexander marched to meet Ptolemy in battle. Ptolemy came out against him with a strong force and routed him. 16 While Alexander fled into hiding in Arabia, King Ptolemy reached the peak of his power. 17 Zabdiel the Arab cut off Alexander's head and sent it to Ptolemy. 18 Ptolemy, however, died on the third day thereafter, and his men occupying the strongholds were massacred by the native troops in the strongholds. 19 As a result, Demetrius became king in the year 167.

NOTES

11:1–11. Our author is consistently sympathetic to Alexander and to his son, Antiochus VI, the benefactors of Jonathan, and here he presents Alexander as the victim of Ptolemy VI's premeditated treachery. On the other hand, Onias IV, the admirer of his own benefactor Ptolemy VI, is the probable source of the account in J. *AJ* xiii 4.5–7.103–10. Josephus chose here to follow Onias IV rather than our author because Onias' attitude toward Alexander and Ptolemy VI matched the one prevailing among Greek and Roman historians (Polybius xxviii 21.4–5; Diodorus xxxiii 1.3, 12.1; Justin xxxv 2.2; Athenaeus v.211a). See my article, "The Tales of the Tobiads," in *Studies Smith*, Part III, p. 111.

The account in Josephus has Ptolemy VI marching into the Seleucid realm to help Alexander fight Demetrius II, only to come near being killed through a plot of Alexander's against him. Only then, according to this account, did Ptolemy turn away from Alexander to support Demetrius. Diodorus (xxxii 9c) presents a third account: Ptolemy entered Syria to help Alexander, but on discovering Alexander's complete incompetence, he fabricated the story of a plot against him and turned to back Demetrius II. Diodorus' source was probably Polybius (Volkmann, *Klio* 19 [1925], 408–9).

However, even an impartial contemporary could not read Ptolemy's mind, and we have no means of determining now what was the truth. The Ptolemies from the first coveted parts of Syria, and so did Ptolemy VI (Otto, *Zur Geschichte*, pp. 121–22). Though Alexander was in a precarious position as regards Demetrius II, he may well not have welcomed Ptolemy's intervention, even if it came as fulfillment of their alliance. A plot to assassinate Ptolemy VI at a time when a large Egyptian army was within the Seleucid realm was not necessarily the wild idea of an incompetent. Many Ptolemaic soldiers who had supported the claims of Ptolemy VI's brother, the future Ptolemy VIII Euergetes II, might welcome the death of Ptolemy VI. Indeed, the survivors of the expeditionary force to Syria seem to have championed the cause of

Ptolemy VIII against Ptolemy VI's widow and his young heir. Ptolemy VIII invaded Egypt by landing at Pelusium, at the east end of the delta (Albert Rehm, "Der Brief Ptolemaios VIII. Euergetes II. an seine Wehrmacht auf Kypros," *Philologus* 97 [1948], 271). He probably joined forces there with the survivors (Volkmann, PW, XXIII [1959], 1726). As for the attitude of the Seleucid army toward Ptolemy VI's intervention in Syria, it can be judged from what happened later (vs. 18). Hence, either king or both may have been guilty of plotting against the other.

As for the date of Ptolemy VI's expedition, the events of vss. 1–19 cannot have taken long, for the provocations were too great for combat to be delayed. Ptolemy's death occurred in midsummer, 145, so that the expedition probably began in late spring.

Verse 4 shows that Ptolemy's march into Syria came very soon after Jonathan's victory at Azotus.

2. *order.* So I have translated the Greek word *entolê,* a technical term for a circular letter addressed to many recipients (here, the authorities in the towns); a messenger would carry the original *entolê,* showing it to each recipient in turn (E. Bikerman, "Notes sur la chancellerie des Lagides," *Archives d'histoire du droit oriental* 2 [1953], 251–59).

3. This posting of garrisons, to anti-Ptolemaic contemporary observers and to our author, was proof of Ptolemy VI's treachery. However, the Philistine towns had strongly supported Demetrius II; see NOTE on 10:69–89. Thus, well might Ptolemy VI secure them for his son-in-law.

4–7. As a good patron of Greeks and of Greek culture (Volkmann, PW, XXIII, 1711; Polybius xxviii 19, xxix 23.7, 24.4 and 12–14; xxxix 7), Ptolemy VI might be expected to show sympathy to Jonathan's victims, Greeks and Hellenized Philistines. Even though he favored Jews, Ptolemy VI might have been hostile to Jonathan, supplanter of the Oniad line of high priests; see Introduction, pp. 57–58. Whatever his motives, however, Ptolemy VI knew how to value any real military power available to him and to Alexander. Our author's purpose in telling of these events is to show that even wicked Ptolemy VI held Jonathan in high esteem and that Jonathan's conduct toward his sovereign, Alexander, was perfectly correct. Thus, Jonathan loyally complied with the circular order mentioned in vs. 2.

6. Though Jonathan did not yet hold Joppe as his own, he now could safely spend the night there.

7–8. Jonathan accompanied Ptolemy all the way through the coastal plain to the Eleutheros river north of Tripolis. See Map 12, p. 536. Ptolemy went on to Seleuceia-by-the-Sea, the port of Antioch, a town which seems to have been conspicuously loyal to Demetrius II (Introduction, pp. 120–21).

8–14. Where were Alexander and Demetrius II when Ptolemy VI sent Demetrius the message from Seleuceia? Demetrius still had reason to assume that Ptolemy was hostile. He could not have been anywhere in Seleucid territory from Seleuceia southward, nor could he have been in Antioch, where he was to be unwelcome even after Ptolemy's overtures to him (J. *AJ* xiii 4.7.111–15; Diodorus xxxii 9c). We must conclude that he was still pressing his claims from Cilicia. It is harder to determine where Alexander was. Our author's narrative last mentions him at Antioch (10:68). The narrative seems to presuppose that Alexander was away in rebellious Cilicia the entire time, for the word order of vs. 14 makes it natural to take the verb there as pluperfect (see G. Bergsträsser, *Hebräische Grammatik*, II, 26–27; GKC, §§ 142a–b), and we can then understand how Ptolemy was able to take the queen and bestow her on Demetrius.

On the other hand, Josephus' account (*AJ* xiii 4.6–7.106–12) says that the attempt on the life of Ptolemy VI by Alexander's minister Ammonius came at Ptolemais, far to the south of the Eleutheros river, yet nothing is said of what Jonathan did during that crisis. Is "Ptolemais" a scribe's mistake for "Seleuceia," by substituting one dynastic name for the other? Thereafter, the account in Josephus says that Ptolemy demanded of Alexander that Ammonius be surrendered to him for punishment. Since nothing is said to indicate that Alexander was away at the front in Cilicia, the narrative seems to assume that the king was in Antioch with Ammonius. Indeed, it goes on to say that the citizens of Antioch were so hostile to Alexander over the misdeeds of Ammonius that they drove the king out of Antioch, and Alexander came as a fugitive to Cilicia. Josephus' account depends on Onias IV, who was a partisan of Ptolemy VI and was an eyewitness, having been in Egypt at the time (J. *Ap.* ii 5.50; see my article in *Studies Smith*, Part III, p. 114, n. 104). It is very unlikely that Alexander would flee toward an area which was the stronghold of his rival, even if rugged mountains do sharply divide Cilicia into regions.

Indeed, the account at Diodorus xxxii 9c says that Ptolemy came to Syria, discovered Alexander's incompetence, and took Cleopatra and pledged her to Demetrius. Nothing is said of Alexander's being present. The account goes on to say that Alexander's commanders in Antioch "despairing of his cause" (*tou Alexandrou kategnôkotes*) roused the people of Antioch to rebellion. Again nothing is said of Alexander's being present. A pro-Ptolemaic writer had an interest in presenting Alexander as being at Antioch, for thus the plot on Ptolemy's life became more credible, as well as the alleged demand for the surrender of Ammonius' person. In such a time of crisis, Alexander may well have kept his whereabouts secret from all except his highest officials, so that neither the Ptolemaic army nor the citizens of Antioch need have known when or why the king left his capital. Thus, our author's account is likely correct, the more so as our author appears not even to have been aware that the rebellious Cilicians were supporting Demetrius II.

Our author probably phrased his version of Ptolemy's letter to Demetrius in a way which also hints that Alexander was absent. Excellent manuscript authority (S*V La^L ^X), which we have followed in our translation, has the letter identify Ptolemy's daughter in vs. 9 by "who was formerly Alexander's wife," using the past tense, though all other witnesses to the text use the present. Even if the queen had not been at Seleuceia on Ptolemy's arrival, it would have been natural for her to come down from Antioch to meet her father. Thus, Ptolemy's ability to take her without opposition has no bearing on the problem of whether Alexander was at Antioch.

13. All accounts have Ptolemy entering Antioch unopposed. All agree that Alexander was now absent, and we hear that the people of Antioch welcomed Ptolemy (J. *AJ* xiii 4.7.113; Diodorus xxxii 9c). There can be little doubt that

Ptolemy VI treated the Seleucid kingdom and the young pretender Demetrius II in the same way as Antiochus IV had treated the Ptolemaic kingdom and the young claimant Ptolemy VI in 169 B.C.E. Antiochus IV, conqueror of Ptolemaic Egypt, had himself crowned king of his second kingdom at Memphis; see NOTE on 1:16–19. Just so, Ptolemy VI, conqueror of Seleucid Syria, crowned himself at Antioch. Both conquering kings knew that the superpower Rome must not be led to think that a new eastern colossus was now rising against her. Antiochus IV had made young Ptolemy VI into a sort of vassal king as his coregent, over whom he claimed to be guardian; see Porphyry FGH 260, F 49, and cf. Livy xlv 11.10. Just so, Ptolemy VI now would bring in Demetrius as "vassal" king. Ptolemy VI in 169 came to hold Egypt no longer as the heir of the Ptolemaic dynasty but rather as the appointee of Antiochus (Livy xliv 19.8–9, xlv 11.5–10; Polybius xxviii 23.4–5). Just so, Demetrius would now hold the Seleucid empire. In 169 the Romans had been tied down by the Third Macedonian War. Just so, the Romans now had to rest their veterans, weary from the Third Punic and Achaean wars, and were having difficulty raising a fresh army to send against a dangerous revolt in Spain (Appian *Ibêrikê* 65). When the Romans would be free to intervene in the eastern Mediterranean, Ptolemy VI would be in a far stronger position than Antiochus, who had to meet the Roman embassy while he was besieging Alexandria. Antioch had already fallen to Ptolemy VI. Had he lived, he would have met any Roman embassy in Egypt, after having left Ptolemaic troops in Syria to help his "vassal" govern.

Antiochus IV himself was already familiar with the institution of guardianship, from his experience with the young son of Seleucus IV; see NOTE on 1:10. On the position of a coregent, see Bikerman, *Institutions,* pp. 21–24. On the actions of Antiochus IV and Ptolemy VI, see Otto, pp. 51–59, 124–31. The repetition of Antiochus' procedure by Ptolemy VI is the strongest proof that the sources (principally Porphyry FGH 260, F 49) present it correctly, against the doubts of some modern scholars (e.g. Mørkholm, pp. 79–84).

Those now on the Seleucid side who did not desire Ptolemaic domination could also learn from the precedent of the experience of Antiochus IV. The Ptolemaic authorities in Alexandria did their utmost to recover Egypt for the dynasty, eventually succeeding through Roman intervention (Livy xliv 19.6–14, 20.1, xlv 11.1 – 12.8). Correspondingly, the first act of the regime of Demetrius II after the sudden death of Ptolemy VI was to reconquer the Seleucid realm by massacring the Ptolemaic garrisons (vs. 18; J. *AJ* xiii 4.9.120).

Pro-Seleucid sources would not preserve the memory of the brief Ptolemaic rule of their empire. Hence, there is no reference to Ptolemy VI's coronation at Justin xxxv 2.3. Polybius, however, knew of it (xxxix 7.1), and so did the sources who follow him (Diodorus xxxii 9c; Porphyry FGH 260, F 2.7). Pro-Ptolemaic sources, anxious to defend the Ptolemaic empire against Roman suspicions, produced the insistence in Josephus and Diodorus, that the people of Antioch forced the Seleucid kingship upon the reluctant Ptolemy VI. According to Josephus, Ptolemy VI had to persuade the people of Antioch to accept Demetrius, by giving a promise to overrule any misdeeds of his. According to Diodorus, Ptolemy was to retain control of southern Syria and of

Palestine, the areas his dynasty had lost to Antiochus III, leaving only the rest of the Seleucid empire to his "vassal" Demetrius. The Greek at Diodorus xxxii 9c calls the areas by the Ptolemaic term "Syria," not by the Seleucid name, "Coele-Syria." Clearly, Diodorus' ultimate source here was Ptolemaic.

15. The battle occurred on the banks of the Oinoparas, one of the streams flowing into the lake northeast of Antioch (Strabo xvi 2.8, C751), as one would expect, since Alexander marched on Antioch from Cilicia, going around rather than through the rugged Amanus mountains. Justin (xxxv 2.3) reports that Alexander's army deserted to Demetrius but does not say whether the desertion occurred during the battle; he may be referring to earlier desertions. Demetrius may have joined Ptolemy VI before the time of the battle; see J. AJ xiii 4.7.113–16.

16–17. According to Diodorus (xxxii 9d, 10.1), Alexander fled with five hundred of his men to a place called "Abai" in "Arabia," i.e. in Arab territory somewhere reasonably near the battle-site. "Arabia" in antiquity first referred to the northern deserts, and only later to the Arabian peninsula. See Albert Dietrich, "Arabia," Der kleine Pauly, I (1964), 483–84, and Dussaud, Pénétration des Arabes. Diodorus says that Alexander sought the protection of the local sheikh Diokles, to whom he had earlier entrusted his little son Antiochus. Later the child's guardian appears with the Arabic name "Iamblichos." Iamblichos may or may not have been identical with Diokles. The Arabic name could mean "God is king," a reasonable equivalent of Greek "Diokles" ("Glory of Zeus"). See below, on vs. 39. According to Diodorus, Heliades and Kasios, two of Alexander's commanders, in order to save their own skins made and carried out an agreement with Demetrius, that they should kill Alexander. One of the two commanders could have been an Arab with the native name Zabdiel, in which case Diodorus' account would substantially agree with the one here. Josephus (AJ xiii 4.8.118) gives a short form of Zabdiel's name, "Zabeilos" or "Zabêlos." Just so, "Zabdaathês son of Malchus" of P. Dura 101. xxxix 19 becomes "Zabathês son of Malchus at P. Dura 100. xxxix 16.

18–19. Ptolemy VI suffered severe head wounds in the battle on the banks of the Oinoparas (J. AJ xiii 4.8.117; Livy Periocha lii). Though he recovered consciousness on the fifth day after the battle, in time to view Alexander's head (J. AJ xiii 4.8.118), he died when surgeons tried to trephine his skull (Livy Periocha lii). The sources are probably in harmony: Ptolemy could well have died on the third day after Alexander was killed, after viewing Alexander's head on the fifth day after the battle. The latest known date on an Egyptian document from the reign of Ptolemy VI is July 15, 145 B.C.E. The earliest known document from the reign of his heir, Ptolemy VII Neos Philopator, is dated August 21, 145. A week could have elapsed before the news of Ptolemy VI's death reached Egypt, and another week or two before it reached remote parts of the country. See A. Samuel, Ptolemaic Chronology, p. 144.

Hence, Demetrius II's accession as undisputed Seleucid king in 167 Sel. Mac. fell in the summer of 145 B.C.E. On the massacres of the Ptolemaic garrisons, see above, on vs. 13. Josephus adds (AJ xiii 4.9.120) that Demetrius got possession of (Ptolemy's?) elephants; see NOTES on 7:1 and 11:56.

XXV. DEMETRIUS II HONORS
JONATHAN AND THE JEWS
(11:20–37)

11 20 Soon thereafter Jonathan gathered the people of Judaea for a fight to the finish against the Akra in Jerusalem. They constructed extensive siegeworks against it. 21 Thereupon, certain haters of their own nation, lawless men, went to the king and reported to him that Jonathan was besieging the Akra. 22 On hearing the news, the king was enraged. Immediately on hearing it he set out, and on reaching Ptolemais he wrote Jonathan to desist from the siege and to come to meet him for discussions at Ptolemais forthwith.

23 On receiving the message, Jonathan ordered that the siege continue. Then, with a chosen retinue of elders of Israel and priests, he took the risk of going. 24 Taking with him silver and gold and raiment and many other gifts, he set out to meet the king at Ptolemais and won a favorable reception. 25 Wicked fellows from our nation brought complaints against Jonathan, 26 but the king treated him just as his predecessors had, raising him to high rank in the presence of all the King's Friends. 27 Thus, Demetrius confirmed him in the high priesthood and in the other privileges he previously held and had him reckoned among the Friends of the First Rank. 28 Jonathan asked the king to make Judaea free of tribute, together with the three toparchies of the Samaritis, promising him in return three hundred talents. 29 The king consented and had a letter written for Jonathan treating all these points, as follows:

30 "King Demetrius to his brother Jonathan and to the nation of the Jews, greeting. 31 We hereby send you for your information a copy of the letter which we wrote concerning you to our Kinsman Lasthenes: 32 'King Demetrius to his Father Lasthenes, greeting. 33 We have decided to reward for their loyalty toward us the nation of the Jews, our friends who have been steadfastly just in their relations with us. 34 We confirm them in the possession of the territory of Judaea as well as the three nomes of Aphairema, Lydda, and Ramathaim. The nomes and all that belongs to them have been an-

nexed to Judaea from the Samaritis. For all Jews who offer sacrifices in Jerusalem we abandon our claim to all the following: to the value of the royal revenues which the king used to receive annually from the Jews from the produce of the soil and the fruit trees, 35 as well as to what is due us from now on in tithes and what is due us in tolls and the salt pans and what is due us in crown money. 36 Not one of these concessions shall ever be revoked. 37 Take care now to have a copy made of all this, and see to it that it is given to Jonathan and set up within the temple mount in a conspicuous place.'"

NOTES

11:20. The words I have rendered "soon thereafter" literally are "in those days" (Hebrew *bayyāmīm hāhēm*). In biblical Hebrew they are equivalent not to "meanwhile" but to "at that time or a bit later" and often to "under that same regime," "in the course of that reign" (Exod 2:11, 23; Judg 17:6, 18:1, 19:1; I Sam 28:1; II Kings 10:32, 15:37; Isa 38:1; Esther 1:2, 2:21). Jonathan had no reason to think that Alexander would allow him to attack the Akra, a royal Seleucid fortress. If the men of the Akra did not go over to Alexander at once, Demetrius I's offer to cede the fortress to the Jews' high priest (10:32) made them do so. Though Alexander went to great lengths to please Jonathan, he never consented to withdraw the garrison of the Akra. We may thus be fairly sure that Jonathan waited for the deaths of Alexander and of Ptolemy VI before he moved to besiege the Akra. See also NOTE on 10:51–58.

21. See NOTE on 6:18–24. The Greek expression "lawless men" (*andres paranomoi*) usually renders Hebrew *bᵉnēy bᵉlīyaʻal*, "sons of Belial." Our author, however, believes that Jews who refuse to recognize the authority of the Hasmonaeans violate God's will; see NOTES on 5:55–62, 67, and on 7:6–7. Hence, such men violate the Torah and are well described by the Greek translator as "lawless men." Enemies of Jonathan could have some hope that Demetrius would stop him from besieging the Akra.

22–29. Though Ptolemais had been Alexander's stronghold, Demetrius could now use it as a base for exerting pressure on Jonathan. The citizens knew well that they needed Seleucid power to defend themselves against the menace of the Jews; see II 13:24–26. Jonathan was aware of the danger of venturing into Ptolemais (cf. I 12:48). This time he took care to see that he would be able to bargain from the strongest possible position. He kept the Akra under siege, took with him leaders of the nation to demonstrate how solidly he was backed, and brought rich gifts to a king whose treasury had been depleted by war and royal incompetence. Confronted by Jonathan's wealth and tangible military power, Demetrius had little trouble deciding to turn a deaf ear to Jonathan's enemies (see Introduction, pp. 65–66, who also came to Ptolemais. Our author passes over in silence what Jonathan did to let the king save face: nothing is said of the siege of the Akra. From vs. 41 we can tell that it was now abandoned. In order to help Jonathan save face with Jews who longed to eliminate the men of the Akra and in order to fill quickly his own depleted treasury, Demetrius consented to forgo permanently onerous taxes of Judaea in return for a single payment of three hundred talents (cf. II 4:8).

26–27. See NOTES on 7:5 and on 10:16–21, 60–65. There was no abstract rank of "Friend" or "Kinsman" but only the concrete rank of "Friend-" or "Kinsman-of-King-X"; see Bikerman, *Institutions*, pp. 41–44. With Alexander dead, Jonathan becomes a member of the court of Demetrius II. If some doubted the legitimacy of Alexander Balas as king, Jonathan now held the high priesthood from the indubitable Seleucid, Demetrius II. Jonathan seems not to have received from Demetrius quite the distinction he had under Alexander. He was now to be only a Friend of the First Rank, not a Kinsman; see NOTE on 10:89. He retained such privileges as those of levying troops and manufacturing arms (10:6), the offices of *stratêgos* and *meridarchês* (10:65), and the possession of Akkaron (10:89).

28. Although "free of tribute" (*aphorologêton*) might mean free from all taxation, the itemized list (vss. 34–35) in Demetrius' letter suggests that only certain particularly onerous payments were included. Indeed, the Seleucid king was to continue to claim revenue from Judaea; see I 13:15, 34, 37, 41. All manuscripts of First Maccabees have "the three toparchies *and* the Samaritis," probably as the result of a misread or miswritten *w* before "the Samaritis" in the Hebrew original. In vs. 34 it is clear that the three districts were part of the Samaritis and that the Samaritans, who were the majority population in the rest of the province, are excluded from Demetrius' concessions. Josephus here appears to have had a correct Hebrew text, for at *AJ* xiii 4.9.125 he has "the three toparchies of Samaria." However, here, too, Josephus or his secretary did not understand that the three toparchies were part of Samaria and, perplexed, guessed that the "other two" toparchies were Joppe and Galilee, inserting their names into the text; see NOTE on 10:38.

30. For the first time in extant records, we have a document addressed both to the Hasmonaean chief, now high priest, and to the nation of the Jews. Thereafter, documents to the Jewish body politic and also Jewish coins mention both the Hasmonaean chief and the Jewish nation or its authoritative organs.

Was Jonathan's powerful position as high priest something new (cf. Bikerman, *Institutions*, p. 165)? We know very little about the powers of the high priest and to what extent he was the head of the nation during the period of the second temple. On the one hand, the letter here is the earliest extant *government* document to the Jews which so much as mentions the name of the high priest (Bikerman, "La charte séleucide de Jérusalem," REJ 100 [1935], 32). On the other hand, when the Jews of Elephantine needed the help of the Jews of Judaea in 408 B.C.E. they addressed their letter to "Yehoḥanan the high priest and his fellow priests in Jerusalem and Ostanes, brother of 'Anani, and the nobles of the Jews" (Cowley, *Aramaic Papyri*, no. 30, lines 18–19; Pritchard, ANET, p. 492a). Even if the report in the papyrus means rather that the Jews of Elephantine sent several letters to the list of addressees, still the high priest is mentioned first, as the head of the nation. We learn from J. *AJ* xii 4.2.161–63, 3.167, that at least some of the political authority did not automatically come to the high priest by virtue of his office and also that such authority could be abdicated to another, even to a non-priest. The authority conferred by the Seleucid government on Onias III, Jason, Menelaus, and Alcimus appears to have been sweeping, though those high priests found it difficult to exercise in the face of Jewish opposition (II 3:1, 4, 4:1–50, 5:23; I 7, 9:23–27, 54–57). If Demetrius I conceded important powers to the high priest (I 10:32, 38), though refraining from giving his name because of the political situation, surely the high priest was already powerful. Hence, if the high priesthood brought Jonathan wide powers as head of the nation, the fact was nothing new. Moreover, even after Jonathan became high priest, documents of official acts of the Jewish national authorities went out without mentioning either Jonathan (in 143 B.C.E.) or his more princely successor John Hyrcanus (in 124). And those documents dealt with the Hasmonaean festival of Hanukkah! See in AB vol. 41A NOTE on II 1:1–10a.

In the fragmentary state of our knowledge, at least the following facts are established. (1) The high priest early had sweeping powers. (2) Jonathan now held the same sort of power. (3) Still greater power came to the Hasmonaean high priest Simon (I 14:41–47). (4) Not all of Jonathan's and Simon's powers were high priestly prerogatives; Jonathan had been "judge" and commander of a band of armed men, and Simon also bore the titles *stratêgos* and ethnarch (I 14:47). (5) From an early date and well into the time of the Hasmonaean princes, the power of the high priest was limited by the real power of the Jewish aristocracy.

On the title "brother" see NOTE on 10:18–21. On the title "nation" (*ethnos*), see NOTE on 1:4.

31. In the Hellenistic empires, if the king's act of conferring a privilege was carried out through notifying a royal minister, it was usual to give the recipient of the privilege a certificate of the grant in the form of a copy of the message to the royal minister. Cf. II 11:22–26, and see Bikerman, RHR 115 (1937), 191–96.

32. Lasthenes was the mercenary chief Demetrius had secured in Crete to help him press his claims to the Seleucid throne (J. *AJ* xiii 4.3.86). He probably became Demetrius' chief minister (cf. Diodorus xxxiii 4).

"Father" was probably the title given high-ranking persons with the title "Kinsman of the King" who were considerably older than the king. See Bikerman, *Institutions,* pp. 42–43.

33. The purpose of our verse is to flatter the Jews and perhaps to soothe pagan public opinion, hardly to inform Lasthenes. Cf. NOTE on 10:26–28.

34. Antiochus IV's decrees seem to have turned Judaea into unprivileged royal domain; see NOTE on 1:29–40. Whatever the status of Judaea under Antiochus V, Demetrius I, and Alexander, Demetrius II now officially turns Judaea, with its established boundaries, into territory belonging to a privileged *ethnos*. He adds to Judaea the territory of the "three nomes"; see NOTE on 10:38.

The name of the nome of *'Āpārayim* to Greek ears easily became *Aphairema* ("separation"), and that appears to have been its official name in Greek.

Ramathaim ("two heights"; I Sam 1:1) also was known by the form "Haramatha" ("the height"; I Sam 1:19 etc.); the place is mentioned in the New Testament as "Arimathaea" (Matt 27:47; John 19:38). See Abel, *Géographie*, II, 428–29.

For the first and last time in our book, we find evidence of Jewish hostility to the Samaritans. The Samaritans, who offer sacrifices on Mount Gerizim near Shechem, are hereby excluded from the exemptions Demetrius is about to list.

On the revenues from the produce of the soil and the fruit trees, see NOTE on 10:30.

35. On tithes and tolls, see NOTE on 10:31. On the salt pans and crown money, see NOTE on 10:29.

37. There was a common practice in the Hellenistic world of providing the recipient of a grant with a copy of the provisions. Frequently the recipient would see to it that a permanent copy, engraved on stone or metal, was set up in some sacred enclosure. See NOTE on 8:22, and the literature cited there.

XXVI. JONATHAN BREAKS WITH
DEMETRIUS II
(11:38–59)

11 ³⁸ King Demetrius perceived that the land lay quiet under his rule and no power opposed him. Accordingly, he dismissed all his troops, sending everyone home except his mercenaries, whom he hired from the islands of the gentiles. As a result, all the troops who had served his ancestors hated him.

³⁹ There was a certain Tryphon, who previously had served Alexander. Tryphon perceived that all the troops were grumbling against Demetrius. Thereupon, he went to Iamblichos, the Arab who was the guardian of Antiochus, Alexander's little son, ⁴⁰ and importuned him to hand the child over to him to become king as his father's successor. Tryphon told him how Demetrius' decrees had won him the hatred of his troops. There he remained for many days.

⁴¹ Jonathan sent a message to King Demetrius, asking for the expulsion of those occupying the Akra in Jerusalem and those occupying the forts, on the ground that they were waging war on Israel. ⁴² Demetrius sent Jonathan the following reply: "Not only shall I do as you request for you and your nation, but I will also confer distinction upon you and your nation if my cause prospers. ⁴³ Now, therefore, be so good as to send me soldiers to support my cause, for all my troops are in revolt." ⁴⁴ Thereupon, Jonathan sent three thousand valiant soldiers to him at Antioch. On their arrival, the king rejoiced that they had come. ⁴⁵ Then the people of the city assembled in the center of the city, to the number of one hundred twenty thousand men, with the intention of doing away with the king. ⁴⁶ The king fled to the palace, but the people of the city seized control of the city thoroughfares and began to attack. ⁴⁷ The king summoned the Jews to the rescue. They all rallied together around him, and they dispersed throughout the city; they slaughtered on that day in the city a total of one hundred thousand. ⁴⁸ They set fire to the city and took much booty on that day. They had saved the king.

⁴⁹ Perceiving that the Jews were masters of the city and had it at their mercy, the people of the city in their despair cried out to the king, begging him, ⁵⁰ "Grant us an armistice, and make the Jews stop attacking us and our city." ⁵¹ They threw down their arms and made peace. The Jews' prestige stood high with the king and with all his subjects, and their fame spread throughout his kingdom, as they returned to Jerusalem heavily loaded with booty. ⁵² And so Demetrius sat firm upon the throne of his kingdom, and the land lay quiet under his rule. ⁵³ He, however, broke all his promises. He turned hostile to Jonathan and failed to reward Jonathan for the loyal services he had rendered him and caused Jonathan much distress.

⁵⁴ Some time afterward, Tryphon returned, bringing with him Antiochus, who was still a very young child. Nevertheless, he was proclaimed king and was crowned with a diadem. ⁵⁵ All the troops whom Demetrius had heedlessly cast off rallied to Antiochus and fought Demetrius, who fled in utter defeat. ⁵⁶ Tryphon took over the elephants and became master of Antioch.

⁵⁷ A letter written in the name of little King Antiochus came to Jonathan, as follows: "I confirm you in the high priesthood and grant you power over the four nomes and make you one of the King's Friends." ⁵⁸ He sent Jonathan gold goblets and a table service and gave him permission to drink from gold goblets and wear purple and use a gold brooch. ⁵⁹ He also appointed Jonathan's brother Simon *stratêgos* over the area from the Ladder of Tyre to the Egyptian border.

NOTES

11:38. Once securely in power, Demetrius is reported to have turned to dissipation and brutality, leaving the conduct of affairs largely to a dissolute and cruel minister (Justin xxxvi 1.1; Diodorus xxxiii 4). Our author says nothing of such reports. It is true that the cruelty fell mostly on Greeks and that Jewish soldiers were important instruments of the regime in this (vss. 47–48), but our author dislikes the line of Demetrius I and is a moralist. Had he known of such reports, he might well have alluded to them.

Modern states have veterans' administrations to take care of soldiers whose services are no longer needed. Pre-modern economies found such institutions hard to support. In many periods of history there were no such arrangements, and dismissed veterans, cut off from hope of future employment, could be very dangerous to all in their path, not least to their former employers. See e.g. Polybius 1 65–88.

By "the islands," our author probably has Crete uppermost in mind, as Josephus guessed (*AJ* xiii 4.9.129). Other islands were under Roman domination and closed to Seleucid recruiting by the peace of Apameia; see NOTE on 6:29. The Seleucids may have evaded this provision extensively, since it was difficult to enforce.

39. Originally, Tryphon's name was "Diodotus." He was born in Kasiana, a military post in the heavily Greek territory of Apameia, south of Antioch. Raised in Apameia, he became a courtier close to the king. Diodotus' power base in Apameia and her tributary villages served him well now in his revolution against Demetrius II (Strabo xvi 2.10, C752; J. *AJ* xiii 5.1.131).

This Diodotus is surely identical with the man who was one of Alexander Balas' commanders at Antioch (Diodorus xxxii 9c, xxxiii 3; J. *AJ* xiii 5.1.131). Hostile to Demetrius I and II, Diodotus and his colleague Hierax are reported to have crowned Ptolemy VI king in Antioch, rather than leave the way open for Demetrius II (Diodorus xxxii 9c).

"Tryphon" was originally more an epithet ("Magnificent," "Luxurious") than a name; see Julien Tondriau, "La tryphè: philosophie royale ptolémaïque," REA 50 (1948), 49–54. On the use of the epithet in Ptolemaic and Seleucid propaganda, see Otto and Bengtson, *Zur Geschichte des Niederganges des Ptolemäerreiches*, pp. 49–50. Diodotus used the name Tryphon at least from the time in 168 Sel. Mac. (145/4 B.C.E.) when the Greek letters *TRY* appear on the coins of Antiochus VI, surely as the abbrieviated name of the boy king's guardian. See Thomas Fischer, "Zu Tryphon," *Chiron* 2 (1972), 209. The strong-man continued to use the name when he claimed himself to be king of the empire (I 13:32).

On how Alexander came to entrust his child to the Arab, see NOTE on 11: 16–17. Diodorus (xxxiii 4a) followed a source who wrote in Greek, using an alphabet wherein all vowels were expressed. Hence, his version of the name of the Arab is probably correct, "Iamblichos" (=Yamliku). The name is known from the region of Emesa (J. *AJ* xiv 8.1.129; *BJ* i 9.3.188; Strabo xvi 2.10, C753; IGLS 2144, 2320, 2339) as well as at Palmyra (Harald Ingholt, Henri Seyrig, and Jean Starcky, *Recueil des Tessères de Palmyre* [Paris: Geuthner, 1955], p. 173). Emesa, in the Orontes valley, some forty-three kilometers south of Hamath (see Map 12, p. 536), was convenient to Antioch, and the hilly vicinity offered good hiding-places for the child. Palmyra lay about one hundred forty kilometers nearly due east of Emesa. Between Palmyra and Antioch the road was both longer and more difficult. Hence, the district of Emesa is by far a more likely refuge for Alexander Balas and his child.

Our author, on the other hand, used the vowelless Hebrew alphabet, and the witnesses to the Hebrew text found the name *ymlkw* perplexing. It is, indeed an unusual form, probably a shortening (hypocoristic) of a name expressing an act of god, *ymlk'l*, "God reigns" or "God enthrones"; see Ingholt et al., and see S. Loewenstamm, "*Yamlēk*," Enc. Bib., III (1958), 702 (in Hebrew). However, Josephus knew the name from the region of Emesa, yet he did not recognize it here, for he gives the Arab's name as "Malchos." The Hebrew text underlying all the versions must have been confusing.

Perhaps it read '*l ymlkw 'l h'rby* . . . , "to Yamliku, to the Arab. . . ." For the repetition of '*l* with an appositive, cf. Josh 22:9; Gen 32:7. The preposition '*l* has the same spelling as the word for "god" (*ēl* or *il*). A reader accustomed to names with "god" in them could easily misread '*l ymlkw 'l* as containing the name forms *Ilimalchu* (so La^L) or *Emalcuel* (so La^V) or *Malcuel* (so La^X). *Ilimalchu* is equivalent to the Hebrew "Elimelech." The writers responsible for the readings *Emalcuel* (La^V) and *Imalkoue* (S V) apparently gave the first two syllables a vowel pattern like that of *Iramael* (Greek I Chron 24:29). The corresponding form of the verb *mlk* occurs in old Aramaic, Syriac, and Arabic. How the reading of S and V lost the final *l* I do not know. Finally, the *y* of *ymlkw* may have been so small as to escape notice, or it may have been read with the preceding '*l* to yield '*ly*, an alternative form of the preposition, so that for Josephus and SyI and SyIII the name became *Malchos* (*mlkw*), known from Nabataea (J. *AJ* xv 6.2.167, 171, 3.175, etc.). The readings of the Latin versions strongly suggest that the Latin scribes had access to a Hebrew text. Hebrew texts were certainly extant when the Latin translation was made, and the scribes may have consulted one only in rare instances when the Greek text appeared strange, as Josephus elsewhere appears to have done; see Introduction, p. 14.

41. Clearly, Jonathan had abandoned the siege of the Akra; see NOTE on vss. 22–29. The other forts included at least Beth-Zur (see vs. 65) and Gazara (see I 13:43–46), and perhaps also Joppe (see I 12:33–34).

42–43. Demetrius' cause was far from prosperous; see NOTE on vs. 38.

44–51. The narrative indicates that the Jewish troops did not have to fight their way into Antioch. Presumably they were given quarters somewhere near the palace. Only later did the civilian rebels seize control of the thoroughfares. Indeed, in asking for aid Demetrius mentioned only the revolt of *soldiers*.

Josephus (*AJ* xiii 5.3.135–41) here follows a more detailed source. According to his account, on the arrival of the Jewish soldiers, the citizens of Antioch, already hostile to Demetrius, moved before Demetrius should recruit yet more troops. Thereupon, Demetrius called not only upon the Jews but also upon his other mercenaries, but the rebels won in the opening stage of the fighting. However, the tide turned when the Jews went up to the roofs of the palace buildings and by bombarding the enemy from above with missiles drove them away from the ground below and from the adjoining buildings, which were then set on fire. Caught between the Jews on the roofs and the spreading flames, the rebels were hard put even to save their wives and children; many were slain, and the rest surrendered to Demetrius.

In Diodorus' account (xxxiii 4.2–4), sympathetic to the rebel victims, the king crushes the revolt and disarms the citizens by using his mercenaries; many rebels are slain with their wives and children. Only later, when riots break out over the disarming, does Demetrius have the city fired. Diodorus' account had no reason to single out the Jews for mention: the narrative includes them among the other mercenaries, all of whom wreaked havoc upon the rebels.

Our author, interested only in the great deeds of Jonathan's men, may be forgiven for writing as if only they had brought about the king's victory. Our author himself knew that the king retained his mercenaries (vs. 38).

Antioch was a very large city for the time. The number of civilian rebels may have reached a hundred thousand, but it is unlikely that the number of the slain reached that figure, if only because the Jews did not occupy the city long enough to count the dead. Diodorus says (xxxiii 4.3–4) refugees from Antioch spread all over Syria, surely providing fuel for the revolt of Diodotus-Tryphon.

In vs. 47 it is most natural to take "the Jews" as the subject of the verb "they dispersed"; cf. Exod 5:12 and I Sam 14:34. However, in view of Josephus' account, "the rebels" are probably the subject; cf. I Sam 11:11 etc. Our author sometimes makes such an abrupt change of subject (e.g. at 4:20). It would, however, be easy to emend the text by inserting *hoi*, to yield "and the people of the city [*hoi en tei polei*] dispersed." For *hoi en* as "the people of," cf. I 13:45.

51. In the description of the glory of the Jews is there an echo of Greek Isa 52:13–15? Cf. also I 3:9, 14:10.

53. Once the king had crushed the rebellion, perhaps he felt that his security rested with his Greek mercenaries. He may have believed that they would be able to cope with the Jews. Mercenaries, however, require pay; hence, Demetrius probably gave Jonathan more tangible grievances than mere ingratitude. Josephus reports (*AJ* xiii 5.3.143) Demetrius demanded that Judaea pay the established taxes going back to the time of "the first kings" (thus excluding any punitive exactions imposed by Antiochus IV). If such was Demetrius' policy, he did not anticipate the danger of Diodotus-Tryphon's movement on behalf of Alexander's heir.

54–56. For further details, see Diodorus xxxiii 4a and Bevan, II, 226–27.

54. Antiochus VI Epiphanes Dionysus was the son of Alexander Balas by Cleopatra Thea (Appian *Syriakê* 68). Therefore, he cannot have been born before 149 B.C.E.; see NOTE on 10:57. The earliest dated coins of Antiochus VI are of 167 Sel. Mac. (October 3, 146 B.C.E. – September 21, 145) and thus must date from late summer, 145 (see NOTE on vss. 18–19). A child king was in fact helpless in the hands of his guardian, but imperial forms took no note of the reality. Officially, acts of the government were acts of the king, as in vss. 57–59. See Bikerman, *Institutions,* p. 21.

55. One wonders how the regime around Antiochus VI found resources to pay the discharged soldiers when Demetrius II probably could not. We may guess that Diodotus-Tryphon's military revolutionary government squeezed the civilians, already hard hit by Demetrius II's regime. Tryphon's motive in later seizing Jonathan may have been to extort money from the Jews as much as to curb a dangerously independent personality (see I 12:39–48, 13:14–16). Demetrius continued to hold large parts of the empire (J. *AJ* xiii 5.4.145; Bevan, II, 227–28).

56. How did the Seleucid empire again come to have elephants? See NOTES on 7:1 and on 11:18–19.

57. The letter was drawn up for the child king by the government secretaries at the orders of Tryphon. Again our author gives only the gist of the king's

letter. On Jonathan's need to be confirmed in the high priesthood by the new king, see NOTE on 7:5.

Suddenly, in our verse, the three nomes (see NOTE on vs. 34) have become four. Taken strictly, our verse may mean that the nomes were not now to be regarded as annexed to Judaea (contrast 10:38 and 11:34), but only as subject to Jonathan, in a "personal union." We can only guess what area constituted the fourth nome. Nowhere is it named. One might expect it to adjoin the three nomes and, like them, to have hitherto been part of the Samaritis. If so, it might be the Akrabattene (so Abel, ad loc., following Dalman; see NOTE on 5:3). No other evidence tells us that the Akrabattene came under Hasmonaean rule so early. M. Avi-Yonah (*The Holy Land*, p. 57) suggests that the fourth nome was the old Tobiad stronghold in Transjordan, but on poor evidence. He argues that Judaea must have possessed Transjordanian territory before the time of John Hyrcanus because Josephus reports that John Hyrcanus' first conquest was of Medaba but says nothing of the conquest of the territory between the Jordan and Medaba (J. *AJ* xiii 9.1.255; *BJ* i 2.6.63). At best, this is no proof that *Jonathan* held Transjordanian territory. Moreover, John Hyrcanus could have moved on Medaba as easily as the guerrilla chieftain Jonathan had (I 9:36–42). The old Tobiad territory was not attached to the Samaritis but was part of the Ammanitis (see commentary on II 1:7, *Jason . . . Kingdom*).

On the whole, the Akrabattene seems the most likely possibility. Though it was part of the Samaritis, its population, too, may have been heavily Jewish (see *M. Ma'aser sheni* 5:2), especially after Judas smashed the Idumaean enclave there (I 5:3).

Antiochus VI admits Jonathan to the Order of the Friends of the new king; see NOTE on vss. 26–27.

58. Jonathan receives from the king the prerogatives both of a Friend and of a Kinsman, thus recovering the rank he held under Alexander (10:89); see Bikerman, *Institutions*, pp. 42–44.

59. See Maps 5 and 14, pp. 530 and 538, respectively. Our author is careful to note Simon's first receipt of political power from a king. Simon's province as Seleucid *stratêgos* appears to have been limited to the coastal plain; his operations outside Judaea while holding the office are limited to Ascalon and Joppe (12:33–34). By extending as far as the Ladder of Tyre (see Map 14), Simon's province included Ptolemais, which therefore appears as detached from Phoenicia. This situation for Ptolemais may have begun as a privilege under Alexander Balas or as a punishment under Demetrius II.

From the theater of Jonathan's operations (vss. 60–64, 67–74; 12:25–32; see Maps 12 and 13, pp. 536 and 537, and 14), it seems clear that he was *stratêgos* of Coele-Syria without Phoenicia. Demetrius' generals must have controlled at least parts of Phoenicia, but there is some reason to believe that the separate status of Phoenicia began earlier. Again, it may have begun as a privilege under Alexander Balas and may be reflected in the fact that the Phoenician cities were allowed to strike their own bronze coins both on the Ptolemaic and on the Seleucid standard; see Otto, *Zur Geschichte der Zeit des 6 Ptolemäers*, p. 121. Other evidence shows that under the weak regime of Alexander Balas the Phoenician cities enjoyed an astonishing degree of independence; see Diodorus xxxiii 5.

There can be no doubt that in vs. 60, as at 7:8 (see ad loc.), *peran tou potamou* means "the Trans-Euphrates province," rather than "across the river [*sc.* Jordan?]." The verb "make a tour of"="traverse" (Greek *diaporeuesthai;* Hebrew *'br*) takes a direct object, not a prepositional phrase. Our Greek text may be slightly corrupt, since one might expect the Greek to have the definite article (*to*) before "Trans-Euphrates," as at 7:8, but a scribe could easily have confused the article with the suffix -*to* of the preceding verb (the Greek original would have had DIEPOREUETOTO). On the other hand, the article is omitted in the Greek version of I Kings and Ezra 4:10, 11, 17; 5:3; 6:6, etc. For once, Josephus' paraphrase (*AJ* xiii 5.5.148) seems to have a correct translation of the archaic province-name, for it says that Antiochus licensed Jonathan to muster a large force "from Syria and Phoenicia." The use of Ptolemaic terminology is strange (see NOTE on 7:8). Did Josephus draw on the work of Onias IV for his narrative here?

Josephus supplies the missing note that Jonathan accepted the proposals of Antiochus VI and justified his step by Demetrius' wrongful ingratitude (*AJ* xiii 5.4.147). Josephus need have had no source to fill out our author's elliptic narrative here.

Since Jonathan now was the regional commander for Antiochus VI, it is not surprising that the regular Seleucid forces in his province, hostile to Demetrius II, rallied to Jonathan. Ascalon, too, recognized the legitimacy of Jonathan's appointment. Josephus (*AJ* xiii 5.5.148–49) says that the *cities* of Syria and Phoenicia provided Jonathan with no troops, though they showed him respect and eventually consented to Jonathan's pleas that they make alliances with Antiochus VI.

Gaza, however, resisted Jonathan. There is evidence that Gaza strongly supported Demetrius II, though at this time Josephus may be right in reporting (*AJ* xiii 5.5.150) that the citizens deserted Demetrius without going over to Antiochus VI. See Introduction, pp. 120–21, and NOTES on 10:69–89 and 70–73. Since Gaza still proudly bore in 113/2 B.C. the title which probably reflected Demetrius II's privileged institution of Seleucian citizenship (see Hill, *Greek Coins of Palestine,* pp. lxix–lxx), one may be sure that at the first opportunity, with or without the return of the hostages, Gaza rebelled. The expansions in Josephus' narrative here (*AJ* xiii 5.5.151–53) may well be mere inventions of Josephus or his secretaries.

11 60 Thereupon, Jonathan marched out and made a tour of the Trans-Euphrates province, passing through the cities. All the troops of Syria rallied to him as allies. He also marched to Ascalon, and the townspeople received him with honor. 61 From there he marched to Gaza, but the people of Gaza barred their gates, so that he besieged the city, burning and plundering the suburbs. 62 The people of Gaza then asked and received an armistice from Jonathan, who took the sons of their officials as hostages, sending them off to Jerusalem. Thereupon he marched through the country all the way to Damascus.

63 There, word came to Jonathan that Demetrius' commanders had come to Kedes in Galilee with a large force, intending to divert him from his mission. 64 Jonathan marched to meet them.

Meanwhile, Jonathan had left his brother Simon behind in our country. 65 Simon encamped against Beth-Zur and besieged the defenders, keeping it under attack for many days. 66 They asked him for an armistice, which he granted to them. After expelling them, he occupied the town and installed a garrison to guard it.

67 As for Jonathan and his army, they encamped by Lake Gennesar and then made an early morning march to the plain of Hazor. 68 An army of foreigners confronted him in the plain. The foreigners had detached a party to lie in ambush against Jonathan in the mountains while the main body met him face to face. 69 When the ambush party emerged from their hiding place and joined battle, 70 all Jonathan's men fled. Not one of them remained, except Mattathias son of Absalom and Judas son of Chalphi, commanders of the elite troops. 71 Thereupon, Jonathan rent his garments, put earth upon his head, and prayed. 72 On returning to do battle against the enemy, he defeated them and put them to flight. 73 When his own fleeing

men perceived what had happened, they turned back and joined him in pursuit all the way to the enemy camp at Kedes, where they themselves then encamped. 74 The number of foreigners killed on that day reached three thousand. Jonathan returned to Jerusalem.

Notes

11:60–74, introductory NOTE. Here and in 12:1–38 our author or his source may have seen the acts of Jonathan and Simon as fulfilling prophesies of Zechariah: victory through being rescued by God (vss. 70–72; Zech 9:14–17); the intimidation of Greeks (vss. 63–74, 12:24–30; Zech 9:13) and of Philistine Gaza and Ascalon (vss. 60–62, 12:33; Zech 9:5–6); the extension of the territory under the control of the LORD's people to Hamath and Damascus (12:25, 32; Zech 9:1–2), indeed, as far as the Euphrates (vs. 60; Zech 9:10); the diminution of Phoenician Tyre and Sidon (Zech 9:2–4) by the capture of Phoenician Joppe (12:33; see NOTE on 10:75–76); the spoliation of Lebanon (12:31; see NOTE ad loc.; Zech 11:1); the friendly negotiations with gentiles (12:1–23; wᵉdibber šālōm, Zech 9:10); the return of the Jews, "prisoners of hope," for the fortification (biṣṣārōn) of their city and their country (12:35–38; Zech 9:12). One wonders whether Jonathan was tempted to enter Jerusalem riding on an ass as the promised king (Zech 9:9); no Hasmonaean could as yet dare to do so.

60–62. See NOTE on vs. 59.

63–64. Demetrius II continued to control much of the coast from Seleuceia southward through Tyre (Bevan, II, 227–28; see also Introduction, pp. 120–21), though Byblos in 142/1 B.C.E. issued coins of Antiochus VI (Le Rider, Suse, p. 370, n. 2). From Tyre Demetrius' generals could march without difficulty to Kedes (=Cadasa=Kadesh); see Map 14, p. 538, and cf. J. AJ xiii 5.6.154.

The Greek at the end of vs. 63 should not be translated "to depose him from his office." As a rebel against Demetrius, Jonathan no longer held any office from Demetrius. Rather, the generals wished to stop him from organizing the forces loyal to Antiochus VI. Josephus (AJ xiii 5.6.154) probably jumps to conclusions when he assumes that Jonathan went to defend Jews of Galilee from Demetrius' army rather than simply to fight the enemies of Antiochus VI. It is doubtful whether any significant number of Jews remained in Galilee; see I 5:23, 9:2.

64–66. For the pluperfect verb in vs. 64, see NOTE on vss. 8–14. Again our author stresses the role of Simon, founder of the hereditary dynasty. Joseph and Azariah, too, had been left behind in charge of Judaea (I 5:55–62). In contrast to them, Simon was successful, in accordance with his destiny.

It did not matter what Seleucid pretender the Seleucid garrison of Beth-Zur chose to back. Manned partly by apostate and anti-Hasmonaean Jews, it had to resist Hasmonaean Simon, who then, as the agent of Antiochus

VI, was free to besiege and take the "rebel" stronghold. The clemency shown by Simon in granting the defenders their lives (cf. J. *AJ* xiii 5.6.156) is eloquent proof that the Jews among them were not idolaters. Our author would not portray his hero as violating the commandments in the Torah (Exod 22:19; Deut 17:2–7) to kill Jewish idolaters!

67. Jonathan marched from Damascus (see vss. 62–63), going by way of Lake Gennesar (=Sea of Galilee=Sea of Chinnereth) in order to take the easiest road toward Kedes, across the plain of Hazor. See Map 14.

68–70. For our author, the reason for the temporary success of Jonathan's enemies is not Jewish sin but the enemy ambush. Our author singles out for mention the two commanders who stood firm, surely accompanied by some of their subordinates. Only by way of hyperbole could our author assert that they alone stood firm. Josephus set aside the hyperbole and guessed that some fifty subordinates stood firm (*AJ* xiii 5.7.161). In giving the names of the steadfast commanders, our author may have meant to gratify Jewish families powerful in the reign of Alexander Jannaeus. Of a family descended from Chalphi (or Chapsaios, according to the reading at J. *AJ* xiii 5.7.161), nothing further is known. On the possible family descended from Absalom, see I 13:11; II 11:17, 1QpHab 5:9; D. N. Freedman, "The 'House of Absalom' in the Habakkuk Scroll," BASOR 114 (April 1949), 11–12.

For the expression "elite troops" (*ṣᵉbā haggibbōrīm*) cf. I Chron 19:8; Greek *dynamis* renders Hebrew *gibbōr* at Hosea 10:13 and Isa 42:13.

71–74. Our author echoes Josh 7:5–9. The point of the narrative is to show that the prayers of the Hasmonaean commander are answered. The Age of Wrath, during which God would not respond to prayer, appeared to have ended with Judas' victories but to have recommenced with Judas' death, and now again appears to have ended. Indeed, in contrast to Judas (I 9:6–7), Jonathan finds his routed men rallying to him again. Our author may have had in mind Isa 58:9–14: Jonathan rebuilt the ancient ruins and (according to the Hasmonaean teachings) observed the Sabbath, and Israel, having received worldwide glory, in expanded Judaea was at last reaping the fruits of the heritage of Jacob. Cf. also Isa 57:13 and 64:6 – 65:1 and Jer 29:10–14. Josephus (*AJ* xiii 5.7.161) omits the story of the efficacy of Jonathan's prayer, perhaps because he knew that the Age of Wrath still continued in his own time.

Our author probably also intended to echo the achievement of the earlier Jonathan; cf. Greek I Sam 14:21–22.

So complete was Jonathan's victory that he occupied the enemy camp. In control of the battlefield, the victorious Jews could easily count the enemy dead, so that the figure of three thousand should be reliable if the text is correct. Josephus (*AJ* xiii 5.8.163) gives the figure as two thousand.

Having raised a force to support Antiochus VI and having decisively defeated the forces of Demetrius II, Jonathan, his mission completed, felt free to return to Jerusalem.

XXVIII. DIPLOMACY WITH ROME
AND SPARTA
(12:1–23)

12 ¹ Perceiving that time was working in his favor, Jonathan appointed ambassadors and sent them to Rome to confirm and renew the ties of friendship with the Romans. ² He also sent letters to the same effect to Sparta and to other places. ³ The ambassadors journeyed to Rome. On being admitted to the senate house, they said, "The High Priest Jonathan and the nation of the Jews have sent us to renew the ties of friendship and alliance with you as before." ⁴ The Romans gave them letters to the authorities in each place containing instructions to see to it that the ambassadors returned safely to the land of Judah.

⁵ Here is the text of the letter which Jonathan wrote to the Spartans:

⁶ "The High Priest Jonathan and the Council of Elders of the nation and the priests and the rest of the People of the Jews to their brothers the Spartans, greeting. ⁷ Long ago, a letter was sent to our High Priest Onias from Areus who was then your king, saying that you are our kin, as in the subjoined text. ⁸ Onias received your emissary with honor and accepted the letter, in which alliance and friendship were mentioned.

⁹ "Now, although we are not in need of ties of alliance and friendship since we have as our source of courage the Holy Books in our possession, ¹⁰ we venture to send a message to renew our ties of brotherhood and friendship with you in order that we may not become estranged from you. Indeed, many years have passed since you sent us your message. ¹¹ Throughout the years we have unfailingly made mention of you, on our festivals and on the other appropriate occasions in connection with the sacrifices we offer, as well as in our prayers, inasmuch as it is right and proper thus to make mention of brothers. ¹² We rejoice over your eminence. ¹³ As for us, many troubles and many wars have beset us, as the kings in our vicinity waged war upon us. ¹⁴ Now, we did not wish to bother you or our

other allies and friends with these wars, 15 for we have the help of Heaven coming to our aid, so that we have been saved from our enemies and our enemies have been brought low. 16 Accordingly, we have appointed Numenius son of Antiochus and Antipater son of Jason and have sent them as ambassadors to Rome to renew our previous ties of friendship and alliance with the Romans. 17 We have ordered them to go to you, too, and greet you and deliver to you our letter concerning the renewal of our ties of brotherhood. 18 Please be so good as to send us a reply to our proposals."

19 Here is the text of the letter which they sent:

20 "To Onias, Areus King of the Spartans, greeting. 21 In a work concerning the Spartans and the Jews there is a statement that they are brothers and that they are descended from Abraham. 22 Now that we have learned this, please be so good as to write us how you are. 23 We are ready to write in reply to you, 'Your cattle and property are ours, and ours are yours.' We have ordered that you be given a full report on these matters."

NOTES

12:1–23, introductory NOTE. See NOTE on 11:60–74, on the possible fulfillments of prophesy here. Like the story of the embassy to Rome (chapter 8), no one would have missed vss. 1–23 had they been omitted. Our author probably places them here because in fact the victory (11:67–74) prompted Jonathan to send the embassy; see below, on vs. 1. Our author would have found no clear indication of where to place the report of the embassy from the position of Zech 9:10 in its own context and from the position of the embassy in the supposed fulfillments of Zechariah 9.

Antiochus VI's reign began in late summer, 145 B.C.E. Jonathan and the Jews won under Antiochus VI the victories and honors which led them to think that God would allow them to send embassies (see below, on vs. 1). Our author does not tell us how much time elapsed during the events of 11:60–74. Jonathan would be prompt to renew the Roman alliance, as soon as he and most Jews were convinced that God permitted the act. Embassies could receive a hearing at Rome in any season, even when the consuls were absent on military campaigns (see NOTE on 8:17–20), as the consuls were in mid-143 (Münzer, "Caecilius 94" and "Claudius 295," PW, III [1899], 1215 and 2848). Indeed, no evidence suggests that a consul dealt with Jonathan's ambassadors. The embassy to Rome and Sparta must have been sent before the death of Jonathan in late 143 (see NOTE on 13:23) and perhaps only shortly before (see NOTE on 14:16–24k). Our author's sole source for the embassy may well have been an undated copy of Jonathan's letter.

1–4. Confirmation and renewal of ties of friendship with the Romans usually consisted, as here, of an exchange of courtesies during a diplomatic visit; in vs. 17 we read how ties of *brotherhood* were similarly "renewed." The Jews had no need now to negotiate a new treaty with the Romans. The treaty made in the time of Judas (8:23–30) had no time limit, and the Romans had made it with the Jews, not with Judas, so that Judas' death made no difference. Indeed, even a Roman treaty with a king did not necessarily have to be renegotiated when that king died and his successor took over. On these matters of treaties and "renewal of ties of friendship," see Heuss, *Grundlagen*, pp. 25–59; Louis Robert, *Hellenica*, I (1940), 96–97; Klose, *Völkerrechtliche Ordnung*, pp. 162–64. The act of renewal of ties of friendship served to prevent the Romans from forgetting the Jews and would give Tryphon, Demetrius II, and others reason to hesitate before attacking recognized friends of the superpower.

Josephus (*AJ* xiii 5.8.165, 170) takes the trouble to record that the Romans and the Spartans confirmed the ties as requested. However, our text is not defective. Our author knew the institutions of Roman diplomacy. The honorable dispatch of the envoys implies that their mission was successful. The Roman letters left the Jews' situation unchanged; even if the text was preserved, our author did not need to quote it. On letters of this kind, see 14:24c–24k and introductory NOTE to chapter 8. The ambassadors' names are given in vs. 16.

1. *time . . . favor.* In such passages "time" (*kairos*) refers to the periods of Israel's punishment or prosperity. Cf. 2:49, 9:10, 13:5, 15:33–34. Nevertheless, the expression is strange, and we probably have here another of our author's circumlocutions to avoid naming the Deity, so that "time" could well be capitalized; Josephus (*AJ* xiii 5.8.163) supplied a direct reference to God. The Greek verb "work in favor of" (*synergein*) is not found elsewhere in translations from the Hebrew Bible but is used of God's help at Testament of Issachar iii 7 and at J. *BJ* vi 1.5.38. Our author may well have been alluding to Isa 49:8, for under Jonathan the "despised nation" had won the admiration of kings (as at Isa 49:7) and was rebuilding the land and reinheriting the once desolate heritage (as at Isa 49:9).

Our author had no doubt that from the time of Judas the Jews no longer were living through a protracted Age of Wrath; God's wrath was now at most intermittent. As Judas had sent an embassy to Rome on receiving a clear sign of God's favor (see introductory NOTE to chapter 8), so now Jonathan does the same following the astonishing reversal of fortune in battle wrought by his prayer (11:70–74).

2. On the two names for Sparta, "Lakedaimon" and "Sparta," see Bölte, "Sparta," PW, IIIᴬ (1929), 1268–78. Even before Jonathan's time writers frequently called the city "Sparta," though Spartan official documents and Greek diplomats used "Lakedaimon"; in the second century B.C.E. the name "Sparta" even appears on a few Spartan inscriptions (ibid., col. 1273). Similarly, the Spartans are usually called "Lakedaimonians," but "Spartan" (*Spartiatês* or *Spartiatas*) appears on a few inscriptions as well as in Greek writers including

Polybius (iv 7.7, 80.6; xxxviii 2.6, 8; see Bölte, PW III^A, 1280–83, 1291–92). Hence, our author and Jonathan, and perhaps the peoples of Asia generally, appear to have known the city by the name "Sparta." Josephus in his paraphrases, predictably, has "Lakedaimonians" (*AJ* xii 4.10.225–26, xiii 5.8.166, 170).

Our author does not care to specify who were the other recipients of the letters, perhaps because, unlike the Spartans and the Romans, they could not be described as "righteous." See Introduction, p. 12.

3. In quoting the ambassadors, our author can now give the high priest Jonathan and the nation (*ethnos*) of the Jews the honorable titles of their status, in contrast to the situation in the time of Judas; see NOTES on 8:17–20 and 20.

5–23. The letter to the Spartans shows how Jonathan and his diplomatic staff were ready and able to use for their own benefit the established methods of the Hellenistic world as we learn from earlier and later documents. Rome at the time stood as the unrivaled power, but even for her friends Rome might not intervene, unless Roman interests were directly involved. The Romans also had by now several times turned hostile to erstwhile beneficiaries whose loyalty they found reason to question, as Rhodes, the Achaean league, and the dynasty of Pergamum had found to their sorrow. Few, indeed, at this time were the political units who enjoyed unclouded Roman favor; see Bengtson, *Griechische Geschichte*, pp. 501–4. Among the few were the Greek city of Massalia (on the site of modern Marseille), Sparta and Athens in Greece, and later the free Greek city of Pergamum in Asia Minor. On Massalia, see Charles Ebel, *Gallia Transalpina* (Diss. Iowa; Ann Arbor: University Microfilms, 1971), pp. 5–119; on Sparta, Ehrenberg, "Sparta (Geschichte)," PW, III^A (1929), 1445–46; on Athens, John Day, *An Economic History of Athens under Roman Domination* (Columbia University Press, 1942), pp. 50–51, 91, 94, 109–10; on Pergamum, David Magie, *Roman Rule in Asia Minor*, pp. 156 and 1045–46, n. 34, and Stern, *Zion* 26 (1961), 14 (in Hebrew).

Many of the peculiarities of the letter to the Spartans become understandable when compared with the procedures used earlier by the Greek city of Lampsakos. When their city on the eastern shore of the Hellespont was threatened by the ambitions of Antiochus III in 197–196, the people of Lampsakos sought to cope with the situation by sending Hegesias on a mission first to the Roman naval commander in Greek waters, Lucius Quinctius Flamininus; then, to distant Massalia; and finally, to Rome.

To Flamininus, Hegesias' embassy pleaded that the people of Lampsakos were *kin* and friends of the Romans and therefore should receive Roman protection, and also because the people of Lampsakos were brothers of those staunch friends and allies of the Romans, the people of Massalia. The embassy received favorable replies from Flamininus, and the news, on reaching Lampsakos, raised the courage of the people (*eutharsesteros ho dêmos ên*). After their meeting with Flamininus, the embassy took the long journey to Massalia, where they pleaded for and got the despatch of a Massaliote embassy to support their cause before the Roman senate. At Rome, the Massaliotes reminded the senate of their own long friendship and alliance with the

Romans and then pleaded for their *brothers* the people of Lampsakos. Thereupon, Hegesias and his embassy themselves pleaded the cause of Lampsakos, asking that the senate look to the interests of Lampsakos as well as to those of Rome's other close friends, because of the ties of *kinship,* because of the existing kindly sentiments at Lampsakos toward Rome, and because Lampsakos' cause had the backing of the Massaliotes. The results were sufficiently favorable for Lampsakos that the people there set up the inscription honoring Hegesias, from which we derive our knowledge of the whole affair (Syll.[3] 591, to be corrected by Maurice Holleaux, *Études d'épigraphie et d'histoire grecques,* vol. V, part II [Paris: Adrien-Maisonneuve, 1957], 141–55).

The "brotherhood" of the people of Lampsakos and the Massaliotes was a fact of history: both cities were originally colonies founded by Phokaia. The kinship of the people of Lampsakos with the Romans was a fiction. Legend traced the origins of Rome to Aeneas the Trojan, and Lampsakos belonged to a league of cities organized around the temple of Athena Ilias at Ilium, on the traditional site of Troy (Syll.[3] 330); such may have been the basis for the fiction.

At the time of the embassy sent by Jonathan, in the reign of Antiochus VI (after late summer, 145, and before the death of Jonathan in late 143), Sparta was the outstanding example of how the favor of the Romans could bring success. The Achaean league had attacked and menaced Sparta in 148 and 147 and in 146 had again gone to war against her. Quickly Rome came to Sparta's rescue with diplomatic moves in 147 and with her armies in 146, utterly crushing and dissolving the Achaean league (Ehrenberg, PW, III[A], 1444; see vs. 12).

Jonathan and his staff understood the threats posed to them by the hostile Demetrius II and the unreliable Diodotus-Tryphon. As was done in the time of Judas, they had recourse to Rome, but they now understood the difficulties of retaining Roman support. Unlike the Greeks of Lampsakos, Jonathan and his staff found no device for claiming kinship to Rome, though they may have quoted Jewish prophesies of Roman greatness to impress the senate (see NOTE on 8:1–19). Like the people of Lampsakos, however, the Jewish diplomats now sought to have for the future the good offices of a close friend of the Romans, a friend to whom they themselves could claim ties of kinship. Where Massalia served that purpose for Lampsakos, Sparta might serve Jonathan and the Jews. Greek practice required the group claiming kinship or pious friendly relations to furnish proof, if the matter in question was not common knowledge; see Bikerman, AIPHOS, XIII (1953), 31, n. 1. Hence Jonathan and his staff here made use of the letter of Areus and composed a letter to accompany it.

The embassy to Rome in the time of Judas made no claims of kinship and did not need to introduce the Jews to the Romans. Romans had previously had relations with the Jews (II 11:34–38). Hence, no letter to the Romans to accompany the speeches of the ambassadors was needed either in the time of Judas or now. In approaching the Spartans, however, where proof was needed for a claim of kinship, a written communication was desirable. If the Spartans replied while Jonathan was still alive, they did so orally, through the ambassadors. It is, however, much more likely that the ambassadors gained a favorable, written response from the Spartans only after Jonathan's death; see NOTE on 14:16–24k.

Later, the Jews themselves and their Hasmonaean prince John Hyrcanus enjoyed a prestige similar to that of Sparta as Roman diplomatic intervention thrice came to John Hyrcanus' aid; see Stern, *Zion* 26 (1961), 1–22 (in Hebrew, with English summary, p. i). During those years even Pergamum and Athens sought to bolster their favored positions with Rome by currying favor with John Hyrcanus, as Lampsakos had resorted to Massalia and Jonathan had to Sparta. See J. *AJ* xiv 10.22.247–55; 8.5.149–55. Pergamum even claimed friendly ties with the Jews going back to the time of Abraham and said that proof of the fact lay in the local archives; on the possible basis for this fiction, see below, on vss. 20–23.

Thus, the diplomatic moves reported here are credible when seen against the background of the times. But is it credible, as our documents would have us believe, that Spartans would accept a genealogy tracing the common descent they shared with the Jews back to the Israelite Abraham, rather than to some figure of Greek myth? Or that the people of Pergamum would similarly trace their friendship with the Jews back to the time of Abraham? The Greek mind was usually ethnocentric, and all the more so after the Jews and the other peoples of Asia had been the despised subjects of Graeco-Macedonian rule for centuries. In Josephus' time, such gentile tributes to the ancient prestige of the Jews were practically unheard of! See J. *Ap.* i 1.2–5. Few Greeks accepted even the claims of the Egyptians, that from their once powerful and indisputably ancient civilization had stemmed many Greek peoples and heroes; note the skepticism of Diodorus (i 9.5–6, 28.1, 29.5–6), and see Bickerman, "Origines Gentium," *Classical Philology* 47 (1952), 71–73. However, there were periods when Greeks were impressed by the antiquity of Egypt and when reputable Greek historians, such as Herodotus and Hecataeus of Abdera, would give Greek heroes and peoples an Egyptian origin (Bickerman, ibid., pp. 71–72, 74). Do our documents reflect the vogue of ideas like those of Hecataeus of Abdera? See below, on vss. 20–23.

From the time of Homer, indeed, Greeks believed that their own genealogies were connected with those of the Phoenicians, a people with strong claims to antiquity; see Astour, *Hellenosemitica*, index, s.vv. "Phoenicia," "Phoenician," and "Phoenix," and Supplementum Epigraphicum Graecum, II, 330. The connections of the Greeks with the Phoenicians are attested early and probably reflect historical fact, whereas no such early connections are attested for the Jews. Nevertheless, could not Greeks, when prompted by self-interest and by supposed evidence, claim common descent with the Jews, an ancient people neighbors to the Phoenicians?

The Greeks, no matter how ethnocentric, knew the rules of courtesy and rhetoric. Romans long before had accepted their own connection with Greece and Troy; see Bickerman, *Classical Philology* 47 (1952), 66–68; hence the people of Lampsakos could appeal to Greek myth in approaching the Romans. But if Greeks were trying to impress Jews, it would do no good for them to say that Jews were descended from or were friends with the Greek hero Herakles. Rather, they would have to mention a figure with whom Jews were familiar. Cf. Richard Volkmann, *Die Rhetorik der Griechen und Römer*, 2d ed. (Leipzig: Teubner, 1885), pp. 235–36. Hence, the people of Pergamum and perhaps Areus, too, had recourse to Abraham. Just so, Jonathan and his staff could not simply mention Abraham to the Spartans; if they could not bring themselves to mention Danaos or Herakles, they had to have something like the letter of Areus to show that an authoritative Spartan knew of Abraham. The isolation of our texts in which Greeks justify claims of friendship and kinship by naming early non-Greek heroes may simply be due to the rarity of opportunities for Greeks to curry favor with non-Greek peoples who had long genealogical traditions and to the fact that relatively few ancient documents of any kind survive. The Septuagint itself may have been available to the people of Pergamum in the second century B.C.E. and perhaps even to Areus in the third. The work of Hecataeus of Abdera was certainly available in the early third century and may well have mentioned Abraham (see below, on vss. 20–23). Abraham was known to Apollonius Molon (*apud* Eusebius *Praeparatio evangelica* ix 19.2), a contemporary of our author, and later in the first century B.C.E., to Nicolaus of Damascus (FGH 90, F 19). Hence the failure of the documents from Pergamum and Sparta to exhibit the usual Greek ethnocentrism is not a reason to dismiss them as spurious.

Far from being a naive injection of Jewish ways into the Graeco-Roman world, Jonathan's letter to the Spartans represents an adroit adaptation of Graeco-Roman institutions to meet Jewish needs. Jonathan's ambassadors were Jews who spoke Greek and bore Greek names; the letter in its original form surely was in polished Greek, and traces of the fact can be seen even through the retranslation into Greek of our author's Hebrew version of the original; see below, in the commentary to the individual passages. Here we may note the following in the Greek: (1) the greater variety in the connective particles, whereas Greek translations from Hebrew usually have a monotonous successive use of the particle *kai* ("and"); (2) the use of participles, a favorite form in Greek, where Hebrew would use a simple noun or a clause.

Jonathan and his staff might have had good reason to forge the letter of the Spartan king Areus to the Jewish high priest Onias, in order both to influence the Spartans and to quiet Jewish fears that God would disapprove of friendly ties with Greeks. However, a propagandistic forger aims to convince the recipients of his propaganda. As we saw, the people of Pergamum, currying favor with John Hyrcanus, were careful to mention Abraham, and Jonathan's staff was able to produce a letter in polished Greek. The strange Semitic flavor of the letter of Areus, even if some of it is due to the multiple translations underlying our text, guarantees that if it is spurious, Jonathan and his staff were not the forgers. See below, on vss. 20–23.

There is a second guarantee that Jonathan and his staff did not forge the letter of Areus. A forger understands the document he has produced. Jonathan and his staff probably *misunderstood* the letter of Areus, for at vs. 8 they write that the letter to Onias spoke of "alliance"; in fact, "alliance" is nowhere mentioned in the letter. Josephus perceived the incongruity, and in his paraphrase he cleverly omitted all reference to alliance (*AJ* xiii 5.8.167). At the outset, Areus asserts that Jews and Spartans are brothers. Greek alliances (*symmachiai*) were military. Far from being chiefly military, in Greek international relations brotherhood and kinship and friendship were matters of hospitality and cordiality, of the sharing of roads and waterways and economic facilities, of shared participation in religious rites and shared use of sacred equipment, and of diplomatic support. See Syll.[3] 559, 591, and 682; Bickerman in *Mélanges syriennes*, pp. 91–99; Rudolf Herzog and Günther Klaffenbach, *Asylieurkunden aus Kos* (Abhandlungen der Deutsche Akademie der Wissenschaften zu Berlin, 1952, No. 1), nos. 3, 12, and 13; cf. Num 20:14–17. Such ties might be invoked in pleading for an alliance, as in the spurious document at Demosthenes 18.186, but in themselves they did not involve any military obligation. The ties of friendship and kinship were flexible: as long as they existed, the two parties would agree that some of what each held was common (*koina*) to both, in accordance with the Greek proverb, *koina ta philôn* ("What friends hold, they hold in common"; Plato *Republic* iv 424a and v 449c). Each party, however, would presume to use the holdings of the other only with the other's consent, as is clear from the inscriptions just cited, as well as from Num 20:14–17. We shall see (below, on vss. 20–23) that Jonathan and his staff had access only to a Hebrew or Aramaic text of Areus' letter. In Biblical Hebrew and probably also in Aramaic there was no word equivalent to the Greek word "common" (*koina*); the concept could be expressed only by paraphrase, "Our holdings are yours and yours are ours." Thus, vs. 23, too, did not express alliance, but only brotherhood, kinship, or friendship. Had Jonathan and his staff seen a Greek original, *koina ta hêmôn kai ta hymôn* ("What we hold and you hold are now in common"), they might well have understood. On seeing the expression in Hebrew or Aramaic, "Your cattle and property are ours and ours are yours," they read it instead as equivalent to the idiom of military alliance at I Kings 22:4 and II Kings 3:7. Greeks similarly misunderstood Roman usages; see E. Bickermann, "Rom und Lampsakos," *Philologus* 87 (1932), 277–99. Josephus paraphrases vs. 23 correctly in using the Greek word "common" (*AJ* xii 4.10.227).

If Jonathan and his staff did not forge the letter of Areus, could our author have forged both the letters of our passage? Hardly. As we have seen, John Hyrcanus had philhellenic tendencies; Judah Aristobulus was even called *Philhellenos* (J. *AJ* xiii 11.3.318). But our author, with his general hostility to Greeks (see NOTE on 8:9–10, and p. 12), had nothing to lead him to forge a document justifying an exception in favor of the Spartans. When he wrote, in the reign of Alexander Jannaeus, the Spartans were insignificant, and the reigning Hasmonaean prince was far from being philhellenic (except to his mercenaries) and no longer was seeking the support of Rome or of Rome's favored Greek friends. Skeptics may still insist that we know too little of the ancient background to exclude the possibility that a philhellenic Jew, when Areus was long enough dead, forged the letter as propaganda. Such a Jew need not have written before the flight of Jason the Oniad to Sparta (ca. 169), because II 5:9 may represent only an inference of Jason of Cyrene from our letter. On the other hand, if there was a forger, Jason the Oniad is a likely possibility, since he was an extreme philhellene and is the only one reported to have gained material profit from the alleged kinship with the Spartans. One must still ask, Why would a philhellenic Jew forge a letter from a Spartan king in Aramaic or in Aramaic style? There were Greek-speaking and Greek-reading Jews already in the third century! As propaganda to Greeks, the letter should have been in good Greek style. As propaganda by a philhellenic Jew aimed at Jews it should have cited Jewish texts; e.g. Gen 9:27 with 25:3, with an explanation that Dedan is Danaos and that L*ummim* ("nations") includes the Spartans.

The factors I have adduced here and below, on vss. 20–23, suffice to refute arguments that the documents here and the decree of Pergamum in Josephus do not fit Greek patterns and are therefore spurious. For those arguments, see Bikerman, AIPHOS, XIII (1953), 21, n. 3; Abel, pp. 231–32; Burkhart Cardauns, "Juden und Spartaner," *Hermes* 95 (1967), 317–24.

6. The Council of Elders had existed before; see NOTE on 8:15. For the first time, our author presents a Hasmonaean as working in cooperation with the Council of Elders and does so by quoting a document. This suggests that previously the Council had opposed or at least not associated with the Hasmonaeans; Jason of Cyrene is wrong in connecting Judas and the Hasmonaeans with the document addressed to the Council at II 11:27 (see NOTE on I 4:35). As soon as Jonathan became the legitimately appointed high priest, the Council surely had to recognize his authority.

The priests are singled out here under Jonathan as an "estate" separate from the rest of the nation, and later under Simon (14:20, 28, 44). One wonders what institutional arrangements this fact reflects. Priests did have cultic prerogatives, but politically in this period they had no privileges that we know of. See, however, J. *AJ* xii 3.3.142, Diodorus xl 4, and Bikerman, *Institutions,* p. 165.

Jonathan's staff addressed the letter to "their brothers the Spartans" following the instructions given in the letter of Areus (". . . the Spartans and the Jews are brothers. . . . Please write us. . . ."). Areus being long dead, they naturally gave the address as we have it, just as the Spartans in later addressing the Jews (14:20) simply copied the formula at the beginning of our verse. On the use of the name "Spartans" rather than "Lakedaimonians," see above, on vs. 2.

Josephus and his secretaries knew something of the protocol followed at Sparta in their own day, though even on that they were probably wrong; see NOTE on 14:20. Finding the text of the letter here gauche, they changed our verse to read, "Jonathan, high priest of the nation of the Jews, and the Council of Elders and the Community [*koinon*] of the Priests to their brothers the Ephors, Council of Elders, and People of the Lakedaimonians" (*AJ* xiii 5.8.166). Manuscript V of Josephus for "Priests" has "Jews," which may be the text intended by Josephus; Hasmonaean coins bear the legend "X, high priest, and the Community [*ḥbr*] of the Jews." But 14:20 proves Josephus to be wrong on Spartan protocol in the time of Jonathan. If Jonathan's staff or our author had known of a protocol like that assumed by Josephus, they would have jumped at the opportunity to parade the parallel institutions of Jews and Spartans, high priest corresponding to ephors and councils of elders and community assemblies being common to both peoples. Hence, our author's version is surely the authentic one.

Here for the first time the Greek translator has Jews use the Greek word *dêmos* ("People") of their own community (Romans use it at 8:29), perhaps because he sensed how Jonathan's diplomats used the word to give the Spartans an impression of similar institutions. On the *damos* (=*dêmos*) at Sparta in this period, see 14:21–23; IG V 1, 4 and 5: and Ehrenberg, PW, III^A, 1443.

After the salutation Josephus added the stereotyped formula, "If you are well and your public and private affairs are proceeding according to your intentions, it would be as we wish"; cf. II 11:20 and Welles, *Royal Correspondence,* no. 56, line 2.

7–9. The content of the letter begins with the typical Greek explanation of how the letter came to be sent, couched in typical Greek syntax, literally, "Inasmuch as long ago [*epei proteron*] a letter was sent . . . and Onias . . . accepted the letter, now . . . we venture to send a message." The reading *epei* is attested by L LA^B 311, by J. *AJ* xiii 5.8.167, and by the parallel at 14:29, whereas *eti proteron* ("still longer ago"), the reading of S, hardly makes sense and is found nowhere else in Greek translations from the Hebrew Bible.

Convenient in Greek, such long explanatory clauses are quite awkward in Hebrew and Aramaic. See NOTE on 14:29–49. On Areus, Onias, and the early letter, see below, on vss. 20–23.

7. "Who was then your king" is expressed by a participle, natural in Greek, but not in Hebrew, where an appositive, "your king at that time," or a clause would be normal; cf. Num 22:4; I Sam 12:14; and Gen 36:31.

8–9. Again the use of participles for "emissary," "although we are not in need," and "since we have" suggests that the letter was originally written in polished Greek. The relative clause, "in which alliance and friendship were mentioned," also looks Greek, and not like a translation from normal Hebrew. Josephus gives the letter bearer a name (*AJ* xiii 5.8.167); see below, on vs. 23.

9. *have as our source of courage.* The Greek is *paraklêsin echontes;* whatever was our author's Hebrew translation of the Greek, the expression had no parallel in Biblical Hebrew, and again suggests a polished Greek original. It is clear from the context that the noun means, not the "comfort" given to the grieved (cf. II 11:32), but a "source of courage" for men at war, such as the knowledge of being backed by allies; cf. II 15:11 and the use of the related verb at Greek Deut 3:28; I 13:3, and II 13:14. At Deut 3:28 and elsewhere Greek *parakalein* translates the Hebrew root *'mṣ* ("encourage"); a noun from the same root (*omeṣ*, "courage") at Job 17:9 is rendered by the Greek noun *tharsos*. The original Greek here may have had a derivative of *tharsos;* compare *eutharsesteros ho dêmos ên* ("the people's courage increased") in the inscription from Lampsakos (see above, on vss. 5–23). The polished Greek translation of Ezra 7:28 at I Esd 8:27 is similar.

Josephus appears to have perceived how Jonathan and his staff misunderstood Areus' offer to be an offer of alliance (see above, on vss. 5–23) and was also surprised that Jews would silently accept the authority of non-Jewish texts on the alleged kinship. Hence, his paraphrase (*AJ* xiii 5.8.167) alters our verse to read, "Although we needed no such demonstration since the kinship has been proved on the basis of our sacred scriptures, and although formerly we did not think it proper to take the first step in recognizing our relationship for fear of giving the impression of being greedy for the honor you were conferring."

10. The word order of the Greek suggests that it was not translated from a normal Hebrew original. The expression "we venture to send" also may be unhebraic, but cf. Deut 4:34.

As with "renewal of friendship," renewal here did not mean that in the interim the ties had lapsed or that a new agreement was negotiated, but rather that a fresh cordial contact had now been made, newly reflecting the supposed old relationship; see above, on vss. 1–4. For another example of renewal of supposed kinship see Wilhelm Vollgraff, "Inscriptions d'Argos," *Bulletin de correspondence hellénique* 25 (1904), 411–27.

11. Even this verse with its references to prayer, festivals, and sacrifices is an adroit Jewish adaptation of Greek patterns.

"Make mention of" or "remember" reflects a common formula of Greek letter writing (*mneian poieisthai*, changed here through multiple translation into the synonymous *mimnêiskometha;* see Mayser, II^{II}, 211). The thoroughly Hellenized Tubias used it, saying, "I have remembered you at all times as was right" (CPJ 4). Although the Greek expressions can simply mean "remember," rather than "make mention of," there are Greek letters wherein the writer adds the phrase "to the Gods," showing that he is mentioning in prayer, not just remembering (*Berliner griechische Urkunden* 632.5). Greek states, too, continually made mention, over sacrificial rites, of communities that were their kin; see Herzog and Klaffenbach, *Asylieurkunden,* No. 12, lines 19–21, and No. 13, lines 19–21.

The "appropriate occasions" here are probably the Jewish holy days called "appointed days" (*mo'ădīm*), those other than the three Pilgrimage festivals (*haggīm*), and would include the Day of Remembrance (Lev 23:24) now called "Rosh hashanah" and also the Day of Atonement; on the distinction between the two sets of holy days, see Loewenstamm, Enc. Bib., III, 21–22 (in Hebrew). On the efficacy of prayer on a fast-day like the Day of Atonement, see Isa 58:1–9. Prayer on Rosh hashanah was thought to be particularly efficacious (TB *Rosh hashanah* 18a end, commenting on Isa 55:6); cf. Ovid *Fasti* i 165 ff. Nowhere in Greek translations from the Hebrew Bible are "appointed days" translated by the Greek expression used here, perhaps because Jonathan's staff used a different vocabulary, one aimed at the Greek recipients. Josephus' paraphrase (*AJ* xiii 5.8.168) has "on our holy days and on our named days [*epônymois hêmerais*]." By "named days" he probably meant commemorative days of celebration like the Day of Nicanor (I 7:47–49; II 15:36) and the Day of Mordecai (II 15:36).

"Appropriate," "right," and "proper" here again may reflect Greek rather than Hebrew style, because all are expressed by participles.

12. See above, on vss. 5–23.

13. Jonathan's diplomatic staff knew how to evoke the sympathies of the Spartans, who had also been beset by wars, including wars waged by Macedonian Kings; see A. H. M. Jones, *Sparta,* pp. 150–64.

14–15. Whether or not Onias had replied to Areus' letter, the Jews had long had no contact with their "kin." The letter here gives a creditable explanation for such unkinsmanlike behavior.

16. The two ambassadors bear Greek names favored by Jews; see CPJ, vol. III, pp. 169, 179, 186. Of the names here, only "Antiochus" might be unusual for a Jew, but it was a common Greek name. Antipater's father Jason may well have been the ambassador to Rome (8:17); the family appears to have had several generations of service as ambassadors to Rome (J. *AJ* xiv 8.5.146, xiii 9.2.260, xiv 10.22.248). The two ambassadors here were to serve again in that capacity (14:22, 24). Josephus' version of the letter adds that Numenius and Antipater were honored members of the Council of Elders (*AJ* xiii 5.8.169).

17. The word order in the Greek, placing "to you, too" before "to go" is very unhebraic. The Greek has "concerning the renewal and our ties of brotherhood." My translation treats the expression as a hendiadys, as does Josephus' paraphrase (*AJ* xiii 5.8.169).

18. On the Spartans' reply, see NOTE on 14:16–24k.

20–23. For the reasons given above (on vss. 5–23), the letter of Areus here cannot have been forged by Jonathan or his staff. Is it, then, authentic? The available evidence may not suffice for certainty. Let us consider the known facts.

Though the scribes and perhaps the Greek translator, too, had difficulty recognizing the name of the Spartan king, the witnesses to the text here (vss. 7, 21) and at *AJ* xii 4.10.225–26 and the known names of Spartan kings leave no doubt that his name was "Areus." Scholars have noticed that the letter, if authentic, portrays Areus as presumptuously offering to involve the Spartans with the Jews, as if the elected ephors and the other machinery of the Spartan republic did not have to be consulted. See Jones, *Sparta*, pp. 15–30; Ulrich von Wilamowitz-Moellendorf, *Hellenistische Dichtung* (Berlin: Weidmann, 1924), p. 43, n. 1. There were only two kings of Sparta named Areus. Areus II was a helpless child who was nominal king from his birth in 262 B.C.E. to 254. Only Areus I, king from 309 to 265, could have sent the letter. There were two Jewish high priests named Onias whose time of office could have fallen within Areus' lifetime. Onias I was the son of the Iaddus (Yaddua) who was high priest at the time of Alexander the Great (J. *AJ* xi 8.7.347). The only other fact known of Onias I is that he was the father of Simon I (*AJ* xii 2.5.43). Onias II was the son of Simon I, but since Onias II was very young when Simon I died, Simon I's brother Eleazaros and then Simon I's uncle Manasses preceded Onias II in the high priesthood (*AJ* xii 2.5.44, 4.1.157). Onias II is reported to have been an old man by the time of the reign of Ptolemy III Euergetes I (246–221; *AJ* xii 4.1–2. 158–63); see my article, "The Tales of the Tobiads," in *Studies Smith*, Part III, pp. 86–87, 94–99. We have insufficient chronological information to exclude either of these two.

Nevertheless, some factors make Onias II the more probable. Areus I seems to have been very young when he became king in 309; his first reported act is in 280 (Jones, *Sparta*, p. 150). In the later part of his reign he displays abundantly the sort of autocratic traits which are also exemplified in the presumption noted in our letter: action with no regard for the ephors, coinage in his own name, luxury after the pattern of the rulers of the Hellenistic empires (see NOTE on 11:39), etc.; see Ehrenberg, PW, III^A, 1423, and Syll.³ 434–35. Hence, if authentic, the letter was probably written in the later part of Areus' reign, when Onias II becomes much more probable as the recipient than Onias I.

Already at this point we have reason to believe that the letter is authentic. Areus I did act independently of the ephors. The period in the second century B.C.E. during which there were no ephors was probably too short to lead even an ignorant Jew to omit mention of the ephors in a letter forged in the name of a third-century king; see Ehrenberg, PW, III^A, 1441–43, and cf. Bickermann, PW, XIV, 786. Indeed, Areus appears here with his own traits, not those of Hellenistic kings mistakenly transferred to Sparta by a forger, though Wilamowitz thought so (Hellenistische Dichtung, p. 43, n.1). Hellenized Jews were quick to claim that Alexander had taken note of the Chosen People (see Hecataeus of Abdera, FGH 264, F 21–22=J. Ap. i 22.192, 200, and ii 4.42–43; on the authenticity of these passages, see Gager, ZNW 50 [1969], 130–39).

Agis III, king of Sparta in the time of Alexander, was probably more famous than Areus, and had, for Jews who gloried in divine aid against Macedonian kings (vs. 13), the added distinction of having resisted Alexander (Jones, Sparta, p. 150). Closer to the times of Jason the Oniad and our author were Agis IV and Cleomenes III, both of whom had striven to restore the ancient Spartan system of land tenure, so similar to that in the Torah (Plutarch Agis and Cleomenes; Jones, Sparta, pp. 152–55). Jews did not study obscure episodes of Spartan history. A letter to a Jewish high priest by Areus I is unlikely to be a forgery.

A skeptic will still object: Can a Spartan king have sent a letter with so Semitic a flavor? And how would Areus I have got the idea that Spartans and Jews were kin? Let us consider these problems.

Our letter is indeed Semitic in flavor, so much so as to suggest that the original was not in Greek but in Aramaic. See below, on the individual verses. It is, indeed, possible that the Aramaic flavor arose when a Greek letter of Areus was translated into Aramaic for deposit in the temple archives. Then the Aramaic flavor of our version presents no obstacle to believing the letter is authentic. However, Jonathan's staff surely should have been able to turn a Jewish archivist's Aramaic translation back into polished Greek, though perhaps the Greek translator of our author's Hebrew was not so well versed in Aramaic. Hence, on the whole, it seems more probable that the Aramaic flavor reflects an Aramaic original, and Jonathan's staff if they rendered it in Greek did so with extreme literalness so as to avoid any charge of having altered the text.

Strange as it may seem, it is quite possible that Areus I could have had a letter drawn up in Aramaic and sent to the Jewish high priest. Areus had close connections with Ptolemaic Egypt (Ehrenberg, PW, III^A, 1423–27) and knew the facts of how to acquire and use mercenary soldiers in his time (Launey, pp. 115, 251–52, 659). Under Ptolemaic rule in the time of Areus Judaea was a source of soldiers (Launey, pp. 541–45), and Jews were still known to be using Aramaic (CPJ, vol. I, p. 30). From the time of Alexander, scribes who knew Aramaic were available to Greek-speaking governments (Berve, *Alexanderreich*, I, 46); they had been available even in Athens a century earlier (Thucydides iv 50.2, where "Assyrian"="Syrian"= "Aramaic"; cf. E. Y. Kutscher, "Aramaic," *Encyclopaedia Judaica*, III [1971], 266).

A possible proof that the original letter of Areus was in Aramaic exists in the enigmatic note (J. *AJ* xii 4.10.227) at the end of Josephus' version: "The writing is square; the seal is an eagle holding fast to a serpent." The sender of a letter might include a description of the seal so as to assure the receiver that the letter reached him unopened. But there is no reason why the sender would include a description of the handwriting. Hence, the words in Josephus' version can hardly be anything but the note of an archivist who copied the letter for preservation in an archive, presumably that of the temple. The Hebrew alphabet used today by Jews is really the Aramaic alphabet, in contrast to the "paleo-Hebrew" or "Phoenician" letter forms used by the Samaritans. I do not know when the Aramaic-Hebrew letters came to be called "square," as they often are today. Professor N. Allony informs me that the term "square writing" is attested in a Hebrew work of the fourteenth century C.E. and is common thereafter; see Leopold Zunz, *Zur Geschichte und Literatur*, I (Berlin: Veit, 1845), 206. "Square" well describes the rectangular shapes of the Aramaic-Hebrew letters. Were they so described earlier? I have been unable to find any instance in an ancient source. However, the early Syriac alphabet is called *"Estrangelā"* (Greek *strongylê*, "round"), perhaps in opposition to the "square" letters of earlier standard Aramaic. Thus, the archivist at the temple may have used "square" to note that Areus' letter was written in the Aramaic, not in the Greek alphabet. In sending an Aramaic letter, the Spartan king would have been using the same sort of self-interested courtesy as he used in alluding to Abraham; see above, on vss. 5–23.

What motive could Areus I have had, to send such a letter to the Jewish high priest? A very practical one, indeed. Areus' aggressive policies required a militarily strong Sparta. Although Sparta still may have had a good program of military training, in the third century B.C.E. she suffered from a grave weakness: shortage of military manpower (Plutarch *Agis and Cleomenes* 3, 5.4 – 6.1; Jones, *Sparta*, pp. 134–37, 152; Ehrenberg, PW, III[A], 1420). Jews, as we saw, were already famous as soldiers. If the Jews were related to the Spartans, Areus could invite Jews to fill up the depleted Spartan ranks. Such, indeed, may be the meaning of vs. 23; see below, ad loc.

Finally, what written work could ever have suggested to Areus that the Jews and the Spartans were related through Abraham? Practically all the literature of any kind written in Areus' time has been lost. There is no reason why any trace of such a work should have survived for us to see. Nevertheless, rather good clues exist. When Alexander's conquests opened Judaea to the eyes of Greeks, there was a brief fad among Greek intellectuals for admiring and studying the "nation of philosophers." Hecataeus of Abdera published his observations of the Jews and their history easily in time for them to be read by Areus I. See Introduction, p. 141, and M. Stern and Oswyn Murray, "Hecataeus of Abdera and Theophrastus on Jews and Egyptians," JEA 59 (1973), 159–68, especially p. 163.

According to Hecataeus, at the same time that the Jews made their exodus from Egypt, the Greek heroes Danaos and Kadmos were driven out of Egypt and went to Greece (FGH 264, F 6=Diodorus xl 3.2). The descendants of Danaos, the Danaoi, in Greek tradition occupied the Peloponnesus, including Sparta (Pindar *Pythian* 4.48–49). In particular, through Perseus and Herakles the line of Danaos gave rise to both dynasties of Spartan kings (Homer *Iliad* xix 95–133; Herodotus ii 91 and vi 53). Already Eduard Meyer (*Ursprung*, II, 31) saw in the fragments of Hecataeus and in these Greek traditions a probable source for the assertion in Areus' letter.

The name of Danaos was highly suggestive. There was no way of connecting him with the Israelite Dan, all of whose offspring were Israelites. But Abraham by his wife Keturah had a son Dedan (Greek Gen 25:3: *Daidan;* J. *AJ* i 15.1.238: *Dadanês*), and one of Dedan's children was Leummim ("nations"= "gentiles"). The Targum at Gen 25:3 renders *Leummim* by *nagwān,* the word used for the islands of the gentiles-descended-from-Japheth (=Greeks) in the Targum to Gen 10:5. Clement of Alexandria (*Stromateis* v 113.1=FGH 264, F 24) quotes a work ascribed to Hecataeus, *On Abraham and the Egyptians.* The quotation contains verses ascribed to Sophocles which echo principles of Jewish theology. Such forgeries could hardly have existed in Hecataeus' time, so that the work which lay before Clement was certainly spurious and probably was the same as the supposed work of Hecataeus, *On Abraham,* known to Josephus (*AJ* i 7.2.159). But Hecataeus himself may have mentioned Abraham and Jewish genealogies in portions of his authentic works which are no longer extant.

A contemporary of our author, Alexander Polyhistor, quoted the work *On the Jews* by Kleodemos the prophet, who was also called "Malchos." We do not know how much earlier Kleodemos-Malchos wrote. Kleodemos mentioned a descendant of Abraham by Keturah, Aphras or Iaphras, saying that Aphras accompanied Herakles on an expedition to Libya and that Aphras' daughter became Herakles' wife and bore him Didoros (FGH 273, F 102= 727, F 1=J. *AJ* i 15.1.240–41; see Ginzberg, *Legends,* V, 265–66, n. 314). Didoros' name is as close to that of Doros, ancestor of the Dorian Spartans, as Dedan's is to that of Danaos. Josephus (*AJ* i 15.1.240–41) identifies Aphras with Eophren (=Epher), son of Midian son of Abraham by Keturah.

Genealogical accounts such as these may have reached more than one Greek state. Readers at Pergamum in the time of John Hyrcanus could have read Hecataeus and probably also Kleodemos-Malchos and known of Herakles' association with Abraham's children or grandchildren. Pergamus, the mythical hero of Pergamum came to the rescue of the Mysian king Grynos, the great-grandson of Herakles (Euphorion *apud* Servius to Vergil *Bucolica* 6.72; Höfer, "Pergamos 1," in Roscher, III 2 [1897–1909], 1958). Thus the people of Pergamum in the time of John Hyrcanus could claim friendship with the Jews going back "to the time of Abraham" (J. *AJ* xiv 10.22.255).

We cannot tell whether or not Areus could have known of Kleodemos' work, but he could have known of Hecataeus'. In fact, Hecataeus visited Sparta in the reign of Archidamos who was co-king (ca. 305–275; Bickerman, *Chronology,* p. 156) with Areus I (Hecataeus FGH 264, T 4=Plutarch *Lycurgus* 20.3); see F. Jacoby, "Hekataios 4," PW, VII (1912), 2752, and Yehoshua Gutman, *The Beginnings of Jewish-Hellenistic Literature* (Jerusalem:

Bialik Institute, 1958), p. 110 (in Hebrew). Evidence is lacking on the reason for his visit. He may have come on a diplomatic mission for the Ptolemaic government or perhaps to observe the current way of life at Sparta and even to compare it with what he had seen in Judaea. If Hecataeus was Areus' source for Spartan kinship with the Jews and had been a recent visitor to Sparta, Areus in his letter would probably have mentioned Hecataeus' name. Hence considerable time had passed since Hecataeus' visit, and we get one more indication that the letter should be dated late in Areus' reign. Hecataeus himself could have brought his work to Sparta or could have aroused interest in it there during his visit.

Even if Areus did not find the report of Spartan kinship with the Jews in Hecataeus' work, he could have found much else to attract him in the account of the Jews there (FGH 264, F 6=Diodorus xl 3.4–8, and F 21= J. *Ap.* i 22.190–94): the resemblances of the Jews to the Spartans in their strict adherence to traditional law, in their exclusion of foreigners, in their military discipline, and in their system of land allotment. No less attractive would be the fact that the Jews were prolific, in contrast to the Spartans. Cf. J. *Ap.* ii 31.225–31, 36.258–59; and on the authenticity of FGH 264, F 21, see Gager, ZNW 50 (1969), 130–39, and Hans Lewy, "Hekataios von Abdera," ZNW 31 (1932), 117–32.

Josephus presents the letter of Areus in an entirely different context, his account of Hyrcanus the Tobiad (*AJ* xii 4.10.225–27). Most of the differences between his paraphrase and the version here are typical examples of the restyling done by Josephus and his Greek secretaries, but his version of the close of the letter and his quotation of the archivist's note which follows upon it show that Josephus' source was different from First Maccabees. Could Josephus and his secretaries have added the archivist's note in an attempt to convey an impression of authenticity? Hardly. This is the only instance in Josephus of such a note, and Josephus should then have elsewhere called attention to royal seals on royal documents; see Wenger, "Signum," PW, II^A (1923), 2395–96, 2442–43. The description of the seal in Josephus may well be authentic. Eagles and serpents appear to have been heraldic devices used by Spartan kings (Pausanias x 26.3; Apollodorus *Bibliotheca* ii 8.5; Percy Gardner, *Catalogue of Greek Coins: Peloponnesus,* A Catalogue of the Greek Coins in the British Museum [Bologna: Forni, 1963], pp. xlviii, 121, and plate xxiv 3; Gutman, p. 110 [in Hebrew]). The archivist had good reason to record the description of the seal; see Wenger, PW, II^A, 2397–98. On the other hand, the note, "The writing is square," was probably at least as enigmatic to Josephus' Graeco-Roman audience as it is now. It is best to assume that Jonathan's staff omitted the archivist's note from the copy they sent, leaving the ambassadors to make any such explanations orally, and that Josephus had access somehow to the text as preserved in the archives. It is unlikely that he drew upon a copy presented in the work of Onias IV, who surely would not have presented the letter in such a way as to allow Josephus to commit the error of identifying the recipient as Onias III, who lived long after Areus I was dead (but see my remarks in *Studies Smith,* Part III, pp. 119–120). Rather, Josephus found nothing to help him identify which Onias was the recipient, except Jason of Cyrene's report (II 5:9), that

Jason the Oniad took refuge at Sparta, making use of the claim of kinship. Surely, reasoned Josephus, Areus' invitation could not have been ignored for decades—it must have been offered shortly before Jason became the first Jew known to have made use of it! With no leisure to check the chronology of the Spartan kings, Josephus never discovered his error.

20–21. On the use of the name "Spartan," rather than "Lakedaimonian," see above, on vs. 2.

20. The salutation formula in the earliest manuscripts was purely Aramaic in style and puzzled later scribes and translators, who thereupon altered the text. However, the original reading, which I have translated, can still be recovered from slightly distorted versions in the manuscripts. The Greek probably had *Oniai Arês basileus Spartiatôn chairein.* Because the Spartan king's name was given in vowelless Aramaic script as *'rys,* the Greek translator and Josephus did not know the precise vowels of "Areus." They had to guess. Most Greek manuscripts at the beginning of our verse have ONIARÊS or ONEIARÊS. La^L has *Honiarex spartiatarum Honia regi magno salutem,* where *Honiarex* is corrupted from *Honia(e) Ares rex* and *Honia regi magno* reflects a puzzled scribe's addition in an attempt to improve the text. Onias' title is also omitted in the version at J. *AJ* xii 4.10.226, and the variants to the title in the Greek manuscripts of First Maccabees suggest that it is a later insertion.

The scribes were perplexed by the Aramaic word order, which gave the name of the recipient first, though Areus regarded Onias as an equal. On Aramaic practice in letters, see J. A. Fitzmyer, "Some Notes on Aramaic Epistolography," JBL 93 (1974), 211; and on Greek practice between equals, see F. Ziemann, *De epistularum Graecarum formulis sollemnibus quaestiones selectae* (Diss. Halle; Halis Saxonum: Karras, 1910), pp. 253–66.

Onias' title was in the Greek when it was translated into Latin, for the texts of La^−L all have it, and La^L reflects it (*magno*). Even if the title was interpolated, the interpolator's choice of words deserves comment, for it has an Aramaic flavor! "High priest" in Aramaic is *kāhănā rabbā* (literally, "great priest"), and the Greek texts give the title as *hiereus megas* ("great priest"), though the normal Greek expression for the Jewish high priest was *archiereus* (I 10:20, 32, etc.; II 3:1, 4, etc.). However, the Greek translator used *hiereus megas* even when rendering the purely Greek letters of the Spartans and Antiochus VII to Simon (14:20 and 15:2) and also in the date formulas at 13:42 and 14:27. We may conclude that the translator used the two expressions indiscriminately. The supposed interpolator could have been equally indiscriminate. Jews outside Egypt appear to have had no reason to avoid the word *archiereus,* though the translators of the canonical Hebrew books, working in Egypt where an *archiereus* was merely the head priest of a temple, appear to have avoided using it for the Jewish high priest; see Gottlob Schenk, "Hiereus," *Theological Dictionary of the New Testament,* III (1965), 265–66.

21. The bearer of the letter was prepared to give details on what work by which author mentioned the kinship of the Jews with the Spartans, as we learn from vs. 23. "There is a statement," in the Greek is, literally, "It was found"; cf. Ezra. 6:2; Esther 6:2; II 2:1; Polybius iii 38.18, xii 10.3 and 5, etc.

22. *how you are.* The Greek has a literal rendering of the Aramaic idiom, "concerning your peace" (*'l šlmkwn;* cf. Dan 3:31, 6:26).

23. "We are ready to write" in the Greek normally would be expressed by the future tense; here it stands in the present, literally, "we are writing." On the other hand, "we have ordered," reflecting an action performed at the time the letter was sent, normally would be expressed in Greek by the perfect or the aorist; here it stands in the present. See Mayser, II^I, 183–84, 211–12; Abel, *Grammaire*, pp. 256–57, 259–60. Although the present tense could have been used in either case (Mayser, II^I, 133–34, 184), the inconsistent use of the Greek present tense in a single verse suggests an Aramaic original. In Aramaic the participle, which can be rendered by the Greek present tense, serves both for actions performed by the sender of a letter at the time of sending (cf. Ezra 4:16) and for actions which the speaker is ready to perform in the future; see H. Bauer and Pontus Leander, *Grammatik der biblischen Aramäisch* (Hildesheim: Olms, 1962), pp. 291–92.

"Cattle and property" probably translates a technical Aramaic expression for "all property, animate or inanimate," probably *nksyn wqnynyn.* Cf. Emil G. Kraeling, *The Brooklyn Museum Aramaic Papyri* (Yale University Press, 1953), no. 7, lines 27, 29–30, 31, 35). In the Palestinian Targum *nksyn* renders Hebrew *mqnh* ("cattle"), and in Targum Onkelos *qnyn* always renders Hebrew *rkwš* ("property"). In the Greek Bible, the word we have rendered "cattle" often renders Hebrew *mqnh,* and the Greek word we have rendered "property" usually renders *rkwš.* Areus and his Aramaic scribe may have meant only to express the "sharing" involved in kinship; cf. Gen 34:23. It is also possible, however, that Areus meant to invite Jews to settle on Spartan territory, offering them the shares in land and serf labor (and cattle, too?) that were the privilege of full Spartan citizens. See Ehrenberg, RE, III^A, 1381–82, and Jones, *Sparta*, pp. 40–43, and cf. Gen 34:23.

Where our author has "We have ordered that you be given a full report on these matters," Josephus has "Demoteles the bearer of the message is transmitting our letter." He or his secretary missed the point: the Spartans did not put all the particulars in writing but instructed the bearer to give full information (e.g. on the author and title of the work discussing the kinship). Josephus may have derived from his copy of the archivist's version of the letter the fact that the bearer's name was Demoteles. Our author may have omitted the name, thinking it unimportant, or the Greek translator may have done so, finding it difficult to recognize in Aramaic transcription.

Did Josephus borrow the name of the message bearer from Plutarch *Agis and Cleomenes* 28 or from Xenophon *Hellenica* vii 1.32? In the immediate context of the passage from Xenophon (at section 39) appears the sentence, "The Persian *bearer of the message* displayed the King's *seal* and read out *what was written.*" All the italicized expressions recur at J. *AJ* xii 4.10.227. Hence, Cardauns (*Hermes* 95 [1967], 319) inferred that Josephus must have borrowed vocabulary and details from Xenophon in order to create a stronger impression of authenticity. We have already remarked (above, on vss. 20–23) that Josephus had no reason to add the archivist's note. Similarly, nowhere else did Josephus find it necessary to name a message bearer; why, then, would he have bothered to do so here?

Jonathan and his staff found no evidence that Onias sent a written reply, but that fact does not prove that none was sent or that Onias did not reply orally through the message bearer. On the other hand, after treating the bearer courteously, Onias may have sent no reply whatever. The Romans, too, long left diplomatic courtesies of the Greeks unanswered; see Badian, *Foreign Clientelae*, p. 33, n. 1.

XXIX. FURTHER GAINS UNDER
ANTIOCHUS VI
(12:24–38)

12 24 Word came to Jonathan that Demetrius' commanders had returned with a larger force than before to wage war on him. 25 He set
out from Jerusalem and confronted them in the territory of the
Amathitis, giving them no opportunity to invade his own territory.
26 He sent spies into the enemy camp. They returned to him with the
report that the enemy were preparing to attack them that night. 27 At
sunset Jonathan ordered his men to be on the alert and to keep their
arms at hand so as to be ready for battle throughout the night. He sent
out advance patrols to guard the perimeter of the camp. 28 When
the enemy learned that Jonathan and his men were ready for battle,
they were struck with terror, and their courage melted. They withdrew, after leaving fires burning in their camp. 29 Jonathan and his
men did not realize what had happened until morning, for they saw
the campfires burning. 30 When Jonathan did pursue after them, he
failed to overtake them, for they had crossed the Eleutheros river.

31 Thereupon, Jonathan turned aside against the Arabs called
Zabadaeans, defeating them and taking their spoils. 32 On withdrawing from there, he marched to Damascus and made a tour of
his entire province. 33 Meanwhile, Simon marched out and made a
tour of . . .ᵃ as far as Ascalon, including the neighboring strongholds. Simon turned aside against Joppe and captured it, 34 because
he had heard that there was a plot to turn over their fortress to
Demetrius' men. Simon stationed a garrison there to keep watch over
the city.

35 On returning, Jonathan convoked the elders of the people and
in consultation with them decided to build fortresses in Judaea
36 and to increase the height of the walls of Jerusalem and to erect
a high wall between the Akra and the city so as to shut it off from

ᵃ See Note ad loc.

the city and isolate it, so that the occupants could neither buy nor sell. 37 The people gathered to fortify the city. Part of the wall of the eastern valley collapsed, so he replaced it by the structure called Chaphenatha. 38 Simon rebuilt Adida in the Shephelah and fortified it, providing it with gates and bars.

NOTES

12:24–38. See introductory NOTE to 12:1–23.

24. Our author returns to the events of military history which he was narrating at the end of chapter 11. On Josephus' insertion, before paraphrasing vs. 24, of an account of the Jewish sects (*AJ* xiii 5.9.171–73), see Introduction, pp. 65–66.

25–30. As an officer of Antiochus VI, Jonathan could move freely through the lands loyal to the boy-king and could confront Demetrius' commanders far from any Jewish territory, indeed outside the much larger province assigned him by the king; see NOTE on 11:59–62. The Amathitis was the district of Hamath, in the Orontes valley, between the Lebanon and Anti-Lebanon mountains. At this time the area may have been part of the province called the Seleukis or of the province of Apameia; see Bikerman, *Institutions*, pp. 200–1, and René Dussaud, *Topographie historique de la Syrie antique et médiévale* (Paris: Geuthner, 1927), 233–44. There is a prophesy speaking of Hamath as "bordering," at Zech 9:2; see NOTE on 11:60–74. The site of the confrontation must have been somewhere near the Eleutheros river. Had our author known that it was at Lebo-Hamath, the well-known border point of the Promised Land (Num 13:21, 34:8; cf. Ezek 47:15–17, and see B. Mazar, "L^{e}bo Ḥămat," Enc. Bib., IV [1962], 416–18 [in Hebrew]), he surely would have said so. Demetrius' troops must have come from the coastal strip still loyal to that king. Since they retreated back to that territory across the Eleutheros, the confrontation probably occurred at a point near the upper Eleutheros, where it runs from north to south. See NOTE on 11:63–64 and Map 12, p. 536.

25–28. Josephus says (*AJ* xiii 5.10.175) that Jonathan's camp was fifty stadia (about six miles or ten kilometers) from the enemy. He may have guessed the distance from Jonathan's sending of spies and from the visibility of the enemy fires from Jonathan's camp. Josephus adds that captured prisoners supplied the information that the enemy were preparing to attack.

26. All Greek witnesses to the text except Josephus (*AJ* xiii 5.10.175) have ". . . that thus [*houtô* or *houtôs*] they were preparing. . . ." The word "thus" here is pointless, is absent from La$^{L X G V}$, and is hardly conceivable in a Hebrew original. Probably *houtoi* ("they," "the enemy") has been misread as *houtô* or *houtôs*, as is suggested by Josephus' *tous polemious* ("the enemy").

31–32. The Zabadaeans gave their name to modern Zebdani, northwest of Damascus. See Map 12, and Abel, p. 227. Josephus or the scribe who wrote his copy of First Maccabees knew nothing of the Zabadaeans and wrongly read "Nabataeans." The Nabataeans were not situated in the area between the Eleutheros and Damascus. Josephus adds that Jonathan sold his captives and spoils from the Arabs at Damascus (*AJ* xiii 5.10.179).

33–34. Again our author takes care to mention Simon's contemporary feats. See NOTE on 11:64–66.

33. There appears to be something missing after "made a tour of," a noun in the accusative case to go with *kai ta plêsion ochyrômata* (literally, "and the neighboring strongholds"). The noun was probably something like "his territory"; see 11:59. Josephus' paraphrase has "Simon went through all Judaea and Palestine as far as Ascalon and secured all the fortresses" (*AJ* xiii 5.10.180). Although Ascalon maintained correct and peaceful relations with the Hasmonaeans (see NOTE on 8:1–16), there was probably good reason for a demonstration in force; cf. Philo *Legatio ad Gaium* 205. Though Jonathan had captured Joppe (10:76), clearly it was not under occupation when Simon took action.

35–38. Jonathan and Simon may have been acting here to fulfill prophesies of Zechariah; see NOTE on 11:60–74.

35–36. The "elders" (*presbyterous*) are surely the members of the Council of Elders; see above, on vs. 6, and NOTE on 8:15. Cf. *M. Sanhedrin* 1:5. Again, Jonathan tries to starve out the occupants of the Akra. See 11:41 and NOTE on 11:20–29. Demetrius II had treated the men of the Akra as his own garrison and protected them from Jonathan. Therefore, Jonathan, as a commander for Antiochus VI, was free to besiege the citadel.

"Erect a high wall" (*hypsôsai hypsos*), literally is "raise a height," but surely the structure was a wall. Compare the Hebrew and the Greek at II Chron 32:5. The Hebrew text here may have been *lhrym ḥmh rmh* or *lhrym ḥmh*, "erect a . . . wall," misread by the translator as *lhrym rmh*, "raise a height."

37. The eastern valley or gorge is the Kidron. See Map 1, p. 528. Our passage speaks of walls of the city, not of the temple mount.

"Chaphenatha" appears to be derived from the Aramaic root meaning "hunger (*kpn*). In the absence of further information, speculation on why the structure was so named is futile.

38. Again our author takes care to record the contemporary activity of Simon. Adida is a strong point six kilometers east-northeast of Lydda; see Map 13, p. 537, and F.-M. Abel, "Topographie des campagnes machabéennes," RB 35 (1926), 218.

XXX. TRYPHON TREACHEROUSLY
CAPTURES JONATHAN
(12:39–53)

12 ³⁹ Then Tryphon plotted to become king of Asia and assume the diadem by doing violence to King Antiochus. ⁴⁰ Apprehensive lest Jonathan should fight to prevent him, he sought a way to capture Jonathan and slay him. Accordingly, he set out and marched to Beth-Shan. ⁴¹ Jonathan marched out to meet him with forty thousand picked men ready for battle and came to Beth-Shan. ⁴² On seeing that Jonathan had come with a large force, Tryphon shrank from doing him violence. ⁴³ He received him with honor and introduced him to all his friends, giving him gifts and ordering his friends and his soldiers to obey Jonathan as they would himself. ⁴⁴ He said to Jonathan, "Why did you weary all these people when we are not at war? ⁴⁵ Now then, let them go home, pick yourself a few men to accompany you, and come with me to Ptolemais, where I shall turn the city over to you as well as the other strongholds and the rest of the troops and all the officials, and then I shall march back home. Indeed, that is the purpose of my coming."

⁴⁶ Jonathan, trusting him, did as he suggested. He dismissed his troops, who went home to the land of Judah. ⁴⁷ He still had with him three thousand men. Of these, he dropped two thousand off in Galilee, so that his escort numbered one thousand. ⁴⁸ However, as soon as Jonathan entered Ptolemais, the citizens of Ptolemais closed their gates, seized him, and put all who had entered with him to the sword. ⁴⁹ Then Tryphon sent infantry and cavalry into Galilee and into the great plain to slay all Jonathan's men. ⁵⁰ The men, however, came to the conclusion that he had been captured and slain with his entire escort. They put heart into one another as they rallied and marched ready for battle. ⁵¹ Their pursuers, perceiving that they were ready to fight to the death, turned back. ⁵² As a result, the Jewish soldiers all returned safe to the land of Judah. There, as they mourned for Jonathan and his escort, they were struck with great fear. Indeed,

while all Israel was in deep mourning, 53 all the neighboring gentiles plotted to destroy them, thinking, "They are leaderless and helpless. Now, therefore, let us wage war upon them and wipe out the memory of them from the human race."

NOTES

12:39–40. There would have been nothing discreditable to Jonathan if our author or his source had written the probable truth, that Tryphon plotted against Jonathan merely because Jonathan was getting to be too powerful to be trusted by an insecure kingmaker. Even at the time, who could have known Tryphon's inner thoughts? If Jonathan's defenders chose to interpret Tryphon's treachery against Jonathan as treachery against Antiochus VI, they had a polemic purpose: either they were claiming that no obedience whatever was due henceforth to the traitor Tryphon (cf. chapter 13; 15:10–14, 25–27), or that far from being a turncoat in his relations with Seleucid kings (as charged by his enemies), Jonathan died because of his fealty (see Introduction, p. 76). Thus, the connection of Jonathan's capture and death with the death of Antiochus VI may be a fiction.

Our author and Josephus (*AJ* xiii 6–7.187–218) leave no doubt that Jonathan's capture preceded Antiochus VI's death. However, in paraphrasing, just before our vs. 39, Josephus inserts his narrative of how Demetrius campaigned against King Arsakes of Parthia and was captured (*AJ* xiii 5.11.184–86), events which our author does not narrate until 14:1–3. Thus, our author has the death of Antiochus VI (13:31) precede Demetrius' expedition, whereas Josephus (*AJ* xiii 6.1.187 and 7.1.218) has the child king die after Demetrius' capture. Appian (*Syriakê* 67–68) and Orosius (*Historiae* v 4.16–17) present both the accession and the death of Antiochus (whom they wrongly call "Alexander") after the capture of Demetrius. Orosius here was probably following Livy. See Fischer, *Chiron*, II (München, 1972), 204–5. Indeed, as we shall see, in departing from our author's account Josephus, like Appian, was following an account accepted in the Graeco-Roman world. Josephus could not afford to have his narrative, written for a gentile audience, contradicted by a reputable gentile source. In fact, however, Josephus, Appian, and Orosius cannot be right. The evidence of the coins supports our author: the coins of Antiochus VI extend only to 171 Sel. Mac.=142/1 B.C.E., whereas the coins of Demetrius extend from 167 Sel. Mac. (145 B.C.E.) to 173 Sel. Mac. (140/39 B.C.E.). See Henri Seyrig, *Notes on Syrian Coins,* "Numismatic Notes and Monographs," No. 119 (New York: American Numismatic Society, 1950), pp. 12–14. On Josephus' chronology it is also difficult to account for the four regnal years attested on Tryphon's coins; see Schürer, I, 172–73, and Seyrig, pp. 12–17. Finally, from 13:22 and from the document of late 143 B.C.E. quoted at II 1:7–8, one can infer that Jonathan was killed late in 143 B.C.E., when Demetrius II was still reigning; see NOTE on II 1:7. Josephus himself agrees that

Jonathan's death preceded that of Antiochus VI and that it also preceded Simon's accession as high priest in 170 Sel. Bab. (March 26, 142 – April 12, 141 B.C.E.); see J. *AJ* xiii 6.6–7.209–13. Hence, Jonathan's death could not have been as late as 172 Sel. Mac. (October 6, 141 – September 25, 140 B.C.E.), when Demetrius II was still issuing coins. On the evidence of Eusebius, see NOTE on I 14:1–3.

Even the gentile source reflected by Josephus and Appian probably supports our author's account. Josephus and Appian are probably following a misinterpretation of an earlier historical source. If so, this earlier source, without giving dates, first narrated the acts of Demetrius II down to his capture and then returned to narrate the acts of Tryphon down to the rise of Antiochus VII to challenge him. To indicate the transition between the story of Demetrius II and that of Tryphon, a Greek author needed to do no more than to write *Tryphôn de* ("On the other hand, Tryphon . . . ," or "Meanwhile, Tryphon . . ."). Indeed, Pompeius Trogus, who lived near the beginning of the Christian era, treated these episodes, and Justin's abridgment of his account has precisely the same vague transition, "Meanwhile, Tryphon" (xxxvi 1.7: *Dum haec aguntur, interim in Syria Trypho . . .*). Pompeius Trogus probably was following the orginal source and still may not have misunderstood the passage. However, it was easy to suppose that the order of the narrative of these episodes was the same as their order in time. The misinterpretation was all the easier because it seemed so probable: When would Tryphon, the insecure kingmaker, feel able to dispense with the helpless child king? When he no longer had to face Demetrius! In fact, however, Tryphon appears to have been so confident of his hold upon the army that he dispensed with all claims to Seleucid legitimacy. See Bevan, II, 230–31.

Once the misinterpretation of the original source had been made, a writer drawing upon it could easily have gone beyond the vague "On the other hand, Tryphon" to add chronological notes such as those found in Josephus and Appian. Josephus had enough good information to know that Antiochus VI became king before Demetrius' capture, and Pompeius Trogus knew the fact, too, since he used the pluperfect at Justin xxxvi 1.7 ("Meanwhile, in Syria, Tryphon, who *had induced* the people to appoint him instead as guardian of Antiochus. . . ."). "The people" could have "appointed Tryphon *instead*" as guardian of Antiochus VI only after the boy had been taken out of hiding, crowned, and assigned a guardian. Appian went so far astray as to place even Antiochus VI's accession after Demetrius' capture! The first to misinterpret the original gentile source may have been Nicolaus of Damascus, but there is no way of being sure of his identity.

39. Asia was a common name for the Seleucid empire (See NOTE on 8:6). For the expression, "doing violence," cf. Esther 2:21, 6:2.

40. Tryphon marched to Beth-Shan=Scythopolis, a Greek city situated in Jonathan's province, where once the despoiled corpse of an earlier Jonathan had been displayed (I Sam 31:3, 10–12). See Map 14, p. 538.

41–42. Jonathan was powerful enough to confront Tryphon with a formidable force.

43–46. Was Tryphon able to deceive Jonathan because Jonathan expected a fulfillment of Isaiah 60 and saw in Tryphon's behavior and remarks a fulfillment of Isa 60:3, 4a, 5?

43. Jonathan already had the title of Friend of Antiochus VI (11:57). Tryphon, too, had a retinue of Friends. Was the possession of such a retinue already a usurpation?

45. Ptolemais was a strategic point (see NOTE on 10:2) with a population hostile to the Jews (I 5:15, 22, 55, 11:22; II 13:24–26; and NOTE on 11:22–29). The Hasmonaeans long sought to conquer it (J. AJ xiii 12.2–6.324–47) and never succeeded.

46. Did Jonathan fall victim to Tryphon's treachery because he believed prophesies of Israel's glory (perhaps Zechariah 9; see NOTE on 11:60–74) were being fulfilled?

47. We are not told why Jonathan dropped off the two thousand, keeping only an honorable retinue of one thousand. Perhaps he intended the two thousand to serve as garrison in territory he expected to annex to Judaea. The normal route from Beth-Shan to Ptolemais went through the Valley of Jezreel and then northward along the Kishon brook and through the coastal plain. If not the Valley of Jezreel, then the last parts of the route could be called "Galilee." See vs. 49 and Map 14.

48–49. Surely the citizens of Ptolemais acted on instructions from Tryphon, though they were glad to bring about Jonathan's downfall (see above, on vs. 45). Our author took for granted that the reader would understand. Josephus felt he had to make Tryphon's role explicit (AJ xiii 6.2.192). Jonathan's person was potentially valuable, to be used in negotiation, so that he was kept alive. Otherwise, Tryphon and the citizens of Ptolemais sought to eliminate as many as they could of the dangerously powerful Jews.

On "Galilee and the great plain," see above, on vs. 47.

50. The closing of the gates of Ptolemais and the small size of Jonathan's retinue were sufficient to justify the men's conclusion. They had no way of knowing that Jonathan had temporarily been spared. Our author makes his narrative the more tense by not mentioning the fact here. Josephus' paraphrase (AJ xiii 6.2.193) says that the men acted on receiving a rumor (phêmês) of what had happened.

51. Literally, "It was a matter of life for them." The Greek translator used such good Greek idiom that it is hard to guess what the original Hebrew could have been; but cf. Prov 7:23.

52–53. No longer could Jonathan appear as the prophesied bringer of permanent victory to Israel. On the reasons why the Jews expected such extreme hostility from their neighbors, see above, introductory NOTE to chapter 5. Demetrius II had long been an enemy of the Jews; now, clearly, the regime of Tryphon and Antiochus VI was hostile, too.

XXXI. SIMON LEADS THE JEWS TO LIBERTY
(13:1–42)

13 1 The news reached Simon, that Tryphon had assembled a large army, intending to invade the land of Judah and wipe it out. 2 Perceiving the terror and dismay of the people, he went to Jerusalem and called a meeting of the people. 3 He proceeded to encourage them, telling them, "You know all that I and my brothers and my family have done for the sake of our laws and our sanctuary. You know the wars and the troubles we have faced. 4 All my brothers gave up their lives for no other cause than for Israel, and only I am left. 5 Now far be it from me to spare my own life in any time of trouble! I am not worth more than my brothers! 6 Rather, I shall take vengeance for my nation and our sanctuary and for your wives and children, now that all the gentiles in their hatred have assembled to wipe us out." 7 He so revived the spirit of the people, as soon as they had heard these words, 8 that they shouted in answer, "You are our chief, in the place of your brothers Judas and Jonathan! 9 Fight our war, and we shall perform all your commands."

10 Thereupon he assembled all the warriors and made haste to complete the walls of Jerusalem and strengthen the fortifications around her. 11 He sent Jonathan son of Absalom with a considerable force to Joppe, where he expelled the inhabitants and occupied the town.

12 Tryphon set out from Ptolemais with a large force, intending to invade the land of Judah. With him, he took his prisoner Jonathan. 13 Simon thereupon posted himself at Adida overlooking the plain. 14 When Tryphon received the news that Simon had taken the place of his brother Jonathan and that he was ready to join battle with him, he sent envoys to Simon with the message, 15 "Because of money which your brother Jonathan owed the royal treasury in connection with his official capacities we are now holding him under arrest. 16 Accordingly, send now a hundred talents of silver and two of his sons as hostages, so that upon being released he will not rebel against us, and

we shall release him." 17 Though Simon understood that there was treachery in their proposal, he sent an order to get the money and the children. In his mind was the fear of deep animosity toward him among the people 18 should they come to say that it was because I did not deliver the money and the children to Tryphon that Jonathan perished. 19 Though Simon delivered the children and the hundred talents, Tryphon cheated him and refused to release Jonathan.

20 Thereupon, Tryphon moved to take over the country and wipe it out. They took a roundabout route by the road to Adora, but Simon and his army countered his every turn at every point along his line of march. 21 Meanwhile the men of the Akra kept sending envoys to Tryphon to urge him to act quickly and come to them by way of the desert and send them provisions. 22 Tryphon did prepare all his cavalry to make the trip, but on that night there was a very heavy snowfall, so that the snow prevented him from going. He then withdrew and marched into the Galaaditis. 23 As he came near Baskama, he put Jonathan to death, and Jonathan was buried there. 24 Then Tryphon turned and went back to his own land. 25 Simon sent men to take up the bones of his brother Jonathan and buried him at Modeïn, the town of his ancestors. 26 All Israel observed deep mourning for him and were plunged into grief for many days. 27 Over the tomb of his father and his brothers Simon constructed a monument impressive for its height, built of hewn stone on both its front and rear sides. 28 He set up seven pyramids, one in front of the other, for his father, his mother, and his four brothers. 29 For the pyramids he contrived an elaborate setting: he surrounded them with massive pillars on which he placed full suits of armor as a perpetual memorial; besides the full suits of armor, there were carved ships, intended to be seen by all who sailed the sea. 30 This tomb, which he erected in Modeïn, still exists today.

31 Turning his treachery against the very young King Antiochus, Tryphon killed him 32 and became king in his place, assuming the diadem of Asia. His rule was a disaster for his land. 33 Simon built up the fortifications of Judaea, constructing circuits with lofty towers and big walls and gates and bars; he placed stores of food in the fortresses.

34 Simon appointed a delegation and sent it to King Demetrius to ask that the country be made tax-exempt, because all Tryphon's exactions were acts of robbery. 35 Demetrius sent a written reply agreeing to these requests. His letter was as follows:

36 "King Demetrius to Simon, High Priest and Friend of Kings, and

to the Elders and nation of the Jews, greeting. 37 We have received the golden crown and palm branch which you sent, and we are ready to declare a full state of peace with you and to write our officials to grant you exemptions. 38 Our past decrees made in your favor stand. The fortresses which you have built shall be yours. 39 We pardon your errors and violations committed down to the present date. We excuse you from the crown payment which you owed. If any other impost was formerly collected in Jerusalem, it shall no longer be collected. 40 If any of you are qualified to be enrolled in our service, let them be enrolled. Let there be peace between us."

41 In the year 170, the yoke of the gentiles was lifted from Israel, 42 and the people began to write as the dating formula in bills and contracts, "In the first year, under Simon, high priest, commander, and chief of the Jews."

Notes

13:1–42, introductory Note. In the sequence of trouble and terror, salvation, and liberation from the yoke of the gentiles, Simon and our author may well have seen a fulfillment of Jer 30:4–8. See below, on vs. 41.

1. Tryphon probably intended to destroy only what remained of Jonathan's army. As before (7:26), our author identifies the cause of the Hasmonaeans with that of the Jews.

2–9. See Note on 14:19.

3–6. Josephus (AJ xiii 6.3.198–200) expands the speech with rhetorical flourishes.

4–5. Our author presents Simon as believing that Jonathan was already dead. The words I have translated "for no other cause than for Israel" literally mean "for this cause . . . for Israel." Cf. Gen 21:31 and Josh 14:14. In writing "only I am left" and "I am not worth more than . . ." our author echoes Elijah at I Kings 19:4, 10, 14.

6. Cf. Zech 12:3, and note the previous echoes of Zechariah (see introductory Note to 11:60–74).

8. Our author shows the people freely conferring on Simon the title "chief" (hêgoumenos), which previously they had conferred on Jonathan (9:30). See also below, on vs. 42. The Jews were not yet independent, so that under the existing rules only the reigning Seleucid king could make Simon high priest; see Introduction, pp. 75–76.

Most witnesses to the text have, at the end of our verse, "of Judas and your brother Jonathan," which is probably a slip of the Greek translator. In vowelless Hebrew, 'ḥyk can be read either as "your brother" or as "your brothers."

Josephus (*AJ* xiii 6.4.201) has the plural as do La$^{X B}$ SyISyII and some minuscules.

10. Jonathan's fortification projects were not yet complete. Was Simon's fresh effort to complete the fortification an effort to pose as the "second in command issuing directives" (*maggīd mishneh*) of Zech 9:12? See introductory NOTE to 11:60–74.

11. On the family descended from Absalom, see NOTE on 11:68–70. The Hasmonaeans had long distrusted Joppe and now Simon feared that even the Jewish garrison there might not be able to control the townspeople (II 12:3–9; I 10:75–76, 12:33–34). Josephus (*AJ* xiii 6.4.202) adds that Simon feared that the people of Joppe might deliver up their city to Tryphon. On the possible fulfillment of Zech 9:2–4, see introductory NOTE to 11:60–74. Simon may have viewed control of Joppe as vital because through it he could send an embassy to seek help from Rome, as he was quick to do; see introductory NOTE to 14:16–24k.

Josephus was probably mistaken in taking Simon as the subject of *emeine*, the word I have rendered "occupied," and also in interpreting the passage to mean "and Simon stayed behind [to keep guard] at Jerusalem."

12–24. See Map 13, p. 537.

13. On Adida, see NOTE on 12:38. Tryphon first moved as if to take one of the routes to Jerusalem from the coastal plain; see NOTES on 3:13 and 3:40–57. Tryphon's force was large enough to bypass Joppe. The Jewish forces did not venture to engage him in the lowland.

15. Hellenistic kings are known to have exacted fees from holders of high office; cf. J. *AJ* xii 4.1–2.158–61, and see Préaux, *Économie*, p. 404. The money claimed by Tryphon could also have been a crown payment due Tryphon on his accession (cf. II 14:4, and Bikerman, *Institutions*, pp. 111–12) or the three hundred talents Jonathan had promised Demetrius (11:28; see Bikerman, *Institutions*, p. 108). However, Tryphon claims that Jonathan owed the money in connection with his official capacities: it was either a fee he should have paid or tax money he should have collected and delivered. Josephus' interpretation, that Jonathan had borrowed the money from the king (*AJ* xiii 6.5.204) does not fit our author's wording. Josephus may well have misread *chreias*, the word we have rendered "offices," as *chrea*, "debts."

16. The Greek translator appears to have shrunk from asserting that all Jonathan's sons were handed over, though his Greek reflects a Hebrew *šny bnyw*, which would normally be translated "his two sons." Josephus, too, has the ambiguous "two of his sons" (*AJ* xiii 6.5.204). If our author had intended to be vague, he would have written *šnym mbnyw*, "two from his sons," and the "from" would have been reflected in the Greek translation.

18. Although our author has been treating Simon in the third person, he uses the pronoun "I" here because he is giving what he imagines was in Simon's mind.

20. Again our author identifies the Hasmonaean cause with the survival of Judaea; see above, on vs. 1. By countering Tryphon's every move and keeping to the edge of the hill country, Simon made it most hazardous for Tryphon to try the main roads from the lowlands to Jerusalem; even if he should manage to pass Simon, Tryphon would be in the hostile Jewish-held mountains. Hence,

he took the more cautious course of going by way of the road to Adora, through friendly Idumaean territory, avoiding even Beth-Zur, now held firmly by Jews (11:65–66, 14:33). Cf. 3:13 – 4:29, 6:31.

21. The occupants of the Akra surely had looked to Demetrius, who had refused to deliver them over to Jonathan (11:41–53; see NOTE on 11:22–29). They surely had been hostile to Tryphon, creator of the regime which had made Jonathan powerful. Now that Tryphon had turned against the Hasmonaeans, he was a natural ally for the hard-pressed (12:36) men of the Akra, who hastened to suggest a junction of forces against Simon's army.

22. Did Jews at the time see a fulfillment of the prophesy concerning winter precipitation and the failure of gentile (Greek; cf. Zech 9:13) cavalry at Zech 10:1–5? Josephus (*AJ* xiii 6.6.208) may have thought so. Perhaps by marching on through the Galaaditis (=Gilead) instead of turning back through Idumaea, Tryphon avoided the ignominy of retreat and encouraged the gentiles of Transjordan to resist Simon.

23. We can only guess at the location of Baskama within the Galaaditis. The manuscripts of Josephus (*AJ* xiii 6.6.210) have *Baska*. Jonathan's death came in the winter (vs. 22) and before the Feast of Dedication in December, 143 (Bickermann, ZNW 32 (1933), 239–41). Jonathan was high priest from October, 152, to late in 143; see NOTES on 10:18–21, and in AB vol. 41A on II 1:7. On Josephus' figures for the length of Jonathan's high priesthood, see Appendix VI.

Tryphon probably killed Jonathan's sons, too, but our author seems deliberately to have avoided mentioning the fact. See Introduction, Part IV, n. 65.

27. *impressive for its height*. Literally, "and he made it high for viewing." "For viewing" reflects a Hebrew *lmr'h;* cf. Josh 22:10.

28. Our author's description lacks clarity. The seventh pyramid may well have been intended for Simon himself. It is hard to see how one pyramid would have been "opposite" or "in front of" (Hebrew *ngd*) another in an odd-numbered array of pyramids. Perhaps our author means the seven pyramids stood in a straight line. This form of monument was in favor at the time; see J. *AJ* xx 4.3.95 and Abel, p. 240.

29–30. Where I have "elaborate setting," the Greek has *mêchanêmata*. The Greek root renders the Hebrew root *ḥšb* ("devise"); see II Chron 26:15. Josephus does not use so vague an expression: he says the pyramids were surrounded by "porticoes" (*stoas; AJ* xiii 6.6.211). The porticoes were distinct from the massive pillars, which Josephus says were monoliths. Here Simon followed purely Greek forms of victory monuments.

Greeks would set up at the site of a victory in a land battle a *tropaion*, a complete suit of armor captured from the enemy, mounted on a cross so as to look like a man wearing armor. Originally, this was not a monument but a representation of the god who had brought the victory. From the end of the fifth century B.C.E. such *tropaia* or more permanent representations of them in stone or bronze were treated as monuments, and appear in temples of the gods as well as at the site of the victory. The Seleucids are known to have set up such monuments. See Donald E. Strong, OCD² s.v. "Trophies" and Gilbert Charles-Picard, *Les trophées romains* (Paris: E. de Boccard, 1957), pp. 1–29, 43–47, 68–74.

Similarly, among the Greeks there were monuments to sea battles, originally on shore near the battle site and later also elsewhere. These would consist of the prows of enemy ships or, in our period, also of sculptured representations of them. Pillars with such sculptured representations (as here) stood at Rome, and probably also in the Greek world. See Ad. Reinach, "Tropaeum," in DAGR V, 503a–b, 517–18.

The Hasmonaeans had no fleet and won no naval victories. Nevertheless Simon held Joppe as a gateway to the sea (vs. 11; 14:5, 34) and believed that with God's help Jews would rule the seas, too (cf. Isa 42:10–13), and confidently displayed the symbols of future naval victories as a warning to "all who sailed the sea." The monument was still there in our author's time, to predict naval victories that never came. Did Jannaeus pick "Alexander" as his Greek name in the belief that God would make him into a conqueror on the scale of Alexander the Great?

Readers have not understood what our author meant here, especially those who knew that the sea is visible from Modeïn; they jumped to the conclusion that the text asserts, ridiculously, that the sculptured ships were visible to persons aboard ships on the Mediterranean! Josephus, too, appears to have omitted our passage from his paraphrase because he misunderstood it. It is also possible that by his time the symbols of victories by land and sea over Graeco-Macedonians had been destroyed, so that he no longer saw fit to describe them.

31–53. Josephus had to omit from his account all material inconsistent with his false chronology; see NOTE on 12:39–40. Josephus had no secure date for the death of Antiochus VI. His Graeco-Roman sources led him to believe that it lay between the time Demetrius II fell into the hands of the Parthians and the accession of Tryphon as king, which itself was followed by the accession of Antiochus VII as rival for the throne. Accordingly, Josephus omitted our vss. 31–32. A summary of Simon's achievements down to the accession of Antiochus VII could be taken from I 13:33 – 14:49 and made compatible with Josephus' chronology. Josephus does so in AJ xiii 6.7.213–15 beginning. The Roman letter mentions Demetrius II as the reigning Seleucid at 14:24i. The Jewish resolution for Simon does the same at 14:38. Accordingly, Josephus omits both documents. Like some modern scholars, he may even have viewed them as forgeries. From section 215 middle to section 217 he draws on a garbled Jewish tradition; see NOTE on 13:52. Having finished his account of Simon's career down to the accession of Antiochus VII, he found it safe to give at AJ xiii 7.1.218–20 the account he derived from his Greek or Roman source, of how Tryphon had Antiochus VI murdered and became king himself.

Thus, there is no reason to assume that Josephus did not possess a copy of I 13:31 – 14:49 or even of 13:31 – 16:24. The assumption has often been made. For other discussions of the problem, see Ettelson, TCAAS (1925), 264–76; Thomas Fischer, *Untersuchungen zum Partherkrieg Antiochos' VII.* (Diss. Tübingen; order from author, Tübingen-Derendingen, Heinlenstr. 28, 1970), pp. 8–9.

31–32. Reportedly, Diodotus-Tryphon had the boy king killed by surgeons, who were supposed to be operating to remove a stone (Livy *Periocha* lv).

Josephus (*AJ* xiii 7.1.218–19), Justin (xxxiii 28 – xxxvi 1.7), Appian (*Syriakê* 68), and Diodorus agree that Tryphon caused his death. On the date and other problems, see NOTE on 12:39–40, and below, on vs. 41. Antiochus VI cannot have been more than seven years old; see NOTE on 11:54, and cf. Livy *Periocha* lii. Livy *Periocha* lv wrongly gives his age as ten years.

Tryphon made no claim to be a member of the Seleucid dynasty. "Asia" was a common name for the territory which had been ruled by the Seleucids and now was claimed by Tryphon (Bikerman, *Institutions*, p. 5). See also Bevan, II, 230–31.

Tryphon's accession only increased the chaos in the war-torn kingdom (Diodorus xxxiii 28; J. *AJ* xiii 7.1.219–22).

33. Simon took measures to strengthen Judaea against the violent usurper Tryphon.

34–42. Josephus in his paraphrase (*AJ* xiii 6.7.2.213–14) omits all reference to Demetrius; see NOTES on 12:39–40 and 31–53.

Jews in Judaea had recognized Demetrius II as their king already by late November or early December, 143 B.C.E., as Ep. 0 (II 1:7–8) shows. At that date and even later, coins were still being issued in the name of Antiochus VI. Posthumous coin issues are, however, known from the Seleucid empire. See O. Mørkholm, "A Posthumous Issue of Antiochus IV of Syria," *Numismatic Chronicle*, 6TH SERIES, 20 (1960), 25–30, and see below, on vs. 41. Hence, Antiochus VI could have been dead before Ep. 0 was written. But there is another difficulty: our author places the death of Antiochus VI (vss. 31–32) *after* Tryphon's winter attempts against Judaea (vss. 20–22). It seems most unlikely that all the reported incidents could occur between the sudden snowfall (vs. 22) and early December: Tryphon abandons the effort against Judaea, he returns to Antioch by way of the Galaaditis, Antiochus VI perishes, the news reaches Jerusalem, and the Jews choose to recognize Demetrius II as king over them.

Rather, it would seem that our author, ever anxious to display Hasmonaean fealty to the house of Alexander Balas, is concealing facts. Pious Jews by now had learned to regard as illegitimate any regime which made unjust war on them. Even if the minister Tryphon was the real tyrant, Jews (and probably even Simon) felt amply justified in then regarding the regime of the helpless Antiochus VI as illegitimate and in going over to the side of Demetrius.

Demetrius was probably growing in strength, and Simon and the Jews had struck him severe blows, so that Demetrius need not have given them a warm welcome. The negotiations which produced Demetrius' letter of 170 Sel. could have dragged on for months.

If so, pious and probably non-Hasmonaean Jews could have dated Ep. 0 by Demetrius in late 143 B.C.E. even if Antiochus VI was still alive. In the period when Antiochus VI was either dead or regarded as an illegitimate ruler and Demetrius II had not yet accepted the Jews as subjects rather than as enemies, partisans of Simon could have proclaimed Simon high priest. Simon could also have then sent Numenius to Rome, and Numenius would later return with strong assurances of Roman support (I 14:24a – 24k). Indeed, such is the course of events attested by the contemporary document at I 14:35–40.

Our author's desire to conceal Simon's and the Jews' desertion of Antiochus VI's cause would thus explain our author's omission of Simon's earlier appointment by the "people" to the high priesthood. See also below, on vs. 36.

34. *because . . . robbery*. The clause may explain why Simon felt it necessary to seek legal relief for the Jews. It may also explain why the pious Simon saw no religious obligation to be loyal to Tryphon. The word "robbery" translates Hebrew *ṭrph* ("prey") at Nahum 2:13, so that our author was probably punning on Tryphon's name. Simon here may have asked Demetrius merely to do what Antiochus III had done before him, to grant temporary relief from taxation; see J. *AJ* xii 3.3.129–44. However, the result this time was permanent exemption from taxation.

36. A considerable body of the Jews had appointed Simon high priest before Demetrius confirmed him in that status. Our author had reason to omit the fact (see above, on vss. 34–42), but Josephus (*AJ* xiii 6.7.213) feels free to assert it. Another factor in our author's silence may have been the consideration that the body of Jews which first appointed Simon high priest was not sufficiently authoritative and faced too much opposition. See above, on vs. 8. If so, our propagandist, who seeks to prove the legitimacy of Hasmonaean rule, preferred to pass the fact over in silence and rely on the undoubted legitimacy of appointment by Demetrius II, recorded here, and the legitimacy of the act of the great assembly recorded in 14:27–49.

The reading "Friend of Kings" is so well attested that it must have stood in the translator's Greek. Yet Simon is not reported to have been a friend even of Alexander Balas or of Antiochus VI, and Demetrius would not have recognized the legitimacy of those usurpers. If the text is correct, Demetrius II here pretends that his own father Demetrius I and he himself have enjoyed the support of Simon as a "friend" in the literal sense, and that this fact has brought Simon the court title "Friend" of both Demetrius I and Demetrius II. See 10:26, 11:33; NOTE on 10:26–28; and Bikerman, *Institutions,* p. 41.

On the Elders, see NOTE on 12:35–36. Perhaps Demetrius II had revoked the status of the Jews as an *ethnos* ("nation") when Jonathan went over to Antiochus VI. If so, he now restores it to them; see 11:30 and NOTE on 1:4.

37. On crowns, see NOTE on 10:29. Such a crown gift to a king might be accompanied by a gold palm branch, as here and at II 14:4. See Bikerman, *Institutions,* pp. 111–12.

38–39. Though Demetrius II's previous concessions had evidently never been put into effect and had been rendered void by Hasmonaean acts of rebellion (including unauthorized Hasmonaean construction of fortifications), Demetrius here revalidates the grants, retroactively concedes the fortifications, pardons the other acts of rebellion, and exempts the Jews from taxes and dues. Jerusalem is probably mentioned in vs. 39 as the center to which all taxes and dues were brought; Demetrius now exempts not merely Jerusalem, but all Judaea (vs. 41).

40. See NOTE on 10:36–37.

41. As usual, our author avoids speaking of the Deity. The words he uses, however, make it clear that he speaks not merely of a secular act of liberating Israel from taxation: God Himself had declared that the sentence He had imposed upon Israel, of servitude to the gentiles, had at last been served

through to the end. See Deut 28:48; Isa 9:3, 10:24–27, 14:24–27; Jer 30:4–8; Ezek 34:27–28; and NOTE on 8:17–18. Isaiah announced the coming of the Age of God's Wrath (za'am) against Judah and predicted its end (10:5 and 25, 26:22; cf. Dan 8:19 and 11:36; Ezek 23:23–31; and Ps 102:9–14). Now the Age of Wrath was over! Not all Jews agreed; see NOTE on 14:26.

The year 170 Sel. Bab. extended from March 26, 142, through April 12, 141 B.C.E. The date can hardly be 170 Sel. Mac. Demetrius' act of liberation was the starting point for counting a Hasmonaean or Jewish era (see below, on vs. 42), and our author, a Hasmonaean propagandist, therefore surely derived his date from Jewish records, not from a pagan work of Seleucid history. Moreover, royal coins of Antiochus VI were still being issued in 171 Sel. Mac. Known from that year are a tetradrachm minted in Ptolemais (S. Ben-Dor, "Some New Seleucid Coins," PEQ 78 [1946], 43–48) and a drachma minted in Byblos (Le Rider, Suse, p. 370, n. 2). Demetrius' liberation of Israel was an act against King Tryphon and hence followed the death of Antiochus VI. If the coins reflect normal circumstances, Demetrius acted between the end of October, 142, and April 12, 141 B.C.E.

Other evidence suggests that the coins do not reflect normal circumstances. When the Roman consul Lucius Caecilius Metellus in 142 wrote the letter on behalf of the Jews (see introductory NOTE to 14:16–24k), the Romans had already recognized Demetrius II as king (14:24i). In view of the favor they seem to have shown the weak Antiochus VI (Diodorus xxxiii 28a), the Romans probably would not have recognized Demetrius if news of Antiochus' death had not reached Rome beforehand. Moreover, it would be very strange if the anniversary of so important an event as Demetrius' act of liberation did not appear in Megillat Ta'anit, though the sobering fact of Israel's renewed subjection could well have turned the description of the event into something less triumphant than vs. 41. Some scholars have taken 27 Iyyar as the anniversary. Demetrius would then have acted in midspring and not between the end of October, 142, and April 12, 141 B.C.E. According to Megillat Ta'anit, on that day "crown [dues] were lifted from Judah and from Jerusalem"; cf. vs. 39, and see Lichtenstein, HUCA 8–9 (1931–32), 286. Why, however, should the crown dues be the only tax mentioned in Megillat Ta'anit in connection with the day? One can hardly say that crown dues were the only Seleucid taxes still being levied upon the Jews (see vss. 34 and 39 and 11:34–35, and above, on vs. 15).

An alternative possibility in Megillat Ta'anit is 3 Tishri. It, too, presents chronological difficulties: "On 3 Tishri mention [of the name of the reigning king] ceased in documents." See Lichtenstein, HUCA 8–9 (1931–32), pp. 282–85. In the ancient Near East law had long required that legal documents be dated by giving the name of the reigning king, as can be seen from the fact that often the first evidence of a revolt is the change of the name of the king in the dates of documents. See Bikerman, Chronology, pp. 65–66; Porten, Archives from Elephantine, pp. 25–27; Parker and Dubberstein, Babylonian Chronology, pp. 10–24. Hence, Jews recalling the stages of their national liberation would view the omission of Demetrius' name from the dates of their legal documents as even more significant than exemption from a single onerous tax. The trouble is that the dated coins of Antiochus VI, if they reflect normal circumstances, show him to be still alive in Tishri, 171 Sel. Mac., so that Demetrius' act of liberation, which followed the death of Antiochus VI, could not have been as early as 3 Tishri (October 20, 142 B.C.E.). Perhaps Phoenician Ptolemais and Byblos felt special loyalty toward the house of Alexander Balas (see NOTES on 10:1–2, 39, 53–56, 68) and granted recognition to King Tryphon only after some time had elapsed in the year 171 Sel. Mac., though Antiochus VI was already dead. In the interim the mints there may have gone on issuing coins in the name of the dead Antiochus VI. Indeed, the coins of Antiochus VI are otherwise relatively abundant, yet for 171 Sel. Mac. only the two examples have been found, a fact suggesting that the two coins known from Ptolemais and Byblos were minted there by die-hard opponents of both Tryphon and Demetrius II.

42. On the legal requirement that documents be dated by the name of the reigning king, see above, on vs. 41. Hence, here Simon may receive a royal prerogative (but see below); he still does not dare to take the title "king" (*melek*). Though Simon and his contemporaries may have seen a fulfillment in their time of Jer 30:4–8 (see above, on vss. 1–41), they did not go so far as to seek a fulfillment of Jer 30:9 by viewing Simon as the promised King David. The sovereign people saw no impediment, however, to confirming the titles of "high priest" and "commander" (*stratēgos*) which Simon already had received from Seleucid kings. In place of the title "king" Simon bore one which the Greek translator rendered by "*hēgoumenos*." In Greek translations of the Hebrew Bible, this word corresponds to *nāśī'*, *nāgīd*, *śār*, and *rōš*. To judge from the Hasmonaean coin legends, *Yᵉhōḥānān rōš ḥeber hayyᵉhūdīm* (see A. Kindler, "Rare and Unpublished Hasmonaean Coins," IEJ 2 [1952], 189), the Hebrew word was *rōš* ("chief"). However, "*śar-'am . . .*" ("prince of . . . nation"), if that is the correct reading at 14:27, would indicate that *hēgoumenos* here reflects *śār* ("prince"), as would the title *ethnarchos* ("prince of the nation") at 14:47, 15:1–2, and J. *AJ* xiii 6.7.214 and xiv 8.5.148; see the Hebrew and the Greek at Esther 3:12. As long as they did not dare to assume the title "king," the Hasmonaeans were glad to be called either *rōš* or *śār*. The Jews thus had their own reasons to avoid the use of the title "king." The avoidance did not imply their continuing recognition of Seleucid overlordship.

More likely, the dating formula here and at 14:27 does not yet come near treating Simon as a king. At first the Jews may have intended to count an era of their own liberation rather than to number the years of Simon's high priesthood. The Tyrians and Sidonians had such eras of their own freedom from Seleucid rule; see Bickerman, *Chronology*, pp. 72–73. It was very common to give, as here, first the designation of the year and then the name of a priest then in office; the official's name would appear in the genitive case preceded by the preposition *epi;* see M. Holleaux, *Études*, III, 170, n. 4, and Welles, *Royal Correspondence*, pp. 183–84. If so, one might translate, "In the first year [of the freedom of the Jews], under Simon. . . ." Similarly one might explain, as a correct date according to the era of the freedom of the Jews, the strange date given at J. *AJ* xiv 8.5.148 for the document quoted ibid., §§ 145–48; the date there, "under Hyrcanus, high priest and prince of the nation, in the ninth year, in the month Panemos," would then be equivalent to late spring, 134 B.C.E. The document at J. *AJ* xiv 8.5.145–48, is indeed of 134

B.C.E.; see Stern, *Zion* 26 (1961), 3–6 (English summary, p. i). There is another reason to suppose that the era in these passages is that of the freedom of the Jews. In normal Greek one did not indicate the regnal year of the king by using the preposition *epi* followed by the genitive (see e.g. Greek Esther 1:1a). However, our Greek text is a translation from the Hebrew, and *epi* with the genitive is used at Greek Hag 1:1 to give a regnal year. The dating formula of John Hyrcanus given at TB *Rosh hashanah* 18b may be of John Hyrcanus II; cf. J. *AJ* xvi 6.2.163.

Josephus in his paraphrase (*AJ* xiii 6.7.214) omits the preposition *epi* and unequivocally makes the year a year of Simon: ". . . the . . . first year of Simon, the benefactor and ethnarch of the Jews." Perhaps he omitted "high priest" and "commander" as not befitting Simon's near-royal rank, and correspondingly, added the royal epithet "benefactor" (cf. Luke 22:25).

On the expression used here for "high priest," see above, on 12:20.

XXXII. FURTHER VICTORIES UNDER
SIMON
(13:43–53)

13 43 At that time Simon besieged Gazara, surrounding it with camps. He built a movable tower, and by bringing it up against the city he overwhelmed an enemy tower and took it. 44 The men in the movable tower surged into the town, where panic began to reign. 45 The townspeople with their wives and children came up onto the wall with their garments torn and cried out loudly, imploring Simon to grant them a truce. 46 They begged, "Look not to our wickedness in treating us, but to your mercy." 47 Simon came to terms with them and ordered his men to cease hostilities. However, he expelled the people from the city and saw to the purification of the buildings in which there were idols. Having accomplished all that, he entered the city singing hymns and praises. 48 After removing all impurity from the city, he resettled it with men who observed the Torah. He also improved the fortifications and built himself a residence within.

49 The men of the Akra in Jerusalem were now blocked from leaving it to go out into the country to buy and sell. They suffered grievously from hunger, and a considerable number of them died of starvation. 50 They cried out to Simon for a truce, and he consented, expelling them from the citadel and purifying it of the abominations. 51 Simon's men entered the citadel on the twenty-third day of the second month, in the year 171, with utterances of praise and palm branches and to the music of lyres and cymbals and lutes and hymns and songs, because a great enemy had been smashed and driven out of Israel. 52 He decreed that the day be observed annually with rejoicing. He also improved the fortifications of the temple mount running along the Akra and began to dwell there himself with his retinue. 53 Observing that his son John had reached maturity, Simon appointed him chief of the entire army. John began to reside at Gazara.

NOTES

13:43–53, introductory NOTE. In Judaea proper, two hostile enclaves remained: Gazara (see 4:15, 9:52) and the Akra in Jerusalem. Simon proceeded to conquer both.

43. The chronological relationship between the letter of Demetrius and the siege of Gazara is vague. The town may well have fallen just before the people's nomination of Simon as high priest. See NOTE on 14:34–35.

Only Josephus (*AJ* xiii 6.7.215; *BJ* i 2.2.50) preserves the correct reading, "Gazara," here. The other witnesses to the text have "Gaza," which cannot be correct, for otherwise our author would have no narrative of the capture of Gazara, presupposed by vs. 53 and by 14:7 and 34, 15:28 and 35, and 16:1, 19, and 21. Gaza did not fall to a Hasmonaean until Alexander Jannaeus took it (J. *AJ* xiii 13.3.358–64).

The movable tower is called in Greek *helepolis*, the name of the type of movable tower for use in sieges invented at the end of the fourth century B.C.E. by Demetrius Poliorcetes. Demetrius' movable tower is said to have been forty-five cubits square and ninety cubits high, to have been mounted on four wheels eight cubits high, to have contained catapults and battering rams, and to have been manned by over two hundred men (Diodorus xx 20.2–3; Plutarch *Demetrius* 21).

44. Although the Greek translator's word for "panic" (*kinêma*) nowhere else is used to render Hebrew *mᵉhūmāh*, our author was probably imitating I Sam 5:9, 11.

46. Cf. Dan 9:18.

47–48. The removal of an idol in itself might be a metaphorical "purification," but our author's choice of words suggests an idol was believed to be a source of uncleanness. Cf. M. *'Abodah zarah* 3:6–7; *Shabbat* 9:1; TB *Shabbat* 82; Maimonides, *Mishneh Torah, Taharah, Hilkot abot hatum'ot,* 6:1–6. Priests had to avoid uncleanness. Since Simon was high priest and surely had other priests with him, he could not march into Gazara before the purification had been carried out. For this reason I have translated the Greek *ekatharise* "he saw to the purification of," rather than simply "he purified."

Other sources of uncleanness might bar pious Jews and their high priest from residing at Gazara (corpses, unclean animals, etc.). Simon was determined that pious Jews should hold the former Seleucid strong point, and he built himself a residence there. Accordingly, he had to remove all such sources of uncleanness.

What R. A. S. Macalister, the excavator of Gazara (=Gezer), thought was Simon's castle now is recognized to be a much earlier gateway; see Y. Yadin, "Solomon's City Wall and Gate at Gezer," IEJ 8 (1958), 80–86. However, on a building stone found in the debris near the gateway in the course of Macalister's excavations, an ancient enemy of Simon, perhaps a gentile laborer forced to work on Simon's construction, scratched an imprecation in Greek, *Pampra Simonos katopazê p[yr] basileion,* which Macalister translated, "[Says] Pampras: may fire follow up Simon's palace" (R. A. S. Macalister, *The Excavation of Gezer, 1902–1905 and 1907–1909,* I [London: John Murray, 1912], 210–12).

49–50. Jonathan's project (12:36) at last achieved its aim. Simon followed the same procedure as at Gazara; see on vss. 47–48. The word "abominations" (*miasmatôn*) probably includes idols as well as sources of ritual uncleanness; see Introduction, Part VI, n. 244. If so, the idols probably were those of the pagan garrison. Pious Simon could hardly have let Jewish idol worshipers depart unmolested (see NOTE on 11:64–66); hence we may deduce that any "apostate" Jews still residing in the Akra were *not* idol worshipers!

51. The date was equivalent to June 3, 141 B.C.E. See also Introduction, p. 124.

52. Accordingly 23 Iyyar appears in *Megillat Ta'anit* as the day on which "The men of the Akra withdrew from Jerusalem."

The Akra lay just north of the temple and could easily be walled so as to be part of the fortifications of the temple mount; see NOTE on 1:33–40.

Josephus' accounts (*BJ* i 2.2.50; *AJ* xiii 6.7.215–17) sharply contradict our verse: far from treating the Akra as part of the temple mount, improving its fortifications, and residing there, Simon according to Josephus completely razed the hated structure. According to the account in the *Antiquities,* Simon even induced the people to cut down the hill on which the Akra stood until it no longer overtopped the temple.

Scholars have ridiculed Josephus' story as an inept and deliberate falsification. See L.-Hugues Vincent and M. A. Steve, *Jérusalem de l'Ancien testament* (Paris: Gabalda, 1954–56), pp. 184–86.

Our author's account here is surely correct. Since the Akra had been a symbol of tyranny and, under the names "Baris" and "Antonia," was to become one again, no pro-Hasmonaean propagandist would have said that Simon preserved it and enlarged it if in fact he had razed it.

I shall explain elsewhere how Josephus came to ascribe to Simon the razing of the Akra and the cutting of its hill, deeds probably accomplished by John Hyrcanus. Again Josephus will prove to have committed a not altogether inept error.

53. Our author takes care to indicate at the first opportunity the distinction of Simon's legitimate successor, John Hyrcanus, the father of Alexander Jannaeus.

XXXIII. SIMON'S GLORY
(14:1–49)

14 ¹ In the year 172 King Demetrius assembled his forces and marched into Media intending to gain reinforcements for his war against Tryphon. ² However, on hearing that Demetrius had invaded his territory, Arsakes, king of Persia and Media, sent one of his commanders with orders to capture Demetrius alive. ³ The commander marched, defeated Demetrius' army, captured him, and brought him to Arsakes, who held him under guard.

⁴ The land had peace as long as Simon lived.
He sought the good of his people.
They welcomed his rule
and his glory as long as he lived.
⁵ By means of all his glory he captured Joppe to be a port
and secured access to the islands of the sea.
⁶ He proceeded to extend the territory of his nation
after conquering the land.
⁷ He collected large numbers of prisoners of war
in conquering Gazara and Beth-Zur and the Akra.
He eliminated the unclean things from the Akra
and there was none to oppose him.
⁸ The people farmed their land in peace,
and the land gave forth its produce
and the trees of the fields their fruit.
⁹ The old people sat in the town squares,
all chatting about their blessings,
while the young men put on the glorious raiment of war.
¹⁰ Simon supplied the towns with food
and equipped them with weapons for defense,
so that his glorious renown reached the end of the earth.
¹¹ He established peace in the land,
and Israel rejoiced exceedingly.
¹² Everyone sat under his own vine and fig tree,
with none to make him afraid.

13 No longer was there anyone on earth waging war against
them.

The kings had been defeated in those days.
14 Simon supported all the poor of his people.
He sought to fulfill the Torah
and wiped out all the impious and wicked.
15 He glorified the temple
and added to its furnishings.

16 The news of Jonathan's death spread (to Rome and) even
as far as Sparta. The Spartans were deeply grieved, 17 but when they
heard that his brother Simon had become high priest in his place
and had won control of the land and of the cities within it, 18 they
wrote to him on bronze tablets, seeking to renew with him the relationship of friendship and alliance which they had established with
(Judas and) Jonathan, his brother(s).ᵃ 19 The inscribed tablets were
read at Jerusalem in the presence of the assembly. 20 The following
is a copy of the letter sent by the Spartans: The magistrates and city
of the Spartans to their brothers the High Priest Simon and the Elders
and the priests and the rest of the People of the Jews, greeting.

21 The ambassadors whom you sent to our People gave us a report
on your present glory and prestige, and we were delighted that they
came. 22 We have recorded the contents of their speeches in the *Proceedings of the People* as follows:

"Numenius son of Antiochus and Antipater son of Jason, ambassadors of the Jews, came before us with the intention of renewing
their ties of friendship with us. 23 The People resolved to receive the
men with honor and to place a copy of their speeches in the volumes
of the People's archives in order that the People might have a record.
The People of the Spartans sent a copy of the foregoing to the High
Priest Simon."

24ᵃ(24) Thereafter, Simon sent Numenius to Rome with a large
gold shield weighing a thousand minas in order to confirm the alliance with the Romans.ᵇ

(15)   24ᵇ(15) When Numenius and his staff returned from Rome,
they bore a letter to the kings and to the countries, which read as
follows:

ᵃ See introductory NOTE to vss. 16–24k, end.
ᵇ All witnesses to the text contain a dislocation at this point. In the commentary I
explain why 15:15–24 originally were intended to follow 14:24. For convenience I
have renumbered 14:24, 15:15–24, as 14:24a–24k.

24ᶜ(16) "Lucius, consul of the Romans, to King Ptolemy, greeting. 24ᵈ(17) Ambassadors of our friends and allies the Jews, commissioned by the High Priest Simon and by the People of the Jews, came to us to renew their longstanding relations of friendship and alliance. 24ᵉ(18) They brought a gold shield of one thousand minas. 24ᶠ(19) Accordingly, we resolved to write to you kings and countries to refrain from attempting to harm them and from making war upon them, their towns, and their territory and from acting in alliance with those at war with them. 24ᵍ(20) We have decided to accept the shield from them. 24ʰ(21) Now, if any traitors have escaped from their territory to yours, deliver them up to the High Priest Simon for him to punish in accordance with their law."

24ⁱ(22) He wrote the same letter to King Demetrius and to Attalus and to Ariarathes and to Arsakes, 24ʲ(23) and to all the following countries: to Sampsame and the Spartans, to Delos and to Myndos and to Sikyon and to Karia and to Samos and to Pamphylia and to Lykia and to Halicarnassus and to Rhodes and to Phaselis and to Kos and to Side and to Arados and Gortyna and Knidos and Cyprus and Cyrene. 24ᵏ(24) They wrote a copy of the letter for the High Priest Simon.

25 When the People learned of these achievements, they said, "How shall we show gratitude to Simon and to his sons? 26 He arose with his brothers and his family and fought off the enemies of Israel, and they gained freedom for our people!" They drew up a document on bronze tablets and set it up on stone slabs on Mount Zion. 27 The following is a copy of the document:

On the eighteenth of Elul in the year 172, which is the year 3 under Simon, high priest and prince of God's People,ᵉ 28 at a great assembly of priests and people and chiefs of the nation and the elders of the land, the following was brought to our attention:

29 "Whereas: at a time when our land was repeatedly afflicted by wars, Simon son of Mattathias of the clan of Joarib and his brothers exposed themselves to danger and resisted their nation's foes, in order that their sanctuary might survive, and the Torah; they won great glory for their nation; 30 Jonathan rallied his nation and became their high priest and then passed away; 31 thereupon their enemies desired to invade their country in order to destroy it and violate their sanctuary; 32 then Simon arose and fought for his nation and spent large sums of his own money, providing arms for the men of the army

ᵉ See second NOTE ad loc.

of his nation and paying their salaries; 33 he fortified the towns of Judaea, including Beth-Zur on the border of Judaea, where previously there had been an enemy arsenal, stationing there a garrison of Jews; 34 he also fortified Joppe by the sea and Gazara on the border of Azotus, previously inhabited by our enemies, settling Jews there; whatever was needed for removing impediments to pious Jewish life in those towns, he provided; 35 observing Simon's fidelity and what he had accomplished and the glory which he proposed to bring upon his nation, the people appointed him their chief and high priest because of all these achievements of his and because of his righteousness and his uninterrupted fidelity to his nation, as he sought in every way to exalt his people; 36 thereafter, during his time of leadership, he succeeded in expelling the gentiles from his people's land and in expelling the inhabitants of the City of David in Jerusalem, who had built themselves a citadel from which they used to go out and commit acts of defilement in the vicinity of the sanctuary and gravely impair its purity; 37 Simon stationed in the citadel Jewish soldiers and fortified it for the sake of the safety of our country and our city; he built higher walls around Jerusalem; 38 moreover, King Demetrius in view of all this has confirmed him as high priest 39 and admitted him to the ranks of his Friends and conferred great distinction upon him; 40 indeed, he heard that the Romans had given the Jews the titles "Friends and Allies (and Brothers)"[d] and that they had treated Simon's ambassadors with honor—41 therefore,[e] be it resolved by the Jews and the priests: that Simon be chief and high priest in perpetuity until a true prophet shall arise, 42 and that he be commander over them (and that he have charge of the sanctuary)[f] so as to appoint on his own authority the officials responsible for services,[g] for the countryside, for armaments, and for fortifications, 43 and that he have charge of the sanctuary, and that all persons obey him, and that all contracts in our country be drawn up in his name, and that he wear purple robes and gold ornaments. 44 No one of the people or of the priests shall have the power to annul any of these provisions or to oppose any of his future commands or to convoke a meeting in our country without his permission or to wear purple robes or use a gold brooch. 45 Whoever acts contrary to these provisions or annuls any of them shall be subject to the penalty of death."

46 The entire people resolved to grant Simon the right to act ac-

[d] See commentary.
[e] See commentary.
[f,g] See NOTE on vss. 42–43.

cording to these provisions. ⁴⁷ Simon accepted and agreed to serve as high priest and to be commander and prince of the nation of the Jews and of the priests and to preside over all. ⁴⁸ They ordered that this text be drawn up on bronze tablets and set up in the precinct of the sanctuary in a conspicuous place ⁴⁹ and that copies of the tablets be placed in the treasury so as to be available for Simon and his sons.

NOTES

14:1–49, introductory NOTE. Our author gives in vs. 1 the correct year, 172 Sel. Mac. (October 6, 141 – September 26, 140 B.C.E.), for Demetrius' departure on his expedition eastward; see NOTE on 12:39–40. Our author appears not to have realized that the date for the expedition, which he took from a pagan source, was on a different basis from the date, 18 Elul, 172 Sel. Bab. (September 13, 140 B.C.E.), of the document at vs. 27; see Introduction, pp. 21–25. In fact, throughout the events narrated in vss. 16–48 Demetrius was still reigning, and many of them occurred before Demetrius had made Simon high priest (see vss. 24c, 24i, 38–40). Our author placed Demetrius' expedition here because he knew that the normal campaigning season was in the spring (see II Sam 11:1 and introductory NOTES to 3:27–37 and to chapter 5). Moreover, the fall of Demetrius, king of Assyria and Babylon, into the hands of Arsakes, king of Media, would signal for Jews the complete liberation of Israel in fulfillment of Isa 10:24–27, 13–14, and Jer 50–51. Hence, the ode to Simon in vss. 4–15 follows naturally, and our author may well have failed to perceive the chronological implication of vss. 38–40. If so, he may have assumed that the fall of Demetrius was one of the events which led the Jews to pass the decree quoted in vss. 27–49.

On the other hand, Simon and our author surely had learned from the sad experiences of Judas and Jonathan not to jump to conclusions about the imminent fulfillment of prophesies. Our author did not follow strict chronological order in his treatment of Judas. His ode summing up Judas' achievements (3:3–9) precedes the detailed narrative. See also introductory NOTE to chapter 5. Hence, we need not be surprised to find departures from chronological arrangement in his treatments of Jonathan (see end of introductory NOTE to 12:1–38) and Simon. With all three, our author may well have followed a partly topical order, placing diplomatic activity just before last battle and death. Our author could well have been reluctant to trouble himself over establishing the precise chronology if his sole sources for Jonathan's and Simon's contacts with the Spartans were undated copies of the letters and his sole sources for Simon's contacts with Rome were an undated copy of the Roman letter and the document at vs. 40.

1–3. Demetrius II's territory in the west of the Seleucid empire had been squeezed close to the Mediterranean coast, including Cilicia and strips from Seleuceia-by-the-Sea through Tyre. Tryphon had controlled inland Syria including Antioch and Apameia and surely had at least a corridor running to Judaea and to Ptolemais on the coast. See 12:40 – 13:24 and Bevan, II, 227–28. How could Demetrius either leave behind so powerfully situated a rival or pass through to Media? There is some reason to seek the truth in a badly confused passage in the Armenian version of Eusebius' *Chronica,* which may well be based on Porphyry (FGH 260, F 32.6): "When Demetrius son of Demetrius came out from Seleuceia and Antiochus son of Alexander came out from Syria and the city of Antioch and the two met in battle, Demetrius was victorious and gained the kingdom in the first year of the one-hundred-sixtieth Olympiad [140/39 B.C.E.], and in the next year [139/8] he raised an army and marched against Arshak [=Arsakes] to Babylon and the inland regions." The dates in the whole passage are at least a year late, and the fragment is written as if Antiochus VI were still alive and ignores Tryphon; see Jacoby's comments, FGH, vol. IID, pp. 873–74. One can easily imagine Eusebius or his source misconstruing a pronoun or "the king" to refer to Antiochus VI. If so, the ultimate source would have had Tryphon rather than Antiochus VI as Demetrius' opponent, and here would be the evidence for a victory which both shut Tryphon in his strongholds of Apameia and Antioch, where he could be reduced by arduous and expensive sieges, and also laid the way open to the east. There in the east, much of it still loyal to Demetrius' house, lay resources which could help in the final struggle against Tryphon. Such a victory of Demetrius' would also have attracted the support of other power figures in the chaotic empire, including Simon. Thus Demetrius could have been confident that his forceful wife Cleopatra Thea, left behind in Seleuceia-by-the-Sea, would have ample forces to hold off Tryphon as long as the eastern campaign should last (see J. *AJ* xiii 7.1.221).

If Tryphon was now almost helpless, there were pressing reasons why Demetrius should march eastward. The rising Parthian empire around this time undid the work of Demetrius I. Demetrius I had regained Media for the Seleucid empire in the winter of 161/0 by crushing the rebel satrap Timarchus; see NOTE on 7:1. Now the Parthians had overrun Media and were pouring into Babylonia. Cuneiform documents indicate that on March 1, 142 B.C.E., Babylonia was still subject to the Seleucid empire under Demetrius II but that at the end of June or the beginning of July, 141, the great city of Seleuceia-on-the-Tigris had fallen to the Parthian king Arsakes, though Olmstead's restoration of the broken clay tablet has Demetrius already counterattacking in Media. Other cuneiform documents show the Parthians holding Babylonia later in the year. See Olmstead, *Classical Philology* 32 (1937), 12–13; Neilson C. Debevoise, *A Political History of Parthia* (University of Chicago Press, 1938), pp. 21–23. On the evidence of the coins, see Le Rider, *Suse,* pp. 150–53, 363–73. Though Parthian policy soon came to win considerable favor among the subject peoples (Diodorus xxxiii 18), at the time of the Parthian advance there was still loyalty to the Seleucid dynasty and some hostility to the "cruelty" of the Parthians. The Greek and Macedonian settlers urged Demetrius to make war on Arsakes (Justin xxxvi 1.3; J. *AJ* xiii 5.11.185).

All Parthian kings on accession took the name of the founder of the dynasty,

Arsakes. Their original personal names could be used outside official documents to distinguish which Parthian king was meant. The Arsakes of vs. 1 is Mithradates I. The sequence of the Parthian kings is uncertain, but it is customary to number Mithradates I as Arsakes VI (see Strabo xv 1.36, C702; E. Bickerman, "The Parthian Ostracon No. 1760 from Nisa," BO 23 [1966], 15–16, and Richard N. Frye, *The Heritage of Persia* [Cleveland and New York: World, 1963], p. 282). Mithradates I began the great expansion of the Parthian empire by conquering Media and Babylonia. See Justin xli 6.1, 7; Édouard Will *Histoire du monde hellénistique*, II (Nancy: Faculté des lettres et des sciences humaines, 1966–67), 338–39, and above, introductory NOTE to this chapter.

1. *gain reinforcements*. The Greek translator used idiomatic Greek (cf. Polybius i 6.5., ii 21.3, etc.); our author may have borrowed the word "gain" (*mšk*) from Judg 4:6.

Our author writes as if the objective of Demetrius' expedition was only to recruit, not to repel the Parthians. He may have been ignorant of the Parthian advance as well as of the probable victory by which Demetrius confined Tryphon to his urban strongholds. If so, our author naturally assumed that Demetrius would not willingly add to the number of his enemies.

2–3. Arsakes is reported to have left the scene of the campaign in Babylonia and to have gone far eastward, to Hyrcania (around the southeast corner of the Caspian Sea), surely to deal with pressing problems. The defense of Media and Babylonia he left to his army commanders. After winning several victories, Demetrius was captured and exhibited as an object lesson to the peoples under Parthian rule who had supported him. We hear that the Parthian king was still in Hyrcania when Demetrius was brought to him. Thereafter, Arsakes treated his royal captive with honor, giving him his own daughter in marriage. See Justin xli 6.6–7, xxxvi 1.1–6, xxxviii 9.2–3; Appian *Syriakê* 67; and Debevoise, pp. 21–25. On the title given Arsakes here, see NOTE on 1:1, *smote . . . place.*

4–15. Knowing Simon's sad end, our author remains cautious insofar as he refrains from explicit claims that Simon's achievements were fulfillments of prophesy. Nevertheless, the abundant echoes of prophesies in the poem here are intended to suggest to the Jewish reader that the age of fulfillment of the prophesies of Israel's glory had begun in the years of Simon's rule.

4. *The land . . . lived*. Our author uses of Simon language similar to that used of Solomon at I Kings 5:5.

He . . . people. Cf. Esther 10:3; Amos 5:14.

They . . . rule. Cf. Esther 10:3.

5. For "glory" as political and military power, cf. Gen 45:13; Isa 8:7. Hitherto, Phoenician Tyre and Sidon controlled the access to the sea (Ezek 27:3), as had the Philistines. Now, Phoenician Joppe (see NOTE on 10:75–76) is settled by Israelites, in fulfillment of Ezek 28:25 and Zeph 2:5–7.

6. Cf. Exod 34:24, Deut 19:8. Simon reconquered territory Jews regarded as their own; cf. vs. 17 and 10:52 and Josh 18:1.

7. *He . . . and the Akra*. The second stich, with its reference to largely gentile garrisons, shows that our passage does not refer to the repatriation of

Jews. Further proof is given by Hab 1:9, the sole biblical parallel, on which our author may well have drawn. The events are recorded at 11:65–66, 13:43–50.

In his summary of our author's account (see introductory NOTE to 13:31–53), Josephus adds that Simon took Jamnia (*AJ* xiii 6.6.215; *BJ* i 2.2.50). If Josephus is correct, he drew on another source, and our author omitted Jamnia because Simon thereafter lost the town (15:40), which is not reported again in Jewish hands until the reign of Alexander Jannaeus (*AJ* xiii 15.4.395).

On the other hand, Josephus' addition of Jamnia can easily be explained as a mistake. Josephus' copy of First Maccabees may already have contained the corruption "Gaza" for "Gazara" at 13:43 (see Niese's apparatus to *AJ* xiii 6.7.215, vol. III, p. 191, line 3, and to *BJ* i 2.2.50, vol. V, p. 13, lines 10–11). A scribe seeing that Simon held "Gaza" and Joppe may well have inserted Jamnia which lies between the two. If so, Josephus, knowing the uninterruptedly gentile character of Gaza, accepted "Gazara," the correct reading still available in some copies, but failed to think of suppressing the erroneous interpolation, "Jamnia."

and there . . . him. As promised at Deut 7:24 and 11:25 and also to Joshua at Josh 1:5.

8. In fulfillment of Lev 26:4 and Zech 8:12 and Ezek 34:27.

9. In fulfillment of Zech 8:4 and Isa 52:1 and perhaps of Isa 61:10, though not quite of Jubilees xxiii 28–29.

10. Perhaps our author saw a fulfillment of Ezek 36:33–35. Cf. II Chron 11:5–12. Simon's acts reflected here are reported at 12:38, 13:33, 52. The biblical histories take care to record corresponding achievements of the kings of Israel and Judah (I Kings 9:15–19; II Chron 8:3–6, 26:6–15, etc.). Greek communities often voted high honors to persons who assured their food supply (see e.g. Pseudo-Plutarch *Vitae decem oratorum* 851b) and to donors of arms and to contributors of money for munitions. See below, on vss. 32–34. On Simon's renown reaching the end of the earth, cf. II Chron 26:15, and see NOTE on 3:9.

11. Does our author allude to Isa 27:5–6? Cf. Ps 37:11.

12. As in the days of Solomon (I Kings 5:5) and in fulfillment of Micah 4:4; Zech 3:10.

13. Cf. Pss 8:3, 46:10; Isa 14:4. The kings are the rulers of foreign empires to which the Jews had hitherto been subjected by God's sentence; see NOTE on 8:4, and *Mekilta, Baḥodesh,* 9, vol. II, p. 268 Lauterbach, and TB *Berakot* 12b.

14. Simon fulfilled Isa 11:4 and equaled the achievement of Solomon (Ps 72:4). Cf. also Pss 105:45 and 118:34, along with the Greek version of the verses. The Qumran sect spoke of its own members as the "poor" or "humble" and called one of its own important figures *dōrēš hattōrāh,* "he who sought to fulfill the Torah," or "the interpreter of the Torah"; see Cross, ALQ, pp. 84–85, and CD 6:7, 7:18. Our author here may be attacking the sect for its opposition to the Hasmonaeans: Hasmonaean Simon is the true *dōrēš hattōrāh,* and the true "humble" are not his opponents but his beneficiaries. Our author, who avoids naming the Deity, may also use "he sought to ful-

fill the Torah" as a substitute for "he sought the LORD"; cf. II Chron 19:3, 22:9, 30:19.

15. Simon's donations parallel both those of Solomon (I Kings 6–7) and of Greek communal benefactors (e.g. Pseudo-Plutarch *Vitae decem oratorum* 852b).

16–24k. These verses narrate events of the immediate aftermath of Jonathan's death, events which preceded those of vss. 1–3 and even preceded many of those reflected in vss. 4–15. In the crisis which followed Tryphon's capture of Jonathan (12:53 – 13:33), Jewish authorities were probably quick to seek the aid of their friends in Sparta and Rome. John Hyrcanus similarly was to be quick to apply to Rome in the crisis which followed the death of Simon; see Stern, *Zion* 26 (1961), 1–6 (in Hebrew, with English summary, p. i). Simon's struggle against Tryphon came in the winter. His ambassador to Rome probably left on the first available boat to set sail after the end of the winter storms (see introductory NOTE to 8:17–20, and NOTE on 13:41). The consul Lucius Caecilius Metellus may have been able to write the letter of vss. 24b–24k at any time during the year, since he is not reported to have gone on military campaign (introductory NOTE to 8:17–20; Münzer, "Caecilius 83," PW III [1899], 1208).

The text and chronology of the letter of the Spartans here present difficulties. The Spartans could address a letter to Simon as high priest only when they knew Jonathan was dead, but in the text of their letter there is no suggestion that Simon himself sent an embassy. Despite vs. 18, it is hard to see in the letter of the Spartans anything but a reply to the letter and embassy sent by Jonathan. Thus, the ambassadors are the same as Jonathan's, and their message is identical with his (compare vss. 21–22 with 12:9–17). It may well be that no official embassy but only a private Jewish traveler brought the news to Sparta and that Jonathan's ambassadors were still there and asked the Spartans to address their letter now to Simon.

Jonathan was killed well before the Feast of Dedication (December 21, 143 B.C.E.). Because of the Jews' good reasons for haste in seeking the aid of friendly powers, the news could hardly have reached the Jewish ambassadors at Sparta as late as October, 142, the earliest possible date for Demetrius' letter recognizing Simon as high priest. Yet the letter of the Spartans addresses Simon as high priest (*hierei megalôi*). There are several possibilities. The Spartans may have been the ones who jumped to the conclusion that Simon was high priest. Or "great priest" (*hierei megalôi*) here may be used in the more general sense of "distinguished priest" or "member of a high priestly family" (see Bauer, *Wörterbuch*, s.v. *archiereus;* the corresponding Hebrew term, *kōhēn gādōl,* may also have had a more general sense [see *M. Ketubot* 13:1–2 and *M. Ohalot* 17:5 and Alon, *Meḥqarim,* I, 61], and if so, there is no error in the prayer *'Al hannissim* when Mattathias is called *kōhēn gādōl*). The more general use of the term could easily have reflected a status of Simon as acting high priest. It is also possible that Simon and his adherents before October, 142, already viewed Seleucid rule over the Jews as illegitimate and that Simon had taken the title high priest. If so, the step would have been viewed as invalid by Jews who believed that God's will still subjected them to foreign rule. Those Jews could have come to accept Simon as high priest only when he was confirmed by Demetrius II; see Introduction, pp. 75–77.

Not merely Simon's adherents but the bulk of the nation passed the decree in vss. 27–48. We shall see that the text of the decree displays several compromises between political factions. One such compromise may be reflected in the failure of the decree to mention the diplomatic contacts with Sparta, in which Simon may have "usurped" the high priesthood.

Josephus' summary of Simon's reign in *AJ* xiii 6.7.213–15 (beginning) is a summary of our author's account through vs. 15, as *AJ* xiii 7.3–4.225–28 is of 15:38 – 16:22. But *AJ* xiii 6.7.215 (middle)–7.2.223 (beginning) and section 224 (end) clearly come from other sources. The brevity of the summary and the presence of the other sources have led scholars to think that Josephus ceased making any use of First Maccabees after vs. 15 and that he did not possess the remainder of our text. For the history of the problem and a refutation of these views, see Ettelson, TCAAS 27 (1925), 255–341.

The scholars and Josephus were right, however, to be suspicious of the text which lay before them. Beyond the difficulties we have noted (introductory NOTES to 13:31–53 and to this chapter), the versions of all witnesses to the text are in disarray but can be restored to order by a simple procedure. One need only note that the passage 15:15–24 is out of place. For no good reason, these verses interrupt the narrative of Antiochus VII's war against Tryphon, and 15:22 (=vs. 24i) shows that not Antiochus VII but Demetrius II was the reigning Seleucid, as far as the Romans knew. Demetrius II was king down to 140/39, but 15:16 (=vs. 24c) shows that the Roman consul of the year had Lucius as his first name (*praenomen*). The only such consul between 143 and 137 B.C.E. was Lucius Caecilius Metellus, consul in 142; see Broughton, *Magistrates*, I, 471–84, and Menahem Stern, *The Documents on the History of the Hasmonaean Revolt* pp. 128–29 (in Hebrew). The rest of chapter 15 treats events of 139 B.C.E. or later. No event of 142 belongs in chapter 15, much less the letter of Lucius, written for the departing Jewish ambassadors. Indeed, the ambassadors were unlikely to leave Rome during the autumn and winter storms on the Mediterranean (see Theophrastus *Characters* 3.3; Vegetius iv 39).

In fact, 15:15–24 should come after 14:24. Without that passage, 14:25 dangles. Not the mere despatch of an embassy to Rome but rather its successful return would motivate public gratitude. Moreover, vs. 40 speaks of the successful return as past. The displacement was recognized by Abraham Kahana, *Ha-sᵉfārīm ha-ḥīṣōnīm*, II (Tel-Aviv: M'qoroth, 1937), 171.

It is easy to imagine how vss. 24b – 24k=15:15–24 came to be displaced: sheets of text were pasted together in the wrong order to form a scroll. In Kappler's edition, the displaced passage contains 1005 Greek letters, about three full columns to judge by the displacements in Josephus' paraphrase of chapter 1; see Appendix V. A three-column sheet could have been common. See J. D. Barthélemy, *Les devanciers d'Aquila*, VTS, X (Leiden: Brill, 1963), pp. 163–65. The Codex Vaticanus of the Greek Bible has three-column pages (William H. P. Hatch, *The Principal Uncial Manuscripts of the New Testament* [University of Chicago Press, 1939], plate XIV).

Two facts suggest that the displacement goes back to the assembling of the original Hebrew roll. First, the passage between the proper place of the dislocated verses and their present position in the manuscripts (14:25 – 15:14) would not occupy an integral number of hypothetical three-column sheets or even of columns in Greek, but about 4½ sheets or 13½ columns. Assuming a ratio of Hebrew letters to Greek of 8 to 15, the Hebrew text of vss. 24b – 24k would contain 536 letters, which could well have occupied two columns while 14:25 – 15:14 occupied nine columns. However, there is no way of being sure of the size of the columns of the archetype; our inference from Josephus' paraphrase of chapter 1 is merely a guess. On the other hand, Josephus evidently did not know how to repair the error here though he may have had access to a Hebrew text, and that fact would suggest that the error goes back to the original Hebrew roll.

Josephus' false chronology forced him to discard the letter of the Romans (vss. 24b – 24k) and the Jewish resolution (14:27–49); see above, introductory NOTE to 13:31–53. He still found a way to insist on Simon's ties to Rome without giving an embarrassing date (AJ xiii 6.7.217). Above we found difficulties even in the letter of the Spartans, though it consists of insignificant civilities. Hence it is no wonder that Josephus found this dislocated part of our author's narrative extremely improbable and preferred to pass it over in silence.

The words in parentheses in vs. 16, "to Rome and," are probably a mistaken interpolation. In vs. 24a we learn that not the Romans but Simon took the initiative in the diplomatic contact, as one would expect in relations between a superpower and a barely independent small nation. Our author goes on in vs. 20 to quote only the letter of the Spartans. Sparta is closer to Judaea than Rome is, so that with the words "to Rome" the text is illogical. Even the Greek looked so bad that scribes tried to correct it. La^B has only "The news of Jonathan's death was heard in Rome"; L' has "Those in Rome heard of Jonathan's death, and the news was heard as far as Sparta." In Hebrew the expression "was heard in [="spread to"] x and as far as y" is unparalleled; "from x and as far as y" would be normal, as would "as far as y" (Neh 12:43, Ezra 3:13; Isa 15:4). Why should Romans go to the expense of drawing up on bronze tablets a mere polite communication, which was no treaty? It was only the Spartans who could have viewed as so important their acknowledgment of "friendship" and "brotherhood" with the Jews. The scribe who made the insertion may well have felt that our context ought to have a firm reference to Rome, for reference to Rome was all but missing after vss. 24b – 24k were displaced.

I have placed parentheses in vs. 18 around "Judas and" and around the "s" of "brothers" because I believe the words were added after "to Rome" was inserted in vs. 16 (in vowelless Hebrew, "his brother" and "his brothers" are both spelled '$\hbar yw$). Not Sparta but Rome established relations with Judas. On the other hand, our author is probably wrong about Jonathan, too, since the ambassadors probably did not return in Jonathan's lifetime and brought a letter addressed to Simon.

17. Our author appears not to perceive the chronological difficulties connected with the Spartans' letter which we noted above. If "the cities" here include Gazara and the Akra (cf. 15:28), he is probably guilty of anachronism;

Simon probably captured them long after the emergency which produced the diplomatic activity was over.

19. In Chronicles "assembly" (*ekklêsia, qāhāl*) frequently means "mass meeting"; see e.g. I Chron 29:1, 10, and II Chron 29:28, etc. The assembly here may have been more than that, as a republican institution of the Jews; see 13:2–9 and see NOTES on 4:59 and 5:16. The body which passed the decree honoring Simon (vss. 27–49) is not called *ekklêsia* but *synagôgê* (vs. 28).

20. Our verse would indicate that official communications of the Spartan state now went out in the name of some presiding elected officials and in the name of the city. Modern writers usually call such officials by the Roman word "magistrates." We have very little information on the political institutions at Sparta in this period. The Greek translator here uses the vaguest Greek word for "officials" (*archontes*). The vague word may cover any or all of the Spartan titles "ephor," *gerôn* ("elder"), or *patronomos;* see Ehrenberg, PW IIIᴬ, 1450, and Jones, *Sparta,* 165–66.

On the forms of address used with Simon, see above, on vss. 16–24k, and NOTE on 12:20. On the title "brothers," see NOTES on 12:5–23 and on 12:6.

22–23. Where I have *"Proceedings of the People,"* the Greek text has *en tais boulais tou dêmou,* which might be rendered "in the presence of the councils of the People." However, no other source on Sparta speaks of "the councils of the People." Moreover, the Greek is a retranslation of our author's Hebrew version of the original Greek, and in Greek translations from the Hebrew Bible the plural word *boulai* always means "counsel," "the results of deliberation," reflecting the Hebrew *'ēṣāh* or synonyms, and never designates political bodies or meeting places (Pss 12[13]:2, 32[33]:10, 65[66]:5; Prov 1:25, 30, 11:13; Job 5:12; II Chron 22:5; cf. I Esd 5:73; Judith 8:16; Tobit 4:19). Hence, it is better to translate as I have. The *Proceedings* would be the same as the volumes mentioned in vs. 23.

Ancient records of diplomacy carefully called attention to honorable treatment of ambassadors; cf. 12:8 and Sherk, no. 9, etc. It was common to set up a permanent record, in the host city, of an important diplomatic contact and to send a copy of the proceedings to the party which sent the embassy; see e.g. Sherk, no. 26, column b, lines 11–23, and cf. vss. 48–49.

Where I have "People's" in vs. 23, the Greek has *apodedeigmenois tôi dêmôi,* "assigned to the People." The expression is awkward, and one wonders what our author's Hebrew was. The same Greek participle renders *rᵉ'ūyōt* at Esther 2:9, where with the words which follow it it might be rendered "assigned to her." The Greek translators of the Hebrew Bible nowhere use the adjective *dêmosios* ("public," "belonging to the People"); it does occur at II 6:10 and III 2:27, 4:7). They may well have avoided deliberately the use of the Greek technical term. In that case, the awkward phrase here is a substitute, and I have translated accordingly. In Greek, *dêmosia grammata* is a common expression for "public documents" or "archives"; see Syll.³, vol. IV, p. 264b.

From this time on, the prestige of Judaea probably stood higher than Sparta's, so the Jews felt no further need to seek Spartan support, and our author reports no further contacts (hence, the objections of Cardauns, *Hermes* 95 [1967] 321, have no weight).

24a. On Numenius, see NOTE on 12:16. One thousand minas is approximately fifteen thousand ounces or four hundred fifty kilograms. The shield thus represented a huge amount of gold for a small struggling nation. Indeed, it dwarfed similar gifts to Rome by Demetrius I (Polybius xxxii 2.10) and Tryphon (Diodorus xxxiii 28a.1). In 134, however, John Hyrcanus equaled Simon's gift (see above, on vss. 16–24k beginning), if the gold pieces at J. *AJ* xiv 8.5.147 are staters. The urgency of the crisis facing the Hasmonaean rulers would explain the magnitude of the gift accompanying each petition for renewal of the alliance with Rome. Cf. also Cicero *In Verrem* II iv 28–29.64–67. Simon and the Jews did not waste their gold. There is no reason to doubt the public declaration of the Jews in vs. 40, that the renewal of the Roman alliance influenced Demetrius II's decisions in favor of Simon. The Jews' appeal may have been a factor in the refusal of the Romans to recognize Tryphon as king (Diodorus xxxiii 28a). On ornamental and ceremonial shields, see Maurice Albert, "Clipeus," DAGR, I, 1258b–1259a.

24b–24k. Our author probably drew on the copy sent to Simon, which quoted the version to Ptolemy VIII Euergetes II, who was then reigning in Egypt. Ptolemy VIII may well have been viewed as the strongest power in Simon's vicinity. The method of informing Simon of the Roman's actions, by sending him a copy of one example of the text of a letter sent out to many addressees, was a common practice. It was also common to give each such addressee a copy of the entire list of recipients. Thereby the addressees would know how comprehensive a policy was being set by the letter. See Bikerman, RHR 115 (1937), 191–96; and for lists of addressees, Y. H. Landau, "A Greek Inscription Found Near Hefzibah," IEJ 16 (1966), 54–70.

Josephus (*AJ* xiii 7.3.227) makes the barest of allusions to Simon's alliance with Rome and omits our document. The chronological connection of the embassy to Rome with Demetrius II was embarrassing for Josephus (connection: vs. 24i; see NOTE on 13:31–53); and the document seems almost contemporary with that at *AJ* xiv 8.5.147, which Josephus dated in 47 B.C.E.

24b. As usual in our book, the Greek plural *epistolai* is to be translated here as singular, "letter." The ambassadors brought back with them only the copy sent to Simon.

Hellenistic kings in diplomacy were treated as identical to the state, so that diplomatic correspondence was addressed to them personally. See Anneliese Mannzmann, "Basileus," Der kleine Pauly, I (1964), 834–35. Different forms of address were used with other kinds of political units, here called "countries." The two categories of recipients are addressed separately in vs. 24f and listed separately in vss. 24i–24j.

24c. Such letters were often sent out by a consul on behalf of the senate. Cf. J. *AJ* xiv 10.15.233 and Sherk, nos. 1, 20, 38. The original Roman text of the letter of the consul Lucius Caecilius Metellus probably did not omit his family name (*nomen*), "Caecilius." Greeks and Jews, however, were accustomed to having persons bear only one name, and Greek historians commonly refer to Romans by the first name (*praenomen*) only, so that our author or the translator or a scribe could easily have omitted "Caecilius." The text of the document at J. *AJ* xiv 10.12.225 gives only one of the names (the cognomen) of Publius Cornelius Dolabella.

24d. On the title "friend and ally," see NOTE on 8:19–32. The Roman document here attests Simon's political position in the Jewish state; contrast the situation in the time of Judas (see NOTE on 8:17–20). The old ties here renewed, however, are those made in the time of Judas. On "renew," see NOTE on 12:1–4.

In the Greek text, the ambassadors, not the Jews, are described as friends and allies, contrary to sense and Roman practice. The usual Roman formula is "the A-ians, B and C . . . , ambassadors, men good and true and friends, from a people good and true, our friend and ally"; see Sherk, no. 7, lines 40–44, no. 9, lines 16–18, no. 10, B, line 5; no. 12, lines 3–4; no. 58, line 77. The Hebrew translator of the original Greek document or the Greek retranslator may have been confused by the repetitions, so that he telescoped the formula to read "ambassadors of the Jews, our friends and allies" (cf. the Syriac *sb' dyhwdy' rḥmyn wm'drnyn*), and the Greek retranslator made the error of construing "friends and allies" with "ambassadors" instead of with "Jews."

24e. See vs. 24a.

24f. No one is to join Tryphon against the Jews, in particular neither Demetrius II nor Ptolemy VIII. The reference to towns and territory and the precarious position of Simon and Judaea make it likely that the ambassadors sought protection for Judaea and that neither they nor the Romans thought of protecting Jews living in the diaspora, though later Hasmonaeans successfully appealed to the Romans on their behalf (J. *AJ* xiv 10.11–12.223–27, 20.241–43).

24g. By accepting the shield, the Romans signified their intention to give the Jews tangible aid in return. The instructions in the letter were not to be viewed as empty words.

24h. We have few parallels for Roman support of demands by their allies for the extradition of fugitives. By the Peace of Apameia, Antiochus III was required to deliver up to Rome's allies any of their deserters (Livy xxxviii 38.7; Polybius xxi 43.10 Buettner-Wobst=42.10 Paton). The privilege granted here to Simon was granted by Augustus to Herod (J. *BJ* i 24.2.474).

Against whom was this privilege of extradition directed? Simon probably felt no duty to pursue idolaters outside the confines of the Promised Land (see 2:44 and Deut 4:25–28). The political and religious regime of which he was the head, however, faced opposition from both "apostates" and pious Jews. "Apostates" had certainly emigrated (2:44, 11:65–66 with 10:14, 13:50) and could be expected to plot against the regime. As for non-apostates, there was the Oniad party in Egypt; see NOTE on 6:63, and my article, "The Tales of the Tobiads," in *Studies Smith*, Part III, pp. 85–123. Surely there also were Pietist emigrés. The Qumran sect may well have gone to Damascus (see Introduction, Part IV, n. 21) and plotted against Simon, whom they probably viewed as "the Cursed Man."

"Traitor" (*loimos*) here literally means "plague." Greek uses *loimos* (Demosthenes 25:80; Aelianus *Varia historia* xiv 11: Acts 24:5; cf. I 15:3 and Libanius *Oration* 1.186) and *nosos* ("disease"; Plato *Protagoras* 322d) to refer to persons dangerous or subversive to a community. It is used in similar contexts in Greek translations of the Hebrew Bible (I Sam 10:27; Dan Th. 12:14; cf. I 10:61, where I have translated *loimoi* as "factious").

24i–24j. Apart from the classification of recipients into "kings" and "countries" there seems to be no principle of arrangement in the list of recipients. Ptolemy VIII and Demetrius II were powerful enough and close enough to Judaea to be objects of the warning in vs. 24f. They as well as Arsakes ruled over considerable Jewish populations, so that their territories were areas where anti-Hasmonaean emigrés would tend to settle, and we may guess that the same was true of all the other recipients in the list. For the locations, see Map 15, p. 539.

24i. The only Demetrius reigning around this time was the Seleucid Demetrius II. Hence the letter must have been written before the news of his capture by the Parthians reached Rome. See above, introductory NOTE to chapter, and on vss. 1–3.

Attalus II was king of Pergamum from 159 to 138 B.C.E. and ruled much of western Asia Minor.

Ariarathes V was king of Cappadocia from 163 to 130. On Arsakes, see above, introductory NOTE to vss. 1–3.

24j. The first of the non-royal countries was so little known as to puzzle the scribes. *Sampsamê* is the reading of SVq, supported by *Samsani* of La^B and *Samsamae* of La^V and *smsnws* of SyIII. A and L have *Sampsakê*, supported by *Sampsace* of La^X and by SyI and SyII. Scholars since Michaelis, following the hint of SyIII, have identified the place mentioned here with Samsun on the Black Sea in modern Turkey. In Greek sources ancient Samsun was called "Amisos," but some Greek coins of the city bear the legends *Samisoês* or *Samisou* (Head, *Historia Numorum*, p. 497); initial *s* was lost in many Greek dialects, so that the place could well have been known to our author as something like "Samsam." Amisos was not subject to the kingdom of Pontus at this time; see Rostovtzeff, SEHHW, p. 578. On the importance of the city, see ibid., index, s.v. *Amisus*.

The Spartans. This friendly city had already harbored at least one Jewish refugee whom Hasmonaeans would view as an enemy, Jason the Oniad (II 5:9). Even a Hellenized Jewish high priest might want the amenities of a Jewish community in his place of exile.

Delos. This tiny island in the middle of the Aegean was a free port under Athenian rule at this time, with a highly mixed population; see W. A. Laidlaw, *A History of Delos* (Oxford: Blackwell, 1933), pp. 169–231. It is strange to find Delos present in the list and Athens absent. There was a local government on Athenian Delos (Laidlaw, pp. 173–81) and the free port of Delos, rather than Athens, may have been a focus for Jewish immigration. Athens later was to curry favor with John Hyrcanus; see NOTE on 12:5–23. A Jewish settlement on Delos at this time is attested by inscriptions and by the ruins of a building which probably was a synagogue. See Laidlaw, pp. 215, 268–69, and Abraham Schalit, "Delos," Enc. Jud., V, 1482–83.

Myndos. Near Halicarnassus, on the southwest coast of Asia Minor. It was independent at this time (Magie, *Roman Rule*, pp. 108–9).

Sikyon. In Greece, on the south shore of the Gulf of Corinth. At this time the city was free and probably enjoyed Roman favor; see Charles H. Skalet, *Ancient Sicyon* (Johns Hopkins University Press, 1928), p. 90.

Karia. North of Lykia, in the southwest corner of Asia Minor. The Romans in 167 B.C.E. had set free large parts of Karia and Lykia (Polybius xxx 5.12–16, 21.3–5, 31; Livy xlv 25), which could therefore be recipients of the Roman message. The independent state of Karia was completely distinct from the Greek cities of Myndos, Halicarnassus, and Knidos, enclaves within it.

Two excellent witnesses to the text, A and La^G have "Karis" instead of Karia (they are supported by La^X *ceridam*). Stephanus Byzantius lists an obscure town Karis in Phrygia, and Ephorus *apud* Athenaeus iii 105d mentions another, in Chios. The form "Karis" as a name for Karia is nowhere else attested. However, there was no reason for the Romans to send the letter to such obscure places, and it was common in Greek to use the feminine adjective ending in *-is* with the definite article as a synonym for the territorial name ending in *-ia*. Just as *hê Iônis* (*chora*) means "Ionia", so *hê Karis* here means "Karia."

Samos. The important island city off the southwest coast of Asia Minor. It, too, was free at this time (Magie, *Roman Rule,* pp. 107–8, 473).

Pamphylia. The middle part of the southern coast of Asia Minor. The Romans appear to have declared the area free in their settlement of a dispute between Eumenes II of Pergamum and Antiochus III over the meaning of the territorial terms of the Peace of Apameia of 188 B.C.E. See Magie, pp. 279–80.

Lykia. See above, on Karia, and Magie, pp. 954–56.

Halicarnassus. See above, on Myndos, and Magie, p. 108.

Rhodes. The important free island city off the southwest coast of Asia Minor. See Isaiah Gafni, "Rhodes," Enc. Jud., XIV, 145.

Phaselis. A free Greek city, an enclave in Lykia. See Magie, pp. 516, 1370–71.

Kos. An island city off the southwest corner of Asia Minor. The coinage indicates that Kos was free at this time; see Bürchner, "Kos," PW, XI (1922), 1480, and introductory NOTE to chapter 8.

Side. An independent city, an enclave in Pamphylia. See Magie, pp. 261–62.

Arados. The northernmost of the Phoenician cities, on an island off the coast of modern Syria. Its almost impregnable site made it nearly independent under the Seleucids; see Diodorus xxxiii 5, Bikerman, *Institutions,* p. 140, and H. Seyrig, "Antiquités syriennes 49," *Syria* 28 (1951), 206–20. Phoenician cities were under the control of Demetrius (Bevan, II, 228–29). On the privileges which Arados and Tyre were to gain in the course of the struggle between Demetrius and Tryphon, see Seyrig, *Notes on Syrian Coins,* pp. 17–22.

Gortyna. An important city in southern Crete. See Bürchner, "Gortyn," PW, VII (1912), 1665–71; Simon Marcus, "Crete," Enc. Jud., V, 1088.

Knidos. At the southwest corner of Asia Minor. See Magie, pp. 108–9.

Cyprus and Cyrene. It is strange to find these two areas mentioned in the list, since both were under the rule of Ptolemy VIII Euergetes II; see Volkmann, PW, XXIII, 1725–26, 1735. A learned scribe may have emended the text by conjecture on perceiving the difficulty, for manuscript V has "Smyrna" instead of "Cyrene." However, in the reign of Ptolemy VI the Romans had tried to weaken the Ptolemaic empire, by working to split Cyrene and Cyprus off from Egypt. Already in his lifetime Ptolemy VI had made his son, the future Ptolemy VII, king of Cyprus, probably acting to please the Romans (ibid., cols. 1712–15). When Ptolemy VIII upon the death of Ptolemy VI moved from Cyrene to seize power over Cyprus and Egypt in the summer of 145 (ibid., cols. 1725–27), the Romans could hardly have been pleased, and we have no evidence of friendly contacts between Ptolemy VIII and Rome before 139 (ibid., col. 1728). Hence, the Romans may have addressed separate letters to Cyrene and Cyprus because they still refused to recognize Ptolemy VIII's right to rule the two regions. Both areas are known to have had Jewish populations (Lea Roth, "Cyprus," Enc. Jud., V, 1181; Isaiah Gafni, "Cyrene," ibid., cols. 1183–84).

25–26. The document in vss. 27–49 is probably our author's sole source for these two verses. Cf. Esther 6:3, 6.

25. For "People" here, the Greek translator used *dēmos*, the Greek word for the totality of the adult male citizenry acting as a political unit. Elsewhere he used it only in quoting the correspondence with the Romans and the Spartans. In Greek translations from the Hebrew Bible it occurs in the sense of "people" only at Dan LXX 8:24, 9:16, 11:32.

26. My translation here departs from all witnesses to the text. Of the Greek manuscripts, A has "he strengthened" (*estērisen*), S has "he was strengthened" (*estēristai*), and *L'* has "they strengthened" (*estērixan*). Nowhere in translations from the Hebrew Bible is the Greek verb "strengthen" used intransitively. It usually renders the Hebrew root *smk*, which is utterly unidiomatic in our context. On the other hand, La^{L X} have "he established" (*statuit; Greek estēse*), which again does not fit the context. All witnesses to the text, however, share the letters *estē*, which spell the Greek word "he arose." Indeed, our verse should echo vs. 32, where "arose," not "strengthened" occurs. Greek scribes are known to have turned the verb of *estē* into the other readings. The words *estē* and *estēse* are two forms (second and first aorist) of one verb. Translators or scribes of Greek versions of Hebrew texts wrongly give it in the first aorist instead of in the second at Sir 45:23 (where A has the correct reading) and at Isa 44:11 (where B and S have the correct reading). At Prov 15:25 only S has the probably correct *estēsen*, whereas all other witnesses have *estērixen*. Hence, the original reading here was probably *estē*.

There should be no period between "Israel" and "and they gained." Kappler so punctuated, apparently because he took the pronoun *autôi*, which I have translated "for our people," to refer to Simon. If so, Kappler wrongly followed I Sam 28:25 so as to construe our passage to mean "they [the People] conferred freedom upon Simon." Far from conferring mere freedom, they conferred near-royal power.

Conspicuous by its absence from the document in vss. 27–49 is any reference to the liberation of Israel by the Hasmonaeans. Clearly, at least one of the Jewish parties whose influence is reflected in the document refused to believe that the age of subjection to foreign empires was over, surely on the ground that the glorious prophesies still remained unfulfilled in large measure. Quite apart from religious factors, such Jews may have regarded as significant the absence from Demetrius' letter at 13:35–40 of the clause (11:36) which would have made his concessions irrevocable. See Note on 13:41, and below, on vss. 27–49.

27–49. Our author used the document here as a source, but at many points it is at variance with his narrative. See above, introductory Note to vss. 16–24k, on vs. 26, and below, on the individual verses of our passage. Whereas our author was an ardent partisan of the Hasmonaeans, our document clearly represents compromises between them and other factions among the Jews. On Josephus' omission of our document, see Note on 13:31–53.

Our document has many parallels in Greek honorific inscriptions and surely imitates them in many respects. Nevertheless, the original was written in Hebrew and drew very much on Hebrew and Aramaic patterns. We have very few examples to tell us how the Semitic peoples drew up communal resolutions. Of the parallels, only Nehemiah 9–10 is probably free from Greek influence. Also important for our purposes are the Greek document of Hellenized Idumaean refugees living in Egypt, OGIS 737, of 112 B.C.E. (see U. Rapaport, "Les Iduméens en Égypte, RPh, 3D SERIES, 43 [1969], 73–82), and the resolution in Phoenician drawn up by the Sidonian community of the Piraeus in Greece, in 96 B.C.E. (G. A. Cooke, *A Text-Book of North Semitic Inscriptions* [Oxford: Clarendon Press, 1903], no. 33=Herbert Donner and W. Röllig, *Kanaanäische und aramäische Inschriften,* 2d ed. [Wiesbaden: Harrassowitz, 1966–69], no. 60; photograph: E. Renan, "Inscription phénicienne et grecque," RArch 3D SERIES, II [1888], plates II–III).

27. Our document, like its parallels, begins with a date; the document envisioned by the author of Nehemiah 9 probably did so, too (see Neh 9:1). 18 Elul, 172 Sel. Bab., was September 13, 140 B.C.E.

which is . . . People. See Note on 13:42. "High priest" here is literally "great high priest," but the translator probably has been guilty of a slip of the pen, first writing the ordinary Greek word for "high priest" (*archiereus*) and then the adjective "great" derived from the Hebrew idiom for "high priest," *khn gdwl* ("great priest"). The last two words in the Greek text, which I have translated "and prince of God's People," are difficult. SVLLa[L X V] have *en asaramel.* All other significant witnesses to the text have *en saramel. En* would normally be the Greek preposition ("in"); if so, the words would give the place of the transaction dated in our verse and would mean "in (A)saramel." Several facts make this hypothesis unlikely. Though the place where a decree was voted was often given in the document reporting it (as in OGIS 737), the place did not stand immediately after the date, as it would here, but after the note that a meeting was held (which here stands in vs. 28); cf. OGIS 737. We hear nowhere else of a place (A)saramel. The place name should have a meaning, perhaps as *ḥăṣar 'am ēl,* "the Court of God's People." If so, however, why did the translator transliterate it instead of translating it? Moreover, to construe the words as giving the place would render the dating formula here inconsistent with 13:42, where Simon bears not only priestly but also political titles.

The translator of the Syriac version probably faced the same enigmatic Greek text but perceived what was required. Neglecting the letters *en,* he rendered it *rb' b'sryl* or *rb' d'sryl,* "prince of Israel." Syriac *rb'* renders Hebrew *śar* ("prince"; e.g. at Ecclus 10:24). If we can explain away the presence of the letters *en* and the *a* of *asaramel*, we would have *šar 'am ēl*, my "prince of God's People," still not precisely what stands at 13:42 but easily compatible with it, since "commander" (*stratêgos*) there may well be a survival of Simon's title under the Seleucid kings and Simon and the political authorities of the nation at this time may have chosen to exchange the original titles for those which appear here. Perhaps Simon himself wished to be mentioned even in Greek texts by his Hebrew title. That preference would explain why the translator transliterated here. On the other hand, at vs. 47 he translated so that the Greek reader would understand what office Simon received. At 15:1–2 in the letter of Antiochus VII the translator simply gave the word "ethnarch" customarily used by Greek speakers.

If our words give Simon's political title, one would expect *kai* ("and") instead of *en*, and that is how I have translated the passage. There is more than one way to exlain how *kai* could become *en*. It is not inconceivable that careless phonetic spelling (or hearing, if the translator worked by listening to a reader of the Hebrew) turned a Hebrew *w-* ("and") into *b-* ("in"). See M. H. Segal, *A Grammar of Mishnaic Hebrew*, §§ 48 and 58, Hebrew edition (Tel-Aviv: Dvir, 5696), §§ 44, 47, and 51, and Kutscher, *Tarbiz* 21–23 (1952), 12 (in Hebrew). At Isa 47:2, 1QIsᵃ has *šwlyk* ("your skirts") for *šbl* ("robe"?), but this is probably the substitution of a common word for a rare one (so Kutscher, *Language and Linguistic Background*, p. xi). A translator confronted with the enigmatic reading containing *b-* could hardly do anything but translate *b-* as "in" and transliterate *šar 'am ēl*.

Nevertheless, it is hard to see how such a slip in the Hebrew could have been made here. More likely, the error arose early in the transmission of the Greek version. In some Greek hands of the period, *k* could be misread as *e*, and *n* as *ai*. See Viktor Gardthausen, *Griechische Palaeographie*, 2d ed. (Leipzig: Veit, 1911–13), vol. II, Tafel I, cols. 7 and 8. As for the *a* of *asaramel*, scribes with some knowledge of Hebrew, on being puzzled by *en saramel*, may have guessed that *ḥāṣar 'am ēl*, "the Court of God's People," was a suitable place name.

Our author would then appear to have abandoned here his usual reticence with terms naming the Deity, but he never shows such reticence with names of God when they form part of the name of a human being; he may have regarded Simon's title as similar to a name. He was still less inclined to alter it since it stood in a quoted document. Even so, Simon's title itself displays Hasmonaean reticence. One would expect, not "God's People," which never occurs in the Hebrew Bible (it does occur at 1QM 1:5, 3:12), but "the LORD's People" (cf. I Sam 6:21; II Kings 9:6), which occurs frequently (Num 11:29; I Sam 2:24; II Sam 1:12; Zeph 2:10), as does *šar 'am* (Ezek 11:1; Esther 3:12; Neh 11:1; I Chron 21:2; II Chron 24:23, 36:14).

28. Parallel ancient documents, after the date, commonly record the identity of the body which passed the decree; so does Neh 9:1, 4 (see also Neh 10:1–29). The nature of a (or the?) "great assembly" (*kᵉneset gᵉdōlāh*) is a vexed question because we lack information; see Baron, I, 367–68, and Daniel Sperber, "Synagogue, the Great," Enc. Jud., XV, 629–31.

On this occasion, the great assembly included priests, ordinary Israelites, important national officials, and the local leaders ("elders") of Judaea outside

Jerusalem. For similar assemblies in the Hebrew Bible, cf. Exod 19:1-9, 24:1-9; I Kings 20:7-8; Ezra 10:9-14; and Neh 9:1 with Neh 10:1-29.

No voting or debate is ever reported in connection with these Israelite assemblies. In every case, one or more figures having or representing authority address and inform those assembled, who then "all" respond "with one voice." Cf. 13:2-9 and Acts 15:6-29. Voice-voting, at least in elections for the ephors (Aristotle *Politics* ii 9.23.1270b), and absence of free debate were features of the Spartan constitution; see Jones, *Sparta*, pp. 20-25. Compare also the procedure of religious assemblies in Ptolemaic Egypt, OGIS 56, lines 3-5, and OGIS 90, lines 6-8.

The last two words of our verse in Greek puzzled the scribes and have been a problem for scholars, but they seem to reflect similar Israelite procedure. The original and difficult reading in the Greek, *egnôrisen hêmin* ("he informed us") still stand in most witnesses to the text, but L' has *egnôrisamen hymin* ("we informed you"). Probably the translator has made a mistake: in vowelless Hebrew, *hwd'* can mean either "he informed" or "was brought to the attention of." The translator should have picked the other alternative. The proposal to confer sweeping powers on Simon, surely drawn up by the leaders of the nation, was phrased as objective fact and was probably broadcast to the assembly by a loud-voiced herald whose name was of no importance. Hence, the draftsman of the decree used the passive verb, "was brought to our attention," using the first person plural as at Neh 9:9, 16, 32-34, 36-37, and 10: 1-40. The verb here thus refers to the information laid before the assembly, not to the assembly's act of decision.

29-49. The syntax of our verses has been distorted by what are probably scribal errors in vs. 41; see ad loc. We have here the regular form of a resolution, a long "whereas" section followed by a "therefore be it resolved" section, as is common in inscriptions reporting the decrees of Greek states. Greek grammar has no trouble accommodating a long series of "whereas" clauses before the verb equivalent to "be it resolved," and in those Greek inscriptions, "whereas" is almost always *epeidê*. See A. G. Woodhead, *The Study of Greek Inscriptions* (Cambridge: University Press, 1959), pp. 38-39. At least two things are strange in our document. First, the Greek translator instead of beginning the "whereas" clauses with *epeidê* uses the synonymous *epei*. Second, in Hebrew it would seem extremely awkward to have a long series of "whereas" clauses precede the verb equivalent to "be it resolved." Indeed, in the Phoenician inscription, Cooke, no. 33, the "whereas" clause follows the verb.

In fact, however, the draftsman of our document was not trying to force Hebrew into the mold of Greek syntax (as Meyer, *Ursprung*, p. 265, n. 1, supposed); rather, he used good Hebrew idiom to express the series of "whereas" clauses. The translator's *epei* here represents Hebrew *hen* or *hinnêh* ("behold"), as at Job 13:15; Ps 77[78H]:20 (cf. Gen 15:3, 18:31, 19:19). For *hinnêh* as "whereas," motivating a decision, see Gen 37:19-20; Exod 1:9-10. In Nehemiah 9-10, the long confessional prayer (Neh 9:5-37) serves as the "whereas" section for the covenant decree in Nehemiah 10. In the document envisioned by the author of Esther 9:23-28, the procedure was probably similar, with *kī* in Esther 9:24 performing the function of *hinnēh;* see Appendix IV.

29. Two things are conspicuous by their absence from our verse. Judas' name is not mentioned, and no event narrated before chapter 9 is included. Though our author takes pains to record Simon's acts during the career of Judas, the authorities who produced our document did not wish to take those acts into account. Perhaps many Jews still regarded the persecution and the other events of 167–160 B.C.E. as having cosmic importance. To concede that Simon, like Judas, was a direct instrument of God in those events might confer upon Simon too much religious significance. Simon and his adherents did not demand such recognition but compromised with other Jewish parties. Such a compromise would explain why the "many wars" here are only those narrated from chapter 9 on and why Judas' name is absent. The authorities who produced our document were willing to regard Demetrius I, Demetrius II, and Tryphon as enemies. Some Jews may not have so viewed Antiochus V, who ended the persecution. Such Jews may well have preserved the documents quoted at II 11:23–33.

On Simon's ancestry as traced here, see Introduction, pp. 16–21.

his brothers. Besides Simon, both Jonathan and John (9:35–36) lived to participate in the events.

their sanctuary . . . Torah. The authorities who produced our document agreed that the temple and the Torah had been menaced, at least by Demetrius I's support of Alcimus (9:1–57; 10:46) and by Tryphon and by the hostile gentile neighbors of Judaea (vs. 31 and 12:53 – 13:6).

30. Jonathan's career gets a summary, though a brief one. His priestly and political offices were precedents for Simon's, even in the eyes of those who did not share the Hasmonaean view, that the high priesthood and princeship over the nation were now the legitimate heritage of the Hasmonaeans, by God's will (see Introduction, pp. 7–12). Significantly, our document does not give Jonathan a political title; contrast our author's account at 9:30. I have translated "passed away," where the Greek has, literally, "was gathered unto his people."

31. See 12:53 – 13:6 and above, on vs. 29.

32–34. See chapter 13. Our author left it to the quoted decree to mention Simon's contributions of his own money. The source of his vast and growing wealth was probably the booty from his successful warfare. Roman Augustus was to do the same, on a much vaster scale. Public gratitude for such out-of-pocket contributions is very common in parallel texts; see Pseudo-Plutarch *Vitai decem oratorum* 851a–852c, OGIS 737, and Cooke, no. 33.

33. See vs. 10 and 11:65–66, 13:10, 33, 48, 52. Our verse does not say that Simon *captured* Beth-Zur after Jonathan's death.

35–36. Kappler's edition in vs. 35 follows ASLa$^{L X B}$ in omitting "and what he had accomplished" (*kai praxin*); then the repetition of "fidelity" (*pistin*) is awkward. *L* omits the first "fidelity." My translation, with both expressions, is based on V alone. It is easy to understand how a scribe could have omitted one or the other of the two similar words *pistin* and *praxin*. For a Greek scribe to have interpolated either seems unlikely, especially since Greek idiom uses not the singular *praxin* but the plural *praxeis*. The singular does occur in translations from the Hebrew (Symmachus Pss 27[28H]:4–5, 89[90H]:17; Eccles 12:14).

Both expressions are, indeed, required. In our verse the draftsman of the document first gives as a historical fact the perception which motivated the people to confer on Simon a previous grant of powers, one which we may assume was recorded in a document. The draftsman then goes on to quote or paraphrase the part of that earlier document which presented the people's motivation. Cf. Esther 9:20–25: in Esther 9:20–22 the narrator explained how the Jews perceived (through Mordecai's letter) the events which led to the Purim festival; in Esther 9:23 he reported that the Jews were thereupon motivated to adopt the festival; in Esther 9:24–25 he quoted or paraphrased the part of the resulting document in which the Jews' motivation was presented. The facts of the motivation should be the same both in the narrative part of our verse and in the paraphrase of the document: fidelity, past accomplishment, and intentions for the future; and so they are, in the reading here adopted. "Righteousness" in the paraphrase is probably no more than a stereotyped pendant to "fidelity." Cf. Ps 109:75, 138; I Sam 26:23.

All parties involved in the decree could agree on the achievements of Simon listed above, on his righteousness and faithfulness, and on the fact that his policies, if not fulfillment of prophesy, at least aimed at glory for the Jews. Vs. 35 reports that the people themselves, before the capture of the Akra, made Simon chief (hêgoumenon) and high priest. Not every Jewish party would recognize such an appointment unless it was ratified by the king then ruling over the Jews; see above, introductory NOTE to vss. 16–24k, and NOTE on 13:36. Hence, the authors of our document intended Demetrius' ratification, reported in vs. 38, to be understood as having occurred shortly after the nation's nomination of Simon. Cf. 13:8, 36, 42.

A difficulty arises from the mention of Gazara in vs. 34. In our author's narrative (13:43) the siege of Gazara seems to follow Demetrius' confirmation of Simon in the high priestly office, whereas in our document it would appear that the fall of Gazara motivated the people to nominate Simon for the office in which he was then confirmed by Demetrius. The contradiction can be resolved: our author's "At that time" in 13:43 is vague enough to permit the successful siege to have preceded the appointment of Simon. Our author may have wished to organize his narrative there topically, grouping the capture of Gazara with the capture of the Akra.

34. *Joppe.* See vs. 5 and 13:11.

Gazara . . . Azotus. See vs. 7 and 13:43–48. Gazara did lie in the territory of Azotus; see NOTE on 5:68.

whatever . . . provided. See 13:47–48. The Greek word *epanorthôsis* (literally, "correction") surely translates a Hebrew word like *hkšr* ("the procedure of making kosher"), and I have translated accordingly.

36–37. Conspicuous by its absence is reference to liberation of the Jews from the shame (cf. 4:58 and Ezek 36:2–6) of foreign taxation. Some Jewish parties were reluctant to regard Simon's regime as having fulfilled Zech 9:8. See above, on vs. 26. All could agree, however, that Simon had glorified Israel by removing the shame of foreign occupation and especially the shame of the garrison in the Akra. Another glorification of Israel was Simon's improvement of the fortifications of Jerusalem. See vss. 7, 13, and 13:49–52. On "City of David," see p. 218.

The complicated Jewish laws of purity left many opportunities for a hostile garrison in the Akra to commit acts of provocation, quite apart from the extreme act of defiling the area with the slain corpses of pious Jews. See 1:36–37; *M. Kelim* 1; J. *AJ* xii 3.4.145–46 with Bickerman, *Syria* 25 (1946–48), 67–85.

38. See above, on vss. 34–35. The word order, with the subject before the verb, also suggests that the draftsman intended to indicate that Demetrius' confirmation of Simon in the high priesthood came before the fall of the Akra; see p. 426. My use of the present perfect tense here is meant to reflect that possibility.

The obscure phrase *kata tauta*, which I have translated "in view of all this," may also have been intended to give the time of Demetrius' action. It would then mean "during the same time" and would refer back to the phrase at the beginning of vs. 36. The obscure phrase here did puzzle the scribes. The Syriac versions omit it, and q^{-71} reads *kata panta* ("in view of everything"?). Grimm (ad loc.) suggested that *kata panta* would mean "in every respect." Simon would then be said to have received all the prerogatives of a high priest. This would fit the idiom *lkl dbr* in tannaitic Hebrew, but were high priests at this time restricted in some of their prerogatives?

For *kata* with the meaning "during," "at the time of," see Johannessohn [cited in NOTE on 3:48], p. 251, and cf. Polybius i 25.6. The difficulty then would be to imagine what Hebrew would underlie the Greek. Would a Greek translator use *kata* instead of *en* to render *bzh* (cf. Esther 2:13) or *bz't* (cf. II Chron 20:17)? A Greek translator did use *kata* instead of *en* with *nouns* meaning "time" at Hosea 2:9 and Num 22:4. I find it difficult, however, to imagine what the original Hebrew might have been no matter what meaning I assign to the phrase. Why did the translator use *kata* and not *epi* if the Hebrew was *'l* ("in view of all this")? If the phrase meant "On the same terms" (Hebrew *ken?*), one would expect to find it at the beginning, not at the end of our verse.

The draftsman need not have written standard biblical Hebrew, and the translator may well have felt no need to render his words in stereotyped biblical Greek. The idiom here may have been similar to the peculiar *'al kākā* at Esther 9:26, which the Greek renders by *dia tauta* ("on account of all this").

39. See NOTE on 13:36.

40. The Jews did not regard the Romans' diplomatic acts in their favor as empty words. Manuscripts of the class q omit the words "and Brothers," but all other witnesses to the text have them. Romans did not confer the title "Brother" on anyone, though in one instance they agreed to enter a relation of brotherhood offered by the Gallic Haedui; see Otto Hirschfeld, "Die Haeduer und Arverner unter Römischer Herrschaft," *Sitzungsberichte der Könglich preussichen Akademie der Wissenschaften zu Berlin*, 1897, pp. 1106–11. Surely the Romans did not confer the title upon the Jews, although the Spartans did.

It is hard to see how the draftsman in a public document could have made the error of including the words "and Brothers." Are they the marginal note of a reader who had read the Spartan letter and let his faulty memory trick him into thinking that the Roman letter also contained the word "Brothers?"

41. On the titles "Friends and Allies," see NOTES on 8:1 and 19–32.

41. The syntax of the whole decree was obscured by scribal errors in our verse. All witnesses to the text, except one minuscule manuscript (71) have at the beginning of our verse *kai hoti hoi Ioudaioi kai hoi hiereis eudokêsan tou einai . . . Simôna,* "and that the Jews and the priests resolved that Simon be. . . ."

The scribe of 71 and many modern scholars are right to omit the word *hoti* ("that"). With the word, our document becomes extremely awkward, for then vss. 41–43 continue to explain why Demetrius honored Simon. Thereby, the most significant actions of the Jews to confer power on Simon are left in the past. The only fresh provisions in Simon's behalf become those in vss. 44–45. But such irrevocability and penalty clauses customarily stood at the end of a document recording a political act and were not in themselves the main content of a political act; see below, on vss. 44–45, and cf. 11:36. Moreover, the word *hoti* makes vss. 41–43 superfluous and out of place. The Jews' *de facto* appointment of Simon to office has already been alluded to in vs. 35 and perhaps again in the words "in view of all this" in vs. 38. The added details in vss. 41–43 should then have stood in vs. 35. Finally, with *hoti* our document lacks a "be it resolved" clause to introduce something new, beyond the earlier prerogatives of Simon mentioned in the "whereas" clauses. If *hoti* is omitted, vss. 41–43 do confer new privileges: office *in perpetuity* and also probably all the provisions in vss. 42–43, at least as grants now conferred by the nation rather than by the foreign king.

The reading *hoti* is so universal that it must be a very old corruption, probably a contamination introduced from the two occurrences of the word in vs. 40. The original had either *kai* alone at the head of the verse, or, better, *kai nyn* ("and now," "therefore"). In a context replete with occurrences of *hoti, nyn* could have been misread as *hoti* because in many scribal hands *y* and *t* look alike. The corruptions probably arose in the Greek, not in the Hebrew, since "and" in Hebrew is a prefix (*w-*), whereas "and that" (*wky*) is a separate word.

Even when *hoti* is omitted, our verse is strangely phrased, because the verb is in the past tense, "the Jews and the priests resolved." Thus our document would lack a "be it resolved" clause and would have two clauses saying "the people resolved" (our verse and vs. 46). It is possible that the Greek translator misread the Hebrew verb form. If the root was that used at Esther 9:23 and 27, he would have misread *wīqabbᵉlū* ("be it resolved by") as the past tense, *wayqabbᵉlū*, both forms being spelled *wyqblw* in vowelless Hebrew. The error may, however, belong to an early Greek scribe, who became confused with the imperative followed by the definite article, *eudokêsatôsan tou* and wrote the past tense followed by the definite article, *eudokêsan tou.* On the form of the third-person plural imperative, see Abel, *Grammaire,* pp. 91–92.

Simon receives the princeship and the high priesthood in perpetuity, that is to say, his heirs are to inherit them after him; cf. Exod 32:13 and II Sam 7:12–13. His son, John Hyrcanus, had claims to being a true prophet (Introduction, Part I, n. 8). The proviso, "until a true prophet shall arise," represents a compromise between the Hasmonaean party and other sects. The other sects may have looked for a miraculous reappearance of the dynasty of David, as predicted by the prophets or perhaps for Daniel's "Son of Man" (cf. Enoch xc 37). There is a similar compromise at Ezra 2:63 and Neh 7:65.

The proviso here also surely reflects the practice in the time of the Israelite kingdoms: the founder of an Israelite dynasty should receive designation from a true prophet. In Simon's time, no true prophets were known to be alive.

42–43. Hitherto Simon may have borne the title commander (*stratêgos*) as an official of the Seleucid empire (see above on vs. 27). "*Stratêgos* and high priest" is known as the title of several provincial governors under the Ptolemies and Seleucids; see OGIS, index, p. 706. Now Simon receives the title from the Jewish nation.

The repetition in our verses of "and that he have charge of the sanctuary" is extremely awkward, whether it arose accidentally from scribal dittography or from a mistaken scribal interpolation; cf. Grimm, ad loc. It is not analogous to the stylistic repetitions noted above (introductory NOTE to 1:1–10 and NOTE on 8:2). The first occurrence of the clause seems the more intrusive, coming between the word "commander" and the listing of areas over which the commander (*stratêgos*) may appoint supervisory staff: labor, the countryside, munitions, and fortifications. All these areas in the Hellenistic monarchies were under the control of men bearing the title *stratêgos*. Cf. Bengtson, *Strategie*, II, 125–44, 166–69; III, 40–64, 71–86. Although the temple had a *stratêgos* (probably the second-ranking priest; see in AB vol. 41A, NOTE on II 3:4) and services or labor projects, it did not have a "countryside," and its munitions and fortifications probably were not separate from those of Judaea. If the words did not wander into vs. 42 by dittography from vs. 43, why would a scribe have added them?

One factor in the context may have induced a scribe to do so. The word I have translated "services" (*ergôn*; Hebrew *'ăbōdāh* or *mᵉlākāh*) in the Hebrew Bible refers mostly to the labor and service of the temple, and I Chron 25:1 may have been in the mind of the possible interpolater. Accordingly, an early scribe, thinking that the context should mention the temple, may have interpolated the intrusive words. If so, he was almost surely wrong. "Service" in the Hebrew Bible can also be secular, as at I Chron 26:30 and II Chron 12:8, and especially at I Sam 8:16. The draftsman and our author probably saw nothing wrong in Simon's use of the power given kings at I Sam 8:16, to conscript men and animals for *his* service. Two minuscule manuscripts (93 and 96) do have a reading which can be rendered "his service" (*ton ergon autou*). Cf. Dan Th. 2:49, 3:12, and Greek III Kings 5:30, 9:23. On the other hand, the translator or an early scribe may have found incredible the use by heroic Simon of so tyrannical a prerogative and accordingly may have interpolated the intrusive words and changed "his" to "its" (*autôn* with antecedent *ta hagia*); by so doing he would have Simon here as in vs. 43 attending to the service of the sanctuary, not conscripting labor for his own purposes. I suspect, however, that the erring scribe is also responsible for introducing the possessive adjective *autôn* into the text and that the reading of 93 and 96 is a learned scribe's correction. Therefore, I have omitted the possessive adjective and translated simply "services."

43. One would expect the high priest to have full control of the sanctuary, but Onias III faced the opposition of Simon of the clan of Bilgah (see NOTE on II 3:4), and Sadducean high priests later were curbed by Pharisaic supervisors (To. *Yoma* 1:8; TB *Yoma* 19b). Here the people give Simon full power over the temple.

Simon now receives from the people the royal and noble prerogatives of being obeyed and of wearing purple and using a gold brooch. See on vs. 44 and Bikerman, *Institutions*, pp. 32, 42–43.

The practice of using Simon's name in the dating formula of documents, mentioned already at 13:42, may have been voluntary. Now the people make it compulsory.

44. The grants by the people to Simon and his heirs are irrevocable (cf. 11:36). Simon's future enactments are to have the force of law. To prevent subversion, all meetings in Judaea must have his permission. The privileges of wearing purple and of using a gold brooch, shared in the Seleucid empire by courtiers (Bikerman, *Institutions*, pp. 42–43), are given by the Jews here to Simon alone.

45. The people place the penalty of death on those who would violate the provisions of the document; cf. Ezra 6:11 and 7:26 and Wilhelm Larfeld, *Griechische Epigraphik*, 3d ed. (München: Beck, 1913), pp. 408–9. The Greek *enochos estai* (literally, "shall be liable") means the death penalty, as is clear from the use of the same Greek expression at Lev 20:9, 11, 12, 13, 16, 27.

46. The message broadcast by the herald (see above, on vs. 28) ends with vs. 45. The draftsman goes on to report that the people consented to the broadcast proposal; cf. Esther 9:23, 28, as explained in Appendix IV.

47. Since the people's grant to Simon gave him not only privileges but heavy responsibilities, his consent had to be recorded. On Simon's titles, see above, on vs. 27, and on vss. 42–43.

48–49. At the end of parallel documents stand similar provisions for permanent copies of the document to be placed on public view and for a copy to be delivered to the beneficiary. See Larfeld, pp. 410–16; Cooke, no. 33, lines 4–5; and OGIS 737, lines 20–22. The treasury here is probably the temple treasury. See NOTE on II 3:6.

XXXIV. SIMON IS BOLD TO
ANTIOCHUS VII
(15:1–36)

15 ¹ Antiochus son of King Demetrius sent a letter from the islands of the sea to Simon, high priest and prince of the nation of the Jews, and to the entire nation. ² Its content was as follows:

"King Antiochus to Simon, high priest and prince of the nation and to the nation of the Jews, greeting.

³ "Whereas: certain traitors have seized power over the kingdom of our ancestors, and I am determined to assert my claim to the kingdom in order to restore it to its former state; I have raised a large force of mercenary soldiers and have had warships fitted out; ⁴ I intend to land in our territory in order to punish those who have ruined our domains and laid waste many cities in my kingdom— ⁵ therefore, I now confirm for you all the exemptions conceded to you by the kings who preceded me, and all other awards which they conceded to you. ⁶ I grant you permission to strike your own coinage as currency for your country. ⁷ Jerusalem and the temple are to be free. All the armaments which you have fabricated and the fortifications which you have built and now hold shall remain in your hands. ⁸ From now on and for all time you are released from any debt to the royal treasury and from any future royal dues. ⁹ When we shall have established our rule over our kingdom, we shall confer great honor upon you and your nation and your temple, so that the whole land will know of your distinction." ¹⁰ In the year 174, Antiochus came ashore into the land of his ancestors. All the troops rallied to him, so that only a few were left with Tryphon. ¹¹ Antiochus pursued Tryphon, who fled to Dora by the sea, ¹² for he knew that his position was desperate since the troops had deserted him. ¹³ Antiochus laid siege to Dora with a force of one hundred twenty thousand warriors and eight thousand cavalrymen. ¹⁴ He surrounded the town, while his ships joined the siege on the sea side. He pressed the town hard by land and by sea and allowed no one to leave or enter,

$$15=14{:}24b \qquad 20=14{:}24g$$
$$16=14{:}24c \qquad 21=14{:}24h$$
$$17=14{:}24d \qquad 22=14{:}24i$$
$$18=14{:}24e \qquad 23=14{:}24j$$
$$19=14{:}24f \qquad 24=14{:}24k$$

25 (. . .) as he brought his forces up against the town continually and constructed siegeworks.[a]

26 Simon sent a force of two thousand picked men to assist him, along with silver and gold coin and considerable equipment. 27 The king, however, refused to accept them and repudiated all his previous agreements with Simon, treating him with hostility. 28 Indeed, the king sent Athenobius, one of his Friends, to hold discussions. Athenobius brought the following message: "You are holding Joppe and Gazara and the Akra in Jerusalem, cities of my kingdom. 29 You have laid waste their territories and caused grave damage in our domains, and you have seized many districts of my kingdom. 30 Accordingly, deliver over to me the cities you have captured and the taxes of the districts outside the borders of Judaea over which you have seized control, 31 or else pay five hundred talents of silver as compensation for the territory and five hundred more talents for the damage you have done and for the taxes due from the cities. Otherwise, we shall come and make war on you."

32 When Athenobius, the king's Friend, came to Jerusalem and saw Simon's splendor, the gold and silver drinking vessels on his sideboard, and his numerous retinue, he was astonished. When he had delivered to him the king's message, 33 Simon replied, "We have not taken land that is not ours nor have we conquered anything that belongs to others. Rather, we have taken our ancestral heritage which had been unjustly conquered by our enemies using one opportunity or another. 34 Now we, seizing our opportunity, lay claim to our ancestral heritage. 35 As for Joppe and Gazara, which you demand, those cities were causing grave damage to our people and our country. In payment for them we are ready to give a hundred talents.

Athenobius gave him no reply, 36 but angrily returned to the king and reported this conversation to him, telling him also of Simon's splendor and of all that he had seen. The king was furious.

[a] On the displacement of vss. 15–24, see introductory Note to 14:16–24k. On the manuscript readings of vs. 25, see Note ad loc.

NOTES

15 1-14, 25-26. Josephus stopped drawing on First Maccabees after 14:15 and turned to other sources. See introductory NOTE to 14:16-24k. With our passage, Josephus (*AJ* xiii 7.2-4.223-29) may well have resumed paraphrasing First Maccabees. The narrative he drew from elsewhere focused on Seleuceia and the actions of Antiochus VII (see below, on vss. 1 and 10). Hence, Josephus narrated first Antiochus VII's acts up to the siege of Tryphon in Dora and then turned back to mention Antiochus VII's letter to Simon and Simon's aid in response to it. Thus, Josephus may have believed that the order of the events was the same as given here by our author. The fact that Josephus or his secretary used the present tense to express Demetrius' sending of the letter and Simon's acceptance of it does not prove the contrary. On the use of the present tense for the perfect or pluperfect, see Raphael Kühner and Bernhard Gerth, *Ausführliche Grammatik der griechischen Sprache: Satzlehre,* 3d ed. (Hannover and Leipzig: Hahn, 1898-1904), I, 136. Otherwise, Josephus' narrative becomes very improbable. Once he had defeated Tryphon and put him under siege, Antiochus VII was unlikely to make the sweeping concessions offered in vss. 5-9. Josephus' ambiguous use of the present tense here may have been deliberate. It left Josephus contradicting neither our author's account nor his own at *BJ* i 2.2.50-51, where he said that Simon's aid helped in the defeat of Tryphon.

1-2. Antiochus VII Euergetes was the younger son of Demetrius I and was the younger brother of Demetrius II. According to Justin xxxvi 1.8, Antiochus VII was still a "boy" (*puero admodum*) when he defeated Tryphon. He certainly was quite young, since Demetrius I married at some time after his accession in 162 B.C.E. Antiochus VII's popular nickname was "Sidetes," a reflection of his having grown up in the Pamphylian city of Side (FGH 260, F 32.17). He bears the cult-epithet Euergetes on his royal coins. Only Josephus gives him the epithets "Soter" (*AJ* xiii 7.1.222, 10.1.271) and "Eusebes" (*AJ* xiii 8.2.244). The news of the capture of Demetrius II reached Antiochus at Rhodes (Appian *Syriakê* 68). In Hebrew, the expression "islands of the sea" refers to the islands and coastlands of the Aegean and eastern Mediterranean, mostly those inhabited by Greeks; see NOTE on 8:11. Antiochus VII was the last Seleucid to prove himself an able king. On his reign (139/8-129 B.C.E.), see Bevan, II, 236-46, and Thomas Fischer, *Untersuchungen zum Partherkrieg Antiochos' VII.*

Already in the letter, Antiochus VII has usurped the title "king." His brother's fall into the hands of the Parthians left the succession to the Seleucid throne even more uncertain than it had been after the murder of Seleucus IV, when there was Seleucus' helpless little son Antiochus in Antioch, and Seleucus' older but still very young son Demetrius as a hostage in Rome, and Seleucus' adult and able brother Antiochus in Athens. There was also Seleucus' murderer, the powerful minister Heliodorus. See NOTE on 1:10. Now, Demetrius II was not dead and could be released at any time deemed expedient by the Parthian king. Back in Seleuceia-by-the-Sea were the forceful queen Cleopatra Thea and her children, among whom there were two sons (see Justin xxxix 1.9). Cleopatra had the support of an army (J. *AJ* xiii 7.1.221; Diodorus xxxiii 28; Poseidonius *apud* Athenaeus viii 333c–d; Strabo xvi C758). Tryphon still held much of Syria (J. *AJ* xiii 7.1.222). On succession in the Seleucid empire, see Bikerman, *Institutions*, pp. 17–20.

Antiochus could not enter a struggle with such many sided potentialities unless he had ample resources and backing. On his possible resources, see below, on vs. 3. Against Tryphon, what better backing could he seek by offering concessions than the backing of the Jews? The Jews had learned to hate the deceitful murderer of Jonathan and had balked Tryphon's campaign in their own country.

On Simon's titles, see NOTE on 14:27. Though the Greek in vs. 1 has "priest" (*hiereus*), not "high priest" (*archiereus*), there can be no doubt that the text means "high priest," as at Diodorus xxxiv–xxxv 1.3 and Neh 13:4. Accordingly, Antiochus VII here recognizes Simon's titles as well as the status of the Jews as a privileged *ethnos* (see NOTE on 1:4, *nations*).

3. The Greek translator here has chosen the most usual Greek word (*epeidê*) to express "whereas" (see NOTE on 14:29–49), though the word seems not to have been so used elsewhere in the epistolary style of the Hellenistic kings. See Welles, *Royal Correspondence*, index, s.v. The equivalent word *epei* was so used by the Pergamene and Pontic chanceries (Welles, nos. 67 and 73), and very common in royal letters are Greek participial expressions of the sort that would emerge as "whereas" (*epeidê*) clauses on being translated into Hebrew and retranslated into Greek (see Welles, nos. 9, 22, 36, 70).

traitors. See NOTE on 14:24h. Antiochus VII refers to Tryphon and his regime as well as to the Parthians.

I have raised . . . fitted out. How did Antiochus VII carry out these costly enterprises? It is unlikely that anything was left of the treasure Demetrius I had sent to Knidos (see NOTE on 10:67–68). Perhaps mercenaries and investors were attracted to Antiochus' risky bid for power by the prospect of sharing in the wealth of the Seleucid empire. Had the young man already been successful as a condottiere? Did he draw on the experienced sailors of his adopted city of Side (see Livy xxxv 48.6)? Had he been successful as a pirate operating from that notorious base (see Strabo xiv 3.2, C664)?

4. Antiochus in his propaganda assumes the posture of avenger of wanton injustice. Simon and the Jews had ample reason to welcome a power who would punish Tryphon.

5. Antiochus confirms here only concessions made to *Simon* (*soi*) by previous kings; thus he can still claim he did not cede Ptolemais (offered by Demetrius I to Jonathan at 10:39) or the Akra (offered by Demetrius II to Jonathan at 11:41–42) or Joppe or Gazara; cf. vs. 28.

exemptions. I follow here the reading *aphemata* of AS*V (cf. La$^{X V}$ *oblationes*). Kappler wrongly accepted the reading *aphairemata* ("deductions") of A (cf. La^{L} *ablationes*), which is probably an early scribal error, a result of the common use of the latter word in the Greek Pentateuch (Exod 29:27, etc.). Cf. 10:28, 13:37.

6. The privilege of issuing coinage was no longer rare in the Seleucid empire; see Introduction, pp. 115–18, 120–21, and NOTE on 14:24j, *Arados*. Within the empire still only the king could coin in silver or gold. If Arados began to coin in silver from 138/7 B.C.E. the fact shows that the city was independent. See Bikerman, *Institutions*, pp. 231–35; Seyrig, *Notes on Syrian Coins*, pp. 17–18. Antiochus VII here (in the following verse, 7) frees only Jerusalem, not Judaea, and silver is not mentioned. Hence, surely he gives Simon only the right to coin in bronze.

There is no evidence Simon ever made use of the right of coinage, which Antiochus VII was probably quick to revoke. See B. Kanael, "The Beginning of Maccabean Coinage," IEJ 1 (1950), 170–75, and "The Historical Background of the Coins 'Year Four . . . of the Redemption of Zion.'" BASOR 129 (February 1953), 18–19. Perhaps Simon also had to face the opposition of Jews who held that the Decalogue prohibited Jews from making coins for themselves (Exod 20:4; Deut 5:8). The whole line of Hasmonaean rulers may have abstained from coining in silver because of religious scruples if they held that Haggai 2:8 forbade Jews from doing so without express permission from God.

7. "Free" as applied to a community was a vague term, ordinarily accompanied by more specific words defining its content, such as "autonomous" (having its own local government under its own laws and its own freely chosen native authorities), "tax-exempt" (*aphorologêtos*), "exempt from garrisons" (*aphrourêtos*), "sacred" (*hiera*), and "having the right of asylum" (*asylos*). See NOTE on 10:31, and Bikerman, *Institutions*, pp. 133–56. Such privileges could be simultaneously conferred on a temple and on the community containing it; see Welles, *Royal Correspondence*, no. 70 (cf. Welles, no. 69, and Syll.³ 781).

However, one wonders if the text here is correct. Demetrius I offered to make Jerusalem "sacred and tax exempt" (*hagia kai apheimenê*) at 10:31 (the use of *hagia* instead of *hiera* is a peculiarity of biblical-translation Greek). In our verse, too, the translator may have written *Ierousalêm . . . kai hagia einai kai eleuthera*, "Jerusalem shall be both sacred and free" (La^V has "Jerusalem shall be sacred and free," and La^X has "Jerusalem shall be free and sacred"). An early scribe may have misunderstood and gone on to produce the reading *Ierousalêm . . . kai ta hagia einai eleuthera*, "Jerusalem and the temple shall be free." If so, I suspect that in the original Greek of Antiochus' letter, "free" was *asylos*, "having the right of asylum," which could easily become "free" after being translated twice. "Sacred and having the right of asylum" is a common formula in this period. See Bikerman, *Institutions*, pp. 149–56.

Antiochus' choice of words here leaves him the right to retain any forts which Simon had built and then lost. Jamnia may have been such a fort; see NOTE on 14:7.

8. Antiochus renounces the right to make claims such as Tryphon made at 13:15–16. Such renunciations, however, could be canceled by the king, especially in the absence of an irrevocability clause (cf. 11:36, and see Bikerman, *Institutions*, pp. 137–40). Antiochus soon asserted the sort of claims he here renounces (see vss. 28–31).

10. The year 174 Sel. Mac. ran from October 15, 139, through October 4,

138 B.C.E. The dated coins of Antiochus VII begin immediately, in 174 Sel. Mac. (Seyrig, *Notes on Syrian Coins,* p. 13). Our author passes over Antiochus' difficult struggle. At first, Tryphon's control of the coastal cities was sufficient to bar Antiochus from access to Seleucid territory. Evidently, even Cleopatra Thea in Seleuceia at first was hostile to his claims (J. *AJ* xii 7.1.221). Finally however, Cleopatra and her supporters decided that the safest policy was for her to admit Antiochus to Seleuceia, recognize his claims, and marry him (ibid., section 222). Indeed, Antiochus' accession in Seleuceia brought about a mass desertion of Tryphon's troops to the legitimate Seleucid claimant.

11. Dora (Dor) was a Phoenician town, south of Mount Carmel; see Map 14, p. 538, and M. Avi-Yonah, "Dōr," Enc. Bib., II (1954), 580–81 (in Hebrew). Cf. J. *AJ* xiii 7.2.223: "Antiochus . . . set out to fight Tryphon, defeated him in battle, drove him out of inland Syria into Phoenicia, whither he pursued him and besieged him when he took refuge in Dora, a fortress difficult to take." Tryphon and the house of Alexander Balas appear to have had the sympathies of Phoenician Dor, Ptolemais, Byblos, and Orthosia, although Sidon and Tyre were loyal to Demetrius II; see vs. 37 and NOTES on 11:63–64 and 13:41.

13. The numbers are probably vastly exaggerated; see Bikerman, *Institutions,* p. 67. Nevertheless, Antiochus' regular Seleucid troops could well have been augmented by large forces contributed by towns and peoples who had learned to hate Tryphon.

14. See vs. 3.

15–24. See introductory NOTE to 14:16–24k, and NOTE on 14:24b–24k.

25. I have omitted from my translation part of our verse although it stands in all witnesses to the text. They all have "King Antiochus encamped against [="besieged"] Dora in the second [*en têi deutêrai*], continually bringing up his forces against the city and constructing siegeworks and he shut Tryphon up so that one could neither leave nor enter." The main burden of our verse would then be superfluous after vs. 14. Why should our author repeat that Antiochus VII put Dora under close siege?

The words *en têi deuterai* ("in the second") are also puzzling. If they mean "in the suburb" (cf. Zeph 1:10), our verse would imply that Antiochus VII moved his siege camp from one site near Dora to another, in the suburb. But in biblical style, when a camp is moved, the author says so explicitly. Since no month or year is given, the words cannot be part of a date. To interpret them as meaning "on Monday" would also leave them pointless in our context. *"Deuterai"* is a feminine adjective, and in Greek translations from the Hebrew Bible, the feminine adjective without a noun is never used to express "for the second time," "in the second instance." However, a similar expression with a feminine adjective occurs frequently in papyri from Ptolemaic Egypt (*eg deuteras;* see Mayser, II¹, 26–27). This would suggest that a hand other than our Greek translator's added the words. Indeed, the original reading of our verse probably had only the words represented in my translation. When 14:24b–24k were displaced into our context, the participles, which originally depended on the verb "pressed hard" in verse 14, dangled. An early scribe, believing that words had fallen out, supplied by conjecture words to complete the "mutilated" verse. If so, the displacement of 14:24b–24k probably occurred not with the Hebrew original but with the Greek translation. Other-wise, the Greek translator probably would not have left the participles dangling and would have written *to deuteron* or *en tôi deuterôi* (Greek Job 33:14), not *en têi deuterai* in filling out the problematic text.

26. Here, if not before, Simon signified his acceptance of Antiochus VII's overtures in vss. 2–9.

27. The king no longer needed to make the sweeping concessions offered in vss. 5–9 and retracted them all. See above, on vss. 5, 6, 8.

28–29. On the office of Friend, see NOTE on 2:18. Since Joppe and Gazara and the Akra are said to have territories and since a Greek is speaking, "cities" here is probably a technical term, not a mere synonym of "town." A city (*polis*) was a privileged urban unit with its own local government and with control of its own rural territory; see Bikerman, *Institutions*, pp. 141–63. On the Akra as a *polis*, see Introduction, pp. 118–19, 123–24.

Beyond the three cities, Simon held districts which were outside Judaea as defined by the Seleucid authorities. These included at least Akkaron (10:89) and Adida (12:38, 13:13), and the fourth name (11:57). The first three names had been ceded by a legitimate Seleucid (11:34).

30–31. Antiochus does not demand the taxes formerly paid by the in-habitants of Judaea as it was defined by the Seleucid authorities. Simon is only to pay back the fruits of his "aggression." The sums demanded are large, but Simon could probably have paid them. See 11:28 and NOTE on 14:24a.

32–36. Our author's language may reflect the prophesy at Isa 52:13–15.

32. *gold and silver drinking vessels*. The Hasmonaean princes had received the right to use them only from Antiochus VI (11:58) and perhaps from Alexander Balas (see NOTE on 10:89), whose reigns Antiochus VII viewed as illegitimate.

retinue. So I have translated the obscure Greek word *parastasin*. The related word *stasin* is similarly used at I Kings 10:5 ("the attendance [of his ser-vants]"), and Symmachus uses *parastasin* to render *ṣābā* ("service") at Num 8:24.

33–34. Greek international law recognized the right to retake one's ancestral heritage which had fallen into the hands of others; see E. Bickermann and J. Sykutris, "Speusipps Brief an König Philipp," *Berichte über die Verhand-lungen der Sächsischen Akademie der Wissenschaften zu Leipzig: philologisch-historische Klasse*, vol. LXXX (1928), Heft III, pp. 27–29, 40. Seleucid kings had insisted on that principle as well as on the right of possession by con-quest; see Livy xxxiii 40 and Polybius xxxviii 20.6–8. The Jews' claims based on divine promises to their ancestors and on previous conquest should have had at least equal validity.

For *kairos* (Hebrew *'ēt*) as "opportunity," cf. Ecclus 12:16.

35–36. As a good diplomat, Simon does not attempt to argue that Joppe and Gazara lay within the confines of the promised land or once belonged to Solomon (II Chron 2:15; Josh 21:21; I Kings 9:15–17). The Seleucid authorities might not have conceded the validity of the evidence. Simon claims the cities by right of conquest in just wars of retribution, a principle recognized in Greek international law. See Bickermann and Sykutris, pp. 27–28.

The Greek in vs. 35 is ungrammatical, whether through a slip of the translator or through a small scribal error. The sense, however, is clear.

Simon's offer was large enough so that if accepted by the king it would give the Jews a claim to have made restitution, yet so small that it amounted to defiance.

XXXV. SIMON AND SONS ROUT
KENDEBAIOS
(15:37–16:10)

15 [37] When Tryphon embarked on board a ship and escaped to Orthosia, [38] the king appointed Kendebaios commander-in-chief of the coastal region and gave him forces of infantry and cavalry, [39] with orders to establish bases against Judaea. In particular, he ordered him to fortify Kedron and Shaarayim[a] and to wage war on our people. Meanwhile, the king undertook the pursuit of Tryphon. [40] Kendebaios came to Jamnia and began to harass our people by invading Judaea and kidnaping and murdering our people. [41] On fortifying Kedron, he stationed there cavalrymen and troopers to make sallies as highwaymen on the roads of Judaea in accordance with the king's commands.

16 [1] John came up from Gazara and reported to his father Simon the outrages being perpetrated by Kendebaios. [2] Thereupon, Simon summoned his two eldest sons, Judas and John, and said to them, "I and my brothers and the older generations of our family have fought the enemies of Israel from my youth down to the present day, and many times have we succeeded in rescuing Israel. [3] Now, however, I have grown old, whereas you, thanks to His mercy, have reached the age of competence. Take my place and the place of my brothers. Go, and champion the cause of your nation, and may the help of Heaven be with you." [4] Simon raised from the land a force of twenty thousand picked warriors and cavalrymen, and they marched out against Kendebaios. They spent the night at Modeïn. [5] On rising in the morning, they marched out into the plain. There, a large force of infantry and cavalry confronted them. Between the two armies there was a rushing brook. [6] Simon and his army halted opposite the enemy. When Simon saw that the people were afraid to cross the brook, he plunged across first. When the men saw him, they plunged across after him. [7] He distributed his army, assigning cavalry to each infantry unit, for the

---

[a] See NOTE on 39–41, middle.

enemy cavalry were very numerous. [8] They sounded the trumpets, and Kendebaios was routed with his army. Many of them fell slain, and the survivors fled to their fortress. [9] Though John's brother Judas was then wounded, John pursued them as far as Kedron, which Kendebaios had fortified. [10] The enemy fled to the forts in the open country around Azotus. John set fire to it. Two thousand of the enemy fell. John returned safe to Judaea.[b]

NOTES

15:37–39. Ancient warships were crowded and uncomfortable, and the crews had to put into shore frequently, so that even the best blockade might be evaded. See F. E. Adcock, *The Greek and Macedonian Art of War* (University of California Press, 1967), pp. 37–38.

Orthosia was a Phoenician city; see Map 12, p. 536 and NOTE on 15:11. If our text is sound, our author neglected to tell of Tryphon's end. Generally, our author does not follow the pattern of works on the deaths of persecutors. Nevertheless, we are nearing what was the end of the ancient scroll, and material may have been lost by tearing or friction. We learn elsewhere that Tryphon before reaching Orthosia passed through Ptolemais (Charax, FGH 103, F 29). From Orthosia he turned inland to his original base of popularity, the region of Apameia (see NOTE on 11:39, and introductory NOTE to 14:1–3). There, after a siege by Antiochus VII, he perished (J. *AJ* xiii 7.2.224; Appian *Syriakê* 68; Justin xxxvi 1.8; cf. Frontinus *Strategemata* ii 13.3), by suicide according to Strabo xiv 5.2, C 668. The omission by Josephus of Orthosia joins the omission in our text of Tryphon's end, to suggest that matter was indeed lost at this point from the scrolls of First Maccabees before the time of Josephus.

38. The name "Kendebaios" has close parallels in Thrace and Asia Minor; see A. Wilhelm, "Griechische Grabinschriften aus Kleinasien," *Sitzungsberichte der Preussischen Akademie der Wissenschaften, Philosophisch-historische Klasse,* 1932, p. 858. Josephus adds that Kendebaois was a member of the Order of the King's Friends (*AJ* xiii 7.3.225). He need have had no other source than First Maccabees. It was legitimate to infer that one who received the high post of commander-in-chief of the coastal region was a Friend of the king.

With the interior of southern Palestine north of Idumaea now under Simon's control, Kendebaios' province was naturally restricted to the seacoast, much of it still in hands loyal to Antiochus VII. Nevertheless, Kendebaios' province probably was not a new geographical unit. Simon's office at 11:59 suggests that the same unit existed under Antiochus VI. See Bengtson, *Strategie,* II, 178. A "commander in chief" (*epistratêgos*) is nowhere else attested in

[b] The text may be slightly disarranged. See NOTE ad loc.

extant records of the Seleucid empire. In the Ptolemaic empire beginning in the second century B.C.E. a man bearing that title had charge of the entire territory (*chôra*) of Egypt except for the few Greek cities. The *epistratêgos* there had under him the governors (*stratêgoi*) of the districts (*nomoi*). See Bengtson, *Strategie*, III, 121–27.

39–41. Our passage implies that Kedron was near Jamnia. Abel identified Kedron with the modern village of Qaṭra near the brook Sorek and thus on a good route into Judaea; see Map 13, p. 537.

Where I have "and Shaarayim" in vs. 39, the Greek text literally has "and to strengthen the gates" (*kai ochyrôsai tas pylas*). Hebrew idiom would require "its gates" if the gates were those of Kedron. Alert scribes seem to have been puzzled: ALaL X have *poleis* ("towns") for *pylas,* but they are unlikely to be correct, since one would then expect the towns to be named. The translator has probably taken the proper noun "Shaarayim" and mis-read it as $\check{s}^{e\prime}\bar{a}r\bar{\imath}m$ ("gates"). The two words are spelled identically in vowelless Hebrew. Shaarayim was near Kedron, along the brook Sorek. See I Sam 17:52; Josh 15:36. In my translation I have omitted *ochyrôsai* ("strengthen") as a mere synonym of "fortify." The echo of I Sam 17:52 in 16:9–10 suggests that our author indeed meant to write "Shaarayim."

Our author uses language connoting crimes and provocative acts to describe Kendebaios' operations.

16:1–7. If Kendebaios had driven John from Gazara, our honest author would probably have said so, especially since John later won glory in driving Kendebaios from the entire area. Rather, it seems that John was wary of entering on his own authority a war against a royal Seleucid army and "came up" (to Jerusalem) to consult his father. Thereupon, aging Simon invited his sons to assume such authority and also to take over from him the task of leading the army in combat. He did not, however, abdicate any of his own authority; see 16:14.

Our verses have been misconstrued by *L* and by modern commentators as meaning that the sons took full charge of the campaign against Kendebaios. Our author was a careful writer, and the third-person singular subject of the main verbs in vss. 4, 6, and 7, unspecified in Greek, remains Simon and does not become John. Our author first shows how vigorous old Simon was and then goes on to show how his two obedient sons did take over from him the task of leading the army in combat. Only when a wound removes Judas from combat (vs. 9) can John enter as the subject of a verb in the third-person singular.

Josephus' version (*AJ* xiii 7.3.225–27) is partly in accord with this inter-pretation. However, at *BJ* i 2.2.52–53, Josephus had given Simon the chief role in combat. Probably in that passage he was writing from memory; see Intro-duction, pp. 59–61. Now, in writing his later account he corrected errors in the *War* only when he thought it necessary. Even if he perceived the full implications of our text, he probably took vs. 3 as mere rhetoric and did not bother to paraphrase it. He simply reproduced his own earlier account, which in his haste he may have viewed as consistent with our author's.

2. From the order of the names here, Judas might seem to have been

Simon's eldest son. Nevertheless, John is the first son recorded to have held a responsible post (13:53). One could explain that fact through our author's special interest in the father of his patron Alexander Jannaeus. However, the word order may not signify the ages of the sons; perhaps our author as in 16:14 mentioned first the name new to his readers.

older . . . family. Literally, "my father's house," the members of generations older than Simon's sons'.

enemies. A S^c V L' read "wars."

3. "His mercy" and "Heaven" are substitutes, in our author's usual manner, for "God."

The Greek has "my brother," a slip of the translator, since "my brother" and "my brothers" are both '*ḥy* in vowelless Hebrew. Our author and Simon had no reason to refer only to Jonathan here.

4. Simon now has full power and is probably backed by the majority of the people. His forces raised from Judaea dwarf those of Judas. Jonathan's army of forty thousand (12:41) may well have included contingents from outside Judaea, if the figure is trustworthy. Here, for the first time, we hear of Jewish cavalry. One would like to know how Simon got around the strong disapproval of cavalry in biblical sources (Deut 17:16; Isa 2:7, 30:16; Hosea 1:7, 14:4; Micah 5:9; Zech 9:10, etc.). Did he use Zech 14:20 and write pious inscriptions on the horses' equipment? Did he explain that unlike King Solomon, he would not be led astray into tyranny and foreign practices? Probably he acted to fulfill Jer 17:24–25 and 22:3–4.

4–5. Our author does not name the battle site. If the battle took place near Kedron, Simon's army had to march for several hours from Modeïn before reaching the site, and the brook would be the Sorek. If Kendebaios had been threatening Gazara, the battle could have been farther north, near the brook of the valley of Ayyalon, a short march into the coastal plain from Modeïn. See Map 13, p. 537. The second alternative seems by far the more probable.

7. Vigorous old Simon distributed (*dieile;* cf. 6:35) his forces over the battle line. Literally, the Greek has Simon placing the cavalry "in the midst of" the infantry. It is most unlikely that our author believed the cavalry was posted in the center of the line, where it would only be hemmed in by the slower infantry and in a headlong charge would surely have been skewered on the spears of the opposing infantry. In warfare of the Hellenistic age, cavalry was posted on the wings of the battle line in order to harass the flanks of the massed infantry formation of the enemy and break it up; even the unusual tactics at 6:35–38 follow this pattern. In Roman warfare, on the other hand, each legion was a mixed unit, not tightly massed, having its own cavalry. The more flexible Roman tactics had by now prevailed many times over the Graeco-Macedonian patterns. Thus, our author probably means that Simon did not mass his infantry in a single phalanx but, in a manner similar to the Romans, divided his battle line into multiple units, each having its own cavalry. Presumably the terrain made it possible for Simon thus to protect the flanks of each of the units of his line from the superior enemy cavalry. After the enemy was routed, the cavalry of each Jewish unit could press the pursuit.

On the patterns of Hellenistic and Roman warfare, see Adcock, *Greek and*

Macedonian Art of War, pp. 26–27; W. W. Tarn, *Hellenistic Military and Naval Developments* (New York: Biblo & Tannen, 1966), pp. 11–19, 26–30, 61–71; Kromayer and Veith, *Heerwesen*, pp. 121, 136, 144–45, 257–67.

8. *their fortress*. Kedron, as in vs. 9.

9. *as far as*. The scribes were puzzled by the translator's use of *heôs elthein* (the original reading, preserved by A 62 46 106 311), which translated the biblical idiom *'ad bōăkā* (cf. Greek Judg 6:4). The variant readings reflect their puzzlement.

Our author borrows the language of I Sam 17:52, a context which contains *'ad bōăkā* and also involves Shaarayim. See above on 15:39–41.

Our author took care to define Kedron by a clause, "which he [sc. Kendebaios] had fortified" because "Kedron" commonly referred to the gorge east of the temple mount in Jerusalem.

10. The antecedent of "it" is obscure, but from the position of the word one would expect the antecedent to be "Azotus." However, Azotus was a walled town, full of property. It is hard to see how John could have penetrated the walls and set fire to it or, if he penetrated the walls, why he did not take spoils. Earlier Hasmonaean attacks on Azotus present a normal picture: Judas harried the territory of Azotus outside the walls (5:68), and Jonathan penetrated Azotus, fired it, and took spoils (10:83–84). La$^{X\,V}$ have John burning "them" (*eas*), i.e. the forts, but if that had been the original reading, it would be hard to see how the reading "it" of all other witnesses to the text arose.

Since we are near the end of the ancient scroll, where the text could suffer damage, the text may well have been tattered and reassembled in the wrong order. If so, the original probably had "John set fire to it [sc. Kedron]. The enemy fled [from burning Kedron] to the forts in the open country around Azotus. Two thousand of the fugitives fell. John returned safe to Judaea."

Towers in the open country around Azotus are pictured on the ancient mosaic map of the Holy Land found at Medaba in Transjordan.

XXXVI. SIMON'S DEATH
(16:11–24)

16 ¹¹ Ptolemy the son of Abubos received the post of commander over the plain of Jericho, and he had much gold and silver, ¹² for he was the son-in-law of the high priest. ¹³ Intoxicated with his success, he formed the desire to seize control over the country and treacherously plotted to do away with Simon and his sons. ¹⁴ Simon was conducting a tour of inspection of the towns of his country and looking to their needs when he came down to Jericho with his sons Mattathias and Judas, in the year 177 in the eleventh month, which is the month of Shebat. ¹⁵ The son of Abubos treacherously received them in the castle called Dok, which he had built; there he concealed men while he set a sumptuous banquet before his guests. ¹⁶ When Simon and his sons became drunk, Ptolemy and his men emerged from hiding, seized their arms, and rushed into the banquet hall upon Simon and killed him and his two sons and some of their servants. ¹⁷ Thus Ptolemy committed high treason and returned evil for good.

¹⁸ He then wrote an account of what he had done and sent a messenger with it to the king, asking the king to send him troops to assist him, offering to deliver to the king the cities and the taxes. ¹⁹ He sent other men to Gazara to do away with John, and to the regimental commanders he sent letters to come to him, intending to bribe them with silver and gold and with gifts. ²⁰ Others he sent to seize Jerusalem and the temple mount. ²¹ However, a man ran up to John at Gazara and informed him that his father and brothers had perished and told him, "He has also sent men to kill you." ²² On hearing the news, John was stunned, but he seized the men who had come to kill him and slew them, for he knew that they sought to do away with him.

²³ As for the remainder of the history of John, his wars and his valorous deeds and his wall building and his other accomplishments, ²⁴ all these are recorded in the chronicle of his high priesthood, from the time he succeeded his father as high priest.

Notes

16:11–17. On the probable allusions to the murder of Simon and his sons in the literature of the Qumran sect, see Cross, ALQ, pp. 144–52.

11–12. Our author takes care to tell why Ptolemy should have been grateful to his benefactor Simon.

11. Ptolemy bears a Greek name, as did other adherents of the Hasmonaean cause; see NOTE on 12:16. The ambiguities of transliteration into Greek leave many possibilities for the name of Ptolemy's father; the most likely, supported by the Syriac version, is Ḥābub ("beloved"). According to Starcky, the name appears in ancient inscriptions from Palmyra in Syria; see F.-M. Abel and Jean Starcky, Les Livres des Maccabées, p. 215, n. b. The name might be Arabic, but in view of the great variety of the names borne by Jews in this period, one need not infer that Ptolemy or his ancestors were proselytes. Would the powerful Hasmonaean high priest have given his daughter to a person of such descent?

commander. The Greek has stratêgos. One cannot tell whether Simon's regime now gave officials Greek titles or whether stratêgos here translated a Hebrew word. The fertile oasis of Jericho and the surrounding plains were now firmly in Jewish hands (cf. 9:50, 10:12–13). We may assume that the stratêgos had civil as well as military authority. On the history of the district of Jericho around this period, see Avi-Yonah, The Holy Land, pp. 22, 73, 84, 95.

14–22. Our author takes care to distinguish Simon the benefactor, whose dynasty survived, from King Elah son of Baasha, who perished similarly and whose dynasty was exterminated in fulfillment of prophesy (I Kings 16:1–13). We need not doubt that prophesies circulated predicting the doom of Simon, the Cursed Man. See Cross, ALQ, pp. 144–52.

14. On the journey which took him to his death, Simon was not a sinner, but a benefactor of his people.

Since Judas was older than Mattathias (see NOTE on 16:2), perhaps our author mentions Mattathias first as the name new to the reader.

The day of the month is not specified, perhaps because it was the day of the new moon, perhaps because Simon's opponents may have celebrated the date as a festival. Shebat, 177 Sel. Bab., was January 27 – February 25, 134 B.C.E. On the designation of the month both by name and by ordinal number, see Introduction, p. 23.

15. Our author takes care to say that the castle was built by Ptolemy, perhaps to refute the sectarian teaching, that Simon the "Cursed Man" and his sons fulfilled the prophesy at Josh 6:26 (4Q175=4Q Testimonia, lines 21–30; Cross, ALQ, pp. 148–52).

The castle "Dok" has been plausibly located at the summit of the Mount of Temptation; see Abel on our verse and Géographie, II, 307. The mountain has been called *Jebel ed-Dūq* by Arabs, and Byzantine lives of saints speak of a monastery *Douka* on the mountainside, and a spring near the mountain is still called *'Ain Dūq*.

Josephus (*BJ* i 2.3.56; *AJ* xiii 8.1.230) says that Ptolemy fled from the vengeance of John to Dagon, "one of the defense works overlooking Jericho." Nothing compels us to identify Dagon with Dok. It is possible, however, that the site originally bore the pagan name "Dagon" (cf. 10:84), and that Jews with scruples against speaking the names of foreign deities changed the name to the inoffensive "Dok."

As the root meaning of the words in Hebrew and Greek (*mišteh*, *potos*) implies, a "banquet" always involved the drinking of liquor.

16. The word order suggests that Ptolemy and his confederates took their own weapons into their hands, though the words could also mean that they took away the weapons of their unsuspecting victims.

Our author surely means what he says in reporting that the two sons were killed at the same time as Simon (cf. vs. 21). Is he, however, telling the truth? Josephus reports (*BJ* i 2.3–4.54–60; *AJ* xiii 7.4–5.228–35) that Ptolemy long held John's mother and John's two brothers as hostages, that by torturing them before John's eyes Ptolemy forced John to give up the siege of Dagon, and that then Ptolemy killed them.

In neither case could John bear any responsibility for the deaths; contrast Simon's role at 13:14–23, where our author shrank from reporting the fate of Jonathan's sons. Hence, it is hard to see any propagandistic interest behind the discrepancy between our author's account and Josephus'. Do we have here another instance in which Josephus in his haste failed to perceive that his own faulty account in the *War* was at variance with our author's account and thereupon went on to reproduce the account he had given in the *War?* If so, perhaps Ptolemy's only hostage in actual fact was John's mother.

17–20. Far from being "just retribution upon the Cursed Man," Ptolemy's act was a heinous crime, involving treason against the free nation of the Jews. We need not doubt our author's account, that in return for Seleucid support of his own bid for power in Judaea, Ptolemy promised Antiochus VII delivery of the very things Antiochus had fruitlessly demanded of Simon (see 15:30–31). There were probably still Jews who held that God had not signified that His sentence of servitude upon the Jews had been served through to the end. They would view Simon as presumptuous and would tend to back Ptolemy's act of submission to Antiochus VII. On the other hand, most Jews surely welcomed freedom from Seleucid taxation. To face their opposition, Ptolemy would need Seleucid troops.

Ptolemy's project required the elimination of John, Simon's surviving heir. Ptolemy could not hope for mass backing, but he saw a chance to win the army over by offering them rewards.

"Regimental commanders" literally are "commanders of thousands," as at 3:55, Num 31:48, etc.

Not surprisingly, mass hostility foiled Ptolemy's plans to seize Jerusalem and the temple mount (J. *BJ* i 2.3.55; *AJ* xiii 7.4.229).

18. My translation follows the argument of De Bruyne (p. x). He reconstructs the original text to be as I have translated, from the reading of La^B,

et traderet ei civitates eorum et tributa ("and he would deliver to him their cities and the taxes"). La$^{L\ X}$ support La^B except for omitting *ei* ("to him"). It is easy to explain how other readings arose. Our author intended "the king" to be the subject of "send" but "Ptolemy" to be the subject of "deliver." Greek scribes failed to perceive the change of subject. Since it was absurd to speak of the king delivering taxes to Ptolemy, the Greek scribes wrote "territory" (*chôran*) instead of "taxes" (*phorous*). With De Bruyne's reading, Ptolemy promises to fulfill the demands Antiochus VII had made on Simon (15:30–31).

22. John killed the assassins without a trial. He was entitled to do so by Jewish law (TB *Sanhedrin* 72a, "If anyone should come intending to kill you, act first and kill him").

23–24. Our author concludes his book using the style of the books of Kings; cf. II Kings 20:20, etc. See Introduction, p. 62, on the wall building; see NOTE on 1:33–40. John had at least to rebuild the walls of Jerusalem destroyed by Antiochus VII (J. *AJ* xiii 8.3.247; Diodorus xxxiv 1).

One is somewhat surprised to find our author omitting explicit mention of John's claims to have received prophetic power (see Introduction, Part I, n. 8). But there was nothing of the kind in the passages of the books of Kings which served as his models, and he could also assume that his readers could learn of those claims from the chronicle of John's high priesthood.

MAPS

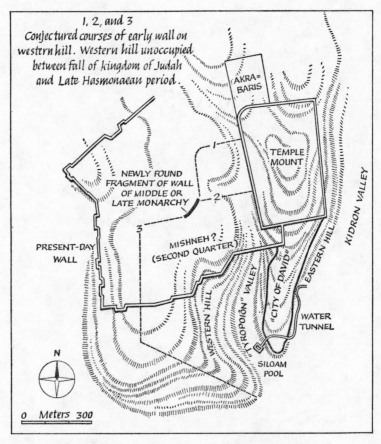

1. The walls of Jerusalem, the "City of David," and the eastern and western hills

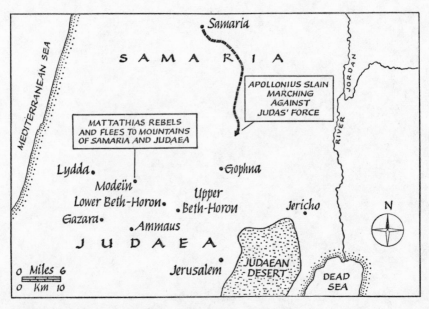

2. The beginnings of the Hasmonaean revolt, 167–165 B.C.E.

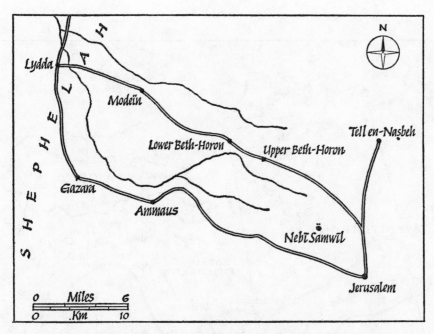

3. The battles of Beth-Horon and Ammaus, between 166 and 164 B.C.E.

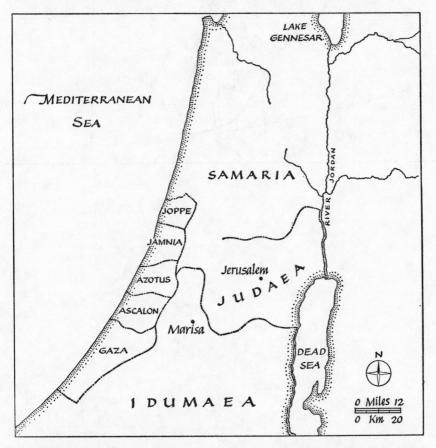

4. Political divisions of territory around Judaea at the beginning of the Hasmonaean revolt, 167–165 B.C.E.

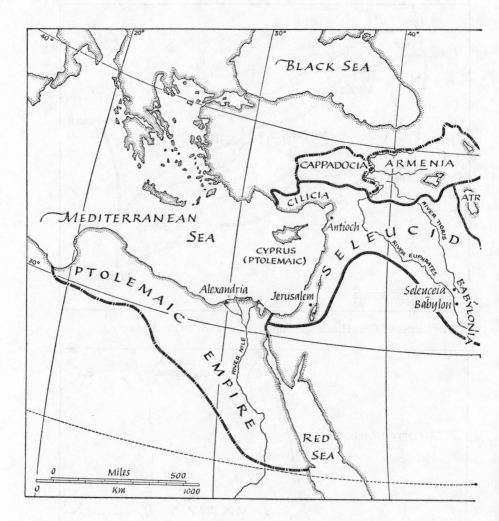

5. Areas important during the last campaigns of Antiochus IV, summer, 165–late autumn, 164 B.C.E.

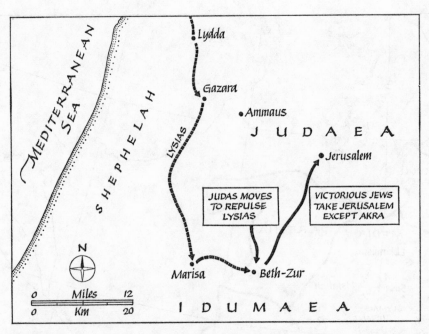

6. The first campaign of Lysias by way of Beth-Zur, 164 B.C.E.

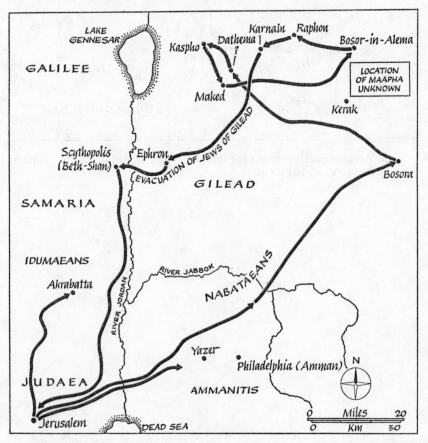

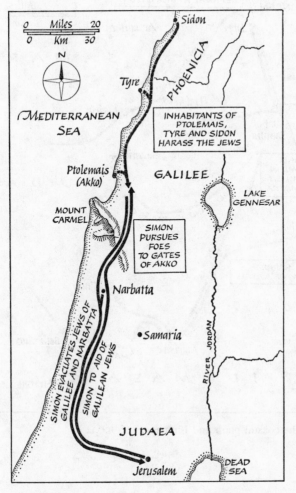

8. Simon's expedition to western Galilee, 163
   B.C.E.

7. *Opposite:* Judas' campaigns against Ammonites and Akrabattene (location of Baianites unknown); the campaign of Judas
   and Jonathan in Galilee, 163 B.C.E.

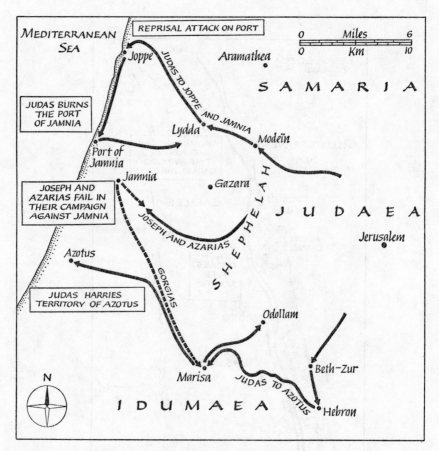

9. Judas in the coastal plain and Idumaea, 163 B.C.E.

10. *Opposite above:* The battle of Beth-Zechariah, 162 B.C.E.

11. *Opposite below:* Sites connected with Judas' last battles, 162–161 B.C.E.

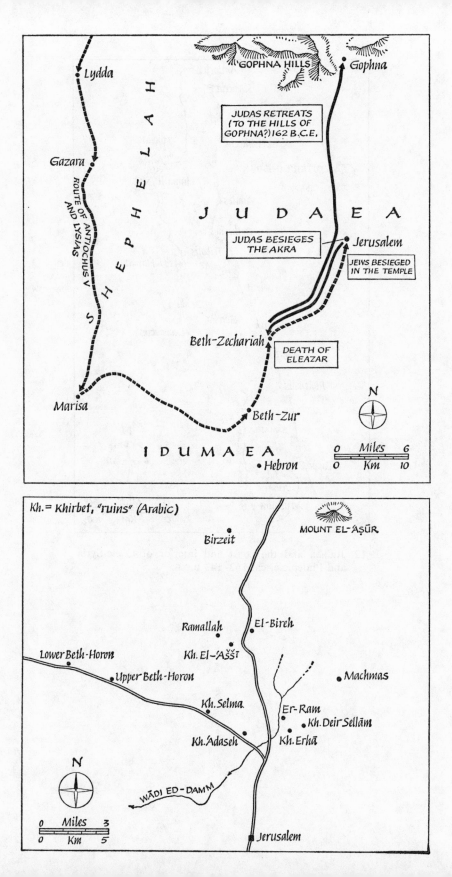

Top map labels:

Lydda

GOPHNA HILLS

Gophna

JUDAS RETREATS
(TO THE HILLS OF
GOPHNA?) 162 B.C.E.

Gazara

S H E P H E L A H

ROUTE OF ANTIOCHUS V
AND LYSIAS

J U D A E A

JUDAS BESIEGES
THE AKRA

Jerusalem

JEWS BESIEGED
IN THE TEMPLE

Beth-Zechariah

DEATH OF
ELEAZAR

N

Marisa

Beth-Zur

I D U M A E A

• Hebron

0   Miles   6

0   Km   10

Bottom map labels:

Kh. = Khirbet, "ruins" (Arabic)

MOUNT EL-ASŪR

Birzeit

Ramallah

El-Bireh

Lower Beth-Horon

Kh. El-ʿAṣṣī

Machmas

Upper Beth-Horon

Kh. Selma

Er-Ram

Kh. Deir Sellām

Kh. ʿAdaseh

Kh. Erhā

N

WĀDJ ED-DAMM

0   Miles   3

0   Km   5

Jerusalem

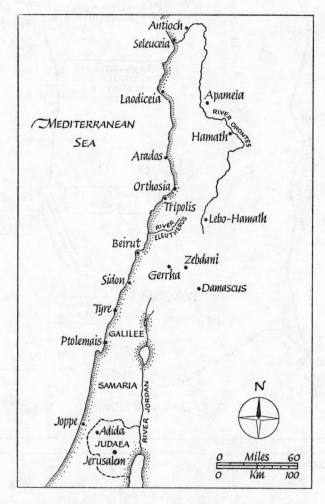

12. Judaea and the coast and interior of Coele-Syria
and Phoenicia, ca. 162–143 B.C.E.

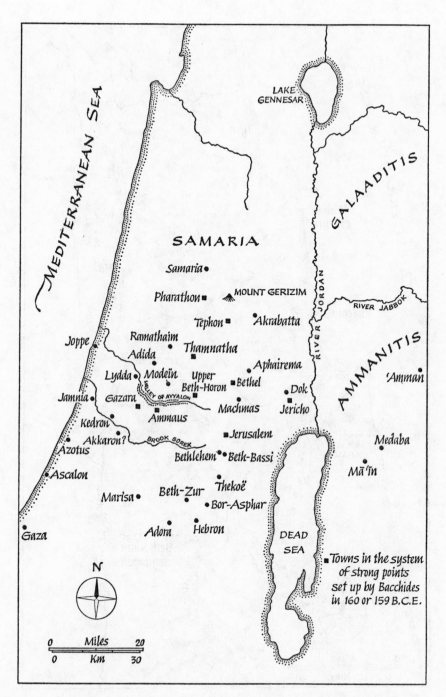

13. Important places in Judaea and her neighbors during the careers of Jonathan and Simon, 160–134 B.C.E.

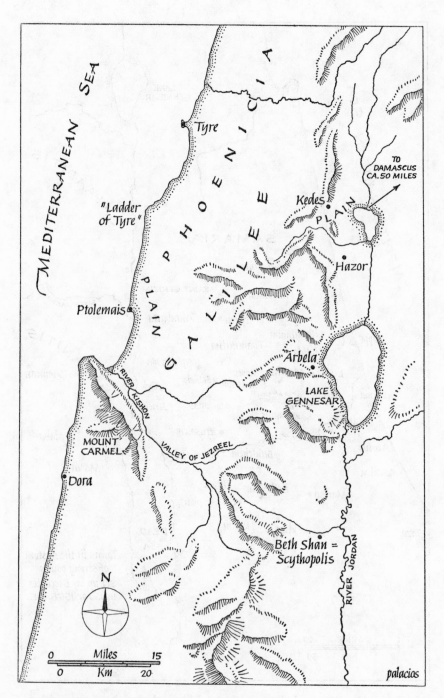

14. Phoenicia, Galilee, and the upper Jordan Valley

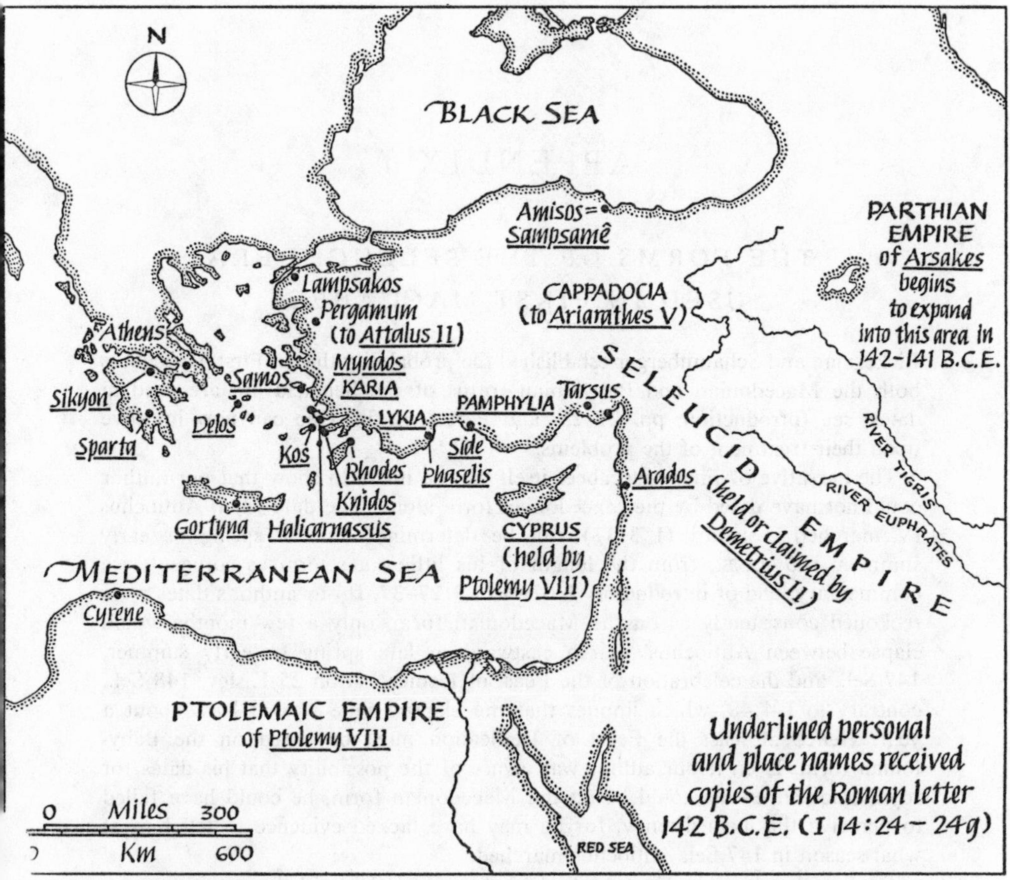
N
BLACK SEA
Amisos=
Sampsamê
PARTHIAN
EMPIRE
of Arsakes
begins
to expand
into this area in
142-141 B.C.E.
Lampsakos
Pergamum
(to Attalus II)
CAPPADOCIA
(to Ariarathes V)
Athens
MynDos
Samos
KARIA
Sikyon
SELEUCID EMPIRE
(held or claimed by
Demetrius II)
Delos
LYKIA
PAMPHYLIA
Tarsus
Sparta
Kos
Side
Rhodes
Phaselis
Arados
RIVER TIGRIS
RIVER EUPHRATES
Knidos
Gortyna
Halicarnassus
CYPRUS
(held by
Ptolemy VIII)
MEDITERRANEAN SEA
Cyrene
PTOLEMAIC EMPIRE
of Ptolemy VIII
Underlined personal
and place names received
copies of the Roman letter
142 B.C.E. (I 14:24 – 24g)
0 Miles 300
0 Km 600
RED SEA

15. Recipients of the Roman letter of 142 B.C.E. and other important contemporary centers in Greece, Asia, and Africa

APPENDIX I

THE FORMS OF THE SELEUCID ERA
USED IN FIRST MACCABEES

Bickerman and Schaumberger established the probability that in First Maccabees both the Macedonian and Babylonian forms of the Seleucid era are used in dates; see Introduction, pp. 21–25, and Part I, n. 54. One can now improve upon their treatment of the problems.

The narrative of First Maccabees itself can be made to show that our author could not have dated by the Macedonian form alone. The date when Antiochus IV marched eastward (I 3:37) can be determined as late spring or early summer, 165 B.C.E., from the length of his little son's term as coregent; see commentary, end of introductory NOTE to I 3:27–37. If our author's dates were reckoned consistently as on the Macedonian form, only a few months would elapse between Antiochus' march eastward in late spring or early summer, 147 Sel., and the celebration of the Feast of Dedication on 25 Kislev, 148 Sel., contrary to I 4:48, which implies that the elapsed time was at least about a year. Hence at least the Feast of Dedication must be dated on the Babylonian form. Even if our author was aware of the possibility that his dates for royal Seleucid events could be on the Macedonian form, he could have failed to perceive the inconsistency, for he may have lacked evidence to tell him at what season in 147 Sel. Antiochus marched.

Two of the dates in First Maccabees for royal Seleucid events, if correct, must be on the Macedonian form. At I 6:16 we learn that Antiochus IV died in 149 Sel. If the date is Babylonian, the year would be from April 16, 163, to April 4, 162; if it is Macedonian, from September 22, 164, to October 9, 163. According to a cuneiform tablet, the news of Antiochus IV's death reached Babylon between November 20 and December 18, 164 B.C.E. (Sachs and Wiseman, *Iraq* 16 [1954], 204, 208–9). Surely the king's death, known in Babylon, could not have been hidden from the Jews for five months. In fact, from Dan 8:14, 25, and from *Megillat Ta'anit* 12 Adar one can deduce that the news of Antiochus IV's death was published in Jerusalem ca. January 28, 163 B.C.E., long before the beginning of 149 Sel. Bab.; see Introduction, p. 43, and Part II, n. 14. On the date at I 7:1, see Bickermann, PW, XIV, 783.

What is the situation with dates of local Jewish history in First Maccabees? Besides the date for the Feast of Dedication, consider the dates in I 10. At I 10:1 our author dates the accession of Alexander Balas in 160 Sel. He goes on (I 10:2–20) to tell first of the efforts of Demetrius I to bid for Jonathan's support, next of Jonathan's use of Demetrius' offers in order to recover hostages from the Akra and fortify Jerusalem and cause the flight of gentile garrisons, and finally of Alexander Balas' bid for Jonathan's support. All these events took time. Thereafter, says our author (I 10:21), Jonathan was invested as high priest on the festival of Tabernacles in the *seventh* month of *160* Sel. Quite apart from the ordinal number of the month, which could have been derived from the biblical verses concerning Tabernacles, the author could not have been using the Macedonian form of the Seleucid era wherein the year number changed with the coming of the autumn month of Tishri, in which Tabernacles falls. Hanhart (*Untersuchungen* p. 61) and Meyer (*Ursprung*, II, 255, n. 3) suggest that our author's 160 could still be 160 Sel. Mac.: we do not know the exact date of the royal Seleucid new year's day and varying intercalation practices could make the royal Seleucid new year begin after Tabernacles. The suggestion is barely possible, and we also have the evidence that our author must have dated the Feast of Dedication in 148 Sel. Bab. Hence, it is best to assume that all dates for events of local Jewish history are on the Babylonian form of the Seleucid era.

A problem arises from the mention of the sabbatical year at J. *AJ* xiii 8.1.230–34. According to I 16:14–16, Simon and two of his sons were murdered in the month of Shebaṭ in the year 177 Sel., a date which should be 177 Sel. Bab.=January–February, 134 B.C.E. However, Josephus reports that John Hyrcanus, the surviving son, who was thirsty for vengeance, was impeded from pressing the siege and capturing the murderer by the advent of the sabbatical year. Before the discovery of the Qumran scrolls, this report was puzzling for a reason other than its chronology: How could the advent of the sabbatical year prevent John from waging war? See e.g. Schürer, I, 35–36. Indeed, after Simon's prosperous reign Judaea must have been well stocked with food. Now, however, we know that the Qumran sect held warfare to be forbidden during the sabbatical year (1QM 2:8–9; cf. Jubilees L2–3, 12–13; and see Yigael Yadin, *The Scroll of the War of the Sons of Light against the Sons of Darkness* [Oxford University Press, 1962], p. 20, n. 1). I shall show elsewhere that in the early years of his reign John Hyrcanus probably tried to win and keep the loyalty of as many Jewish sects as possible. Hence, though Judas Maccabaeus surely waged war in a sabbatical year (I 5–6), John Hyrcanus let a sabbatical year prevent him from taking vengeance on the murderer Ptolemy.

The story at J. *AJ* xiii 8.1.230–34 implies that Simon found time to seek vengeance, between the death of Simon and the beginning of the sabbatical year. We have established the most probable cycle for the sabbatical years; see NOTE on I 6:20. Accordingly, the nearest sabbatical year to Simon's death ran from autumn, 136, to autumn, 135, and the next one ran from autumn, 129, to autumn, 128. Should we make the date of local Jewish history at I 16:14 to be 177 Sel. Mac. (=autumn, 136, to autumn, 135)? Or should we say that vengeful John Hyrcanus waited five years to attack the murderer?

Bickermann (*Gott*, p. 157, n. 2) tried to solve the problem by suggesting that here Josephus departed from his Jewish source to follow a pagan one, and the pagan author had erred on the cycle of sabbatical years. However, one could then ask why even a pagan, if he knew enough to mention the sabbatical year, would make such an error or would even be interested in a local feud of John Hyrcanus and his brother-in-law. Schaumberger, *Biblica* 36 (1955), 430–31, tries to solve the problem by assuming that Josephus was careless when he wrote at *AJ* xiii 8.1.234 that the sabbatical year "began" in the course of the siege when actually Simon's vengeance was frustrated by the dearth which resulted from the aftermath of the sabbatical year. However, scholars have been too ready to assume that Josephus was careless.

The solution probably lies elsewhere. Josephus' source on John Hyrcanus' attempt at vengeance was probably Jewish. If that source gave no dates, the problem is easily solved. Josephus assumed that the warlike prince immediately attempted to avenge his father and brothers, but John Hyrcanus was in no position to do so. Antiochus VII Sidetes was quick to invade (J. *AJ* xiii 8.2.236; 4Q Testimonia as cited in Cross, ALQ, pp. 148–52). Even the threat of his invasion would have kept John Hyrcanus from concentrating his limited forces against the murderer, who had been quick to seek Sidetes' favor (I 16:18). Hence, the attempt at vengeance probably came after Sidetes was no longer a threat.

During the year 130/29, Antiochus Sidetes was away fighting the Parthians. Although John Hyrcanus accompanied Sidetes on the march eastward (J. *AJ* xiii 8.4.250–52), he probably returned westward before Sidetes fell in battle in 129 B.C.E., for Josephus reports (*AJ* xiii 8.4.253–9.1.254) that John Hyrcanus "heard" the news of Sidetes' death and "immediately marched out" to conquer Syrian cities. If John Hyrcanus "heard" of Sidetes' last battle, he was not present at it, and if he "immediately marched out" to conquer, he was then at a secure base, surely his own Judaea. Probably his first target for conquest was his treacherous brother-in-law, upon whom he sought to wreak vengeance. However, Jericho had been fortified and supplied, and the coming of the sabbatical year 129/8 was an added impediment, as we learn from Josephus' narrative.

Josephus himself appears to have been conscious of the difficulty. He may have tried to conceal it; see Appendix VI, near the end. He may also have tried to solve it, in both the *War* and the *Antiquities*. At *BJ* i 2.8.68 he gives the length of the reign of John Hyrcanus as thirty-three years instead of the correct 31 (134–104/3). If John became high priest and prince two years earlier, in Shebaṭ, 175 Sel. Bab.=January–February, 136 B.C.E., he could indeed have been foiled in his quest for revenge by the coming of the sabbatical year 136/5.

When Josephus wrote the *Antiquities*, he knew that John Hyrcanus' tenure of thirty-one years, attested by the high priestly list, was not to be altered; see Appendix VI. Greek historians in his time usually dated by the cycle of Olympiads. Easy computations could be used to connect the cycle of sabbatical years with the cycle of Olympiads. The Olympiad cycle is easy to understand. The first Olympic games, according to tradition, were in 776/5 B.C.E. Accordingly, 776/5 was Olympiad 1, year 1; 775/4 was Olympiad 1, year 2; 774/3 was Olympiad 1, year 3; 773/2 was Olympiad 1, year 4; 772/1 was Olympiad 2, year 1, and so on. A year on the Olympiad system is a sabbatical year if four times (Olympiad number) plus (year number) minus one is divisible by seven. No one could readily compute whether a year was sabbatical from the names of Antiochus VII and John Hyrcanus plus the numerals of their regnal years. Hence, Josephus may have acted deliberately at *AJ* xiii 8.2.236 in dating Antiochus VII's invasion of Judaea in Olympiad

162 (=132–128 B.C.E.). By so doing he could put the interruption of John Hyrcanus' siege of Ptolemy in the sabbatical year 129/8 and solve the problem. In the same passage, however, Josephus also dated Antiochus VII's invasion of Judaea in the fourth year of Antiochus and in the first year of John Hyrcanus, so as to make it come in 135/4, in the immediate aftermath of a speedy attempt by John to avenge his father and brothers. Was Josephus aware of the discrepancy between the date 135/4 unequivocally designated by the regnal years and the date between 132 and 128 indicated by the Olympiad? Few if any readers would have noticed the discrepancy.

APPENDIX II

THE FORM OF THE SELEUCID ERA
USED IN SECOND MACCABEES

According to II 14:3–4, Alcimus came to Demetrius seeking confirmation as high priest in 151 Sel. We do not know how far the irregularities in the Jewish calendar had been corrected by the beginning of 151 Sel. Mac. (September 29, 162 B.C.E.); see NOTES on I 4:36–54 and 7:43. If the date is on a completely uncorrected local Jewish version of the Babylonian Seleucid era, Alcimus waited at least until January 26, 161, before approaching Demetrius. If the date is on a correct Babylonian calendar, Alcimus waited until March 25, 161. But Demetrius became king already in the autumn of 162 (Bickermann, PW, XIV, 783), and since the appointment of the high priest even under the current Jewish law was a royal prerogative (see Introduction, pp. 75–76), Alcimus needed confirmation as soon as Antiochus V ceased to rule. Hence, the Seleucid date at II 14:4 must be on the Macedonian form of the era. This argument refutes the effort of Schaumberger, *Biblica* 36 (1955), 429, to regard the Babylonian form as a possibility.

According to II 13:1, Lysias and Antiochus V invaded Judaea in 149 Sel. According to I 6:49, 53–54, the campaign occurred during the sabbatical year, which probably ran from autumn, 164, to autumn, 163 (see NOTE on I 6:20). Jason of Cyrene had good reason not to mention the sabbatical year; see Introduction, pp. 47–48, 53. On the other hand, the pious author of First Maccabees would not have invented his reference to the sabbatical year, especially since it contradicted his own erroneous date for the siege of the Akra; see NOTE on I 6:20. Furthermore, by June 27, 163, Lysias and Antiochus V seemed to have victory in sight; see Introduction, pp. 43–44. Hence, the campaign may well have begun after 1 Nisan (April 16), 163, at a time when 149 was the number both of the Macedonian and of the Babylonian Seleucid year. There was a still longer period during which the Seleucid year 149, on the unintercalated calendar probably being used by the Jews, coincided with the Macedonian year 149, for 1 Nisan on the unintercalated calendar was February 16; see NOTE on I 4:36–54.

In the case of First Maccabees there are compelling reasons to assume that the author used dates based on two different forms of the Seleucid era. No such reasons exist in the case of the abridgement of Jason's work, so we may assume that both his Seleucid dates follow the Macedonian form, as one could expect from a man of Greek culture who knew much about Seleucid institutions (Bickermann, *Gott,* p. 147) and came not from Babylon or Judaea but from Cyrene.

APPENDIX III

EPISTLE 2

Epistle 2 (abbr. Ep. 2) cannot be what it claims to be: a letter of the Jews in Jerusalem and Judaea, the Council of Elders, and Judas (Maccabaeus) sent to the Jews of Egypt after the death of Antiochus IV and before the Feast of Dedication, asking the Jews of Egypt to celebrate the event simultaneously. The strange account of the death of Antiochus (II 1:13–16) is not an obstacle to the authenticity of Ep. 2. The first reports of the king's death to reach Jerusalem could well have been distorted by rumor, especially with the precedent of the death of Antiochus III (Diodorus xxviii 3, xxix 15; Justin xxxii 2.1–2). The decisive point is chronological. Antiochus died in 164/3 (Bickermann, *Gott*, p. 14, n. 2). His death became known at Babylon in the ninth month of the Babylonian year (British Museum cuneiform tablet BM 35603, published in Sachs and Wiseman, *Iraq* 16 (1954), 204, 208–9), or between November 20 and December 18, 164. Necessarily, Antiochus' death became known at Jerusalem later than at Babylon (see Introduction, p. 43). A festal letter to a large and fairly distant community had to be sent out well in advance. Hence, if the ninth month at Babylon coincided with the ninth Babylonian month (Kislev) on the calendar used at Jerusalem, there would certainly be no time to send Ep. 2 as a festal letter to Egypt.

On the local Jewish calendar at Jerusalem, the ninth month need not have coincided with the ninth month at Babylon (see Introduction, pp. 22–23). In fact, there is evidence to show that the ninth month fell earlier in Jerusalem than it did in Babylon, since the Babylonian calendar had had an intercalary month in 166 (Parker and Dubberstein, p. 41) and the Jews had been unable to intercalate their calendar since 167 (see NOTE on I 4:36–54). Both First Maccabees and the abridged history place the king's death well after the Feast of Dedication, which occurred at the end of the ninth month. Surely, then, the news could not have reached Jerusalem in time to be included in a festal letter like Ep. 2.

One cannot save the authenticity of Ep. 2 by viewing it rather as an invitation to celebrate the first anniversary of Judas' dedication, though the past tense of "he has purified" (aorist: *ekatherisen*) at II 2:18 might so indicate (cf. Kolbe, *Beiträge*, pp. 116–17). Long before Kislev of 163 the Seleucids were besieging Judas' men in Jerusalem (see Introduction, pp. 43–44, 52–53; Appendix II; and NOTE on I 6:20). The siege was long. It ended shortly before 28 Shebaṭ March 2, 163 (*Megillat Ta'anit* 28 Shebaṭ; Bickermann, *Gott,* p. 159), long after the Feast of Dedication. No letter could have been sent from Jerusalem during the siege, and certainly not one like Ep. 2.

Finally, if Ep. 2 had truly been a public letter which reached Egypt before Ep. 1, Ep. 1 would have to alluded to it, not to the obscure Ep. 0 (see Introduction, pp. 35, 36–37).

One may plead that Aristobulus, to whom Ep. 2 is addressed, for some reason refrained from publishing it in 164, but there is no visible reason why Jews living under Ptolemy VI in 164 should not celebrate a Seleucid defeat, so why would Aristobulus have held the letter back from circulation?

In fact, Ep. 2 bears clear signs of being later than Ep. 1. Wherever Ep. 1 is cryptic, Ep. 2 explains matters for a later generation. Jason the Oniad, still notorious in 143, by the time of the pro-Hasmonaean propaganda in Josephus was a mere name unconnected with the wicked apostates. Even in 124 few Egyptian Jews reading Ep. 1 could fully have understood the reference to him in the letter of 143. Hence, the description of the persecution in Ep. 0 as "the events beginning with Jason's rebellion," was paradoxical. The chief villain to posterity was Antiochus IV, not the Jewish sinners against whom he was "the rod of God's wrath." Accordingly, the author of Ep. 2 presents Antiochus IV as the villain and does not mention Jason the Oniad.

The author of Ep. 1 was content with quoting Ep. 0, which strangely omits all mention of dedication or rededication, as if the festival commemorated a mere resumption of interrupted ritual rather than the dedication of a new altar to replace one defiled or the rededication of a desecrated sanctuary. Ep. 0 here may well be deliberately avoiding mention of embarrassing facts; see NOTE on 4:36–54. However, the audience of Ep. 2 was accustomed to the Feast of Purification and Dedication, to the Feast of Lights. To them the reference to the "Festival of Tabernacles in the month of Kislev" was not only obscure; it was incomprehensible. Accordingly, Ep. 2 carefully explains and connects all these appellations ("purification": II 1:18, 36, and 2:16; "dedication": 2:9 and cf. "be sanctified" at 2:8; "lights" connected with dedication: 1:18–36; "Tabernacles" connected with dedication: 2:8–12, and see commentary ad loc.).

Ep. 1 comes from an anonymous group, perhaps to avoid the necessity of seeking the approval of the Hasmonaean prince John Hyrcanus (see I 14:43–45). Ep. 2 comes from the official organs of the Jews in Jerusalem and from the hero Judas.

Furthermore, Epp. 0, 1, and 2 can all be shown to be anti-Oniad propaganda; see Introduction, pp. 34–36, and Bickermann, PW, XIV, 790. Ep. 0 makes the Oniad, Jason, the cause of all the disasters. Ep. 1 condemns the Oniad temple. Ep. 2 is pointedly addressed to a member of the "stock of the anointed priests," i.e. of the Zadokite-Oniad line. To see further how Ep. 2 fits into this sequence, we must consider its probable background in religious and political struggle. Ep. 2, despite its chaotic appearance, is a reasoned attack upon challenges to the holiness of the second temple prevalent at the time; see pp. 40, 58–61, and Cross, ALQ, pp. 101–2. Even loyal adherents of the holiness of the second temple recognized that it lacked important attributes of the first temple. Rabbinic lists of items missing from the second

temple include all but one of those mentioned here in Ep. 2 (the altar of incense).[1]

Onias IV and the partisans of the temple of Leontopolis surely did more
than quote Isa 19:18–19 (see J. *AJ* xiii 3.1.64, 68, 2.71). They must have
claimed that insecure Judaea and the contemporary temple of Jerusalem,
lacking the sacred attributes, were no longer "the rest and the inheritance"
or "the place which the Lord will choose," and hence, that the Oniad temple
of Leontopolis was at least equally legitimate; see Deut 12:8–14; Jer
7:3–15; Ezek 24:21; Lam 2:7; and cf. *M. Zebaḥim* 14:4–8 and J. *AJ* xiii
3.1.65–66. Indeed, they surely claimed their temple was more legitimate, since
it was the seat of the legitimate high priestly line.

The author of Ep. 2 knew that the prophet Jeremiah was much respected
in Egypt, where his prophetic career ended; cf. Philo *De cherubim* 49. The
author of Ep. 2 alludes to the Epistle of Jeremiah at II 2:2, surely because the
Epistle was popular among Egyptian Jews. The literate Jewish community
of Egypt followed with respectful interest the publication of texts from the
authoritative collections at Jerusalem (II 2:14; cf. Bickerman, JBL 63 [1944],
339–62).

The point of the legends of the miraculous fire in the time of Nehemiah
(II 1:19–36) and of the hiding of the tabernacle, ark, and incense altar
(II 2:4–8) is to show from authoritative tradition that the second temple,
whatever its deficiencies, still is chosen and favored by God, who in His own
time will restore what is lacking.

The author of Ep. 2 is neither modest nor cautious in countering the claims
of the Oniads. He boldly asserts that by the time of the purification of the
temple in 164 God restored to Israel four precious gifts: the "kingdom"
(*basileion*), the "inheritance" (*klêronomian*), the "sanctification" (*hagiasmon*),
and the priesthood (*hierateuma*). On the term for "kingdom," cf. Dan LXX
4:34 in Rahlfs' edition and Greek Exod 23:22. Daniel predicted the restoration
of the "kingdom" at 7:22. On the "inheritance," see Deut 12:9. On the priesthood, cf. Exod 19:6 and Greek Exod 23:22. Conspicuously absent in 164 was

---

[1] Fire, ark, cruse of anointing oil, Urim and Thummim, Holy Spirit: TP *Ta'aniyyot*
2:1, p. 65a; *Makkot* 2 end, p. 32a; *Horayot* 3:3, p. 47c; *Shir ha-Shirim Rabbah* to
8:9, par. 3.

Fire, ark, Šᵉkīnāh (Divine Presence), Holy Spirit, Urim and Thummim: TB
Yoma 21b.

Tabernacle and its furniture, ark, vessel of manna, cruse of anointing oil, Moses'
rod, Aaron's rod: *Abot de-Rabbi Nathan*, version A, 41, p. 67a.

Ark, manna, anointing oil, Aron's rod, and the box which the Philistines used to
return the ark: To. *Yoma* 2:15; TB *Yoma* 52b, *Horayot* 12a, *Keritot* 5b; TP *Sheqalim*
6:1, p. 49c; *Soṭah* 8:3, p. 22c.

It is strange to find the altar of incense mentioned here in II 2:5 after no mention
of it in II 2:4. It is just possible that there is a trace here of an otherwise unat-
tested belief that the absence of the original altar of incense impaired the complete-
ness of a Jewish temple. There may be another trace of such a belief in Ep. 1, where
mention of incense is conspicuous by its absence from II 1:8. Elsewhere, Judas and
his followers do not hesitate to construct a new altar of incense to replace the one
taken by Antiochus (I 1:21; 4:49–50; cf. II 10:3), and rabbinic sources take for
granted the validity of the altar of incense in the temple of Jerusalem; see Schürer, II,
342–43, n. 17.

the restoration of an Oniad as high priest. Further to stress the point, at II 2:18 the author twice calls the temple of Jerusalem "the place" (cf. Deut 12:11, etc.). Also conspicuously absent from Jewish history, at least to the reign of Aristobulus I and perhaps to the reign of Alexander Jannaeus was the restoration of the kingdom (J. *AJ* xiii 11.1.301; Strabo xvi 2.40; on the coins the title "king" appears first on those of Alexander Jannaeus). The letter thus recognizes the royal claims of the later Hasmonaeans even as it ignores the victories of Judas Maccabaeus. In the last years of the second century B.C.E. Judas' victories lay far in the past, but Aristobulus' and Jannaeus' claims to be king were burning issues of the present. (On the allusion to Exod 19:6, see AB vol. 41A, NOTE on II 1:10b – 2:18 and NOTE on II 2:17, *the kingdom . . . Torah.*)

Here is one clue to date Ep. 2 within those two reigns. There are others. Ep. 2, like Ep. 1, seems to hold forth the hope of divine aid to the distressed Jews of Egypt (II 1:11, 17, 25, 27–29, 2:18). The Jews of Egypt who received Ep. 1 in 124 had good reason to fear Ptolemy VIII Euergetes II when he and his sister-wife Cleopatra II made peace. Hence the anti-Oniads of Jerusalem found the time opportune to send Ep. 1. See my article in *Studies Smith*, Part III, pp. 113–16. However, there were few opportunities after 124 for a propagandist to fabricate an anti-Oniad letter to console a menaced Egyptian Jewry. The fears of the Egyptian Jews in 124 were not fulfilled. Sweeping amnesties helped quiet the country, which stayed at peace until Euergetes II's death in 116.

For a brief period after his death, the aged pro-Jewish Cleopatra II held considerable power (Otto and Bengtson, *Zur Geschichte des Niederganges des Ptolemäerreiches*, pp. 112–36). Even her sudden death between December, 116, and March, 115, brought no danger to the Jews. Cleopatra III, widow of Euergetes II and daughter of Cleopatra II, at first dominated the government. She took over the cult names, Philometor Soteira, of the mother she hated, using this peculiar means to inflict *damnatio memoriae* upon Cleopatra II (Otto and Bengtson, pp. 136–44). Cleopatra III hated her own son, Ptolemy IX, with whom she shared the throne. Ptolemy IX may well have been hostile to the Jews from the beginning of his reign (cf. J. *AJ* xiii 10.2.278 and Otto and Bengtson, pp. 166–67). In any case, Cleopatra III soon displayed the pro-Jewish policy and firm alliance with the Oniads that Ptolemy VI Philometor and Cleopatra II held. Cleopatra III's trusted commanders were Chelkias and Ananias, sons of Onias IV (J. *AJ* xiii 10.4.285), and thereafter the Jews were secure as long as Cleopatra III was the dominant figure. Egyptian Jews knew only too well the hatred toward them in past years on the part of supporters of Euergetes II. They may have known already of the hostility toward them of the coregent Ptolemy IX. During this period Egyptian Jews could hardly have listened to Jewish propaganda attacking their Oniad protectors; still less would they have preserved it.

However, in 103/2 a grave menace came upon the Jews of Egypt from which the Oniads appeared powerless to save them. Cleopatra III had been holding her own in her war with Ptolemy IX, until the king in 103 landed in Coele-Syria and threatened to overrun Judaea and invade Egypt (J. *AJ* xiii 12.2.328 – 13.1.348). Worse yet, Ptolemy X, Cleopatra's new coregent, to whom she had entrusted part of the conduct of the war, broke with her for a short time in 103/2 (J. *AJ* xiii 13.1.350; Justin xxxix 4.3.; J. Cohen, "Ad Justini XXXIX, 4," *Mnemosyne,* 3D SERIES, 10 [1941–42], 229–30). At this point Ptolemy IX actually invaded Egypt, surely much to the consternation of the Egyptian Jews. The Oniad commanders were far away in Coele-Syria. One of them, Chelkias, had been killed while pursuing Ptolemy IX (J. *AJ* xiii 13.1–2.351–52). However, the threat quickly dissipated. There was a reconciliation between Ptolemy X and Cleopatra (Justin xxxix 4.4–5; Cohen, *Mnemosyne,* loc. cit.), and Ptolemy IX's attempt was repulsed (J. *AJ* xiii 13.2. 352; Hans Volkmann, "Ptolemaios 31," PW, XXIII^{II} [1959], 1745; Otto and Bengtson, pp. 190–91). Winter had barely begun, for Josephus *AJ* xiii 13.2.352) reports that Ptolemy IX on withdrawing spent the winter at Gaza. Only during the dark days of Ptolemy IX's invasion of Egypt in 103/2, when the Oniads appeared powerless to help, could there have been a ready audience among Egyptian Jews for anti-Oniad propaganda stressing the sole legitimacy of the temple of Jerusalem and calling for observance of the Hasmonaean and Jerusalemite Feast of Dedication. No such propaganda could have been written later, for in 102 Ananias, the ranking Oniad, in effect gave up his claim to the high priesthood by supporting and preserving the Hasmonaean Alexander Jannaeus' claim to the kingdom of Judaea (J. *AJ* xiii 13.2.353–55; cf. xiv 6.2.99 and 8.1.131 and *BJ* i 8.7.175 and 9.4.190) Thereafter there is no trace of any attempt to assert for the temple of Leontopolis sanctity rivaling that of the temple of Jerusalem. So faithful were the Jews of Egypt to the temple of Jerusalem that even rabbinic texts could concede a limited legitimacy to the temple of Leontopolis (*M. Menaḥot* 13:10; TB *Menaḥot* 109a–110a; see Schürer, III, 146–48).

I shall argue elsewhere that the news of the death of Antiochus IV became known at Jerusalem on 12 Adar (see now, above, pp. 166 and 43; the anniversary of the date was celebrated by the Jews of Judaea). Thus, a Jew of Judaea might not have misplaced the date of the arrival of the news of the death of Antiochus IV. Hence we may guess that an Egyptian Jew wrote Ep. 2 and published it in the dark days of November or early December, 103. The addressee, Aristobulus, probably is intended to be the Jewish philosopher who wrote under Ptolemy VI (see Schürer, III, 512, n. 38). Ep. 2 ascribes to him kinship with the Zadokite-Oniad priestly line. If so, he was an appropriate addressee for such a letter. His pious philosophical exposition of the Torah may have been aimed against the Hellenizing policies of his kinsman Jason and of Menelaus.

As the interpreter in Greek of the Jewish religious calendar (Anatolius *apud* Eusebius *Historia ecclesiastica* vii 32.17–18), he would be a logical recipient of a letter establishing a new festival. The author or publisher of Ep. 2 may well have been a descendant of Aristobulus. Such a person could circulate the letter without being suspected of forgery. In any case, by late 103 so much time had elapsed that the addressee and his contemporaries were dead and few if any were left in Egypt to take exception to the blatant errors concerning events of sixty years before.

The practice of Hellenistic scribes was to place at the end of a document earlier documents which were evidence or provided motivation; see Bikerman,

RHR 115 (1937), 192–95. Having fabricated Ep. 2 to have an earlier date than Ep. 1, the author of Ep. 2 may well have appended it to a copy of Ep. 1 and published them together. In any case, the content of both letters was timely, teaching that God would always defend and avenge Jews who kept the Torah and were loyal to the temple of Jerusalem. Readers of Ep. 2 would know that recently the Oniads themselves, despite their sin, had rescued the righteous Jews of Judaea from the atrocities perpetrated by Ptolemy IX (J. *AJ* xii 12.4.336 – 13.1.351), though in so doing Chelkias had lost his life, perhaps because of his sin of pressing the claims of the temple of Leontopolis. By observing the Feast of Dedication and by due reverence to the temple of Jerusalem, the Jews of Egypt, too, along with the surviving Oniads, could hope for deliverance from peril. It may have been Ep. 2 and the reaction it aroused in the Jewish community of Egypt that drove Ananias to give up a possible Oniad restoration to Jerusalem and instead to support the claims of Alexander Jannaeus. From this point on, if not before, Jannaeus, supported by the adherents of the line of Onias and Zadok (=Ṣaddūq) could be called a "Sadducee"; see Introduction, pp. 68–71.

APPENDIX IV

HOW EPISTLES 1 AND 2 CAME TO STAND
AT THE HEAD OF SECOND MACCABEES

Since both Ep. 1 and Ep. 2 are incompatible with the narrative of the abridged history, one would like to know how they came to be prefixed to it. The key to solving the problem lies in understanding the structure of the book of Esther as described in Esther 9.

The narrative of the book of Esther is called a "letter" (Hebrew *iggeret;* Greek *epistolê*) at Esther 9:26 and in the colophon to the Greek version of the book (Greek Esther 10 end); cf. TB *Megillah* 19a end and the customs reported by the Geonim collected at B. M. Lewin, *Otzar ha-Gaonim* (Jerusalem: Hebrew University Press Association, 1932–), V, *Megillah,* pp. 18, 25.

In fact, the author or final editor of the Hebrew Esther claimed that his work essentially reproduced the text of a letter of Esther and Mordecai, in which an earlier letter of Mordecai was quoted. To understand the writer's procedure, we must know the rules which he took for granted. Biblical writers of history or historical fiction proceeded not unlike modern historians: they drew, or pretended to draw, on earlier historical works and official documents. Historical works were written in narrative form and, with the exception of autobiographical memoirs like those of Nehemiah, were cast in the third person. Official Persian and Israelite royal edicts were cast in the first and second person; see e.g. Ezra 1:2–6 and II Chron 30:6–9. A chronicler using an official document as a source had his choice of several procedures. He could quote the document verbatim as at Ezra 7:11–27; he could render its content in an indirect quotation, turning the first and second person into the third and often using infinitive verbs, as at II Chron 30:1; or he could narrate the events which the document recorded, as at Ezra 6:1–2, where the narrative in the third person surely is a paraphrase of the rescript of Artaxerxes in the first person, the end of which is quoted verbatim at Ezra 6:6–12.

There were other standard procedures which ancient scribes and authors followed in writing and quoting letters. At the head of a message, whether oral or epistolary, customarily stood a formula of greeting, "peace" or "health" (e.g. Hebrew *Šālōm;* Aramaic *Šᵉlām;* Greek *chairein*), which was usually a mere piece of conventional politeness. To mark the transition from such conventionalities and other preliminary matter (e.g. the prayer at II 1:2–5) to the real business of the letter, the scribe would use the formula "and now" (Greek *kai nyn;* Hebrew *w'th;* Aramaic *wk'nt* or *wk't;* see e.g. II Sam 2:6; II Kings 5:6, 10:2; Ezra 4:10, 11, 17, and 7:12). If an earlier letter was quoted in a later official document, both the greeting and the formula of transition were omitted, for only the real business of the letter was of interest;

cf. Driver, *Aramaic Documents of the Fifth Century B.C.*, letters III, IV, VIII,
XII, and see Bikerman, RHR 115 (1937), 192. Quotation of an earlier letter
in an official document could be either direct (as in Driver, letters III, IV,
VIII, XII) or indirect (as in Driver, letter XI, line 2).

On the other hand, in a historical narrative, the introductory formulas could
be of interest, for inclusion of the formula of greeting in the original message
signified a friendly attitude of the sender to the recipient (Deut 2:26;
Judg 21:13; II Kings 9:18–22) and omission of it signified a hostile relationship (e.g. Judg 11:12). The Jews, who had been declared public enemies,
stand only a short time later in the document at Esther 9:30–31 as friends of
the queen and vizier; the writer includes the formula of greeting to dramatize
the change (cf. Esther 10:3 end, and on the formula see in AB vol. 41A NOTE
on II 1:10b). When a chronicler cited either the greeting formula or the
gestures of friendship which accompanied the message, he might include the
formula of transition to indicate the chief purpose of the mission (II Sam 2:6;
II Kings 5:6). If the sender of the message was in a hostile relationship to the
recipient, the chronicler might include the formula of transition in the absence
of a greeting formula, to signify that hostility (II Kings 5:6, 10:2). Otherwise,
the chronicler would omit the formula of transition.

We can now understand Esther 9:20–32. Esther 9:20–22 explains that Esther
1:1 – 9:19 was incorporated in Mordecai's festal letter on Purim, sent to all
Jews in the Persian empire. The author of Esther intended to reflect either of
two possibilities: either the entire narrative stood at the head of the letter, as
II 1:7–8 probably stood at the head of Ep. 0; or a brief allusion to the
content of Esther 1:1 – 9:19 stood at the head of the letter, with a note that
the full narrative was appended below. See Bikerman, RHR 115 (1937),
191–96. Esther 9:21–22 goes on to give in indirect discourse the request
to observe the festival, which, like II 1:9, was the main purpose of the letter.
Absent from the quoted text of this first letter are the formula of greeting
and the formula of transition; the author or final editor presents the text as if
he had found it quoted in the second letter, the one sent by Esther and
Mordecai.

It is easy to reconstruct the appearance of the second letter as envisaged by
the author or final editor. After the formula of greeting the letter proceeded
to quote the earlier letter of Mordecai, omitting the formula of greeting and
transition but repeating in full Esther 1:1 – 9:19. We may guess that in the
second letter Esther 9:21–22 was already cast as an indirect quotation. At
Ezra 5–6, only material from Darius' rescript is turned into third-person narrative (Ezra 6:1–2), not the letter to which the rescript replied (Ezra 5:7–17).
This instance suggests that an ancient chronicler would recast in the third person
only material that was the main message of the document lying before him
and would render verbatim the earlier material as quoted therein. For our
purposes, it makes no difference whether the author or final editor envisaged
himself or Mordecai and Esther as casting 9:20–21 in indirect discourse.

After quoting Mordecai's earlier letter, the letter of Esther and Mordecai
continued with a note that the Jews had formally signified their compliance with
Mordecai's orders (Esther 9:23). A quotation, direct or indirect, followed of
the Jews' formal resolution, which now stands in indirect discourse at Esther

9:24–28, complete with its motivating clauses, Esther 9:24–25; cf. the motivating clauses, I 14:29–40. There is a lacuna between 9:24–25, where Esther must have been mentioned, as is clear from the feminine singular at the head of vs. 25, "When she came before the king."

Thereupon the letter of Esther and Mordecai, like II 1:9, used the formula of transition and turned to give in the first and second person the request which was the purpose of the letter, to observe annually also the fasts and prayers. This request the author or final editor has turned into indirect discourse (Esther 9:30–31), preserving the formula of greeting but not the formula of transition.

One can translate Esther 9:32, "A decree of Esther's rendered these observances of Purim binding and was included in the text of the letter." The last word of the Hebrew text, *bspr*, is ambiguous. That the singular, *spr*, can mean the text of a letter sent in copies (*sprym*) to more than one recipient is clear from II Kings 10:1–7; see also Loewenstamm, *"Mikhtabh,"* Enc. Bib., IV (1962), 966–67 (in Hebrew). The next to last word, *wnktb*, should probably be vocalized *w*ᵉ*nikhtōbh*, as an infinitive consecutive, a much used construction in the book of Esther. Cf. Esther 2:3 and 6:9 (vocalize probably at both places *w*ᵉ*nittōn*), 8:8, 9:6, 16, 18; and see GKC, § 113z, p. 345.

The author of Esther 9:32 probably believed that a Persian queen could issue decrees on her own authority. Indeed, the "queen's word" at Esther 1:17–18 and "Esther's word" at Esther 5:5 appear to be analogous to the "king's word" at Esther 1:13, 2:8, 4:3, 8:17, and 9:1. I have been unable to find direct confirmation elsewhere, but Achaemenian queens, especially Parysatis, took forceful action on their own authority; see J. Miller, "Parysatis I," PW, XVIIIᴵᴵ, Part 3, (1949), 2051–52. Early Sassanian queens, independently of the king, could claim title to property (TB *Giṭṭin* 86a).

My rendering of Esther 9:32 disagrees with the Greek translation, on which see below. Still another interpretation is possible, though less likely. If Esther as queen had power of her own to issue decrees whereas Mordecai held only delegated authority, the letter sent in her name and Mordecai's could properly be called "Esther's decree." Then we might vocalize *wnktb* of Esther 9:32 as the first-person plural *qal* imperfect with *waw*-consecutive, *wannikhtōbh*, and translate, "Esther's decree rendered these observances of Purim binding, and it we have been quoting in this our book." Cf. Josh 24:26; Jer 32:10 and 36:4, 18, 32; for the interchangeability of *'al* and *bĕ-* in these expressions, see Jer 25:13 with II Kings 23:3.

The facts of Esther 10 the author or final editor attributes no longer to official correspondence but to the Chronicles of the Kings of Persia and Media.

The Greek translator of Esther understood at least some of these principles of style. Clearly he understood that the narrative of Esther 1:1 – 9:19 was included with the letter of Mordecai described in 9:20–22. It is doubtful, however, whether he suspected that in Esther 9:23–28 the writer intended to quote the formal document recording the Jews' assent rather than merely to report the event.

The translator might well have understood the intent of the author or final editor to reproduce the content of the letter of Esther and Mordecai in 9:29–32. However, evidently the text which lay before the translator was defective and prevented him from doing so. The unintelligible Greek vs. 30, "And Mordecai and Queen Esther enjoined upon them for themselves and then having laid down upon their health and their counsel," could hardly have resulted from scribal errors in the Greek. After vs. 29, the Greek text omits Hebrew vs. 30, and Greek vs. 30 begins with "Mordecai and Queen Esther enjoined upon them [. . .] for themselves" from Hebrew vs. 31, then has words which render the Hebrew "as they had laid down upon" (words which originally stood where I have placed the brackets), then passes to the "health" which renders the "peace" of the greeting formula at the end of Hebrew vs. 30, and finally speaks of "their counsel," which probably represents a misreading ('ṣtm) of one or both of the last two words of Hebrew vs. 31. At the end of chapter 9, after presenting the unintelligible Greek text, minuscule manuscripts 93 and 583 present the Hebrew text from 9:30, "truth," to the end of 9:32, but they reflect not the original Greek translation but Hexaplaric correction on the basis of the Hebrew text. See Esther, ed. Robert Hanhart, Septuaginta: Vetus Testamentum Graecum Auctoritate Academiae Litterarum Gottingensis editum, vol. VIII, 3 (Göttingen: Vandenhoeck & Rupprecht, 1966), 60–81, 205. Such disorder in the translator's Hebrew text is not surprising. The ends of ancient scrolls tended to suffer mutilation because they were so frequently pulled by the readers and because, normally left on the outside of the scroll, they were subjected to friction.

Such being the case, it is also not surprising that the translator failed to understand Esther 9:32 as we have. According to him, a decree of Esther's confirmed the matter of the second letter in perpetuity, and the decree was entered "in a record book of the [royal] archives" (eis mnêmosynon); cf. Greek Esther 6:1 and Bickerman, Four Strange Books of the Bible, pp. 203–4. However, an archival record in Hebrew is spr zkrnwt or spr dbry hymym, not the simple spr of Esther 9:32. Exod 14:14 and Ezra 6:2 both have zkrwn or dkrwn in the context and are therefore not exceptions to this rule.

Even so, the translator and his readers, the Greek-speaking Jews of Egypt, clearly could understand the documentary forms of Esther 9:20–32 enough to perceive that Esther 1:1 – 9:19 was supposed to have stood in a festal letter of Mordecai.

Indeed, in some ways Greek-speaking Jews may well have understood Esther 9:20–32 better than Jews who spoke Hebrew and Aramaic (cf. Bickerman, Four Strange Books of the Bible, p. 204). The Jews annually celebrated one great commemorative festival of deliverance, the Passover. Its history, too, was narrated in a book. But there is no trace of any other such observance among Jews before the institution of Purim and the Feast of Dedication and the Egyptian Jewish festivals of deliverance reported in Third Maccabees (6:36–40; 7:19–23). Never, before these later examples, are the Jews asked to ratify the observance of a festival. On the other hand, annual commemorative panhellenic festivals of deliverance adopted by the deliberative body of the individual states were common among the Greeks of the Hellenistic age and before; see Plutarch Aristides 21 and Pfister, "Soteria 2," PW, IIIᴬ (1929), 1221–31.

Greek-speaking Jews might also understand the formulas of Esther 9:20–32 better, though in part the contractual forms are paralleled in the Hebrew Bible.

Jews knew of covenants and oaths with motivating clauses, and these agreements could be entered into freely, as with the letter of Mordecai, or under command, as with the letter of Esther and Mordecai. The most vivid parallels are at Joshua 24 and Neh 9:6 – 10:40. Neh 10:33, "We . . . have laid upon ourselves" (*wh'mdnw 'lynw*), even gives us a parallel for the formula "The Jews ordained" (*qymw . . . 'lyhm*), since the two Hebrew roots are synonymous. See also Exod 19:3–8, 24:3, 7–9; Deut 5:2–24, 29:9–14; Josh 23:16; II Kings 17:35–39, 23:1–3; Jer 34:8–15; Ezra 10:3–14; II Chron 15:8–14, 34:30–32. Nevertheless, in none of these cases is a festival adopted. In every case the covenant is to observe part or all of the Torah. Moreover, the technical language of Esther 9:20–32 makes no use of the Hebrew terms for "covenant" and "oath." Aramaic *qym* is used in the Targum for "vow," but the use of the verb at Esther 9:29 and 31 in the senses "confirm" and "keep" shows that no vow is intended in our context; indeed, at Ps 119:106 *qym* in connection with an oath means "fulfill," not "swear." The technical terms *qym* and *qbl* do not occur anywhere in connection with the covenants and oaths we have cited as parallels. These formulas of Esther 9:20–32 may have had parallels in non-Greek communities such as Sidon and Tyre and Judaea, but no evidence survives of them. However, the formulas have exact parallels in Greek documents establishing panhellenic commemorative festivals of deliverance. For messages parallel to the letter of Mordecai and motivating clauses parallel to Esther 9:24–26, see Syll.[3] 398.1–14 (of 278 B.C.E.), 402.1–11 (of 277/6); H. Pomtow, "Delphische Neufunde," *Klio* 14 (1914–15), 271, inscription 2, lines 3–12. In Esther the Jews "ordain," presumably by vote of their deliberative bodies, and "accept" the proposals of Mordecai and Esther (Esther 9:23, 27, 31); exact parallels stand at Syll.[3] 390.36 (of ca. 281/0); 402.9, 10–11, 13, 15, and esp. 23; 408.5–11, 16 (of ca. 275/4).

We return now to the problem of the presence of Ep. 1 and Ep. 2 at the head of Second Maccabees. The Greek Esther was brought to Egypt in 78/7; see Bickerman, JBL 63 (1944), 346–47. Thereafter, Egyptian Jews who observed the Feast of Dedication and the Day of Nicanor probably would want to have for those days a text like Esther for Purim and like Third Maccabees for their own festival of deliverance. Such tales of deliverance were popular among gentiles as well as Jews. See Nilsson, *Geschichte der griechischen Religion*, II, 2d ed., 53, 225–29; and cf. Deut 32:7–14; Judg 6:13; Pss 44:2–4, 71:18–24, 78:1–72, 79:13, 145:4, 11–12. The book of Esther validated itself by reference to official documents, and Third Maccabees did so by reference to monuments in Egypt (III 70:20). The Feast of Dedication and Day of Nicanor, commemorating events outside the Ptolemaic empire, could not be validated by Egyptian monuments, but only by official documents. Two such documents by now circulated in Egypt, very likely together (see Appendix III). Egyptian Jews would readily prefix them to a narrative of the new festivals even if neither document alluded to such a narrative. They would do so the more readily to Jason's narrative or its abridgement, because of the similarity of II 10:3, 5 end–6 to Ep. 1 (II 1:8–9); see Introduction, pp. 35–36.

However, if Epp. 1 and 2 were so prefixed to a narrative, it is most unlikely that the narrative was the voluminous unabridged work of Jason, which could hardy pose as matter sent along with a festal letter. Moreover, the account of Antiochus' death in Ep. 2 blatantly contradicts that in II 9. If the abridger had found such a contradiction lying before him, he might well have tried to hide it. Hence, the letters were probably attached by an unsophisticated Egyptian Jew to the abridged history.

If Ep. 1 and Ep. 2 were not already circulating together, the same Egyptian Jew now appended Ep. 2 to Ep. 1 in accordance with Hellenistic documentary procedure; see pp. 549–50.

The probability that Epp. 1 and 2 were thus prefixed to the abridged history becomes a near certainty if the ritual of reading the book of Esther on Purim was already being observed in Egypt in the first century B.C.E. I know of no Greek parallel for this ritual of reading a full narrative text on a commemorative festival of deliverance, though a city might require the public herald to proclaim on the festival the reason for its observance (see Syll.[3] 398.39–40). Only rabbinic texts purport to discuss the origins of the ritual reading; the authorities named in them are all of the third century C.E. The discussion at TP *Megillah* 1:5, p. 70d, begins with a question of when the ritual reading of the book of Esther should take place in an intercalary year and without further mention of ritual reading goes on to discuss the problem posed by the letter of Mordecai and Esther for the sages of their time, among whom there still were prophets. The sages finally accepted the proposals of the letter, despite the innovations they made in Jewish law. At TB *Makkot* 23b the ritual reading is clearly ascribed to the time of the recipients of the letter of Esther and Mordecai, though at the parallel, TP *Berakot* 9:8, p. 14c, it is not clear whether the ritual reading is included or only the observances of Esther 9:21–22. At TB *Megillah* 2a the anonymous discussion by inference, not by citing tradition, concludes that regulations about the ritual reading must go back to the Men of the Great Synagogue. At TB *Megillah* 19b a rabbi of the third century C.E. is reported to have called the ritual reading an "innovation of the Scribes." The identity and time of the Men of the Great Synagogue and of the Scribes are matters of controversy, and so is the reliability of rabbinic attributions of institutions to them. At any rate, as far as the early *amoraim* of the third century C.E. knew, the ritual of reading the book of Esther was considerably older than the rise of the Hasmonaean dynasty. There is a text which discusses the relationship of the ritual reading to the temple service (TB *Megillah* 3a); and Zechariah, the butcher's son, who lived at the time of the destruction of the temple, gives rulings on the reading of Esther (TB *Megillah* 1:6). Hence, the ritual was certainly long-established by the first century C.E.

Biblical texts cited above (p. 555) show how the Jews felt a duty to tell how their God had delivered them from evil; in the case of their deliverance from Egypt, divine commandments obligated them to do so (Exod 13:8, 14–15; Deut 6:20–25; cf. Deut 26:3–10). Since as told in the Torah the story of the deliverance from Egypt is long, already in Judaea under the rule of the Ptolemies a shorter text for telling the story, the *Haggadah,* had come into being; see Louis Finkelstein, "The Oldest Midrash," HTR 31 (1938), 291–317, and "Pre-Maccabean Documents in the Passover Haggadah," HTR 35 (1942), 291–332, and 36 (1943), 1–38. It would not be surprising if Jews in Judaea and in the diaspora thereafter, as soon as they adopted a new festival of deliverance, would feel the need for a ritual recital of the story behind the festival. The book of Esther with its manageable length readily lent itself to such use. However, not all Jews shared the sectarian abstinence in the Hebrew book of Esther from all mention of God; see Introduction, pp. 12–14. The Greek book of Esther with its copious references to God makes good the lack, and perhaps the Greek translator had ritual use of the book in mind when he made his additions. Once the Egyptian Jews had accepted the new festivals of the deliverance of the temple as well as the ritual reading of the Greek book of Esther, they all (except perhaps a few sharp-eyed critics) would find the abridged history, with Epp. 1 and 2 prefixed, a perfect ritual text analogous to Esther. It, too, was of manageable length; its theology was acceptable; and its narrative in two sections treated each of the two festivals as a climax.

Ancient texts seem to recognize this composition as a "Hanukkah scroll" analogous to the Purim scroll, for the Codex Alexandrinus at the end of Second Maccabees gives the book the title "Letter of the deeds of Judas Macc[abae]us," analogous to "Letter of Phrouraia [=Purim]" in the Greek colophon of the book of Esther, and Clement of Alexandria writes (*Stromateis* i 21.123.2), "Among this captivity [the Babylonian] were Esther and Mordecai, whose book, like the Maccabaean History, is read widely [*pheretai*]." Clement calls Second Maccabees "the epitome of the Maccabaean History" at *Stromateis* v 14.97. The widespread reading referred to by Clement might mean mere private reading, but by his time (fl. late second and early third century C.E.) the ritual reading of the book of Esther certainly existed, and hence his remark suggests the existence also of ritual reading of Second Maccabees.

Since the abridged history with the prefixed letters was in Greek, it never became a liturgical text in Judaea, but the felt need for a "Hanukkah scroll" did give rise to the medieval *Megillat Antiokhus;* see Introduction, Part I, n. 58.

At first, perhaps, the contradiction between Jason's account of the death of Antiochus IV and the account in Ep. 2 passed unnoticed. Ultimately, however, it became intolerable and was removed by rearranging the abridged history, placing II 9 in its present position instead of after II 10:8. See introductory commentary to II 9. The rearrangement left the contradictions in the details of the narrative of the death of Antiochus IV unresolved.

Our study has led to the following important conclusions: Epp. 1 and 2 were probably added to the abridged history soon after the Greek book of Esther was brought to Egypt in 78/7 B.C.E. The ritual reading of the book of Esther in Egypt had probably developed by the time the letters were added to the abridged history. Soon thereafter in Egypt probably came the ritual reading of the resultant text, which came to be our Second Maccabees.

APPENDIX V

HOW JOSEPHUS INTERPRETED DANIEL AND
REWROTE FIRST MACCABEES 1:20–64

Josephus' account of the events covered by First Maccabees for the most part is a mere paraphrase of that work. His narrative of the events covered by I 1:20–64 clearly draws on those verses but strangely distorts them. Let the reader compare I 1:20–64 in my translation with the following translation of Josephus' version (*AJ* xii 5.3–4.246–56). The footnotes indicate the passages in First Maccabees drawn on by Josephus.

(3.246) While returning from Egypt because he had been intimidated by the Romans, King Antiochus marched against the city of Jerusalem. On reaching the city in the year 143 of the Seleucid dynasty,[1] he took it without a battle, for his supporters in the city opened the gates to him. (3.247) After taking Jerusalem in this manner, he killed many members of the faction opposed to him[2] and took much money as loot and then returned to Antioch.[3]

(4.248) Two years later,[4] in the year 145, on the twenty-fifth day of the month called by us "Kislev" and by the Macedonians "Apellaios,"[5] in the one hundred fifty-third Olympiad, the king marched against Jerusalem with a strong army, and by the treachery of feigning peaceful intentions he captured the city.[6] (4.249) This time, because of the wealth in the temple, he spared not even those who let him enter[7]; rather, driven by his greed, inasmuch as he saw much gold in the temple as well as the other kinds of extremely expensive ornamentation there in the form of dedicatory offerings, he stooped to violating his treaty obligations with the Jews in order to plunder it.[8] (4.250) He stripped the temple, carrying off the vessels of God, including golden candelabra and a golden incense altar and a table and the other altars; he even took the curtains, which were made of fine linen and scarlet. He also emptied the hidden treasuries, leaving absolutely nothing behind.[9]

Thereupon, he brought further great sorrow upon the Jews,[10] (4.251) for he made them stop offering the daily sacrifices which they were accustomed to offer to God in accordance with the Torah,[11] and after looting the entire city,[12] he killed some of the people[13] and took others captive along with their wives and children, so that the number of the prisoners came to some

[1] 1:20.   [2] 1:20a.   [3] 1:24.   [4] 1:20.
[5] 1:54 and 59.   [6] 1:29, 30 beginning.
[7] 1:30 end.   [8] 1:24 end.   [9] 1:21–23.
[10] 1:25.   [11] 1:45.
[12] 1:31 beginning.   [13] 1:30 end.

ten thousand.[14] (4.252) He set fire to the finest parts of the city and after destroying its walls[15] rebuilt the citadel (the Akra) in the lower city, for it was on high ground and overlooked the temple. Accordingly, he fortified the citadel with high walls and towers[16] and stationed there a Macedonian garrison. Also given residence in the Akra were those of the people who were impious and of evil character. At their hands their fellow Jews were to suffer many atrocities.[17]

(4.253) The king also built an illicit altar upon the sacrificial altar[18] and slaughtered swine on it, though the offering of such a sacrifice is contrary to the laws and ancestral traditions of the religion of the Jews.[19] He forced them to abandon the religion of their own God and worship the gods in whom he believed.[20] They were to build illicit temples and illicit altars to those gods in every town and village and to sacrifice swine upon them daily.[21] (4.254) He also commanded them not to circumcise their children,[22] threatening to punish anyone found violating his orders.[23] He appointed supervisory officials to assist in compelling them to carry out his commands.[24]

(4.255) Many of the Jews, some willingly, others out of fear of the threatened punishment, complied with the king's orders,[25] but the worthiest and those of noble character paid him no heed and regarded the ancestral customs as of more weight than the threatened punishments for disobedience. Consequently daily they suffered maltreatment and were cruelly tortured to death. (4.256) Indeed, they were whipped and mutilated, and while still alive and breathing,[26] they were crucified.[27] Their wives and their children, whom they had circumcised contrary to the king's will, the king's agents strangled, hanging the children from the necks of their crucified parents.[28] Anywhere a sacred book or copy of the Torah was found, it was destroyed, and the persons with whom it was found, poor wretches, were wretchedly put to death.[29]

The important departures of Josephus from I 1:20–64 are the following:

1) Though Josephus knows of a sack of Jerusalem in 143 Sel. Bab. (169 B.C.E.), he says nothing of a plundering of the temple in that year.

2) Josephus connects the sack of Jerusalem in 169 B.C.E. with Antiochus IV's withdrawal from Egypt under Roman pressure.

3) Josephus takes details which in I 1:20–64 belong to two separate expeditions, one of Antiochus IV in 169 and one of the Mysarch in 167, and also details of the persecution of 167–164 and blends them to produce a single campaign of Antiochus in 167, in the course of which the king is said to have begun the persecution.

---

[14] 1:32; cf. II 5:13–14.   [15] 1:31 end.
[16] 1:33.   [17] 1:34–37.   [18] 1:54 and 59.
[19] Josephus appears to have interpreted "Abomination of Desolation" as "altar-for-swine-sacrifice-to-idols." Josephus may also have derived the sacrifice of (inherently unclean) swine upon the temple altar from I 1:46.
[20] 1:41–42.   [21] 1:47.   [22] 1:48.
[23] 1:50.   [24] 1:51.
[25] 1:43 and 52.   [26] 1:62–63; cf. II 6:29 – 7:42.
[27] Cf. Test Moses viii 1, and see my article in *Studies on the Testament of Moses*, p. 48.
[28] 1:60–61.   [29] 1:56–57 and perhaps also 1:64.

4) Josephus fails to reproduce the information at I 1:41 and 51, that the king's messages were sent not only to Judaea but to all his kingdom.

5) Whereas the author of I 1:63 fails to describe the tortures suffered by the martyrs, Josephus gives details reminiscent of II 6:18 – 7:42.

Three factors will account for all Josephus' departures from I 1:20–64: his belief in the veracity of Daniel 7–12, his belief in the value and efficacy of martyrdom, and his intention to write his work in good Greek rhetorical style.

The author of First Maccabees took delight in exposing what he saw as the falsity of Daniel 7–12 (see Introduction, pp. 45–48). Therefore, as a believer in the veracity of Daniel, Josephus could not accept his account unmodified (see Introduction, pp. 56, 58–59).

How did Josephus interpret the obscure words of Daniel? Josephus' account at *AJ* xii 5.3–4.246–56 and 7.6.320–21 shows he believed that Antiochus IV twice came in person to attack Jerusalem: once after being forced out of Egypt by the Romans and a second time three years before the Feast of Dedication which occurred in 164. In connecting the former attack with the forced withdrawal from Egypt, Josephus in part may have been following the ambiguous words at II 5:1; but unlike Jason of Cyrene, Josephus was not wary of giving a date in 169 (taken from I 1:20) for a withdrawal from Egypt which occurred in 168 (see Introduction, pp. 50–52). He seems to have been unaware of the discrepancy. Moreover, unlike Jason of Cyrene, Josephus does not say that the king plundered the temple when he attacked Jerusalem on his way back from Egypt. There was only one source which seemed to connect an attack on Jerusalem by Antiochus IV with the king's withdrawal from Egypt and yet did not mention a spoliation of the temple: Dan 11:30, "And ships of Kittim [i.e. Rome] shall come against him so that, depressed, he shall turn back and let his wrath fall upon the Holy Covenant, and he shall act."[30]

As for Antiochus IV's "later" attack on Jerusalem, Josephus himself lets us know that he derived it from Daniel (*AJ* x 11.7.271, 275–76; cf. xii 7.6.321–32). The summary of Daniel's oracles in *AJ* x 11.7.269–75 is strange. In writing the *Antiquities* Josephus possessed copies of all his scriptural sources. He can hardly have been writing an inaccurate account from memory. Rather, he knew that the Feast of Dedication occurred in 164, three years after the desecration of Kislev, 167 (*AJ* xii 7.6.320; I 4:52, 54), an interval nowhere predicted by Daniel, who repeatedly speaks of three and a half years (7:25, 9:27, 12:7, and perhaps also the 1290 days of 12:11, which Josephus may have viewed as a round approximation of the 1298 days of two intercalary lunar years plus one and a half ordinary lunar years). Though once (8:14) Daniel speaks of 1150 full days, which could equal three intercalary

---

[30] I translate here in accordance with Josephus' apparent interpretation of the verse. On the true meaning of Dan 11:30, see commentary, NOTE on I 1:29–30.

Josephus was deceived by appearances in interpreting Dan 11:28 and 30. Dan 11:28 was intended by its author to refer to the sack of 169 (see NOTE on I 1:20, *with a strong army*). To Josephus, the ambiguous verse with its vague "and he shall act" and with its lack of a reference to the king's fury seemed to mean that the king did not attack Jerusalem at the end of his first campaign in Egypt. For still another erroneous but natural interpretation of Dan 11:28 and 30, see Introduction, pp. 44–47, and Jerome's commentary ad loc.

lunar years, three consecutive intercalary lunar years were an impossibility.[31] Hence, in *AJ* x 11.7.269–75 Josephus seems to have tried to synthesize from the obscurities and inconsistencies of Daniel 7–12 a single oracle which would predict the correct interval and would be more likely to impress his Graeco-Roman audience.

As usual, Josephus' vast project left him insufficient time to solve the (truly insoluble) difficulties. Though he appears to have interpreted the 1150 days of Dan 8:14 as three years (*AJ* x 11.7.275), he also quotes a figure of 1296 days (*AJ* x 11.7.271), presumably a variant of the figure at Dan 12:11. In his last allusion to the topic (*AJ* xii 7.6.321), Josephus seems to shrink from asserting to his Graeco-Roman audience that Daniel predicted the interval; rather, he is content to say that Daniel merely predicted that Antiochus IV would "devastate" the temple.[32]

Josephus sincerely believed in the veracity of Daniel. How he explained away for himself the extra half year of Dan 7:25 we cannot tell, but the crucial part (*AJ* x 11.7.275) of the Daniel-oracle Josephus synthesized is clearly derived from Daniel 7. "A king who would make war on the nation," if derived from Daniel, can come only from 7:21, ". . . shall make war on the Saints." The next words in the synthesized oracle, "and their Laws and would abolish the way of life based upon them and would despoil the temple," can come only from Dan 7:25, which Josephus seems to have rendered, "he shall think to change the times [i.e. to substitute other observances for the observances of the Sabbath and the festivals] and the Law, and everything shall be delivered into his hands [including the spoils of the temple]."[33] The next words in the synthesized oracle, "and shall put a stop to the offering of sacrifices for three years," are derived from Dan 9:27, but the three years reflect the three and a half years of both Dan 7:25 and Dan 9:27, as well as the 1150 days of Dan 8:14.

In Dan 7:21 and 25 the war and the attendant atrocities are reported as acts of Antiochus and as the starting point of three and a half years in which the Saints are to be left in the power of the king. The seer, who knew that the Mysarch acted under Antiochus' orders and that the decrees came in the king's name, did not need to mention the Mysarch in Daniel 7; the war and the atrocities were acts of Antiochus even if he did not come in person to Jerusalem. The murderous expedition of the Mysarch (early spring, 167) was indeed close enough in time to Antiochus' decrees that the seer could mention the two in the same breath.[34] With good information independent of Daniel, the author of I 1:29–51 pointedly fails to connect the two, and Jason of Cyrene explicitly states that the two were separated by an interval.[35] Without that good information, Josephus naturally assumed that if the atrocities

---

[31] Cf. To. *Sanhedrin* 2:8, TB *Sanhedrin* 12a.

[32] Dan 9:26 was originally intended to describe the death of Onias III, the coup of Jason the Oniad, and the ensuing war, with no direct allusion to Antiochus IV; see in AB vol. 41A NOTE on II 4:34. Josephus, however, may have seen an allusion to Antiochus in the "chief who came" (*nāgīd habbā*) in Dan 9:26.

[33] The old Greek version of Daniel (Dan LXX) also renders *wytyhbwn bydh* as "everything shall be delivered into his hands"; cf. I 1:24.

[34] See Introduction, p. 42.

[35] On Jason of Cyrene's interpretation of the 3½ years, see pp. 52–54.

are mentioned in Dan 7:25 as the starting point for a period of three or three
and a half years, the atrocities all occurred together.

In the light of this interpretation of Dan 7:25 Josephus read Dan 11:31–33.
After the "first sack" of Jerusalem in Dan 11:30, the seer spoke of a series
of atrocities all ascribed to Antiochus IV: the plundering of the temple ("And
arms shall arise from him and violate the sanctity of the temple"), the
suspension of the regular temple sacrifices and the imposition of an idolatrous
cult ("Arms . . . from him . . . shall remove the continual offering and set
up the Abomination from Desolation"), the protection of the wicked who
later were to be sheltered in the Akra ("And he shall flatter the evildoers of
the Covenant with deceits"), the slaughter and captivity of pious Jews and
the plundering of their city ("But those who bring understanding to the
People shall instruct the Many, but they shall fall to sword and fire and
captivity and spoil for some days"), and, evidently somewhat later, the building of the Akra (Dan 11:39; see commentary, NOTE on I 1:33–40). On reading
Dan 11:31–33, 39, Josephus again judged that all the events except the building of the Akra were nearly simultaneous.

Thus, for Josephus, the text of Daniel seemed to prove that Antiochus twice
attacked Jerusalem in person and that the true course of events was quite different from the accounts of both I 1:20–64 and II 5:1–26.

On approaching I 1:20–64 with such preconceptions, Josephus found many
puzzles in the passage. Verse 29 seemed to be utter nonsense. To judge by
the extant Greek text of vs. 29 (see commentary, NOTE on I 1:29–40), the
translator and perhaps Josephus, too, read the Hebrew as saying, "Two years
later the king sent a tax gathering official against the towns of Judah. . . ."
"Tax gathering official" (*śar missīm*) is the same expression as that used for
"taskmaster" at Exod 1:11. On seeing the expression, Josephus like any educated
Jew would immediately think of Exod 1:11. The context in First Maccabees
shows that Antiochus, unlike Pharaoh, did not exact labor from the Jews.
No one could doubt that the Jews paid taxes to Antiochus, so what could be
unusual or cruel about the sending of a single tax official or even the sending
of a single taskmaster imposing forced labor? On the other hand a single
official in charge of taxes or forced labor would not command a large army
or direct a large-scale military operation to punish a rebellious people. S and
La^L and SyII try to solve the problem by having the text speak of plural
"tax officials." To Josephus, the narrative was embarrassing even where it
was comprehensible since it provided for only one visit by Antiochus IV to
Jerusalem. Hence, Josephus welcomed the incomprehensible passage as a sign
the whole context was corrupt, and he was ready to use the drastic methods
of our modern biblical critics.

Josephus proceeded from his belief in the veracity of Daniel, not simply in
an effort to deal with an unintelligible text. To cure the text without any
transpositions he could have omitted the word "tax" or excised the entire
clause mentioning the tax official. Nothing could override Josephus' faith in
Daniel. Even Mattathias seemed to confirm the veracity of Daniel's book
(I 2:59–60).

Josephus appears to have assumed, first, that a stupid worker had wrongly
pasted together the columns of a torn text. The "unintelligible" passage

Josephus regarded as either hopelessly corrupt or as an interpolation of a stupid scribe. If Josephus had both a Hebrew and a Greek text of First Maccabees, he assumed that the pasting error occurred in the Hebrew before the Greek translation. Josephus appears to have proceeded similarly elsewhere; see commentary, NOTE on I 9:34–53. Josephus also seems to have assumed the Jason of Cyrene drew on the same interpolated account. For Josephus, Jason's interpretation of šar missīm as "Mysarch" was incorrect, since it did not allow for a second attack on Jerusalem by Antiochus IV.

Josephus found it fairly easy to "restore" our author's account to its "original" form from the "corrupt" text which lay before him. On the basis of First Maccabees and the end result of Josephus' labors we can easily determine the "uncorrected" text which lay before him and then see how he worked.

The block 1:21–23 (paraphrased in J. *AJ* xii 5.4.250) is the longest block which appears in Josephus' version intact but surrounded by transpositions. This fact suggests that in Josephus' copy of First Maccabees it occupied a full column. If so, a full Greek column contained about 357 letters, perhaps about thirty lines of about 12 letters per line. For an ancient Greek literary text, especially one intended to appear biblical, the proportions are correct.[36] Josephus may have looked into a Hebrew text here. If so, he assumed that the pasting error occurred with columns of the Hebrew. To judge by the undisturbed block 1:21–23, as reconstructed in Hebrew by A. Kahana, the original Hebrew would contain about 192 letters, a figure which is not unprecedented in ancient Hebrew manuscripts.[37]

Josephus' procedure in reconstructing the text would be the same whether he operated on the Hebrew or upon the Greek. Hence, in the remainder of our discussion we shall reconstruct his procedure on the basis of the Greek rather than on the basis of a hypothetical Hebrew. To estimate his operations on a Hebrew text, one need only reduce the letter counts per column in a proportion of $192:360=8:15$.

Accordingly, if vss. 21–23 constituted a complete column in Josephus' uncorrected copy, then 1:24 stood at the head of the next column. See

---

[36] Very fine manuscripts had 9–15 letters to the line; see W. Schubart, *Das Buch bei der Griechen und Römer*, 3d ed. (Heidelberg: Schneider, 1962), p. 59. We have only a few Greek biblical rolls which predate Josephus and are Jewish in origin. The Qumran Leviticus (4QLXX Lev^a) has a column of 28 lines, with about 27 letters per line; see P. W. Skehan, "The Qumran Manuscripts and Textual Criticism," VTS, IV (1956), 157–60. The Greek version of the Twelve Prophets from Naḥal Ḥever (Hev XII gr) has about 42 lines per column and 22 letters per line (Barthélmy, *Les Devanciers d'Aquila* [VTS, X (1963)], 164). *P. Fouad* Inv. no. 266, of the late second or early first century B.C.E., has a column of 20 lines with a maximum of 33 letters per line; see W. G. Waddell, "The Tetragrammaton in the LXX," JTS 45 (1944), 160 and facing plate. The conservatism of the scribes makes Christian codices relevant for comparison. *Chester Beatty Papyrus* III of the third Christian century, of Rev 9:10 – 17:2, has about 28 letters per line and 23–30 lines per column. The *Sinaiticus* has 12–14 letters per line and 48 lines per column. See William H. P. Hatch, *The Principal Uncial Manuscripts of the New Testament* (University of Chicago Press, 1939), plates x, xv.

[37] The only close Hebrew parallel I have found for a column with so few letters is the Qumran copper scroll, 3Q15, cols. v–viii (DJD, III, 289–92), with 14–16 lines per column and 14–15 letters per line. The Habakkuk commentary, 1QpHab, has 16–17 lines per column and about 30 letters per line.

Figure E. I 1:18–32 as they appeared in Josephus' copy of First Maccabees

[Vss. 21–23]

BY/ANTIOCHUS
PTOLEMY/FLED
AND/MANY/OF/HIS
TROOPS/FELL/SLAIN.
19THE/FORTIFIED
CITIES/OF/EGYPT
WERE/CAPTURED
AND/ANTIOCHUS
TOOK/THE/SPOILS
OF/THE/LAND/OF
EGYPT./20WHILE
RETURNING/FROM
HIS/CONQUEST/OF
EGYPT/IN/THE/YEAR
143/ANTIOCHUS
MARCHED/AGAINST
JERUSALEM/WITH
A/STRONG/ARMY.
20aTHE/PEOPLE/IN
THE/CITY/OPENED
THE/GATES/TO/HIM
AND/HE/ENTERED
THE/CITY/AND/TOOK
IT,/KILLING/MANY
ISRAELITES

End of vs. 18–vs. 20a
constitute a column of
359 letters in Greek

[Vss. 21–23]

Vss. 21–23 constitute
a column of 357
letters in Greek

24.1WITH/ALL/THIS
LOOT/HE/RETURNED
TO/HIS/OWN/COUNTRY.
24.2HE/POLLUTED/HIM-
SELF/WITH/MASSA-
CRES/AND/UTTERED
WORDS/OF/GREAT
ARROGANCE.

[Vss. 25–28]

Vss. 24–28 constitute
a column of 345
letters in Greek

29TWO/YEARS/LATER
THE/KING/SENT/A
MYSARCH/AGAINST
THE/TOWNS/OF/JUDAH
AND/HE/CAME/AGAINST
JERUSALEM/WITH
A/STRONG/ARMY.
30TREACHEROUSLY/HE
ADDRESSED/THE/PEO-
PLE/IN/PEACEFUL
TERMS/SO/THAT/THEY
TRUSTED/HIM/AND
THEN/HE/HIT/THE
CITY/HARD/WITH/A
SURPRISE/ATTACK
KILLING/MANY
ISRAELITES.

[Vs. 31 and begin-
ning of vs. 32]

Vss. 29–32 (through
"took captive") con-
stitute a column of
347 letters in Greek

The columns of the
text as they appeared
in Josephus' copy of
First Maccabees. I
have simulated the
Greek script with
English capitals and
have left no space
between words. Old
Greek manuscripts
neither space nor
insert word-separators.
I have followed my
own translation
and used the word
"Mysarch" instead
of "tax-gathering
official" in vs.
29.

Figure F. I 1:18–32 as "corrected" by Josephus

[Vss. 21–23]

[Vss. 25–28]

[Vs. 31 and begin-
ning of vs. 32]

The columns of
the text as Josephus
imagined they must
have been before
they were torn
and then were
"wrongly" re-
assembled by a
scribe. Even after
restoring the
"correct" arrangement,
Josephus found
vs. 29, "sent . . .
Judah and," in-
comprehensible and
deleted the words
as hopelessly
corrupt.

BY/ANTIOCHUS
PTOLEMY/FLED
AND/MANY/OF/HIS
TROOPS/FELL/SLAIN.
¹⁹THE/FORTIFIED
CITIES/OF/EGYPT
WERE/CAPTURED
AND/ANTIOCHUS
TOOK/THE/SPOILS
OF/THE/LAND/OF
EGYPT./²⁰WHILE
RETURNING/FROM
HIS/CONQUEST/OF
EGYPT/IN/THE/YEAR
143/ANTIOCHUS
MARCHED/AGAINST
JERUSALEM/WITH
A/STRONG/ARMY.
²⁰ᵃTHE/PEOPLE/IN
THE/CITY/OPENED
THE/GATES/TO/HIM
AND/HE/ENTERED
THE/CITY/AND/TOOK
IT/KILLING/MANY
ISRAELITES

End of vs. 18–vs. 20a
constitute a column
of 359 letters in
Greek

24.1WITH/ALL/THIS
LOOT/HE/RETURNED
TO/HIS/OWN/COUNTRY.
²⁹TWO/YEARS/LATER
THE/KING/SENT/A
MYSARCH/AGAINST
THE/TOWNS/OF
JUDAH/AND/HE/CAME
AGAINST/JERUSALEM
WITH/A/STRONG/ARMY.
³⁰TREACHEROUSLY/HE
ADDRESSED/THE/PEO-
PLE/IN/PEACEFUL
TERMS/SO/THAT/THEY
TRUSTED/HIM/AND
THEN/HE/HIT/THE
CITY/HARD/WITH/A
SURPRISE/ATTACK
KILLING/MANY
ISRAELITES.
24.²HE/POLLUTED/HIM-
SELF/WITH/MASSA-
CRES/AND/UTTERED
WORDS/OF/GREAT
ARROGANCE

Vss. 24.1, 29–30, 24.2
constitute a column
of 328 letters in
Greek

Vss. 21–23 constitute
a column of 357
letters in Greek

Vss. 25–28 and 31–32
(through "took
captive") constitute
a column of 365
letters in Greek

Figure E. Josephus appears now to have assumed the following:

1) In the text which lay before the hypothetical foolish paster, the column of about 360 letters containing vss. 21–23 was loose from the scroll as was the column of 345 letters containing vss. 24–28.

2) Verse 24 (84 letters) was not attached to vss. 25–28 (262 letters), but had been torn off from its context and had been split into two loose scraps.

3) Also torn off as a loose scrap of uncertain origin were vss. 29–30 (244 letters).

Josephus assumed that the stupid worker had then reassembled the scraps and columns in the wrong order, and Josephus "corrected" the "error" as shown in Figure F.[38] He also cut out the incomprehensible clause.

Josephus' assumptions were not farfetched, though he was mistaken here. Josephus failed to correct the real dislocation in the text of I 15:15–24= 14:24b–24k. See commentary, introductory NOTE to 14:16–24k.

At this point Josephus had what he wanted: two expeditions of Antiochus against Jerusalem, in agreement with his own interpretation of Daniel. The text in *AJ* xii 5.3–4.246–52 (beginning) corresponds quite closely to that in Figure F. Nevertheless, the hypothesis of a stupid paster did not solve all of Josephus' problems. He had to make further modifications in the text. In his view, the atrocities of 167 occurred together, over a short span of time; hence, it was particularly awkward to let the date dangle farther along in the narrative, at I 1:54. In writing *AJ* xii 5.4.248, Josephus moved the date into what was left of I 1:29[39] and added a few words of explanation, correct in his time, for his Graeco-Roman audience.[40] Josephus felt he was only making the text clearer when he transposed the date to I 1:29.

If he had stopped there, Josephus and his reader would have faced a puzzle. In Josephus' time the day of the month given in vs. 54, that of the first act of desecration of 15 Kislev, meant nothing. All Jews knew that the Feast of Dedication came on 25 Kislev, the "anniversary of the desecration" (see commentary, NOTE on I 1:54–59). Hence, Josephus instead took the day of the month from I 1:59. Thus, his section 248 came to contain the two-year lapse of time and the events (though not the Mysarch) of I 1:29–30, and the year and month of I 1:54, and the day of the month given in I 1:59. He probably viewed the "15" in vs. 54 as a scribal error for "25," and took the "repeated" date in vs. 59 as a typical piece of Hebraic redundancy.

Josephus was convinced that Antiochus violated his treaty obligations and sacked an innocent city out of greed (Ap. ii 7.83–84). Since no motive was

---

38 The variation in the number of letters per column is well within the limits of ancient scribal practice. See the examples in the previous two notes.

We can get a more detailed picture now of the original manuscript which lay before Josephus. Assuming 360 letters per column and assuming that our restoration of vs. 20a is correct (see commentary, NOTE on I 1:20, *with a strong army*), we find that the text of I 1:1–20a would fill about six columns.

39 He probably took the *kai* at the head of 1:54 as equivalent to *kai gar*. Then, in the context of 1:53, the date in 1:54 could indeed be applied to the whole of Josephus' revised version of 1:29–53.

40 The one hundred fifty-third Olympiad did include 167 B.C.E. on Josephus' equation of Kislev with Apellaios, see Bickerman, *Chronology*, p. 25.

given at I 1:20a–24, Josephus mentioned the breach of faith and supplied the motive of greed in his section 249.

The poetic amplification at 1:26–28 Josephus simply omitted. The passage *AJ* xii 5.4.251–56 also contains drastic rearrangements of I 1:30–64. We might again imagine Josephus pasting together a reconstructed text of vss. 30–32, but from vs. 30 on, Josephus does not seem to have treated the text as corrupt but rather to have reorganized it either to conform more closely to Dan 11:30–33 or for greater rhetorical effectiveness. In Dan 11:30–33 as read by Josephus, the order of atrocities after the sack of the temple was suspension of the temple cult (and imposition of an idolatrous one), slaughter, fire, captivity, and spoil. Accordingly, Josephus' narrative in section 251 paraphrases I 1:45 beginning (suspension of cult) and then I 1:30 end (spoil), 31 beginning and 32 (slaughter and captivity).[41] Josephus or his Greek secretary allowed the paraphrase of I 1:30 end to precede that of vs. 31 beginning and vs. 32 for the sake of elegant Greek word order in an elegant participial construction. Josephus put fire (I 1:31 end) last in section 252 because the burning and destruction of Jerusalem's buildings and walls left the Akra to become the sole local fortification, and Josephus thought that at least a day or two elapsed before the Akra was built.

Writing in Greek, Josephus felt free to condense the somewhat redundant patterns by which Hebrew historians first narrated a king's commands in detail (as in I 1:44–51) and then told of their execution (see commentary, NOTE on I 1:52–64). He could merely paraphrase I 1:33–37 and leave out the end of vs. 37 as superfluous in view of vs. 54 and again omit poetic amplification at I 1:38–40. From Antiochus' heinous destruction of the status quo, Josephus passes to still more heinous innovations. To Josephus, the information in vss. 41 and 51, that the king's messages were sent not only to Judaea but to all his kingdom seemed incredible. How could such messages to Babylonia, with its large Jewish population, have failed to leave traces in history, of Jewish resistance there or of Jewish martyrs? Josephus also failed to perceive the true meaning of vss. 41–43 and believed that those verses represented Antiochus' imposition of impious religious innovations in 167.[42] He made the passages "credible" by presenting the innovations reported in vs. 41 as imposed only upon the Jews and by omitting the beginning of vs. 51. Verse 44 thus became a redundant duplicate of vs. 41, to be omitted.

In detailing the heinous innovations (*AJ* xii 5.4.253–56), Josephus again follows Daniel and his own rhetorical preferences and places first the most dreadful, the desecration of the altar (I 1:54), then lesser violations of Jewish law (1:47–48, 50–52), and finally the persecution (1:60–63, 56–57). He had no idea that the desecration of 15 Kislev was distinct from the monthly sacrifice

---

[41] Josephus regretted that the author of I 1:32 gave no figure for the number of captives, whereas Jason of Cyrene at II 5:14 had given an incredibly inflated figure of forty thousand. Josephus appears to have taken Jason's figure and reduced it to a credible ten thousand (4.251).

[42] On the true meaning and credibility of the passages, see Introduction, pp. 119–21 and NOTE on I 1:51.

on the twenty-fifth (see commentary, NOTE on I 1:54–59) and so blends
I 1:54 with I 1:59.[43] He saw no reason to record that even heroic Jews could be
frightened into hiding and so omitted I 1:53. The description at I 1:62–63, of
the courage of the martyrs, was too cool for Josephus. Into *AJ* xii 5.4.255–56
he inserted a brief summary of II 6:29 – 7:42 and a report of the use of
crucifixion which he probably derived from the Testament of Moses.[44]
Josephus' other changes in *AJ* xii 5.4.256 probably reflect only his rhetorical
preferences.

Thus, there is no reason to assume that Josephus used any other source for
his narrative here than Daniel, the Testament of Moses, and First and Second
Maccabees.[45]

The editor of the Latin text of Josephus' *Antiquities* perceived the difference
between Josephus and First Maccabees and began to emend the text of
Josephus! He placed part of section 249 into section 247, to yield, ". . . he
killed many of those who were opposed to him. In so doing he spared not
even those who had let him in, for he was intent on the wealth in the temple.
Having taken large sums of money as spoil from the city, he returned to
Antioch."

[43] See above, n. 19.
[44] See above, n. 27.
[45] Correct accordingly Bickermann, *Gott,* pp. 18, 21–24, 33–35, 41, 163–68.

APPENDIX VI

WHY JOSEPHUS DEPARTED FROM THE CHRONOLOGY OF FIRST MACCABEES 7–16

Josephus in his *Antiquities* follows so closely upon I 7–16 that most of his narrative is mere paraphrase. Nevertheless, repeatedly he departs from our author's chronology. Josephus seems to have been unaware that our author drew on sources which used two different forms of the Seleucid era. Hence, in this appendix, I generally shall give Seleucid dates as "Sel.," without specifying whether they are Sel. Mac. or Sel. Bab.

Our author does not mention Menelaus. Josephus took delight in exposing the iniquities of that non-Hasmonaean high priest; see Introduction, pp. 58–59. To do so, he had to use other sources. From one of them he learned that Menelaus was high priest for ten years (*AJ* xii 9.7.384–85). Josephus holds that Menelaus' term ended with his removal and execution in the course of the withdrawal of Antiochus V from Jerusalem, but Josephus gives no dates.

Again Josephus departs from I 7:5–9 to use another source (Onias IV; see commentary, NOTE on I 6:63). Thus he brings Alcimus on the scene as high priest already in the reign of Antiochus V, immediately after the deposition of Menelaus. Again, Josephus gives no date for the investiture of Alcimus (*AJ* xii 9.7.385–87).

Josephus omits (*AJ* xii 10.1.389) the year of the accession of Demetrius I, though I 7:1 gives it as 151 Sel.

Josephus places Alcimus' death before the treaty with the Romans and gives no date but does give the duration of his high priesthood as four years (*AJ* xii 10.6.413); whereas our author places Alcimus' death well after the treaty, gives 153 Sel. as the date, but says nothing about the length of his high priesthood (I 9:54). Josephus had second thoughts and later reckoned Alcimus' term as three years (*AJ* xx 10.3.235–37).

Josephus omits (*AJ* xii 11.1.421) the date in Nisan, 152 Sel., for Bacchides' arrival at Jerusalem, given at I 9:3. Though Josephus gives (*AJ* xiii 2.1.35) the year 160 Sel. of Alexander Balas' accession (as at I 10:1), he omits (*AJ* xiii 2.3.46) the year of Jonathan's investiture as high priest, though it had the same figure and was given at I 10:21.

Our author does not call attention to the interval between Alcimus' death and Jonathan's investiture, though it could be reckoned from the dates he gives as seven years. Josephus takes care to mention the interval, and though he treats the interval in two different ways, the length is always seven years. In his first effort, Josephus divided the seven years into a term of three years for Judas as high priest (*AJ* xii 11.2.434) and then four years when the office was vacant (*AJ* xiii 2.3.46). At that point Josephus should have asked himself why our ardent pro-Hasmonaean author passed over in silence the first term of a Hasmonaean as high priest. Josephus did discover his error. At *AJ* xx 10.3.237 he says there were seven years without a high priest between Alcimus and Jonathan.

Josephus omits (*AJ* xiii 4.1.82) the year 162 Sel. of the wedding of Cleopatra Thea and Alexander Balas (I 10:57) but includes (*AJ* xiii 4.3.86) the year 165 Sel. of Demetrius II's accession as pretender (I 10:67). However, he omits (*AJ* xiii 4.8–9.119–20) the year 167 Sel. of Demetrius II's accession as sole king of the Seleucid empire (I 11:19).

Josephus places (*AJ* xiii 5.11.184) Demetrius II's campaign against the Parthians before the deaths of Jonathan and Antiochus VI and gives no date, whereas our author gives the opposite sequence and dates the campaign in 172 Sel. (I 14:1).

Josephus gives the wrong figure, four years, for the duration of Jonathan's term as high priest (*AJ* xiii 6.6.212). From our author's dates (I 10:21, 11:19, 13:41) it could be reckoned at more than seven and less than eleven years. Even in his second thoughts (*AJ* xx 10.3.238), Josephus gives Jonathan only seven years as high priest.

Josephus gives (*AJ* xiii 6.7.213) 170 Sel. as the beginning of Simon's "years of high priesthood." He calls attention to no gap between Jonathan's death and Simon's investiture, unlike our author, who also describes the "era" which began in 170 Sel. somewhat differently (see I 13:1–42 and NOTE on 13:42), Josephus omits altogether the document of the resolution of the Jews and its date in 172 Sel. (I 14:27–49).

Josephus omits (*AJ* xiii 7.1–2.222–23) the year 172 Sel. of the accession of Antiochus VII (I 15:10). He also omits (*AJ* xiii 7.4.228) the date in 177 Sel. of the death of Simon (I 16:14).

For the most part in his *Antiquities* Josephus continues to paraphrase I 7:16 as closely as he followed I 1:6. Hence we are led to believe that all the above-mentioned departures from our author's chronology are deliberate. Why did Josephus distrust our author's generally excellent data? Indeed, Josephus copies only some Seleucid accession dates and the beginning of Simon's high priestly years. Pagan sources could surely confirm the former. As for the latter, business and government documents, dated (like I 14:27) according to both "Simon's high priestly years" and the Seleucid era, probably survived along with other material and let Josephus once again trust our author's figure. If Josephus' trust is based on confirmatory evidence, perhaps his distrust arises from one or more conflicting sources.

Josephus' departures from our author's account give good clues about one possible conflicting source. Repeatedly, Josephus gives figures for tenures of the high priesthood and for periods when that office was vacant. Even when he has second thoughts, Josephus modifies these figures only slightly. We may thus assume that before Josephus there lay a list of high priests from Menelaus through Antigonus, the last Hasmonaean. The list gave the number of years of the tenure of each. Josephus presented the list, with slight modifications, at *AJ* xx 10.3–4.235–46. If so, the list was not drawn up by a partisan of the Hasmonaeans. Such a partisan would have counted both Menelaus and Alcimus as illegitimate.

It is hard to see how Jonathan came to be credited with only four years as high priest. But if the compiler of the list did not recognize Alexander Balas as a legitimate king and believed that the "era of Simon's high priesthood" began as soon as Jonathan was killed, all becomes easy. Then only Demetrius II could legitimately appoint Jonathan high priest. Demetrius II acceded as sole Seleucid king in early summer, 167 Sel., and the "era of Simon's high priesthood" probably began in autumn, 170 Sel. (see commentary, NOTE on I 13:41). The compiler of the list, too, could have had access to Seleucid accession dates and to the months and days of the festivals in *Megillat Ta'anit*. Jonathan, then, would have had a term of three years plus several months, which a chronicler would reckon as four years (see in AB vol. 41A Appendix VII).

Let us now examine how Josephus used his various sources.

Josephus may have learned from Onias IV that Antiochus V appointed Alcimus high priest (see NOTE on I 6:63). From calculations based on Dan 11:24 and his own date for the deposition of Menelaus (see in AB vol. 41A commentary on II 13:3–8), Josephus could have placed Alcimus' appointment to the office as early as October, 163, with what he supposed was the end of the sabbatical year. In fact, however, Josephus had to date Alcimus' appointment later, for he insisted on retaining our author's erroneous date in 160 Sel. for Judas' siege of the Akra; see NOTE on I 6:20. Indeed the siege had provoked the expedition in the course of which Antiochus V made the appointment.

Now, the high priestly list which lay before Josephus when he was writing *AJ* xii 10.6.413 gave Alcimus' tenure as four years. Even the three-year figure the historian later adopted would have been awkward in the context of Josephus' convictions:

1) Josephus believed that the high priestly list was largely reliable, though it might exhibit a few data to be rejected as arising from an "erroneous" (i.e. non-Hasmonaean) political view.

2) Josephus was convinced that Judas had held a term as high priest in the reign of Demetrius I; see NOTE on I 8:19–20. The story of the death of Alcimus in office was famous. Alcimus could not have been deposed. Judas must have outlived him.

If Alcimus became high priest well into 150 Sel. and served for three or four years until he died, his death can hardly have come before Nisan (April), 152 Sel. Yet Judas was killed in or just after Nisan, 152 Sel. Even if Alcimus had died at the beginning of Nisan, 152 Sel., Judas in his few remaining days, hard-pressed by Bacchides, could not have taken the drastic steps Josephus ascribes to him, of deciding to make an alliance with Rome and sending an embassy for the purpose (*AJ* xii 10.6.414–19; see commentary, introductory NOTE to chapter 8).

Josephus could not solve these difficulties. He tried to conceal them by giving no dates during the period. He is especially careful to give no information allowing one to come close to the precise date of Judas' death (see *AJ* xii 11.1–2.420–34) and of course gives no dates for the deposition of Menelaus or the death of Alcimus.

Josephus was even forced to omit (*AJ* xii 10.1.389) the accession year, 151 Sel., of Demetrius I, for it was incompatible with his convictions. Our author (I 7:1) had given the accession year and had regarded it as the year of the victory over Nicanor (see NOTE on I 7:43). In order to make room for a term for Judas as high priest, Josephus moved Alcimus' death back in time, to the aftermath of Nicanor's defeat (*AJ* xii 10.6.413). Trusting the high priestly list, Josephus insisted that by then Alcimus had been high priest four years. Yet four years (and even three years) cannot be squeezed into the time between well into 150 Sel. and the aftermath of an event in late winter, 151 Sel. Hence, Josephus prudently omitted the accession year of Demetrius I. As for Josephus' second thought concerning the length of Alcimus' tenure, see NOTE on I 9:55–56.

I do not know why Josephus chose to give Judas a term of three years when one of a single year would have been much less difficult chronologically. Perhaps three years was Josephus' estimate of the "brief period" mentioned at I 7:50. His paraphrase, however, suggests nothing of the kind (*AJ* xii 10.5.412).

The high priestly list displayed a seven-year period between Alcimus and Jonathan without a high priest (J. *AJ* xx 10.3.237). Josephus seems to have believed that the compilers of the list denied the legitimacy of the appointment of the first Hasmonaean high priest. Well might they do so, if, as Josephus believed (*AJ* xii 10.6.414), Judas received his appointment from the people, not from a king ruling over Judaea. See Introduction, pp. 75–76, and see also NOTE on I 14:34–35. Many Jews long after Judas' time stubbornly maintained that only the foreign king who was master of the Jews had the power to appoint the high priest. At this point, Josephus ignored such "sectarian" views. But chronology was an equally difficult obstacle to asserting that Judas had a respectable term as high priest. Josephus was forced to omit from *AJ* xii 11.1.421 the date, Nisan, 152 Sel., of Bacchides' arrival at Jerusalem (I 9:3). Bacchides' arrival came shortly before Judas fell in his last battle. In no way could a term of four years for Alcimus plus a term of three years for Judas as high priests begin in 150 Sel. and end in (or shortly after) Nisan, 152 Sel.

Josephus showed his confidence in the basic reliability of the high priestly list. Since he had given Judas three of the seven vacant years, he left a vacant period of four years before Jonathan's high priesthood (*AJ* viii 2.3.46). Later, Josephus' second thoughts convinced him that a credible pro-Hasmonaean history neither required nor allowed a term for Judas as high priest. Accordingly, he went back to quote the unaltered high priestly list, at *AJ* xx 10.3.237.

Josephus felt safe in giving the accession year of Alexander Balas as 160 Sel., in accordance with I 10:1. Even if that king was quick in making Jonathan high priest, how could it embarrass Josephus if someone should reckon backward, into the little-known reign of Demetrius I, to find that Judas, if so, became high priest in about 153 Sel. and was killed in about 156 Sel.? The approximations involved in reckoning fractional years would then even allow of Alcimus beginning a "four year" term in 150 Sel.! Thus, by selective omission of our author's dates, Josephus produced the kind of pro-Hasmonaean account he desired, one in which Rome acted benevolently toward a legitimate Jewish regime headed by a Hasmonaean (*AJ* xii 10.6.414–19). Later, in his second thoughts, he must have gained more respect for our author's account in the same way as we saw him returning to the high priestly list. Egotism or death prevented Josephus from a more open acknowledgment of his errors here.

Perhaps there is no ulterior motive in Josephus' omission (*AJ* xiii 2.3.46) of the year 160 Sel. of Jonathan's investiture as high priest. The reader could easily infer, correctly, that the time was near the accession of Alexander Balas. But Josephus may well have been puzzled by the discrepancy between our author's chronology and the four-year term reported for Jonathan in the high priestly list. Our solution of the problem above may not have occurred to Josephus. If so, he would have been glad to conceal his difficulty by omitting the date of the investiture.

Similarly, the marriage of Alexander Balas and Cleopatra Thea came in 162 Sel. (I 10:57), after Jonathan's investiture but more than four years before Jonathan's death. Again, to conceal the same problem, Josephus had good reason to omit the date from *AJ* xiii 4.1.82.

Mere pretenders could well lack power to appoint a Jewish high priest. Even without this factor, the date of Demetrius II's accession as pretender in 165 Sel. appears to have posed no difficulties for Josephus. He included it at *AJ* xiii 4.3.86.

Again, Josephus may have had no motive in omitting (*AJ* xiii 4.8–9.119–20) the year 167 Sel. of Demetrius II's assumption of power as sole king. Indeed, at that point Josephus is clearly not using First Maccabees as his source. He may well have been paraphrasing the work of Onias IV (see Introduction, pp. 57–59, and my article in *Studies Smith*, Part III, pp. 85–123), and Onias IV at this point may have given no date. More likely, however, Josephus again omits a date to conceal a difficulty: according to the high priestly list, Jonathan was high priest for four years; Josephus believed Alexander Balas appointed Jonathan to the office; yet Alexander Balas was dead at Demetrius II's accession in summer, 167 Sel.; Jonathan was dead by the time of the beginning in 170 Sel. of "Simon's high priestly era." Jonathan, if so, could have served as high priest under Alexander Balas for only one year. How could all the events of *AJ* xiii 2.2.45 – 4.8.128 have occupied only one year when Jonathan was serving as high priest *before* Demetrius II became pretender in 165 Sel.? Hence, if he lacked our explanation of Jonathan's four-year term in the high priestly list, Josephus had good reason to omit either the year of Demetrius II's accession as pretender or that of his accession as sole king and chose to omit the latter. Even by omitting both dates, Josephus would have difficulties remain: Alexander Balas' marriage was later than the investiture, and there was a child of the marriage who was not newborn when Balas was killed. With his limited time for his huge work, Josephus probably judged he had done his best.

On Josephus' dislocation of Demetrius II's Parthian expedition, see commentary, NOTE on I 12:39–40. On Josephus' omissions in *AJ* xiii 6.7.213–15, see NOTE on I 13:31–53.

Josephus probably omits (*AJ* xiii 7.1–2.222–23) the accession year of Antiochus VII merely because at that point he was not paraphrasing First Maccabees but another source, where that other source gave no date. See NOTES on I 15:1–14, 25–26.

Josephus may well have omitted the date of Simon's death to conceal the difficulty of the story: how the sabbatical year prevented John Hyrcanus from taking vengeance. See Appendix I.

Josephus' second thought (*AJ* xx 10.3.239) is puzzling. In correcting the high priestly list, why does he give Jonathan only seven years instead of our author's approximately ten? Josephus may at this point have discovered our solution, that the four years are the years under Demetrius II, counting appreciable fractions of years as whole years. The figure for Jonathan under Alexander Balas, calculated in the same manner (160 Sel. – 167 Sel.) would be seven years. Perhaps in a mental lapse, Josephus took the figure in the high priestly list for Jonathan under Demetrius II and merely replaced it with the figure for him under Alexander Balas, instead of calculating a new combined figure for Jonathan under both kings.

On earlier efforts to solve these problems, see Ettelson, TCAAS 27 (1925), 267–68, 276–77.

THE JEWISH MONTHS

Month	*Normal Equivalent*
Nisan	March–April
Iyyar	April–May
Sivan	May–June
Tammuz	June–July
Ab	July–August
Elul	August–September
Tishri	September–October
Marḥeshvan	October–November
Kislev	November–December
Ṭebet	December–January
Shebaṭ	January–February
Adar	February–March
Second Adar (in intercalary years)	

INDEXES

I. TOPICAL INDEX TO THE INTRODUCTION, COMMENTARY AND APPENDICES

II. INDEX OF REFERENCES TO THE BIBLE,
THE APOCRYPHA, AND THE PSEUDEPIGRAPHA

Listed in this index are passages which (a) receive interpretation in this book, (b) are mentioned as having had an important influence on the course of the history, or (c) served the author of First Maccabees as models and as foundations for his thesis, that God had chosen the Hasmonaean dynasty to lead Israel. Excluded are passages which are cited merely as evidence or as illustrations.

KEY TO THE TEXT

DATE DUE

5/Aug/76			